THE

Vanderbilt
Women

Dynasty of Wealth,
Glamour, and Tragedy

Also by Clarice Stasz

THE AMERICAN NIGHTMARE: Why Inequality Persists

AMERICAN DREAMERS: Charmian and Jack London

SIMULATION AND GAMING IN SOCIAL SCIENCE

SIMULATION GAMES FOR THE SOCIAL STUDIES TEACHER

SEXISM: Scientific Debates

FEMALE AND MALE

THE SOCIAL CONTROL OF DEVIANCE

THE

Vanderbilt Women

Dynasty of Wealth, Glamour, and Tragedy

by

Clarice Stasz

ST. MARTIN'S PRESS NEW YORK

Design by N.S.G. Design

Library of Congress Cataloging-in-Publication Data

Stasz, Clarice.
    The Vanderbilt women : dynasty of wealth, glamour, and tragedy / Clarice Stasz.
        p.   cm.
    ISBN 0-312-06486-1
    1. Vanderbilt family. 2. Women—United States—Biography. 3. Upper classes—United States—Biography. 4. United States—Social life and customs—20th century. I. Title.
    CT274.V35S83   1991
    929'.2'0973—dc20   91-21611
                                                                  CIP

First Edition: November 1991

10 9 8 7 6 5 4 3 2 1

CONTENTS

EARLY VANDERBILT PATRIARCHY

JAN AERTSEN VAN DER BILT
(?–1705)

ARIS VAN DER BILT
(1653–1715)

JACOB VAN DER BILT
(1692–1760)

JACOB VAN DER BILT II
(1723–1766)

CORNELIUS VAN DERBILT
(1764–1832)
m. Phebe Hand (1767–1854)

CORNELIUS "COMMODORE" VANDERBILT
(1794–1877)*

m1. Sophia Johnson (1795–1868)
m2. Frances "Frank" Armstrong
Crawford (c. 1839–1885)

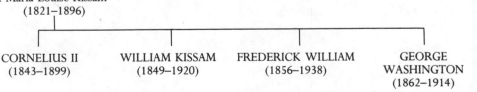

WILLIAM HENRY
(1821–1885)*
m. Maria Louise Kissam
(1821–1896)

CORNELIUS JEREMIAH
(1830–1882)

GEORGE
(1839–1863)

CORNELIUS II
(1843–1899)

WILLIAM KISSAM
(1849–1920)

FREDERICK WILLIAM
(1856–1938)

GEORGE
WASHINGTON
(1862–1914)

*Genealogy omits female descendants

CORNELIUS VANDERBILT II FAMILY*

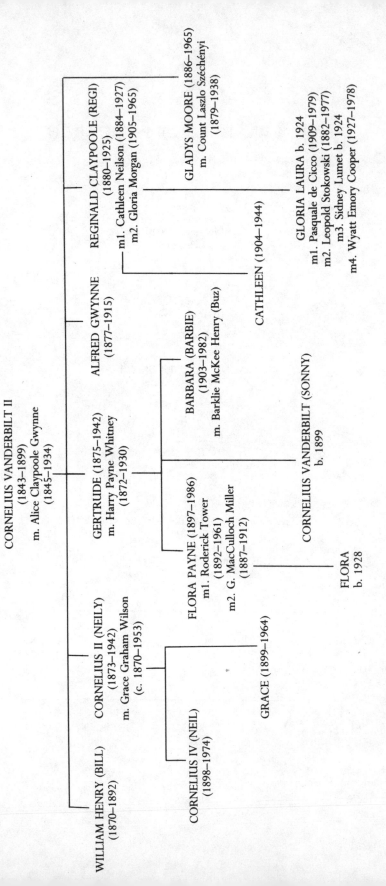

CORNELIUS VANDERBILT II
(1843–1899)
m. Alice Claypoole Gwynne
(1845–1934)

WILLIAM HENRY (BILL)
(1870–1892)

CORNELIUS II (NEILY)
(1873–1942)
m. Grace Graham Wilson
(c. 1870–1953)

CORNELIUS IV (NEIL)
(1898–1974)

GRACE (1899–1964)

GERTRUDE (1875–1942)
m. Harry Payne Whitney
(1872–1930)

FLORA PAYNE (1897–1986)
m1. Roderick Tower
(1892–1961)
m2. G. MacCulloch Miller
(1887–1912)

CORNELIUS VANDERBILT (SONNY)
b. 1899

FLORA
b. 1928

BARBARA (BARBIE)
(1903–1982)
m. Barklie McKee Henry (Buz)

ALFRED GWYNNE
(1877–1915)

CATHLEEN (1904–1944)

GLORIA LAURA b. 1924
m1. Pasquale de Cicco (1909–1979)
m2. Leopold Stokowski (1882–1977)
m3. Sidney Lumet b. 1924
m4. Wyatt Emory Cooper (1927–1978)

REGINALD CLAYPOOLE (REGI)
(1880–1925)
m1. Cathleen Neilson (1884–1927)
m2. Gloria Morgan (1905–1965)

GLADYS MOORE (1886–1965)
m. Count Laszlo Széchényi
(1879–1938)

*Genealogy is abbreviated to highlight descendants mentioned in the text.

WILLIAM KISSAM VANDERBILT FAMILY

WILLIAM KISSAM VANDERBILT I
(1849–1920)
m1. Alva Smith (1853–1933)   [m. Oliver Hazard Perry Belmont (1858–1908)]
m2. Anne Harriman Sands
Rutherford (1860–1940)

CONSUELO (1877–1964)   WILLIAM KISSAM II
m1. Charles Spencer-Churchill   (1878–1944)
9th Duke of Marlborough   HAROLD STIRLING
(1871–1934)   (1884–1970)
m2. Louis Jacques Balsan (1869–1956)

JOHN   IVOR (1898–1956)
10th Duke of Marlborough
(1897–1972)

PREFACE

*The study of history is useful to the historian by
teaching him his ignorance of women; and the mass of
this ignorance crushes one who is familiar enough with
what are called historical sources to realize how few
women have ever been known.*

—**Henry Adams**

Yet another book on the Vanderbilts? It
seems totally unnecessary.

Indeed, during my final year of writing this volume, five more appeared.
Louis Auchincloss, patrician lawyer and novelist who married into the family,
presented charming sketches from the lives of its Gilded Age members and their
associates. Alfred Vanderbilt, Jr., produced a lengthier history emphasizing the
decline of the family over the generations. Two colorful coffee table volumes also
appeared: Robert D. King's guidebook to many of the noted mansions built by
family members and Jerry E. Patterson's overview of the family. John Foreman
and Robbe Pierce Stimson reviewed the various architectural projects sponsored
by the family between 1879 and 1901. To these add a list of several dozen
previous works by both family members and other writers. Certainly the reading
public should have its fill for the time being!

Despite this shelf-bending collection, the family story remains oddly defi-
cient and distorted. Bluntly, many writings on the family fall under the theme
of "the rich and the shameless." Although tabloid writing is uncommon, tabloid
themes prevail: cantankerous and thieving Cornelius, the patriarch; his unbending
son William and the nasty public feud over the Commodore's will; mean and
manipulative Alva Vanderbilt forcing her innocent daughter Consuelo to marry a
money-hungry duke of Marlborough; hapless Neily, tossed out of the family for
loving the unwelcome Grace Wilson; cold-hearted Gertrude Vanderbilt Whitney
and her niece Gloria, "the poor little rich girl" who made a business fortune off
her signature. These and other tales feed a moral need to see the well-to-do as
variously unhappier than, unkinder than, or more sinful than the average person.

Although these yarns all have elements of truth, they have become more
caricatured with each retelling, making family members ever more objects of
buffoonery and ridicule. The stories *are* dramatic and intriguing—their very retelling proof of their allure. Still, they exaggerate the personalities of the players and

take them out of historical context. Treating personal squabbles and troubles of a hundred years ago like today's *National Enquirer* scoops, mere truncated gossip, belittles the participants.

Some writers want this belittlement, of course, and so do many readers. John Kenneth Galbraith praises Alfred Vanderbilt, Jr., for "a superior account" of the family's "unparalleled self-gratification and, very often, rather forthright stupidity." For Galbraith and other critics of certain features of capitalism, the Vanderbilts have been convenient proof of the injustices of our economic system. The accusation is oversimplified.

My quarrel is not with the social injustices, to which several Vanderbilts certainly contributed, but with the accompanying bad history. Rarely are individuals totally virtuous or despicable. If the rich can be stupid and self-satisfying, they can also be creative and empathetic—and like so many Americans they can exhibit both sets of traits simultaneously. Although the Vanderbilts had wastrels, even a scoundrel or two, they also included members who made significant contributions to the public welfare. Consequently, to maintain the rich-and-shameless theme, writers have often simply left out or mocked praiseworthy acts. For example, Alfred Vanderbilt simply omits Gertrude Vanderbilt Whitney's impressive role in American art and burlesques Alva Vanderbilt Belmont's suffrage activity.

The women have particularly suffered in these depictions. Subtleties disappear. Alva is a bulldog, Consuelo faultless, Gertrude twisted, Gloria superficial. In many sources they have little existence apart from their roles in scandal or sensation. Yet what distinguishes the family from others of their class is the deviance of these women (and several others in the line who have retained privacy); they have refused to submit to their friends' and relatives' expectations of them as society matrons. They would not limit their lives to a seclusive circle of family, the "right kind" of social events, and approved charity work.

It is tempting to think of unconventional behavior as based solely in personality, a matter of a rebellious temperament. Such tendencies reveal themselves over generations of Vanderbilt blood—more proclivity for risk taking, less need to fit into the crowd. Yet temperament is potential, a leaning in a direction; environment must provide the resources and opportunities to move. Each of these feisty and unusual women was presented with unlimited resources to achieve whatever she desired, but history provided unique opportunities that sent each in very different expressions of that unconventionality. No one has yet addressed this story, this unfolding of female rebellion from one generation to the next.

More puzzling, the contributions of the two most notable women, Gertrude Vanderbilt Whitney and Alva Smith Vanderbilt Belmont, receive short shrift or misrepresentation even in the feminist histories. Although Gertrude was a sculptor of note in her day, a patron of artists, and the founder of the Whitney Museum, she seldom earns more than a couple of lines, if that, in most books on women artists by feminist art historians. This neglect has been despite the highly detailed chronological biography by B. H. Friedman and Gertrude's granddaughter Flora Miller Irving [Biddle]. Even Avis Berman's meticulous rendering of the origins of the Whitney Museum, *Rebels on Eighth Street,* should really be titled *Rebel,* for it virtually neglects Gertrude in favor of her partner, Juliana Force. And while Alva played so significant a role in the National Woman's party as to share equal responsibility with Alice Paul for that group's actions, she earns brief and scattered comments that fail to honor her full contribution. One suspects feminist scholars have bent to the same prejudice that has struck so many other observers, that because these women were rich, they could not have done anything worthwhile.

The family itself has contributed to the skewed telling. Fond of diaries, bent toward confessional writing, and assured of their historical prominence, various members over four generations have chronicled this or that part of their lives for public scrutiny, and several others have left behind as yet unpublished memoirs or private papers. Given such juicy firsthand accounts, writers have gratefully expropriated the stories for their own benefit. Unfortunately, too often the retold versions ignore T. E. Lawrence's reminder that the documents lie.

The errors proliferate and reproduce. The trivial ones, which show up even in standard reference works, are easy to catch through the normal verification procedures. Gertrude was born in 1875, not 1877, the latter inaccuracy the result of her fudging a passport. Alva was never a member of the American Insitute of Architects, let alone the first woman member of that prestigious organization.

More vexing are stories told by only one participant, then accepted as the whole truth. Most notable here is Consuelo's moving account of being forced to marry the duke of Marlborough. The more I examined this narrative, indeed her entire memoir, the less credible it became in light of other information. In old age, when she published her version, Consuelo was so gracious and regal that to doubt her would be to seem dastardly, and even Oxford-trained scholars dropped their normally acute discrimination to defer to her account. The evidence now suggests that a lie once told in private, and later exposed, forced her to continue the deception. Consuelo was much more complex than the goody-two-shoes her memoir paints.

Just as dubious are the recollections of Gloria Vanderbilt's mother, Gloria Morgan. Ghost writers served her well in providing Hollywood quality melodrama, and that is the way to take her story. More interesting are the omissions and emphases, for example, the almost total lack of reference to her child contrasted with pages filled with names of party guests and wearing apparel. Though more accurate, Gloria Vanderbilt's autobiographical writings have telling omissions.

While documents lie, they retain their value if read circumspectly and checked against other available information. This puzzle reconstruction is complicated by the errors and misrepresentations in newspapers and other individuals' accounts of events. (Barbara Goldsmith's exposé of the untruths in news accounts of the Gloria Vanderbilt custody trial is a good model here.) The findings of social historians help in sorting out what makes sense and what does not. Furthermore, the Vanderbilt memoirists were not fabulists and fabricators—their lives were too public for much invention. Rather, they sometimes played with motives or conveniently left information out of their accounts, the normal and small deceptions of autobiographers. Although I have attempted the most sensible interpretation of this sometimes confounding material, I respect my sources enough to know they may have yet duped me here or there. That is one reason there will always be room for yet another Vanderbilt book.

PROLOGUE

The soothing waters of Bailey's Beach in Newport were unusually deserted on the afternoon of August 14, 1895. A scattering of toddlers romped in the shoreline riffles of Rhode Island Sound, with an even smaller array of nurses keeping vigilant watch from under the shade of sun umbrellas. For once the gulls could plod on the sand undisturbed by either the boisterous running and shouting of the older children or the more tentative frolic of flirtatious young adults.

Any flirtation on this date in Newport was being held in reserve for later that evening at the great ball at the Breakers, where the richest family in the United States, that of Cornelius Vanderbilt II, was spending the summer season. True, not all Newport society would be in attendance, but those who were not invited found convenient reasons to stay away from the beach, the tennis courts, and golf links, where their presence would advertise their exclusion from this major event in society circles, not only of the year but of the decade so far. Actually, it would not have mattered if they had ventured out, because most wise guests were also indoors, napping in preparation for the all-night affair.

The busy people that day were the servants. Despite its palatial size, the Breakers was not designed for house guests; consequently out-of-towners, who were numerous, stayed at the hotel or, if more fortunate, found bed and board at another mansion along Bellevue Avenue. Visitors brought their own maids, who jostled with one another at ironing tables and competed to reserve one of the too few bathrooms for a mistress's convenience. Chefs worried in the kitchens, eyed the day's roasts and fowls closely, smiled if the quality was right, and shouted a few more orders in frustration at the scullery help if it was not. The ball would not start until after eleven, so even though a dinner would be served there, guests would need fortification before arrival.

It was the Breakers staff who would be most pressed, and not just because this was the site of the evening's festivities. Their mistress, the incomparable Alice, could spot a dust mote, a slightly misaligned bibelot, from across the room. With florists setting up immense vases of American Beauty roses and decorators adding gold ribbons to the perimeter of one hundred chairs around the ballroom, the possibility of collision and unseemly mess was high. By Newport standards, the ornamentation was understated—"Mrs. Vanderbilt made no great effort at floral display," the *New York Times* would review—but then Alice knew the rooms themselves needed no artificial sparkle to add to their luxury and grandeur. What mattered to her was that there be sufficient fragrance to mask the sweat and perspiration of the dances, for deodorants had not been invented yet.

The most nervous person on the island that day might have been Gertrude

Vanderbilt, whom Cornelius and Alice were formally presenting to society at the event. More likely, Gertrude was just tired. Since the debut marked her official availability on the marriage market, during the months leading up to it, young men of her set competed for her favor. They appeared after church to walk her home, vied to be seated beside her at a dinner, accompanied her about museums, sought her as a partner for tennis and golf, and dropped in during afternoon visiting hours. Some days she would come in from a walk with one swain, and have barely enough time to change for her social appointment with another. By this late point in the summer she was looking forward to the fall, when her family chose to remain in a deserted Newport to rest before the more clamorous and formal winter season in New York.

Though her social calendar suggests a gregarious nature, Gertrude was in fact most solitary by temperament and exuded the kind of shyness that is often mistaken for snobbery. During the final hours leading to the party, she doubtless stole to her room on the second floor of the massive imitation of a sixteenth-century Genovese palazzo, where her windows looked out on the Atlantic below, giving one the sense of being in the snug, luxurious stateroom of a ship. Of all the moments in the day, the ones she most treasured were those spent in this quiet retreat, away from the watchful attention of servants and more judgmental scrutiny of her parents.

Now twenty, her height was five feet, eight inches, very tall for a time when the average man's height was five-foot-seven. Her slim, willowy body and erect posture added to the impression of height, but without making her seem overbearing. Her light brown hair, sensuously wavy, crowned a long face that was not beautiful but, rather, alluring and mysterious. The green of her eyes distracted from their smallness, the elegant shape of her nose from its length, and the fullness of her lips from the slightly receding chin underneath.

Gertrude's very divergence from the more petite standard of beauty of the day doubtless attracted suitors as much as her wealth. Gertrude herself was not so certain that this was the case. It was only of late, that she had been permitted to have visits with young men, and, given the etiquette of the day, she had yet to be kissed by one.[1]

In recent months she had filled pages of her diary with the confused and precipitous emotions familiar to today's young adolescent girls. She had experienced crushes, only to lose interest. She had played cool to tease a suitor. Some afternoons she had spent in bed crying, and at several dinners she had annoyed her mother by leaving her plate full. Cousins married, leaving her longing for a similar state, only to be followed by fantasies of being a governess, free from the burden of wealth. Though the men were of the acceptable mold—heirs to great fortunes, educated at Yale, sporty with horses, knowledgeable in the arts, facile in conversation—they did not occupy the pinnacle Gertrude's family did—a pinnacle shared with very few other families. Indeed, the only men also at Gertrude's level seemed to be her very brothers!

On this afternoon, Gertrude was playing with the idea of marriage to lawyer and Rhinelander fortune heir Lispenard Stewart, who, at forty, was much older than her usual beaus. "He likes me very much because I am not clever or pushing or poor," she had recently jotted. "He knows I would not marry him for anything except love because I have everything else. And he has always been more or less afraid of that. His feelings are not very deep, and he could get to love me as much as was necessary."[2] Stewart's very lack of ardor was a relief following the more eager attention of men her age. Although Gertrude did not yet realize such, she desired a relationship in which comfortable intimacy did not smother each partner's independence.

If Gertrude had any case of nerves on this day, it was out of concern for her mother. She knew the true reason for the ball was less her own belated debut than that of the building itself. This was the family's first summer in the Breakers, which had been built to replace the earlier shingle "cottage" of the same name that had burned down in 1892. The Vanderbilts had signed architect Richard Morris Hunt to design a large, solid home to overshadow any other in that town of sumptuous and often overdressed mansions.

Hunt's preferred scheme was of a three-story French Rennaisance château, whose turrets, dormers, and complex roof would best disguise the extensive warren of servants' rooms on the top floor. The Vanderbilts insisted on the more massive Italian structure, which forced Hunt to add a fourth story, a move the family later regretted. They also insisted the house be as fireproof as possible, which explained the absence of any wood in the construction (save some oak parquet) as well as the placement of the heating plant at several hundred feet from the main building.

Despite the limitations placed on Hunt, he produced one of the finest houses of his long and accomplished career. The seventy-room house (thirty-three of which were for servants) was magnificently situated on its twelve-acre site overlooking the Atlantic. The ground floor was arranged symmetrically around a central great hall of light French Caen stone rising through the second floor to a height of forty-five feet. There tonight's guests could gaze up at the ceiling, where a massive carved and gilt cornice surrounded a painting of blue sky.

Several years later expatriate Henry James would refer to "this miniature spot of earth, where sea nymphs on the curved sands, at the worst, might have changed to the shepherds, as a breeding ground for white elephants."[3] The family did not agree, particularly Gertrude, whose bedroom in the smaller Breakers had been used to store visitors' coats. However uninviting the house looked to James, a man more accustomed to the cozier homes of Boston and London wealth, it was what the Vanderbilts were used to, for their house in New York City was another massive citadel.

Although Alice Vanderbilt had little to fear of the opinions of the evening's three hundred guests, she was anxious nonetheless. Tonight was simply one in a long series of many based on competition with her sister-in-law Alva, wife of Cornelius' younger brother, William K.

One would think that after more than twenty years of rivalry Alice would relax. After all, Cornelius was the first son and the richest (though not by much). And Alice, unlike Alva, had made social arbiter Ward Mcallister's list of The Four Hundred (which actually numbered almost a hundred less). Nor did Alice leave behind her as Alva did a trail of gossip and rumors. Alice was proud of her piety, propriety, and primness, whereas Alva—well, Alice was too correct to even think of Alva's free-spirited character in any detail! When Alice had ordered that a nude in a mural for the billiard room at the Breakers be draped by the painter, she suspected that Alva in the same circumstances instead would have ordered the clothes removed from the remaining garbed figures.

As Alice prepared with her family for the pre-ball dinner, an intimate affair for thirty of Gertrude's closest young friends, she had good reason to worry. She knew that Alva looked upon society, indeed all of life, as an adventure, whereas Alice viewed it as a haven to be protected and preserved. Alva played by the rules only when it suited her to do so, thus she never took the game seriously. The latest example was her insistence on being accepted by society despite her recent divorce. For Alva, technically speaking, was now Alice's ex-sister-in-law, having successfully sued Willy K. in March of that year. Alice and all the other Vanderbilts immediately ostracized Alva, but that would not prevent her from making a mark on tonight's event.

By eleven, the official starting time of the affair, a parade of black victorias was streaming down East Narragansett Avenue, through the black wrought iron gates of the Breakers. Blank-faced footmen, dressed in the traditional Vanderbilt livery of maroon with white wigs, stepped forward to assist the young women, who nervously grasped bouquets in one hand and swept up their billowing trains in the other to alight. Their jeweled tiaras, dog collars, and stomachers sparkled in the warm glow of four immense outdoor bronze chandeliers.

Hunt's understanding of the drama possible through thoughtful design was manifest. The guests' excitement increased as they passed through the great oak entrance doors of the mansion, down the marble passageway, through another set of wrought iron doors, where a short flight of marble steps led to the galleried great hall. There four enormous crystal chandeliers showered the room with flickering soft gaslight, leaving each woman to feel shown off at her best.

Before joining the party, the women, accompanied by their personal maids, ascended a great hanging marble staircase with a filigree ironwork ballister at one end of the room to the balcony, off which dressing rooms were located. Here, while bodices were supposedly being straightened and locks of hair put under control, the young women actually stole quick glances at others' apparel and jewelry. Some left the room and swept back down the staircase more confident than others.

Meanwhile, the male guests had completed their toilette in dressing rooms on the lowest floor. The men had less need to compare appearance, for this social event, like all others in society, was where their wives and daughters competed for the family honor and glory. The men were dressed alike, the shiny shirt fronts and fresh glacé gloves in stark contrast to their black evening wear. Their job was to be unobtrusive background for the ladies, to be necessary props for the most showy part of the contest, as cavaliers on the dance floor, cleverly positioning one's partner as though she were the most exquisite woman in the room.

Many of the men shared Cornelius's view of the whole shebang, that it was stuff and nonsense. These great titans of industry and graft, these men who could in a single financial transaction bring joy or hunger to the families of workingmen throughout the country, fell to their knees when it came to the women's sphere. They became guests in their own homes.

Of course it was also highly practical to let the women reign in the social arena. For one, it kept the women busy at frivolous ventures, and prevented them from meddling in the men's serious concerns. And, because of a quirk in demography at that time, the men were fewer in number and could enjoy the benefits of rarity. Thus young men at the courting stage need spend little money for extravagant entertainment, for invitations from hopeful mothers would cover the expense. And once married, they need only make their ritual appearance and could do what they wanted the rest of the time.

So on this sultry, perfect evening the men more likely sighed in resignation before making their entrance. With luck there would be several graceful dance partners, few exchanges with dull conversationalists, perhaps a most understated titillation of one sort or another. Since this was Alice's party, one could not hope for as delicious a spread as at, say, the Astors' or Belmonts'. Alice and Cornelius could never be credited as being sensualists or gourmands. Still, the women were lovely. . . .

The ceremony began with greeting the debutante of honor. Alice and Gertrude had selected for this ritual the brightly colored music room, with its dazzling gold and silver highlights heightened by the scarlet of the upholstery. Mother and daughter sat stiffly in high-backed chairs resembling thrones, while Cornelius positioned himself beside. The butler stood at the entrance to announce each guest.

A difference in temperament between the mother and daughter would be immediately apparent. Alice was tiny, rather stern, not one for easy quick talk. Neither her glowing red satin gown nor her pounds of jewels could warm her personality. Still, though guests might feel a bit stiff around Alice, they respected her forthright morality, her devotion to family and charity. Visitors approached Gertrude, lovely in white chiffon, with less trepidation. Although her face revealed some of her mother's strong will, her more animated body language confirmed her to be able to enjoy a good time. She was the kind of wholesome girl young men of her set admired, and a loyal friend to the other girls in her crowd, one who would never steal a beau away from someone else.

The three hundred guests were a predictable lot: many from the Four Hundred, some titled Europeans from Russia and Hungary, representatives from embassies or legations of England, France, Spain, and Belgium. Among the family's closer friends were Newporters Edward Wharton and his wife Edith (known within the set as "Pussy"), who was to memorialize this social stratum and era in her novels. Few people were strangers to one another. The premier rule of the wealthy then as now is play only with people of one's class to protect one's interests, save for a few outsiders allowed to play the role of joker. No jokers were present this evening.

While the minutes passed and Alice greeted the cream of society, her nagging worry became more insistent. One group had yet to arrive, that known to be dining with Alva. This was curious because Alva had been a leader in introducing the "short meal." Soon upon becoming Mrs. Willie K. Vanderbilt she had decided the custom of three- and four-hour repasts where a guest literally expanded as one rich course followed another, must be tossed aside in favor of the more Continental custom of the one-hour dinner. Her innovation proved so sensible that even the most conservative families, the Old Money Knickerbockers, sighed with relief and followed suit.

Tonight, as Alice feared, Alva had a plan up her sleeve. It was bad enough that Alva would worry Alice by delaying the guests at a later than respectable time. When they belatedly appeared, full of apologies, they could not help but share the latest gossip, dropped very casually from Alva's lips during the leisurely repast. It seemed one could expect an announcement soon of the engagement of Alva's daughter Consuelo to the ninth duke of Marlborough! Of course, the chattering about this social coup spread from one to another through the ballroom, drawing attention away from Alice and her family. There could be no better humiliation of a woman so devoted to keeping her place at the top of the social pinnacle.

Gertrude's cousin Consuelo could not appear at the ball because the casting out of Alva applied to her as well. While she must have missed participating in her cousin's debut, she had an exciting future to anticipate. And being cut off from the family at this point would make the permanent move to England that much easier. (And since Consuelo was considered the most beautiful of the younger Vanderbilt women, Alice, may have been just as happy with her absence.)

But Alva's machinations proved to be minor compared to a romance that flared during that long night. Just when it happened is not known. It may have started at the midnight supper, where guests dined around small tables covered with silver ornaments and pink shaded lamps. It likely developed further during the dancing, with music led by Mullaly's Orchestra and Sherry's Hungarian Band. The style of dance then was the cotillion, a complex, formalized set of figures that could go on without break for two hours or more (hence the need for two orchestras). With its weaving in and out, greeting and separating of partners, it was the ideal dance for flirtation. Likely at one point the young lady involved demurely played with the French fan given out as a favor. There would not be, as today, a slipping away to a dark corner of the colonnaded porch overlooking the sweep of lawn to the ocean, and that inability to talk privately only added to the mystery and appeal of the attraction.

The woman was arguably the most magnificent of the young beauties at the party, the stunning Grace Wilson; the man, Cornelius III. A more attractive couple could not be imagined.

Neily, as he was called to distinguish him from his namesake parent, was a tall and clean-cut figure, whose strong Vanderbilt facial features were softened just enough to make him handsome. His full, thick, and curly hair beckoned one to run fingers through its glossy brown locks. Although he had a history of chronic illness, in recent months he had strengthened and appeared vigorous. With his regular church going, good school record, and generally sweet personality (save a temper few experienced), he was to Cornelius and Alice a perfect child.

Grace seemed a virginal princess in her white chiffon gown intricately embroidered with pearls and appliqued flowers of satin. A small ivory fan hung on a diamond chain from her waist. Her face was of classic beauty, haloed by honey-gold hair, marked by dark-lashed chameleon eyes that changed from gray to violet to green and back. Her fine-boned movement was gentle, unforced, so poised that no woman in the room could question her good blood.

Neily and Grace had seen each other during the summer, in the company of others, properly chaperoned of course, but on this evening, under this gas light, to the strains of this Hungarian melody, an understanding was reached.

Nothing explicit was stated. A time traveler from today's society listening in would not have guessed the monumental import of the exchange that was passing between their lips. In that society one "lived in a kind of hieroglyphic world, where the real thing was never said or done or even thought, but only represented by a set of arbitrary signs."[4] Thus, somewhere in the muddle of talk of tennis and friends and the lovely roses, Neily paid Grace a compliment which she returned, then the discussion continued on to golf links and party favors. But each knew through a particular glance accompanying the interruption that they had become betrothed.

If custom demanded the couple dampen their celebration over the agreement, their affection was nonetheless visible to onlookers. Two in particular followed the pair as it glided by, studied vigilantly for the tiny signs that would give away the smoldering passion passing between these handsome dancers. The proof was clear in the quick smiles, the darting eyes, the waist held a bit too tightly. By party's close, Cornelius and Alice were troubled, yet not too worried. Their son would surely listen to their wise counsel. This was, after all, his first real flirtation, the first of many such an agreeable young man could expect to experience before taking a wife.

What mattered was that Gertrude be enjoying herself, and she was. Lispenard Stewart had her eye, and they were matched as partners together for the start of the cotillion. Nor did she mind that the rules of society forbade him to monopolize her on the dance floor. So many adoring young men flocked about her, competed for her favor, men who had sent her violets, not to be forgotten, who had asked hostesses to seat them beside her at dinners, or even merely to include them at the table. Tonight they all had an equal chance to attend to this heiress referred to in the press as an "American princess."

The party did not end until the rise of the sun, when the youngest and most sturdy guests remained to watch the first peach and orange rays while taking breakfast from tents on the lawn. They agreed with the newspapers' later summation that it was "a grand ball," indeed.

For many contemporary readers of the chronicle of this event, the story of yet another opulent society entertainment was not viewed with envy. The country had been in a severe depression since bank failures and the panic of 1893. In 1894 a strike by railroad workers, who had experienced wage cuts of twenty-five percent, ended with federal troops called in to quell the revolt. An army of unemployed men marched across the country to make a noisy outcry in Washington for public works jobs.

Just a few years earlier, common talk blamed a man's poverty on himself, on his laziness, or on lack of salvation. Now people noticed that many hardworking men had become poor. Worse, women and children were forced to work twelve-to-fifteen hour days in factories while husbands and fathers went without jobs. It did not take long for people to question the morality of extravagance. For a number of years the rich had been a major national entertainment, its great stars and personalities, but now ministers, social workers, Socialists, labor leaders, and novelists were suggesting the adulation was undeserved.

Society itself was unaware of these developments. Wealth brings insularity, an ability to buy symbolic and real fences to block out the unattractive, the unseemly. Although the Vanderbilts were charitable, more so than most of their wealthy friends, their recognition of great need did not lead them to question their daily choices in life-style. So even on the night of this great ball they could dance without care, as if the great cement and steel bulk of the Breakers could shield them from history.

But history is no respecter of class. The Gilded Age, which the family had come to rule, was over. For the women in particular, those traits and attitudes they had passed down from one to another, that feminine circle of safety and predictability, was about to be broken. Some members would fight this loss, their struggle to rebuild and maintain the old ways resulting in near self-destruction. Others would find the broken circle an invitation to move beyond and express themselves in ways previously forbidden. Two in particular would make lasting marks on the country's well-being. Yet on this perfect, sultry evening in Newport, it seemed impossible that the pattern could ever change, for just as the tide and sun are predictable, so then seemed the rule of society.

P   A   *1*   R   T

The nearest thing to a royal family that has ever appeared on the American scene was the Vanderbilts. Their palaces and summer palaces, their balls and routs and banquetings, their royal alliances and their vendettas, their armies of servitors, partisans, and sycophants, their love affairs, scandals, and shortcomings, all were the stuff of an imperial routine.

—LUCIUS BEEBE

1

1647-1849

A Hearty
Stock Takes Root

On May 11, 1647, the plucky settlers composing New Amsterdam gathered at the Battery piers to glimpse the arrival of the recently appointed director general of New Netherland, Peter Stuyvesant. He strutted down the ramp "like a peacock, with great state and pomp," his artificial leg, its ornate silver adornments glittering in the sunlight, thumping a staccato that would soon become a familiar approaching warning to the onlookers. A tough, virile, willful man, Stuyvesant was typical of many of those under his rule. One such subject, who would step onto the same Battery piers in 1650, was Jan Aertsen Van der Bilt.

Just why the Van der Bilts, or any Dutch for that matter, chose to settle in a wilderness three thousand miles across the ocean is an enigma. Unlike England, Holland was a land of religious tolerance and a thriving economy. This is not to say there were no poor. Indeed, during the early seventeenth-century boom brought by international trade and industry, the number of starving people in the population actually increased. The government responded with repressive poor laws that called for the arrest of the indigent. If willing to search for new hope, however, down-and-outers found ready welcome in neighboring European countries, who admired their abilities as farmers, their skills in certain trades, and their reputation for hard work. Still, some dared to try the New World, particularly those ruined by "tulipomania," a crazed speculation in tulip bulbs that resulted in a collapse of the market during 1636–37. It took a special breed, one more confident and willing to take risks, to move to what was considered a hostile and savage-filled world.[1] Such was the case for Jan Aertsen Van der Bilt.

Opportunity, not escape, attracted Van der Bilt, who came with sufficient financial resources to ensure his family would thrive in New Amsterdam. His first child, Aris, was born on American soil in 1653, with others soon to follow. The colony did not so flourish. Unable to attract or retain settlers, in 1664 the Dutch were humiliated by their bloodless surrender to an English fleet. Soon afterward, Van der Bilt proudly registered ownership of a considerable portion of the forests surrounding Midwout, later known as Flatbush, better known in modern days as Brooklyn.[2] In 1667, son Aris married Hilletje Vanderbeeck and soon joined his father and brothers in adding the family name repeatedly to the land deeds of that wilderness area. Owning land meant clearing it for pasture and planting, a task that could take several years of work with oxen and field hand to complete. Talented and civic minded, the Van der Bilt line gained prominence in the community. One family member was an elder in the local church, and still another contributed a fine bell imported from Holland for its steeple.

During the initial rule of that sparsely populated colony by the English, the governing duke of York had been liberal in his tolerance of Dutch ways. He granted the early settlers their forms of local government, their land titles, and even the right to support their churches with tax revenues. York's tolerance also meant the Van der Bilts were able to practice their old country ways and language in the company of fellow Dutch farmers. Thus Jan and Aris soon had friends with whom to share a drink in the village tavern following a long day's labor in the fields, or with whom to race horses, a favorite Dutch pastime, on a rare free afternoon. Hilletje and other wives found their kitchen gardens as fertile as in Holland.

York's control was interrupted briefly in 1783, when six hundred Dutch men easily took back New York from the control of the English and renamed it New Orange. Optimistic messages sent to the home government encouraged settlers to take advantage of the agricultural promise of the area that could become "for Fatherland, a granary and magazine of many necessaries which are ordinarily imported [from outside Holland]."[3] Unfortunately, the return to Dutch rule lasted little more than six months, but the brief time of glory encouraged a mass of new Dutch immigration that may have put pressure on the Van der Bilts to seek new land.

The Van der Bilts' gamble was paying off. Like their fellow countrymen they were imbued with values of thrift and hard work; more uniquely, they were of sturdy and hardy physical stock. Because Dutch families were both large in number and successful at farming, the time would come when part of a community would have to splinter off and resettle land farther out, or as they would put it, "start a new hive." Thus it happened that Aris Van der Bilt was able in 1715 to provide his son Jacob with a large tract on Staaten Eylandt. Although only five miles from the southern tip of Manhattan, this island was neither very civilized nor promising as farmland. Only recently had the justifiably angry natives quit their raids on the white intruders. Hilly and densely forested down to the shoreline, except where marshes intervened, the soil proved highly variable in fertility. Thirteen hundred people lived widely scattered about the island. Jacob received sixty acres of upland (now part of the Moravian cemetery), eight acres of swampy meadow, and ten acres by the shoreline at the Great Kills.

The closest hamlet was New Dorp, a frontier community in the forests south of Dongan Hills. Practically every man in the area was busy extending clearings on his property by cutting down trees, burning out shrubs, grubbing out remaining stumps, carting boulders, and spreading manure to make fields for crops of wheat and Indian corn. Jacob's holdings being split into several locations was not unusual, for marshes were used to grow salt hay to feed the cattle during the winter months. The work was so arduous that many families purchased a slave or two, although unlike the English, the less color-conscious Dutch masters worked alongside their slaves in the field and were less brutal. Within a few years thrifty Jacob added further acreage to his original plots and may well have had a slave to help him.

Jacob's wife and daughters would have a day of steady labor as well. In an economy that was self-sustaining, the women were required to tend the kitchen garden and the pigs as well as attend to the cooking, cleaning, laundry, and child care. (Dutch doors offered a convenient way to toss garbage out to the pigs without leaving the house or letting the animals into the kitchen.) The worst taskmasters for women of the time, however, were the spinning wheels, the small foot-powered wheel for linen and the larger one for wool. Whereas children found its steady hum soothing, for most women it was the despised low wail of tedium. Beating hemp for fibers was another hated chore in the preparation of homespun cloth, hence allotted to a slave when possible.

Not long after Jacob arrived, New Dorp attracted the followers of John Huss, called Moravians (later known as United Brethren), who had escaped religious persecution and torture in Europe. The Van der Bilts and many of their fellow Dutch joined this sect and its stalwart people. Staunch converts, the Van der Bilts led the community in building a ship to bring yet other Moravians from Germany. From their homes on the green hills looking down toward the Narrows, the Moravians were satisfied to live austere lives, worship often, and die in grace to reach heaven. Like Dutch throughout the middle colonies, they were clannish, avoided other ethnic groups, and avoided intermarriage. (Indeed, people of German, Swedish, or English background living around the Dutch often accommodated them and joined in their ways.) The fleets of masted ships that spread over the northern bay surrounding the port of New York never tempted them to explore other lands.

As was common with members of this sect, the Vanderbilts, as they came to spell their name, multiplied in biblical fashion. One of Jacob's twelve children, Jacob II, married Mary Sprague, of English blood, and had seven of his own. The Revolution had little effect on the family, apart from the British having burned down a new church building. It was even rumored that some Vanderbilts were moderate Tories, who helped provision the troops of General Howe and provided temporary housing for him and his staff. The Rose and Crown, a tavern owned by Jacob II, was a popular watering hole for British officers.

Jacob II and Mary's youngest son was named Cornelius Vanderbilt. Tragically, his parents died soon after his birth, and as the youngest he was also landless, so he was forced to make his way in life by hiring out to other farmers. Cornelius apparently did not care much for the heavy labor—some called him a ne'er-do-well—but he was clever enough to search for another source of income. By now New York City was the primary market for island farmers. Scraping together enough coins for a rickety boat, he instituted what was the equivalent of the first Staten Island ferry, offering regular service through the Narrows and Upper New York Bay to the wharves at the tip of Manhattan.

In choosing such an occupation as ferrying, Cornelius was announcing himself a defector from his community, yielding the spiritual life for the commercial, so possibly his poor reputation reflects that insult. He was certainly not the only deviant in the neighborhood at that time. With the arrival of independence, the firm center of Dutch ethnicity began to give way. The churches switched the language of their services to English, and the wealthiest families sent their children to New York for short stays to learn more genteel manners and behaviors. These were small signs that the community was taking on a new identity, that of Americans. Little could Cornelius guess that his mild rebellion would serve his own son a model for great risk taking, that this same son would do much in his century to redefine the very identity of "American."

If Cornelius was wise to see a better future away from farming, he was wiser still in his choice of a mate. Phebe Hand was of a good family of English stock whose patriotism had proved its downfall. Like other supporters of independence, the Hands had invested their money in Continental bonds, which proved after the war to be worthless. Left to her own support, she moved from Rahway, New Jersey, to nearby Port Richmond on Staten Island to serve the family of a clergyman. It was there she met Cornelius and agreed to marry him. Of high and strong character, she provided a ballast to her husband's impulsiveness and gambling urges. Despite her British heritage, she was temperamentally well suited to adopt the ways and preferences of Dutch-American culture, so the Dutch influence prevailed in family practices and values.

A Plucky
Child Appears

The year 1787 was an inauspicious time to start a family. The economy was in disarray following the war, the many currencies of dubious value. Optimistic nonetheless, the newlyweds settled in Port Richmond, where they lived like many Americans at the time in little more than a shack. Very quickly their tiny cottage began to fill with squawling babies. Their fourth child and second son, Cornelius, Jr., was born on May 27, 1794, during the administration of the first president of the new nation, George Washington. This timing of his arrival proved felicitous, as he would come to maturity during a period of unique opportunity in the youthful nation.

Eventually Cornelius settled his family in a sturdier house in Stapleton, on the northeastern coast of the island where his ferry pier was located. The family cottage retained a Dutch manner, with its white clapboard, highly sloping modified gambrel roof, and great hearth at one end.[4] Typical of homes of the day, the kitchen was in a shed area attached to the rear, the outhouse nearby so one would have little exposure to the elements on the walk to its convenience. A porch running across the front was also characteristic, for the Dutch enjoyed sitting out in the evenings with family and neighbors smoking, drinking, conversing, joking, and playing cards. While the adults sat and gossipped, the children chased about the field below.

To modern eyes this five-room structure seems cramped for a family that would eventually grow to nine children. Phebe would likely not have agreed. Few Americans, the elite really, lived in the large Colonial homes that stand restored today and are not representative of how average people lived. The Stapleton home was a typical middle-class dwelling. Phebe knew that had Cornelius remained a farmhand they would be living under rather wretched conditions, for the single-room house was the common abode for many early nineteenth-century Americans.

Furthermore, privacy did not hold the value it does today, primarily because it was impractical. Life was corporate, its activities carried out in the sight and hearing of others. With no electricity or gas, family members centered around the great room hearth, with its warmth and evening glow. Sharing beds in unheated attic rooms with siblings, servants, visitors, and travelers seeking overnight stay was a necessity. Phebe and Cornelius likely slept in the parlor, which contained the family's most valuable possessions (the bed the most important of them). Otherwise the parlor would be reserved for important entertaining and ceremony.

Non-Dutch visitors were often struck by the tranquillity of Dutch interiors. Unlike homes of English design, the walls were whitewashed and free of wallpaper, allowing light to reflect on the highly polished woods and pewter ware. The low mudded ceilings added to the feeling of coziness and domesticity. Children's and guests' beds were enclosed in cabinets so they would not be visible during the day. Fireplaces usually had the familiar blue and white tiles to brighten the mantle. What the visitors did not reflect upon was the very untranquil activity that produced this amicable setting.

If Phebe was lucky, an odd unmarried female relative or domestic helper also lived in the home, for her household labor was unimaginable to modern eyes, especially considering a babe was often whining for her breast or a toddler pulling at her gown. Daily the cow needed milking, which was followed by butter churning, a task of dexterity, strength, and good eye. Since the family was of Dutch background, she made cheeses as well. Then there was bread baking in the hearth oven, along with the back-wrenching stooping and lifting of heavy iron pots over the fire. Because refrigeration did not yet exist, she needed to keep up a steady line of salting, pickling, smoking of meats, and of preparing vegetables for root storage. Her spices and coffee came whole, leaving her to grind them by hand before use. She also had to haul all the water, slaughter the chickens, and keep the children from breaking the eggs or falling into the fire.

Clothing was a particular burden. While Phebe was possibly freed from the daily spinning and weaving poorer women still practiced, she nonetheless faced the cutting and stitching by hand of every article of clothing for her family's backs. (It is hardly surprising wardrobes were small those days, often a costume for the week, one for church, and no underwear.) Worse was the burden of laundry. Whereas non-Dutch settlers, being less fussy about personal cleanliness, might handle it only once a month, Phebe would demand more frequent sudsings of her family's clothes. It was a day to shush the children away, have the older take the younger ones on a long walk, while she lugged the pails of water, filled the iron pots, heated them to near boiling, loaded the tubs, and plunged her arms into the brew to scrub away with homemade soap. Dainty hands were not common then among women of her class.

Unlike their fellow English settlers, Dutch women held a more equal position in their households. The duke of York had allowed them to continue both their practice of owning property after marriage and inheriting, rights no woman of English descent had ever enjoyed. By now, with the formation of the new country such legal freedoms had been eliminated; still, within Dutch-based communities the status of women had not deteriorated. Wives of village shopkeepers were partners in business with their husbands, and wives of farmers held a strong voice in the management of money. Consequently, Cornelius would have consulted with Phebe about his small ferry service. Should that young man down the road be hired? Should we raise the fare for a bundle of wheat? Neighbors considered Phebe the more competent adult in the family, more resourceful and industrious than her husband. She grew cabbages and turnips for the Manhattan market and kept the proceeds as her own, accumulating a sizeable nest egg. One story asserts that on a day the improvident Cornelius appeared in the kitchen and confessed to considerable betting debts, frugal Phebe pulled $3,000 out of a secret cache in a grandfather's clock and paid them off.

Typical of Dutch parents of the day, Phebe was permissive. Both visiting foreigners and Yankees criticized the Dutch for giving their children too free a hand, for not restricting their impulses. Thus Phebe neither cowed her children into submission, the New England practice, nor drilled them into decorum, the preference in the South. Nor would she, like Yankee women, supervise too closely, frown upon too much frivolity, or keep the sexes separate at play. The sight of her boys and girls together picking berries in fields, skating on frozen farm ponds, and bowling in freshly mown fields would bring a smile, not a switch. The result was a highly congenial family life, where the children, lacking fear of the harsh physical punishment common elsewhere in the young nation, were loving and respectful of their parents.

While Phebe saw to the children's religious education, the church was a less dark and foreboding version of Calvinism. Despite centering their community around the local church, the Dutch were less rigid about Sunday attendance and evidence of true devotion. The family would attend regularly, but if a Sunday came when the weather tempted sitting on the porch instead, an activity not forbidden by Sabbath rules, it would be entered without guilt. The children's catechism was essentially rote learning of creed and biblical passages, with little emphasis on proof of faith.

Nor did the Dutch place much value on education or culture. The local church controlled the schoolroom, where supplies were sparse and the schoolmaster so poorly paid that he would pick in the fields after hours. Hard benches and flogging were poor competition for the tempting opportunities of field, creek, and forest. Many adults were illiterate and showed little interest in painting or music, arts much admired in other parts of the colonies. Except for the wealthy, their speech was notably ungrammatical and crude, given to colorful oaths. Cornelius, Jr., joined his friends in flouting authority and playing *hoekies* from school. He was an obstinate and disobedient boy who preferred the outdoors, becoming an expert bareback rider, swimmer, oarsman, and rock climber by the age of ten. He was so barely literate that throughout life he kept business matters of the most complex accounting in his head and depended on secretaries to handle both reading and writing of letters.

The lad likely read one book, or at least looked at its illustrations: *Aristotle's Masterpiece,* perhaps the most prominent underground text of the day. Written anonymously in seventeenth-century England, its pseudomedical descriptions of sexual intercourse and woodcuts of the female body drew a furtive readership. His sexual education would also have been expanded by a rich oral tradition of the bawdy songs, jokes, and poems that children then, as now, joyfully shared among one another. (The foreign travelers who commented upon the Americans' straitlaced sexuality had simply missed this flourishing private ribaldry.) Given the boy's later strong erotic drive, one suspects he was sexually active as an adolescent.

The boy's real education may have ended in 1805, when he was eleven. That year his oldest brother died, and a mourning Phebe channeled all her lost affection the more onto this second and surviving son. Whereas before she indulged, now she coddled. He adored her in return and became something of a mama's boy, with one exception—he did not care for the farm work she expected of him. But apart from that, until her death at age 87, in 1854, her word was the only one he would ungrudgingly obey. As he matured, with his heavy-lidded eyes and drooping underlip he came to closely resemble this favorite parent.

Young Cornelius wanted to join his father, who gave his now-eldest son lessons in cleverness and manipulation. Knowing the boy was anxious for the chance to sail the family produce boat that carried corn and hay to Manhattan, one day his father told him to show up at the wharf early the next morning with a friend. They arrived, excited over the good times ahead of them in the city, only to hear his father order them instead to pitch hay and pile it on the wharf in exchange for the promise of a future trip. This lesson in double-dealing stuck with the boy, who would recount in old age how he and his friend had fun that day but "were just as tired that night as if we had been working."[5] In fact, however much he found pleasure in sport and play, the young Cornelius did not stint work. With a ne'er-do-well for a father, he was quick to find odd jobs to help the family survive the inevitable periods when his father would either earn no money or lose it. At that time, the law allowed whatever income children earned to be possessed by the parents, and the boy handed his money over as his rightful duty and without resentment.

Living on the waterfront, the boy grew impassioned about the sea. His first application of his prodigious memory, which would serve him well throughout his life, was in the identification of sailing craft. He amazed neighbors with his ability to identify the type of craft and owner of all the ships moving in and out of the harbor beyond. By age sixteen, unhappy with farm labor and his father's refusal to let him have a major responsibility on the ferry, the tall, muscular, and ruggedly handsome Cornelius, Jr., could wait no longer for his maturity. He asked his mother's permission to go to sea. The sailor's life was particularly difficult in those days because the British navy, suffering a severe shortage of men as a result of its poor food and brutal discipline, had taken to stopping American ships and forcibly removing sailors whom they claimed to be British subjects. Pirates also roamed about the ocean waters, pillaging ships and murdering crews. Fretting for her son's welfare, Phebe urged him to find another way to satisfy his longing and was pleased when he returned to request a loan to buy a periauger, a two-masted sailing barge he planned to convert into a ferry. Phebe agreed on condition he plow, harrow, and plant eight acres of untilled land within the next few weeks. By hiring friends to help him, he met the deadline and bought the boat. Thus on the 27th of May, 1810, Cornelius Vanderbilt, Jr. (though he often spelled it Van Derbilt), became self-supporting, his own man.

The Commodore
Creates Himself

That Cornelius, Jr., was a visionary is evident. The clannish Dutch ways could not hold this youth, who scanned the Narrows waters and masted crafts sailing upon them and who understood the role of the boats carrying raw materials, goods, and people up the rivers, through inlets, and along the coastline of the growing nation. He discerned that whereas his mother and neighbors were bound to the soil, his father's sight limited to get-rich schemes, other Americans were not so immobile. They would need transportation not only to move their food and merchandise but to stock new settlements.

He picked a good time to enter the business. At first he served the larger estates on the islands, sailing from New Dorp through the Narrows between Staten Island and Brooklyn and up to the Battery. New York City, then with a population of 96,000, had great need for the foodstuffs and hay he piled on the wharves, and Staten Islanders were beginning to travel to the city to shop or in a few cases commute to work. He became known for the punctuality of his service and his skill in getting people across the waters in the fiercest storms. At the end of the first season he was able to repay his mother the $1,000 for the periauger and $1,000 besides. For himself he kept only half the money earned on nighttime freight runs. Nonetheless, soon he had three ferries that could move larger amounts of goods and people more safely than the little periauger.

History assisted when war provided the circumstance to accelerate his profits. Forts were going up around the bay to protect the city from the British, who were angry over President Madison's refusal to stop trade with France. He gained not only exemption from military service but also the lucrative contract to supply the six forts during what became known as the War of 1812. During this time the young man also gained a reputation for courage and daring. He delivered messages and goods in weather others avoided; he sailed unsafe craft to turn a profit. He was a colorful figure on the waterfront, known to face any challengers and overcome them through sheer force of personality and a barrage of profanities. The word compromise was not in his vocabulary; he was rude, un-civil, and tactless with his customers. The bullheaded self-confidence that was to serve him well later became the dominant feature of his character. The waterfront salts responded by dubbing him the Commodore, a nickname that stuck as he became more successful (and which we shall use to refer to him from this point). Following the conflict's close, he expanded his line to include shipping along the Atlantic Coast, delivering food to cities and towns that could not get it as quickly in any other way.

To seal his final independence from his parents, the young entrepreneur decided he must start a family of his own. His heart led him to a cousin, Sophia Johnson. When he made his desire to marry her known to his mother, she objected, arguing that the consanguinity would not be healthy for any offspring. With his usual winning ways, he persuaded Phebe to grant her approval. Thus at age nineteen on December 19, 1813, he wed Sophia in a simple ceremony. There was no honeymoon. He promptly made her pregnant, a state she was to experience thirteen times.

Proof of the saying "Anonymous was a woman," Sophia left behind for the curious little evidence of her temperament or feelings. Only one likeness survives, that taken in her later years. Hence one can only surmise how it was for her to live with her in-laws and husband's five younger siblings in that small Stapleton cottage. Despite the myth that has come down concerning early American life, it was neither common nor accepted for two generations of the same family to live under the same roof. Phebe would have run the household and, given her strong will, may well have treated her daughter-in-law Sophia as a convenient addition to the domestic service staff. A devoted family member, for many years following his marriage the Commodore continued to provide for the support of his parents and siblings, particularly his brother Jacob, who also entered shipping.

Fortunately, the postwar boom boosted Sophia's fortunes. Although no engineer or draftsman, the Commodore had a talent for boat design and commissioned several ships ranging from twenty-two to thirty-two tons for use as ferries or short coastal runs. These sloops and schooners took such loads as machinery from the north to bring back melons from South Carolinia, or barrels of salted shad from the Delaware River to sell in North Jersey. Although most of the money went into expanding the business, not improving the living conditions of the growing family, Sophia shared her husband's natural prudence and belief that such investment would pay in the long run.

In 1818, the Commodore reflected on the state of shipping and determined it was time to sell the sailing ships and move to steam. In 1807, when Robert Fulton took his steamboat *North River* from Albany to New York, shaving twenty-five hours off the thirty-hour trip, the death knell for the masted ships began tolling. Steamers soon proved effective on the Mississippi and the ocean. The young venturer also foresaw the impact canals would bring on trade. Although the first attempt, between the Santee River and Cooper River in South Carolina, ultimately failed, others succeeded in providing more efficient routes for the new faster boats. In 1817, Governor De Witt Clinton of New York authorized construction of that major transportation link across the state, the Erie Canal. That connection would ultimately secure for New York City its role as the major port in the nation.

During these initial years, indeed for many to come, steamboats were unpredictable, often dangerous craft. Boilers would explode, the resulting shrapnel maiming and killing and the steam searing people alive. Cautious, not willing to follow the more foolhardy, the Commodore entered the service of Thomas Gibbons in order to learn more about this unstable infant technology. At that time Robert Fulton and Robert Livingston had gained exclusive rights from the New York legislature over steam traffic in New York waters, including the right to collect royalties from approved vessels and the prerogative to seize any vessel they did not license. Gibbons's line thus ran between New Brunswick and Elizabeth, where passengers from Philadelphia and points south who had come by way of the Raritan Canal or by stagecoach then transferred to monopoly-approved boats for the remainder of the trip to New York.

Gibbons had been a wealthy lawyer and planter who left Savannah to settle in Elizabeth, New Jersey, where he entered the steamboat business. An eccentric, he once sued his son-in-law for refusing to make a public statement that he had not seduced his daughter before their marriage. The daughter sided with her husband, both sides spreading stories and threatening libel suits against one another for years. The Commodore's relationship with Gibbons was rather formal, as this excerpt from a letter indicates (and aptly demonstrates his illiteracy):

Sir the reason of my writing you of this business now is that I have sean Lawance

& Co and if the boat is to be dun this winter they must no as quick as possible so that they may prepair Stuff in time. You will reccolect the bellona must be halled up weather you have hir 12 feet longer or no inorder to repair hir bottom that is if you do hir Justice I understood from William that She would be halled up at al events if you was willing.[6]

Though both men were equally stubborn and obstinate, somehow they forged a congenial working partnership.

As part of the arrangement, the Commodore took over an inn named Bellona Hall at the New Brunswick terminus, putting Sophia in charge of its daily operation. Thus encumbered by two small daughters, she took on the tasks of food preserving, sewing, cooking, cleaning, and laundering for not only her family but also for guests. Her firstborn son, William Henry, was born there in 1821.

Sophia's management was highly capable, and the inn brought good profit for the first time in its history. Considering the state of such establishments in those days, the task may not have been very difficult. Complaints about filthy beds swarming with bugs and other vermin not on the bill of fare were familiar lines in traveler's letters and diaries. The simple addition of more frequent scrubbing and laundering—such innovations as heating stones for the beds and tasteful cooking, not the begristled, bony, insect-laden stews travelers found elsewhere—put Bellona Hall well ahead of its competitors. The establishment was so successful that Gibbons agreed to expand the building with an addition of fourteen rooms. With three guests to a room (and as was the practice then, often strangers in the same bed), the inn added quickly to the family's prosperity. Thus, the base of the eventual Vanderbilt family fortune was built from Sophia's labor as well as that of her husband.

The Commodore was proving profitable as well for his employer. Very likely the more timid Gibbons had hired the Commodore in the hope that the blustery young man would effectively challenge the New York monopoly. If so, he got his wish. In defiance of Fulton and Livingston, the Commodore regularly sailed the steamers *Mouse* and *Bellona* directly into New York City. For several dozen trips he eluded the lawmen waiting at the dock by hiding in secret compartments as the ship pulled into port. Making game of the dare, he once left his crew at the final New Jersey stop and put a woman at the helm. And he must have had a good laugh upon hearing her describe the flabbergasted look on the arresting officers' faces. Another time he submitted to officials, but when testifying at Albany produced paperwork to show that on the particular day in question his ship was licensed to a subcontractor of the monopoly. As if these maneuvers were not enough, he regularly flew a "NEW JERSEY MUST BE FREE" banner from the *Bellona*. This successful jockeying exhilarated the young steamboat captain, who found his calling in life as a result: he would steal power from the already powerful.

Law suits ensued. In 1824 the case was argued before the United States Supreme Court in *Ogden vs. Gibbons.* (Aaron Ogden, a licensee of the New York monopoly, had once been Gibbons's competitor in New Jersey and had been engaged in a fierce battle with him for years.)[7] Daniel Webster argued on behalf of Gibbons before the great jurist and then head of the Court, John Marshall. The issue was whether the state of New York could restrict trade and thus impede nationwide commerce. Marshall ruled in favor of Gibbons. He concluded that although the federal government could not interfere with the internal trade of states, one could not conceive of a system for regulating commerce that did not include navigation. Because the monopoly interfered with coastwise shipping, the Constitution prevailed. Gibbons's ships were properly registered with federal authorities, noted Marshall, consequently the means by which they were propelled should be of no concern to the state of New York. The opinion was one of the most significant in Supreme Court history. In one swoop it disrupted an unpopular monopoly, prevented the fragmentation of commerce by states, deterred states from impeding a new technology, and most important, legitimized the notion of interstate commerce regulated on the federal level.

If the young Commodore played a major role in this landmark decision to expand federal powers over the economy in the promotion of business enterprise, he was less likely concerned with the principle than with the result. Within a year forty-three other steamers ran the waters once reserved for the New York monopolists, many of them belonging to Gibbons.

Unfortunately, Gibbons did not live long to enjoy the fruits of victory. He died in 1826, and the Commodore continued to run the line for his heirs until 1829. At that point, he decided the profits of his labor should go to him alone.

The Family
Fortunes Expand

Now thirty-five, the Commodore, with Sophia's wise management, had saved enough money to start his own steamboat line, which for the next twenty years would radiate out from New York. His very entry into the commerce drove out some competitors, while others bribed him to keep out of their territory. He soon came upon tactics that proved unbeatable. He would depress rates until his competition could not hold on, then buy them out; or he would cut service and wages to a minimum to reduce costs. Finding cheap ticket fares and even free meals on some lines, travelers crowded onto his decks.

Starting his own business meant moving the family from New Brunswick to New York City so he could be close to the waterfront. Although household servants eased Sophia's toil, she was not happy to leave Bellona Inn for a virtual tenement on Stone Street in the Battery, to be followed by a small house on East Broadway. Always happier in clannish communities, she found living conditions in New York to be, for the most part, unappealing.

With its population increased by recent spurts in immigration, the city was now home to more than a quarter of a million souls, most living below Twenty-third Street. Then as now, it was a city devoted to progress, to destroying its past to make room for the new. "The whole of New York is rebuilt about once in ten years," remarked one mayor of the time.[8] Consequently, a mansion might adjoin a farmhouse and barn, which would soon be replaced by other brown-stones, which in a few years might be torn down to make way for stores and boutiques. Nonetheless, the hills, oaks, elms, and grassy plots and fields retained the mark of nature in the bustling citizenry's lives. However noisy and crowded some streets, the changing foliage and seasonal habits of the birds marked the passage of the seasons and added to the pleasantness of a stroll. Indeed, so lush was the greenery that it was known as the Garden City of the nation.

It was not a place for people who preferred uniformity and pattern to their lives. In the streets, pigs; chickens; ice men; porters wheeling handcarts; horse-drawn gigs; phaetons, and carriages; and pedestrians all competed for space. Wandering through this confusion, boys hawked newspapers, milkmen called "Milk, ho!" 'bakers announced their wares, and peddlers sang their individual songs of their exquisite clams, strawberries, pineapples, or sweet potatoes. The pavement stones, polished to a sheen from all this traffic, also tendered piles of steaming manure and garbage to sully the soles of the top-hatted gentlemen and the hems of the ladies' silk skirts. So picturesque was the crowd that visitor Charles Dickens exclaimed that he had never in his extensive travels seen such a rich display of color and luxury. As a modest and unaffected countrywoman, Sophia had little interest in such showing off.

In June of 1832, a calamity occurred that may have provoked the family's decision to live on Staten Island. Cholera had struck. That month, a mother who was healthy in the morning could be dead by sundown, having suffered acute diarrhea, uncontrollable vomiting, violent abdominal cramps, chilled extremities, and the delirium of dehydration before succumbing. Because those who were better off normally drank bottled water, they were much less at risk to the disease. Nonetheless, they panicked and fled to the surrounding countryside, leaving the poor in a ghost town where, by July, grass sprouted on once-crowded boulevards.

The Commodore and Sophia had the old family homestead to return to, and Phebe was still alive (Cornelius, Sr., having recently died), albeit in a nicer house her favorite son had built especially for her on the property. He may have set the family up in the farm cottage while a new residence was being built nearby. In 1839, Sophia took her brood to their new home.

The structure testified to the family's tremendous prosperity.[9] Adult children raised in the farm cottage or the inn returned to visit their parents in a mansion; the youngest children grew up in a comfort that only the wealthiest in the country could experience. The house had much to recommend its being dubbed the finest residence on the island. As the Commodore was not known for notice of his surroundings, Sophia was likely the guiding figure in the design and decor. Certainly it suggests the attraction to art and architecture later to emerge in the family line was linked to her influence.

Coming up the walk, a visitor faced a fifty-foot square structure with forty-foot high fluted Grecian columns along the front portico, a favorite decoration of the period. The business of the owner was marked by a glass painting over the front door of the Commodore's favorite boat, the *Cleopatra.* Once inside, the guest entered a central hallway made resplendent by the graceful lines of a spiral staircase that culminated in an oval on the top floor. The doors to the parlor were rosewood, with handmade English silver knobs and steel locks. The parlor itself, like all the other rooms, had a twelve-foot ceiling, and it boasted a fireplace mantle of imported Egyptian marble. The rarest imported woods were used throughout the interior, with perfect fitting done by English carpenters brought over for the job.

The grounds were as gracious as the interior. The house was set on a rise from which one could see beyond the surrounding stone and iron wall to the bay beyond. Gardeners planted mature horse chestnuts and linden trees about the property to frame the view.

Certainly the Commodore was not present very much, for he maintained offices in the city and may well have spent nights there when convenient. When he did appear at home, both the children and Sophia stifled any natural enthusiasms, for his breeding was clearly more the result of erotic relief than an interest in offspring. He was not the kind of father who would make moral homilies at the dinner table and read Bible stories before the fire on Sundays. Instead, he would bully and shout, intimidate and mock. He cared more about his horses than his own flesh and blood.

He probably ignored the eight girls, to their advantage. His attitude best expressed itself years later the day he told one daughter that he did not consider her children, all girls, to be Vanderbilts because they could not carry on his name. (As will be seen, his final testament would bear further proof of his unconcern for his daughters.) That they grew up to make contented marriages suggests Sophia may have been the key in nurturing their self-esteem and stability.

One feature of the family stands out: it resisted the tumultuous cultural currents affecting so many other families of the day. They lived unmarked by the great reforms, the efforts to reduce alcohol consumption, to open more schools to educate poorer children, to remove unsanitary conditions from the cities, to take a stand against slavery, to press for women's rights. Nor had they much use for culture, of sharing literature and music. The prints and paintings on the walls were of landscapes or of patriotic themes hung for ornamental purposes, a reflection of the family's commitment to national values.

Rather, it was under Sophia's influence a most domestic family, inturned, content to stay within the insularity of home. She exemplified what historians would later call the Cult of True Womanhood. According to these precepts, the ideals every woman should attain were purity in thought and action, piety, submission to father and husband, and domesticity. These ideals reflected a considerable shift from the 1700s, a time when it was possible for a woman to be described as strong, tough, independent, and hardy, without implying any criticism (Phebe being a good example). By the 1800s, any attributes shared between the sexes were forgotten; differences were emphasized. Consequently, Sophia and her friends learned from magazines, newspapers, and everyday talk that the true woman was delicate, timid, modest, sweet, and required protection. Such women, whose sphere of activities was confined to the home, were called "ladies," whereas those who strayed were deemed "unsexed," a fearsome epithet.[10]

Further proof of Sophia's commitment to the cult of domesticity is her having brought so many children to term. Birth control was widespread at the time, the most widely used practices being *coitus interruptus* and rhythm. If a woman was married to a man like the Commodore, a man unlikely to subdue his sexual passion, then abortion was readily available and acceptable. Besides surgical abortions performed by doctors, over-the-counter potions were readily available and folk methods of self-induction well-known. A well-to-do woman like Sophia could also choose to go to a spa, where a special regimen of repeated hot baths, massage, and douching might provoke spontaneous abortion.

Eight daughters only added to feminization of the family. If True Womanhood isolated women from the rest of the world, it recompensed some by encouraging congenial and convivial relationships among women. Consequently, mothers and daughters then knew little of the emotional tensions found in modern times. Because motherhood was a woman's most important job, daughters, facing a similar future, in turn devoted themselves to their mothers. This little circle of sweet and pious Vanderbilt women drew tight to protect one another from the fierce paternal temper.

Rage struck most of all at the sons. Two of them particularly bore the brunt of their father's arrogant and nasty disposition. Eldest son William H. was not fast enough on his feet for his father, who was quick with mockery and ridicule.[11] If anything saved William H., it was his plodding, patient, phlegmatic temperament. While his father wailed and belittled, he stood quietly with only a slight high whine from his breath to give away his suppressed discomfort. This seemingly passive temperament riled the father even more, provoking yet a longer string of colorful condemnations. Yet oddly, as will be shown shortly, William did not turn to his mother for protection, for he shared his father's poor estimate of her.

William H.'s behavior disguised a will as strong as his father's. In his late teens he became a bookkeeper for the banking firm of Daniel Drew (who was to become his father's major nemesis in later years). Impressing Drew with his methodical and meticulous service, he saw his salary climb from $300 the first year to $1,000 the third, several times the wages of a craftsman of the time. A pious man, he was attracted not to the brightly dressed young women who delighted Charles Dickens but to a demure and plainly adorned Maria Louis Kissam, the daughter of a noted Brooklyn clergyman. She had many of the same qualities as his mother and his sisters, a devotion to domesticity and godliness.

They married in 1841. Unfortunately, despite his great earnings, William H. had not saved much money. Upon hearing of his son's spendthrift ways, the Commodore refused the couple any assistance, so they took a small furnished room on East Broadway. However, in 1842 William H. collapsed in severe mental exhaustion from his banking job, and his father sent him to manage the farm in Staten Island. There he again figured the son who "didn't amount to a row of pins" would barely make do. In fact, William H.'s attention to detail ensured prosperity, and the fields burst forth with approval. His fertility extended to the home, where Maria would bring forth eight children.

While William H. quietly went about earning his own fortune, his younger brother Cornelius Jeremiah set on a path of perpetual waywardness. "I'd give a hundred dollars if he'd never been named Corneel," his father is said to have remarked.[12] The lad, born later into the family when money was freer, became an itinerant gambler, a frequenter of faro tables, fancy restaurants, and the brothels on Greene Street in the city. In his various callings he failed as a law clerk, leather merchant, farmer, and revenue agent. Given this record it is hard not to brand him a wastrel, as his father was quick to do.

"He is a very smart fellow, but he has a cog out," the Commodore frequently observed. The missing cog, however, was epilepsy. Unlike Sophia, the Commodore was unwilling to make any move to understand or sympathize with the affliction, which was severely disruptive in the absence of anticonvulsive drugs. Instead, he berated and accused the young man, held him responsible for his fits, and periodically ordered him carted him off to an asylum. Seen in this light, Cornelius Jeremiah's failed attempts to settle in an occupation were understandable. (While the crusty father cursed this troubled son, others took to him sympathetically. In later years Horace Greeley, the kindly editor, regularly lent Cornelius Jeremiah funds. Furious over this benefaction, the Commodore one day confronted the editor and warned him not to expect any payment back from his quarters. "Who the devil asked you?" Greeley shot back. "Have I?")[13]

Indeed, only one child of the twelve surviving to adulthood was to soften the Commodore's heart, his youngest son, George Washington. From earliest days George exhibited none of the faults of his older brothers; he was quick minded, lively, attractive, and physically adept, the closest in appearance and temperament to his talented father. Though he was last in line, the Commodore clearly had him marked to be his heir. As the baby, he was also Sophia's pride.

In 1844, to the surprise of Sophia and the children, the Commodore sold his ferry business to the Staten Island Warehouse Company and moved his family once again to Manhattan. His success was now public knowledge. By the 1840s the word *millionaire* was a familiar term in the American vocabulary. It was probably first applied to tobacconist Pierre Lorillard, but within a few years it was so common a term as to be used without quotes. The 1845 edition of *The Wealth and Biography of the Wealthy Citizens of New York City* credited banker August Belmont with $100,000, shipowner E. K. Collins with $200,000, and merchant A. T. Stewart with $400,000. But that of the Commodore was placed at $1,200,000, "of an old Dutch root, Cornelius has evinced more energy in building and driving steamboats and other projects than ever one single Dutchman possessed. It takes our American hot suns to clear up the vapors and fogs of the Zuyder Zee and wake up the phlegm of a descendant of old Holland."[14] Still, this was paltry income in light of real estate magnate John Jacob Astor, who jounced the scales at $20 million.

Despite his wealth, the Commodore felt the sting of exclusion from the Knickerbockers, that self-selected society descended from seventeenth-century Dutch settlers.[15] The Vanderbilts along with the Schylers, Schermerhorns, and Livingstons had entered this country with colonial Dutch land grants, but unlike the latter, the Vanderbilts had stayed on the land. Most important, they failed to resettle in Manhattan after the Revolution, to buy up property for development, and to acquire the manners of genteel society. That the Commodore exuded the outlandish individualism and crudeness of the countryside was too much a reminder of the Knickerbockers' actual roots. So while his family was part of that four percent of New York City that owned eighty percent of its individual wealth, the Vanderbilts were not welcome in the brownstone parlors of the Breevorts or Van Rensselaers.

The persistance of certain Dutch ways on Knickerbocker life-style in the mid-1800s was evident. The women were less likely than wives and daughters of middle-class merchants and craftsmen to parade in the colorful silks Dickens admired, but wore simple untrimmed dresses and shawls, the effect of which was to completely conceal "any charm of figure or grace of outline . . . a timid maiden might possess."[16] Their bonnets, which resembled coal scuttles, and their heavily fringed parasols further obscured their faces from view of passers-by. For men, the only proper dress on any occasion, be it office, church, parlor, or ball, was a high beaver hat, white, stiff-collared shirtfront, black frock coat, tight black pantaloons, high, narrow pointed boots, black gloves, and black cane. Mood and manners matched these funereal figures. They distrusted fancy food, waltzing, and fine art. They were cultish, constructing within that polyglot city a neighborhood of sameness, where neighbors grew up together, went to school together, married one another, grew old together, and were buried together. They retained old Dutch virtues of thrift, industriousness, modesty, and sobriety, while they condemned idleness, luxury, and ostentation. They greatly feared outsiders, be they Bowery Boys, Irish laborers, or newly arrived rich, such as the Vanderbilts.

The Commodore's desire to be accepted can be seen in the design of the home he ordered to be constructed at 10 Washington Place, a stark and unadorned brick four-story townhouse. Though more costly than the Staten Island mansion, it followed the practice of understatement that was common to the old-line Knickerbockers. The interior fourteen rooms were decorated in a cluttered, unostentatious late-Federal fashion. Moldings and mantles followed the spare and elegant lines of Greek revival, with an American eagle here and there to proclaim patriotic pride. Without this move he would have remained a millionaire, albeit a small one. One wonders what impelled this man at the half-century mark to foresake his more luxurious family homestead and enter into a life of much-heightened activity. Little is known of his inclinations at this time, save evidence he was not happy with Sophia. Perhaps that personal disgruntlement, and not solely the needs of business, was the motive.

Sophia once again objected to the move. She preferred the countryside, with its congenial community, its Dutch values, the Moravian congregation. The city was even noisier than in the early 1830s, dirtier, with pigs roaming freely to scavenge the garbage, and despite the cholera epidemics, still rather lacking in municipal water delivery and sanitary improvements. Prostitutes strolled even the best streets, and within a short walk of their affluent neighborhood were hovels filled with hoodlums and immigrants, stinking tanning establishments, and fly-attracting slaughterhouses. Piles of manure still baked in the streets (Vanderbilt scows carted it to Staten Island to fertilize the fields), while the profusion of caterpillars eating the shade trees overhead frequently dropped on the pedestrians below, causing them to squirm and squeal.

The Commodore could overlook these deficiencies because of New York's development into a city of unique and distinct personality in the growing nation. A comparison with Boston emphasizes its uniqueness. That venerable bay community had long served the model for other cities in the colonies. Boston was born of the Puritan fathers with their dream for close-knit communities where love of God united neighbor over selfishness. Rich and poor alike shared in politics at the town meeting, and the rich were careful not to hide their advantage behind restrained dress, dislike of flashy decor, and homes with simple facades to mask the comforts within. Boston's values emphasized respect for learning, as shown by the speedy establishment of Harvard College in 1636, and the printed word, as evidenced by its being the center of publishing.

New York, by contrast, was settled by an assortment of people for whom profit came first—pirates, smugglers, slave traders, and royal appointment seekers. Virtue was neither a common nor praiseworthy word in their vocabulary. The remarks of Bostonian John Adams fifty years earlier remained true. If he admitted the people were hospitable, he approved less of their extraordinary display of wealth, their frequent and tiring socializing, and their general lack of good breeding. "They talk very loud, very fast, and altogether," he opined.[17] When they were not rushing off to visit one another, they were busy shopping or selling. And most striking, not a single New Yorker thought to direct Adams to view a college, church, or bookshop.

Whereas Bostonians worshiped the moral and well-considered life, New Yorkers were frankly and unashamedly devoted to the art of making money by any means. And if the city pressed its men to grab and acquire, the city, state, and federal governments all operated as if to send out invitations: "Rob the public!" The Commodore joined many other businessmen in accepting the welcome.

By the time he resettled in New York, the Commodore had ocean steamers running up and down the Atlantic coasts, including some runs meeting contracts to carry mail. The postal system then was essentially private, with Congress underwriting all the capital expenses. Thus the steamship owners bought or built boats and established new lines without financial risk while the tax-paying public received no share in the profits. A steamer carrying mail, after all, also carried fare-paying passengers and goods. Politicians supporting this system argued that establishing such transportation routes was necessary for building commerce in the new nation, the advantages of speedy mail delivery being payment enough to the citizenry. Ignoring the costs to social equality, they were right. It was a good time for men like the Commodore.

A Grievance Is
Made upon Sophia

Now beyond childbearing age, Sophia no longer suited her husband's carnal needs. Household servants fled from from his grasping hands and puckering lips. In 1846, rumors spread around New York that he had fallen madly in love with young George's governess. Wishing Sophia out of the way, the Commodore urged her to travel to spas to handle her "change of life." She happily packed her trunks and took off, but the governess wisely refused to stay in the house in Sophia's absence. It was William H., the only child not to object to the Commodore's actions, who found a more agreeable young woman to satisfy his father's wishes. "The old man is bound to have his way, and it is useless to oppose him," he remarked when questioned about his complicity.[18]

When Sophia returned from her pilgrimage, however, the Commodore decided she was insane and confined her to an asylum in Flushing. (Such incarceration was then a convenience affluent men used to dispose of unwanted wives.) To his dismay, the physicians pronounced Sophia of sound mind and refused to keep her locked up, and, worse, Phebe gave him a terrific scolding for his chicanery and cruelty. How Sophia reacted to this ill treatment is unknown. It was outspokenness over the move to the city that had gotten her in trouble, so perhaps she simply shut up. Possibly the other children swooped around and let their father know he had been out of bounds. Whatever, in later years her husband would use the asylum as a punishment only for Corneel. It is hard to believe relations in the family could be peaceable following such a brute show of authority on the patriarch's part.

It appears a *modus vivendi* was established, whereby the Commodore did what he wished and let the family go about its own ways. Thus when he went to Nicaragua to set up his western passage there (gaining several days off his competitors' crossing of Panama), he departed without informing Sophia and neglected to communicate with her while he was gone. If he found other outlets for his carnality, they were kept secret. Meanwhile, Sophia took consolation among her many daughters, most now married and bringing grandchildren to visit her.

During these visits, one wonders if the conversations took into account certain sensational ideas being decried in the New York press. Up and down the coast in recent years, certain women had been shocking the public with their claims for women's equality. In 1845, Margaret Fuller wrote of the decline of women's position in the United States, "Now there is no woman, only an over-grown child."[19] In 1848, the first women's rights meeting in the United States was held in Seneca Falls, New York, during which a proclamation was drawn up, declaring that the "history of mankind is a history of repeated injuries and usur-pations on the part of man toward woman." In 1849, Lucretia Mott decried that woman had been so long "degraded by personal bondage, she hugs her chains."[20]

The Vanderbilt daughters, gathered about in a parlor to talk free of hus-bands' and father's influence, must have discussed these ideas in their conversa-tions. As properly reserved gentleladies of the day, they would seem inclined to question and discredit the charges of the outspoken women activists. But they were also of Dutch heritage, which was more felicitous toward the notion of female competence, and they had in their mother and grandmother two strong examples of such. That some of the Commodore's daughters were swayed by this new feminist influence would emerge in their later actions.

2

1849-1869

The Family Fancies
Itself Aristocracy

In the spring of 1849, an event erupted in New York that dramatized the growing gap between rich and poor in the nation. The circumstance concerned a theatrical feud focused upon William Macready, a British actor who liked to affect aristrocratic airs offstage, and Edwin Forrest, an American blood-and-thunder thespian who drew huzzahs from the working class and the Bowery Boy gangs. Thinking Macready's fans were trying to form an aristocracy in America, on May 7, 1849, Forrest's fans attended a performance of *Macbeth* and threw eggs, lemons, apples, pennies, and chairs at "the English hog." Forced to leave the theater, Macready vowed to return on May 10, and did so. By then, rumors and handbills had stirred up a mob of between ten and twenty thousand outside the theater. The militia was called, which exchanged bullets for the rioters' rocks. By evening's end, thirty-one people lay dead, and more than a hundred had been injured.

In its editorial about what became known as Massacre Place, the *Herald* deplored the wealthy, who shocked "our plain American notions of decency and propriety, as they flaunt their finery in the voluptuous movements of some newly imported meretricious dance" and imported "the same offensive system which prevails in the aristocratic capitals of Europe."[1]

Neither the Knickerbockers nor the Vanderbilts paid any notice. Indeed, in 1853, the Commodore determined to one-up European aristocracy in the form of taking his entire family, with the exception of an ailing Phebe, invalid daughter Frances, and renegade son Cornelius Jeremiah, on a fairy tale journey across the Atlantic for the Grand Tour. His proclaimed purpose was a patriotic one, to demonstrate to the Old World that "the real character of our people has been misunderstood."[2] He wished to demonstrate the optimism of the proud young country, now enjoying a prosperity to be envied in the old homelands. He shared with public opinion of the day a belief that fashion would soon desert the passé capitals of Europe to reestablish itself in New York. The Commodore determined to lead the way in that shifting of social power and recognition, as well as to upstage the Knickerbockers by being the first wealthy American family to be acknowledged by the old aristocracy.

To ensure Europe would pay attention, the Commodore built for this voyage the *North Star,* a private yacht to outclass all others on the seas. Following a tour of the cabins, New York reporters gushed over the likely effect of a mere private citizen of the United States sailing into a major port in a ship as large as major European naval vessels. As sumptuous as it was large, the *North Star* started what was to be a long and acclaimed family tradition in yachting. Two nations were represented in its decor. First, the United States, of course, was evident through such ornamentation as the dining saloon's ceiling with its medallion paintings of the essential and by now mythologized Americans: Columbus, Washington, Franklin, Clay, Calhoun, and Webster. Second, France predominated with its Louis XV furnishings, silk lambrequins and lace curtains, tapestries, and sculpture. Although the mass of the American population was descended from the British Isles, the Revolution was too close in mind to honor the designs of that nation. Wealthy Americans looked instead to Paris for their aesthetics as a way of both snubbing the English and honoring the French, who had figured so large in assistance toward the end of the Revolution.

As soon as the *North Star* slid into port, the London press dashed aboard and quickly conveyed their astonishment. Noting that the splendor of the yacht exceeded that of the queen's, the *Daily News* claimed the Vanderbilts were a sign of the times, America's replacing of the old aristocracy with *parvenus.* As a working-class paper, it was quick to make political play of their appearance. What the Vanderbilts proved, the editors suggested, was the "vicious condition of English society" in which "the cold shade of aristocracy" made those who had earned their own fortunes ashamed of such. "It is time that the *millionaire* should cease to be ashamed. It is time that the [English] middle classes should take the place which is their own in the world which they have made. Let them take example from America."[3]

True to form, the English ruling class for the most part avoided this "vulgar" family. The wealthy tradesmen did not. If the Vanderbilts did not meet English royalty directly, its members did have a chance to observe them at such events as the opera and at Ascot. They were not impressed. One family member sniffed how "divested of their rank and privileges, they [the royals] were only common clay after all."[4] It was a most American evaluation.

For the remainder of the summer the *North Star* steamed about European ports, drawing more public attention and acclaim, as well as invitations from major and minor aristrocrats. The family wandered through the Baltic Sea to St. Petersburg, then back to Copenhagen, down to Paris, through the Mediterranean with many island stops, ending at Constantinople before turning back. During visits to ruins and museums, family members developed a new interest in the visual arts, and William H. in particular realized he could own works for his everyday enjoyment.

Despite the impression the *North Star* voyage made abroad and at home, the Vanderbilts remained anathema to old society. While the girls found affluent mates, their new, English names reflected that exclusion: Cross, Allen, Thorn, Williams, Osgood, Torrance, La Bau, Barker, and Clark. It would take another generation before the word "Vanderbilt" was penned in an elegant hand on an invitation to a societal ball, and it would take a woman marrying into the family to accomplish the coup.

A Spirited Southern Belle Vexes Her Parents

While the *North Star* toured the European ports of call, the Vanderbilts would have been dismayed could they have known that the person who was to bring them their longed-for acceptance was just being born. Even more astonishing would have been the news that she was a Southerner, the latest addition to an affluent cotton-growing family. The babe's mother, Phoebe Ann Smith, a society matron in Mobile, Alabama, would have been similarly suprised, though delighted, could she have foreseen her daughter's future prosperity and fame.

The infant, named Alva, was the family's seventh child. In those days of high child mortality, a popular saying went that the seventh child would be the strongest, the mainstay of the family. This would prove to be the case for Phoebe Ann and her husband Murray. Four of their nine offspring died in infancy, and the others, except one, did not live to old age. But that one, Alva, was to live to eighty and fill each of the days of her fourscore years as though it were the only one. She was to become the mainstay for members not only of her parental family but of many others whose lives crossed hers, including those of the Vanderbilt family.

In 1853, when Alva was born, her birthright was that of any well-to-do southern female, and enough dash of romance filled her background to make her boast immodestly after she learned of it. Her father's line was originally of the Scottish Stirlings. Her great-grandmother, Margaret Stirling, had been raised by uncle James Erskine, Lord Alva, and his wife but was cast out of the family when she disgraced them by falling in love with a man beneath their class, Doctor Murray Forbes. The lovers eloped and settled in Virginia, where one of their daughters, Delia, married into the eminent Smith clan. Her son Murray became a lawyer who found himself a promising client in Robert Desha, who convinced the young man to leave the bar and manage his cotton exports.

Kentuckian Desha had that important souce of male southern pride, military accomplishment, in this case gained in the War of 1812. He was elected twice to the House of Representatives (although it must be remembered such elections then were less the voice of the people than the handpick of the powerful few) and managed a thriving cotton plantation. Joseph Desha, his brother, became governor of Kentucky.[5] Robert Desha provided Murray Smith with more than profitable work; he introduced him to granddaughter Phoebe Ann, who saw in the clever lawyer promise of social ambition to match her own. Spoiled and strong willed, she resolved to propel the family line into even greater prominence.

With the bride usually came wealth, for the law of the day gave a woman no existence apart from her husband. Once she left the church door, any money in her name was no longer hers. Phoebe Ann's father was a liberal-minded man, however, and gave her only slaves, not money, as a wedding gift. Instead, he set up a trust, of which she could control the income, with the principal to pass on to her children. This grant gave Phoebe Ann more power in relation to her husband than married women of the day normally held. It may explain the frequent evidence of her breaking away from expected behaviors. Although she wanted to succeed in high society circles, she never did so at cost to her individuality.

The Smiths moved to Mobile, the major exit point for cotton export. Bales from family lands filled barges floating down the Tongigbee, Mobile, Alabama, and Tensaw rivers to be loaded on the docks and shipped out from Mobile Bay, through the Gulf of Mexico, and on to be milled in England. It was a lucrative business.

The Smith home there, which would leave a lasting impression on Alva, was a classic southern city mansion, with spacious rooms, wide halls, casement windows, magnolia trees, and a separate bathhouse of marble. The way the light fell through the windows, the classic sense of proportion, the impression of nobility, all etched a model of security she was to seek out in later years. One of her earliest pleasures was going alone into the library, where she would take the large volumes of books and stand them this way and that, like blocks, forming imaginary buildings.

Alva was also particularly blessed, she would say in her old age, by her traditional well-to-do southern upbringing. She and her siblings had the run of the house and were not shut up away from their parents with nurses or governesses, as was common among the rich up north. The children took meals with their parents, slept near to them, and joined in conversation when other adults came to visit. There were nurses, likely slaves, but they did not supplant the companionship of adult relatives. Where the Commodore's grandchildren were being taught to be silent, to assent, to suffer quietly, to rein in passion, to practice piety on every day of their lives, not just on Sunday, Alva was permitted to ask questions at dinner and to disagree, to explore, to poke about the house and grounds and neighborhood, to come up with her own plans and ideas, to honor the Christian faith as a philosophy more than as a guidebook for daily living.

Still, the Smith children were not spoiled. Certain rules were inviolate, such as punctuality and honesty. Punishment could be harsh, and many times Alva went to bed with the bruise of a horsewhip on the back of her legs. But she did not resent the beatings, for she felt they were deserved.

And not just her parents helped shape her opinions. Significant was her godmother, who was invested in a ceremony of impressive solemnity and afterward took an active role in directing Alva's maturation. Every Sunday after church she arrived in an open barouche pulled by two long-tailed well-groomed horses led by coachman and slave. (Though a youngster, Alva had the discerning eye to notice the driver's livery was ill fitting.)

Alva accepted her privilege as a matter of course. She took for granted that some were put on this earth to serve and others, such as herself, to be served. On Sabbath afternoons she joined her godmother's son in tyrannizing slave children. She despised people who lived uncomplainingly with meek submission, and since this was her perception of slaves, she felt they deserved their poor position in society. In contrast, she respected the Indians who came to the city to sell their herbs and handmade goods because they presented themselves with pride and independence. (Alva overlooked that the Native Americans, however exploited, were not enslaved.)

Like other wealthy southern families, the Smiths escaped to the comforting breezes of Newport in the summer, not only for the cooler temperatures but to protect themselves from malaria and related mosquito-caused diseases that afflicted the swampy delta areas of the South. Now in its final days of importance as a port, Newport was a charming town of old Colonial homes and Victorian cottages, where pretenses were few even among the rich. It was a setting congenial to wild Alva, who dashed about the fields and shoreline with her siblings and friends without having to encounter the sour faces that would censure them on the streets of Mobile.

The Smith family also traveled to spas in Belgium and Hamburg, a practice that surprised their friends, who would leave the smallest children behind during European jaunts. The trip was not an easy one—fourteen days to Liverpool on a wooden paddle steamer of modest arrangements, one large center cabin for a general sitting/dining room, surrounded by small staterooms with bunked berths, a washbasin, and "seat." That gentleman's necessary, the smoking room, was a collection of chairs placed on deck around the smokestack. European trains had no drawing rooms or dining cars to ease comfort. Nonetheless, the Smiths took their entire brood, including their dog and caged birds.

In rejecting fashion, which emphasized protectiveness, Phoebe Ann sought to broaden her children's minds and give them opportunities to learn to handle emergencies. Of very independent temperament, Alva thrived under this care, which produced a girl of confidence, self-reliance, and sense of personal responsibility untypical of the more delicate-appearing girls around her in that Mobile neighborhood. She was frankly a terror, and the neighborhood children were probably relieved the day six-year-old Alva told them sadly the family was moving far away, to New York City.

The Smiths Test
New York Society

The smell of Civil War propelled Murray Smith north, for while he loved the South he could not support ceding from the Union, which he treasured even more. He believed southern land without slavery would be worthless, and he argued that if slavery was to be abolished, which appeared necessary, it must happen gradually to allow the economy time to adjust. Thus, like similar escaping southerners, he brought the Mobile house slaves north with the family.

It was not a particularly good time to arrive. In the fall of 1857 a predictable crash in the economy had occurred, the result, as one prescient editor predicted beforehand, of "government spoilations, public defrauders, paper bubbles, a general scramble for western lands and town and city sites, millions of dollars, made or borrowed, expended in fine houses or guady furniture."[6] As rumors of default or embezzlement spread, people crowded into banks to demand gold for their paper currency. Railroads collapsed. The Smiths would find signs of the crash on every street, buildings half constructed, others deserted.

Characteristic of such declines, those few with large reserves of capital were able to buy up failing businesses at cheap prices, holding on to them despite lack of profits until the economy improved. The Commodore was among these elite and foresaw that the future of transportation would rest with the railroads. For many years, a personal experience in 1833 had left him mocking the value of the iron horse. That October he had boarded the Amboy Railroad in New Jersey for a trip to Philadelphia. Traveling twenty-five miles an hour, quite fast for that period, an axle broke, pitching the train's cars off the tracks. The Commodore was tossed out of the window and plummeted down a thirty-foot embankment, breaking three ribs, which punctured a lung, and sustaining other severe internal injuries. Several weeks of bleeding, then a common medical practice, could not have helped his recuperation. He did heal, but having been in this accident, the first in the nation to result in passenger fatalities, he felt the railroad too risky a venture and so remained in shipping. By the 1850s, however, he saw that the technology had improved and that the system, a motley collection of tiny lines with incompatible equipment, required centralization. The crash was an opportunity to begin this consolidation.

Also untouched by the debacle, the Smiths were affluent enough to ignore the ruin. Thanks partly to the steamboat and railroad men like the Commodore, New York had at half a million inhabitants taken its place as the nation's largest city. Phoebe Ann was anxious to join among the growing numbers of *nouveaux riches* clamoring for higher status in society. She was aware one such person had recently made it to the pinnacle, although she could never imagine that her own family would one day be linked to this notable exception.

August Belmont has been described as "the last Jew to enter the arcana of smart New York Society before the bars went up."[7] Of modest German family, Belmont was fortunate to start out a career with the famed Rothschild banking firm. After proving his knack for finance, he became U.S. representative for the company, eventually leaving to found his own financial house and become a citizen, rising so quickly to prominence that he was appointed consul-general to Austria between 1844 and 1850. Belmont's limp, the result of a dueling wound, and his continental manner, learned at the feet of the elegant Rothschilds, offended the puritanical Knickerbockers, who determined that money should buy no luxury or pleasure. To their horror, he rejected the evening meal's plain roasts, game birds, and puddings in favor of the fancier sauces, greater variety of meat prepartion, and elaborate pastry desserts that were characteristic of European cuisine. Just as repugnant, he had these elaborate foods served on gold-plated rather than simple china. He was also a connoiseur of paintings, porcelains, horse-flesh, and, some whispered, women's flesh.

Why then should the Knickerbockers grudgingly open their doors to this somewhat tainted and not very attractive man? Money may well have had an influence—his skills in helping the rich multiply their money. Furthermore, while they equated European ways with decadence, they grudgingly allowed some interest in the arts of the Old Country, and Belmont was proficient in his knowledge of such topics. Finally, he courted and won the eminently acceptable Caroline Slidell Perry. She was the niece of Oliver Hazard Perry, war hero of Lake Erie in the War of 1812, and daughter of Commodore Matthew Perry, who had opened Japan to American commerce. These impeccable patriotic credentials, combined with her singular charm and beauty, further eased the Belmonts into Knickerbocker society, which came to admit it liked some of the sauces and spices of the fancy European dishes.

The Smiths astutely placed themselves in a prime spot for advancing in this social game, chosing as the locale for their first New York home a house at Twenty-sixth and Fifth, overlooking Madison Square. That plot's six acres had once been in turn a pauper's burial grounds, a circus site, playing turf for the city's first baseball club, and a location where certain ladies would stroll in the evenings for assignations of a commercial nature. Despite the Square's previous disreputableness, it sufficed for August Belmont's best friend, Wall Street speculator Leonard Jerome, as the site of his new mansion. Promising his wife Clara a palace, he agreed to a six-story, redbrick version of Napoleon III's home in Paris. The mansard roof, tall windows, and delicate ironwork drew pointed disapproval from the Knickerbockers.

Jerome's daughter Jennie was a year younger than Alva, and like her a rebellious sort. Though they would have made congenial playmates, they had little opportunity to meet, a fact that must have amused them years later when a surprising circumstance drew their lives together. Unlike Alva, Jennie and her sisters were being raised by maids, nurses, and teachers and were paraded out like silent dolls when company was around. While Alva found ways to sneak out of the house alone and was often successful at cajoling slave Monroe Crawford into taking her shopping with him, Jennie was kept at home, restricted to certain areas, and forbidden from attending society children's activities such as dancing classes. Their paths more likely crossed in Newport, where both girls were known for their wild and rambunctious horseback riding and where even the Jerome sisters were allowed to grub about for a few weeks each year.

Yet even had Alva met Jennie Jerome on the cliffs, it is unlikely she would have wanted to spend much time with her. Except for dolls, her one obsession besides constructing buildings with books and blocks, she loathed any play identified with the feminine and had not one close girlfriend. Consequently, at Newport, as everywhere, Alva preferred the company of boys, who were not fenced in like their sisters. Boys had access to what she considered to be the prerogatives of all human beings: adventure, excitement, liberty. When taunted by them that she couldn't do something, Alva grew enraged and fiercely moved to disprove the sneer. One day a boy pulled the ladder away from a tree Alva had mounted and threw apples at her as she clambered down, tearing her hands on the rough bark. As soon as she hit the ground she ignored her bleeding hands and pounded on him so severely she had to be torn away.

Alva's favorite companions at the summer resort were the Yznaga children. Antonio Yznaga del Valle had been a well-to-do Cuban merchant in Natchez who married a planter's daughter. A little rock island sat ashore just beyond their Newport lawns, and Alva was one day struck by hunger for construction. With Fernando Yznaga she hauled boulders and stones to erect a bridge on which it seemed to her it was possible to pass from shore to island as dry shod as the Israelites when they passed through the Red Sea. Upon completion, an epiphany occurred, during which she sensed the thrill of good workmanship and connected it to God's satisfaction following the six days of Creation. That she would have no trouble identifying herself with God hints at her remarkable self-confidence.

Very likely the Smith adults became acquaintances of the Jeromes' and Belmonts'. Caroline Belmont and Phoebe Ann would find in discussing their children, who were within the same age range, that they shared similar circumstances. In both families, all the children but one were well-behaved and easy to manage. Just as Phoebe Ann was frequently vexed by Alva, Caroline had difficulty controlling her youngest son, O.H.P., called Harry. Caroline, however, was having less success in maneuvering her wayward boy into using his talents. Despite her disciplinary measures, the temptations of the easy life were too strong. The rebellious Alva could be tamed, but Harry gave every sign of becoming a ne'er-do-well. But though she would be cordial to Phoebe Ann Smith at social gatherings, Caroline Belmont would not have invited her to her home, the ultimate sign of acceptance into Knickerbocker society. In fact, despite her husband's dealings with Leonard Jerome, it is likely his family was not welcome either.

The Smith's direct entree into the newcomer society was A. T. Stewart, who had revolutionized merchandising by creating the department store. His block-square Italianate iron front at Broadway between Ninth and Tenth was the terminus for many a female pilgrimage to buy Belgian carpets, Irish linens, French gloves, and English woolens all under one roof. Stewart won the affection of the middle classes, who previously could not afford, nor even receive entry into, the small exclusive shops that previously traded in imported luxuries. Despite his wealth, Stewart was shunned by the Old Society for being a "mere tradesman." This blemish did not dissuade the "Upstarts," as social climbers were called. They were not scandalized that Stewart would host a dinner on Sunday night and shared his appreciation for culture. Though reputed to be rather cool and antisocial, he made a strong impression on young Alva, because "in every way he sought to encourage and foster the arts, to make life more agreeable, and homes more beautiful."[8] Like Belmont, he was among the first New Yorkers to amass an enormous private art collection and with him would be among the founding trustees of the Metropolitan Museum of Art.

That the Smiths were quick to be accepted among those knocking at the Knickerbocker gates can be seen in their receiving invitations to attend the Prince of Wales Ball in October of 1860. This being the first visit of royalty to the United States, all New York was agog and pressing for an invitation. They saw no contradiction in considering Europe's aristocratic system to be inferior to America's democracy, yet rushing to honor the prince. Alva's later memory was that her mother was among the few chosen for the receiving line at the Fifth Avenue Hotel before the ball started, but this honor was unlikely. More certain, Phoebe Ann and Murray were part of the four thousand who wrangled an invitation solely to the ball. As it was, this left three hundred thousand on the streets the night of the event to watch the prince's carriage and those of the lucky few pass by. At the gala the crush was so horrendous that a floor actually collapsed, though with little harm. (The crush would have been further exacerbated by the hoop skirts, which ladies had recently adopted in relief that they need no longer haul several pounds of underskirts beneath their dresses.) The prince himself saw that he was later taken to a more private entertainment at one of the fancy brothels.

Besides obtaining the right invitation, the right church was a necessary membership for an ambitious family. One not only chose carefully, in this case Episcopalian, but went to services several times a week. Alva sensed a "great determination to frighten [one] into religion," for many activities were deemed sinful.[9] At a dancing class Phoebe Ann sponsored at her home, Alva felt sorry for the the Presbyterian children who had to sit out any dances requiring partners to clasp each other. They could do only square, not round, dances. She realized in later years that the narrow-minded bishops had shaped her to think snobbishly toward others.

Yet it was through church that young Alva felt rise up in her a militancy that was to become the strongest mark in her temperament. Among Phoebe Ann's own determination to follow her own beat and not that of others was dressing the children in Parisian clothes from the house of Olympe. This was a day when modishness was condemned by society—one's new clothes were kept in their boxes for several years so they would be sufficiently out-of-date to be acceptable. Consequently, other children frequently teased the girls for their fresh style. One morning during Sunday school a boy jeered at Alva's funny hat and made faces at her throughout the lesson. Controlling herself in the presence of grown-ups, Alva held her temper. But once outside, she shoved him in the gutter so forcefully that he never picked on her again. Indeed, no member of the male sex would ever be able to push her around.

Her self-control during the lesson was unusual. For the most part, Alva was a difficult and insubordinate child with a quick and loud temper. "There was a force in me that seemed to compel me to do what I wanted to do regardless of what might happen afterwards."[10] She was horsewhipped for taking a horse from the stable and riding it bareback. She harassed her teachers, whom she despised for being lenient with her. When she decided she was too old to sleep in the nursery, she took a towel and smashed all the china ornaments. Though severely whipped, she won her way, for she had learned that by standing up to repeated beatings she would simply wear her mother down and eventually get her way. She was a law unto herself.

Though disobedient, she was her mother's favorite, perhaps because both shared a streak of rebelliousness. Phoebe Ann understood the way to the girl's heart was to break her in without destroying her spirit, much like one would train a fine thoroughbred. Alva loved her mother passionately in return, but not enough to accompany her on mother's daily carriage ride, which followed Fifth Avenue past the reservoir between 40th and 41st streets, beyond the cattle yards that bounded the fifties, into the rocky hillsides of Central Park covered with squatters' shanties. This daily ride between four and five in the afternoon was *de rigueur* for anyone considering themselves society. The Knickerbockers hid their identity within closed, grim carriages, their coachmen and footmen in somber livery like funeral directors. The younger smart set, which would include Phoebe Ann Smith and Caroline Belmont, showed off the latest Parisian fashion from their barouches or even drove their own light, swift phaetons. Mixed in the crowd were such men as the Commodore, Belmont, Jerome, and even Dr. Henry Ward Beecher, the eminent Brooklyn clergyman, who took their trotters up to Harlem Lane for daily races. Though now in his late sixties, the Commodore remained the predictable favorite in these contests. Fancying horseback riding over sitting in a carriage and showing off, Alva early learned to bribe her sister to take her place on this duty.

There was additional reason to cleave to her mother's bosom: her father alienated her at an early age. When her younger brother Murray died, Alva observed her father grieve much more than when her sister had died and was both puzzled and shocked by his behavior. While it was some years before she connected his deeper mourning with woman's subjugation, the episode echoed in her memory, a reminder that to be female in the society was to be less valued. Following that day, she felt it impossible to be close to him. Although he was always kind to his girls, she observed him conveying the message that it was the sons who best represented the family. Sadly for him, none of the boys survived childhood, so the children's number was eventually reduced to four girls.

With the Civil War under way, life for Southerners in New York became increasingly difficult. Jennie Jerome recalled that "every little Southerner I met at dancing school was 'a wicked rebel,' to be pinched, if possible."[11] At the outbreak of the war, the city rallied about with a revival of patriotism. By 1863, however, dissension spread particularly among the immigrant quarters, where the Irish, composing one-fourth of the city's population, said they did not come to this country to free its slaves. Unfortunately, the draft regulations then provided a man could buy his way out of military service for three hundred dollars, in effect exempting the prosperous from fighting. A summer of rioting followed. Thousands took to the streets, destroying telegraph lines, looting stores, and attacking blacks, the police returning with firepower. At riots' end, twelve hundred people lay dead, with many more wounded. Street barricades around better neighborhoods saved the Smiths, and their well-to-do Northern neighbors remained strong in their support for the Union.

Even the ministers stirred up anti-Southern hatred. The rector of their own congregation so offended Southern members that the Smiths joined in withdrawing their membership. Later, following Lincoln's assassination, Phoebe Ann was quick to put up black bunting to avoid ink pots being tossed through the windows and took the children to view his funeral train.

Alva Thrives
in Paris

At war's end Murray Smith went abroad to Liverpool to see to the business from that end of the trade (the English had been supporters of the South during the war, so connections with that important trading partner had continued). Phoebe Ann took Alva and her three sisters to Paris.[12] Murray stayed in Liverpool, which could be taken as a sign that the marriage in trouble. More likely the separation was a practical one for the girls' sake.

Paris's brilliant flowering under the rule of Napoleon III and Empress Eugenie attracted many wealthy American families following the war. Many of these were newly rich (or richer, as in the case of the Smiths) from war profiteering, and they sought in Paris to acquire an aristocratic veneer, as well as a way to avoid the shortages and inflation wracking the States. It was also considered somehow more patriotic to align with the French, who had supported the American Revolution and paid the further compliment of taking inspiration for its own democratic upheaval. Still, the nobles had not been vanquished completely, and though their titles meant less and they were poorer, their style of life—more vivacious, urbane, and wordly than the country-oriented British—became the model of comportment for the socially ambitious. In return, the French noble families, with their declining fortunes, were only too happy to extend hospitality to the Americans in the expectation that a fortunate marriage would bring funds to shore up their crumbling châteaux.

Phoebe Ann selected an apartment on the Champs-Elysées and once again easily ingratiated herself with the more select crowd. To her surprise, Alva suddenly took to her schooling. The French system of education cut through the girl's usual defiance because it made so much more sense to her than the American approach. In particular she was drawn in by the method of "universal history," where one started with biblical times, not of a single country but of several in interrelationship. In addition, literature and art were interwoven with history, not treated separately. "History taught in this way is colorful and dramatic; it unfolds with the natural continuity of relative events," she discovered, and her passion for this integrated form of French history would absorb her into old age.[13] In contrast, in the States history was taught backward, beginning with American history, followed by European and classical periods. And by extracting the arts and literature, it was a lifeless and confusing chronology.

One period in French history was particularly entrancing, that of the medieval days. Tales of knights and castles flourished in her imagination, to be heightened further by the sight of armor and châteaux. But where other girls would identify with the ladies of the romances, the virginal mistresses patiently weaving tapestries while their beloveds fought for their lords, their king, and their God, Alva's heroine was the Maid of Orleans, Jeanne d'Arc, inspired by the Holy Spirit to don armor and lead men into these battles. There was no comparable female icon in American history, and no better model for a high-spirited rebel like Alva.

At first Alva studied with her sisters and their governess. Once a week a professor from a university came by with an outline he would test them on the next week. This requirement kept the governess on her toes and stimulated competition among the pupils. Alva then went to a private boarding school, that of Mademoiselle Coulon in Neilley, a suburb of Paris. She desired it not for its educational reputation but "because of the romantic beauty of the place."[4] To her surprise, she admired the French emphasis on good writing, set herself to win a prize, and did so. The school also taught her to rein in her exuberance through discipline and concentration. Students could not fidget through the many church services as they did in New York but had to take notes on the sermon. Consequently, she thrived in the regimen that allowed the girls release from school for only two occasions—the weekly bath and church. Hard work and discipline appealed to her, so long as the goal of the effort was a noble one, and French teachers exuded noble principles.

Apart from studies, Alva retained her stubborn preferences, playing up her reputation as an "American savage." Whereas the French children would eat what was before them, she objected to vegetables. She would climb a walnut tree to the top and refuse to come down, no matter how long the gardener (the only man allowed on the grounds) pleaded with her. On Sunday evenings, when the girls gathered for instruction on social behavior, she was extremely bored and unafraid to express such disdain. One evening she purposely loosened her hair, allowing it to fall from its clips and cascade to the ground, a gesture associated with boudoir sexuality. "O tempora. O mores. Shocked etiquette did not recover during the evening, but the girls enjoyed it."[15] She stayed at the school only one year, both her family and the teachers agreeing that her life there "was merely a wild career and must come to an end."[16]

In Paris, Alva did submit unhappily to a rite of passage for young women of the day: ear piercing. She equated the act with the bodily torture women in other cultures endured in order to be attractive to men—the foot binding in China and the nose piercing in India. She also hated the daily toilette surrounding the care of her hair, which in fashion of the day had never been cut.

Now fully mature, her buxom shape and vivacity soon attracted a caller, one Marice de R., who initially had come to visit her mother and older sister but soon turned his attentions to Alva. Their courtship consisted of hours spent poring over her stamp collection and discussing the various countries and cultures represented on the tiny, colorful squares of paper. "So it was on a mental basis I made my first close man friend. I mention this because it has been characteristic of all my later important contacts with men."[17]

William H. Vanderbilt
Succeeds as Well

W hile Alva was delighting herself along the broad boulevards of Paris, little could she dream that her future husband, a Vanderbilt no less, was also completing his education in nearby Geneva. Born in 1849, William Kissam was called "Willie" or "Willie K." to distinguish him from his father, William H. Vanderbilt. Despite being a grandchild of the Commodore, his early years' experiences were modest. His parents' first home on the farm in New Dorp was a modest two-story with kitchen lean-to. He was six when it was enlarged and a tower added to give the Italianate look so fashionable then.

By the time of Willie's appearance in the family, his father had made a quick success of the farm. William H.'s approach to the soil was at odds with fellow Dutch in the area. During these years he amused neighbors with his custom of sitting on the rail fence to watch his workers to make sure they put in a full day's work. The other farmers held that the best way to motivate farmhands was to work hard beside them. When the favorite sitting rail broke one day under the strain of William H.'s growing poundage, a farm hand replaced it with a sharp-edged board. Whether William H. stopped fence-sitting at that point is unknown, but the board remained.

Unlike his father, William H. was above all a family man, who shared wife Maria's religious devotion and interest in the children's welfare. Like other parents of Dutch extraction, they believed their children had rights and sought to develop each one's individuality. Perhaps recalling his father's brusque and blunt manner, William H. was notably kind, indulgent, and conciliatory with his own offspring. He and Maria also preached modesty. "Our money doesn't make us better than anyone else" was a frequent maxim, and in that regard, the children were warned not to fall for people who were adventurers, who put on airs, or who were foreign nobility. As they approached marital age, they were encouraged to pick mates of their own chosing, and not for their social status. Years later, this would lead the *New York World* to approve that the William H. Vanderbilt children "have fallen in love and married like the boys and girls of any American mechanic."[18]

The parent's openhandedness was evident in their different treatments of Willie and his brother Cornelius II, six years his senior. Cornelius II shared his father's temperament, being very methodical, even plodding, in his everyday actions. Like many first children, he had a strong drive to achieve, to perform beyond normal standards of behavior. Part of this drive was stoked by a strong conscience that allowed little room for leisure and nonproductive activity. Those who met the lad commented on his upright, correct manner. Willie, on the other hand, was handsome and athletic, ready to take risks for the excitement they would bring. Though quicker-minded than Cornelius, he suffered from a melancholy disposition that was given to quick tempers and just as rapid depressions, which made him unpopular with his peers. Unlike his elder brother, he grew bored easily and disliked repetitive chores.

Aware of the two differing dispositions, William H. and Maria set the boys out for different educations. Cornelius II by the age of 18 was working at the New York Central Railroad in the treasurer's office. His devotion to duty showed particularly the day an uncle urged him to take a leave of absence from work and join him for a summer tour of Europe, and upon learning he could leave but would lose his hundred dollars in salary, Cornelius II declined and stayed at his desk. Willie would have grabbed such an opportunity, and his parents knew so. Setting him on Cornelius II's path would have been a mistake for so sensitive a son, and Europe was a wise solution. There he could gain an excellent education away from the pressures of the Vanderbilt name.

Sending Willie abroad for his final schooling may also have reflected a shift occurring in William H.'s life, that toward a more cosmopolitan outlook. By the 1850s, the Commodore had grudgingly come to recognize his stolid son's business acumen and brought him into railroad development. Given the bankrupt thirteen-mile Staten Island Railroad, William H. quickly reorganized the company and turned it into a money-maker. He did so well that he could relocate his family to a home in the fashionable area of Fifth Avenue and Fortieth Street in New York. The farm continued to be profitable, its produce being sold during the Civil War to the Union government to feed the troops. With that move he was able to indulge two passions, the opera and fine art. As the family fortunes increased, he became a frequenter of the studios of New York artists, where he bought cheerful genre scenes, romantic landscapes, and anecdotal depictions, and unlike many who sat in the boxes at the Academy of Music, he actually enjoyed the trills and arpeggios of the singers. The Commodore considered such cultural interests sheer frivolities, for they had no profit, but William H. was his own man now and could not be ridiculed into forsaking these pursuits.

Yet William H.'s success came at personal loss, for he was too detail oriented, insisted on looking at every check, voucher, contract, and bill that came into the offices, and went out into the sheds to examine equipment, monitor repair costs, and oversee maintenance. A suspicious man, almost to the point of paranoia, he could not delegate authority, hence he often expended his health through overconcern with minutiae. The Commodore, however, was most gratified with his eldest son's accomplishments and was heard at last to make begrudging statements of praise.

The Civil War Adds to
the Vanderbilt Vaults

The Civil War increased the Commodore's bounty. Even those who like to idealize the history of free enterprise in the United States admit business went very askew during this conflict. In fact, businessmen were no less moral than in the years just before or after the conflict, for at no time during those decades did they recognize any connection between business and morality. Their exploiting of government treasuries was an established and acceptable technique. Munitions makers manufactured guns so worthless they had to be thrown away new. For example, one set of 4,000 rifles made by the Philip Justice Company was so dangerous that "at target practice so many burst that the men became afraid to fire them."[19] Congressional investigations pointed to muskets being sold at twice the peacetime rate. Uniforms, blankets, and shoes were delivered shoddy and ill made. Sickly horses were doctored up to appear healthy. Food supplies were maggotty and vermin infested.

Yet press and pulpit idolized capitalists during this period, thus contributing to the myth of their patriotism, the Commodore being among those most lauded. His steamers had provided cheap transport to California, his trains meant fresher food on the tables of city dwellers and more markets for manufacturers. Average people concluded the benefits of his transportation system outweighed its flaws. His workers, often squeezed for wages, were not as sanguine, nor were many of his freight contractors, who decried his manipulation of charges. Those cavilers aside, he was very much a hero of his age, becoming a new model for the meaning of the word *American*.

Appropriately, then, at the break of war, government officials courted the Commodore. They knew his capacity for sharp dealing and greed, yet trusted he would place private interest second to the needs of the Union. What their offer did, however, was simply bring new opportunities for his rapacity. Asked to help provide ships for transporting and supplying Union soldiers to New Orleans, the Commodore selected a ship broker who negotiated exorbitant rates on a commission business. Although aware many such craft were unseaworthy, he personally passed approval and blocked attempts by the Senate to require inspections. One ship, the *Niagara,* was found to be a freshly painted rotten hull that barely made safe harbor following a harrowing trip from New York. Following a Senate investigation, many involved in the transactions were charged with negligence of duty. Despite criticism of the Commodore throughout the hearings, once again he escaped without a single word of censure.

Vanderbilt family fortunes gained as well by a curious exemption in the exceedingly mild income tax charged to pay for the war. Railroad dividends were among the exclusions. Consequently, the net taxable income for the family was well below their actual intake.

Sometimes the Commodore's egomania served the Union well. The U.S. Sanitary Commission was an organization of predominantly women who greatly served the survival of Union soldiers by seeing to improvements in the sanitary conditions of camps, the provision of nutritious diets, and the availability of medical care. Hearing that merchant A. T. Stewart intended to endow the Commission, the Commodore pledged to give as much. Each upped the ante in turn, with a result that they gave $100,000 apiece to this lifesaving service.

His next ploy, though unsuccessful, was to collaborate with a group of other millionaires who sought to turn the U.S. Treasury into a stock company. They would assume the national debt in exchange for exemption from income and estate taxes. He also offered his transatlantic steamships for sale to the government, but it refused, fearing at war's end the Commodore's children would make claims for further compensation.

In a more curious expression of ego, the Commodore offered his namesake steamer to defeat the marauding *Merrimac*. Granted a personal visit with President Lincoln, he guaranteed success on condition that the government provide a crew for a ship that the Commodore would personally captain. "Only let me be free from the control of your Navy Department, and I'll answer for it that the 'Merrimac' won't pass Old Point Comfort."[20] Wily in his ability to deal with what he perceived to be sleazier members of the republic, Lincoln approved, possibly to keep the old manipulator from doing more serious kinds of damage to the Union cause. Thus the Commodore, almost seventy, took his chance to be a war hero. To his dismay, the Confederate craft declined to meet the challenge, and despite months of patrolling, the *Vanderbilt* never won a naval battle. In 1864, after Congress passed a resolution honoring the Commodore's contribution of his ship to the cause, the Commodore sniffed, "Congress be damned. I never gave that ship to Congress."[21] While he accepted the honoring medal with a letter responding "no pecuniary sacrifice is too large to make in [the nation's] behalf," he remained bitter for years afterward. What he never told those listening to his rampage was that he had garnered over three hundred thousand dollars in profits from the government before donating her.

It would be wrong to assume the Commodore's participation in war efforts was solely pecuniary. However much he disapproved of Lincoln—and he had much company in the North—he championed the Union cause. (Later critics implied otherwise, without providing any proof.) He had commandered the *Vanderbilt* sincerely out of confidence he could undo the Confederate menace on the seas. He was also most proud that his favorite child, George, had been a great success at West Point and promised to bring glory to the family name. Following the war, he personally honored Grant by providing the late commander of the Northern armies a private train of the Harlem Railroad. American flags decorated the locomotive, and a portrait of George Washington, the great national icon, replaced the reflector of the engine lamp.

In the midst of the war years, 1863, an unusual event occurred for the Vanderbilt family, a reunion in honor of the parents. To celebrate the fiftieth anniversary of his marriage to Sophia, the Commodore invited two sons (George being on active duty), eight daughters, eight sons-in-law, two daughters-in-law, thirty-two grandchildren, one brother, three sisters, and numerous neices and nephews to celebrate. "Brothers and sisters," advised Cornelius Jeremiah, "let the spectacle presented tonight inspire us with a firm resolve that while we may not hope to live so long nor near so usefully as our parents have already lived, we shall at least so act henceforth as to leave no stain upon the spotless names, no tear to the eyes of those we have so many reasons to revere or bless."[22] It was a speech to be recalled with irony more than twenty years later.

Unfortunately, soon after this joyous event George came down with tuberculosis and was discharged from the army. William H. accompanied him to the Riviera, where it was hoped he would heal. To everyone's shock and sorrow, the fair-haired son, the Commodore's main hope for the future, died in 1864.

The Commodore
Memorializes Himself

By the end of the war, now 71, the tireless Commodore turned more to railroads, where descriptions of his crafty tricking of other speculators won the public's heart even more. Over the next few years, through bribes to state legislators and New York City councilmen, and through outwitting voracious but less clever competitors, the Commodore took control of the Harlem Line, the New York and Hudson, and the New York Central. He became adept at stock watering, which occurs when a capitalist evaluates his property as worth more than previously set. Those defending the practice, point to the farmer who gets a sickly cow and nurses it back to health. In one deal sanctioned by the New York legislature he ordered the printing presses to run off certificates worth $180 for each current $100 share. The extra $80 represented a total theft of $54 million from the company. The debt would really be paid by the passengers, through higher rates, by businesses through higher freight costs, and by railroad workers through depressed wages. As the major stockholder, the Commodore essentially printed for himself $26 million. One night he actually left with over $6 million in fresh greenbacks from the company office as part of his booty. (In those days the average male worker took home ten to twelve dollars a week.)

Middle-class merchants and factory owners objected to and complained about the Commodore's tactics but could do little to stop him. For one thing, they were no less guilty in their own business doings. These were the men who turned laws harshly against the woman who begged or the man who stole a potato for his hungry family, yet obstructed attempts to stifle their abuse of consumers. They wanted no regulation, for example, of scales that measured meat or inspection of drugs to be certain they lacked poisonous compounds. Bluntly, business worked on the principle of fleecing anyone—supplier, customer, worker—for the game of profit. Now these businessmen watched in horror and helplessness as the Vanderbilt lines crossed state boundaries and acquired exclusive control over large territories. Cornelius was king at despoiling the despoilers, and he could extract any price from them for the use of his rails.

In 1868, at age seventy-four, the Commodore decided his accomplishments deserved a memorial. Consequently, he commissioned a massive monument to grace the western wall of the new Hudson River Railroad Depot. The 150-foot-long bronze bas relief included allegorical symbols to celebrate both the achievements of the Commodore and the growth and prosperity of the American republic. In the center was a twelve-foot-high statue of Van Derbilt in heavy fur-trimmed overcoat, his right hand inserted beneath his vest Napoleonically. The surrounding relief incorporated marine elements (Neptune, a sea monster, a racoon, his childhood periauger, and the *North Star*) and rail (an engine, switchmen, passenger cars). American symbols included Liberty, a rural scene of cows in a field, beehives of industry, and, to represent prosperity, a dock overflowing with goods.

The majority of Americans thought this self-aggrandizement fitting. Parents held the Commodore up to their children as proof of the ranks one could achieve through hard work. Little more than a decade later in Illinois, future poet Carl Sandburg was deeply impressed by a biography of Vanderbilt included in a series of cigarette premiums. In a country born out of the crushing of aristocracy, the name *Vanderbilt* was proof of the wisdom of the common man, his ability to rise in the world.

This being the United States, there was vocal dissent from a minority. On the day the monument was dedicated, a group of stockbrokers staged a ceremony in which an actor posing as a statue of the Commodore held a watering pot labeled "207," the price he had paid for New York Central shares at its consolidation. A speaker noted his "use of water, not as a beverage, but as an element of wealth," a reference of course to stock watering.[23] The *Nation* remarked that there was something essentially laughable in a man's erecting his own memorial, adding "the tendency to-day in this country is to count up our list of peculiarly American virtues as consisting of audacity, push, unscrupulousness, and brazen disregard of other's rights or others' good opinion."[24] The Commodore, along with most other businessmen, and indeed many middle-class people, would have agreed: audacity, push, and guile *are* virtues.

That year the Commodore was more moved by this monument than by Sophia's death from a stroke. Horace Greeley and A. T. Stewart served as pallbearers at her funeral, where the noted editor praised her as having "lived nearly seventy-four years without incurring a reproach or provoking an enemy."[25] While the children mourned their devoted and self-sacrificing mother, the widower paid only the most cursory respects. Any emotional ties he had felt for her had long been broken, and he was never the man to feign an attitude for propriety's sake.

While the Commodore's fortune grew, so did his parsimony. He viewed anyone soliciting a donation as either lazy or a drunkard. A man who lives by a fierce competitive ethic can trust no one, and he was no exception. His few pleasures were card games at home or trotting his horses. Turning over most of the details of his businesses to William H., the Commodore now began his day with a visit to his stables, and whenever the weather was conducive he would tear down the avenues to Harlem Lane, where the most ferocious races and betting took place, favorite competitors including August Belmont and Leonard Jerome. Smart people always bet on the Commodore: it was about the only way the common person could profit from his activities.

Freed from the eldest son's special burdens, Willie K. modeled himself more on his grandfather's playful side. Upon returning from school in Geneva, he too joined the New York Central Railroad offices. While his brother Cornelius II mimicked their father's devotion to work, Willie would take off to accompany his grandfather to the stables, acquiring from him the sharp eye for horseflesh he would exhibit the rest of his life. He also shared his grandfather's daring and inventiveness in business decision-making, so the family tolerated his escapades. He might not be at the desk every day, but when he was there he was a brilliant tactician. Nor did he show much interest in taking a wife, as his brother had already done in 1867, when he married Alice Gwynne, whom he met while teaching Sunday school. As lusty as his grandfather, Willie K. saw no reason to rein himself in with domesticity.

The Smiths Return to New York and Face Misfortune

Following the war, Alva Smith had returned to New York with her family, but it is unlikely she paid attention either to the hoopla surrounding the Vanderbilt Memorial or to Sophia's obituary.[26] The girl was broken hearted, finding everything American crude and raw in contrast to France. Even the French furniture brought over to decorate their rented home at 14 East 33rd Street could not compensate for the ugliness of the city. Her heart would soon break over more profound events.

Phoebe Ann's health began to fail, and in 1869 she died at age forty-eight.[27] In old age Alva reminisced that nothing in modern childrearing nourished the kind of bond she had for her mother, who was lenient, kind, and allowed great liberty while insisting on right and moral choices. She felt she owed her mother a great debt and pledged in memory of her to always do her best. Throughout her life she often sensed her mother was present in the room with her, and this impression fed her persistent drive for excellence.

Mourning sent the family into seclusion for the appointed year, during which time more ill fortune struck. Murray Smith's business dealings resulted in repeated losses, and while the girls tried every economy, they noted how their father's constant worry was destroying his health. They discussed starting a boardinghouse, and perhaps indeed the girls kept one.[28] Although Alva was not the eldest daughter, she felt responsible for the family, probably because her other sisters were so much more conventional and "educated for nothing but the drawing room."[29] She determined to save her family in the only way available to a young woman of the day, by marrying a man with the means to assist relatives. It would take several years to succeed, but the search would end all the family's worries.

3

1870-1879

"Do As I Do,
Consult the Spirits"

A
lthough the word *feminist* did not exist
in Alva Smith's day, she was from child-
hood conscious of the particular restrictions placed on females in American
society. A woman fascinated with history, she could not help but note the latest
activities of the suffragists.[1] Throughout the Civil War, women in both the North
and the South had been loyal and essential supporters of the military effort. They
disbanded their equal rights' campaign to attend to the nation's crisis. They took
over men's jobs in government offices, stores, munitions factories, and farms.
They gathered to make bandages, stamp blankets or towels, quilt blankets, can
preserves, dry fruits, pickle vegetables, knit stockings, and sew shirts. Some went
to the encampments to nurse wounded or console those healthy in body but not
in spirit. They were scouts, couriers, smugglers, sabateurs, and spies (their hoop-
skirts, bustles, and hairpieces convenient hiding places for messages). Women in
the battle areas of the South did whatever was necessary to keep the fields productive, the homestead, however tiny, preserved. Proud of their vital contributions, women's rights leaders were certain men would reward them with the
vote, possibly at the same time former black slaves were granted citizenship and
suffrage.

Yet the war's end introduced a difficult time for rebellious women. Disappointment soon emerged when it became apparent that the Fourteenth Amendment would apply citizenship to men only. Even abolitionist Frederick Douglass,
a noted supporter of women's rights, advised that it was "the Negro's hour,"
meaning Negro *men*. Other commentators urged women to forget the male tasks
they had taken over during the war and return to domesticity. In their much-
discussed *Principles of Domestic Science,* Catherine Beecher and sister Harriet Beecher
Stowe argued women's profession was child care, nursing, household budgeting,

and the training and control of servants. Although most women by default returned to full-time housekeeping, they found it difficult to resume the submissive, passive attitude that was part of True Womanhood.

Not only were proponents of abolitionism excluding women from their concerns, the women's advocates disagreed among themselves as to how woman suffrage might best be achieved. In 1869, Elizabeth Cady Stanton and Susan B. Anthony had formed the National Woman Suffrage Association in Washington. Excluding men from membership, its primary goal was a federal amendment granting women the right to vote, although it also supported equal pay for equal work, more equitable divorce laws, and even child-care centers for working mothers. Deeming that organization too radical, Lucy Stone and others responded by creating the American Woman Suffrage Association, headquartered in Boston, which encouraged male members and sought to get the vote within each individual state before seeking a federal amendment. This split in organizations and tactics would undermine the women's suffrage cause for fifty years.

Although Alva Smith did not enter the suffrage fray at this time, she was inclined toward the harder, more demanding views of Stanton and Anthony. Their self-confidence and assertiveness was congenial with her nature, and their courage planted a seed in her mind that would lie dormant many years. While scanning the papers, besides reading of these well-known leaders, she also became familiar with another figure whose more idiosyncratic actions would strike an important, to many shocking, signal of what was rightfully due to the female gender in the United States. Curiously, none other than Cornelius Vanderbilt, the remarkable Commodore, would be the major underwriter of this colorful personality's efforts for women's rights.

The precipitating circumstance was death. Mesmerism (which we know as hypnotism) and séances had been in vogue since the tour in the late 1840s of the prescient Fox sisters, who could summon up fortune-telling voices through rappings on tables and walls. Women down on their luck found quick income as spirit mediums, and while some were conscious frauds, others were sincere believers. Convinced of the truth of occult practices, Vanderbilt sought séance specialists to invoke the presence of his mother. He was soon devoted to one Mrs. Tufts, who besides levitating tables and sending messages to and from the dead, was also a magnetic healer who believed health was a matter of controlling invisible physical forces that could corrupt the body. One of the remedies the Commodore gratefully accepted from her was to place salt cellars under his bed as "health conductors." Similarly, he had his barber sweep up his hair clippings and give them to him, lest they fall into strange hands who could practice black magic on him.

Vanderbilt's loyalty to Mrs. Tufts ended on a day in 1868 when two vivacious, sexy sisters appeared at his door, claiming to be able to materialize ectoplasm. He was quick to try their proposals. The elder, Victoria Woodhull, lithe and graceful, was the talker of the two. She made her point with frank, bold speech, which for the Commodore only added to her appeal. Younger sister,

Tennessee, with her petite, overripe plumpness was considered the more beautiful. Where Victoria attracted men with her intelligence and way with words, Tennessee tempted men with her flamboyant gaiety and proclivity to stand very close to them during a conversation, closer than a lady should. Adding to that forwardness were her quick hands, which would emphasize a phrase by patting or caressing a gentleman with most pleasing results.

Born to Buck Claflin, a shrewd, scheming father, and Roxanna, a fiery, opinionated mother, the sisters grew up in a large, noisy, and quarrelsome clan. Buck was a peripatetic luck seeker who invaded various Ohio towns for a deal here, a card game there, more often than not leaving local businessmen richer and his own pockets empty. The girls' spiritual interests came from mother Roxanna, who was addicted to the traveling evangelical revival meetings that set up tents and called for repentance. That she spoke in tongues or danced in a trance at church meetings was nothing out of the ordinary—many townsfolk did so. The problem for neighbors was that she carried these actions out of the sanctuary of church and revival tent into her home and on the streets. She also took up mesmerism before it had become fashionable and was said to hypnotize any child, her own or not, at the first sign of illness.

Victoria was clairvoyant from the age of three, her first noted experience that of falling into a swoon after a neighbor died. She felt herself being carried off by angels to a beautiful otherworld where a Grecian man in a tunic predicted, "you will know wealth and fame one day. You will live in a mansion in a city surrounded by ships and you will become ruler of your people."[2] By age six, Tennessee also showed second sight. Word spread about the town of her predicting a fire in a local seminary, and, later, of her identifying the location of a lost calf. She frightened playmates with her astute reading of their minds, and Victoria scared schoolmates with her fervent imitations of local preachers' descriptions of the fiery flames of hell and the devil she actually saw at times lurking behind a nearby oak tree.

In 1852, Buck read in the papers of the Fox sisters, whose profitable séances were praised by such responsible public figures as publisher Horace Greeley, a devout believer in the girls' insights. The press generated near mania around the youngsters, who traveled the countryside collecting medals, awards, and a great deal of cash wherever they went. Eyeing fortune in his own household, Buck set up Victoria and Tennie in the parlor of a boardinghouse and advertised their future-telling abilities. There Victoria, fourteen, instructed her six-year-old sister in the secrets of the darkened room, the tappings and sudden shrieks that upset the other boardinghouse occupants. Their customers, however, were most satisfied and left in admiration of the sisters' devotion to one another.

Alas, the gold in Buck's mine was thin veined. Just a year later, perhaps to leave her father's control, Victoria married Canning Woodhull. He was the perfect combination: a handsome doctor. He was also, Victoria sadly learned too late, a drunkard who was too dissipated to carry on a medical practice. Soon after the birth of son Byron, Canning deserted her, and she traced him to another boardinghouse where he kept a mistress who went by the name "Mrs. Canning." Victoria was all-forgiving; she pulled the lout from his love nest and took on the job as main support of the family. Determined "to find fame and fortune," she found some success in the theater and traveled as far west as San Francisco with troupes. When Byron became a "near-idiot" as a result of a fall, she determined to have a daughter, and had one, Zulu Maud, who was to be devoted to her mother for life.

Meanwhile Buck billed Tennessee as "the Wonder Child" in a traveling medicine show he organized under handbills advertising "Dr. R. B. Claflin, AMERICAN KING OF CANCERS." In Ottowa the family set up an infirmary, but when a patient died, local doctors pressed to have Tennessee charged with manslaughter. She never went to trial: "Sudden Disappearance of Tennessee Claflin" announced the Ottowa *Free Trader* in June of 1864.

Eventually the sisters reunited to sell their services as clairvoyants. A key figure herein was Colonel James Blood, a free-love advocate who was for a time their manager and Victoria's lover. (Whether they legally married is in dispute—their own testimony is contradictory.) Canning remained in the picture; Victoria saw it her duty to support him along with her children. The motley group lived a carefree gypsy life around and about the Midwest until one day in 1868 when Victoria had another major vision. This time an ancient spirit told her to go to 17 Great Jones Street in New York, where she would find a house waiting for her. The spectre then displayed the interior of the commodious dwelling and pointed to a marble-topped table, where its finger wrote the glowing signature "Demosthenes." Victoria dropped everything, hurried to New York, and found the house exactly as portrayed in her vision—and available for rent, furnished. On the very same marble-topped table she found a single bound volume entitled *The Oracle of Demosthenes*. That was all she needed to convince her to settle in. Always the loyal family member, she moved in not only her children, Tennessee, and Colonel Blood, but her parents, assorted siblings and other relatives, and eventually, ex-husband Canning, now a morphine addict.

Being a segment of Third between the Bowery and Broadway, 17 Great Jones was an easy walk to the Vanderbilt house. Unpretentious and unaffected by social strictures, the Commodore welcomed any stranger for company so long as the visitor briskly stated his business and expected no small talk. Very likely he changed his rule about small talk when these sprightly young women entered the room. Tennessee, with her healing hands, completely captivated him. "My little sparrow," he called her. It was not long before her tickles, squeezes, and pats reawakened youthful lust, and servants gossiped over the nestlings and rustlings in their master's bedroom.

If Tennessee revived the Commodore physically, Victoria regenerated his mind to the playfulness of financial competition. By now William was running the businesses, at last to his father's approval and praise. Still, the old man found the hours too many to fill with horse racing and whist, and on Victoria's promptings he took up stock dealings again. People argued as to whether he sought tips from her spirit guides or he leaked insider information to her. Whatever the case, the many residents at 17 Great Jones shifted their bickerings and worries from the source of the next meal to arguments over which items of a limitless bounty to place on the table.

The Vanderbilt offspring were obviously not pleased with the sisters' influence on their aging father and suspected Tennessee was out to take the family fortune by the more conventional method of marriage. It seemed they could do nothing, for their father had never cared a a whit for their opinions. If he would not listen, they must use less direct methods. Consequently, in early 1869 they managed to arrange the visit of distant relatives from Alabama, a Mrs. Crawford and her daughter Frances, a divorcée who not unlike other similarly named women of the day went by the nickname of Frank. (Although the Crawford women had been friends of Phoebe Ann Smith, whether they visited her during these, her final days, is unknown.) The mails must have been filled with messages passing among the Vanderbilt daughters for information on possible signs that their father was taking to the winsome Southern widow. And they must have noted with dismay the day the mother and daughter without notice departed and headed for home. Worse, the Commodore then offered his hand to Tennessee. To everyone's surprise, she refused him.

If the children sighed over the good news, it was not for long, for the Alabama relatives reappeared. One day they were stunned to learn the Commodore was on a train to Canada with Frank Crawford. When asked why he chose the younger woman and not the mother, who was attractive and more fitting a man of his age, Vanderbilt replied, "Oh, no! If I had married her, Frank would have gone off and married someone else. Now I have them both."[3]

Despite the forty-five year difference in age, the union was apparently more satisfying to both sides than their previous marriages. Gossips noted the Commodore spent fewer evenings out at euchre and more in his parlor with his wife. Tall, refined, graceful, and intelligent, Frank was the only person outside of his mother to ever tame this American titan. Still, it is questionable that she was able, as her minister Reverend Deems claimed, to rescue from the "burden of worldliness the intrinsic goodness surviving in his soul, and to inspire benevolent deeds that crowned his days."[4] Always tight with a penny, and notably uncharitable, he gave grudgingly, and did not slow down his financial wranglings.

Nor did Vanderbilt's marriage loosen his bonds to the Claflin sisters. While honeymooning, he learned that financiers Jim Fisk and Jay Gould had cornered the gold market, almost undermining the country's financial structure, causing a "Black Friday."[5] The Commodore abruptly returned home and advised the sisters to follow his lead in buying up depressed stocks at remarkable lows, which would soon rise again.

Even more unconventional for a man not known for special kindness to friends, he set the Claflins up in an office at 44 Broad Street as the country's first "Lady Stockbrokers." The men who flocked to the building, first on the Commodore's recommendation, then on the word of satisfied clients, entered an elegant lobby gleaming with black marble counters and warmed by multipatterned Oriental carpets and black walnut furnishings. Scrapbooks invited glances at clippings attesting to the women's accomplishments. Magnums of champagne in silver buckets caused some clients to linger longer before stating their business. For convenience the sisters also hired Parlors 25 and 26 at the Hoffman House on Madison Square. This hotel, with its infamous Bouguereau nudes, was to that point off limits for ladies (if not other females). Visitors to the inner sanctum of Parlor 26 found peering down upon them in judgment a large portrait of Cornelius Van Derbilt, the best seal of approval any stock manipulator could have.

During 1870 newspapermen repeatedly delighted in the "Bewitching Brokers," as they called them, and overlooked any questions concerning the sisters' amazingly rapid rise to wealth. In the parlors of Old New York, however, Schylers and Livingstons clucked their tongues over stories that the newly married Commodore seemed to be spending a lot of time with Tennessee, while Victoria, that most horrific of creatures, a divorced woman, gathered friends in her home to preach free love. Reporters ignored possible scandals, preferring to emphasize the women's "intelligent, business-like manners" and earnest commitment to women's rights. "I despise what squeamy, crying girls or powdered counter-jumping dandies say of me," asserted Tennessee to a reporter. "I think a woman is just as capable of making a living as a man."[6]

The Commodore Assists
the Women's Righters

Victoria and Tennessee were typical of those who insisted then that women had a right to an equal economic role with men. Their success not only built their confidence but alerted them to other women's rights that were being neglected as well. New York City presented a particular situation that stirred Victoria's feminism. Though church bells rose a din every Sunday morning and ministers were an elite who competed for the contemporary equivalent of stardom, streetwalkers paraded Broadway from Canal Street to Madison Square. In 1866, when Bishop Simpson protested this immorality from the pulpit, the superintendant of police responded that his count showed only 621 houses of prostitution, 95 houses of assignation, and 75 concert saloons of ill repute. But the statistics were irrelevant, for it was the sheer visibility and variety of the immoral commerce that shocked visitors and many residents. Women loitered by the finest shops, before the entrances of luxury hotels, under the marquees of theaters. Victoria watched these women and concluded it was not their fault, that they should not be condemned as sinners. Rather, she blamed society as the culprit in failing to provide the means by which women from poor or tragic circumstances could find a decent wage or charity.

It is not known what Vanderbilt thought on April 2, 1870, when Victoria, spurred on by her fellow salon intellectuals announced herself a candidate for the presidency of the United States. He must have approved, for his relations with the women remained on such good terms that his money helped support *Woodhull and Claflin's Weekly,* the liveliest woman suffrage paper of its day. Despite her audacity and radical views on sex, Victoria in person showed such devoutness to the cause and power in oratory that more conservative suffragists bowed to her will. So effective was she that in December of 1871 she achieved the unprecedented honor of speaking on woman suffrage before the congressional judiciary committee, where she argued the Fourteenth Amendment already included women, and sexual equality should therefore be enforced. Her courage and conviction at this event garnered the official support of the National Woman Suffrage Association.

Just her speaking out in public to mixed-sex groups broke barriers. Prior to the Civil War, for a woman to do so was considered "promiscuous." When Dorothea Dix wanted to plead her case for hospital reform, and Catherine Beecher hers for equal education, they handed their speeches to men to read. When they spoke before all-female gatherings, it would be in the informal setting of sewing circles or discussion groups. Although a few suffragists spoke out to larger groups following the Seneca declarations of 1848, none captured the national spotlight as Victoria did. Commanding the podium was a challenging political act, an assertion women would no longer be silenced.[7]

In 1872, Victoria created the Equal Rights party to nominate herself as candidate for president, with abolitionist Frederick Douglass—without his approval—on the ticket as Vice President. Testing the Fourteenth Amendment that November, Susan B. Anthony and a group of followers who attempted to vote in that election were arrested.

When more pious suffragists attacked Woodhull's morals and support of free love, movement matriarch Susan B. Anthony commended Victoria as "a beautiful woman, refined in appearance and plainly dressed with a clear, musical voice" that captivated both men and women.[8] Elizabeth Cady Stanton was blunter. "We have had women enough sacrificed to this sentimental, hypocritical prattling about purity. This is one of man's most effective engines for our division and subjugation."[9] Despite the backing of movement leaders, many suffragists were nervous. They had been fighting the tough daily skirmishes for twenty-five years, and now this charismatic dynamo of suspect past was threatening to take over the movement. Lucy Stone, whose retaining her maiden name after marriage had led to others doing the same and becoming "Lucy Stoners," privately charged the sisters were untrustworthy blackmailers.

Ultimately the Claflin sisters' messy private lives caught up with them. Novelist Harriet Beecher Stowe had not been able to come up with anything as popular as *Uncle Tom's Cabin* and saw in these two upstarts an opportunity to grab the reading public's interest once more. Her device was a serial (in the *Christian Union*) whose main character, modeled on Victoria, served to mock liberal feminist causes. The weekly appearance of this ridicule stirred growing resentment among the conservative supporters of woman suffrage who wished women the right to vote but not to deviate from the Cult of True Womanhood.

Stowe made great fun when the sister's mother provided a convenient twist in the plot. A vexatious and discontented woman, Roxanna Claflin went to court to charge Colonel Blood with threatening her life and destroying the daughters' affections for her. Out of the trial came word both Blood and Canning were living under the same roof at the sisters' new mansion on 38th Street. This curious menage did not disturb the Commodore. What did shock him was Tennessee's confession of hornswoggling him. In seeming defense of Blood, she let her voluble tongue go too far in saying, "I have power and I know my power. Commodore Van Derbilt knows my power. I have humbugged people, a great many rich people—Van Derbilt included—I know."[10]

It was easy at this point for Frank to break her husband's fascination with the sisters. Frequent visitors to the lady stockbrokers' mansion noticed treasured objects disappearing, sold to bring food to a once-again troubled table.

Yet further events added to Frank's confidence that her husband would not forgive his protégées and welcome them back into his life. One was Victoria's role in the notorious Beecher-Tilton scandal. Henry Ward Beecher, the most popular preacher in the land, had for some years been philandering with female parishioners. One of them, Elizabeth Tilton, eventually confessed the adultery to husband Theodore. Although he forgave her, he grew obsessed with the episode and could not stop talking about it, so that in time many tittle-tattles passed on the story. Eventually Victoria became privy to the tale and was tempted to go public to shame Beecher for his hypocrisy. Others, including suffragist Elizabeth Cady Stanton, urged her to be silent for the sake of other innocent parties who would be drawn into the scandal. Victoria kept silent, even after Beecher spoke out from the pulpit against her curious household. Remarkably, she even befriended and had love affairs with both the cuckolded Tilton and cuckolder Beecher!

Yet the sexual charms (or lack of them) of these two men did not satisfy Victoria. Frustrated by the spiraling losses of income and reputation, one evening during a speech at a Spiritualist convention, she felt inspired to go public and confessed all she knew about Beecher's adultery with Mrs. Tilton. But that was not all: "He preaches every Sunday to dozens of his mistresses, who are members of his church, sitting in their pews, robed in silks and satins of high respectability."[11] The reason for her exposé, she stated, was that she believed in free love and it was now time for hypocritical Beecher to admit the same. So powerful was the preacher that only one newspaper in the country, the Memphis *Appeal,* identified him by name in reporting the story. Frustrated by the press censorship, five months later Victoria wrote a detailed version of the adultery in her *Weekly,* which soon became a runaway best-seller and forced the city papers to follow up what became the most sensational story since the assassination of Lincoln.

Tilton sued Beecher. Through the resulting publicity and trial Victoria was able to get even with both Beecher and his sister Harriet for their earlier condemnation of the Claflins. Although Tilton's lawsuit resulted in a hung jury, many newspapers determined the minister clearly guilty, a "divine seducer." The case affected more than those directly involved; suffragism was split over the case and suffered as a result. Beecher had once been president of the American Woman Suffrage Association, so conservatives had ready proof that woman's rights would bring lax morals. Susan B. Anthony, heading the National Woman Suffrage Association, came under attack for her earlier affiliation with Victoria Woodhull and her defense of Elizabeth Tilton, who under existing social customs had been forbidden to appear at the trial in her own defense. Members of the two competing organizations had even less in common now, and each organization lost members as a result of the persuasive criticism of antisuffragists.

Victoria and Tennessee drew the wrath of the most determined conservative, self-appointed censor Anthony Comstock, who had the sisters jailed for sending obscenities, their *Weekly* with its columns on free love, through the mail. Though the case was eventually dismissed, they lost their final shreds of acceptability, even among the most loyal suffragists, and found themselves cast out of respectable society, while Beecher seemed untouchable behind the shield of his Bible and his loyal congregation.

By 1874, the onetime belles of the financial world were penniless, ill, and worn down by family feuds. Victoria appealed to Vanderbilt for financial assistance, not for themselves, but for the woman's movement. Recalling his earlier support of their activism, they urged him to become "Patron Saint of this great cause." He did not answer. Ailing and now compliant to Frank's charge, he instead agreed with her request that he endow $1 million upon the university that bears his name today. It was his one noted act of charity. While this request was the sisters' final communication with the Commodore, it was not the end of their seeking benefit from the Vanderbilt family. There was one more hand to play, and they held the aces.

Alva Takes a Vanderbilt

Also in 1874, another woman would be more successful in exploiting the family gold. Despite her recent impoverishment, Alva Smith had maneuvered to maintain connections with *nouveaux riches* society. While the Smith's table fare was plain, their mother's French furniture and bibelots rendered a semblance of success. The eldest daughter, Armide, took over as their father's hostess for her younger sisters' debuts. Alva soon found herself with a passel of well-connected friends, including Mamie Paul (the future Mrs. William Astor) and Minnie Stevens (the future wife of Almeric Paget and favorite of the Prince of Wales). These daughters of Upstarts were determined to break into society whatever the expense.[12]

Her closest friend was Consuelo Yznaga, sister of her childhood playmate Fernando. A dainty blond with dark eyes, Consuelo had also lived in Paris, where with her two sisters she became a center of Empress Eugenie's court. Among Consuelo's noted charms was her banjo playing in accompaniment to American folk songs. When the Prussians invaded in 1870, the Yznagas settled in London but often returned to New York. A warm and fun-filled family, the Yznagas took the motherless Smith girls under their social protection. Alva's sister Jennie was courted by and eventually married Fernando Yznaga, and it was Consuelo Yznaga who one day in 1874 saw to it that young Willie K. Vanderbilt attend a Smith reception.

Willie was unusual for a Vanderbilt offspring; he eschewed the dour piety forced on him by his parents. He was a nice, moral, upright fellow but he didn't think such virtues should get in the way of enjoying life. Possibly his European education played a role in shaping his more frank hedonism. He was also more handsome than other men in the line, with flashing green eyes, a ready smile, and quick with humor. Alva, whose later pictures do not do justice to her youthful beauty, had the luxurious strawberry blond hair, marble-fine complexion, and buxom figure so admired then. More the passive sort, Willie was likely bowled over by Alva's sharp wit and unwavering opinions. Despite his *bon vivant* appearance, his actual nature was rather one of melancholy and confusion. He was a young man ready to be led, and Alva was his natural leader.

The courting followed the pattern of the day: Alva could not be unchaperoned, and Willie was required to execute a series of carefully prescribed ritual acts and sayings before striking a proposal. He was to chase, and he did, all the way to the lighthearted resort of Greenbrier at White Sulphur Springs, where she had gone for the annual spa treatment. The staging area for display of southern belles, the Springs had a series of paths appropriately named Lovers' Walk, Lovers' Rest, Courtship Maze, Hesitance, Acceptance Way, Paradise, Rejection, and Lover's Leap. Alva doubtless led Willie down most of the paths before acceding to his request for marriage.

In fact, she was rather desperate for the bargain. Her father lay dying and was tormented by the thought that his daughters would be left penniless and adrift. Finding him too sick to attend the wedding, Alva sat at his sickbed and promised to look after her sisters. (She did, seeing to the lifetime support of Armide, who never married.)

In 1875, Alva and Willie K. wed at Calvary Church, then the most fashionable in New York. Claiming her Parisian gown had not arrived on time—when in fact none had been ordered—she had her mother's wedding flounces made up into an appropriate dress. So many onlookers came out that mounted police cleared crowds from the door of the church and along the procession route. A private train conveyed the newlyweds like royalty to Saratoga, the traditional honeymoon resort for the wealthy.

The nuptial night was apparently nightmarish for Alva, who had never been

instructed on sex. Forty years later she would cry when describing her humiliation to poet Sara Bard Field, who was assisting on her autobiography. "The agony
of suffering ... this she will not let me write [in the memoirs]. The children
would object, and the Vanderbilts, too. It is the sacred confidence of a woman's
inner heart—a heart that could have been loved into beauty but that has been
steeled against its own finer and softer emotions," Field wrote in a letter to a
confidante.[13] Apparently the sexual relation never flowered, to the eventual bitterness of both partners.

The couple returned to a house on Forty-fourth Street, a gift from her
father-in-law. Alva easily gained acceptance from the most important member of
the family, the Commodore himself. It aided that the Commodore's wife Frank
had been a close friend of her mother's. More significant, the old man and young
belle shared in having feisty, clever, and energetic minds that created a natural
sympathy between the two. Alva thought the Commodore one of the most handsome, intelligent, and interesting men she had ever met. Her never holding anyone in awe ingratiated this figure who had so successfully terrorized and cowed
his first wife, most children, and most business associates. When he learned she
enjoyed the country, he gave her his childhood house in Stapleton, which she
doubled in size and renovated. (And when the notorious mosquitoes drove her
off, she was clever enough never to inform him of her deserting the place.)

Similarly, her in-laws warmly welcomed her despite her unwomanly streak
of independence. As had been anticipated, Murray Smith had not lived long after
the wedding. After the funeral, William H. went over to Alva and said, "My
dear, you have lost your father. You are now my daughter. I want you to come
to me on any and all occasions of need."[14] She did, and she often found him
supportive to her ideas. Her sincere Christian devotion and strong commitment
to Christian virtues also compensated in their eyes for her more showy behavior.

Alice Vanderbilt Shuns
Her New Sister-in-Law

Other Vanderbilt kin were less sanguine
over Alva's joining the clan, notably
Willie's older brother Cornelius and his wife, Alice. Cornelius shared his father's
stolidity and coolness under fire but was a harder worker and esteemed to have
a better intellect than either his father or grandfather. From his mother he acquired a devotion to religion and good works. He was to set a style common
with most Vanderbilts today of the anonymous donation or quiet beneficence.
Whereas other noted families attached their names to foundations and institutions, except for the case of the university in Tennessee, the Vanderbilts eschewed
publicizing their charitable works.

Alice was as quick to spout off her bloodline as was Alva, and she took it more seriously by joining the elitist Daughters of the Cincinnati and the National Society of Colonial Dames. Her ancestors included James Claypoole, who had arrived in Philadelphia in 1683 and become treasurer of the Free Society of Traders of Pennsylvania, Captain Abraham George of the American revolutionary army, and David Gwynne, an officer during the War of 1812. She was born Alice Claypoole Gwynne in Cincinnati to the lawyer son and heir of considerable real estate wealth. After her father died in 1863, her mother moved the children to New York City, perhaps to improve the chances on the marriage market of her four daughters. Alice did not disappoint.

Unlike Alva, Alice easily submitted to the notion of True Womanhood. Her model of feminine heroine would be her own mother-in-law, Maria, who spent her days in her home, overseeing her children's moral development and ventured out only for church activities or a visit to a relative. She would have considered Jeanne d'Arc a sadly deluded young woman who only got what she deserved for her improprieties. Proud and doctrinaire, she shared her husband's constricted and narrow worldview.

Cornelius and Alice made a physically imposing couple, both of stiff posture, long and often unsmiling faces, darkly shaded and undecorative clothing. They were throughout their lives deeply compassionate people when it came to social need, be it a new church building, hospital wing, school equipment, or settlement house. They took their Christianity seriously in that regard and were much admired as models of civic duty by those who knew of this dedication.

Unfortunately, they also subscribed to rigid rules and rituals when it came to the matters of daily intimate life. They loved their children but were of the school that believed to show affection would be to spoil. In the larger social world, Alice was particularly sensitive to the fact that the name *Vanderbilt* would not yet get her into all the sitting rooms of Fifth Avenue. Even though her father-in-law William H. had raised a model family, sent his children to the right schools, amassed a respectable and praiseworthy art collection, and gave generously to New York charities, neither he nor his well-behaved offspring's families were admissable to the old guard.

The rejection infected Alice, who became obsessed with propriety. It was as though she believed she could open the doors by behaving in so scrupulous and correct a manner that the Knickerbocker matrons would have no choice. Or perhaps she thought to one-up society by appearing so much more the grand dame than they. In sum, this strategy meant stretching the WASP code to an extreme, to show no emotion, to speak in elliptical phrases, to attend carefully to caste markings, to discipline oneself to stifle any wayward impulse. Surely the spontaneity, frankness, and playfulness of Alva and Willie must have at times embarrassed both her and Cornelius.

Though the facts of her education are lost to history, it is evident Alice had a sharp mind. Unlike other women of her class, she took much interest in her husband's job as Treasurer (and later President) of the New York and Harlem line. This shared concern, along with their spiritual devotion, forged a bond unusual among such executive couples then. This was after all an era when rich men's duties to family were limited to siring an heir and supporting the wife's social aspirations. Compatibility and companionship were not required. The husbands more often sought sexuality in the better bordellos or with mistresses. (Saratoga's popularity was partly due to its providing separate cottages which granted privacy to assignations with mistresses. One wag who noted a line in the hotel register stating "Wall and Valet" signed himself and lady friend in as "McCarty and Valise.") Though unromantic in appearance, Cornelius and Alice were a rare romance among their set.

The Commodore Leaves
This World—and a Will

While Alice kept her distance from her new sister-in-law, she could not avoid her as much as she would have liked. The Commodore's health was failing in fits and starts, as if he almost wished to tease them as to the time of his death and the state of their inheritance. Consequently, the family was often called together for this or that "last scene," which would prove to be premature. Aware of Alva's popularity with the old patriarch, Alice was concerned that her sister-in-law would have influenced him to give Willie special favors in his will. As events later proved, Alice was overlooking Alva's persuasive powers with another member of the family.

Since the spring of 1876, when word of the Commodore's imminent death first appeared in newspapers, businessmen had kept a wary eye on the stock market in fear the Commodore's actual demise would send investors into a tizzy. Yet the crusty old man rallied repeatedly and warned he was not ready to leave the mortal coil just yet. To assist his recuperation he often called upon Dr. Frederick Weed, a magnetician, whose glass bottles failed to dissipate the sickly humors. It was a gruesome dying, all his major organs gradually failing, the pain so great at times that he threw his hot water bottles at whomever happened to walk into the room. For weeks, a twenty-four hour vigil of reporters kept guard at Washington Place, sending rumor and invention to secure their easy post with their editors. By December the final turn came. Each small decline and rally was headlined on the front pages as if the country were losing one of its greatest heroes and leaders.

On January 4, 1877, the doctors knew the predicted day had finally arrived. The scene, described in extraordinary detail in the evening news, easily brings to mind a Victorian steel point drawing. The Commodore lies in bed, propped up to view his surrounding kin. The young wife weeps while the aging daughters sing "Come Ye Sinners, Poor and Needy." The minister reads from the Bible. William H. stands in the background, ready to take the reins of the family, in law as well as in fact. Cornelius Jeremiah, back to his discrediting ways, paces the floor of a downstairs parlor expectantly. For the past several months he has been forbidden by Frank to see his father. "I don't want to see Corneel whether I'm dead or alive," the Commodore had ordered.[15] One can almost hear the violins and the piano playing a mournful accompaniment and see several gossamer angels hovering overhead.

As he wished, Vanderbilt's funeral was brief, simple, and solemn. Parson Deems described the holy atmosphere of the death chamber as proof the Commodore was now at peace with the angels. (In another pulpit, Henry Ward Beecher was more acerbic. "I am very glad he liked those hymns when he died; but if he had sung them thirty years ago, it would have been a good deal better for himself and many others."[16]) The funeral cortege proceeded down Broadway to the Battery, crossed by ferry to New Dorp, and there by carriage to the family burial plot in the old Moravian cemetery. (Being seven months along in pregnancy, Alva was unable to attend.)

The body buried, the family was quick to attend to the disposition of the wealth. The next day the surviving children, now eight daughters and two sons, and Frank gathered to hear the reading of the will. Few left satisfied. As a result of a prenuptial agreement, Frank received the house and stables, along with a half million in U.S. Bonds. Five daughters received a quarter million's worth apiece of bonds of the Lake Shore and Michigan Southern Railroad Company. The other three daughters were given U.S. Bonds in amounts of $300,000, $400,000 and $500,000, respectively, which were bound up in trusts. In effect, they could take only the yearly income during their lives, and the principal would pass on to the residuary heir of the estate. That legatee, it was now clear, would be William H., who was now the richest man in the country. His brother Cornelius Jeremiah, in contrast, was to get only the income from $200,000 in U.S. Bonds, which the trustees were warned to dispense cautiously provided Cornelius's behavior remain exemplary. Furthermore, if Cornelius were to in any way assign or encumber this income, he was to lose its use entirely.

The will further spurned the Commodore's daughters by ignoring their sons. Of his sixteen male grandchildren, the Commodore left money only to the four sons of William H. Alice was delighted to learn her husband, the eldest, would come away with $5 million whereas Willie and the other two brothers received $2 million. The message was clear, that one day her husband would be the residuary heir to his father's estate, and her position as *the* Mrs. Vanderbilt was secure.

Curiously, the Claflin sisters were not overlooked. Tennessee was bequeathed the painting *Aurora,* a life-sized Venus with a film of gauze draped around her middle in a hint of modesty; the work's value was placed at $2,000. In addition, he provided money for a trust to be managed by the women toward the furthering of Spiritualist practices.

The children should not have been surprised by the various designations. Their father's pride in his fortune was always evident, that he would want to preserve it should have been predictable. His disdain for Cornelius Jeremiah and lack of concern for the daughters was common knowledge. One can even imagine his glee in the commotion the document would provoke.

The Heirs Argue
over the Spoils

Thus, with the reading of the Commodore's will, began the first of the great Vanderbilt scandals. Two months after the Commodore's death, Cornelius Jeremiah and two of his dissatisfied sisters, Ethelinda Allen and Marie Alicia La Bau, notified the surrogate that they intended to contest the will's validity. Their charge was that the will had been colored by the fraud, circumvention, and undue influence pressed against their father by none other than their brother William H. and unspecified others.

On March 13, 1877, gapers and the curious pushed into the New York courtroom to hear the formal objections filed. Rumors flew throughout the gallery: Did you hear that Jay Gould was supporting the contestants in hope he could finagle control of the New York Central? Did you know certain gamblers had threatened Cornelius J. with his life if he did not press the suit? The room hushed when the surrogate entered to hear from ex-Congressman Scott Lord, chief counsel for the contestants. His statement stunned the listeners: his clients had decided to withdraw their objections from the will. He was still in shock from their decision, perhaps because, as a colleague exclaimed to a nearby reporter, "It's highway robbery. It robs the profession of a million dollars!"[17] If the public and lawyers were disappointed by that news, they would soon be repaid. In May, Cornelius J. filed a complaint with the state supreme court, claiming William H. had promised him a million dollars to drop the suit, then reneged on delivery of the money.

William H. may have followed through on the delivery of hush money to his sister Ethelinda, for she suddenly withdrew her criticisms of the will. Marie Alicia would not be stilled, however, and demanded that probate be reopened. Throughout the long spectacle that was to follow she made clear to onlookers her indignation over the inequities of her father's will. Among the youngest children, she had come of age just as the women's rights activists were rising to prominence, and was apparently less willing than her older sisters to accept a subordinate status.

In this day before baseball and movies, the courtroom provided popular entertainment. Lawyers enjoyed the celebrity of later ball players or movie stars and were followed by fans knowledgeable of cross-examination strategies. Thus readers around the country were quick each morning to scan the newspaper for the latest turn in this impending drama. If in the course of being entertaining the lawyers bent the truth, few cared.

This case, with its notable jurists, promised to be the hit of the season. William's team was headed by Henry Clinton, notable for his ability to obtain acquittals for bloody handed clients. His strategist was George Comstock, ranked by many the greatest legal mind of the day. Marie Alicia, the contestant, had an experienced will breaker in Scott Lord. For eloquence, they could count on Jeremiah S. Black, a magnificent speaker in an age of great speakers, whose argument could be measured by the number of spittoons he filled during the oration.

When the case opened in earnest on November 12, Lord argued he would use all three grounds available to break a will: first, to show Vanderbilt had been of unsound mind at the time; second, that he was subject to undue influence; and third, that a fraudulent conspiracy had been at work. Although the state supreme court appeal kept Cornelius from being a formal party to the case, Lord made clear he would play on the "vassalage [of Cornelius] so odious that every instinct of his manhood revolted against it."[18] Public sympathy quickly rallied around Cornelius and the sisters, less because they gained too little from the will than because William H. profited so much.

If the public wanted drama, surprise, gossip, and titillation, they were not to be disappointed. The lawyer for the complainants was like a feisty Pomeranian. Outweighed by the reputation of the defense counsel, Lord used his energy and persistence to wear them down. By constantly snapping at their ankles, he preoccupied them with numerous annoyances, thus drawing their attention away from their intended goal.

Lord's first strategy was to bring forth witnesses testifying that Vanderbilt had been of unsound mind at the time of the signing of the will. He had three arguments here. First, that the Commodore's various illnesses were such that he could not have maintained his sanity. Second, that the millionaire was so smitten by Spiritualism that his logic was affected. Finally, he hoped to show that anyone as monomaniacal about seeking wealth and fame as Vanderbilt was necessarily off balance (a claim, that if successful, would have indicted all the robber barons of the age and later).

The first witnesses, the various doctors who had attended Vanderbilt's final days or participated in the autopsy, did not help the case. True, they noted, the Commodore's autopsy showed virtually every organ in his body seriously diseased. Oddly, his heart, which was unusually small for a man his size, was still in good condition at death. Clinton had no problem objecting that the decrepitness of Vanderbilt's body drew no conclusion on his mind. Furthermore, the will had been drawn two years before his death, when he was in more vigorous shape.

The key witness to the Commodore's excessive Spiritualism was one Jennie W. Danforth, who described at length various meetings with Vanderbilt, where he called upon her ability to call up dead spirits as well as to heal. One day she described with particular clarity an encounter when he asked her to contact his first wife, Sophia. Apparently, the spectral Sophia refused to talk to her husband because she wasn't happy with his will. Moved by the medium's message, the Commodore promised Sophia he would make amends and rewrite it. Overall, Mrs. Danforth made a most favorable impression on the gallery, which was inclined to accept Spiritualism as a reasonable and intelligent philosophy. The problem for Lord was that she was too convincing. If so many people accepted clairvoyance and Spiritualism, then how could one say such beliefs were signs of mental instability?

Significantly absent from this list of witnesses were the Claflin sisters. What Surrogate Black did not know was that they had dangled blackmail before William, who had taken the bait. Specifically, upon hearing that William had inherited ninety-seven percent of the fortune, which some siblings were disputing, they somehow "discovered" $70,000 due to them from the Commodore, which with compounded interest would come to $100,000. They further informed him they had left $10,000 with his father in 1871 for speculation. When in 1873 they asked for their earnings, the Commodore responded he would not return it unless the sisters promised to build a home for their mother, Roxanna, who conveniently would swear to this fact. Also, he promised to leave them $500,000 in his will. In order to keep their compromising presence out of the courtroom, William tried to settle for $15,000, but it was likely more.

In August of 1877 the sisters and their entire extended family sailed for England. There Victoria wed a scholarly gentleman and banker, John Biddulph Martin. Tennessee learned of a wealthy widower, Lord Cook, who was interested in Spiritualism and took to him the message from beyond that he was to marry her. He did. Both women lived most comfortably from that point, but it was not the last Americans would hear of Tennessee.

Left to his final argument, that Vanderbilt was a monomaniac about money, Lord called upon phrenology, another well-accepted "science" of the day. According to this system, various areas of the skull represented different virtues, temperaments, or inclinations. A bump or lump in a particular area was sign of possible weakness. Sanity depends upon balance, intoned Lord, but Vanderbilt's "bump of acquisitiveness" was chronically inflamed. "Morally and intellectually his mind was a howling wilderness. His love of money amounted to a mania, which would render any act of his void if it could be shown to be the offspring of the delusion under which he labored."[19] Despite his magnificent oratory, Lord failed to sway Surrogate Black, who simply ignored it. The fact is, he concluded, Lord had failed to bring forth any witness to show that the Commodore was actually insane during the period in question.

Clinton summarized more pointedly: "Counsel seeks on behalf of a crazy client and through a crazy witness to influence this court to let in all kinds of crazy testimony."[20]

Craziness excluded as a defense, Lord suddenly shifted his tactics. In mid-December, the trial a month old and spectators growing bored, he perked them up one day by seeking to add to the list of conspirators Frank Vanderbilt, the widow, and her mother, Mrs. Crawford. This move was particularly worrisome to William H. and Clinton because it presaged the introduction of much private familiar matter into the trial. Nonetheless, they lost their appeal to prevent the addition of the two women into the charge, and the newspapermen breathed a sigh in knowledge they would now have juicier bits to fill their columns.

Cornelius Jeremiah Maligns
His Brother's Motives

Lord's chief witness in this move was none other than Cornelius Jeremiah, the Commodore's much aggrieved son. Although he could not be party to the trial, he could testify as to the possibility of fraud or coercion in the making of the will. It did not matter that only his sister Marie Alicia was the sole challenger, for if she won, all the Vanderbilt offspring, save William H., could count on gains. Were any reporters snoozing during the day's proceedings, they certainly roused at word Cornelius J. was taking the stand. As he passed by his older brother, observers could see at once a difference in personality and temperament of the two men. William H. was conservatively dressed, portly, his ruddy complexion framed by large curly mutton chops. His strong features were to repeat often in later generations: broad cheekbones with strong nose, full lips, and eyes with a hint of Asian influence, sometimes romantically and dubiously attributed to a Dutch sailing ancestor's mating with an Indonesian. It is a face one cannot call particularly handsome—the individual elements each a bit too bold. But taken together they command attention, suggest the classic beauty is superficial, vapid. Cornelius J. was taller, thinner, and finer boned; he carried himself in the languid manner that was characteristic of dandies of his class. Though only forty-six, he gave off little impression of the vigor and energy characteristic of his older, more temperate brother.

As all present expected, Lord's opening questions led the disgruntled heir through a quick review of his life, his leaving home at eighteen, his marriage, the various amounts of monthly allowances his father provided through the years. He sidestepped reference to Cornelius J.'s mercurial work history, indebtedness, or epilepsy, knowing full well this would come up during cross-examination. Instead, he moved quickly to establish the presence of fraud in the will.

To demonstrate William H.'s manipulativeness, Lord questioned Cornelius J. at length concerning an episode from January of 1854. On that day the twenty-three year old was dressing for a supper engagement when police burst in and took him protesting to the Bloomingdale Asylum in the country area of Morningside Heights. In consulting with Dr. J. Tilden Brown, director of the asylum, Cornelius J. discovered the commitment papers were flawed. He was stunned to learn that a cosigner to the commitment paper was his own older brother, William H. Dr. Brown agreed to support him in asking the court for a writ of *habeas corpus*. At the hearing, William H. pulled his younger brother aside and warned him to withdraw his writ, else suffer arrest for forgery against a downtown merchant. To add force to his argument, William H. pointed out that their father was very ill and would immediately disinherit Cornelius J. if he learned the young man had been arrested. Cornelius J.'s testimony brought down the courtroom when he recounted how he told his brother that he would rather be considered a damned rascal than a damned lunatic.

Cornelius J. testified further how he then got his writ and visited the merchant, who told him simply to pay up an old debt, that he had no forgery complaint. Some months later the incident came up again during a rare visit home. Somehow, perhaps through William H., the Commodore had learned of his wayward son's trip to the asylum and spewed his ritually well scripted torrent of invectives at the young man. Suddenly Sophia burst out in tears, shouted at her husband to stop being a fool, that William was the instigator of his incarceration. She said she loved all her children but had to bring into the open William H.'s scheming to keep Cornelius J. and his father apart. Handkerchief in hand during this retelling, Cornelius J. sniffed as he noted how his father suddenly grew silent and no longer taunted him.

Lord then jumped forward to 1874, and asked many questions to establish that Cornelius J. never gambled, whored, or drank during October and November of that year. Clinton objected strenuously: this information had no bearing on the will. The surrogate agreed, and asked for an explanation. Lord said he intended to show William H.'s role in a conspiracy to mislead the Commodore, hence shape the will. Surrogate agreed that if any part of the will could be shown to have been obtained fraudulently, even though it be unrelated to Marie's claim, the entire will would be invalidated.

Clinton had a go at cross-examination, a predictable march through Cornelius J.'s illnesses, proclivity for leaving jobs following only a month or two, numerous arrests, and debts. Cornelius J. suffered convenient memory losses on the stand. He admitted to leaving unpaid loans in Utica, Rochester, Cincinatti, San Francisco, and Philadelphia but could not be sure as to Baltimore, Chicago, or Saint Louis. And if he borrowed money from gamblers, it was not for gambling, he explained. Only $10,000 of his $90,000 in debts were for gambling. And where did Cornelius J. ever expect to get the money to pay these bills off? Why, from the same source his brother William H. was counting on, he responded. Despite four days of facing skillful and demanding questions, Cornelius J. held up well. It is uncertain how many spectators left agreeing with Clinton's conclusion, "Here was a son worthless and dissipated."[21]

It was now time for Lord to establish the conspiracy of 1874. William H. must have been nervous, for professional witnesses paid for their testimony were a common legal ploy. For several months Lord called up obscure and irrelevant witnesses to the stand, none of whom addressed the fall of 1874. It was March before Lord was able to bring forth affadavits on the claim. The key witnesses, he claimed, had fled to Chicago following numerous threats and attempts at bribes by William H.

The affadavits suggested the following. A well-dressed man, later identified as the Commodore's right-hand man, Chauncy Depew, asked a detective firm to watch a man pointed out in a hotel lobby to be Cornelius J. The surveillance noted a daily pattern of discreditable habits. Upon hearing the report, William H. was said to be outwardly sorry while constraining delight. One detective accompanied Depew to give the report to the Commodore, who finally said in the middle of it, "Go away, go away, and never let me see you again."[22] Then, three years later one of the detectives was with an acquaintance who pointed out Cornelius J., who proved not to be the man he had tracked those two months. He decided to write Cornelius J. and inform him of the nefarious plot.

Following weeks of delays and no witnesses, on the 11th of June, Lord reported to the court he had received a letter from the detectives denying their earlier statements. The real plotter, they discovered, was Cornelius J. himself! Despite Clinton's objections, the surrogate permitted the original statements to be read into the court record. While the clerk droned on, William H. sat rigidly while his sister shook an angry fist at him. Also read were the denials, and Cornelius J.'s denial of the denials. Then came affadavits from Depew and William H., along with a flowery speech by Clinton indicting the honesty of any professional detectives.

A Judge's Slip Brings
Sudden Resolution

The trial was now more than a year old, and neither side had presented a strong case. Observers wondered who was telling the truth concerning events in 1874. Had there been a conspiracy involving William H. and Chauncey Depew to undermine Cornelius J.'s reputation? Or was their lawyer's version correct, that the story was an invitation of Cornelius J.'s to besmirch his brother? Only the principals knew the truth, and courtrooms in that day were like the entertainment that later replaced them—utterly untrustworthy as vehicles for truth.

Following a summer break, the trial lurched on with several highly colorful and amusing witnesses who told inventive stories later shown to be perjuries. It was not until November 18, 1878, that the defense could commence its presentation, which brought numerous men of repute to testify to the Commodore's acumen. For the most part, Lord did not cross-examine. Then one day he caught Clinton off guard. Bishop Holland McTyeire of the Southern Methodist church was commenting on the praiseworthy character of Frank, who was the cajoling force behind the Commodore's gift of $1 million toward the founding of Vanderbilt University. Are you aware, interrupted Lord, that said Frank had an ex-husband? A lightening bolt could have struck the defense. They had opened the one fatal vulnerability that could threaten their case.

Judge Black quickly brought the matter into the open for those spectators too obtuse to understand the import of Lord's remark. "Here is a man eighty years old marrying a woman fifty [sic] years his junior, who came here a stranger, after separating from a husband who is still living." This should cause bitterness among the children, and it did so, he observed. Save one, he added, William H., who encouraged the marriage. Now besides the fact that Frank caused hatred and distress, and as a consequence held undue influence over the Commodore, there was a suggestion the marriage was unlawful, "unholy." Choking on his words, Judge Black became even more frank, to the defense's horror. "That a stranger should sell herself to this old man for his money, taking advantage of that weakness of his nature, is not a reason why a will made under such circumstances should be allowed to stand."[23]

Despite the surrogate's attempt to regain poise and set the trial back on course, everyone knew it was over. William H. could not risk further public aspersions on his stepmother, whom he needed to keep on his side. (After all, she could just as easily turn tail and go after the money as well.) The defense continued its case with little interruption from Lord. Meanwhile, the press leaked stories of compromise.

The surrogate's decision against the claimants on March 19, 1879, was irrelevant. The Commodore had been an astute and talented man, he concluded, "but lacking in the amenities of education and culture and a delicate respect for the opinions of his fellow man."[24] His remarks mattered little to the complainants, who celebrated their gain. Although the exact figures disappeared from the records, most likely both Cornelius J. and Marie Alicia received substantial "gifts" from William H. The lawyers, all of whom billed William H. as part of the agreement, did almost as well. Clinton alone was rumored to get between $300,000 and $500,000.

But if two Vanderbilts celebrated, the clan as a whole was not joyful. The Commodore had left a regrettable legacy, one of furious family in-fighting that encouraged extreme positions, stubbornness, obstinacy, and pride. Parent could cut off son; brother could fight brother; the women did not matter. Blood connections, those elemental sources of trust and security, were weakened for the sake of preserving the family trust. The more perceptive members of the family must have shuddered at the *New York Tribune*'s editorial righteousness. "[R]ivers of gold will not wash out the stain. The name Vanderbilt will disappear in shame and ignominy."

The *Tribune* was wrong, of course. The very qualities that made for bad family relations ensured success in other endeavors. Sophia and the Commodore's genes promised strength, courage, determination, and quick minds. Later Vanderbilts would make up for the shame of the Great Feud for decades afterward, with some placing significant and positive marks on society. But the heritage of this public exposure would haunt, and try as they would to avoid further notoriety, as if cursed, descendants could not help but repeat their ancestors' script. It had its most sorry consequence on April 2, 1882, when William Henry's maroon coupe alighted at the vestibule of the Glenham Hotel, where his brother Cornelius Jeremiah was sprawled on the floor, dead of a self-inflicted gunshot wound.

1880-1885

Alva Discovers
Architecture

The public feud over the Commodore's will hardened society's low estimate of the Vanderbilts. When William H.'s daughter Florence married Hamilton Twombly of Boston in 1877, so staid a paper as *The New York Times* ran a mocking account of the ritual. It described the affair "a circus," with ticket takers (invitation collectors actually) at the door of the church shouting to gain guests' attention, crowds "pressed against the canopy," guests threatened by unruly carriage horses. The guests themselves were described as including Wall Street brokers, members of German banking houses, women of a class that would not be expected to receive invitations, and among the ushers, five Boston men nobody seemed to know. Three years later a pseudonymous novel appeared, *The Vanderdorps*, based much upon the scandalous dispute over the will. Of a bride in the story, obviously Florence Vanderbilt Twombly, one character cheekily remarks, "Fanny is a good enough sort of girl, but I think her charms lie mostly in the Vanderdorp gilding."

To William H. and Maria, such insult and exclusion did not matter much. But to daughters-in-law Alva and Alice, it was a constantly burning insult. For both, breaking into society, indeed dominating it, became a magnificent obsession. Unfortunately for the older Alice, Alva had more spirit and grace for the game.

The path began simply enough. In 1877, Alva gave birth to her first child, Consuelo, and was soon pregnant again with Willie K., Jr. She and Willie now desired a country home on a thousand acres they had purchased on Long Island near Oakdale, where he was a member of the South Side Sportsman Club. Improvements in road and rail meant more of the well-to-do were building houses on the Island, not as in the past, simple spacious summer cottages, often without plumbing or heating, but as "half-homes," fully equipped for use in all seasons.

Long Island's appeal attracted horsemen for its varied landscape of hill and wood that called for skillful and daring riding. Theodore Roosevelt thought riding to the hounds in Long Island the "most exciting and perhaps the manliest kind of amusement to be found east of the Mississippi."[1] With the streets of New York now marching farther north and much of the Manhattan countryside being flattened in preparation for yet further expansion, fox hunting on the Island proved a ready substitute for trotting.

In a rare expression of compatibility, Willie and Alva agreed there was only one architect for the job: Richard Morris Hunt. It proved an auspicious choice for architectural history.

Hunt, then fifty-one, was the son of early New England stock traceable to Jonathan Hunt, who had stepped foot on the shores of Massachusetts Bay Colony around 1630 and founded a prosperous line. When Hunt was just a toddler, his father died suddenly, leaving his mother to cast about New England with her brood of five for a decade. Noting "his distinguishing quality, from a very early age, was his persistent industry," Jane Hunt was not surprised to see Richard take several honors at Boston Latin School.[2] In 1843 she took the family to Italy, where it was hoped another son's respiratory ailments would find cure, but settled in Paris. Following more schooling there and in Geneva, Richard entered the Ecole des Beaux Arts, the preeminent school of architecture in the world.

Paris in the 1840s was still a medieval city, where poorly lit twisted streets lined with rotting garbage posed many dangers to hapless walkers. Fresh water and modern sewage removal were available to few. Still, unconventional Americans were enthralled by the very messiness, which was compensated for by the spirited, cheerful temperament of the city dwellers and the elegant variety of the buildings. No drab New England salt boxes here! And thanks to Louis Phillipe, the king who wanted to link his monarchy to the glories of the Napoleonic empire, an architectural renaissance brought frequent new delights. Young Hunt saw the Arc de Triomphe de l'Etoile and the Church of the Madeleine in their pristine states. New lamp standards and fountains graced the Place de Concorde and Champs-Elysées. The restoration of the Palais du Louvre was under way—Hunt would later design some working plans of details for the reconstruction—along with new iron and glass railroad stations, such as the Gare Montparnesse.

In 1856, Hunt returned to New York, the first in a long line of Beaux Arts students to practice architecture in the United States. His move was a risky one, for Americans were not used to hiring a professional to design their buildings. Urban homes were the expressions of the craftsmen hired to build them, who for expertise relied upon published handbooks of designs and engineering specifications. So Hunt knew he would have a selling job to do, and he found business slow at first. To achieve his aim, he drew the public's mind away from a conception of architecture as engineering to place it in the province of art. In doing so, he connected the activity with one of the most honorable careers of the day, one aligned closely to the religious vocation in moral and spiritual values. At that time, Americans then viewed art to be a necessary function in society, and artists agreed, holding their work to be service to national glory, an expression of the best of American virtues. One might study in Europe to learn from the old masters but should complete one's mature work at home to share in and with the community good by celebrating the nation's best qualities.

In the summer, Hunt would join his mother and siblings in Newport, where the family had a retreat. His brother William set up his studio there, and at one point instructed a young William James in the craft. William Hunt had chosen Newport for its moderate Gulf Stream climate and its artistic intellectual colony, which attracted such diverse notables as Louis Agassiz and the poet Longfellow. Hunt found commissions in Newport, and to his greater satisfaction, wife Catherine Howland, daughter of a prominent shipping owner who shared his preference for bohemian friends. Their home, Hill Top Cottage, became a center for Newport cultural life. So it is possible Alva as a girl had seen the man who was to bring her so much fulfillment.

By the time Alva and Hunt met professionally, he had acquired both fame and notoriety. His ten-story New York Tribune building was one of New York City's first skyscrapers. His Stuyvesant apartment building on East Eighteenth Street was the first multiple dwelling designed to dissociate itself from the tenements of the poor, hence attract the middle class to apartment living. His simple and modern Neo-Grecian town houses inspired copies in many cities. But his Lenox Library, which after demolition was recognized to have been one of his greatest creations, disturbed the press and public for its classic Grecian influences and Parisian floor plan. The ponderious High Victorian Gothic, which he disdained, was more popular. Then his proposed designs for gateways into Central Park caused such a stir for their being reminiscent of Napoleon III, hence too imperialistic in tone for a democracy, that the contract was canceled. (He would come into better public favor later when he designed the pedestal for the Statue of Liberty.)

Alva would most certainly have been on Hunt's side during the various controversies about his work. A fellow Francophile, she mocked the know-nothing insensibility of those who stopped his Central Park plans. That he continued to buck trends and introduce elements of European classicism in his works would only add to his appeal. She realized he was as determined, opinionated, and perfectionist as she was.

Hunt was, of course, no stranger to socialite women, for he and wife Catherine, unlike the Vanderbilts, were welcome guests at the home of Caroline Astor, the arbiter of who was "in" or "out." When Alva was still a girl, Caroline Schermerhorn had married the younger son of William Backhouse Astor, hence was outranked by her brother-in-law John Jacob Astor III. Fortunately, that man's wife had rather unconventional views, for example, that it would be interesting to include artists and writers at her dinner table. Another of her innovations was *Les Causeries de Lundi,* a weekly women's group who met to hear the reading of very intellectual papers. Art and ideas being anathema to society, Caroline Astor was able to upstage her sister-in-law by moving society into a more opulent entertaining. Building upon August Belmont's ice-breaking introduction of European luxury, she made gastronomy a cult through her weekly dinner parties, where she dared to serve on gold plate. There the conversation was careful not to tax vacant brain cells, being limited to sauces, wines, horses, yachts, cotillions, marriages, Newport, and Saratoga. Society followed partly because its fortunes were so immense, partly because with each generation the Dutch names reflected less of that culture's modest preference.

It was Caroline Astor, *the* "Mrs. Astor," who had been primarily responsible for the exclusion of the Vanderbilts from society. In fact, the Astor family had acquired its wealth during the same period as the Vanderbilts, only in fur trading, the main difference being its members earlier settled in New York City and took on the accoutrements of society. As the major real estate holders in New York City, they were also its greatest slumlords. By the 1850s the Vanderbilts were wealthier than any of the Knickerbockers, yet still considered Upstarts. Born a Schermerhorn, part of Mrs. Astor's drive may have come from the knowledge she had married beneath herself.

So unrivaled became her authority that she was dubbed the Mystic Rose, evidence she had transformed society into a secular religion. Through her indomitable efforts, she also expanded and elevated the role of women in society, which would have continued its dull and doughty act without her leadership. One of the results was their greater activity in the architecture and design of the houses many were building farther up Fifth Avenue. (In 1871, the Old Society's greatest and most conservative arbiter, elderly Mary Mason Jones, had dared to put a flagrantly Parisian-style mansion up in the netherlands of Fifty-eighth Street, the only outspoken act of her long life.) Hunt did not generally find such women congenial clients, for while they accepted him as an equal socially, they were imperious when it came to his role as designer of their buildings. Such matrons were considered to be that scorned yet essential client who, while knowing little about architecture, are quick to impose little fussy changes that compel large and troublesome adjustments upon the designer and builders.

Only twenty-five, vivacious Alva appeared one day at Hunt's small office and presented herself. There she squarely faced this man of medium height and strict bearing, red necktie to warn of his temper, a big black cigar in his nondrawing hand. Expecting an order to draw up a set of plans, his deepset eyes could hardly contain his astonishment over her subsequent request. She wanted him to design her a house, true, but in the process she wanted to learn architecture, to be a kind of protégée. That meant accepting her presence at his studio, observing and practicing, seeking his instruction. Like so many who came across demands from this indomitable personality, he agreed.[3] They became fast friends, their hotheadedness well matched. The studio oftened resounded with their shouting matches over tiny details. "Damn it, Mrs. Vanderbilt, who is building this house," he would yell. "Damn it, Mr. Hunt, who is going to live in this house?" she would holler back.[4] Despite the constant disagreements, they held firm to one another, for they shared a common goal, excellence. "Work, work, keep on going; that is the best you can have," was his motto, a philosophy she shared.

The Oakdale house was purposefully undistinguished, a rambling clapboard and shingle reminiscent of European half timber houses and chalets. When the main house was completed, for years afterward Alva kept the Hunt studio workers busy with orders for dependencies, including a gardener's cottage, a hothouse, an entrance gate, a bowling alley, and a stable for thirty horses with living quarters for twelve grooms and keepers.[5] The point was to emphasize the role of the home with nature surrounding, a place in service of outdoor activities. A statement of distinction was to be reserved for another home she and Willie asked him to build at 660 Fifth Avenue, a palace really, from which Alva could stake her claim on the heights of society, a position from which she could metaphorically look down upon Mrs. Astor and the other grande dames. Alva always set her mind on the best, and nothing could prevent her from getting it.

Alva and Hunt
Create 660 Fifth

Alva knew the way to stand out was not to build the largest or the most ornate house. Already numerous massive homes with eye-numbingly opulent interiors commanded Fifth Avenue. The trick, she understood, was to put up a structure that broke tradition and set new standards for elegance. She wanted to show that money and poor taste did not necessarily go together, however much current New Yorkers proved otherwise. The project was to become in her eyes her "fourth child," and attended to with all the considerable care she gave to her real children.

Alva saw her aspirations as curiously fitting in the democratic tradition. Since this was a time when art was held to express the great virtues of the country, she felt it incumbent upon the wealthy to erect homes that the public could learn from and admire. The rich had a responsibility to build monuments representing "not only wealth, but knowledge and culture, desirable elements for wealth to encourage."[6] Her inspiration was the Medici family, which had left the permanent imprint of beauty and art on Florence. Like the Medici, she also saw her building as an "expression in outward and visible terms of the importance of the Vanderbilt family."[7]

Hunt responded in kind to these high ideals. Alva told him he could chose any style, Norman, Italian, or Spanish, so long as it was medieval. If there was any irony in Alva claiming feudal symbols to represent American democracy, it eluded her. She should likely have responded that it was beauty and its spiritual accompaniments that was the point, not the display of great class differences.

Fortunately, Hunt's response was vigorously on the side of art, not material display. His inspiration was the sixteenth-century Loire Valley Chateau du Bois, skillfully reinterpreted and adapted to a millionaire of the late nineteenth century. His design extended beyond the exterior to include meticulous renderings of interior elements—fireplaces, panelings, carvings. Hunt's life philosophy that work is the best rest one can have is apparent in the fastidious renderings he presented to Alva. His mind generated multiple versions of this wall or that fireplace mantle for her to choose from.

It took two years for imported Italian stonecutters to frame the granite foundation, place the Indiana limestone blocks, and carve the intricate tracery panels bordering the window and the balustrades of the third and fourth stories. To the blue slate roof with copper cresting they added griffins, unicorns, sea serpents, and cupids. The entrance pavilion featured the *fleurs de lys,* along with acorns and oak leaves, which had been fashioned into a coat of arms for the Vanderbilt family, great oaks from tiny acorns the obvious message.[8] While this hulk was going up, New Yorkers gathered on the street corner to argue over the effect, which overwhelmed the chunky flat-topped brownstones alongside. (Although Hunt had urged Willie K. to buy up the entire block frontage so the house would be better sited, he refused, a spurning he much regretted later.) Indeed, some of society actually shunned Alva for using Indiana limestone.

Although the exterior of 660 Fifth was sixteenth-century French, a guest passing through the interior public rooms encountered different themes: the library was French Renaissance, the billiard room Moorish, the salon Louis XV. (Adding to the eclecticism, several years later Alva had the French walnut panels of the parlor redone in the style of seventeenth-century England.) Throughout, one's eyes were delighted by the Boucher tapestries and magnificent French furniture, some of which had belonged to Marie Antoinette. Unlike her father-in-law's copious and derivative collection of oils, Alva's paintings were fewer and at times more discerning. They included Rembrandt's *The Noble Slav,* Greuze's *Broken Eggs,* and portraits by Joshua Reynolds and Thomas Gainsborough. Perhaps the most famous room, the two-story dining hall, was Henry II, with walls of Caen stone and oak wainscoting. Diners sat in the glow of massive stained glass windows and were further dwarfed by the immense double fireplace with its elaborate carved niches to hold life-sized statues and large porcelain vases. It was a humbling space, reminding guests they were not so important, that the works of art would outlast them.

Alva dominated the second-story private space, her dressing room alone being larger than her husband's bedroom. Her bedroom was as large as the grand salon below, 38 by 25 feet. There hung Boucher's sumptuous *Toilette of Venus,* believed to have been painted by the artist for Madame de Pompadour. The image of the nude goddess, perched self-satisfied while cherubs adorn her with jewels, was an apt portrait of Alva's contented success. Consuelo was placed on the third floor, a corkscrew stairwell in the tourelle connecting her to her mother's room underneath. Adjoining Alva's bedroom was not Willie K.'s room, as would be typical in such homes, but that of the boys. The provider of the purse for this immensity was relegated to a corner across the hall.

Other Vanderbilt Mansions
Rise Along Fifth Avenue

I t should be no surprise that with the Commodore's inheritance fast in hand, the other Vanderbilts were on a building spree as well. Most active was William H., who ordered a "Triple Palace" at 640–642 Fifth, on the block south of Alva and Willie K.'s. The triplet provided one section for himself and Maria and two others for two daughters. Learning that marble would force a long construction period, William H. chose the more malleable brownstone for the facade, and had more than seven hundred laborers, along with sixty foreign sculptors, rush the task. Following his father's model of self-puffery, he authorized publication of *Mr. Vanderbilt's House and Collection,* which claimed "Like a more perfect Pompeii, the work will be the vision and image of a typical American residence, seized at the moment when the nation begins to have a taste of its own."[9] With its hodge-podge collection of antique furniture of assorted eras, its dark woods and date palms, its art gallery with oils hung like puzzle parts to cover every inch of wall, it only too unfortunately exhibited the banal popular taste of the day.

Apart from his financial prowess, William Henry was now acclaimed to be the most noted art collector in the city. Although he had started by collecting American art, in 1874 an incident embarrassed him into shifting his interests. That year Seymour Guy borrowed his group portrait *The William Henry Vanderbilt Family* to hang in an exhibition at the National Academy of Design. When the critics ridiculed the work, William sought out art dealer Samuel P. Avery to direct him in purchasing art considered beyond reproach, in other words, European art. Avery observed that he was kind and generous with the artists, even raising the price on a work he thought deserved more. When his companions sometimes objected to his lack of economy, he would respond that "the pleasure of possession ought to be taken into consideration."[10] He was particularly attracted to rural scenes and landscapes, nostalgic reminders of his own early pastoral days, and was quick to point out accuracies and errors in the depictions.

Significantly, he collected contemporary works from artists he could visit and talk with, names familiar today, such as Bonheur, Millais, Theodore Rousseau, or Corot, and many less recognizable, such as Goupil or Frere. His sympathy for the artist was well known. He liked to tell how Rosa Bonheur, in her eighth decade, remarked how upon hearing the lumbermen "cutting down trees in the forest ... every blow of the axe hurts my heart." When Meissonier mourned that his favorite painting, *Le Renseignement,* was in Germany and the owner would not sell it so it could hang once more in France, William H. quietly set to work. He sent wife Maria and a friend to Dresden, where they simply started placing bank notes on the table until the painting's owner said, "Stop—take the picture." Maria carried the canvas back to France, where it was set up as a surprise for Meissonier. The news of his kindness brought the name of Vanderbilt much good will in the Paris art world thereafter.

William H. also went far to correct his father's noted miserliness when it came to good works. In addition to providing for special cases who came to his attention, such as elderly neighbors from his days on Staten Island, he was profligate with his contributions to various Episcopalian missionary and service activities, the YMCA, the General Theological Seminary of New York, and the Metropolitan Museum of Art, which would become the eventual beneficiary of his collection. His most visible contribution stands today in Central Park, Cleopatra's Needle, actually the obelisk of Thothmes III, which he paid to have transported and erected there for public enjoyment.

Having decided to build homes for two daughters, he ordered two more mansions for his remaining daughters placed at 680 and 684 Fifth. The results only added to a view of New York so adeptly opined by Edith "Pussy" Jones, a friend of Alice Vanderbilt's whose family was among the most exclusive in society. One of her most depressing recollections of her youth, she later recalled, was the "intolerable ugliness of New York, of its untended streets and narrow houses, so lacking in external dignity, so crammed with smug and suffocating upholstery." She wondered how the owners, who had seen the elegance of London, Rome, and Paris could continue to build on "a cramped horizontal gridiron ... without towers, porticoes, fountains, or perspectives" and in that "universal chocolate coating of the most hideous stone ever quarried."[11] The houses were as cramped inside as out. If rooms were large, they were so crammed with Victorian excess that the spaciousness was imperceptible. The room arrangements also prevented privacy, for rooms opened upon one another through large portals, and eyes were ever present to watch what was going on. It is no wonder people spoke in veiled terms.

Not one to be left out of the latest family mania, Alice decided she better make her mark on the street as well. She and her family had been living at Fifth Avenue and Thirty-second Street, an area losing in social prominence. In 1878 she and Cornelius selected an unremarkable brownstone at 742 Fifth, then gradually acquired 744 and 746, along with the corner of 1 West Fifty-seventh Street, the total price for these parcels coming to $900,000. For her architect she chose a onetime student of Hunt's, George B. Post, to design a castle for the site, which was completed in 1882. That French Renaissance edifice of pressed brick and light Bedford stone showed the student had little of the graceful line or conceptual clarity of Hunt.

Alice was quite pleased, however, and proceeded to decorate it as a monument to expensive mediocrity. The foyer, with its excessively massive stairwell, prominently displayed portraits of the Commodore and her father-in-law William H. One room, a kind of bepillowed and heavily draped Turkish harem room, was so ungainly that even Alice's children in later years would futilely urge her to redo it. The result may have been the inspiration for art critic Charles Caffin's comment that the American rich "prefer a room in which every detail is dryly imitated from a dead period to one animated by the art spirit of to-day. So they take their morning coffee *a la Louis Quinze;* their luncheon in a Dutch kitchen; drop into an affectation of Japan for a cup of afternoon tea; dine in the splendour of the *Grand Monarque;* sip their liqueurs in Pompeii; and rest at length from this jumble of inert impressions in a chamber *a l'Empire.*"[12] This uninspired vision was regrettable, because if uninspired with his exteriors, Post was renowned for his cohesive and inspiring interiors, and he had incorporated an elegant backdrop that was haplessly ignored by its owners.

Not all in the house was a loss, of course, for many individual objects were significant and would bring pleasure to family members. Most notable here was Turner's splendid depiction of *The Grand Canal, Venice,* purchased in 1885 from the earl of Dudley. (And in his usual charitable way, when Cornelius spied Rosa Bonheur's *Horse Fair* at an auction, he sent it directly to the Metropolitan Museum of Art.) Yet it would take concentration to rest upon this or that particular masterwork amid the general jumble of a room.

Not only did the house fail to satisfy the eye, it lacked the most important need, a ballroom. It seems the building plot was not deep enough to include one, so Alice had to open the doors between the parlors on ball nights and place folding camp stools about to accommodate her guests. This deficiency irked her, for once Alice recognized her mother-in-law had no interest in social recognition, she took it as her duty to advance the Vanderbilt name in society, to become known as *the* "Mrs. Vanderbilt." Cornelius provided the resources, though one must suspect it was not always ungrudgingly, for he was shrewd with his money and, as a deacon of his church, most familiar with the biblical passages concerning the ultimate meaninglessness of wealth or fame. But Alice seemed to have a demon in her concerning propriety and respectability. Possibly the scandalous newspaper reports during the great will feud made her particularly sensitive to reputation. A woman of many private and praiseworthy virtues, she was unable to rechannel or inhibit this egotistic impulse, which grew stronger and increasingly destructive over the years.

It was not so much that society rejected her, for she knew the subtle rituals and rules of the inner circle and made them her own, indeed seemed born to them. She was not too European, like Alva, who required her family converse with her at dinner in French. Nor was she excessively buoyant or expressive, too direct and frank in stating an opinion (again unlike Alva). She was a handsome woman, understood the importance of dressing stylishly and expensively without crossing over the line to ostentation. Still, she was not included in Mrs. Astor's airy crowd nor in the Four Hundred (which counted several dozen less than that, in fact). What she failed to see was that numerous other wealthy women were also clamoring for a place on that height, and she was simply too indistinguishable from the rest.

Alva Brings
Mrs. Astor to Kneel

Alva understood that only a daring and even defiant act would force society to open its doors to the Vanderbilts.

The very building of 660 Fifth itself accomplished much. Upon seeing its exceptional taste and talent, the powers that be deemed the Willie K. Vanderbilts worth an invitation to the 1881 Patriarch's Ball. This annual event, begun in 1872, was to introduce to old New Yorkers the "adopted citizens, and men whose ability and integrity had won the esteem of the community."[13] The ball was a place where people like the Goelets, Cuttings, and Astors could look over an Avenoodle without having to ask them into their homes. Invitation to the Patriarch's Ball did not mean acceptance; what mattered was the invitations to private events that followed—or not. Alva and Willie K. passed, but not enough for Caroline Astor to open her home to them. A more audacious move was required for that attainment.

It is doubtful she had the goal of forcing Mrs. Astor's hand in mind when she first planned the event that would set her in the public's mind as *the* "Mrs. Vanderbilt." Her good friend Consuelo Yznaga had come for a long stay at 660 Fifth soon after it opened, and by her presence she provided the perfect excuse to inaugurate her ballroom.

After seeing Alva married off in 1875, Consuelo had managed to land herself a British title. On a trip to Saratoga she met Viscount Mandeville, son of the duchess of Manchester. Spying a potential husband, the Yznagas invited him to their country home, where he promptly came down with typhoid. Consuelo saved the day with her banjo picking, and he rewarded her with an engagement. Unfortunately, the duchess was none too pleased but had no choice in the matter. She herself was rather notorious for her gambling and parties at which guests carried on with one another's spouses. Raised by such a mother, the viscount's reputation was too racy to satisfy other British aristocratic mamas. Consuelo was therefore a bargain.

The duchess of Manchester was also a leading player in the prince of Wales set. After his father died in 1861, and his mother Queen Victoria went into permanent mourning, Albert Edward, or Bertie as his intimates referred to him, had established his own separate court. Defying his mother's wishes, he aligned with the fashionable set, that collection of aristocratic families Victoria disdained as wretched, ignorant, decadent beings who lived only to kill time. The fun-loving prince particularly took to the frank and less inhibited American heiresses appearing at London social events and soon brought several of them into his inner circle, which became known as the Marlborough House set. Consequently, three girls from Alva's past were now among the prince's favorites: Jennie Jerome Churchill, Minnie Stevens Paget, and Consuelo. (Gertrude Atherton would describe their lives in her unfinished novel, *The Buccaneers*.)

It was good Consuelo made such important friends, because her husband, now Lord Mandeville, lived up to his profligate reputation. Reckless with money and attracted to dance house girls, he forced her to seek the better life in the company of generous friends—hence the long visit with Alva that winter. Aware that society lusted after the chance to touch hands with a titleholder, Alva was ready to throw her ace.

It was the quadrille that gave Alva her unexpected opportunity. Once word went out that twelve hundred people were to be selected for invitations, the crème de la crème immediately set about putting the best seamstresses and jewelers to work. One of these, Carrie Astor, youngest and favorite daughter of the dowager queen, called together seven other friends to practice the Star Quadrille. Alas, when the invitations were known to have been sent out, the Astors found none delivered to their doorstep. Mrs. Astor let her puzzlement be known through friends. Alva sweetly observed that she could hardly invite Carrie Astor or any Astor for that matter because they had never paid her a call. Upon receiving this message, and swayed by Carrie's tears, Mrs. Astor swallowed her pride, donned a Worth afternoon gown, ordered a carriage, and dropped her calling card on the plate at 660 Fifth. In short order a footman arrived in a Vanderbilt carriage at the Astor residence to deliver an invitation to the ball. The Astor seamstresses must have been relieved their recent work was not in vain.

Always alert to timing, Alva chose as the date of the ball March 26, right after Easter and its six weeks of Lenten sobriety. It was also a Monday, Mrs. Astor's traditional night for entertaining. The hour was set for the usual 11:30 P.M., but an hour before then Alva and Lady Mandeville discovered guests were actually arriving early and rushed to take their places at the head of the receiving line in the great entrance hall. There, Alva, costumed as a Venetian Renaissance princess after a painting by Alexis Cabanel, positioned herself under a full-length portrait of herself. Her tawny blond hair was crowned by a Venetian cap covered with encrusted designs of jewels. The deep square decolletage of her dress was draped in multiple strands of pearls and a double-strand diamond necklace, the gown constructed of brilliantly colored and embroidered fabrics, with transparent gold tissue hanging over her unsleeved arms. Willie K. stood beside her in yellow silk tights, yellow doublet and trunks, and a black velvet cape embroidered in gold, a replica from a painting of the duc de Guise. William Henry stood nearby, the only attendee not in costume, with Maria garbed as a lady-in-waiting to Marie Antoinette.

Alva was right to feel great pride in what she had accomplished. Guests soon understood the real victory was not the petty social one over Mrs. Astor but that of setting a standard of irreproachable taste over every detail of the event. Alva was often quoted as saying that being a society woman was one of the hardest jobs imaginable, the reason being she planned, controlled, and watched every preparation. Like Richard Morris Hunt with his architecture, Alva was a historicist when it came to entertaining. She would strike a theme, research, and create a dramatic, often surprising interpretation. This was immediately apparent to guests in her choice of dress.

The court of Louis XV would have admired her tour de force for the event, the "Hobby-Horse Quadrille." For this dance she had constructed costumes in which the dancers, dressed in riding habits, appeared to be sitting on hobbyhorses. With real hides, bright eyes, and flowing manes and tails, and false legs hung on the outside of richly-embroidered blankets, the horses appeared almost lifelike. Yet these apparatuses were so light and comfortably attached that the wearers could move with grace and security. Then Carrie Astor and her friends were invited to perform the Star Quadrille they had practiced so hard. In accord with the theme, their variously colored dresses were covered with a silver gauze embroidered with stars, and they carried a star-tipped wand. To complete the effect, each had attached to a forehead band a large star of clustered diamonds. Following yet another quadrille, the guests were free to try the new Ticklish Water Polka or waltz in the Louis XV salon, with its Gobelin tapestries and wainscoting taken from an old Loire chateau.

Supper was served in the third-floor gymnasium (actually an enormous two-story indoor play area for the children so they could skate and race about in bad weather). In the recreation of a tropical garden replete with orchids, palm fronds, and bougainvillea, diners could chose from a sumptuous buffet or an eight-course served meal. There former President Ulysses S. Grant (whose costume was not recorded) found himself in a line with Daniel Boone (a Senator Wagstaff), Queen Elizabeth I (Mrs. Paran Stevens), Father Knickerbocker (Vanderbilt lawyer Chauncey Depew), gypsies, witches, cats, Romeos and Juliets, and multiple Madame Pompadours. Among the many French personages, no Napoleons sat at the dinner tables. As one guest observed, "The beauty of the women was perhaps not enhanced by their costumes, for American women are always beautiful. But the beauty of the men was very much improved by the glory of the costume. It shows us how much men lose in the ugly dress of the nineteenth century."[14]

Mrs. Astor must have had special difficulty moving about, weighed down by a heavy dark velvet gown thickly embroidered with pearls, the bodice of which was almost fully blanketed by her usual complement of diamonds, said to be worth more than $200,000. Guests keeping a close eye on relations between Mrs. Astor and Alva were surprised to see the two in lengthy, apparently amiable conversation. Despite her hauteur, Caroline Astor was renowned for her kindness and lack of maliciousness toward others. She never made catty gossip and may have surprised Alva with her gentle charm.

If Mrs. Astor sought to stand out by blinding people with her fossilized carbons, Alice Vanderbilt chose a less costly but more spectacular solution, the illuminated costume. Twenty years earlier Mrs. Pierre Lorillard Ronalds had astonished her guests by appearing as Music, a tiny harp in her hair illuminated by tiny gas jets. The age of Edison and batteries introduced a safer alternative, so Alice came as Electric Light, her white satin, diamond betrimmed gown reflecting the sparkling flutter of her headdress. Cornelius joined in the spirit of the day by coming as Louis XVI, in fawn-colored brocade edged with lace of real silver, and a diamond-hilted sword. How he managed the sword during dancing, the one frivolity he greatly enjoyed, is unknown.

Even Alice and Cornelius's three young children attended, an unusual inclusion for youngsters who were usually expected to be behind the scenes when adults were around. Although Alice, knowing Alva's victory extended to the ascendency of all the Vanderbilts in society, should have felt some gratitude, it is unclear exactly what her feelings were. People noticed the costume, not the behavior or talk of the woman wearing it.

The impact of this ball lasted for years in the lives of participants. As they aged, recounting that evening became a favorite story. In her memoirs years later, Catherine Hunt was able to call up precise details about the costumes and decor. "It was the best of its kind," they said, somewhat wistfully, although one later admitted such events were often a bore, for society people were uncomfortable as fancy dress characters.

The expense of the ball in terms of individual costumes, decoration, and food was at least a quarter of a million dollars (or in today's terms, at least three million) and the newspapers made great play of the opulence displayed. In the sense that it was so conspicuous a display, the ball marked the zenith of the Gilded Age, or what historian Vernon Partington more astutely dubbed the Great Barbecue, fifteen years or so of riotous and extravagant entertaining in society. Others erred in thinking they need only spend money as freely as Alva and Willie K. to repeat that success. But few hostesses had her clever mind, her curiosity, her love of history, to match her artistic taste. Alva's entertainments would remain a rare bit of gold in that time of glitzy showing off.

Alva Bullies to Bring the
Metropolitan Opera About

Alva's victory over the waning Knickerbocker aristocracy was not yet complete. That group, whose motto was "If we don't all stand together, there'll be no such thing as Society left," had one last stand, the Academy of Music.[15] The academy, on East Fourteenth Street, though chartered by the State of New York as a quasi-educational institution, became best known as the opera house, the most fashionable public setting for old New York. It was small, with an interior very much like the noted Academy of Music in Philadelphia, small enough to prevent the addition of the new people "whom New York was beginning to dread and yet be drawn to."[15] Like the Philadelphia twin, it had superb acoustics, which mattered to only a few. Opera, after all, was simply a convenient excuse to be seen and visit with friends.

On a special night, as when Adelina Patti would be singing, what the newspapers would describe as "an exceptionally brilliant audience" drove up in commodious family landaus or smaller Brown coupes, the equivalent of hired limousines in those days. And, of course, one arrived late and left early, for the brilliance of the audience applied to its jewels, not its artistic acumen. Since the unquestioned law of that musical world required that "the German text of French opera sung by Swedish artists should be translated into Italian for the clearer understanding of English-speaking audiences," one generally ignored the activities on the stage except for favorite arias. The music and drama were noticed no more than in a cocktail lounge today.

Arriving late also meant one had less time to sit until the most important activity of the event, the intermission. With the lights on, the occupants of the shabby red-and-gold boxes played their intricate game of social chutes and ladders. Alva claimed her family owned a box at the academy when she was a small child, but that is doubtful. More likely her visits took her to the netherland of the orchestra section, from where she could look up and observe the visitings, the passing of messages back and forth; possibly during such envious visits she determined to have a box of her own one day.

During the 1879–80 season, Alva sought her claim, without success. Singer Lilli Lehmann later recalled, "As, on a particular evening, one of the millionairesses did not receive the box in which she intended to shine because another woman had anticipated her, the husband of the former took prompt action and caused the Metropolitan Opera House to rise."[17] William Henry also made an offer of $30,000 for a box and was frostily turned down. During early 1880, a Vanderbilt-connected lawyer, George Henry Warren, called upon the head of the Academy of Music's board of directors, August Belmont. Warren warned Belmont that Vanderbilt and several other newcomers were willing to build their own opera house if the academy could not find boxes for them in its current space. On April 3, Belmont reported that the board had agreed to remodel the interior of the academy to add twenty-six new boxes.

This wasn't enough for Alva. On April 7, Warren informed the *New York Times* that he and a group of associates had already obtained $800,000 in subscriptions to purchase a site and build a new opera house. The group, which eventually expanded to sixty-five founding members, included not only newcomer Vanderbilts but also cotton broker R. T. Wilson, financier J. P. Morgan, oil magnate William Rockefeller, and William C. Whitney, Cleveland's secretary of the navy. While it is the men who are identified as the founders, informal history places much responsibility for the actual fund-raising upon Alva, who fearlessly approached similarly snubbed archmillionaires to solicit their participation.

Alva's hand is shown in the eventual appearance of the Knickerbockers into the scheme. Most notably, following the ball, Mrs. Astor announced that she stood to join behind the new Metropolitan, where she was rewarded with box 8, from thereafter known as the "social throne" of the Met. Alva was next to her in box 7, one of four Vanderbilt boxes. At the opening night performance of *Faust* on October 22, 1883, two queens oversaw their joint rule. Society was no longer the old New Yorkers holding back the Invaders. It was simply society.

The origins of the building, which was derisively called "the yellow-brick brewery," explain some of the idiosyncrasies of that now-demolished structure. Architect Joshiah Cleveland Cady's original design was for a large plot later found to have deed restrictions excluding its use for places of entertainment. The Broadway site then bought was both smaller and irregular, forcing Cady to cut and trim. Placing storefronts on the Broadway side further sliced into useful space, but the millionaires wanted some way of getting a return on their investment, so they insisted on that commercial intrusion. And while the investors got their boxes, three tiers of thirty-six, the performers faced a shortage of rehearsal rooms, studios, and practice stages. The chorus rehearsed in the ladies' parlor or smoking room of the Grand Tier, while the ballet practiced nearby in what was later to become Sherry's Restaurant. A visiting prima donna was shocked to find a cramped dressing room with unenclosed toilet and poor heating. The stagehands had to build and store sets elsewhere. Yet most artists decided the remarkable acoustics made up for these many inconveniences. Although they could not hear themselves, they quickly learned that without strain they could be heard well by every seat in the house.

Ironically, the Met board also learned that first season that it had approved too many boxes, and not enough millionaires could be found to pay the $60,000 fee. Thus they ordered elimination of the top tier, leaving the middle one, dubbed the Golden Horseshoe, and the lower one, the Diamond Horseshoe. What with the hall's deep sides and numerous pillars one could not see the stage well, the critics argued, and they were right, completely missing the point.

A Belmont Son Brings
Shame upon the Family

August and Caroline Belmont found the Metropolitan debut a convenient opportunity to squash a recent family scandal involving their youngest son, O. H. P., who went by Harry. As they had feared might happen, age did not bring him maturity. When in childhood he showed an interest in the sea, his parents were hopeful he would follow in the steps of his illustrious namesake. But Harry was so lackluster a student that August Belmont had to use his personal influence to get him admitted to the U.S. Naval Academy, where he was thrown out, readmitted (again on his father's pressuring of authorities), and took six years to graduate. The Belmonts demanded too much of their children, and they always presumed it was the children who were weak or wrong. An easygoing sort who aped his father's love of luxury and culture, but not his work habits, Harry gave up most often and most visibly and hence became singled out as the family rebel.

His rebellion peaked when he showed up in Paris and surprised his mother, who thought he was on a naval cruise, to announce he was through with the navy. The reason was Sara (Sallie) Swan Whiting, a high-spirited and flirtatious member of Newport society, where her family owned Swanhurst. Believing Harry was merely infatuated and did not really love the girl, his parents asked him to prove the worthiness of the affection by working in a Bremen bank for two years and agreeing not to see Sallie during that time. He capitulated. Content they had nipped his impulse in the bud, his parents took a long cruise on the Nile.

Quickly bored by Bremen, after several months Harry left Bremen for Paris, where Sallie's family soon appeared. August was furious and withdrew his conditional consent to the engagement. None of the family believed Sallie loved Harry either, for it was apparent that her mother was aggressively pressing for a wedding and had almost gone to the Nile herself to intercept the Belmonts and argue her case. She waited instead until Caroline was back in Paris, then doggedly pursued her. Though Caroline evaded them at the dressmaker's and restaurants, she was finally caught at home one day. Advising August, she wrote, "And tho' Sallie has very bad manners, she is liked, and said to be very amiable, and has money, which will be absolutely necessary for Oliver [Harry] with his extravagant tastes. The great objection in my eyes is that he is too young and does not yet know how to take care of himself, but I don't believe he ever will."[18] Although she continued to question Sallie's suitability—there was a story of her staying at a hotel under questionable circumstances—Harry's charm and nagging won her over. There was yet another benefit in agreeing, for he could better enjoy himself "with a wife than bothering us."[19] Tired of so many years of correcting and advising him, Caroline gave Harry permission to marry at once.

The wedding took place in Newport in December of 1882. Immediately afterward the couple returned to honeymoon in Paris, where Sallie's mother and two unmarried sisters soon moved in with them. Frustrated by Sallie's overdependence on her family, Harry insisted they move away and be on their own. She refused. Furious, he stomped off and traveled through the south of France, Spain, and Tangiers without her, and rumors came back that he was accompanied by a French dancer. Sallie took comfort in the company of Pussy Jones, whose engagement to Harry Stevens had just been postponed by his mother. Sallie realized she was pregnant, and when Harry heard the news he immediately returned, only to discover that his wife and her family had departed for England just a few hours before his arrival. He pursued her but was told at the door she refused to see him.

Most likely, Sallie's mother was the instigator and fed her mind with proof of Harry's bad character. Before he had left, he must have shown some temper, for Sallie wrote Caroline Belmont of his mean and violent ways. Caroline could not understand this complaint at all, for Harry had always been too lazy to fight back, having found he could get further by coaxing and flattering his adversary.

The Whitings returned to New York, where upon their appearance on May 15, 1883, they started a propaganda blitz against Harry. Where previously Caroline had overlooked her daughter-in-law's insulting implications, which had been expressed only in private letters, she now hardened. However, to avoid scandal, when Harry soon arrived, she coached him to write a letter to Sallie in which he demanded "as your husband by all the ties that bind us that you return to me at once."[20] Held back by her mother, Sallie refused. Public disgrace followed, most of it heaped on Harry. Over the following months, Caroline and August successfully wooed their old friends over to their side, with the Metropolitan debut providing the most visible proof of their continued favor.

Ultimately, however, Sallie Whiting came off the poorest. She gave birth to a daughter, Natica, whom Harry was never allowed to see, and lived the rest of her days under her mother's fanatically possessive power. (Years later, when Natica was a young married matron, she took a book to bed and fell asleep with the gaslight on. A gust of wind dampened the flame, and the resulting fumes killed her.)

Harry settled in at the family farm near Newport, to spend his days lolling about smoking, sometimes sporting about with other men of leisure. Caroline and August Belmont despaired Harry would ever turn to be of any good but admitted their role in spoiling him. Being easygoing and good hearted, he had little trouble befriending others. Willie K. shared Harry Belmont's hedonism, his love of men's clubs and horses, yachting and mistresses, and Alva found his boyishness appealing. Consequently, he became a favorite guest of theirs and one of their most intimate friends, much to his parents' dismay.

William Henry Leaves a
Solomonic Will

Having achieved their goal of acceptance into society, Alva and Alice need no longer make a prominent mark in the public eye. Their Fifth Avenue mansions were up, their children in need of their guidance. Their only fears being that death would snatch away one of their children, as it had already done to Alice's first daughter. Indeed, as proper societal matrons, it was now their duty to keep out of the papers, the only appropriate mentions being one's birth, marriage, and death, with exceptions for such events as a child's debut.

While the Vanderbilts lived like European aristocracy, indeed better than many titled people abroad, for average Americans, these had been troubled years. In 1881, President Garfield died of blood poisoning weeks after being shot by an unhappy federal office seeker. His death raised the clamor to remove the spoils system, bribery, and graft rampant in politics. Ironically, an enormous surplus in the government treasury brought high unemployment, because federal borrowing, an important outlet for private investments, was unnecessary. Agriculture was in a slump as well. It did not help the nation's mood when the presidential candidates for the 1884 election invoked slurs, scandals, and slander, making it one of the dirtiest campaigns ever in the country's history. (In the midst of this mudslinging, Susan B. Anthony and her followers were little able to bring woman suffrage into the debate.) Insulated from the political discontent and the suffering of the unemployed, the Vanderbilt family fortunes projected steadily upward under the clever contrivances of William Henry.

On the afternoon of December 8, 1885, the family patriarch arose early. He had a busy day ahead, discussing railway matters with his agents, followed by a sitting for his portrait at the studio of sculptor J. Q. A. Ward. He had much to be satisfied with in his life. He enjoyed his mansion, which received as guests people who once turned their backs upon him and whose art gallery drew personal contentment as well as praise from others. Though less happy with the home, which she found too ostentatious, wife Maria continued to be the devoted center of the family. His children were all well married, save George, the youngest son, who was tending the old farm at New Dorp. Cornelius II and Willie K. proved creditable additions to the railroad executive offices. And thanks to Alva's social acumen and Alice's charitableness, the Vanderbilt name was no longer a source for ridicule in society.

In the other society, that of the working people burdened by repeated economic upsets, the Vanderbilt name was often prefaced with vulgar and obscene adjectives. In 1879 the Hepburn Committee of the New York State legislature had exposed the secret agreements between railroad heads such as Vanderbilt and oil refiners like Rockefeller, whose collusion insured the elimination of small-time oil refiners and great profit to themselves.[21] New stories charged that the high cost of milk was due to William, who extracted exorbitant fees for its transport. Merchants and small manufacturers decried his manipulation of freight rates, where a short haul across several counties was often more costly than a cross-country one.

This was the time of the great trust builders, who tricked apparent friends, bribed politicians, undercut labor, and abused social welfare in the course of building massive fortunes. Thus he was hardly alone in his pressing the "free market," a cynical term considering that politicians were quick to use public funds and resources to lubricate the wheels of private industry. But Vanderbilt earned special rebuke. When asked by a cub reported why a mail train had been eliminated he responded, "The public be damned. I am working for my stock-holders. If the public want the train why don't they pay for it?" What most of the public saw in the papers was only the first four words (not that the remaining statement exempted him from criticism). Consequently, in a time of economic roller coaster, Vanderbilt became the critics' symbol of rapacious and destructive capitalism.[22]

As with the other robber barons, he generally deserved the rebukes. One of the rare instances where he showed unusual restraint had been during the railroad strikes of 1877. Other rail line owners destroyed their own property, blamed the destruction on the unionists, and thus quickly obtained military support to attack the strikers. In contrast, Vanderbilt reversed the wage cuts previously implemented on his lines and avoided decisions that incited violence. Nevertheless, William now regularly found himself reviled by editorial cartoonists as a moloch, a pirate, or a monster preying on the helpless through his endless greed for more railroads, more property. His mail contained death threats from labor activists, letter bombs, and packages with insulting contents. His staff marveled at his fearlessness in the light of clear danger. Part of his apparent courage was that unflappable confidence so common to the wealthy, who can afford to design lives of guarded isolation. But part of his indifference to lurking terrorism was a belief he would not live to old age anyway, that he had not inherited a sturdy constitution.

December 8 would fulfill William Henry's prophecy. Following lunch he invited his guest, Baltimore & Ohio capitalist William Garrett, to discuss business before the fire in his library. In the course of their conversation, William suddenly turned purple, his speech garbled, and he fell over dead.

As was characteristic of Vanderbilt funerals, the ceremony was simple and unassuming. The loss was deeply personal for the family, certainly more so than when the Commodore died. Widow Maria was so griefstricken that she could not attend the church services. During the funeral, observers noted the many sons and daughters and their families weeping openly. The body was taken to the Moravian Cemetery in Staten Island to be placed to rest in the family mausoleum designed by Richard Morris Hunt. There a lone watchman would punch a timeclock every fifteen minutes, to protect against the kind of ghouls who had absconded with and held for ransom the remains of A. T. Stewart. Stewart's body was never retrieved, and the Vanderbilts wanted no such defilement of their kins' remains.[23]

Then came the will. The public waited expectantly: Would it result in another family feud? William and Maria had been taking care for some years that such an eventuality would not occur; their strong parenting abided no sibling antagonism. Still, when brothers and sisters gathered to hear the readying of the lengthy document, there must have been memories of their father's earlier lawsuit, some unstated fear family history would repeat itself.

The early sections of the bequest were predictable: the assignment of various homes to their occupants, the distribution of more than a million dollars to various charities and art institutions, the various trust funds in the forms of railroad stocks and bonds to the daughters and sons, the smaller gifts to more distant relatives and friends. It was the twenty-second item they most awaited, the disposal of the "rest, residue, and remainder" of the property, the bulk of the estate. This was bequeathed not to Cornelius, the eldest son, but to both him and Willie K. and their heirs "in equal shares." The amount, they were informed, came to about $65 million apiece. The slow "blatherskite" son of the Commodore had doubled his father's fortune in eight years, proof to some of his financial acumen, to others of his deserving the editorial cartoonists' blasphemies.

The reasoning behind the division, an insider slipped to a *New York Times* reporter, was William's conclusion that the two sons were differing in kind but equal in value. Cornelius's conservative and deliberate business approach would be enlivened by Willie K.'s brilliance and decisiveness.[24] (One suspects as well that he anticipated the fury that a neglected Alva would have released.) With each of the other children getting more than $5 million each, along with real estate and trust funds, no family fuss followed. Instead, the name *Vanderbilt* disappeared from the public scene for several years, in appropriate and heartfelt mourning.

5

1885-1893

An Artist Comes
into the Family

The requisite period of grief may have been a welcome respite for Alva and Alice, for whom childrearing took on a larger role. Between them, Alice and Alva had four daughters. Alice's first child was her namesake, Alice Gwynne. Two sons, William and Cornelius, followed. Then Alice Gwynne died at age five. The following year, 1875, Gertrude was born, then two more boys, Alfred and Reginald, and finally change-of-life Gladys in 1886. Alva's daughter Consuelo, born in 1877, was followed by two sons, William, Jr., in 1878 and Harold, in 1885. Both Gertrude and Consuelo were to gain public attention in later years, and it is they who thus most interest us here. For reasons that will become clearer later, Gladys was to leave less of a public mark as a Vanderbilt woman.

Alva and Alice understood well their charge, to rear their sons to manage the family businesses and trusts, and their daughters to marry men of great wealth. Both had strong, distinct ideas about how best to go about these aims and were varyingly successful in accomplishing them.

From an outsider's view, it would appear Alice was the more domestic and maternal of the two women. She had the larger brood, and apart from inconspicuous charity work was less given to the social and public activities of Alva. Her husband shared her vision of continuing a dynasty, of shaping their children's character so their activities in the practical world would always be guided by strong Christian piety and virtues.

Alva, on the other hand, was much busier with her constant stream of architectural projects and discovered within several years of marriage that her husband was, like many of his class, a philanderer. Yet Alva's southern heritage impelled her to be much more involved in the daily raising of her children than was typical of wealthy northeastern families of the day, and she scorned women who left their children to be raised virtually by surrogates, the nurses, maids, and governesses. Furthermore, Alva's maternal instinct expressed itself strongly in early childhood through an obsession with her dolls and their care. Discovering she was pregnant was "a moment of truly religious joy." She also perceived that men deprecated maternity as a way of oppressing women, and worse, that women of her class were quick to adopt that estimate and thus gave lesser value to mothering than to other activities. In defiance, Alva always lunched at home to be with the children, whereas other women of her set might not see their off-spring apart from tea- or dinnertime. Indeed, later she would reflect that she had sacrificed too many of her personal needs and intruded too much in her children's lives.

Of all ten cousins, Gertrude was, at an early age, to show evidence of a most distinct and promising individuality. Unfortunately, her temperament rubbed against the grain of what was expected of young women of means and in particular against her parents' conception of what a Vanderbilt woman should be. For one, she was alert to all the sense-data of life, the tiny details of shape, texture, and movement around her. A visit to a battlefield in France, for example, conjured up the sound of cannons and men's shouts, the rivers of blood. She was just as exquisitely attuned, too much some might say, to her internal sensations and feelings. This hypersensitivity could bring about a clarity of vision, an ability to separate cant from substance, but more often it presented a confusing press of conflicting impulses. With so many seductive winds to buffet her about, she was continually searching for moorings to stabilize her identity.

Imagine such a girl in the family of Cornelius and Alice. Visualizing them-selves as custodians of the dynasty, they did not encourage creativity or risk. While knowledgeable about art, they valued more industry in business and charity in the community. They were essentially good and decent people, who earned much deserving respect from society, but they were not the sort whose dinners were valued for their witty banter. Unlike his namesake grandfather, Cornelius was the kind of father to gather the children about after dinner for prayer and moral stories.

Young Gertrude was pious, industrious, and charitable, but she was also *passionate,* and there was simply no room in that Vanderbilt household for strong emotion. Though no words stated such, she understood she was not to express the haunting perceptions, moods, and impulses that pulled at her throughout the day. Alice was often put out by this child, whose sulkiness was taken to be a lack of respect for parental authority.

Of course the boys in the family were somewhat cosseted, but they lacked Gertrude's sensitivities and found the bonds less troublesome. More important, they were boys, so in all situations they were permitted more freedom of thought and activity than she. They could also look into the future with some vision of a day when they would be independent, in control of their lives, freed by the advantages of the family wealth. Little were they aware of the pitfalls and traps inherited riches set before the male, that the freedom was illusory.

Surrounded by four brothers, Gertrude astutely perceived the difference. One of her first self-conscious desires was of wanting to be a boy.[1] At age four, pushed by this impulse, she crept unseen into her mother's room, found a scissors, and cut off her curls. "Only girls have curls," she had heard her parents say, so in her child's magical thinking, no curls, no girl. The magic did not work, and Alice punished her severely. Still, Gertrude continued to observe the privileges of her brothers and mimicked them whenever she could get away with it.

Childhood fiction repeated this theme. Among one of the earliest stories she wrote, the daughter of a rich banker has a brother who is stolen and never found. Other childhood writings bespoke distant and cruel fathers, men who "love women purely for the pleasure they derive from them. As soon as they have drunk their fill of these, the woman is cast aside."[2] Her distrust of adult men came from observations of other men in society, who frequently kept mistresses. Her own father, whose coolness she may have mistaken for lack of love, was a loyal and devoted family man, so this perception must have come from eavesdropping on adult gossip. Perhaps she heard of her Uncle Willie and his mistresses.

It would be wrong to interpret Gertrude's unhappiness as due solely to a delicate nature; history played into the hand as well. While perceiving herself to be different, she found no concepts in the culture to validate her view. The idea of raising boys and girls separately was so taken for granted that no one in her sphere questioned the pattern. The other girls Gertrude knew were like her cousin Adele Sloan, whose mother, Emily, was one of the four daughters of William H. Vanderbilt. Adele's diary expressed little of the anguish found in Gertrude's. She delighted in the benefits of privilege and took pride in developing her intellectual abilities. But she also looked forward to being able "to take the back seat" to a man. "As for being a genius, you know I don't believe in genius for women; as none of them have had it yet. *I* will certainly not be an exception." She embraced the notion of living a "humdrum" life, a future Gertrude foresaw with terror.[3]

Often visionaries neglect to see that they are just that, and instead turn society's condemnation on themselves. Gertrude responded similarly. Failing to find confirmation from her parents or society in general, she turned inward to seek consolation. To give affirmation to her thoughts, she used up hundreds of bottles of ink, and filled shelves with journal and copy books over her lifetime, talking to herself as if a best friend. Unlike Adele, whose diary seldom recorded introspection, Gertrude made minute analyses and criticisms of her thoughts and actions. She even wrote poems on this theme:

> I sometimes wonder when alone within my chamber
> When other minds prepare to rest
> Why God loves his erring daughter.[4]

She was often restless, seldom satisfied with her own behavior.

To keep such a diary was in itself an act of rebellion. Like others of her background, her childhood was one completely organized and scrutinized by adults. There were nurses to attend to her physical needs and governesses to direct her mental ones. She could not eat, dress, bathe, or take a walk without a servant being present. Until her marriage, she could not go anywhere without a chaperone. (She felt very daring one day in New York when she slinked out to visit a fortune teller, but even then she felt compelled to take her maid along.) Along with this constant presence of eyes went her parents' emphasis upon meaningful activity, and sitting alone in one's room scribbling fantasies and intimacies into a diary did not count as meaningful. A few minutes in a daybook, yes, but not these long solitary hours of writing. Indeed, one suspects Gertrude invented headaches or reasons to be sent to her room simply for the opportunity to be left alone with her thoughts.

Gertrude Grows Alienated
from Her Mother

Until she was seventeen, the only real and significant loss Gertrude experienced was that of the bond with her mother. Since we have only Gertrude's side of the story, it is hard to tell exactly why this breach occurred. It is clear, though, that by adolescence Gertrude resented Alice, documented grievances against her, and withheld affection. Once when the children came back late from an outing to a farm, Alice refused to let them go again. "Mama was angry and Papa sorry." A few days later, when Gertrude had a bad cold, Alice forbade her to go out riding. Following her recuperation, Gertrude one day joined her brother Alfred on horseback. When Alice reprimanded Gertrude for being "a naughty, naughty child," she almost wanted to laugh aloud. Then Alice added that Gertrude "did it because [she] thought I would not know," to which the girl pointed out she had admitted the trip. Denying that confession, Alice went on to berate Gertrude in front of the family for lying, "and I am very glad to say that none of you—boys have ever told one [lie]."[5] Gertrude fled to her room, sat at her desk, wrote out the incident, and consoled herself thinking that God at least saw the truth.

It could not have helped that Alice had a fetish for privacy and as a result kept Gertrude's life more closed in than that of cousins such as Adele. Rather than mingle with strangers at a shop, however exclusive the clientele, Alice insisted the goods be brought to her home for consideration. This meant Gertrude missed the mother-daughter bonding built on such mundane shared acts as going to a store together. While attending the opera or a ball, if she spied a news photographer in the vicinity, Alice would order her chauffeur to grab the camera and smash it to bits. In light of previous Vanderbilt scandals, her avoidance of newspaper notoriety was sensible, but it also increased the air of regal artificiality about the household.

Unable to show her animosity toward her mother directly, Gertrude allowed it to surface in her youthful fiction. One untitled story concerned a girl being told by her mother she was to marry an Englishman.[6] The girl is astonished by her mother's cold-blooded tone, which always reminds the girl how she has had every advantage: "What had I to wish for. Absolutely nothing." As a result of this double message, that she has everything but lacks any freedom, the girl decides to hide her feelings. "I did not wish my mother to know me," says the fictional heiress, just as Gertrude in her journal repeated "I don't tell my thoughts or feelings to anyone." More directly she allowed, "If I have children of my own, they will tell me everything because they know I will understand and sympathize, yes, if my prayer is granted, I will live over my youth with them and God will help me, for He is good."[7]

To be fair, Alice had a fearsome task. As her granddaughter Gloria would one day observe, "In the beginning a child believes that all other children are in the same world that she or he inhabits. That is how a poor child defines all others, and that is how a rich child defines all others."[8] Alice had the problem of rearing the richest girl in the nation, a girl she felt would be prey to fortune hunters, when for that girl being the richest was just a simple fact of life. Adele Sloan and other Vanderbilt relations adapted more easily. When she first realized what it mean to be an heiress, Adele was "terribly unhappy" and wished to be poor so people could love her for herself. Then she became "used to the thought," declaring, "and I face it boldly."[9] But Adele's mother had inherited one-eighth the amount from William H. that Cornelius had, so she was not "the richest girl in the world," nor did Adele have any emotional complexity.

In fact, Alice was an affectionate and loving woman, if not directly expressive of such. Her other children even found her doting, and none expressed the resentment Gertrude felt. Their devotion was lifelong, a fact outsiders often commented upon. So it does not seem fair to conclude she was, as Gertrude's pained expressions sometimes suggest, a mean woman. Possibly she was harder on her oldest daughter, but it could also be that Gertrude interpreted normal parental disapproval as more harsh than it was meant to be.

So self-effacing and insecure was Gertrude that she developed a habit of writing in her journal imaginary letters to people she wished to confide in, then creating imaginary responses from those recipients. An early "recipient" was her English teacher, Miss Winsor, whom she much admired and from whom she wanted special recognition.[10] After a long stumbling apology, she moved to the core of the missive: that she had held Miss Winsor in her affections for five years, yet kept these feelings quiet. "I hope you have not been bored, and that you will believe in the sincerity of everything I have said." She added to this unsent letter a self-effacing postscript promising to never trouble Miss Winsor this way again. That confession entered in her journal, she composed Miss Winsor's response, which assented to getting to know Gertrude better. Unfortunately for Gertrude, the real Miss Winsor never knew of her pupil's longing for deeper communion.

Gertrude's Cousin
Consuelo Worships Alva

I am not exactly the same as all the other girls," Gertrude accurately wrote.[11] But she did have a female cousin near her age who experienced similar circumstances—Consuelo.

Although the girls were close relations and lived a few short blocks from each other in New York, they did not see each other often. Their mothers ruled the domestic sphere, and the uneasy truce between those very dissimilar matriarchs meant infrequent family gatherings. Also, the families had country homes in different locations. Cornelius and Alice chose Newport, where they purchased a 160-foot wide Queen Anne mansion, the Breakers, from Pierre Lorillard. (Country homes had names, not addresses, as though to set their status apart from those of average people in their communities.) Although Alva and Willie K. did the late summer season in Newport each year, renting a house for the purpose, throughout the year they took their children to Idlehour, their Richard Morris Hunt home in Oakdale, Long Island.

Had the girls been able to develop an intimacy, they would have found much in common to commiserate about. As it was, from what little Gertrude saw of Consuelo, she deduced her cousin was having a much harder time. Although Gertrude disliked her own mother's intrusions, she counted herself blessed not to have Alva for a mother.

Simply put, Alva was a martinet. Her temper was awesome, quick, furious, and tending toward physical expressions, such as the throwing of a convenient piece of porcelain at a hapless servant. She insisted on absolute obedience from everyone around her, brooked no contradictions, no talking back. If the riding whip had kept her rebellious spirit down as a child, then it would serve her own children. Consuelo took these punishments stoically, and rather than rebelling, bent herself more to her mother's will. In later years, she would reflect that this harsh discipline, though too severe, was better for developing her character than the laxity she saw in other homes.

Worse than the private punishments was public ridicule. Consuelo sat in humiliation through many teas while Alva and her friends discussed the girl's nose, which they thought too upturned, along with other physical characteristics they deemed unfavorable.[12] To improve her daughter's posture, Alva made her wear a back brace (with a stiff iron rod that extended up her spine), which succeeded in producing Consuelo's remarkable carriage. And if she had known the pain of her own mother forcing her to wear unusual and attention-getting clothes, Alva forgot the experience when it came to dressing Consuelo, who was given no choice in the matter. As a result, the child, who was to become a handsome and striking woman, reached adolescence shy, hypersensitive, and like her mother, quick to temper (though not against her mother).

One suspects Alva was not the only source of the girl's introversion. Her quick and lively imagination fed her timidity. Climbing the rather dark stairway of 660 Fifth, she was frightened by the flickering shadows of the gas lamps. Her Christian education stimulated a scrupulous conscience and melancholy over others' suffering. During the time she studied for her confirmation, she imagined becoming an Anglican nun, and at night, after her personal servant had left the room, slipped out of bed to sleep on the floor as an act of penance and ascetic practice.

Despite Alva's authoritarian rule, Consuelo was deeply attached to her mother, and, however thoughtlessly Alva acted, never quit that loyalty and affection. How is it that Gertrude in effect deserted her mother over what many would consider normal and reasonable discipline, whereas Consuelo frankly loved cantankerous and egotistical Alva? The answer may have to do with Alva's rich individuality. Alva's energy, imagination, and individuality delighted her daughter. Though only six when the great ball of 1883 took place, Consuelo read the newspaper stories on the event with pride. As she matured, she shared her mother's superb taste for antiques and design and accompanied her during shopping trips in Europe to buy furnishings and art. From her first visit she preferred Paris and found her mother's requirement that French be spoken at home in the evening a pleasure, not a burden. She also shared her mother's criticism of a society that left so many families struggling in poverty, the women in particular overburdened.

Just as she shared her mother's values, which were more unconventional and daring than those of Gertrude's, Consuelo also felt secure in her mother's love. For Alva would follow her sudden outbursts of fury with just as quick and intense expressions of affection, virtual confessions of remorse. And during peaceful periods Alva was as charming and entrancing to her children as to adults who found her mercurial temperament exasperating yet beguiling. She could turn a sail on a pond into an imaginary ocean crossing to Europe, teaching Consuelo geography in the process. At the dinner table, Consuelo's and her brothers' thoughts on topics were sought and respected. (As men, Alva's sons would become known for their unpretentious ways and egalitarian values.)

But what most held Consuelo loyal was her mother's courage. It was not just that Alva challenged conventions and dared to express herself where others in her class hid behind tradition, it was also her physical courage.

One day when she was nine, Consuelo was driving her pony cart when the young steed went wild, heading for a water hydrant. Foreseeing a serious accident, Alva ran and threw herself on the animal, seized its bridle, and averted disaster just in time. Consuelo never forgot her mother's quick and unswerving rescue. It is because of such faith and confidence in her mother that Consuelo took Alva's criticisms to heart, and did not question them as Gertrude did her mother's.

Disciplined, the Girls
Look beyond Luxuries

It would be wrong to conclude that the Vanderbilt cousins were "poor little rich girls." True, they were often lonely, but other children face that fate. They entered adolescence shy and insecure, but some might say that is a definition of puberty. Alice was not as open and warm as Gertrude would have wished, but she was not coldhearted or hostile. Alva was not as gentle as Consuelo would have wished, but she was not vindictive or purposely cruel. Separation of self from mother is not easy in this culture, and many women today would find the perceptions of these nineteenth-century heiresses familiar to their own experiences.

Being among the richest families in the world, the Vanderbilt girls had benefits few other children then would know. All were quick to rejoice at the departure from New York to the country or to Europe. Newport and Long Island meant the chance to play in ways unavailable in the city. There were pony carts and beaches, play houses, woods for picking berries, and fields to run about for playing games inspired by the frontier novels of James Fenimore Cooper. Their play houses were actually full-sized cottages with working kitchens, where the children could learn to cook, and, in the case of Willie's children, the boys could learn carpentry. They could come in from a day's play with clothes torn and knees bruised. And during visits to France, play meant a Parisian carousel, a Punch and Judy show on the Champs-Elysées, and sailing miniature boats on the Tuileries garden ponds.

It must be remembered that this was still a time when going to high school was not yet a typical experience for boys, let alone girls. Both Gertrude and Consuelo were taught at home in their early years by governesses, then sent to private girls' schools during adolescence. There girls were humbled, discouraged from developing a sense of themselves as superior because of their class. They were to dress simply to avoid competition with one another in jewelry or fashion. Such restrictions suited Gertrude and Consuelo. Both had only kind feelings toward their various teachers, and each took her studies seriously. Studies continued year-round, including during travels, when governesses were a necessary part of the entourage, responsible for taking the girls to museums and historical sites and for improving their conversation in foreign languages. "Vacation" was not in the vocabulary of these budding socialites.

The content of education was more important to cosmopolitan Alva, who hired French and German governesses so that Consuelo was able to read and write in both languages by age eight. (Consuelo also gained her noted tact by dealing with the often contradictory requirements of governesses from these two antagonistic nations.) That linguistic competence meant she was soon reading European classics in the original tongue, the French and German fairy tales at first, then poetry, and eventually philosophy. On Saturdays, Alva expected her and her brothers to recite from memory lengthy excerpts or stanzas in the appropriate language. Consuelo became an avid student whose dream was to attend Oxford, a most unusual goal for any young woman of her day. (Of course, had she gone, she would not have been allowed to sit for a degree, for Oxford barely tolerated select women in attendance at lectures.)

It was not family members but women staff who opened for each girl the door to her individuality. Consuelo was later able to identify the precise moment her particular enlightenment occurred. While still a child, one day she happened upon the Bohemian gardener, observed he was looking sad, and inquired as to the matter. He explained that his ten-year-old daughter was sick, a cripple condemned for life to her bed. With her nurse's encouragement, Consuelo went to visit the girl, finding her "in a miserable little room on a small unlovely cot." That moment awoke her commitment to social justice and charity, which she attributed to her nurse's wise model. Alva, who was becoming increasingly liberal in her political orientation, further encouraged this humanitarianism.

For Gertrude, the opening was more gradual, growing out of her exposure to art. During visits to Europe, she spent long hours of each day out with "Madame," her governess, stalking the museums for examples of "excellence." Without consciously recognizing such, she became enthralled with painting and particularly sculpture. On first seeing Michelangelo's sculptures, she wrote, "That a mere boy could put into his work that something which generations would seek in vain. I met the Master for the first time face to face and in future the hem of his garment was not too lowly to kiss. He could cover all provinces with deft fingers, fashion worlds past, present, and to come." She grew so certain of her evaluations of various works that she would even argue with her father. Disagreeing with him about the *Dying Gladiator,* she said it lacked feeling, that "a leg, an arm, a hip, can be done with such feeling as to make the whole beautiful."[13] Thus, while other girls were filing away names of artists and works to retrieve during some future dinner table patter, Gertrude was cultivating an aesthetic eye of her own, and more important, attempting to reach into the mind of the artist, to think about the creator and act of creation.

Gertrude was also more self-reflective than Consuelo or other young relations about the psychological consequences of being a Vanderbilt. Traveling through Italy in particular made her aware that there was not necessarily one way to behave and express oneself. The Latin races, she observed, flickered like sparrows, where her heritage, the Anglo-Saxon temperament, "is the real construction of high fences and in consequence the clipper and restricter of wings."[14] This image of a bird unable to fly was to reappear in her journals, in one case the vision being that of a bird released from a cage and not realizing until that point of potential freedom that the wings are clipped.

The Wayward
Harry Belmont Falls for a
Vanderbilt Woman

I t was not only the competitiveness and distrust between Alva and Alice that prevented the cousins from knowing each other better. Following William Henry's death and receipt of their patrimony, the differing temperaments of Willie and Cornelius separated them further. William Henry had in effect removed any reason for the two to continue being involved in Vanderbilt business interests. He had seen that affairs would really be in the hands of Chauncey Depew, who was eminently capable of controlling the investments. Never attracted to business, Willie grabbed the opportunity to use his time for leisure, particularly horse racing, along with yachting and traveling abroad. He became what was known at the time as a sporting man, convivial, honorable, and quick to pay his debts, a gentle hedonist whose carefree ways hurt few. The more puritanical Cornelius, however, felt the weight as titular head of the family and went to the office each day, often arriving before the lowliest clerk. His favorite leisure activities were serving his church as an elder and Sunday school teacher and attending the meetings of various charitable boards.

Consequently, the family of Cornelius Vanderbilt II was not present in 1886, when Alva's sister christened a 285-foot steam yacht, the *Alva,* then the largest of its class in the world. True to her namesake's preferences, the ship was decorated with a simple French elegance the *Times* praised as a necessary corrective in a day when impractical ornateness tossed upon the ocean waves. Though the staterooms were pleasant and practical, the craft itself was like a tired tug, slow to respond and clumsy. The crew, apart from the captain and first mate, were Scots, Swedes, and Norwegians. When the duchess of Sunderland asked Alva why this was so, she replied, "Why, Duchess, there are no American sailors. They are all captains!"[15]

For Consuelo and her brothers, the word of yet another romantic cruise, to Egypt or Turkey or Italy, brought only anxiety, for the reality would be days of seasickness or, worse, injury from being thrown against a cabinet during a lurch. While Alva and Willie K. dined and danced in the salon with friends, the children kept lengthy diaries of the experience, to be examined carefully by the parents as proof of hard study. (Here again Gertrude could be grateful, for her family went abroad first class in passenger liners.)

Preoccupied with her unsettled stomach or endless studies, Consuelo was unaware of a certain relationship that slowly and quietly took shape over several of these voyages. As in her youth, Alva preferred male companions and always invited several sporting bachelors to add to the conviviality. In 1887, one such guest was O. H. P. "Harry" Belmont. Though now thirty years old, he still vexed his parents with his complacency. Compared to brother Perry, who had just served three terms in the U.S. Congress and was about to become a minister to Spain, he was an utter failure. (After death, his reputation was to gain from Perry's success, when some later commentators, unaware O. H. P. went by Oliver or Harry, sometimes attributed Perry's accomplishments to him.)

After Harry returned from the 1887 cruise, August feared his frivolous son was infatuated with the older Alva, which was true. If gossips tittered over the flirtation, it did not seem to bother Willie K. or Alva, who continued to invite Harry over. August Belmont was just as displeased when Harry returned to New-port to tend his horses. "I am glad that he has some amusement and relaxation after his ardous work of last year," he remarked.[16] But he was furious when he learned Harry had accepted an invitation for the 1888 cruise. "I feel very bad about [Harry], which I would not if I loved him less," wrote August to another son. "He is preparing a very unhappy future for himself." As with so many of August Belmont's predictions concerning his children, he was utterly wrong.

Alva Conquers
Newport

Spring and early summer was the cus-tomary time for the annual escape to Europe. Winter and early spring were for New York City and the social season tied to opera and balls. That left late summer for Newport.

What had once been an unpretentious resort town favored by southerners and New England bohemians was now a national enclave for the cream of society from Philadelphia, Chicago, and Washington as well as New York. Newport pro-vided all the requisite needs: harbor and ocean for yachting, pleasant weather for golf and tennis, and ample space for raising and riding horses. The Newport Country Club became the site of the first American amateur golf championship, and the Newport Casino hosted the first Tennis Hall of Fame. The casino, de-signed by bon vivant Stanford White, was the creation of publisher James Gordon Bennett, Jr., a yachtsman who wanted an exclusive private club commensurate with his high self-opinion. The block-long complex, still in use today, provided a charming shingled and multigabled two-story structure enclosing a courtyard with a clock tower, horseshoe piazza, and several latticed porches. Within, social-ites could dine, play and watch tennis, and attend concerts, theatricals, and dances. The Reading Room was the male preserve, where little reading went on. The most exclusive club, however, was the Spouting Rock Beach Association, the formal name for the rather austere eighty-one cabanas rimming the tiny, seaweed-ridden Bailey's Beach.

With the prosperity of the Gilded Age, the scions of finance, industry, and transportation left the management of their capital and trusts to lawyers and trusted managers, allowing them more time for leisure. Willie K. could spend his days on the *Alva,* the most expensive yacht of its day, with his boys, the youngest of whom, Harold, would become the most famous yacht racer of his age. Nearby would be J. P. Morgan's *Corsair,* with its crew of eighty-five, the Drexels' (of Philadelphia) *Sultana,* and Bennett's *Lysistrata,* equipped with a turkish bath and miniature dairy. But it was Mrs. Astor who added her imprimatur to the town by setting up court summers there at her cottage, Beechwood, to which she added the town's largest ballroom, while her husband tinkered about on *Nour-mahal.*

While Newport would seem to outsiders to provide a relaxing break in the country, for its participants it was, apart from children, a place with rigid and utterly inflexible schedules, events, and manners. Where only several decades earlier Americans had thumbed their noses at European formalities and deport-ment, indeed were refreshing in their informality, that very unpretentiousness had brought so much criticism from foreign observers that now society overcom-pensated. In Newport, society was the only game; there being no offices nearby for men to escape to, women set the rules. By spelling out meticulous, often baffling regulations of great subtlety, they were able in the first seconds of an encounter to designate a stranger as either In or Out. Consequently, the newly rich Kansas meat-packing family would find itself relegated to driving its carriage under the elm-lined canopy of Bellevue Avenue, wistfully hoping for an invitation to dine or dance within the mansions.

For the In, stamina was as much a requisite for success as money and manners. On a typical day, a woman would dress in a morning gown and go to the dining room for an English breakfast, a sideboard teeming with eggs, sausage, cereals, kidneys, and such. Then she would change into her riding habit and take her morning ride. After that she donned her day dress and drove in a phaeton to the casino, where she could watch a tennis match or visit the Worth boutique. As Consuelo noted, "My dresses had high, tight, whalebone collars. A corset laced my waist to the eighteen inches fashion decreed. An enormous hatpin adorned with flowers, feathers and ribbons was fastened to my hair with long steel pins, and a veil covered my face. Tight gloves pinched my hands and I carried a parasol."[17] Next would come ladies' swim time at Bailey's Beach, where fully clad in a heavy dark blue alpaca dress, woolen drawers, and black silk stockings, with a large hat to protect her skin from the sun, she would bob in chest-deep water and gossip with friends. (Socialite Tessie Oelrichs horrified the others one day when on discovering that her stockings had been left at home she dared to bathe barelegged.) Luncheon, with a friend at home or perhaps on the family yacht in harbor, was the first point in the day when she could don her sapphires, rubies, and turquoises. There might follow a visit to the polo field to watch her father, brothers, and friends play.

Another change of dress brought the major daytime event, the afternoon promenade between the hours of three and five, when she left her visiting card at the house of a friend, who would not be at home because she, too, was out delivering cards. During this silly ritual it was important to follow the social pecking order, seeing to it that one's impetuous coachman would not speed up and trot one's carriage past a woman of higher standing. As coaches passed one another on the ten-mile route, each woman would stiffly nod her head in greeting while scanning the other's dress and jewels. The wise woman would take care never to be seen in the same frock during that season more than once, with the result that the maid of a girl like Consuelo would have over a hundred dresses to attend to during the six or so weeks of the season. (For all these numerous changes, her maid developed strong calves during her many climbs up and down the stairs to the closets in the floor above Consuelo's bedroom.)

On some days a coaching parade would take place instead, wherein the men could take control of the pedigreed horses pulling their highly polished phaetons, victorias, landaus, barouches, and four-in-hands. Flowers would decorate the necks of the high-stepping lead horses, whose heads would rise haughtily, while the wheelers behind them anchored the coach by stepping with their hooves low to the ground. Wives and daughters would add flowers to their apparel as well, and ride proudly behind the patriarch.

Following the drive would be tea, and if the women were lucky, a nap. The evening would mean more changing, first into attire appropriate for a light supper, then into a formal ball gown or costume for the evening party, which normally started at ten or eleven and went all night, followed by breakfast at dawn. Such balls would be held every night of the week at the season's height.

The purpose of all this ritual was more than the establishing of social boundaries and hierarchies; it was primarily to create an insular marriage market. Only at Newport could the mothers exclude undesirables their daughters might meet in the more inclusive parties of their home cities or during trips abroad. They could allow their carefully taught daughters to attend picnics or golf or tennis, properly chaperoned (or *matronized,* as the term went), without concern that ineligible men would incite a forbidden romance. Eligible young men, it should be apparent, had a much easier day, spent on the golf links, the tennis courts, their male-only swim hours at Bailey's, and the male-only smoking rooms at the casino. They were also spared anything equivalent to the buyings, fittings, and donning of the dozens of different dresses and outfits to be shown off throughout the day.

Gertrude had a rousing good time in Newport. Being somewhat athletic, she enjoyed the many outdoors sports and play. Consuelo, on the other hand, found herself with less free time. While Gertrude was out playing tennis and golf in the afternoons, Consuelo faced lessons in deportment. While Gertrude had lunch with friends at their house or hers, Consuelo's only social activity of the day was lunch with her mother and her mother's older friends. Furthermore, she was discouraged from participating in the conversations. (She did, however, enjoy outspoken Mamie Fish, who when told by one luncheon hostess, "And this is my Louis Quinze salon!" responded "And what makes you think so?"[18] Consuelo's early connoisseurship in art made her as intolerant as Mrs. Fish of those wealthy who measured the value of a work by its cost.)

Clear that her daughter should have the catch of the day, Alva determined that the family, which up to this point had rented a place in Newport each summer, must have its own home. Furthermore, it must provide a setting so extraordinary that the list of men who concluded themselves eligible to marry Consuelo would be very small indeed. Her inspiration for the exterior, taken from a cruise to Greece, was the Acropolis, but given her love of French architecture, she accepted Richard Morris Hunt's derivation of the neoclassical Petit Trianon at Versailles. Although Marble House, as it came to be known, was actually to be a birthday gift from Willie K. to his wife, she once again orchestrated the project. Its site was on the cliffs overlooking the Atlantic, and it was bounded to the west by Bellevue Avenue, the mansion row of that seafaring town. From 1889 to 1892 workmen labored behind high fences to shield the progress from onlookers. Newporters said that workmen in various phases of the job were sworn to secrecy so that no leaks about its design would appear in the press.

When unveiled, the secrecy proved deserved. Niece Adele Sloane, one of the first allowed in, gushed, "No description can possibly give one an idea of how marvelously beautiful it is. It is far ahead of any palace I have ever seen abroad, far ahead of any I have ever dreamed of!"[19] Once again the team of Alva and Hunt outdid anything going on in that time of castle-building along the shore. Hunt was delighted to be working closely with Alva again, for he found her the most congenial and knowledgeable of his several Vanderbilt clients.[20]

The first shock for Newporters was the presence of a marble wall. For people used to old-fashioned and unfenced lawns, this barrier was an abrupt symbol of exclusiveness, that "white fence around the Vanderbilts!" They could not complain so readily about the house itself, however. Stepping up the slate walkway, one approached an immense marble portico, supported by enormous Corinthian columns. The intricate doors of gunmetal steel over thick glass, though one and a half tons each, had no handle on the outside nor any visible hinges. Instead, an ever present maroon-liveried servant stood by to open them, their mass swinging easily on pivots built into the frame.

Inside, the visitor confronted room after room of richly colored and decorated interiors reflecting Alva's admiration for and control of French design. The leading inspiration was Louis XIV's architect, Jules Mansart, whose portrait was placed in bas-relief over a window in the entrance hall. Rare marbles sienna, rose, and gold, mirrored doors, gilt bronze and ormulu decorations on the walls, Gobelin tapestries, cherubs and gods holding light standards, rococo woodwork, and furniture designed by Freres Allard in Louis XIV style were arrayed to form a flawless impression.

For guests, the Gold Ballroom epitomized the Gilded Age. There, wood-carved and gilded gods and goddesses shone down from wall panels bordering the several mirrored French doors. Twinned chandeliers of massed cupids, repro-ductions from the Chateau Maison la Fitte, were fitted for both gas and electric-ity. Perched on the mantlepiece were life-sized figures of Old Age and Youth, in between them an unusual timepiece, a glass globe of the earth circled a crystal globe to mark the month, day, and hour. A large mirror above the mantle dou-bled the sparkle from the chandeliers. Virtually the only color was from the Savonnerie rug, with its depiction of the coat of arms of Louis XIV, the coat of arms of Paris, and that of France.

Alva's favorite room was one that her family, and no doubt some guests, found gloomy: the haunting Gothic Room, with its characteristic arches, ribbing, figurative carvings, and stained-glass windows.[21] Its fifty-by-thirty-foot extent held a virtual museum of pre-sixteenth-century artifacts, the renowned collection of M. Gavet. Although Gothic rooms were common then in the homes of the rich, they were more stage sets than attempts at authenticity because their owners lacked Alva's drive for historic research and accuracy. Pleased with the success of this room, she was to continue collecting from the period and would be building further Gothic rooms over the years to contain her growing medieval armory.

The sheer eye-blinding opulence of the interior camouflages that this was a home. It is difficult today, strolling through the unsullied dining room adapted from the Salon of Hercules at Versailles to imagine odors of roast and pheasants, cauliflower and carrots, sounds of tinkling crystal, of wit and laughter. The solid bronze chairs, one is told by the docent, are so heavy that footmen were needed to adjust them for the sitter. The modern middle-class viewer, used to dinner in the family room, perhaps even on a sofa with the television on, cannot imagine comfort in such a setting. But in fact Marble House was above all else an abode, a place for intimate and domestic life. Consider the furniture. The great accom-plishment of the French craftsmen was not simply in the designs with their pleasing sculptures and curves many moderns find too fancy. It was in their understanding the human body, its requirements for restful sitting or writing at a desk. Thus Alva's women guests, tightly corseted under their Worth silk gowns, would feel at least the furniture was not also adding to their unease.

It was not guests who mattered to Alva, it was her family, whose privacy was her guiding rule. To this end, only one guest room was allowed in the design, and tradition holds that only one particularly eminent guest was ever allowed to stay in it overnight. Further, the servants were to be out of the house as much as possible. To prevent unwanted intrusion, a heavy door in the basement separated servants from the main rooms, and a man at the portal kept watch that a minimum of staff were upstairs, and then only for absolute necessities.

Finally, there are the proportions of the rooms themselves. Only the public rooms are large, and even they are not of the imposing, overpowering scale found in some other Newport houses. The private rooms could be even cozy, notably the studies for Alva and Willie twinning the top of the staircase. Despite the palatial glitter, Marble House was, for Alva, a home.

Alice Seeks to
Even the Score

A short walk away from the Marble House site was the brick-and-board Breakers. Though it had the many rooms needed for a family with many growing children and their complement of servants, it lacked good public spaces for entertaining. Indeed, when guests came, Gertrude had to give her room over to the ladies' cloaks. In August of 1892, when Marble House was finally unveiled, Alice had other, more serious problems than that of being upstaged once again. She experienced the worst loss one can ever know, that of a child.

It happened so suddenly. Catherine Hunt's memoirs recorded those bad seasons when scarlet fever, rheumatic fever, or typhoid would strike and carry away friends and, more often, their children. It was, after all, the infectious diseases of the summer that started the habit of the rich moving temporarily to the country, where fewer people and better sanitation lessened risk of illness.

This time it was typhoid. William, the kind of child who surpassed his parents' highest hopes, came home from Yale for Easter vacation and was struck down. By May 6 he was dead. Just weeks before he had purchased a 46-foot sloop and was planning to enjoy the summer sailing the waters of Narragansett. He was about to be inducted into the most elite Yale society, Skull and Bones. He had inherited all the best Vanderbilt traits—intelligence, charity, courage—and was likely the most handsome man to ever come from the line. Now, where his voice should be delighting parents with his plans and promise, was emptiness.

The family's grief was so great that even Gertrude's prolific diary habit was stunted. A "gloom" descended, was all that she noted. There must be two years of mourning, complete with dark clothes, little jewelry, avoidance of large-scale entertaining or attendance at such.

There could, however, be small gatherings with a few friends. On November 25, a cold, windy afternoon, Alice welcomed Pussy Jones, now wed to Edward Wharton. While they gathered, quietly talking, an unexpected racket arose from the servants' quarters. The house was on fire, the voices shouted; they must flee immediately. Playing outside, Gertrude and Gladys ran across the lawn to investigate the commotion, found their parents, and watched them during the painfully slow minutes while the fire engines made their, some would later say, tardy arrival. The cause was lost—the water pressure was too low to save any part of the building. Priceless furnishings, tapestries, and artworks became ash within an hour.

Cornelius was philosophical, blaming no one for the fire except a design that would allow a defective heating plant to spread so easily. Consequently, he immediately hired Richard Morris Hunt to replace the Breakers with a new building, stipulating that the heating source be in a separate structure some distance away. Hunt was also working on other Newport mansions: Belcourt, for Harry Belmont, and Ochre Court, for Ogden and May Goelet. He was to find working with Alice very different from his collegial relationship with Alva. Catherine Hunt observed of Alice and May Goelet, "as neither of these ladies practiced the courtesy to which Richard hitherto had been uniformly accustomed, he chafed under their unconscious rudeness. It made the work occasionally trying, not only for him, but for their husbands."[22] Indeed, Hunt's health deteriorated badly during this time, and Catherine Hunt intimated that "these two exacting ladies being insistent in their demands" contributed significantly to his premature death from exhaustion soon after the jobs were completed.

Though not his best work, the Breakers became his most popular. One would not guess from the public rooms on the first story that Cornelius Vanderbilt was a man of modest and plain preferences. The Great Hall with its wall of windows looking beyond to the ocean teases with its many delights, from the impressive grandeur of the sheer size of the room, the delicately carved cream-colored Caen stone, the filigree iron balcony carvings, the gilt-corniced ceiling painted like a fresh summer's day, the massive bronze chandeliers and free-standing candalabras. The gracious oval-shaped music room contrasts with its rich colors and allegorical paintings. The two-story dining room overwhelms with its high reliefs, painted panels and ceiling, its chandeliers with thousands of crystals. The second and third floors, with interior designs by Ogden Codman (who had been introduced to Alice by Edith Warton), startle with their neoclassic, understated simplicity and better reflect the values of the owners. There on the bedtables of Cornelius and Alice rested well-worn copies of the Bible.

When the work on the Breakers began, Alice treated Hunt as a social equal, for his family joined hers on a trip to Europe. For wealthy families to travel together was not unusual then, and since this visit included the purchase of furnishings and art for the new Breakers, it was natural the Hunts come along. Among the Hunt children was Esther, who was Gertrude's age. Perhaps the animosity Alice later showed toward Hunt was less out of dissatisfaction with his architectural work, than out of disapproval of his daughter.

Gertrude Gains a
Girlfriend—and More

With her somewhat bohemian upbringing, Esther Hunt was the perfect friend for Gertrude. Consequently, Gertrude found in Esther a soulmate for endless conversations about art and life. Esther also shared Gertrude's passionate temperament, with one important exception: she was willing to express her feelings frankly, too frankly for the Vanderbilts. Esther had a crush on Gertrude, played it out, and successfully entranced Gertrude emotionally—not an easy task, considering her mercurial, hesitant temperament. They spent hours together, with friends on picnics and rides and country jaunts, and alone, on a sofa in a bedroom, arms surrounded. At age 19, Gertrude was to write, "I can count the thrills of my life, they are so few and far between. Once it was when Sally (dear old Sally whom I don't care very much for now) took my hand. Again when Esther kissed me."[23]

Esther kissed her many times, with the result that Gertrude was doubtless sexually aroused. Gertrude kissed back, driving Esther "crazy" with thoughts of her mouth. But so, too, could Gertrude feel rapture hugging her little sister Gladys. Gertrude was so restricted from any physical expression of affection that just the accidental brushing of a shoulder against a man could cause a paragraph of epiphany in her diary. They teased one another with lightly jealous remarks. The more solicitous of the two, Esther promises she "will not let her [Kitty] hold my hand if you mind, I don't care and I don't like you to hold anyone's really I don't anyhow you can't kiss anyone the way you kiss me."[24] To summarize the relationship as lesbian, as modern readers are apt to do, is to overlook its context and meaning for the participants.

Significantly, the context for same-sex relationships was very different from today. Separate spheres for men and women still held, with the consequence that one looked to members of one's own gender for most intimacy and companionship. Women friends in particular, even after marriage, would confide to one another as they never would to a fiancé or husband. Embraces, hugs, and kisses were a natural accompaniment. Gertrude noted in her diary, "I don't say talk [during the long visit] because sometimes we hardly speak at all. Esther puts her arm about my waist and I put my head on her shoulder and we are happy. We remembered all the time, though we tried to forget, that it would be six weeks before we saw each other again." Such a description women of Gertrude's day would find normal, indeed admirable.[26] Accordingly, the modern mind can read too much into Esther's effusive letters, "Take care of yourself my own Sweetheart—I love you and I love you with all my heart and soul I love you."[26] Such sentimentality was common in the culture.

One wonders what else they could have done with their adolescent hormonal surges. They could not touch men, unless coming upon it innocently by accident; they would not masturbate (and had they learned what they were doing, would have quickly stopped it in horror); they were not hugged by parents. Gertrude and Esther were eighteen when the crush started, and it would continue for two more years, even though both would be at the same time flirting with young men. And in Esther's case, the flirting included other young women, even Adele Sloane, whose own diary remarked about "having so often loved women myself when they cared very little for me."[27] Indeed, for a time Gertrude and Esther would be attracted to the same man, Moses Taylor, who had been William Vanderbilt's roommate at Yale, and would playfully vie for his attention.

While Gertrude was delighted with Esther ("tall—pretty—a flirt—charming when she wants to be—airs—light brown hair—blue eyes—attracted—affected"[28]), Alice was not. Two modern Vanderbilt descendants separately writing of this episode cited lesbianism as the reason. But the cause was likely simpler, that Esther was too effusive, too artsy for Alice to want around. At Esther's house Gertrude would be more likely to meet men not fully acceptable to Vanderbilt society. And, not incidentally, Esther's father was in the employ of Cornelius. Given the higher social status of the Hunts prior to Alva's breaking down the barriers, the fact of employment as a basis for her snobbishness was ridiculous, but just the sort of distinction Alice would make.

Among the first signs of Alice's displeasure was in September 1893, when Gertrude returned home late in the afternoon following a long drive with Esther. Alice called her errant daughter into the parlor and questioned her severely, rejecting her explanation, a truthful one, that they had turned down a wrong road. She then forbade Gertrude to see Esther for a month, a punishment she retracted after dinner. But if Alice could not keep the girls apart, she did not stop her campaign to end the relationship. Two months later Gertrude prayed that she "never by word or deed may offend or hurt" her future children. She asked forgiveness for not sharing feelings and thoughts with her parents. Her supplication was followed by sorrow and bitterness: "Sit by and hear your best friend picked to pieces or the fact of your having three letters from the same girl in the same week laughed at and mockingly alluded to. Listen to your friend being called a runner after rich girls, with a knowing look in your direction."[29]

Despite being in mourning over William, Gertrude continued a lively, if less public, social life that extended to about two dozen acceptable young women and men (ninety-two parties, balls, and operas noted in 1894). Alice's disapproval only fueled her daughter's independence. In April of that year Gertrude made an entry describing a confrontation with her mother over the latter's demand that she once and for all stop seeing Esther. "You think you can twist me around your finger, and let me tell you that the only thing you have succeeded in making me do is in telling you less and less about myself, and my affairs and something else I think I had better not say."[30] The women would continue to meet, and on her twentieth birthday in January of 1985, Gertrude would unwrap an inscribed leather-bound album:

To Gertrude
To see her is to love her,
And love her forever,
For nature made her what she is
And never made another.
I have gathered a posie of other men's flowers, and
nothing but the thread that binds them is my own—
Esther[31]

1893-1895

Mother and Daughter
Each Find Romance

When Alva was planning Marble House, as she had done with 660 Fifth Avenue, she once again approved a feature of the design that today's tourists often comment upon: she consigned Willie to a tiny bedroom, smaller than that of his children. That subordination accurately reflected her feelings for him; the marriage had been a shambles for some years.

It is easy to blame Alva. Consuelo found her father sweet and gentle, playful and full of jokes. She saw him beset upon unfairly by her intemperate plate-tossing mother, her childhood ruined by the dread of noissome fights. She was frustrated that her parents, whom she loved individually, were unable to love one another.

Yet there is always a story the child does not see. In the case of Willie, he neglected his family in the pursuit of pleasure—pleasure that included other women. He was simply not around much and left the disciplining to Alva. Toward the children he was like a modern weekend divorced father, the one to have fun with because there are so few hours to spend together. Compared to a mother with horsewhip and sharp tongue, he was easy to idolize and idealize.

Nor was Willie's character so jolly as his worshipful daughter perceived. Andrew Croffut, the only biographer who personally knew him, described him as the least popular of William Henry's sons, given to sullen and dark moods. Far from being bad for the Vanderbilt heir, Alva knew exactly how to cajole him, to raise his spirits, claimed Croffut. Later in life Willie would show his melancholy in a much-quoted remark to a reporter, "My life was never destined to be happy. Inherited wealth is a real handicap to happiness. It is as certain death to ambition as cocaine is to morality."[1] (In fact, in the years following this comment, with a more compatible wife and life in France racing horses, he was rather content.)

With the marriage in turmoil, it is a puzzle why the couple chose in late 1893 to sail to India, a journey that would take many months, unless perhaps they hoped for a reconciliation. This time the yacht was the *Valiant,* for the *Alva,* in an event ancients would have taken as an omen, had sunk in a collision near Boston. The new ship carried a crew of seventy-two and a French chef. Besides the family (excluding son William K. II, now at boarding school), a doctor, a governess, and three male guests were aboard, two of whom were to make a special mark on the journey. One was attorney Winthrop Rutherfurd ("Winty"), the other was Harry Belmont. (August Belmont had died in 1890, and despite his constant dismay over Harry's lackadaisical ways, had left his wayward son well provided for.)

As may be expected, Alva and Consuelo sketched different memories of the journey. Once the yacht pulled into Bombay, a private train carried the group all about India, eventually ending the journey in Calcutta, on the opposite shore.[2] Initially, Alva reacted with a characteristic Western response, fascination with various temples and sites but revulsion "of deplorably poor and sick people frightened into superstitious submission by their priests." Bodies of babies tossed into a crocodile-ridden river and animals sacrificed at a Temple of Kali were not comprehensible acts to her. On the other hand, she concluded from the Taj Mahal and the goddesses of its religion evidence of Indian respect for women. That a man would so honor his wife with a building like the Taj stirred her feminism. The Taj "was a challenge to my own woman's heart and to all other women's hearts to lift up her head and take her place side by side with man as he was decreed from earliest legend, 'Male and female made he them and he gave *them* dominion over the earth.'"[3] Consuelo did not recall the temples so much as the shabby treatment of women, the *veiling,* the noisy crowds, the fear of attack from violent-looking men, the bad food.

It is a wonder the women later recalled any facts concerning the various stops on the journey, as the real adventure was an intimate one. Somewhere on this curious jaunt mother and daughter fell in love, fortunately with different men.

Harry Belmont, five years Alva's junior, finally won her hardened forty-two-year-old heart. Why should she be drawn to this man whose own parents thought him an indolent wastrel? He was after all as much a sporting man as Willie. The Belmonts' censure was ironic—Harry more than any of their offspring had grasped August's lessons in refined connoisseurship, so much so that he thought a life built upon the expression of beauty and perfection was in itself worthwhile. Where his parents saw frivolity, he saw the creation of a well-bred horse, a sensually appealing meal, a room filled with objects to stimulate the mind. His particular aesthetics, such as his attraction to the French Gothic, matched Alva's, and with her he insisted on flawlessness in craft, whatever the expense of labor.

His rebellious individualism must also have added to his appeal. Years of nagging and threats from his parents had failed to break him into submission to their more bourgeois wishes. His refusal to be swayed by society is evident in the design of Belcourt. There, one entire wing of the first floor was reserved not for salons and library, but for his horses. This clever eccentricity, which would shock other women for its implication that the horses deserved first place, may have secretly delighted Alva.

Harry's other allure was his politics. During dinner conversations, August Belmont had preached to his children a gospel of free market, which meant that the multitentacled monopolies of the day must go. Older brother Perry had won a seat to the U.S. Congress on such a stand, and Harry was as avid a true believer in his desire to fight "trusts, monopolies, and the money power on behalf of the common people."[4] Given her progressive ancestors, Alva was always ready to challenge the very people who had provided her sumptuous life-style—so long as she could keep her mansions and bully her servants. During the mid-1890s, Harry even published a magazine of political opinion, *The Verdict,* much of which supported Democrat Williams Jenning Bryan, who attacked supporters of the gold standard as elitist oppressors of the debt-ridden masses. (In 1896 Bryan's opponents would refer to his stand as a "foul pit of repudiation, socialism, [and] anarchy.)

While Alva and Harry secretly met, or played cards with Willie and the anonymous male guest, Consuelo found herself in the company of Winty Rutherfurd. Society deemed the Rutherfurds, descendants of Peter Stuyvesant and John Winthrop, to be of impeccable pedigree, certainly better than the Vanderbilts. Winty's father was Lewis Rutherfurd, a lawyer who became Lincoln's secretary of state, then devoted himself to photographic astronomy. He developed the spectroscope, and his pictures of the planets and the moon brought him fame in his new profession. Besides being intelligent, rich, and "of good blood," the Rutherfurds were known for their breathtakingly good looks (again placing them above the Vanderbilts). Impeccably garbed and mannered, he became for neighbor Edith Wharton "the prototype of my first novels."[5] A noted dog breeder, his favorite sport was riding to hounds with such friends as Theodore and Elliot Roosevelt. It was likely through a shared interest in horseflesh that he was befriended by Willie. At thirty-one, still a bachelor, Winty was a catch many mothers would fight over, one the daughters would fight over as well.

Since Consuelo was only sixteen, Alva probably never thought a romance was possible. A storm in the North Atlantic disproved her, for Winty's gentlemanly offer of an arm to steady Consuelo on the pitching deck aroused the girl's heart. He seemed to her the perfect man, the knight to free the unhappy princess from her tower.

Alva Seeks a
Noble Connection

Unfortunately for the love-struck child, the party's visit with Viceroy and Lady Lansdowne at Calcutta House set Alva's mind on an intractable goal. Lady Lansdowne was the daughter of the duke of Albercorn, her sister the mother of the duke of Marlborough. Never much of an Anglophile, Alva's look at the pampered life at Calcutta House destroyed her prejudices. She decided it would be best if Consuelo married "in the Anglo Saxon race."[6] An aristocrat, of course, and preferably one of two available men: the Lansdowne's son or the duke of Marlborough.

During her adolescent years in Paris, Alva had observed how wealthy or aristocratic parents chose their childrens' mates, and she concluded the method was a sensible one for her to follow with Consuelo.[7] The marriages of youth, often founded on mere physical attraction, did not seem wise to her. American enough not to want a forced marriage or a loveless one, she decided to use that society's more subtle route: propinquity. Namely, allow a daughter to meet only pre-approved men, and you control her choice of mates.

As she considered Consuelo, she was gratified to find a child with many admirable qualities: well informed, a love of learning, a high sense of service, and strong moral character. On the other hand, she was docile and tractable, easily bending to other's pressures. Alva did not see that an American mate would do here, for they seldom possessed the sense of family purpose and historical mission found in the great lines of Europe. Instead, American men of wealth and their wives led lives lacking in public mindedness. Endless leisure with its accompanying impulsiveness destroyed good minds. Thus, when the romance left the marriage (as it surely would, Alva believed) there would be no meaningful mutual interest to take the relationship to a new level of maturity. She did not want Consuelo to end up like some of her friends, so witless that they were unable to write a check and proud of that ignorance.

Although marrying a wealthy American daughter off to an English title had been going on for two decades, the origins of the practice left a disreputable air. For all her beauty, Alva's childhood neighbor Jenny Jerome, the first to make such a tie, had problems finding a respectable spouse among the Knickerbockers because her father's more than professional interest in opera singers tainted his daughters. Her marriage to Randolph Churchill in 1874 earned only a sentence in the New York papers, where it was embedded in a general news release from Paris, the site of the wedding. In 1876, Alva's best friend, Consuelo Ygnaza, had wed Viscount Mandeville in New York before 1,200 guests, initiating a new style in extravagant ceremonies as a result. Yet the *New York Times* headline was "Lord Mandeville Married," for the bride, described as a mere banjo-playing southerner, was not considered worth mention.[8]

Since then, however, other *arrivistes,* and eventually even daughters of Knickerbockers, set up household in the British Isles. Many of these marriages were to lesser members of the aristocracy, a younger brother, a third son. Back in the States, the old prejudice remained. Once the prince bemusedly shared with a friend, "Whenever I ask Consuelo, Duchess of Manchester [nee Yznaga], about an American lady I am invariably told, 'Oh, sir, she has no position at home; out there she would be just dirt under our feet.'"[9]

What Consuelo Vanderbilt never realized until too late was Alva's ultimate purpose for the trip: to groom her in Paris so she would make so strong a mark on English society that the lords would rush to beg for the girl's hand. Even following a horrible quarrel that resulted in Alva and Willie's final separation, Consuelo was too mesmerized by her infatuation with Winty to perceive Alva's plans. For her, Paris was the consummation of the trip, even though Winty (and Harry Belmont) had left the party. Innocently, Consuelo attended the Theatre Français, the Comedie Française, the Paris Opera, radiant in white Worth gown, jewels purposely left out, to draw attention to the wearer not the dress. The young woman lost some of her shyness and welcomed all the attention. She was, to her own surprise, having a good time.

The ruse worked. Titled and questionably titled men from throughout the Continent circled around this tall beauty with the swanlike neck, to seek her and, more important, her mother's favor. Of five marriage proposals, the one most attractive to Alva was that from His Serene Highness Prince Francis Joseph of Battenburg. Repulsed by his Teutonic imperiousness, Consuelo was most relieved when her mother decided a title unaccompanied by palaces and servants was not adequate, however esteemed the line. A French aristocrat with more gold to back up his name also seemed a possibility, until Alva decided the political situation of the country was too unstable. No, it must be an Englishman after all.

Alva Defies
Convention

W hen not chaperoning her daughter to prominent events, Alva was engaged in her final battle with Willie, who had set up separate quarters in Paris. Even Cornelius joined the act, leaving the office to cross the ocean and serve as personal intermediary to save the marriage. He was unsuccessful. Not only had Willie's philandering become too public, he had even brought his mistresses into their homes for assignations, Alva charged. Against her lawyer's advice, Alva decided to sue for divorce on the basis of adultery.

Alva's decision was an unheard-of and glaring defiance of custom, her first of many public contributions to woman's rights. Echoing her niece Gertrude's observations of marriage, she noted, "All around me were women leading these half lives, practically deserted by their husbands who not only neglected them but insulted them by their open and flagrant and vulgar infidelities."[10] Some of these men, such as John Jacob Astor, were known to hold orgies, whose scandalous details were passed word-of-mouth throughout society. So public were affairs that there were rules about how to acknowledge a man passing by in a carriage with a woman who was not his wife. The Riviera was especially notorious for its demimondes. There a society woman might well find herself humiliated to cross a hotel lobby past a friend's husband who was accompanied by one of the infamous French mistresses. Should she execute a "cut direct" and insult the man or greet him and in effect give recognition to his disreputable partner? And while it was never spoken of or written down, these wives must have worried about syphilis, which was rampant then, untreatable, and was sometimes spread to the innocent partner. (Jennie Jerome Churchill had just lost her husband to the dreaded disease.)

Over the years Alva had studied the women of these unhappy arrangements, their isolation and eventual banishment from the world. While the husbands maintained their public stature, the women had to swallow their pride and accept the patronizing attitude of others who knew the truth. The wives were to sustain the moral image of the family by pretending the marriage was intact and successful, all the while subordinating their own personal needs. They could not assert their right to a lover or be free to develop other contacts in the outside world.

To seek a divorce was sensational, but to charge the husband publicly with the actual reason, adultery, was beyond the pale. Aware that social osctracism would result, Alva charged ahead, determining it was "a question of social injustice not only to myself but other women situated as I was."[11] She was not surprised when her lawyer fought with her night after night, trying to convince her to forgo the divorce. He had no chance, for she had concluded that as "a true representative of Organized Wealth" he understood the threat to wealthy men were she successful.[12]

Willie quickly demurred, granting her full custody of the children and munificent support. She refused his offers of 660 Fifth Avenue and Idlehour, taking instead a town house at Fifth and 72nd for her New York base. Since it was a gift, Marble House was already in her name. Willie also agreed to "provide cause" by participating in a hotel room encounter with a hired stooge, one Nellie Neustretter brought over from Nevada. For Alva to come away with so many benefits suggests she had something sensational in her pocket. If this were not the case, why would Willie K. capitulate so readily? It was unlikely, as Consuelo rationalized that he was easily owed for he could afford the best lawyer. The shadow figure in this affair may have been none other than Consuelo Ygnaza, duchess of Manchester, once Alva's dearest friend. Rumors spread about the Continent that Willie K. was having an affair with her. One indication that the stories were true . . . that after the divorce she was conspicuously absent from Alva's and Consuelo's lives.

While Alva expected ostracism as a result of her decision, she found its sting similar to the lashings she had received as a child. "So I bared my back to the whipping of Society for taking a freedom which would eventually better [women]."[13] The Sunday after obtaining her divorce, no one in Trinity Church in Newport spoke to her. At dinner parties, often the only woman to chat with her would be the hostess, that rare friend who supported her cause. She would walk into a room to find that all the women would suddenly hush, gather their skirts, and walk out without recognizing her. The men continued to be friendly because, she concluded, their wives and daughters behaved appropriately in shunning her.

The divorce charge gave Alva her first taste of harnessing her naturally rebellious spirit for the good of others. She would benefit financially from the divorce, yet she envisioned herself as a Jeanne d'Arc, riding into battle for a noble cause, willing to suffer personally for the final victory. She felt tremendous satisfaction in subsequent years as she saw other women, not only of her class, but of modest means, follow her model and break out of abusive marriages.

Consuelo Meets
a Duke

With legal matters set in motion, Alva took Consuelo to London, where they settled in Brown's Hotel on Dover Street, a haven for American heiresses. Consuelo found the rooms "frowsy in the true English sense."[14] From that staging area, Alva's major plan was implemented. It began with a visit to her old friend Lady Paget, who agreed that Consuelo should be mated with Charles Richard John Spencer Churchill, the ninth duke of Marlborough. Sunny (as he was known because of his title of Lord Sunderland) was twenty-two and in need of money for his beloved Blenheim Palace. A dinner was arranged for the two young people to meet.

Still unaware of the matrimonial plot, and excessively modest about her looks, Consuelo felt gawky and embarrassed when Lady Paget ordered her to wear a dress showing plenty of bosom, of which she did not have much to display. Alert to the scheme, Sunny prepared for the event expecting to be disappointed and was nonplussed upon arrival to find otherwise. Consuelo's famed neck, hair, and complexion pleased him. She admitted to finding him good looking and intelligent, if young for his age, his nose a bit large, and his attitude toward his well-shaped hands "inordinately proud."[15] Given his meticulous, at times persnickety nature, his mood did not live up to his nickname. She was impatient to return to the hotel suite to read Winty's latest love letter.

When the London season closed, Alva settled all three children with her in a country house on the Thames, where Consuelo was kept to her usual heavy schedule of studies. There she passed the Oxford examinations with high scores, but her formal learning would end with that achievement. No offer came from Sunny, only from some obvious dowry hunters.

Gertrude Meets a Lord, *But Mocks Him*

Consuelo was not the only Vandervilt daughter to be noticed by British society that summer season. It was also Gertrude's first time there as an adult, free to join in the dancing at balls, luncheons at elegant clubs, and the dress parade at Ascot. It was in the stands at Ascot that she attracted John Francis Hamilton Sinclair Cunliffe Brooks Forbes, better known as Lord Garioch, a tall, ruddy-faced redhead who talked easily to Gertrude about hunting, fishing, shooting, horse racing, and the season. ("Yes, get a man to talk about himself and, unless something is radically the matter, you will get on beautifully," she wrote her favorite teacher about the encounter.[16]) Meanwhile, she later learned, his relatives, the count and countess of Mar, had invited her family to lunch. When Alice and Cornelius consulted with a confidante about the invitation, they were advised to make apologies that the family, despite its being the oldest Scottish earldom, was not worth their time. The countess charmingly deflected their refusals, and so the family members of Cornelius Vanderbilt II found themselves with an appointment they did not desire.

In the days leading up to the luncheon, the family found much amusement in the situation. "What have you done to him?" her father quipped one afternoon. Laughing, Gertrude responded that she was sure she was not the attraction, although she secretly feared otherwise. In the meantime, she imagined the scene, creating an episode fit for Jane Austen. The house would be small, with hints of shabbiness. The countess would appear dignified in her black silk dress, the earl slightly bent with age and with old-fashioned manners. Lord Garioch would talk on and on about anything she encouraged. She would catch them appraising her family, reaching the surprising conclusion that the Vanderbilts were after all well-bred and accomplished conversationalists.

In a more impish daydream, she considered finding herself alone with Lord Garioch, on a sofa or in a conservatory, where she would tease and flatter him, lean toward him, lower her voice to make him thrill to her. "I will go so far as to take the most tremendous interest in his little finger. I will not omit to ask him how it happened that he became a little deaf in one ear." She would press him to the point where he would ask for a stroll. And at the point where they seemed to be "on dangerous grounds," she would burst out laughing and say she had been fibbing all along. He would chuckle with her, she supposed. In another version of this story, he would seize her hand, try to put his arm around her waist. She would struggle, blame him, and scold him, until he apologized. Then they would become fast friends.

The actual luncheon was much as she imagined, but more subdued. His mother, dressed in black, was much younger than Gertrude anticipated. Gertrude did encourage Garioch to talk about Scotland, where her family was about to visit. He asked if he could see her upon her return, and she agreed, all the while barely able to control her giggling amusement. As they were about to leave the house, he appeared with a single red rose and gave it to her. She thanked him graciously, then climbed into the carriage and fell into a fit of hilarity with her parents.

A few days later Gertrude caught the measles from her brother Regi, thus she had a ready excuse not to see Garioch. Once she recuperated, she developed a crush for Regi Ronalds, an American related to the tobacco-wealthy Lorillards. She had been interested in Regi since meeting him at Newport previously, and at dinner one evening she practiced the wiles she had playfully considered using with the Scottish suitor. Englishmen had no chance with this Vanderbilt heiress.

Consuelo Defies
Her Mother

In the fall of 1894, Consuelo was thrilled to be packing for the trip home. She missed her friends, looked forward to her debut before American society, and most of all, longed for the arms of her distant love. Alas, she found instead she was cut from a large part of society, the result of her mother's divorce action. When she returned from those parties that allowed her presence, Alva conducted what seemed like an inquisition, a sign of her desperation to control her daughter's objects of affection. Who was there? With whom did she dance? Any mention of Winty brought sarcasm and jibes. Didn't Consuelo know he had a reputation for breaking women's hearts, that he had affairs with married women, that madness ran in his family?

While decades later Consuelo portrayed the Alva of this time as a heartless, mean-spirited mother, the image is not fully credible. For one, Alva permitted Consuelo to see Winty and even invited him to the house. Possibly Consuelo was projecting some of her anger over the divorce upon her mother. Certainly Alva had sharp remarks for her daughter, but they were motivated by a genuine if misguided attempt to see Consuelo fulfilled in marriage. Alva may have concluded correctly that Winty, while a delightful first infatuation, should remain just that. Indeed, it is hard to imagine Consuelo being contented on the countryside estate of Allemuchy in northern New Jersey while Winty tended to his obsession, his foxhounds.

What Consuelo also could not appreciate were the other stresses on Alva during this period. She had refused the ostracism of divorce, demanding that her friends and even Vanderbilt relatives retain their allegiance. The Vanderbilts understandably all stood behind Willie, with hard consequences for the three children, who missed their cousins, aunts, and uncles. Even the southern Smith relatives drew back in horror over their cousin's behavior. And then there was impatient Harry Belmont, with whom she must manage a discreet relatonship without losing his affections. He must wait until Consuelo was married, she pled. And perhaps the worst frustration for Alva was having to face for the first time in her life a peevish daughter instead of the sweet and compliant one she had known.

One afternoon during an outing accompanied by Alva and others, Winty actually proposed.[17] As the group cycled up Riverside Drive, a fad of the time, he pressed faster, urging Consuelo to join him in pulling out of earshot of the crowd. In those few minutes of privacy he offered his troth, which she accepted. Unfortunately, she and her mother were set to sail for Europe the next day, so when Alva cycled up furiously to disrupt the privacy, the lovers had no chance for a farewell.

Although Consuelo said nothing to Alva of the discussion, her behavior must have given the secret away. From that day she received no letters from Winty, for they were intercepted, and she did not know he had been refused at the door when he followed her later to Paris. She felt what any heartbroken adolescent experiences, "an automaton . . . steered into a vortex that was to engulf me."[18] Familiar with Juliet, she must have identified strongly with the romantic fate of that and similar tragic heroines.

A brief stay with Lady Paget in London brought the return of Sunny. By now totally with confidence, bewildered over her lover's silence, she welcomed the duke's cool interest. Yet following a visit to Blenheim, she questioned the wisdom of marrying him. He was too proud, too ambitious, she concluded.

An Uncertain Sunny
Capitulates

U nknown to Consuelo and Alva, Sunny was in love with another woman. She was not in a position to bring a fortune to the marriage, however, and Sunny was under great pressure from his family to preserve the estate. The strongest inducement to find a wealthy wife, though, was his own passion for Blenheim, which had become the object of his childhood affection when his parents neglected him. While growing up, he had watched his grandfather and father struggle to keep its fabled walls from collapsing into ruin.

In 1873, just after Sunny's birth, farm income in England began to slide. Tenant farmers moved to the city, fields lay fallow. Noble landlords, suddenly without profit, were often forced to sell treasured heritage, such as the priceless manuscripts and rare volumes of English literature that settled in the collection of railroad magnate Henry Huntington in California. Youngest sons were virtually impoverished, whereas their eldest brothers inherited leaky-roofed, crumbling plastered, musty ancestral seats filled with worm-eaten furniture, moth-eaten draperies, and soot-tainted oil paintings.

Blenheim was the only nonroyal palace in the land, a gift of Queen Anne to the duke in honor of his defeating the French in 1704. This magnificent dwelling, a favorite among tourists today, had turned into a voracious money eater. There were so many windows that it took a man a year to wash them all, at which point he must start over again. The grounds, designed in the natural style by acclaimed Capability Brown, were growing wilder than that tolerant landscaper would have preferred. The fourteen acres of roof was a sieve. The estate was not just the palace, but the surrounding tenancies, the farmers and village people to whom the family had many social responsibilities.

Beginning in 1874, Sunny's grandfather had started selling off whatever could be spared to pay the bills. He first released the estates of Wichendon and Waddesdon, which were purchased by Baron Ferdinand de Rothschild. In 1875 the Marlborough gems went on the block at Christie's. During 1882 and 1883 servants packed the books and manuscripts of Sunderland Library and sent them off to various buyers. The biggest sale was the Blenheim Enamels, which earned £73,000 in 1883. Yet when the Duke died, his will left only £7,000.

Sunny's father, better known as Blandford, immediately started another round of auctions, this time including treasured paintings by Titian, Rembrandt, Rubens, Watteau, and Van Dyck. That other aristocrats were selling their family treasures was no solace. By 1888 he decided the only long-lasting solution would be to marry an American heiress. Thus he sailed to New York, where Leonard Jerome prepared to provide the introductions.

There was one serious hitch. The eighth duke of Marlborough was *persona non grata* to New York society. He was known to be a *roué*, certainly not an unusual role for an English aristocrat, but he had made the unforgivable mistake of letting his pecadilloes be known publicly. As one newspaper wit put it, "Everything His Grace of Marlborough brought with him was clean, except his reputation."[19]

The breaking story had occurred in 1876. Blandford's amorous ways with Lady Edith, wife of the earl of Aylesford, were perhaps more successful than he wished, for she foolishly informed her husband she intended to elope with her lover. When the earl threatened to sue for divorce, the prince of Wales stepped in, rebuking Blandford for provoking two marital breakups. (Blandford himself was also married to Sunny's mother at the time.) At that point the duke produced for the prince a set of letters addressed to Lady Edith during an earlier time. They were written on royal stationery in the royal hand and expressed very unroyal remarks. Furious over the blackmail attempt, the prince ostracized the entire Churchill family. Lady Blandford left her husband, later to sue for divorce in 1883. Lady Edith, whose husband retracted his suit, was to bear Blandford an illegitimate son.

Although London society and the prince eventually forgave Blandford, the more puritanical New Yorkers could not. Fortunately for Blenheim, one woman did not mind meeting this notorious womanizer—or possibly she was ignorant of his reputation. Lily Hammersley, a rich young widow was only too happy to buy a title, the duke only too pleased to provide it. Following the wedding, even so conservative a paper as *The New York Times* remarked cynically on the match as an exchange of convenience. Lily's fortune helped treat some of the rising damp of Blenheim, and she looked away when the profligate Blandford went about with Lady Colin Campbell. Alas for the estate, Blandford died only four years later in 1892, and Lily, finding nobility congenial, married Lord William de la Poer Beresford in 1895, with Sunny giving her away.

Thus Sunny had no stronger a role model than his own father to encourage a "sacrifice," for it would not be a great one if he were also to follow his father's wandering and adulterous ways afterward. That early summer of 1895 he was not ready to commit himself, however, so Alva and Consuelo returned to the States to bide their time at Marble House. Sunny indicated he would follow in six weeks, the unstated implication being a proposal was on the way.

While Sunny faced many pressures to marry well, there was no reason he should either marry immediately or marry Consuelo. He was young, and as first son from one of only twenty-seven ducal families, was a catch for many anxious mothers from better-heeled parts of the British aristocracy. Because aristocratic sons could marry down, as it were, to women in the gentry, whereas daughters could not, the market for marriageable men in this class was tight. This imbalance impelled wealthy fathers, if they could, to sweeten a daughter's marital appeal with promise of a settlement. And understandably, the rash of men choosing to overlook the isle's own and take a bride from overseas provoked much criticism from aristocratic women. Very likely Sunny's own two unmarried sisters held the common opinion that American heiresses were "forward hussies" and adventuresses. Thus London society resented this trend as much as Americans did (although British-bashing Yankees assumed otherwise). Seen in light of this backdrop, Sunny's seeming procrastination in the matter of proposing to Consuelo makes much sense.

There was another reason for his caution. His scoundrel father had alternately bullied and neglected the youth, forcing him, for example, to attend Trinity College, Cambridge, rather than the traditional Churchill family choice of Oxford. With a brooding, insecure temperament, Sunny sought solace from women like his sisters or Aunt Jennie Churchill, and he was so dependent on feminine opinion for his self-worth that he went to great lengths to understand the feminine mind.[20] But Consuelo had been cool to him, and he required more assurance of her interest before he would commit himself. Without evidence of support and attention from her, he could look for another bride of fortune, though none would likely bring so much with her as a Vanderbilt.

Consuelo
Gives In

According to Consuelo, once back in Newport she became a virtual prisoner, the house porter and her governess having been ordered to prevent the young woman from going out alone. Raised to be compliant, she accepted their orders, never considering that, if she really tried, she could escape. Alva was a hovering chaperone her few times out. It was on such a date that Consuelo asserted her will. Winty happened to be at the party and managed most of one dance with her before Alva brusquely stepped in, separated them, and dragged her daughter out to the carriage. On the ride home Consuelo finally summoned the courage and asserted her right to choose her own husband, who was to be Winty. Enraged by her daughter's audacity, Alva's shouted invectives rocked the carriage: Winty's search for an heiress was well known. And not only did madness run in his family, he was likely sterile! (Winty's six children later disproved that charge.)

Alva's tactic was no more effective than that of any parent who damns a child's blind choice. The story is an old one, the ending predictable. Consuelo grew more obstinate. By the time the horses pulled up the short curved drive to Marble House, Alva pulled herself up and announced in steely determined words she would *shoot* Winthrop Rutherfurd before allowing him to ruin Consuelo's life! Consuelo ran to her room in tears.

The next morning Consuelo awoke to a maid's shaking her, shouting that Alva was ill. The household staff, normally cool and controlled, were visibly distraught. Late in the day, Lucy Jay, a friend of Alva's, approached Consuelo to report that Alva had had a heart attack, that Consuelo was to blame, that the doctor warned any further scenes could have mortal results. Consuelo had no doubt this was all true. At this point, her English governess sat down with her and painted so attractive a portrait of the social service Consuelo could perform as a duchess that she decided to give in to her mother's wishes.

But was this melodrama true? Alva's condemnation of Winty Rutherfurd was so well known that the gossip columns had chided her for disrupting the romance. But as for locking up Consuelo, the press evidence points otherwise, one reporter observing how she had gone about "all summer [of 1895] in her usual timid, shrinking way, accepting attentions from would-be suitors with a simple, childish artlessness."[21] Furthermore, had Alva so constrained Consuelo, would not Willie have found out and come to his favorite child's rescue? Indeed, it is hard to believe Consuelo's claim that she had no contact with her father at all since the time of separation.

Futhermore, Consuelo's confessed behavior with Sunny further belies the claim she was forced into the marriage. When he arrived, Alva put him in the Marble House guest room, vacant in virginal splendor since its creation for this one perfect guest. Trained since childhood for this eventuality, Consuelo launched into a season of self-admitted gaiety with him as escort, from soirees on famed yachts docked in the harbor, dinners at other mansions, polo games, carriage rides (often with Harry Belmont), and tennis matches. She hoped he found her wit and cheerful spirits amusing. If she pined for Winty, it was not for long.

Consuelo and Sunny would find they had much in common. They had known domineering parents and lonely childhoods. They were both avid horse people, accomplished riders, and shared an interest in interior design and art. They were from prominent families of their respective countries and accepted that birthright as entailing special responsibilities. Reassured by Consuelo's heightened attention, Sunny determined to go ahead with the marriage. Propinquity was working its charm.

Aristocracy deserved a perfect ball, and once again Alva went down in entertaining history, producing what was later agreed to be the best event of its sort in Newport experience. However much society deplored Alva's frankness about her divorce, many of its members could not resist her invitation to meet England's leading duke. By then too Alva had the backing of such society notables as Mrs. Stuyvesant Fish, so meeker members could feel secure in following her lead to Alva's door. They might not reciprocate and welcome her in their homes, but they would drink her wines and brag about meeting Sunny. Thus in late August 1895, over five hundred entered the gold ballroom to meet the guest of honor. They were surprised to find "a pale-faced, frail-looking lad with a voice void of that affected drawl peculiar to the English, and as soft as a debutante's."[22] (This press description hints further at the frequent American put-down of the British.) He was also shorter than Consuelo, who stood regally in her grandmother Smith's white satin and lace gown. The gossipy *Town Topics* concluded, "Winty was outclassed. Six-foot-two in his golf stockings, he was no match for five-foot-six and a coronet."[23] (Gossips also hinted that Sunny preferred Gertrude Vanderbilt, but in fact he never met her.)

Sunny's actual proposal took some time, for the lawyers were busy negotiating the details of the prenuptial agreement. The contract provided Sunny life interest in a trust fund based on Willie's holdings: $2.5 million dollars in 50,000 shares of Beach Creek Railway, with a guarantee of four percent per annum. If Sunny died first, the interest would go to Consuelo. Apart from the agreement, the couple had access to other Vanderbilt money. For example, they later received from Willie a half million pounds to build a house on Curzon Street in London.

Just what this influx was to mean to Blenheim over the years has been disputed, but a reasonable estimate is around $15 million dollars in that day's currency.

The public announcement of the engagement brought a slew of reporters to the door daily. Never one to shun publicity, Alva cooperated in the media circus, whereas Consuelo shuddered to find such items as a sketch of her wedding corset reproduced in one daily sheet. The papers were schizophrenic in their presentation: on the one hand implicitly praising the expense and luxury surrounding the upcoming rite, on the other stirring up sympathy for Consuelo, the American beauty being "sold" to the puny, impoverished son of a man who had just a few years earlier made a similar bargain. "Th' Jook iv Marlburrow is a young lad an' poor. Th' Ganderbilts had th' money an' he was a jook," taunted Peter Finley in his popular "Mr. Dooley" column. Meanwhile, Sunny, who had traveled little in his life, toured about the West, the equivalent for the British of the American Grand Tour circuit abroad.

Years later, Consuelo's retelling of the event itself was notably conflicting in tone. On the one hand, she recalled her "lovely lingerie . . . beautiful dress . . . lovely bridesmaids . . . hymns glorifying perfect love."[24] On the other, she recounted discovering that a footman had been present outside her room all night, supposedly a final insurance on Alva's part that no elopement with Rutherfurd would occur. Her maid helped her into the Parisian gown, ordered months before Sunny's actual proposal, and met her father, who accompanied her to the church to give her away but was forbidden attendance at the luncheon. As the carriage rolled through the streets, Consuelo looked back into the eyes of the gapers lining the streets, who, she said, could not see her tear-stained face through the heavy veiling. Indeed, she was so out of control that she had had her father delay her arrival, holding up the ceremony for twenty minutes. Several blocks from the church a line of policemen held back the crowds, which at past sensational weddings had been known to crush into the basilicas. Despite her sorrow, Consuelo found the scene of her eight bridesmaids and copious sprays of flowers lovely. Near the end of the ceremony, she glanced shyly at Sunny's face, hoping to catch his eyes. They were, she was distressed to find, "fixed in space."[25]

Emerging from the building, the crowd found further reason to mock the event. Elegant straight-backed Consuelo, height emphasized by her high-collared dress, seemed a full head taller than her husband. In truth it was only a couple of inches, but for the American plebians she appeared supreme, a daughter of democracy who deserved better. It may well be that Consuelo felt the same way. Why else, fifty years later in her autobiography, would she take a swipe at Sunny for the fact that her orchid bouquet from Blenheim did not arrive in time for the ceremony? Such a petty grudge hints that she also entered the relationship with an imperiousness that only an obsequious man of lesser status could have managed well.

In later memoirs, Alva recalled a different scene. She remembered the perfection of the flowers and gowns, the extraordinary beauty of the symphony orchestra directed by Walter Damrosch. And when Consuelo did not show up for twenty minutes and the crowd murmured about the delay, she was relieved to learn from Willie that he and Consuelo had been having such a happy conversation that they had simply lost track of the time. She felt great sadness at losing her favorite child and wept at the window when her daughter rode off to leave for England. But she felt secure that encouraging this marriage had been the right choice for her beloved child.

The Duchess Finds
Her Lot a Lonely One

Consuelo's recollection of her wedding night is haunting, with its layers of painful intimation. As to that experience and her first days with Sunny, she reflected, "The problem created by the marriage of two irreconcilable characters is a psychological one which deserves sympathy as well as understanding. In the hidden reaches where memory probes lie sorrows too deep to fathom."[26]

One doubts Sunny would have disagreed. Along with their many common interests, Sunny and Consuelo shared certain personality traits that would make intimacy with anyone difficult. Their parental role models were arrogant, used to ruling with a strong hand, and now, on their own, each soon assumed the same qualities toward the other. They could be moody and hot tempered. Each was eminently confident that his or her way of doing things was the correct way. Neither had much experience in compromise and forgiveness.

In reviewing this early time together, it must be remembered that Consuelo's account was tainted by her later ill will toward Sunny. His side of the story never appeared. Nevertheless, much of her experience was typical for similar American heiresses finding themselves transplanted to the world of English aristocracy. Indeed, one wonders how much the eventual incompatibility was grounded in cultural as well as personal differences.

First, Consuelo soon learned that the relationship between husband and wife was most unlike what she had observed in her own and other friends' homes. If she tried to assert herself with even a fraction of her mother's bluster, she was met quickly with a rebuff. Apart from providing an heir and managing the household, her job as a nobleman's wife was to keep out of his way. She dare not try to "manage" him as American women did with their husbands. This treasured only daughter of an American Midas was to obey this foreigner's commands.

And so it was that the honeymoon was his choice, a lengthy meander around the Continent, Consuelo sulking as they wandered the winter through poorly heated museums in Spain, where the preponderance of inferior paintings bored her. In Monaco their party was a lively crowd, obviously longtime acquaintances of Marlborough, whom she learned were of the *demimonde*. For a woman raised to believe even powder was considered "fast," these stunning, bejeweled mistresses fascinated her. Sunny warned her not to talk to them and to pretend not to know their male companions, several of whom, to her surprise, were men who had pursued her in Paris. One day she was relieved to find another recent bride of English aristocracy, only to be dismayed by the crass materialism of the woman. In Rome, Marlborough deserted her for days, ostensibly to buy art. In Pompeii, she felt humiliated when he left her alone in the ruins so he could look at the notorious erotica. In Paris, he ordered her wardrobe without consulting her. A famous item he bought for her long neck, a nineteen-row dog collar of pearls, proved too obvious a symbol of his chafing rule. Patriarchy did not sit well with Consuelo.

To be fair, Sunny had little reason to behave otherwise. His birthright was to maintain class tradition by ensuring continued supremacy of his family and its estate. One result was an insulation from everyday events that bordered on the ludicrous. Once when his valet was ill, and he went to a house party, he come down in the morning to complain to his host that his toothbrush had not frothed properly. He had to be told that toothpaste must be applied first for that to happen. His cousin Winston never drew a bath for himself. Although wealthy American men had valets, they were not kept so ignorant of personal care.

His upbringing also meant acting in ways an American girl would find arrogant, insufferable, and insensitive (which is not to imply Consuelo was behaving well herself). He was far from the American man of wealth—the sporty, independent, cosmopolitan romantic who approached his heiress lover from below the pedestal with an almost cloying admiration. She could also not understand a system where able-bodied and well-educated men were not supposed to expend themselves in work, as most of her many Vanderbilt male relatives did.

Furthermore, for Consuelo in particular, a man should proclaim the democratic principles and liberal politics both her parents espoused. That one was benefited by accident of birth did not make one naturally superior. Indeed, it brought responsibilities to use one's wealth for the social good. Sunny's attitude toward charity seemed miserly to her, tainted as it was by the English attitude that too much assistance to the poor will only encourage idleness and immorality.

One can only surmise what Sunny's impressions were of his young bride, too quick to state her opinion, too used to being petted, coddled, and spoiled by her family and suitors. He must often have been flabbergasted by her complaints. Simply put, the couple were proof that the differences between British and American society far outweigh the similarity in language. It did not matter that they used the same words—the implications were different.

Consuelo's initial encounters with his family only added to her dislike of English ways and manners. Their ignorance of history, current affairs, literature, and philosophy, especially among the poorly educated women, appalled her. They believed the United States still had scalping Indians and cotton slaves. They confused South America with the southern states. Then there was the matter of the lightly veiled feud between the two branches of the family, the Hamiltons and the Churchills. Sunny's imposing grandmother, the Dowager Duchess, was quick to lecture Consuelo, "Your first duty is to have a child and it must be a son, because it would be intolerable to have that little upstart Winston become Duke."[27] (Since Sunny was an only son, his cousin Winston was in line for the Dukedom should Consuelo bear no heir.)

At least there was Winston, just three years older than she, a delightful, vital young man with a zest for getting the most out of life. His mother, Jennie, welcomed Consuelo despite knowledge her presence would eventually mean Winston's loss of his place in line. Now middle aged, popular with the prince of Wales set, intelligent, gay, well informed, Jennie became a protector for the confused newlywed, especially in the more difficult years ahead.

Another surprise Consuelo shared with similar American heiresses married to aristocrats was the complexity and strangeness of British customs. She must memorize the *Peerage* to understand the proper place of everyone, avoid certain off-limits locations, such as music halls, not dance more than once with the same man, and so on. Combined with these iron-clad rules was what she considered hypocrisy. If one was discreet about one's indiscretions, one could get away with almost anything. (Always the idealistic American, Consuelo failed to consider how her own class in the States was no less rigid and hypocritical.) Nevertheless, she learned to smile and feign so well the charming arrogance required of a duchess that one doubts her later claims to have hated the pretense.

Her major duty, running the household, was quite beyond her ken, as it was for most American heiresses. She had never been in a servant's quarters, let alone been aware of the various functions of the household help and its management. Yet had she known, she would have still run up against what she found to be a curious caste system and eccentricity. Unlike domestic staff Stateside, the English servants viewed themselves as professionals with a code, a set of rules, and a pride no mistress dare disturb. Consuelo later rued the day she asked the butler to light the fire, a job relegated to footmen. Unlike the servants in her family's home, this large and assorted number was often seen *and* heard and quick to draw Consuelo into this or that fray. The chef and housekeeper annoyed her with their ongoing quarrel concerning breakfast trays.

The staff were also talented in that uniquely English way of humiliating the foreigner in a gracious manner, forcing hierarchy to spite the democrat. After all, the newcomer's refusal to play by the rules was to them a slap at their status as professionals. Worst was Consuelo's personal maid, an elderly Swiss woman whose constant hectoring and griping disrupted the sanctuary of the boudoir. Consuelo's reaction to this feisty group was similar to that of another American heiress, Lady Curzon, who once wrote her mother, "English servants are *fiends*. They seem to plot among themselves. I should like to hang a few and burn the rest at the stake."[28]

Reared by a mother who abused her staff, Consuelo was nonetheless sensitive to the plight of the servants. She quickly realized the housekeeper's small crew of maids was very overworked, their life of heavy labor made worse by living quarters lacking in running water. Approaching Sunny to add the plumbing, she was stunned to hear him say they had lived without plumbing satisfactorily for two hundred years, and certainly they could continue to do so. (That she even had to ask Sunny for what her mother would have demanded of Willie must have added to her growing bitterness.)

Then there was Blenheim itself. Although girls in the States envied Consuelo's luxurious life, the reality was otherwise. Marble House had been opulent, and every detail included the very latest technology for the comfort of the occupants. It was, however, a cottage that could fit into a tiny corner of Blenheim. While the palace proved a visual delight to Consuelo's discriminating eye, it was also "Dear Sir John Vanburgh's [the architect's] house of clay . . . a heavy load."[29] Or, as Alexander Pope had observed, "I never saw so great a thing with so much littleness in it."[30] Closets lacked ventilation. Salons and long galleries overwhelmed the solitary visitor with their inhuman scale. Food was cold by the time it crossed the long passageways from the kitchen. The few bathrooms were at the end of long corridors. Every morning Consuelo awoke to face "Dust Ashes Nothing," black letters on the tomblike marble mantlepiece, a decorative selection of Sunny's, a man of deep if private spiritual convictions.

Then there was the English tolerance of personal eccentricities, quirks Americans would little condone among their relatives. Sunny's little oddities infuriated Consuelo. His fastidiousness could lean to meanness, as when he hid a decorative box to test the housekeeper, then purposely accused a maid of stealing it. Most oppressive were the nightly dinners, where after being served, he would push his service away, lean back, and twiddle a ring for fifteen minutes or so while absorbed in thought. When he finally began to eat, he invariably complained about the coldness of the food. Consuelo adapted by taking to knitting between courses, while the butler, waiting in the hall for the sound of the bell, read detective stories.

Worst of all was the plain tedium of estate life, which ran according to almost monastic ritual. Again she was not unusual among American heiresses here, who had caught their mates in London during the lively, overactive social season, then found themselves living in isolated country retreats much of the year. (Their begging letters to papa resulted in the construction of town houses in London, as Consuelo would do, so they could have an escape.) Everyone awoke at the same time, shared meals at the same time, sat in the salon at the same time. At Blenheim, the morning began with prayers in the chapel at nine-thirty sharp. There was none of the pampered spontaneity she had been raised on, the calling of a horse for a ride at any hour of the day, for there was only one hour of the day allotted for such. "From my window I overlooked a pond in which a former butler had drowned himself. As one gloomy day succeeded another, I began to feel a deep sympathy for him."[31]

Yet somehow this nineteen-year-old thrust into an alien environment constructed a life of some satisfaction. Partly it was her training, her years of adjusting to Alva's whims prepared her well for submission at Blenheim. Partly it was her temperament, her ability to find humor in difficult situations, a trait that Sunny at his most hostile admittedly admired. Partly it was Sunny's two unmarried sisters, who despite their poor education, made good companions. Partly it was the visits of eccentric local gentry, such as the pair of mustachioed and enormously fat sisters whose bubbly goodwill brought giggles into dull afternoons.

As Alva had anticipated, Blenheim also offered an outlet for Consuelo's benevolence. Unlike America, where the slightest outside interest of a millionaire's wife (besides quiet and unpublicized involvement in a charity) brought disapproval, in England the nobleman's wife could share in public duties. If he were in politics, she could voice an opinion during a discussion, and he might often seek her advice, as Randolph Churchill had done with Jennie. And if there were a large tenancy, as there was attached to Blenheim, she could gallop out with the estate agents to tend to tenant family needs. Consuelo brightened up on days such as these, when she could visit the old blind woman who asked that she read aloud from the Gospel of St. John. Genuinely good hearted, Consuelo preferred that her charity work bring her in direct contact with the needy.

In time, too, she must have valued the rule saying a noble husband could take off whenever he wished, even for long periods, for it would mean time free of Sunny. She did her duty, in 1897 producing the necessary heir, John Albert Edward William Spencer Churchill, Marquess of Blandford. Her pregnancy and delivery difficult, she welcomed to Blenheim the comforting companionship of the mother who had "forced" this "hapless" marriage.

7

1895-1899

Another Southern Belle
Enters the Scene

The ball for the duke of Marlborough took place in late August 1895, two weeks following Gertrude's coming-out party. If Consuelo missed seeing her cousin's affair, she left no mention of regrets. Gertrude was curiously silent for the several weeks surrounding the event, perhaps too caught up in the preparations to sit down in the rose pink wing chair in her new bedroom with its cabbage rose wall paper, shell pink spread and drapes, and record in her diary this significant social event.

It was Grace Wilson who would most remember Gertrude's belated coming-out ball.

Grace's father, Richard T. Wilson, son of a Scottish tanner, had used his drive, charm, and cleverness to start young adulthood as a traveling salesman in Georgia, eventually to become a multimillionaire financier and railroad owner. A handsome man with a delicious sense of humor, he was later believed by some Southerners to have inspired the character of Rhett Butler in Margaret Mitchell's novel *Gone with the Wind*. Wisely he married no Scarlett O'Hara type but rather the gracious and socially clever Melissa Johnston, whose sweet southern ways softened his brashness. As with the Commodore, the Civil War added to Wilson's fortunes, first from speculating on foreign bonds, which he obtained at thirty cents on the dollar, and then, like Murray Smith, by serving as a middleman in London for cotton growers. Following the war, he did not return to Georgia, which was just as well, as his fellow rebels branded him a war profiteer.

While Wilson's financial finagling increased the family treasury, his wife swiftly moved their social estimate up several pegs. Like other Upstarts, they had lived for a time in London, where Melissa ingratiated herself with the usually resistant British aristocracy. Once back in the States, her social acumen led to the family's being accepted in the drawing room of Mrs. Astor years before that doyenne dropped her calling card at 660 Fifth Avenue.

No family of the era had greater success at arranging socially advantageous marriages. A joke of the day went, "Why did the Diamond Match company fail? Because Mrs. Richard T. Wilson beat them at making matches." Eldest daughter May married Ogden Goelet. She became one of the wealthiest young women in town when Ogden's uncle Peter died and, lacking issue of his own, bequeathed his massive real estate holdings in Manhattan to the young couple. Son Orme married Carrie Astor. This favored pair started marriage with a Fifth Avenue mansion, a house filled with servants, and a million dollars in the bank. Daughter Belle's 1888 prize was the Honorable Michael Herbert, or "Mungo," brother of the earle of Pembroke, who settled her in Wilton House, a four-hundred year-old castle designed for the first Herbert occupants by Holbein. (An English poet once quipped that one found Herberts at Wilton as one found swallows in its village.) The Herberts were at the highest level of English society, and they frequently entertained the prince of Wales.

A change-of-life child, Grace enjoyed all the benefits of arriving late into a loyal, loving, prideful family whose fortunes brought an abundance most Americans would find imaginable only in a fairy tale. Nonetheless, perhaps because of their southern preference for family over social impression, the Wilsons did not live as ostentatiously as their peers. Their first New York home was located "in the country" on Fifth above Fifty-ninth, where squatter shacks perched nearby on rocky outposts. Their Newport cottage remained board and shingle at a time others were tearing down and constructing in cement and marble, and they could give modest calico baskets and ribbon sashes instead of costly pieces of jewelry or imported handcrafts for favors at parties and yet be called charming. Unlike their Yankee neighbors, southern blood ran warm, so ties to one another and to friends were more important than acquisition. Grace's girlhood visits to Tennessee emphasized modest pleasures such as picking blackberries, wading in a creek, and listening to lilting bits of family gossip. She knew none of the loneliness that afflicted Consuelo or Gertrude.

While the Wilsons did not show off at home, they did not stint on comfort for themselves. From the age of eleven, Grace spent large segments of each year in London and Paris. With her sister Belle's marriage into English society, the family's social world widened. May and Ogden Goelet, who frequently lived abroad, joined the prince of Wales's circle, as did Grace by the time she reached young adulthood. Thus in a typical year, Grace sailed for Paris in April to have her summer wardrobe fitted at the House of Worth, joined the Goelets at Beaulieu on the Riviera, a short Mediterranean cruise, then on to Bad Neuheim, with its heated mineral waters, massages, and steam baths. By June, she was in London for the season, after which she returned to Paris for fitting of her winter wardrobe before climbing the gangplank of the ocean steamer home to catch the Newport season. It was a life more frivolous than any Vanderbilt girl of the day had known, where any social claim could take precedence over education.

Spoiled and cosseted, Grace developed a highly skewed vision of the world. When once she cabled her father that it appeared Worth would not have her dresses ready in time for her sailing, he dispatched a male relative over to Paris to harangue the couturier to drop all else. R. T. would allow no one to keep his angelic daughter waiting. Grace's older sisters impressed her with the values of appearance and style above all else. The cut of a dress, the design of a heavily gemmed stomacher, the carefully shaped vowel and choice of word in conversation, the status of one's dinner partner—these were what mattered most in life. Grace's letters were filled with Lord This and Duke of That. That much of humanity worried about the day's food and shelter never occurred to her. But why should it? The last trait the Wilsons wanted to encourage in so cheerful and delicate a young woman would be awareness of political economy.

She succeeded well in learning her lessons. Despite no formal schooling and only intermittent instruction from governesses, she learned to speak flawless French, workable German. Her eye for art was adept, be the object an English oil or a Chinese porcelain. An avid opera goer, she learned by heart the arias of the great masterworks, and she took voice lessons from the Polish tenor Jean de Reszke until he advised her she lacked the vocal instrument for a career. She knew wine vintages, French sauces, the proper way to curtsy, and how to seat eminent guests without insulting anyone. She knew how to flatter, and more important, whom to flatter.

By her early twenties, Grace was living most of the time in Europe, where she attracted numerous suitors with lofty titles. Cecil Baring, son of Lord Revelstoke proposed, but the engagement was short lived, with the couple breaking up in 1893. Gossips said she left Baring because he had lost so much money in the financial crash of that year; others said Lord Revelstoke demanded too high a dowry of R. T., who was unlikely to go along with the popular craze of buying a title. If anything, R. T. would have expected to receive a bride price for the sacrifice of his favorite child. (Baring later did well for himself by marrying a daughter of the Lorillard tobacco family.)

Grace Forces
Her Hand

In 1895, the Vanderbilts had no reason to exclude Grace from their parties. She was of the most exclusive Newport set and a member of the Four Hundred. Furthermore, R. T. was a partner in some of Cornelius's business deals, so they could hardly ban his daughter even if her behavior was occasionally not to their liking. During Gertrude's debut, Grace was too showy, too happy to take center stage—too much like a young Alva? Now twenty-four (and many hinted her age actually several years above that), she seemed too anxious to catch a wealthy mate. Worse, Alice had heard the rumors about the prince of Wales crowd, hints that Grace had "a past." (This could mean merely that she was imprudent enough to be found having an unchaperoned conversation with a suitor—or it could have meant much more.) Yet another, more personal reason set the couple against her. Grace had had a flirtation with their son Bill the year before he died; indeed, some whispered there had been a secret engagement. It was hard for Alice and Cornelius to escape the conclusion that Grace was now using Neily as a substitute to get at the family fortune.[1] Alice and Cornelius were not simply against Grace; they wanted to protect Neily. Unhappily moved into the position of eldest by the tragedy of Bill's death, this son had neither the temperament nor the desire to take over his new responsibilities. Bill had been handsome, outgoing, and athletic, in other words, all the makings for becoming the next head of the family. Neily was handsome but also introverted, physically frail, and scholarly. Whereas Bill's adolescence turned him to sports and girls, Neily's led to test tubes and a screw-cutting lathe. Atypical of other Vanderbilts, he had no use for culture, be it music, art, or literature, and even less for artists themselves. Sent alone to Europe on a chartered boat loaded with fresh produce to improve his health, he was bored once on land. His two passions were science and sailing.

It is to his parents' credit that they did not insist Neily prepare to head the railroad but rather encouraged his intellectuality. (Perhaps they saw in Alfred, correctly, a better choice for Bill's successor.) They must have wondered what their shy and taciturn son could have in common with that frankly superficial older Wilson woman. They believed it necessary to prevent the flirtation from blooming into marriage, which they foresaw would be disastrous for their unusual son.

The week following Gertrude's debut the Wilsons held a gala of their own. While Neily did not attend, he did send a note of apology, explaining that he had a previous engagement. He made up for this absence by squiring Grace to polo matches, tennis parties, and picnics the remainder of the summer.

Ever alert to the unspoken, Gertrude wrote in her diary of a certain tension developing in the family. The conflict came into the open one Sunday when Neily announced he was not lunching at home, but was joining the Goelets, whose only other guest would be Grace. Alice raised her eyebrows, a major sign of anger on her part. Following another meal, when Cornelius asked his son to join him in the library, Gertrude was "terribly excited" he was going to say he had proposed to Grace.[2] If he hinted at such to his father that evening, he must have learned of his parents' disapproval, for he virtually disappeared from the family. He refused to join them for breakfast, slipped out of the house without acknowledging anyone, and stayed away until late at night.

Somewhat to his parents' relief, in early September Neily was struck down by his chronic rheumatism; so they sent him to Hot Springs for a rest. While he was away, Alice accepted an invitation to tea from Melissa Wilson, during which the women discussed the liaison between their children and agreed that the couple should be separated. Neily was to go abroad for a year while Grace stayed behind. Nevertheless, she and Cornelius were not satisfied that enough had been done to prevent the couple from reuniting. Consequently, afterward they charged railroad attorney Chauncey Depew, who often handled delicate public and private matters on behalf of the Vanderbilts, to request an interview with Grace's father about the matter. Indignant, R. T. refused, stating he would talk only to Cornelius directly, not to his intermediary. Cornelius did go, and he informed R. T. that Neily would find his prospects altered if he married Grace. His threat to cancel Neily's patrimony was an implied insult to the Wilson family that then united them behind Grace and her beau. Now the sides were set, and any possibility of cooperation between the two families vanished.

Neily was soon back from Hot Springs, already well informed through the Wilsons' letters of his parents' displeasure and interference. One morning an envelope written in Grace's hand and marked "IMMEDIATE" was delivered to the Vanderbilts' door. Several days later Neily announced he was leaving for Europe. Worse, the Vanderbilts learned that the Wilsons, in defiance of the separation agreement, had decided to send Grace with the Ogden Goelets to Paris. Alice finally clarified the situation to Gertrude, who had been noting in her diary all the strange behavior yet failed to understand it. The Wilsons were "liars and cheats," Alice exclaimed. "There is *nothing* the girl would not do. She is at least 27, he is 22, and [she] has had unbounded experience."[3] Gertrude was stunned to see how happy Neily became as his departure approached, and she was pained over his obliviousness to the effect of his behavior on their parents, who had hardly slept since hearing of his plans. Fond of her brother, yet worried for her parents, Gertrude set upon herself the impossible task of bringing the disputants together for a reconciliation. She was also left feeling more obligated than ever to deliver to her parents an eminently suitable fiancé.

Upon Neily's arrival in Paris a French newspaper soon reported on his visit with Grace and the Goelets at the Hotel Bristol. Subsequent days' stories commented on the warmth the couple displayed while taking long carriage rides about that city so suited for lovers. Probably to protect Grace's reputation, Neily went on to Constantinople to stay with Michael and Belle Herbert, who kept Grace informed of the "visitor's" activities. There his mail was thick with demands from Alice, Cornelius, and Depew, along with pleas from Gertrude, that he give up Grace. One letter from Alice struck Neily as so horrible and mean spirited that he burned it. The family could not have done a better job of ensuring the opposite of their intentions.

Hurt and depressed that his previously loving parents and sister should suddenly turn on him, Neily remained in the welcoming arms of the Wilsons. By late winter he was in Cannes with all three Wilson sisters. Belle wrote her parents in New York, "And try *not* to exaggerate the consequences of the *animosity* of that [Vanderbilt] family. Of course *nothing* could exceed their vulgarity and the dreadfulness of their conduct, but I for one should not be knocked down by anything else they do."[4]

However much the Wilson sisters wished to support Neily, they also had Grace's reputation to consider. After all, Neily had not yet formally proposed. He told them he was inclined to return home and seek his parents' blessings on the arrangement first. Grace pouted, objecting that she must return to the States first so he would have to follow her, otherwise it would appear she was chasing him. Belle, frantic, urged her father to come to France and get Grace so she would not travel home on the ship unaccompanied. Throughout this period, their European and British friends, including the prince of Wales, voiced their puzzlement over the brouhaha, for they thought Grace a superb addition to any family.

As it happened, Neily did return first. Publicly, it seemed a smoothing over had occurred, for the newspapers announced he had accepted a position in the engineering department of his father's railroad. In fact, Cornelius had not forgiven him but instead banished his rebellious son to Newport. The truth of Neily's return is that he was in ill health and wanted to recuperate before marrying Grace. Writing Gertrude to beg her sympathy, he pointed out that their parents' machinations had included persuading the family doctor to write Grace that he was unfit for marriage. Gertrude begged him not to announce an engagement, arguing that were Grace the right girl she would be willing to wait, as Alice had requested.

Gertrude Flirts and
Despairs to Find a Mate

Fortunately, soon after Neily's return, Gertrude provided the circumstance to deflect attention from his waywardness: she had become engaged. This took some of the pressure off him.

The year 1895 had intensified Gertrude's need to find a mate. On her birthday that year she wrote, probably with some intended irony, "Alas, I am out of my teens today! Alas, I am no more very young. Alas, when a girl is twenty she is on the road to being an old maid."[5] The men were quick to notice otherwise, for she was a beguiling young woman, still innocent and playful. They flocked to her at-home hours and kept servants busy arranging their flowers in vases and delivering their messages. Their attention made Alice alert and watchful for signs of inappropriate interest. They were delightful young men, free of worry, blessed with a freedom few ever know. They were the sons who would not have to work, and they could not anticipate how that lack of usefulness could poison later years. They were heirs to fortune, as James Appleton of the Waltham watch works; educated at Yale, as Moses Taylor, her dead brother's roommate; sharp on a horse, as Regi Ronalds. Some days three different men had an engagement with her—for a walk through a museum, a ride through the countryside, a round of golf, a ball, or an opera.

Gertrude met these callers with ambivalence. She received all in a friendly manner, encouraged their affections, yet secretly resisted. For a while she pined for the attentions of Moses Taylor, then suddenly concluded that the thought of making love to him (which to her meant kissing and hugging) would be "abominable." She flirted with Bobby Sands, then flitted off to James Appleton, seeking a way to spurn the former without guilt. The men who most interested her were those who shared her devotion to the arts: Howard Cushing, Rawlins Cottenet, James Barnes. She would be "desperately gone" on a man, then without a sign to him just as precipitately lose interest. She was like a hummingbird flitting about from one attractive flower to another within its narrow territory, never staying too long with one blossom, yet eventually returning to it for another taste of its nectar.

It would be wrong to think that these men's ardor was merely for Gertrude's money, that her own coolness and inconsistency were simply manipulation on her part. During that period men were to be the romantics in courtship, women to be detached and pursued. Many observers deplored this state of affairs, but Charles Dana Gibson captured it best in his drawing in which Cupid is depicted placing a stethoscope to a bored society maiden's bosom, an anxious and hopeful suitor looking on, devastated by Cupid's diagnosis that nothing could be heard. This heartlessness was a useful form of protection for women like Gertrude, who in one fit of frustration observed of heiresses like herself, "The fortune hunter chases her footsteps with protestations of neverending devotion and the true lover (if perchance one exists) shuns her society and dares not say the words that tremble on his lips. And so she sits on her throne, her money bags."[6]

Even if the man were rich, she feared the chances were ten to one that he would chose her to make his own fortune greater. When she was at dinner with Harry Whitney one night in 1894, he frankly affirmed her fears, and she wanted desperately to ask him if he thought any man could ever love her for herself. "Of course that is impossible," she concluded in her diary, but she came away from the conversation thinking him "a great friend" who has "much underneath."[7] But he went off to finish his courses at Yale, and when he came to spend one night at the Vanderbilts' that October, Gertrude was devastated when he showed no interest in spending some time alone with her but went off instead with Moses Taylor. Blaming herself, she wrote, "You are only nice looking, you are not one bit entertaining or amusing, you are stupid, you are conceited, you are tiresome, you are weak, you are characterless, you are cold and reserved . . . your waist is big, your hands and arms badly formed, your features out of proportion, your face red, your legs long."[8] She made up for Harry's nonchalance by adding to her string of admirers.

Soon after Harry's remark, she set a warning for herself. "Keep yourself under control completely. Never for a moment let your feelings get the best of you. You will be sorry and unhappy as well if you do. Don't let yourself imagine things, above all don't exaggerate. People do little things out of politeness or kindness, not out of any deeper feeling. You are Miss Vanderbilt."[9] In following this philosophy, she effectively prevented men who desired her for herself from getting close. Although she developed hard crushes on these handsome swains, she kept her passions to herself and her journal.

Her hesitancy to display any interest in a man was reinforced by her parents, ever hovering nearby, reminding her of her duties. Soon after her twentieth birthday, she concluded her father "hates me" or "does not like me" for reasons she could not understand.[10] She suspected it had to do with his seeing her as a child, one who could do nothing right, when in fact she was now a woman. Her mother would open her mail at breakfast and skim through it before allowing Gertrude to look. Consequently, just when Gertrude could use the counsel of compassionate, wise adults, her parents were unable to provide it. Unaware how harsh she sounded, Alice would make blunt pronouncements about the suitability of this or that suitor or, worse, would leave Gertrude second-guessing her opinions. Gertrude took to the only rebellion available to her, sneaking out with a caller, though she was always sure to have her personal maid go along as a chaperone.

During the spring and summer of 1895 leading to her coming out, Gertrude also closed off her intimate feelings from Esther Hunt. She realized she did not love her as she once had, and she wrote in her journals numerous expressions of guilt over this change of heart. Yet she treated her friend in as fickle a manner as she did her male suitors, hinting at future bliss, then casually changing her mind. (That July the death of Richard Morris Hunt, worn out from overwork in mansion building, revived the bond for a while, for Gertrude was compassionate in response to Esther's mourning.)

The problem was, what to do with the sexual passions now? Here was a highly sensual woman, age twenty, who had never been kissed by a man, spending hours daily in the company of young men, often in physical activities with them or walking beside them with coat sleeve almost but not quite touching. She still spent quiet hours cuddled in Esther's arms, though less frequently. The only person she could make frequent close physical contact with was her adored sister Gladys. "When she is tired and puts two tender arms around my neck and her head on my breast, it makes me feel that here is the pleasure of my life, here is someone who needs and loves to have me."[11]

What Gertrude needed more was the tender arms of an adult male lover, but her erotic needs had to be recast. In a remarkable expression of this desire, she wrote of standing at a wall, her head against the cold wallpaper, her heart burning inside her. "Perhaps the wall had some life in it. She would run her hand down the edge of the curtain perhaps and little tiny thrills would run down her back or up her legs till she realized that it was only the wall."[12] As this erotic passage hints, like the majority of young women of her class, Gertrude was totally ignorant of sexual function. It was said that probably nine out of ten women of her class went to their honeymoon completely unaware of what was to pass on the nuptial bed.

Weddings of cousins and friends only heightened her longing for a mate. In June she was bridesmaid for Adele Sloan, who married James Burden, heir to the iron fortune. Then cousin Alice Shepard eloped with an "unsuitable," a medical student. Alice's audacity stunned Gertrude, and also strengthened her resolve to be a respectful daughter and not shock the family. When her brother fell for Grace, some of her initial hope that he become engaged was likely vicarious. November brought Consuelo's wedding, and although Gertrude did not attend, she must have worried over the prospects of possibly being forced into an uncongenial match. Then days later childhood playmate Pauline Whitney, who lived across the street in New York, married an English title, Almeric Hugh Paget, baron Queensborough. (The Whitney-Paget wedding drew as large a crowd as Consuelo's.)

At the time of her coming out, Gertrude fantasized marrying Lispenard Stewart, an older suitor. She fantasized traveling with him or of sitting on a small sofa with him and how he would say something nice and she would stroke his arm. She wished for a small house, not a big establishment, a cozy place with a library that would be a private room for her and her husband *alone*. No such room existed in the houses she had grown up in. Either rooms were public or separately private, husband and wife with their own bedroom and library. But Stewart, who was not a serious suitor, was soon off with another woman, and Gertrude was back to teasing Moses Taylor.

Poor Moses finally confessed his love, only to face the ignominy of Gertrude's refusal. By early 1896, she was infatuated with James Barnes, though over many months' time she had been "alone" with him a total of only three hours and twenty-three minutes. (Her keeping of accounts of such matters hints at her captivation.) During the week she pined expectantly for his company, which most predictably would be a walk after church, and less predictably sight of him at a dinner or a dance. She wrote of watching him at church, of waiting until others had left and he was the only one in his pew. "I feel so deeply and solemnly that it was more than an ordinary pleasure for me to go through the holy service with him."[13]

Gertrude Falls for
the Boy Next Door

In February, Gertrude took a sudden shift in attitude. "Harry and I are having a desperate flirtation."[14] The Harry was Harry Payne Whitney, who was now attending Columbia Law School. Harry was the son of William Collins Whitney and Cleveland heiress Flora Payne. Both parents were ambitious, intelligent, energetic, and determined. By the time Harry was born in 1872, William C.

Whitney had brilliantly combined his acumen as a corporation lawyer with politics and business investments, becoming one of the most powerful men in the city, exerting his influence in Washington, D.C., as well. Flora's entertainments moved her up as a hostess close to the ranks of Alva and Mrs. Astor. In fact, sensing that the indomitable Alva would crash the gates of society, Flora befriended her so that she could follow close behind, and she urged her husband's sponsorship of the new Metropolitan Opera, where they ended up with box 63, one of the best. But her closest friend was Alice Vanderbilt, who lived across the street on Fifth Avenue.

Their first child having been stillborn, Flora and William C. doted on Harry, "Never came a Baby into the world, more wanted, with more love ready to welcome him than our Boy."[15] Even the birth of other children did not diffuse their ardor, and Flora in particular spoiled him. Harry did not fail her. His easy intelligence took him to second in his class at Groton, and when against his father's will he stated a preference for Yale over Harvard, she backed him up. There he was elected to Phi Beta Kappa and became the editor of the *Yale Daily News,* an accomplished player on various athletic teams, and a member of the elite Skull and Bones. His boyish good looks, hearty laugh, and easy camaraderie added to his popularity. His father, equally proud of him, went abroad to buy polo ponies for his son, an accomplished equestrian. Harry was to all who met him the golden boy who seemed easily able to achieve, even surpass, his father's achievements.

Were he to ape his father, Harry had a daunting model. By 1893 Whitney was such an exemplar of success that Henry Adams singled him out in an astute profile. Explaining why men of greater fortune envied Whitney, Adams explained: "[He] had finished with politics after having gratified every ambition, and swung the country almost at his will; he had thrown away the usual objects of political ambition like the ashes of smoked cigarettes; had turned to other amusements, satiated every taste, gorged every appetite, won every object that New York afforded, and, not yet satisfied, had carried his field of activity abroad, until New York no longer knew what most to envy, his houses or his horses."[16]

But Flora was never to see her favorite child graduate from Yale. In late January of 1893 she suffered a heart attack and died several days later, leaving Harry without the unconditional and ever-present love he had grown dependent upon. At this point, little noted aspects of the father's personality, melancholy and self-absorption, began to express themselves more in the son. He attended law school with little of the fervor toward learning that he had displayed in the past. With his mother dead, Harry seemed to have no reason to succeed in life and turned instead to find a replacement for her. As he came to know Gertrude better, her poise, intelligence, and energy must have reminded him of his mother, and he became determined to have her. Perhaps, too, her elusiveness and apparent indifference to him, a man used to women fawning over him, added to her allure.

Despite admitting the flirtation in her diary, Gertrude was still seeing Jim

Barnes but confided in Harry about the relationship, the way young women often do to platonic buddies. Smitten at last, Harry set out a careful strategy to win her over. He began by sending messages to her on heavily engraved Tiffany paper. These notes, carried across the street by a servant, documented his current invalidisms, various pains, headaches, and fevers likely brought on by the stresses of school and his self-preoccupation. Soon he was leaving his puppy in her company while he went uptown to classes. Cleverly, he accepted her definition that they were just good family friends and confidantes, while dropping hints that she might not really be in love with Jim. In one particularly long letter, he discussed how "The unit of the Creator's Mind is a man & a woman—not only physically but morally, mentally, intellectually, & in every other way. Our *whole* nature yearns for its complement, its other half in every respect."[17] If he did not yet suggest that he was the other half of her nature, he planted a successful suggestion.

Harry's insouciant manner worked. Gertrude began to doubt the value of Jim Barnes, instead determined to "*Make* him [Harry] by being indifferent and oh, various other little tricks that I have learnt in my career."[18] By March 5, she had crossed Jim off her list by scrawling a pithy "The End" to her accounts of their minutes together.

The next day Gertrude boarded a private Vanderbilt train to Palm Beach. Accompanying her were her parents, four girlfriends, her sister Gladys, and six single men. One of the men was Harry. (Neily did not go along, his absence provoking melodramatic comments in the press concerning "his shattered memories" of Grace.[19]) Alice and Cornelius had arranged the trip, probably with the blessings of William C. Whitney, to facilitate the romance.

While the *New York Journal* anticipated "announcements of early Summer weddings with June roses" coming out of the venture, Harry and Gertrude did not cooperate at first in creating that outcome. Both played the same game of being cool and distant until Gertrude, unable to stand Harry's avoidance any longer, wrote him a note asking what was the matter. Once situated at the Hotel Royal Poinciana, the swaying palms, ocean murmurs, sultry breezes, and romantic moon took over. Harry suddenly turned to Gertrude one evening and requested in the veiled language of the time, "Gertrude, shall we not have an understanding?" She was so overtaken she could not speak; she simply let him take her hand, a sign of acceptance on her part. The next day Gertrude, now twenty-one, received her first kiss from a man.

Oblivious to how obvious their quickly heated feelings appeared to others, Gertrude and Harry really believed the engagement would be a surprise to their parents, and they held off saying anything until a week after the trip. Alice's quick praise for her future son-in-law relieved Gertrude: she had saved the day for her parents, who were still smarting from Neily's rebelliousness. Although Cornelius assented to Harry's request for Gertrude's hand, no formal announcement was made, so Harry was forced to behave circumspectly, as though he were simply a suitor. For some reason Gertrude backed away again, and Harry grew frustrated over her coolness. The situation was eventually taken out of her control, and she would soon be impelled to revive the intimacy.

Neily Disdains His Parents' Orders, to Tragic Result

The entire household must have shuddered upon news in May of 1896 that Grace Wilson had returned to New York. Belle advised her sister to "wait a week or two to see if there is any attempt to retreat their [the Vanderbilts'] bitterly insulting conduct" and, if unsuccessful, to go on with Neily, dismissing the outside world.[20] When the paramours failed to appear together in public, rumors spread Neily had given in to his parents' threats of disinheritance.

In fact, the very opposite had occurred. During Neily's absence, the Wilsons and their three daughters had been in constant contact with him to sustain the romance. Consequently, after waiting to see if Cornelius and Alice had relented, and finding that not to be the case, in early June the familiar Vanderbilt maroon victoria was seen carrying Neily and Grace, chaperoned by the highly respectable Mrs. R. T. Wilson. On June 10, 1896, the New York papers prominently displayed sketches of the couple with an announcement their wedding would take place in two or three weeks. One article claimed Alice and Cornelius were canceling a European trip because of the wedding, that they were giving the couple a yacht. The story was a reporter's invention, for by then Cornelius was not even talking to his son. Although both were living in the same house, each rode separately to their offices at the New York Central, and when present in the same room they did not acknowledge one another. When Neily wrote Gertrude of his decision to wed Grace on June 18, her response was so vituperous that he begged her not to write in that tone again. To his future sister-in-law May Goelet, he expressed his joy, "I am sure you are quite as pleased as we are happy that all is settled and arranged, for all our difficulties are forgotten now."[21]

On June 11 the newspapers carried two new stories, juxtaposed to present readers a interesting tale. One pronounced "Miss Vanderbilt Engaged" and stressed the "cordial approval" of all members of the Vanderbilt and Whitney families. The editors approved as well, noting that Harry's fortune meant his courtship of Gertrude must be prompted by sincere liking and affection. The other story headlined "Against His Wish" and quoted Cornelius as being opposed to the marriage "on what grounds I do not wish to discuss." The article then defended the Wilsons through the rhetorical question "Who do these *nouveaux riches* Vanderbilts think they are?"[22] (That the Wilsons were even more *nouveaux riches* was left out.) Alice and Cornelius were especially humiliated by the public airing of private matters, for it smacked too much of the great feud over the Commodore's will.

Grace, on the other hand, was having the time of her life. She adored being in the public eye, no matter what was said, and at this point the saying was in her favor. Reporters followed her doings here and there, followed her preparations for the wedding, described her luncheons with her girlfriends. Her father cooperated further by telling the press he didn't care what Vanderbilt felt, that it would not matter to him if Neily came into the marriage penniless. Further stories came from servants at both houses, who earned extra money for nine days from the bribes of reporters. All of New York was enjoying this excellent scandal, which easily competed with the Republican convention going on in St. Louis.

A Vanderbilt-Wilson feud could not be limited to the family; society must choose sides. Two-thirds of those one hundred and fifty select who received invitations to the wedding suddenly found themselves on trains and boats, departing the city rather than risk being cut off by the Vanderbilts. The rectors of leading churches were also mysteriously unavailable to officiate. Thus while the public supported the Wilsons, society stood behind the Vanderbilts.

On June 16, Alice arrived from Newport, where she had gone with Gertrude ostensibly to plan her wedding, which was to occur after the appropriate six-month interval in November, but also to evade the press. Neily returned from a cheerful gathering at the New York Yacht Club to face a confrontation with both parents. Whatever pressures were brought upon him that evening succeeded, for the next day he did not go outside, and rumors spread that he was ill. R. T. Wilson sent his personal physician to see the young man. Later that afternoon Wilson canceled tens of thousands of roses, lillies of the valley, and orchids and informed the caterer and orchestra that the nuptials were off. The next day newspapers announced that Neily had been struck down with another rheumatic attack, hence he was too ill to go through with the ceremony. The only problem with this story is that the servants did not corroborate it. Furthermore, on June 17 diners at the Metropolitan Club observed the high spirits of Alice and Cornelius, who gave no indication of concern for their son's health. Yet in the past when Neily had been similarly afflicted, they had always expressed distress, as would be expected after having lost two children already.[23]

This time the Wilsons fled to Newport to evade the press.

If Alice and Cornelius mimicked Alva by attempting to dominate their wayward son, the result was far more tragic. While of gentle, sweet temperament most of the time, Neily also had a stubborn streak and once set on a path could be unbending. He seldom showed anger, but when he did it would be ferocious. Within several weeks Neily reconsidered his promise and informed his parents he was going to marry Grace after all. On that fateful July night, just what passed is speculation. Enough stories circulated that Neily struck his father to give credence to them. But simply a loud shout of defiance on Neily's part could have provoked the final result: Cornelius collapsed into a paralytic stroke. Although the doctors said Cornelius might die, Neily went ahead with wedding plans and moved to a small apartment. His behavior sickened Gertrude, who had always held special affection for this brother above her others. Now she did not care if she never saw him again. Alice shared those feelings.

The wedding, a private affair, finally took place in early August at the Wilson's brownstone at 511 Fifth Avenue. "Courtship So Bitterly Opposed by the Young Man's Father Thus Ends with His Loyalty and Scorn or Disinheritance."[24] Cables of congratulation were noted as including the prince of Wales, the earl and countess of Pembroke, and the duke and duchess of Marlborough. Thus Consuelo, who more than any cousin could understand Neily's motives, was the one Vanderbilt to stand publicly behind him. It seemed for the couple as happy a day as the admiring news readers wished. For weeks strangers had been following the pair's tribulations and responded with sacks of letters urging them on, the vote being in favor of romantic love over parental control. Neily and Grace first went to honeymoon in Saratoga, where people followed them on the streets or came up to offer congratulations. Grace wrote home that Neily was "the most darling creature that ever lived."[25]

Gertrude and Harry Wed
Quietly, for Their Set

The marriage of Grace and Neily did not end the scandal. Now the newspapers wanted to know if the new Mr. and Mrs. Cornelius Vanderbilt, Jr., would be in attendance at Harry and Gertrude's ceremony, which had been moved up from November to late August for fear Cornelius would not otherwise survive to see his daughter marry.

There must have been times that tumultuous summer when Gertrude and Harry doubted if the wedding would actually take place. Most of the time they were separated by Harry's interspersing of studies with trips to Long Island, where he would ride, play golf, sail, and play polo, his favorite activity. A friend pointedly told him, "Why I thought you were engaged to sport," a remark Gertrude heard of but did not incorporate into her understanding of her fiancé.[26] He also went camping in the Whitney 70,000-acre compound in the Adirondacks. While Harry wrote Gertrude daily and lovingly, he was not happy and often described various symptoms bothering him. He was frustrated that their few meetings were almost always public. While she could not demonstrate her affection for Harry easily, she felt it nonetheless. From Newport, Gertrude wrote long letters to friends extolling the wonders of love. "Esther, you must get engaged, you don't know what it is to be absolutely happy until you are."[27]

While Harry fretted and pledged his love, one letter hinted at possible future problems. Written right after Neily's marriage, he quoted from a book by Frank Norris, "'Matrimony is a deplorable institution. As a cause of misery I should rank it second only to drink.' And then he agrees with you that love & so happiness can only last a year; or two at most. As to women—'Women are only adjuncts of existence, the world belongs to the men.' (Beautiful, is it not?)"[28] He meant this jokingly, but it would prove significant that he share this particular passage from among his extensive readings. Having little reason to think otherwise, they assumed their marriage would be superior to most, that such was a natural consequence of their special station in life.

On August 25, Harry's frustrations were put to rest. There on a warm, cloudless day in Newport, sixty guests gathered in the grand salon of the Breakers to attend the wedding. Neily and Grace were conspicuously absent. He had continued to communicate with the family through his brother Alfred, who informed him Neily was welcome at the ceremony, but not Grace. *Town Topics* reported there was "no return of the prodigal son, no scene of weeping reconciliation."[29]

After the guests took their places, a servant wheeled in Cornelius, tanned from daily seatings outdoors. He appeared more alert and vigorous than they expected, but was in fact not well. When Gertrude appeared resplendent in white figured satin, he had only sufficient energy to give her away by reaching up and placing her hand in Harry's. At the end of the service, the orchestra played the "Star-Spangled Banner" because the music leader thought it necessary to mark symbolically the rarity of an American girl of fortune marrying one of her countrymen. ("There will be no foreign nobleman in this—no purchased titles," the *New York Journal* approved. "The millions all belong in America and they will all remain here.") Then Cornelius was wheeled to his room away from the wedding party to eat in the company of his mother and his doctor.

Upstairs three detectives guarded the wedding gifts. As was the practice, the predominant gift was jewelry for Gertrude, for it was assumed the couple would have or could easily buy any household items they might desire. The booty included a five-strand set of matched pearls from Harry's grandfather, a set of diamond pins from his father, a diamond and tiara necklace from her father, and a diamond cluster from her uncle Willie. Downstairs, the guests gathered in the dining room for breakfast. The menu, which appeared elegant in its original French version was actually quite simple, including melons, eggs, salmon, beef supreme, lima beans, cauliflower, tomatoes, celery, peaches shaped as wedding bells, fruit, and bonbons. The cake was served in satin-covered boxes decorated with the Whitney monogram.

By mid-afternoon, Gertrude and Harry had changed and stepped into the Vanderbilt carriage for the trip to the railroad station. Their destination was the Berkshires, where William Whitney had recently purchased an 8,000-acre preserve on October Mountain in the Adirondacks, near the town of Lenox. There a two-room cottage was being prepared for the couple. But since it would not be ready for several days, Harry had arranged for a four-room tent furnished in mahogany, the "parlor" decorated in the colors of Delft blue and white. The cottage had coal stoves, oriental rugs, a brass double bed, and exotic floral fabrics.

It was the first time in Gertrude's life she would be alone with a man for a sustained period, for Harry had made sure even servants would not be needed. She wrote Esther, now living in London, "It is impossible to be blue when you *know* that someone really cares and that you really care. I seem to walk on air."[30] Certainly her honeymoon was more congenial than that of Consuelo's. A passionate woman, Gertrude may have found the sexual aspects a delightful surprise, enhancing the state of bliss to be wed to the man she loved, who apparently loved her for herself in return.

In late September they left for Vancouver, the first leg of a trip to Japan, taking "only" twenty-four trunks. While in transit, Harry unexpectedly received a telegram from his father announcing a private marriage to Edith Sybil May Randolph, a witty and beautiful widow. Having been pampered by his mother, Harry wrote a peevish letter home, expressing his dismay that someone else would be in the house "that is so much mamma's."[31] There was more unsaid behind his pique, as he knew his father had become infatuated with Mrs. Randolph during a family trip to Europe in 1890 and that Flora Whitney had been outspoken for months afterward in her anger over the flirtation. (It was not Whitney's first dalliance, so she clearly felt a special threat from this mistress.) Worse, soon after Flora's death Whitney was out again with his old paramour, but Harry had never imagined a matrimony would result.

Harry was not the only one taking umbrage over the sudden marriage. Flora's marriage to Whitney had been the result of maneuvering by her brother Oliver Payne, a partner of John D. Rockefeller, and it was Payne money that set Whitney up in style before he made his own fortunes in city transit. (Some say he ransacked the city of Detroit in setting up the rail system there.) Payne called on his four Whitney nieces and nephews and informed them he would disinherit them if they did not disown their father. Since the Payne fortune was much larger than Whitney's, the offer was tempting. Two children, Payne and Pauline, accepted. Harry, the eldest, and youngest, Dorothy, remained faithful to their father. Needless to say, the opposing siblings no longer spoke to each other.

The Columnists' Rumors Hint at
New Vanderbilt Scandal

B y fall of 1896 Neily and Grace were also extending their honeymoon in Europe. Neily brought from his grandfather's trust an income of $6,000 a year, then twenty times the average working man's wages. Grace's income was $25,000 annually, an amount she was accustomed to spending on clothes alone. Consequently, their combined income forced "severe economies" on them. Her sisters, having no such restraints, must have annoyed Grace in describing their dispute whether to give her a necklace worth $175,000 or $125,000. Cost was not the issue—it was the design and practicality of the setting.

That fall, Maria Kissam Vanderbilt also died, and Cornelius ordered a telegram sent to his son. Grateful to receive this small sign of recognition, both Neily and Grace put on mourning clothes. (Not a Vanderbilt received any of her fortune, which went entirely to her Kissam relatives.) Still in touch with the family through Alfred, Neily reserved a stateroom to return for the services, but the Vanderbilt family doctor reported back that Cornelius did not want him around. Neily remained in Europe and repeatedly cabled his parents to seek their forgiveness. They refused.

In December, Grace's parents sent the couple a mysterious cable speaking of certain "slanderous reports" appearing in the New York press. A later letter explained how rumors reported in the papers intimated that Grace had delivered a baby in Switzerland, certainly the most scandalous news that could be made of the pair at this point. Cholly Knickerbocker had run the story his usual way, that of spreading the tale by denying it, while scattering sufficient clues to point to the identity of those being gossiped about. Although he heartily condemned the "scandalmongers" and "libellous tongues," he had taken a story out of the private clubs and fashionable restaurants and made it daily gossip for the man and woman on the street, who quickly deduced the principals.

When Joseph Choate, the Wilson lawyer, said nothing could be done to force a retraction from the newspaper, the Wilsons appealed to the Vanderbilt physician to approve Neily and Grace's return. Surely, they argued, the couple's mere presence in the States could not harm Cornelius, whom they would not visit. The doctor rejected the proposal and further advised Cornelius to settle in a warm climate for the winter for the sake of his own fragile health.

Neily and Grace were dumbfounded by the rumors. It was not as if they were in an obscure and distant country—anyone in Paris could see she was not pregnant when she arrived, nor was she now. If they returned to New York and any further ill came to Cornelius, they would be blamed. By staying away, the gossips would continue to chatter, and *that* also could precipitate a crisis in Cornelius's health. The stress became so great that Neily fainted one evening during a visit to the opera.

Eventually the Vanderbilt doctor retracted his earlier order and urged the couple to return home so the "business" would be settled. In late January 1897, Grace and Neily disembarked in New York before the eyes of many curious reporters, who were quick to observe her figure was more slender than ever. Her thoughtless cooperation with the press ensured further continuation of the breach between her husband and his family.

Neily commuted from New York to Yale to complete a master's degree in mechanical engineering. His studies completed, he approached the employment office of the New York Central and applied for a job as though he were any young man off the street. He was placed in the motive power and rolling stock department at a modest salary, an assignment that was to inspire the most creative and productive period of his life. His work, which required inspection trips to watch equipment in action, was precisely suited to his tinkerer's mind. He designed a variety of new equipment, the most famous of which, a firebox, provided great cost savings and was soon in place in railroads all over the country. Hailed a "genius" in locomotive engineering, Neily heard no word of praise from his Vanderbilt relatives in the New York Central offices.

Despite Neily and Grace's more subdued life-style, the press used any opportunity at hand to refer to the scandal. When Gertrude gave birth to a daughter, Flora (named after Harry's mother), on July 29, 1897, the newspapers incorrectly reported a reconciliation between Alice and Neily. On April 30, 1898, Grace brought forth a ten-pound son, the fifth Cornelius in the line, known in the family as Neil. Papers asked of this baby, "Will he heal the breach between the families? If they are reconciled he will be worth many times his weight in gold."[32]

Neily hoped this arrival might at last sweeten the bitterness, but his family held firm. Cornelius and Alice, then in Switzerland, instead went to Paris, where George Vanderbilt, the owner of another Hunt mansion, Biltmore, was to marry Edith Stuyvesant Dresser. The guests at that eminent nuptial whispered how deeply the feud was dividing society. In Paris were Sloanes and Whitneys, Shepards and Twombleys. Stateside were Wilsons and Goelets, Astors and Belmonts. The Vanderbilts were said to refer to their first grandson as "that Wilson baby," and as a youth in Newport, Neil heard himself spoken of only as a Wilson by shopkeepers and passersby on the streets.

The Vanderbilts' rejection of their son is as understandable as is his defiance of their demands. Following Gertrude's wedding, Cornelius's health had turned so poor that the newspapers rumored his impending death and later expressed relief over his eventual improvement. In January of 1897, he and Alice had rented a home in Washington, D.C., and when hot weather fatigued him greatly, then moved to Europe for his further recuperation. Despite the best medical care, Cornelius remained paralyzed on the right side, unable to participate in even a few of his beloved charities. Watching her previously vigorous husband dictate letters to twelve-year-old Gladys, then laboriously pen his signature in shaky hand, was torturous to Alice. His mind heavily influenced by the Wilsons, Neily seemed oblivious to the daily consequences of his and Grace's thoughtless behavior on his father.

Gladys proved great solace. Her shy and quiet temperament was a blessing in strained circumstances. Simple, direct, secure, she was devoted to both her parents, whose demands she found natural and reasonable. During her formative years she had watched her parents suffer through the death of Bill, the destruction of the Breakers, the symbolic slap in the face from Alva, and the real slap from Neily. She seemed to develop a compassionate and protective stance toward them, which may have loosened Alice's monumental reserve. Gladys would have found Gertrude's youthful criticisms of their mother incomprehensible.

Unfortunately for Alice, her other children were not so well behaved as sweet Gladys or Alfred, who had competently stepped in as head male. Gertrude had been unhappy to be pregnant so soon after the marriage and extracted a promise that Alice would take care of the baby. Wisely, Alice did not comply, although she did leave Cornelius in Europe to spend several weeks with her daughter around the time of the delivery. Gertrude was not so much uncaring as perhaps relieved to have an ocean separating her from her parents, who could still be intrusive; she reached out to the Whitneys more for family support. And youngest son Regi, now at Yale, where he had arrived with a servant who was promptly sent home, was giving signs of being a reincarnation of the Commodore's hapless son Corneel. Already he had a reputation as a gambler, and unlike his older brothers he showed no interest in gaining honors either in the classroom or on the playing field. In an average family he would have found a trade to keep him content; as a Vanderbilt, he had choices fitting him. Despite deeming him a failure, his parents continued to coddle him with servants and unlimited money to indulge his impulses. Why they did not attempt to rein in his waywardness is a puzzle.

In 1899, the Vanderbilts and Whitneys particularly celebrated when Gertrude gave birth to her second child, Cornelius, known better as Sonny. With his health suddenly improved, the elder Cornelius returned with Alice to the States, where they appeared at parties in Newport for the first time in three years. Alice concluded her numerous prayers had at last been answered, for she could wave good-bye to her husband who now felt well enough for short visits in New York for meetings of various charitable boards, which included the Sloane Maternity Hospital, the New York Home for Incurables, the Hospital for the Relief of the Ruptured and Crippled, and the General Theological Seminary.

On September 11, Alice decided to accompany Cornelius for such a journey, bringing Gladys along. He had a full schedule and arrived so late in the evening at their Fifth Avenue home that he went right to bed. Alice retired soon afterward in her adjoining bedroom. At dawn, she awoke to hear Cornelius calling out her name in an urgent, choking voice. Rushing to his side, he looked at her, said, "I'm dying," and fell into unconsciousness in her arms. He lingered for several more hours before succumbing to a cerebral hemorrhage.

At the funeral in St. Bartholemew's, Bishop Potter praised Cornelius for being "more than his money" and for recognizing his wealth "as a sacred trust for the benefit of his fellow man."[33] This summary was true to a point. Cornelius had been "preeminently a religious man" but not so tied to the idea of sacred trust that he followed the model of Andrew Carnegie, who believed it his duty to dispose of the wealth God had given him for the betterment of society. Cornelius Vanderbilt's estate of more than $72 million left less than two percent to charity.

The family would not know this for some time—Alfred Vanderbilt was in the Orient, a long journey away in those days of steamers and railroads. When the moment came for the reading of the will, the family gathering, which by law had to include Neily, took place in the library of the Breakers. "I give and devise to my beloved wife Alice G. Vanderbilt, for and during the term of her natural life, my dwelling house on Fifth Avenue and Fifty-seventh Street . . ." intoned the lawyer.[34] She also received the Breakers. No one was surprised at this grant, nor of those to various servants, friends, and charities. But Neily reddened upon hearing that Alfred, his younger brother, would get the vast Oakland Farm in South Portsmouth, Rhode Island.

The most important bequest concerned the distribution of the bulk of the estate among trust funds for the children and Alice. The appointed head of the family could be expected to get half, and that, too, was placed upon Alfred. Worse for Neily, where Gertrude, Regi, and Gladys ended up with more than $6 million each, Neily was granted $1 million in trust, the principal never to be disturbed, and an additional half million outright.

Yet the greatest shock to the wayward eldest son came in the final sentence, "I have to this my last Will and Testament set my hand and seal in the city of New York this 18th day of June in 1896.[35] This was the day after Neily had agreed to withdraw from marrying Grace, the day after pleadings and lawyers that ended with Alice and Cornelius dining in celebratory spirits at the Metropolitan Club. This vindictive act was performed after breaking the youth's spirit!

The matter did not end there, however. Upon hearing of the will, the public once again made Neily a hero, sending him letters of support for choosing his heart over his family's wishes. As one letter writer stated, Neily's name would be "handed down for generations as the noble, manly Vanderbilt who sacrificed millions for love."[36] (Grace would keep these letters from the public all her life.) Probably fearing another will feud, Alfred offered Neily $6 million more to bring him into parity with his siblings. While the conservative *New York Times* said this additional grant was an act of generosity, accepted in good spirit by Neily, the less euphemistic *World* reported that Neily had expected more, at least $10 million.

Somehow Alfred and his lawyers prevailed, and Neily did not contest. Seven-and-a-half million dollars tax free was enough to provide his desired style of living, the mansions for Grace, and yachts for himself. For once the family had squelched the public's desire for another Vanderbilt scandal.

P A 2 R T

The Bible of the bluebloods is the
Social Register, a stud book of
mediocrities. There are not a dozen
women in it of the caliber of Mrs. O.
H. P. Belmont and Mrs. Harry Payne
Whitney, the most distinguished
sculptress of her time.

—ELSA MAXWELL

1900-1908

The Progressives
Tempt Alva

The Gay Nineties were over, but for most Americans the gaiety had been sporadic at best. In 1893, the year Alva unveiled Marble House, five hundred banks collapsed, railroads went broke (though not the Vanderbilts'), and stocks fell like meteors to a fizzle. In 1894, while Gertrude and Consuelo took in the London season, unemployed men marched on Washington in protest of economic policies, and the strikers in Pullman, Illinois, one day faced a rain of bullets from federal troops. In 1895, while Consuelo and Pauline Whitney planned their respective marriages to British nobility, wages fell to their lowest point in years, driving desperate men in 1897 to the Yukon in an often hapless search for gold. In 1897 as well the Bradley-Martins in New York held an extravagant dress ball, which instead of gaining praise drew such calumny from the press for its decadent waste of money that the couple fled to England, where they settled permanently.

Prosperity returned in 1898 to a nation more sober yet optimistic. During this troubled decade, immigrants from similarly depressed countries in central and southern Europe had streamed off ships and crowded in American cities in search of new opportunity. Their exotic languages, unfamiliar customs, different religions, and slightly darker complexions stirred apprehensions among many white Protestants. Herbert Spencer's social Darwinism—his claim the Anglo-Saxon represented the "survival of the fittest"—enjoyed a great vogue for both its rationalization of class differences and warnings it stirred that the inferior races of Europe, Asia, and Africa would outpopulate and outvote the ruling WASPS. (Little did they know these peasants and shtetlers found American culture coarse and rude, inferior to that of their home countries.)

Nonetheless, some white Protestants waged an attack on monopoly, materialism, and greed. Some of these Progressives, as they called themselves, took their

Christian gospel to mean they should ameliorate the ills of the city; others of less religious devotion invoked science as the new savior to design more efficient and healthful ways of living. A new breed of fiction, social realism, roused readers with its exposés of corporate evil, while social scientists such as Thorstein Veblen chastised the lower class for its parasitic conspicuous consumption. (Some whispered that Alice Vanderbilt inspired his attack on wealthy women.[1]) It was this progressive spirit that brought hope during a time of bewildering threats within the social order.

For the Vanderbilts, however, these shifts and challenges passed unnoticed, further expression of their self-delusion that they were immune from the currents of history. Their diaries and later recollections overlooked such well-published circumstances as the children losing fingers in factory machinery, the young men—boys really—dying of yellow fever for the sake of imperialism, the mine disasters taking hundreds of lives in a second, the dark and dank tenement lives of immigrants a short trolley ride from the palaces of Fifth Avenue. Presidents came and went, with no notice. The economy swelled and ebbed, with no concern.

The first to be roused from this delusionary outlook was Alva. She had finally married Harry Belmont on January 11, 1896, in a most modest ceremony for a woman of her class. Arranging the service had proved difficult, for the clergyman at Trinity Church in Newport, their preferred location for the rite, refused to officiate on grounds the Episcopal church allowed no marriage between divorced persons. They settled instead for a civil ceremony administered by the mayor of New York at Alva's town house. Although they had wanted the event to go unnoticed, hence invited only a handful of discreet guests, the mayor happened to leave the marriage certificate behind him in the cab. Calling up the livery stables to retrieve it, he warned them not to leak any information. Nevertheless, word naturally got out to reporters used to crossing the palm of cabbies for information.

There was no honeymoon, perhaps because none was needed. The couple returned immediately to Newport, where Alva closed up Marble House and moved into sixty-room Belcourt, patterned after a Louis XIII hunting lodge at Versailles. (Though she did send her servants to do the laundry at Marble House, which she felt had better facilities.) Few buildings so reflect the obsession of the owner, in this case with horses. The first floor entrance was designed so carriages could ride right in, deposit guests in a hall where they climbed a grand stairway to the second floor, while the driver continued to a large inner hallway to park the rig. The other long wing of the building held stalls built with fine imported woods and furnished with gold-embroidered and monogrammed linen sheets for his thoroughbreds. Harry even had two of his favorite horses stuffed and put them on exhibition upstairs.

This strange arrangement did not bother Alva. She was a strong horsewoman, who kept sidesaddles for both left and right sides so she could alternate the distortion that technique forces on women's bodies. Furthermore, she took the living quarters that were only recently finished and tore apart one section and redesigned the other to accommodate herself and her wardrobe. (Unfortunately, with Hunt dead, she had to work with his sons, to much less effect.) Alva left untouched the superb intimate oval dining room with indirect lighting, designed by Thomas Edison, and the imposing Gothic ballroom with its fairy tale medieval splendor.[2]

While he may not exactly have tamed the shrew, Harry Belmont had a more felicitous effect on Alva than anyone imagined could be possible. One suspects part of this compatibility was sexual, for both had been known for their erotic appeal. Surely the major reason for her change was Harry's admiration of Alva's spirit. As a wedding gift he gave her a life-sized statue of Jeanne d'Arc, a copy of one in the Cathedral at Rheims.[3] Where written history has left us little knowledge of Harry Belmont, his sensitive choice of this present says more than pages. Where others mocked or avoided, he honored Alva's visions and courage, her willingness to challenge convention for a higher cause.

In addition, Harry and Alva also shared a playful, thumb-nosing attitude toward pretense. Although her parties continued to be showpieces, they sometimes included amusing novelties. Illustrative here is one breakfast she gave in Newport at which the honored the guest was Consul, a champagne-loving chimpanzee dressed in frock coat and waistcoat. He was said to have deported himself well throughout the meal, using the appropriate utensils, but when offered a cigar, he took one taste and threw it away. He did accept and smoke a cigarette, however.[4] Even the staid *New York Times* could not resist giving prominent space to a tongue-in-cheek report of this tongue-in-cheek event.

Another humorous occasion was a more historic one. Belmont took the lead in introducing "bubbles," or automobiles, to Newport society and held the first automobile parade there, during which "everybody stared and many jeered."[5] The general feeling at the time was that these noisy and ugly monstrosities would remain only novelties. Alva and Harry designed an obstacle course with novel and somewhat sadistic obstacles, such as a woman dressed as a nurse pushing a "baby," a doll in a perambulator, or a liveried servant behind a wooden horse. The scoring was similar to horse-vaulting contests, with points taken off for any obstacle hit.

Alva also accepted Harry's butler, Azar, a tall Egyptian with a penchant for condescension, gold-laden uniforms, and women servants. With his overseeing the liveried footmen, and equipped with the best chef in the city, Alva became noted for her splendid luncheons for the half of Newport that still aligned itself with her. It was, she summed up, "an ideal life, thoroughly refined but full of gaiety and fun but a total lack of anything bordering on fast behavior."[6] She settled down to days of pleasant leisure with her good friends, such as Mamie Fish, who was known for her outspoken ways and manners.

Mamie, more formally Mrs. Stuyvesant Fish, had sponsored the notorious Dogs Dinner a few years earlier during the height of a depression, garnering nationwide criticism for the Gilded Age celebrants who had sent their pets to dine off porcelain place settings. Censure never bothered her. If she decided not to appear at a luncheon she had planned, she ordered her butler to tell the guests to go home. She was the first to include actors and celebrities at her table, where her *bon mots* were famous. "Here you are again," she opined at her opening party one season, "older faces and younger clothes." One evening when Mrs. John Drexel, a widow with a male secretary who was her constant companion, slipped away, Mamie punned that the searchers try "under the secretary." And when Alva once confronted Mamie for telling people she looked like a frog, the reply was, "Not a frog! A toad, my pet, a toad." (For once in her life Alva was apparently speechless.) These two friends gave Newport stuffed shirts constant cause for tittle-tattle.

Alva's building spree did not end with Belcourt. Desiring a new home in New York completely dissociated from her earlier memories of Willie K., she bought a town house between 54th and 55th streets. As with all her efforts, this was photographed and written up for architectural journals. She also wanted another home in Hempstead, Long Island, and had the Hunt brothers design Brookholt, a straightforward, massive Georgian revival.

While Alva remained "kneedeep in mortar," as people commonly noted, Harry decided probably at her urging to take a stab at politics. During the 1890s he had been rumored for mayor of New York. In 1900, *Munsey's* predicted he was a serious contender for vice president on the Democratic party ticket. Instead he ran for Congress in the thirteenth district of New York. His platform was an attack on McKinley's "imperialism and the policy of protectionism to the trusts which he has well-nigh perfected."[7] Thanks to a recent favorable turn in the economy, McKinley was reelected. But Belmont won his seat as well, and he spent one anonymous term in office. He probably found the life of a politician in Washington much less interesting than his horses, club activities, and Alva, who refused to submit to the life of a politician's wife in D.C. His official congressional biography lists not one accomplishment, not even a committee membership. He was not renominated. (The person who should have run was Alva, but she could not vote, let alone hold office.)

When the Republicans had set up McKinley for reelection, they stifled Theodore Roosevelt, outspoken in his demands for regulation of business, by burying him in the vice presidency. Thus, in 1901 the assassin's bullet removing McKinley brought into power the very voice the party had hoped to squelch. Even more surprising to party leaders, the public lauded their new president's progressive views. Press and pulpit clamored loudly for even more changes in a system that allowed one percent of American families to own almost ninety percent of the wealth. In too many households, women and children were working ten to fourteen hour days at wages much lower than men. Too many people lived in dank, dark, crowded, vermin-infested catacombs.

More politically conscious than the other Vanderbilts, Alva was quick to join the progressive social justice activities developing in New York City. This was a time when throughout the country middle-class and some upper-class urban women became more vocal and visible in their humanitarian work. The causes were many, including the elimination of prostitution (where Kit Hepburn, mother of a future actress, was a leader), alcohol prohibition, child welfare, workplace safety, child labor reform, shorter workdays, adequate and hygienic housing, and better education for the poor. Alva began as many well-to-do women are inclined, by giving large donations to charities and serving on boards. But temperamentally needing to be in charge, she soon found that rather passive philanthropy uninteresting. She began to visit settlement houses and charity hospitals, roll up her sleeves, and participate in workaday activities. History beckoned, and she responded, as would Gertrude and Consuelo.

Consuelo Comes into Her Own

When, as happened for the Vanderbilt women, all one's physical needs, all ones impulses can be met many times over, then connections with others become heightened in meaning. When one is used to having one's way, not getting it from intimates poses a major problem. One cannot, after all, simply fire them or buy them off (although, as we have seen, this was tried among the Vanderbilts in several cases). Add to this a training that forbids direct and honest expression of feeling and one has a good recipe for marital discord. Unexpressed anger festers or transforms into passive aggression and manipulation. This defect in intimacy surfaced first and most visibly for Consuelo and Sunny but would appear as well among the other couples.

Despite its practical inconveniences, Blenheim brought heady pleasures to Consuelo during her early years there. Before the age of twenty she was to host a shooting stay of the prince of Wales, who had quickly taken to her quick mind and impeccable manners, and may even had considered adding her to his love list. While she was too tender hearted for hunts, she took easily to other ceremonies of aristocratic life, such as the daily carriage ride during the London season and the weekday round of balls, dinners, and fetes. She must also have shared with Sunny some of the satisfaction of refurbishing Blenheim, both the interior repairs and a tasteful redesign of part of the gardens.

When the Boer War struck in 1899, both Sunny and Winston went to South Africa to fight for the cause. When word came of Winston's capture and imprisonment, Consuelo consoled Jennie. Later released, he caught up with Sunny, and one day the two mounted their horses to single-handedly liberate the camp. Prisoners washing their clothes that morning saw the two gallop into the compound, tear down the Boer flag, and hoist a homemade Union Jack. Consuelo also joined Jennie in a well-publicized project to outfit an American hospital ship to help the beleaguered British troops. Such moves by American heiresses in England intensified feelings of kinship from the mother country toward its former colony. The pragmatism and organizational skills in such Yankee-inspired endeavors began to win over the public, if not always the English women of their class.

Having delivered in quick succession John and Ivor, the requisite "heir and spare," and determined to have no other children. Consuelo moved more freely on her own away from Sunny. She visited her father, who had settled with his new wife in Paris, and stayed in London, where she oversaw the building of a home he had given her, Sunderlund House. In Paris she also befriended painters and bohemians, although she was careful to keep her activities less public so they would not reflect badly on the Marlborough family. In 1902, Consuelo even spent a summer in Newport, where she snubbed the various members of the Vanderbilt family whose carriage happened to pass hers or executed the chilling "cut direct" if they happened to be in the same room at the casino. Her frequent absences from Blenheim were evidence that all was not well in the marriage.

A personal misfortune struck Consuelo that exacerbated her poor relationship with Sunny. During a trip to Russia she contracted a severe ear infection that caused considerable permanent deafness. The best specialists in Europe and the United States did not help. Their attempts at a cure, all horrible to describe—one involving wires snaked up the eustacian tubes without benefit of anesthesia—brought no repair. She took lip-reading lessons with Princess Alexandra, who was also deaf, to little avail. Consuelo preferred to cover her disability, a guise that is seldom successful. Pretending to hear can disrupt the most congenial relationship, and there is no reason to think it did not do so in Consuelo's case. Worse, it forced her further into a certain narcissism, reinforcing belief in the rightness of her way of thinking and doing things, because the voice she heard most often was that of her own mind.

Despite the rancor in the bedroom and over the dinner table, Consuelo's life was not so desperate as she later suggested. If American heiresses marrying peers found one consolation, it was their ability to participate alongside their husbands in politics and community affairs. Unlike in the States, where wealthy women were to keep out of nondomestic life, even to the extent of being criticized for doing too much charitable work, in England the aristocratic woman found that politics *was* life. Thus Jennie Churchill early compensated for the more stultifying social restrictions by campaigning for husband Randolph, making speeches and sharing confidences with political men who valued her opinion. Once widowed, she turned her energies to Winston, and she signed Consuelo up to help in his first campaign for Parliament.

Consuelo's support for Winston was unflagging and conspicuous. Queen Victoria died in January 1901, just before the opening of Parliament at which he took his oath. Where the other women in the gallery appeared in drab and somber mourning dress, Consuelo swept into her seat aglitter with jewelry, including the dog collar of diamonds and pearls Sunny had given her, ropes of trademark Vanderbilt pearls, and a tiara with diamond tips. When the day came for Winston's maiden speech, she once again brought attention to herself through similar conspicuous dress.

Winston held no grudge against the woman who had produced the heir that separated him from Blenheim. Indeed, he found her "one of the most gracious and charming of women" and, more important, realized in her an inquisitive mind, a ready comrade for sharing talk about books and government affairs. Surely he met few women in his lifetime as well read as Consuelo. She in turn was in awe of his energy and remarkable memory, which combined to make him a captivating, if "tremendously self-centered" friend.[8] (Actor Laurence Olivier was once startled during a performance of "Richard the III" to realize that Churchill, sitting up front in the audience, was silently mouthing all the words by heart.) It was Winston who encouraged her to make her first public speech, before a club of blind men in Birmingham.[9] He even helped her write and edit the talk, which she gave despite numbing stage fright. The men's quick and loud applause converted her to a new role. From that day Consuelo accepted the challenge of public appearances for good causes, although she acknowledged that opening bazaars, a typical duchess's duty, could be "successfully done by a moron."[10]

Consuelo slipped easily into the Duchess role in other ways. Where photographs of her before marriage show the shy and self-effacing girl, those afterward depict a woman of elegance, confidence, and poise. She had quickly transformed from a pretty young woman to a stunning, delicate beauty. "I would stand all day in the street to see Consuelo Marlborough get into her carriage," admitted playwright. James Barrie.[11] She also became vain, and she happily spent uncomfortable hours before various artists to have her portrait immortalized. While she later attributed this output of images to Sunny's demands, she sat for more than the "official" paintings. One suspects she enjoyed the company of the artists as much as the finished creation. For a family portrait, John Singer Sargent placed Consuelo in the center on a step above Sunny so that she towered over him and overpowered the scene.

Her celebrity blossomed in 1902, when the coronation of Edward VII took place. His loyalty to his old American friends continued unabated, and their influence was so strong that an enterprising publisher began to distribute *Bancroft's Guide to Americans in London*. By June of that year the Savoy, Berkeley, Carlton, and Claridge hotels were bursting with Stateside society, including Consuelo's brother W. K. Vanderbilt, Jr., and cousin Alfred Vanderbilt. Alva and Harry Belmont were the only Americans present at a dinner given by Lord and Lady Rothschild in honor of the new king and queen. Alva had much to be proud about: Consuelo had been selected as one of the four duchesses to carry Alexandra's canopy, where her stately and glamorous figure stood out even among the other tall beauties so honored. Always the pragmatist, she ordered a candy bar placed in the pocket of her fur-trimmed red velvet robe and wore a specially designed coronet to fit within her tiara so it would slip easily upon her head at the crucial moment in the five-hour service.

However much Consuelo later complained about life at Blenheim, it did offer what Consuelo was used to having in the way of service. Unlike her mother, she turned her sons over to the nanny system and did not, as Jennie Churchill had done with hers, take a commanding and very American role in raising them. The maternal drive was not as strong in Consuelo as it had been in Alva, which is not to imply she was indifferent. She adored her children, but did not need to spend a lot of time with them. She also disagreed with Sunny over their discipline. Convinced her mother's harsh ways had in the long run been best, she wished to exert the same discipline on her boys, but Sunny, recalling his father's similar punishments as needless cruelty, refused her that expression.

While Consuelo could not convince Sunny to fully modernize Blenheim and increase its basic comforts, she did have her father's limitless generosity to compensate her. By 1904, Sunderland House in London was complete. Although publicly explained to be Willie K.'s gift to commemorate Sunny's homecoming from the Boer War, it was in fact Consuelo's private domain. Located on Curzon Street, its five stories incorporated all that wealthy Americans expected in a home, including four elevators, individual bathrooms with the latest fixtures, such as towel-drying racks; kitchens that allowed cooking by steam, gas, electricity, and coal; capacious closets; and its own water towers atop. Of her fifty rooms, the most splendid was the combined ballroom and picture gallery, ninety feet long, twenty-three feet wide, and thirty feet high, which she decorated in the French style. As Alva's daughter, she had an eye for interior design (though not one as original as her mother's) and used many of her trips to Paris to buy the most expensive and finest antiques, paintings, Oriental rugs, and bibelots on the market. However democratic Consuelo thought herself to be, she never gave a thought to living more simply so that the money could be spent to alleviate the needs of the poor and uneducated. While she criticized the English aristocrat's hauteur, her own was even greater in its demands for excessive comfort.

Nor was Consuelo lonely in Blenheim for long. To make life more pleasant she informally adopted an adolescent American belle. Gladys (pronounced Glaydis) Deacon was a child with a troubled and notorious past. Her father had shot and killed her mother's French lover in Paris when the child was eleven. After spending a year in prison, he was pardoned by the president of France and managed eventually to gain custody of Gladys. Mrs. Deacon later kidnapped Gladys from her convent school and took her to Paris again for schooling.

Gladys's rosy complexion and wideset bright blue eyes made up for her irregular features, notably an ill-formed nose. Though ill-educated, she had a gift for language and a superb retention of all she heard or read. Consequently, even as an adolescent she was complimented in French society for her conversational ability, and nicknamed "the marvel." She so attracted art conneisseur Bernard Berenson that soon after his marriage he informed his wife Mary he wished he had wed Gladys instead. Mary was not threatened—she thought Gladys to be sexless, like a hermaphrodite that never matured. Others who befriended Gladys included painter Edgar Degas, playwright Hugo von Hofmannsthal, and poet Rainer Maria Rilke. American expatriate writer Natalie Barney, center of a lesbian social circle, also invited Gladys to her affairs; whether Gladys had intimate relations with women is unclear.

Somehow in 1901 Gladys received an invitation to Blenheim. This opportunity had long been a dream of hers, for she happened to be living in Newport in 1895 when Sunny visited there, and on glimpsing him had written in her diary, "O dear me if I was only a little older I might 'catch' him yet! But Helas! I am too young. And I will have to give up all chance to ever get Marlborough."[12] Gladys charmed both Sunny and Consuelo, who asked that the girl refer to her as "Coon." Gladys spent six months with the couple in 1901, and for similar visits over the next few years. Throughout this period, many visitors to Blenheim fell for Gladys, including Ivor Guest, Lord Francis Hope (owner of the world's largest diamond), Crown Prince Wilhelm of Germany, and the Duke of Norfolk, who pressed unsuccessfully to marry her. Gladys had eyes only for Sunny, who at one point thanked her "for kindness which I believe few men have received at women's hands."[13]

Consuelo called Gladys her little sister, and wrote frankly of her longing and tenderness for her company. The two young women travelled frequently together to Germany and Paris, where Gladys introduced Consuelo to her bohemian friends. Consuelo once confessed to her younger friend that she would have liked to be either a Vestal Virgin or Cleopatra, that she hated her life with its middle course. With Gladys she could lead a secret life in Paris.

Also at Blenheim were the tenants, whose affection for Consuelo became legendary. Part of her appeal was her Yankee practicality. Discovering leftovers at Blenheim were just tossed without care into biscuit tins for distribution to the needy, so that one could get potatoes mixed with fruit, or fish in pudding, she demanded the courses be thoughtfully arranged. In summer she hired roundabouts and provided the tenant children a fair. In addition to the seasonal ceremonies, such as distributing toys at Christmas, she made frequent visits to homes to see what unique need she could fill. The only flaw tenants and villagers found in her was her gullibility, her readiness to believe any story of woe, so that at times clever ones received undeserved bounty.

Consuelo and Sunny
Cause the King Grief

In 1905, an anonymous reporter sketched a profile of Consuelo for American readers.[14] Amidst all the infighting and competition among American women in London, she observed, all agreed that Consuelo was liked by all. Though not as brilliant, talented, or accomplished as some other American hostesses there, she charmed people with her continued ingenue attitude. "The Duchess is not a strongly marked character. Gentleness, submissiveness, an aversion from asserting herself—all those qualities which women seem agreed to call 'sweet'—are rather her characteristics." After praising Consuelo's accomplishments in improving Blenheim, her achieving the impossible by making it look livable, as well as her gracious meeting of her public duties as a duchess, the writer concluded tellingly by remarking on her look of "subdued sadness" and "pretty wistfulness."

That sadness disclosed her real feelings over her lot in life, for late in that year Consuelo decided to leave Sunny. The story she told her family, and later published in her autobiography, was otherwise. At the time, Alice Vanderbilt happened to be in Paris, where she talked to Consuelo, who said Sunny had been impossible for two years. As she was packing to leave for Paris, he reputedly told her not to bother to return to Blenheim. But as London society was well aware, Consuelo was much less innocent than she let on to the family or publicly.

The origin of the eventual breakup of the marriage is not clear. Winston Churchill, who was among those closest to both Sunny and Consuelo, wrote, "To those who knew both him [Sunny] and his wife and their exceptional gifts of personal charm and kindliness the breach that occurred seemed unaccountable. But no one can penetrate the mysterious springs of human nature."[15] While Consuelo blamed Sunny's boorishness, friends in their set found both partners at fault. They picked on each other and argued in public, making nearby diners uncomfortable; they criticized one another behind their backs. In doing so, they violated a major norm of the day: Don't make a fuss about marital troubles in public.

In time, rumors of infidelity accompanied mention of the couple. Later in life, Consuelo remained mute on the subject and implied that Sunny was the sole guilty party. But tongues were wagging about her own extramarital interests before his own philandering was noted. One name associated with her was that of Lord Castlereagh, eldest son of Teresa Londonderry, the preeminent political hostess of the day.[16] Indeed, one story went that Sunny did indeed eject Consuelo from his life, albeit in the form of a telegram sent to her in Paris, where she had gone with Lord Castlereagh. While that aristocrat may not have been the man in her life, Consuelo was clearly devoted to someone else. Whether she left Sunny or he asked her to leave was beside the point.

That Consuelo strayed is hardly surprising. Her prim American upbringing was tested by the sexual practices of the prince of Wales set. One could not entertain that jolly, portly royal, as she did, and not know about both his brief liaisons and his long-term relationship with the Honorable Mrs. George Keppel. It was whispered that the prince had hoped to include Consuelo on his list of liaisons, although he was probably unsuccessful there. Closest female friend Jennie Churchill was also a realist when it came to matters of the heart and the constraints of marriage. It is hard to believe the captivating and sophisticated Jennie would have no sway over her susceptible niece-in-law. In 1900, when Jennie stunned society by marrying the dashing George Cornwallis-West, a man her son Winston's age, Sunny gave her away, and the entire Churchill family attended in a phalanx of support. To demonstrate his own approval of the match, the prince sent her a gold pig to add to her collection of porcine statues. The attitude of the rest of English society, however, was best summed up in the remark of eighty-year old Lady Nevill, who remarked to one friend whom she came across in Hyde Park, "Well, if you want to know, my dear, I am searching in the perambulators for *my* future husband."[17]

That Consuelo and eventually Sunny were unfaithful was hardly a scandal, for one of the unwritten rules of their class was that a spouse should be obliging. If a lord knew the prince of Wales was carrying on with his wife, he graciously accompanied her to whatever country home the prince happened to be visiting and stayed out of her separate bedroom. If his wife had a child whose carrot-red hair resembled his best friend's and not his, no one would make notice of the curious resemblance. The Edwardians cherished their amorous rituals of after-noon tea (where the presence of nosy servants permitted no more than necking); lovers traded heated erotic correspondence and exchanged sentimental keepsakes. Helpful hostesses at country-house parties arranged bedrooms to permit easy noc-turnal visits to one's paramour, a subterfuge aided by the requirement that one must be gruff and rude at breakfast to the person one had just spent the night with. What was unacceptable about Consuelo and Sunny's behavior then was that they took umbrage at one another's dalliances, that they made a fuss about it. For a couple who claimed to dislike one another, this was curious behavior.

Since his coronation, Edward VII continued to be loyal to his fast crowd of friends—so long as they followed the unwritten rules. Royalty was expected to uphold the sanctity of Christian marriage, which meant refusing to associate with separated or divorced couples. Divorce was essentially the charge of a crimi-nal act against the guilty party. A man could divorce his wife on grounds of adultery; a wife her husband only if his adultery involved incest, bigamy, sodomy, or bestiality. Royalty held that during a troubled time it was all the more im-portant to uphold the sanctity of the family as a haven of security. Though privately compassionate toward his two friends, when the king heard of a possible break between the couple, he was quick to exert pressure to keep them together. If they separated, he announced, they would no longer be welcome in his pres-ence. Willie K. and the duke's relatives also brought pressure to bear, with no success.

The person to suffer most from court exclusion would be Sunny. He had watched his father incur a similar fate and was himself very attached to the court society. Despite this unwanted consequence, he signed the separation. In the agreement he split custody of the children with Consuelo, although he would have been expected to seek full custody. This meant the boys, now away at schools, would appear for vacations during the half of the year each held custody. Sunny did not lose financially, for the original prenuptial agreement assured he would continue to receive income from Willie K. Vanderbilt regardless of the condition of the marriage.

Following the official separation, family and royalty continued to press for reconciliation. Edward VII waited almost three years before asking Winston Churchill to notify the duke and duchess that they "should not come to any dinner, or evening party, or private entertainment at which either of their Majesties are expected to be present."[18] This ostracism hurt Sunny much more than Consuelo, who readily found a different set to replace her old court relations. (In 1911, when George V took the throne, Winston successfully appealed on behalf of Sunny to have him included at a convocation of the Knights of the Garter. This exception was made because the king decided that the event was not a regular court occasion.)

By separating, Consuelo and Sunny had accepted legal limbo. Neither could now remarry, and the consequences for them vis à vis society were no less severe than if they had divorced. Consuelo had seen her mother successfully challenge divorce attitudes in the States. But divorce was a much more serious breach in England, and Consuelo was not the radical her mother had been. The only practical gain for Sunny would be some protection of any political career he might wish to pursue.

Both Sunny and Consuelo would make overtures for reconciliation during the next few years, but none took hold. Their stubbornness, oversensitivity to slights, and hot tempers blinded them in the end. The fact is they would have been a smashing pair, for Blenheim and Britain, and likely for each other, had they been able to see they could be superior *together*.

Grace Becomes the "Mrs. Vanderbilt"

The younger Vanderbilt marriages were not faring much better. Since her husband's death, Alice had followed the lead of Queen Victoria and entered into a state of permanent widowhood and mourning. Except for the brief period when daughter Gladys was introduced to society, she avoided hosting or attending significant social events. She wore only black, her famous yards of perfectly matched pearls her sole jewelry. Her homes became mausoleums, nothing touched, changed, or replaced since Cornelius's death.

Gladys was her steadfast comfort. Although society was loosening up, Alice insisted on chaperoning her daughter everywhere. Remarkably, Gladys showed no sign of resentment but instead reciprocated with a fierce loyalty to her mother. Closest of the children to her mother in temperament, she was so restrained as to never wear make-up her entire life. Able to reduce problems to black-and-white, Gladys felt strongly her duty to her mother. And when the time came to let go, when Gladys married Hungarian aristocrat and chamberlain to the Austrian emperor, Count Laszlo Szechenyi in 1908, Alice released her willingly, although it meant seldom seeing her favorite daughter, who would now live overseas. She resigned herself to her two cavernous mansions with the companionship only of her Bible and her large, faithful staff.

Although Gladys was a consolation, there were worries with the other children. Regi, still in his twenties, had chosen the path of dissipation, which even a 1903 marriage to Catholic socialite Cathleen Neilson did not slow down, nor did the arrival soon afterward of daughter Cathleen. Reputed to have dropped several thousand in debts with gambling czar Richard Canfield, a *Town Topics* wit summed up Alice's reaction: "Lo, the poor Reggie, ousted from his fold/For speculating with superfluous gold."[19] In 1904, subpoenaed to appear in a case against the gambler, he eluded detectives and fled to Europe.

Son and now head of the family, Alfred incurred no such notoriety, but this anonymity probably reflected his skill at eluding reporters rather than flawless behavior. (In 1911 his wife would sue him for divorce for having an affair with a Cuban attaché's wife. He would give up $10 million to his ex-wife, but his lover would commit suicide.)

Neily remained the proverbial thorn in Alice's side, primarily because Grace so quickly and brazenly showed off to society. It was not unusual for her to appear drenched in so many jewels that observers wondered how she could walk upright. In many ways Grace's maneuvers were a repetition of Alva's, only with less substance because she took so seriously the notion of being queen of society. (Alva would never weigh herself down with excess gems when a few extraordinary ones would do.) Nothing else got in the way of that coronation, certainly not children Neil and Grace junior, nor husband Neily.

Alice Roosevelt, one of Grace's closest friends, in later years told an adult Neil that he and his sister had been terribly repressed as children. They were forbidden any strong self-expression, no loud laughing or crying; they were to be quick to bow or curtsy, silent unless addressed; they were to speak with a British accent. (A devoted son, Neil took this remark as a compliment, noting, "There are worse systems of education than the cultivation of perfect manners."[20]) Grace let the children see her briefly at nine in the morning, for she stayed in bed until noon, and once again at five o'clock tea. For the most part they were left to the care of a British nanny and French nursemaid.

Although Grace was a neglectful mother in many ways, and became even abusive in later years with her intrusiveness and invasion of their privacy, the children nonetheless treasured these fleeting visits. For one, she seemed to them a fairy in her elegant Worth and Paquin gowns that required special closets where they could be laid flat. Her quick smile, dainty wrists, and halo of silver curls augmented the vision. (Early in the marriage, anxiety over Neily's near-fatal bout with typhoid turned her hair white, and finding the effect stunning, she never dyed it.) Furthermore, even the most careless parent has times when she is sweet or entrancing or loving. Particularly in Newport, Grace could drop all pretense and organize a family crabbing hunt or picnic. She read psalms, sang southern lullabies, and played piano while their father sang. She could be wise. On a ride past a cemetery, she reminded Neil that all the graves were filled with people who had once thought a lot of themselves, that he should have good times in life without hurting other people.

Yet these treasured episodes of family unity were not that frequent. For the most part Grace confused running the household with ruling it. The major victim was husband Neily, who soon discovered that he was utterly incompatible with his lovely wife. Where he was happiest tinkering in his sound-proofed home laboratory, she demanded constant social activity. He took to making the minimal appearance before guests in his own home, then sneaked off to work on a new railroad invention. The children often heard voices raised, doors slammed. Increasingly, their father was simply not at home.

Grace's imperious ways were not atypical. When Henry James returned to the States during this time, he reflected on the unhappy relation of women and men. Nothing so assaults the foreigner, he averred, than the superiority of the women tied unfortunately to the narrow-minded, commercialized, and specialized businessman. The men supplied the canvas, the women the embroidery. He concluded, "The right kind of man for the American woman may really be the man who intervenes in her life only by occult, by barely divinable, by practically disavowed courses."[21] Love became for such men an abnegation of self, a stultifying dependence, which conflicted with the very image of masculinity. (James's biographer Leon Edel adroitly dubbed this the "vampire theme.") Consequently, if the men really did not have to work, they fled the home to club and sport with other men or to their mistresses' apartments.

Neily often escaped to his yacht, another *North Star,* which against his wishes Grace decorated like a French chateau rather than with the nautical simplicity and practicality he preferred. Although she suffered severe seasickness, Grace encouraged his European cruises for the opportunity they offered to mix with European royalty. The children, required by their father to dress in sailor suits, found these voyages no more enjoyable than Consuelo had found hers on the *Alva.* A king, an emperor, or a czar was usually just another funny-looking man to them before whom they must behave particularly well.

While the children were bored by the many munificent "M's in the drawing room," Morgans, Mitchells, Mellons, and such, they adored President Theodore Roosevelt, the only adult who seemed to take them seriously.[22] Despite Grace's threats of punishment, they would bombard him with questions and sit hyperalert to every gesture and response. When he once invited them alone to the White House for lunch, Neily assumed the children had wheedled the invitation and called the president to cancel. He discovered to his chagrin that Roosevelt had initiated the idea on his own. Following the meal, the president took young Neil to the Lincoln study and spoke so inspiringly of the martyred hero that the boy read scores of books on him over the years. (While Roosevelt enjoyed Grace's children, he did not approve of his daughter Alice spending so much time at her well-publicized and ostentatious parties, fearing rightly such actions were not the campaign symbol he wished bandied about in the papers. It helped less when a paper falsely described Alice, garbed in a flimsy chemise, dancing before a group of men on the roof of Grace's house.)

Grace and Neily purposely isolated the youngsters from "commoners" so that they would not learn the facts of Vanderbilt family history, in particular their own parents' scandal. Until he was twelve, Neil believed every family owned a home in Newport and an oceangoing yacht. He was taught to learn the subtle status differences among guests, to recognize that the leading banker deserved fawning attention, whereas the lady with only a side box at the opera deserved mere cordiality.

Neil also discovered that despite its wealth the family was not really free to do as it wished. "No tragedy of the world was permitted to enter our conversation or change our routine until we found out what Messrs. Blank, Blank, and Blank thought of it."[23] The Blanks were the lawyers and accountants who interpreted every move in terms of its consequences for the trust funds and investments. Fortunately, his parents always hired exceptional professionals, who were able to multiply the money faster than even profligate Grace and Neily could spend it. Like other family members, they could also be strangely spendthrift. For example, Neil earned only a quarter a week allowance and was teased by the boys at St. Paul's, who forced him to charge things for them in the family name.

Despite her gaudy extravagance, Grace cleverly took reign of society and was even referred to as its queen. The formative event, which took place in 1902, further illustrates society's oddly un-American determination to align itself with oldtime aristocracy. In February of that year Prince Henry, brother of the German kaiser, came to New York. Honored at a gala opera performance, the prince departed early, but not before stopping by Grace's box to pass a word. The *New York Times* commented, "The recognition was so marked and the signaling out of this young matron so obvious that it took many by surprise."[24] Everyone knew that the still indomitable Mrs. Astor had aspired to entertain His Royal Highness, even to the point of postponing a trip abroad. But Grace had used good manners to outwit the grande dame. Aware the prince was coming, she had written the German ambassador asking for advice. Namely, years earlier the imperial family had been very kind to her during a visit to Potsdam, and she wanted to show her appreciation. Upon hearing of this, Emperor Wilhelm cabled Grace, requesting her to ask his brother to dinner so he could experience "a representative American family." The further result, as gossipy *Town Topics* observed, was "Mrs. CV has become *the* Mrs. Vanderbilt. She is recognized as head of the family by the Kaiser."[25] While Alfred's wife returned to Palm Beach in a huff and Alice fretted over the insult in her mansion, Grace had her dinner, invited Mrs. Astor, and placed her down the table in nobodyland.

To seal her dominance, Grace was determined to prevail at the next Newport season. She did this by throwing what was later referred to as the Fete of the Roses at their Newport mansion, Beaulieu. Her timing was impeccable, the last event of the summer, so it would be the most remembered. The next day the papers gave four times as much space to this festivity as to President Roosevelt's political tour. Only two hundred guests received invitations to this fantasy. First they entered a carnival with booths staffed by fellow socialites. Visiting for the summer, Consuelo dressed up as a gypsy and told fortunes. (Aligning with Grace was of course a slap at her other Vanderbilt relatives.) The highlight was a theater tent, where at midnight the Broadway cast of *The Wild Rose* put on an abbreviated version of that hit show.

As a result of her prominence, Grace became an unofficial head of U.S. protocol for eminent visitors and royalty from abroad. She would entertain in New York or in foreign ports every British monarch from Victoria to George VI, Albert of Belgium, the king and queen of Spain, the king of Siam, Emperor Wilhelm of Germany, the czar and czarina of Russia. She would also live to see a number of these friends find their lives end in tragedy as monarchies fell to democracy or revolution.

It could well have been a party of Grace's that impelled Henry James to pen some of his most stinging criticism of the era. He concluded that however much such hostesses aped European society, they could not match it. Although their homes resembled palaces, their jewels fit for royalty, no substantive social order existed. At eleven, all one could do was go to bed. The men were mere suppliers of the means for the celebration, and during it, were too boring to add to its gaiety. As James wittily summed up, in America the tiara produced the occasion, unlike Europe, where the occasion produced the tiara.[26]

However much Neily might have agreed with James's judgment, he remained loyal to Grace. He had no choice, for to turn against her would be to admit that his rebellion against his family, with its terrible consequences for his father's health, had been in error. Through dogged notes and visits he had won his way back into his mother's affections. Now he wanted her to accept his wife.

At some point in the early 1900s, Alice acceded to allow Neily to bring her grandchildren to visit without Grace. Their young imaginations found the Breakers terrifying with its huge, echoing rooms, towering throne chairs, and scary suits of armor. Tiny Alice dressed in witchlike black greeted them stiffly, asked perfunctory questions about school, but seemed to pay little attention. When the ritual was concluded, she saw they were served French vanilla ice cream with chocolate sauce, the highlight of the experience.

It was Gladys who forced a complete reconciliation. Upon her engagement, she wrote to Grace to ask her to Newport for the public announcement. Unhappy with the family discord, she wanted her wedding to be free of the usual reminders of scandal in the press. Grace complied, but in an indirect way. Neily dropped by the Breakers one day to discuss the upcoming marriage, and Alice mused the family should gather together for lunch. "Why not Beaulieu," Neily quickly offered. The real meaning was clear. Possibly primed by Gladys, Alice quietly responded, "Very well. If Grace will not come to me—then I shall go to her."[27] Following eleven years of snubs, the two women finally met. From that day Gladys, Alice, and Grace behaved as though no breach had ever occurred. Gertrude, however, refused to forgive.

Gertrude Attempts Domesticity

Perhaps it is more correct to say Gertrude could not have cared less about the long festering family dispute. Following her marriage to Harry Whitney, she broke away from her blood kin and reorganized her life around her growing family and other Whitney relations. Although she and Harry accepted as a gift the Whitney family house he had grown up in at 871 Fifth Avenue, she did not spend much time visiting her mother across the street.

Neither she nor Harry had wanted the house. Harry wrote his father from their honeymoon in Japan that they preferred to start with a smaller place, a theme reminiscent of Gertrude's fantasy marriage to Lispenard Stewart several years earlier. They finally assented to the gift on the proviso that they take it over completely and his father make no contributions to its upkeep. The capitulation was probably Harry's, for although he told his father he did not deserve the house, "eminently the home of a prominent citizen, which I am *not* at present," it was his childhood home, and anything less would have seemed a demotion in status.[28]

So almost immediately Gertrude found herself giving up part of her dream. The Fifth Avenue house was "the very same atmosphere in which I had been brought up . . . so I had moved some fifty feet in feeling, environment and period. No more than that."[29] When they settled in, it was fully furnished with antiques and artworks, William and Flora Whitney's acquisitions over the years. The elder Whitney's taste being little better than that of Alice and Cornelius, Gertrude determined to redo the interior to make it her home, not Harry's mother's home.

She also had other properties to oversee. As a honeymoon present, Harry purchased the John Knower house on Bellevue Avenue in Newport, a three-acre waterfront property well-placed between Beechwood, the charming stuccoed home of Mrs. William Astor, and Rosecliff, Stanford White's Grand Trianon adaptation for the Hermann Oelrichs. His father also informed them he was building a "Whitney village" on his Lenox site with its 11,000 acres, which would include space for the couple. Another home for them, Roslyn, would soon go up at the Westbury, Long Island, farm. Whitney owned two other properties where Gertrude would enjoy family outings: a "camp" in the Adirondacks with 70,000 acres of timber and 52 lakes, and a horse farm in Aiken, South Carolina.

Gertrude initially embraced these domestic obligations. For one, she was more free than she had ever been. She had almost never been out of the house alone, never read a book Alice had not approved ahead of time. She had been prevented (as her parents were) from any of the simple ordinary activities tens of thousands of New Yorkers around her experienced. She was delighted to take a bus, to call up a girlfriend and meet her for lunch somewhere with no one to question and judge or forbid. Shopping and decorating were playful, not onerous tasks. She also accepted the conventional demands of entertaining. Like other well-to-do young couples, she and Harry hosted and attended dinner parties, regularly frequented the opera and the theater, and passed weekends at country house parties, their own and others. The world of the wealthy being very narrow and circumscribed, it is not surprising their best friends would be Gertrude's cousin Adele Sloan and her husband Jay Burden. Adele had a zest for fun, with no Puritan guilt about it, while Jay was more serious, being responsible for the family's declining ironworks. Although still shy and uncomfortable with crowds, Gertrude pushed ahead and did her duty as a society matron, partly because these social ties were intricately woven with her husband's career.

Actually, it was not clear to her just what Harry's career was. Soon after their marriage he signed with the prestigious law firm of Elihu Root to complete his law training. However, he never passed the bar, which may explain his accepting an appointment as associate commissioner of the Bureau of Municipal Statistics of New York City. That sinecure lasted seventeen months. His actual work, such as it was, consisted of assisting his father's many business deals and eventually developing his own. A sport, a man's man, Harry fit in well with the older generation, men such as Daniel Guggenheim, with whom he invested in silver, lead, and copper mines out West to great profit.

Although Harry enjoyed meetings and trips with fellow investors, his passion was horses. William Whitney had revitalized Saratoga by building a new racetrack and cleaning up the resort to get rid of its recent honky-tonk image. Harry delighted his father with his ability to judge horseflesh and from the first found his entries in the winner's circle. The Whitney spread in Westbury centered around a stable a sixth of a mile long, steam heated, with electric lights, telephones, and stalls for 116 horses and dormitories for grooms. When he learned a nearby estate was for sale, William Whitney renovated that to add even more housing for horses. Besides raising horses for racing, Harry played polo, and he set his goal on forming a team to one day beat the best in England.

Gertrude was not the sporty sort, so early in the marriage she watched Harry go away alone to the training stables in the country or the tracks at Saratoga and Belmont. Pregnancy tied her down as well, for in those days it was considered a somewhat unnatural condition. Gertrude had returned from the honeymoon three months pregnant, giving birth to Flora (named after Harry's mother) in 1897, then Cornelius, known always as Sonny, in early 1899. She suffered more than the usual discomfort during pregnancy, because, like Consuelo, she was slim hipped, not built for easy delivery. Childbearing also brought on a bout with phlebitis, the chronic recurrence of which would afflict her throughout her life.

By the time Sonny arrived, Gertrude sensed that marriage with Harry was not going to provide the companionship she had observed between her mother and father. The mutual interests simply were not there. Still, she felt no less love for Harry, and she depended upon his intermittent company and attention for her self-esteem. She tolerated his long absences so long as he showed his passion when he returned. Nor did the children bring the satisfaction society told her they should. She had not been happy to be pregnant so early in the marriage, for she was not able to travel. Her life was far removed from her youthful vision of marriage, which was childless, a woman and man sharing intimacies away from the intrusion of anyone else.

Restless, Gertrude began to explore the arts. She received early first encouragement from stained-glass artist John LaFarge, whom she met in 1898 when she was redecorating the Fifth Avenue house. She and Harry visited his studio and came away with three Japanese prints. That purchase was the start of her collection; which would quickly focus on the works of American artists.

More significantly, she began to dabble, first with watercolors, then with modeling. Since childhood she had known Howard Cushing, a painter from a prominent family who had studied in France. (In 1895, Gertrude had been delighted to come across him at the Louvre, where he was copying a Velasquez.) Although he was more interested in art than any of the men in her set, Gertrude had never had a crush on him. She may have been dissuaded by rumors he was "degenerate," a term she entered in her diary while admitting she did not understand what it meant. Possibly because she was now off the marriage market, Cushing showed more interest in her, and the two became fast friends.

Making such artist acquaintances provoked a significant dream, of being in a cellar sculpting the figure of a man. Howard Cushing introduced her to his brother-in-law, sculptor Hendrik Andersen, who "made colossal statues which no one wanted."[30] While he may not have been a great artist, he was an adept teacher whose harsh criticisms reduced her to tears without destroying her faith in her potential. He guided the creation of her first work for exhibition, *Aspiration,* a larger-than-life male nude with arms stretched toward the heavens. She decided to submit it for the 1901 Pan-American Exhibit in Buffalo, where it was accepted under a pseudonym.

Andersen's personality was as colossal as his statues. A distant relative of Hans Christian Andersen, his poor but genteel parents had settled in Newport, where the better-off Cushings took to him and his talented siblings. Later, Hendrik studied at art schools in Boston and Paris. In Rome, he was introduced to Henry James, who was so erotically taken with the youth that he started a correspondence with him and invited him to his home in London. During Gertrude's practice in his studio, Hendrik would read aloud to her from Ibsen and other writers forbidden in her youth. At first seeing her as a source of easy money, he soon became fascinated with her, and he wrote his brother: "For I want to make her excited. *Not myself!* And although she is *very foolish* I will put the *world* in a *new* light for her."[31] To do this he also took her to galleries. He introduced her to Ellen Terry, the most scandalous of actresses because she had borne "unfathered" children. He reached his goal. Gertrude "began to see how many things in life [she] knew nothing about," to feel she had been admitted into a Secret Society.[32] She had never known a bohemian before, let alone an artist who followed his muse despite that no one else liked what that muse inspired.

More importantly, Hendrik Andersen instilled in her the primacy of technique and was unstinting in his criticism. Use you own judgment, let the faults be *your* faults, he intoned. Do not be swayed by other's advice and suggestions. Gertrude soon realized that her initially frivolous attempts could lead to a serious career, though she understood she must apply herself to a disciplined training were she to accomplish anything of value.

Unfortunately, the lessons did not last, for Andersen felt the need to visit James again and spend a winter in Rome for further study. Gertrude took out Arthur Thomson's fig-leafed *Handbook of Anatomy for Art Students* and worked alone in a small studio she had set up in her home. Andersen's departure also meant losing one of the few sources of support for her explorations. Esther Hunt backed her efforts, but she had moved abroad and was no longer available for tête-à-têtes over tea. Interestingly, Alice approved at first and searched to find another teacher for her. Then she saw the tiny fig leaf on *Aspiration* and caustically urged that a scarf be put on the figure for fear it would shock three-year-old Flora. Interspersed with such direct condemnation would be pieties reminding Gertrude of her obligations to her babies, that she should not apply herself too closely to her art. Nor did most of her other friends understand why she would "work," as they called it, when she did not need to.

Gertrude was used to her mother's disapproval, and could overlook that of her friends. Harder to take was the attitude of Harry, the most important judge in her eyes, who was at best tolerant, perhaps grateful she had something harmless to calm her fitfulness. His letters during his many absences were self-absorbed with talk of hunting, adventures with friends, and hypochondriacal complaints. Gertrude clung to the rare sign of affection from him. A characteristic one, "Dearest, I am glad you are doing your duty to the kids & will be back soon & give you a kiss for it" hardly expressed the passionate phantom lover of her premarriage days.[33]

As the century closed for Gertrude, she received two letters that reflected the split in her life. Her father-in-law wrote in a warm, loving manner (certainly more loving than Harry was demonstrating to her), in which he expressed how much he valued her as a daughter-in-law. Speaking from experience, he observed that marriage was "a lottery," where people had to get over illusions "to be broken into life's hard sides." Reflecting on the frequent separations she and Harry underwent, he concluded optimistically that they had not resulted in alienation, as happened with most other couples. Yet he must have sensed some of Gertrude's dissatisfaction, for he advised, "Harry may be supposed not to have done much— But wait until he settles down."[34] The other letter was from Esther: "I feel that things are drifting with you, am I right?"[35] She was.

9

1900-1908 *(continued)*

*Gertrude Discovers
Her Passions*

Gertrude loved Europe, and she was delighted in 1901 when Harry agreed to a trip. She had not been there for six years, and she longed to study sculpture from her more mature perspective. The journey would not be a second honeymoon, however; when they made their way up the gangplank of the ocean liner, alongside them were Adele and Jay Burden and bachelor Jimmie Appleton, one of Gertrude's early suitors. In Italy they were to be joined by Howard Cushing and Rollie Cottenet, another suitor who had bowed out when Harry came on the scene.

Gertrude was to write two distinct accounts of this trip. One was a journal entered intermittently during the actual travel; the other, titled *Travels in Foreign Countries and in the Mind,* was written soon afterward. The first account is similar to her earlier travelogues, with lengthy detailed entries about museums, artworks, dinner conversations, and odd encounters. The second is literature, a poetic reinterpretation of the journey as a metaphor for changes in Gertrude's perceptions of herself and others. What she expected to be the usual Continental tour, rushing here and there with a crush of experiences soon forgotten, became a time of transformation so consequential she would return a very different woman.

London set the tone. She said of the city, it "swallowed and absorbed me so completely that I feel like an atom of the great city—lost, lost in its meshes, ensnared in its charms and loving it all the time."[1] Giving herself up to its overpowering size, she felt it "wiping out all one's personality." Cleansed of past worries, strictures, and fears, she unconsciously opened her mind to see in a new way.

London also spoiled any hope Gertrude may have had for renewed intimacy with Harry. Following fitful attendance at a play, he announced his need to tend to business and visit associates in the polo world. At first Harry seemed happy that Jimmie Appleton was along to supply the companionship he was unwilling to provide; what he did not suspect was Gertrude's fragile self-esteem, her need for masculine attention. Admiring Jimmie's "strong, deep and good" character, his tender heart, Gertrude almost overlooked Harry's slighting of her.[2] Most memorable was an evening they sat in the Poets Corner at Westminster, where Gertrude felt they "seemed alone with a past that had a thousand voices."[3] While part of her was awed by the haunt of the organ processional, the awesome sweep of the Gothic arches, another part was tingling with awareness of Jimmie's presence. "[W]hen two people for a moment, no matter how short, lived a pulse together they were irretrievably linked together were they never to meet or speak again. A pulse—a beat in life—a thing that makes us move forward—a thing that measures time and eternity—for what are events? They pass unnoticed, it is the beating of the pulses which makes us live."[4]

In Paris, she realized she was infatuated with Jimmie and played with the fun of the flirtation. Harry discovered he had to return to England for a week, thus leaving her alone with Jimmie, for Jay and Adele were off on a side trip as well. When she went shopping with Jimmie at the Bon Marché, the clerk's misconception that they were married titillated her. Then Harry finally reappeared. However, instead of saying how he missed her, he picked up on the obvious electricity between the pair and privately accused her of not having good principles. Rather than express guilt or repent, she admitted in her journal, though not to Harry, to a "deviltry that is not altogether safe" and that her conscience was not what it should be.[5] She did not care, for in Paris "they live for the moment."[6]

By the time their train rolled into the station in Italy, she was thinking of Harry as "the other occupant, whose fondness for staying at home was marked."[7] She would refer to him in her later account as "Fatty," and note what she considered to be his various faults—his whining over small discomforts, his arguments with her over works of art, his fast driving. That he was still handsome with his green eyes, youthful looks, strong limbs, his clever and quick mind, only confounded her feelings. She admitted he had generally a cheerful temperament and made for good company. What he most lacked for her was the quality she abounded in, discipline, a legacy from her parents she now admired in herself. She mourned that Harry's lack of character would mean a wealth of natural talent gone to waste. In doing so, she greatly underestimated her husband, who simply had very different goals in life and a more relaxed approach to achieving them.

On the one hand, she was loathe to displease, to misbehave before him and friends by breaking the bonds of convention; on the other, she was anxious to explore her own needs. "A great passion of selfishness swept me before it—*my* life, *my* desires. *I* was to build a foundation for myself. *I* was to gild and varnish rooms in which to live. *I* was to soar into castles untenanted by humanity. *I* was to touch the core of life!"[8]

The image of herself as a fledgling recurred throughout the journey. Rome, for example, was a magic color box where wings were fashioned. Later she wrote of what it was like to live surrounded all one's life by so high a fence that even when let free, "one's wings are so inconceivably weak that though one longs to fly one has abrupt falls which are painful from every point of view." The constructor of the high fence and clipper of the wings was "the Anglo-Saxon temperament," which compared poorly to the Latin races, who sought "the natural outlet of their wants as easily as does the unsuspecting sparrow."[9]

If Gertrude felt herself an empty slate in London, in Rome she saw herself a child responding anew to its mysterious mixture of the ancient, the medieval, and the modern. "Interred among its stones were memories of a warm life. These came to me over the cold stone floor [of St. Peter's] and beckoned me to follow and live and learn."[10] Before Michelangelo's *Pieta* she became swept away by the artist's deft fingers, a flawless technique that left her literally shaken as she turned away.

More than Michelangelo may have stirred her. Because Harry had come down with a cold, she had gone exploring the ruins, museums, and Vatican with Howard Cushing. He had stood before the *Pieta* with her, and she "felt there was no one I would rather see beautiful things with than this man . . . sympathetic and strong and magnetic."[11] Another evening they viewed the Coliseum by moonlight, where on turning a corner "suddenly yet meltingly rows upon rows of seats stood out leaving the rest like a cloud dark and unfathomable."[12] The joy of the vision, the almost painful bliss, was heightened by her awareness that she and Cushing absolutely understood each other. They lingered, talked, refrained from returning to the hotel where the others were chattering over the bridge table. Though part of her response to him was erotic, she declined to express it. When Cushing later left the group, she reviewed how she could never have more than a platonic caring for him, yet that was what made their relationship so strong.

Cushing respected Gertrude's seriousness about sculpture and countered her tendency to belittle herself. Daily confrontation with the masterpieces of classical sculpture left her feeling too old to be embarking on the art form, too lacking in technique. She knew technique meant time, sacrifice of other things that perhaps could not be sacrificed given the strictures of her class position. These strictures were not just practical, most notably the children, but worse for art, emotional. To "rather die than show my real feelings once deeply touched" could not make for good art, she knew. Could she sacrifice what was necessary? Could she unleash the years of suppression with its "inexpressible agony of the 'shut in feeling'"?[13]

Other circumstances served to further the deviltry awakened in Paris. Rollie Cottonet finally appeared to make the party complete.[14] At that point Harry uncharacteristically took over as social chairman, touring the way Gertrude used to enjoy but no longer did—miles of galleries, acres of churches, Tivoli, Fiesole, Florence, Siena. Accompanying this rushing about was frequent drinking and behavior she described as dissolute and degenerate. The degeneracy was probably merely sexual comments, lewd joking, playful eroticism, not acting out. As would be expected with such a mix of coddled people with too much time and money and too much liquor, petty arguments flared.

In Naples, Gertrude dropped a further veil from her dark side. The city's main attraction, she observed, was the immorality of its inhabitants. Rather than finding herself repulsed, she found that "those people racked by many sins possessed for me a glamor which in the wilderness of my mind shone like stars, distant but strangely bright." She questioned how to handle this "morbid" and "evil minded" part of herself.[15] Should she allow her imagination to play in this forbidden garden of exotic flowers or avoid its temptations?

Appropriately, a second motif appeared in her journal, that of the sea. If only one could toss restraints aside, she wished, as waves toss their foam! As if to mirror her inner life, the party boarded a boat, the *Sheelah*, to sail to the island of Sicily, then on to Syracuse and then to Tunis on the African coast. And the real-life sea stirred even further water imagery. The shimmering, changing Mediterranean represented the source of power and passion. "The water surface was alive. It was vibrant with force, exultation and joy in its own beauty. The sea has no clear outline, it falls and rises everlastingly changing its mighty shape as easily and as momentarily as if it were not as eternal as the mountains. It wavers like a shaken curtain. In the tremulous sunlight it glitters so that we dare not probe too deep into its secret. What intensities of feeling rise like sea creatures from the depths to disturb my daydreams."[16] The sea was an Amazon that can never be tamed, she concluded. Gertrude came to meld with that image, to view herself as the sea, "reckless and destructive, her true self."

It was on glimpsing the sea from a road one day that another insight was revealed to her. Watching the waves crash upon the dark rocks and gorges, she concluded that it was human fate to be alone, always. Even love could not remove the last veil covering the soul, no matter how compatible the man and woman. Only art could compensate for that inevitable separateness. "To become steeped in beauty, to make an image in one's heart that cannot be wiped out!"[17] Creativity would affirm her self, provide an immortality relationships with others could not.

Art responded through richer dream and fantasy images, which she recorded in her journal. While absentmindedly looking out the window of a hotel one afternoon, she fell into a reverie where she saw herself walking in a garden of orange blossoms. When her fantasy lover did not appear as expected, she watched herself collapse in sobs before the full golden moon. Then a low sound aroused her, the sea wind, she assumed. The murmur transformed into words of passion, and her lover came out of the shadows to take her savagely. Drifting out of the fantasy, suddenly defining herself (incorrectly) as a woman of neither fire nor passion, she left the window and her dream self, and she went back to her friends, who could not imagine the richness of her secret passion.

Another day brought a vision of Medusa, the vile snakes arising out of her beautiful head. She feared herself corrupted, and did not consider that the corruption was perhaps the emergence of feelings long entombed until this journey. The Medusa image guided her to further awareness that she was on the most difficult journey of all, that into herself. She recognized there could be no short-cuts to this "hidden knowledge of life for which I had been seeking."[18] The trick was to persist in the journey without becoming hardened or callous along the way. She became less fearful of being overwhelmed by thoughts of the weird and exotic.

Again as if on cue, the group moved on into Arab territory, Tunis, whose exotic sights further enflamed her imagination. They visited a snake charmer, who played with his pets and stuck long nails through parts of his face. She watched the women on the streets, treated as beasts of burden and pleasure by the men. This repeated experience incited a despairing vision of an "animal woman," blind, groping, tortured, her "mouth unsatisfied with multitudinous kisses, her body burning with fever."[19] In contrast to this Eastern animal woman was the Western "idol woman," such as herself, who struggled with her mind as well as her body. The animal woman could find no unity because Eastern man tyrannized her.[20]

If Gertrude despised the Eastern male for his gluttony, his heavy body pressing down on his women, she did not think the Western woman, more educated and free, should rush into actions better suited to men. Rather, she believed that a woman should use her intuitive powers to contribute more poetry, music, art, understanding of human nature. No androgeny for her (or for even the most rabid suffragists of her day, who believed medical claims that women were essentially different from men). And if the intuitive were the realm for Western woman, then by implication it was the realm for Gertrude Vanderbilt Whitney.

Every mythical journey of the self has its final thrust into the depths of the inferno, and Gertrude witnessed hers on a hot, dusty day during an Islamic rite, which began with a procession of men who cut themselves with knives and beat themselves with chains as they passed by. Blood streaked their white trousers and yellow skins. Now and then a man would collapse, to be helped to his feet so he might carry on. Following the men came chanting boys in long robes carrying candles. Next came two white horses covered with blood-stained clothes, and on each a blood-stained child. Behind these two steeds massed another crowd of men slicing their heads with glittering long knives so that the fresh orange-red blood streamed like flames down their faces onto their chests and backs.

Walking away from this purification ritual, Gertrude determined to culti-vate a naive and open-minded attitude toward the world. Nothing could be too strange, no deception possible. The hope was to incorporate the Medusa, the vile with the beautiful, into her self-conception.

Harry Disappoints,
and More

Arriving home in the summer of 1901, a five-month absence from the children, Gertrude still felt caught in the tumult and agony caused by the voyage. If she was not clear just who she was, she was certain she could no longer live as she had before the voyage. She had yet to pull together the two sides of her, the "restless, wild person with crazy notions and a dull exterior," but she no longer denied her unconventional impulses.[21] She was ready to sacrifice the part of her world that did not interest, notably much of her social life, in order to have more time with the children and her sculpting. She found a new teacher, James Earle Fraser, famed sculptor of the dying Indian called *The End of the Trail,* and leased one of the Charles Dana Gibson studios on West 33rd Street in New York. She also transformed an unused blacksmith's shop on the Westbury property into a temporary studio while she planned a more permanent structure.

In October she suffered a loss so great she could not write about it for some years. Her trip with Harry and the Burdens had kept Gertrude from attending Esther Hunt's February marriage to George Muirson Woolsey. The couple had gone abroad after the marriage, during which time Esther became pregnant. While in London, one afternoon she collapsed from an internal hemorrhage and died within minutes. She was twenty-seven. The full effects of this loss were to be postponed until a time when Gertrude was more vulnerable and in need of Esther's counsel.

Believing correctly that her efforts in sculpture should be toward building proficiency, which meant many practice models, she turned to writing for freer artistic expression. She worked on *Travels,* in addition to various fictional projects. Unwisely, she decided that to be a sculptor was not enough; she must also be a novelist, she must be published and recognized. This splitting of her attention between two very different media diluted her talent in both. Nonetheless, for the rest of her life she would discipline herself to spend almost as many hours at her desk writing fiction as she would molding clay in the studio. That she did so with much less success and virtually no recognition hints at the powerful drive for self-fulfillment that motivated her.

The predominant theme in her plot notes for her early novels was explicitly autobiographical, an elaboration of her relationship with Harry.[22] In two versions of one story, a man and woman have been married "6 or 7 years." Having married too young to experience much of life, they are now aware of having missed something. They have outgrown each other, although they are still fond of each other. They determine to separate for a year, each to do what he or she pleases. She finds a lover, while he goes to Paris and has a mistress. In the first version, after a year they agree not to reunite. She loses her position in society and eventually her lover; the husband becomes dissipated and settles into becoming a nobody. In the second version, the two come together after a year, neither wanting to renew the marriage, and the wife tells her story first. As the husband recounts his adventures, he becomes disgusted with himself and sees her anew. He convinces her to break from her lover and return to him, which she does. Although she can never forget the other man, her life continues happily, while her husband is more in love with her than ever.

The two versions reflected Gertrude's clutching to a romantic and dramatized view of her marriage. According to the first story, to act on deep feelings of unhappiness and violate society's strictures would bring tragedy to both partners. The second version suggested a hope that once Harry had seen that other men found Gertrude attractive, he would love her passionately as she wished. What is significant about both tales is that the husband is also unfaithful.

In July of 1902, Harry and Gertrude attended the wedding of cousin Lila Sloane. While they were at the celebration, Gertrude happened to notice Harry with a tall and willowy woman the same age as Gertrude. She was the sister-in-law of a Vanderbilt cousin. Unlike Gertrude, she was a prize-winning horsewoman, self-confident, a quick conversationalist, and at ease within their social set, in other words, much more like Harry. From their behavior, Gertrude suddenly understood that they were lovers. That entire night she cried, while lying to Harry and claiming to be upset about Neily. Harry went to Lenox, to be with his mistress, Gertrude knew, while she remained behind, wildly talkative and laughing around friends. Reflecting later, she wrote, "It was the hardest thing I had had in my life then, harder than Papa's death or Bill's or C's [Neily's] troubles. Barbara [her third child] had started then, which did not make it easier."[23] Harry continued to see the other woman, taking a week in December to spend with her in Aiken. (Gertrude knew his romantic intentions because he neglected to take his valet.)

Given such deceit, it is not surprising that her *Travels* manuscript, completed around this time, concluded with harsh words about men. "One day thinking of Paris [when Harry chided her for flirting with Jimmie] made me think that men were tyrants. They wish to become possessed of the soul of woman as well as the body, and having accomplished this foul object they drag her down, down till her vitality is sapped and all her fine possibilities destroyed. Then it becomes necessary if she would to live and enjoy again that she should escape the tyranny of one man."[24] The problem was how to become "untrammeled and free" while "the heavy hand of man rests upon her." Her vision of Western men was ironically modeling that of the Arab men she despised.

Complications with her pregnancy heightened Gertrude's sense of hollowness and worthlessness. Thinking she might die during the delivery, one evening she took out her pen and paper to write a farewell letter to Harry. It was a virtual suicide note. Within it, Gertrude reviewed her flirtation with Jimmie Appleton, her discovery of Harry's infidelity, her realization it was not a mere flirtation. Apparently he had by then agreed not to see his mistress again, for

Gertrude sympathized with the pain that loss was bringing him. She assured him of her forgiveness, and in effect asked for his: *She* was at fault, she emphasized. She could not hold him, she had so much more love for him than he wanted that it choked her, forcing her to flirtations. "Could I have gone on without that for which I pine the most. I doubt it and been a good woman. I know you must have suffered but after this blow [her death] is softened you will be happy and you are not so old. After all you did care for me a great deal and we were very happy."[25] In the final sentences she gave advice on his relationship with the children, pointing out that Flora was a very sensitive child. When she was done she sealed the letter in an envelope and labeled it to be opened only upon her death. He never saw it—yet she never destroyed it, keeping it among her papers.

Gertrude Commits
to Sculpture

Gertrude's self-abnegation continued for several years during which she repeatedly sought to regain Harry's affection. In the summer of 1903, for example, she uncomplainingly accompanied him to Europe, even went with him on his hunting side trips and bit her tongue during his fast driving. Although she was docile and convivial in public, in her journal she protested about Harry's constant "abominable state of mind." It is unlikely he was aware of her real feelings.

Further pressure to submit herself came in early 1904 when Harry lost his truly dearest companion, his father, who died suddenly from peritonitis following an appendicitis operation (a frequent killer in those days prior to antibiotics). In death William Whitney intruded on their lives as he never had when alive. Shattered, Harry determined he and Gertrude should move their family to his father's 68th Street mansion (which they did not) and to his rambling Westbury house (which they did). And they were made guardians of Dorothy Whitney, an addition to a troubled household that could barely manage to do right by its own children at that time. Although Dorothy was now seventeen and had wages for an adult companion included in the will, Gertrude nonetheless agreed when Harry insisted that they see the young woman properly introduced to society. Dorothy was to become an heiress at twenty-one, and Harry wanted her coached and groomed to attain the "right" marriage, a goal his sister Pauline Paget in England also emphasized.

As part of Dorothy's priming, a grand tour was called for, where the trio was expanded by the addition of Alice and Gladys as well. Tall, blue-eyed, smiling Dorothy enthused over her first exposure to London, Paris, the Louvre, and the Loire country. Her bubbliness and girlishness cloaked a streak of independence and social compassion that would later upset Harry. On this trip, though, Harry was delighted with her; indeed, Dorothy could not help noticing that her brother treated her better than his own wife.

Just when Gertrude most needed confidantes, they had disappeared. Howard Cushing, by then a loyal and constant friend, suddenly married Ethel Cochran, whom Gertrude did not find very compatible. Obviously he could no longer write Gertrude frequently or visit her for private chats. Earlier that year her closest female friend, Lena Morton, suddenly died.

As a result of these repeated losses, Gertrude descended into a profound depression. She struggled valiantly. She continued to sculpt and even earned her first commission, bas relief panels for a private house. In June, she decided that her only road to happiness would be to use her position, her wealth, and any special gifts on a special project. After talking with some friends and learning that the country needed a strong architectural training center, she came upon the idea of a Beaux Arts school. Once it was established, she planned that art and sculpture classes would be attached to the institution.

Yet this dream lingered and ultimately languished because she tied it to Harry's approval. The degree of her groveling can be seen in the many days that passed without her being able to discuss it with him out of fear he would belittle the idea. After all, he had no sympathy for her sculpting. "Has Harry always refused to make any effort for me? I think so and yet I am not sure. The same feeling that used to make me take a book when I went out for a long time alone with him assails me now. I feel at times that I must set off a bomb under him or die. Bomb. I must try today and be outrageous. He will not go halfway with me and I starve. The kids help, but—oh well, of course they do not really satisfy at all."[26] All she wanted was one sign that he cared, but instead she felt him putting up blocks whenever she tried to get closer.

Mourning for Lena Morton also revived the loss of Esther. As the summer progressed Gertrude became more despondent, to the point where one day she wished the children did not exist because she had brought them into a world where, given their natures, they could not be happy. She especially worried for Flora, in whom she perceived a sensitive temperament similar to hers. She even mused about drowning them, an act the world would say was mad, when she saw it as simple common sense. Others would wonder how she, granted everything in life others wanted materially, could feel murderous, "a corpse." It was a fleeting thought, one made permanent only because she wrote so honestly in her journal.

While attempting to create her own life as an artist, attending classes, studying anatomy, molding small models based on classical forms, she continued to placate Harry. Berating herself as "stupid and dull," she filled pages lecturing herself to "cultivate a certain amount of conversation," listed topics to discuss, to read up on, opinions to develop, in other words, to be more like her once-rival. She crammed her social calendar with "respectable activities" for the days he would be away to show him she was no different from his friends' wives. The rare happy family outings with Harry, the small hint of approval from him, were entered as if gold stars.

The determination to mold herself to what she believed to be Harry's ideal woman failed. If it seems she was too servile, one has to consider Harry's responses to her. He was not a cruel or cold person. Although Gertrude was not what he wanted in a lover, Harry was by temperament a kindly, generous man whose treatment of her was decent. He was not like some other men who mistreated their wives to assuage their guilt over their own failures toward them. When he mentioned in his letters how he missed her, he was honest—he just didn't miss her passionately, the way she wanted. He was also a loving father, an enthusiast for picnics and playtimes with the children. Spoiled himself, he was quick to spoil his own. If only he had been a cad, a drunk, a degenerate, how much easier for Gertrude. His innate sweetness only confounded her feelings because she took it as a sign he would once again return to her with the enthusiasm shown in their early months of marriage.

On October 22, 1904, Gertrude sat with her journal, and came to a conscious awareness that she needed to shift her perspective. There she acknowledged that she disliked the people she was required to mix with socially, that being a society matron was not congenial. "I cannot be the sort of a person which my life demands me to be—so why not try and be my own self. That is something I have never tried to be."[27] She vowed that she must throw aside her masquerade even though that meant disappointing Harry. Even then she could not face his not being in love with her, and rationalized that perhaps he might respect her more were she to follow her heart.

As is common with major psychological changes, Gertrude's accepted this shift intellectually before she did emotionally. Consequently, her actions continued to be ambivalent. Thus she organized a successful charity benefit, but instead of seeking self-satisfaction from the accomplishment, undertook it in hopes it would "elevate me in the eyes of H. P. W."[28] And despite her recognition that society did not interest her, she jammed her daybook with guests and visits to others. Her journal lectured her to "try to see something of Mr. McKim [the architect], St. Gaudens [the noted American sculptor] and any other artists that you can. Have two dances, a musical and some bridge evenings, opera dinners and a few large dinners. Take Tuesday nights and have dinners with something always doing afterwards. According to the crowd."[29] Indeed, until April of 1907 her life retained the old pattern: winter and spring in New York/Westbury, late summer in Europe touring, intermittent trips to Aiken and Newport. Harry remained cordial yet unresponsive. He made love to her infrequently, but just enough to keep her longings alive.

Somehow in this overburdened schedule she squeezed hours in the studio shaping clay into figures for exhibition. Her early works chose topics popular with sculptors of the day: mythical figures (*Pan*), children (*Boy with Parrot*), and allegory (*Paganism*). Although tentative, such initial attempts hinted at the main strength of Gertrude's mature style, a nervous vitality and intensity of emotion. However, as she later acknowledged, her self-doubt and preoccupation with false social values at this point kept her from developing her art as rapidly as she might had she made a clearer commitment. Nevertheless, it was a start.

Just as important to her as steady work at her craft was her decision to allot more time to be with fellow artists. Most were men at all stages in their careers who respected Gertrude's discipline, her openness to criticism, and her relentless pursuit of technique. Some were blatantly attracted to her money and hoped to benefit from her largesse. Others were attracted to her sexually, to which she responded with playful flirtation. It was wonderful for a woman who had felt her life almost over at thirty, who considered herself ugly, to discover she had physical appeal. (Her poor estimate of her looks was not totally imaginary. She did not have "good bones," so when she lost her slight adolescent plumpness to become excessively thin, the skin on her face drooped and over time formed deep crevices.)

One of her earliest influences was Robert Henri, informal leader of a group of painters commited to discovering beauty in commonplace scenes in the city around them. These American Realists reached back to Manet, Goya, Velazquez, Hals, and Daumier for inspiration in technique. As such, they were not radical in their departure from the mannered salon style so prevalent then, yet they were nonetheless considered beyond the pale by influential critics. Being a traditional sculptor of her day, a modeler of familiar and mythical beings, Gertrude was more attracted to these rebels than that another coterie of painters that was breaking more rules, hinting at abstraction.

She first met Henri in 1906 in Aiken, where he was on a working vacation to paint a portrait of Mrs. George Sheffield. "Today Mrs. Harry Payne Whitney is come to see [the portrait]. I believe she is the one who is interesting herself in sculpture and decoration," he noted.[30] He was to raise his estimate of her in the future. The tall, dashing, haunting-looking Henri so captivated Gertrude that she started to follow his career in the newspapers and pasted in her scrapbook the clippings concerning his frequent attacks on traditionalists in American art. Although it would be some time before he became a friend, Henri's philosophy, like a "rock dashed, ripping and tearing, through bolts of patiently prepared lace," excited her, increased her natural enthusiasm for dissent.[31]

Another significant early supporter was Robert Winthrop Chanler, a wealthy descendant of Dutch patroons who was a painter, womanizer, and county sheriff. A blond giant with a Whitmanesque personality to match, Gertrude admired his frankness and expansiveness. "I would like to see you go to the Devil," he admitted, to which she merely smiled. Though she knew he was in his own way "a fraud and a flirt," she recognized he had much of value to teach her about art. She must use him: "Vampire. Oh what does that matter. Take what you can, you need not think men cannot take care of themselves."[32] They attended exhibitions together, where his comments spurred her development of a more critical eye.

A third figure, who would grow more significant as the years passed, was sculptor Andrew O'Connor. The son of an American sculptor, O'Connor had left home at age sixteen, and following some wandering, he apprenticed with the painter

Sargent in London. Sargent sent him to study the Greek statuary in the British Museum to perfect his sculpting technique. He later returned to the States, where his gifts were recognized early. Following the death of Gertrude's father, Alice decided a fitting memorial would be to donate doors to the family church, St. Bartholemew's. Her architect, Stanford White, selected O'Connor to create the bronze reliefs for these great doors, and the family was most pleased with the results. O'Connor, only a year older than Gertrude, impressed upon her the necessity to develop a strong classical technique.

Splitting her life between what she considered false, conventional behavior and the more genuine and artistic sent Gertrude into wide mood swings. Depressions recurred, her solution being to make yet one more futile effort to be a sparkling, sophisticated socialite.

It is difficult perhaps for the modern observer to appreciate the ostracism Gertrude faced from friends and the disapproval from Harry, for wishing to spend a few hours a day in her studio. Had she dabbled in watercolors or china painting, they would have been more tolerant—barely. But she was one of a number of women artists of the day who rejected those acceptable feminine outlets for a medium historically associated only with men. Consider the tools of the trade: the mallet, chisels, the calipers, and the medium, earth and metals, all associated with the masculine. The artist must be roughly and loosely clothed, uncorseted, to move easily on and around the projects. Sculpture was physical, messy, and worse, necessitated the use of live models; the implication of unrestrained sexuality was too obvious. There was no way Gertrude could express to family or friends her delight in anticipating an afternoon in the studio with model Edgar McAdams, "his beautiful bare body will be more beautiful than ever and I will look at him and be glad that I am alive and that my heart beats now quickly."[33] Their worst unstated suspicions would come true: she would one day do more than merely admire his body.

The artistic profession as well discouraged women. Young male artists could apprentice by working in architectural firms or the studios of established sculptors. Neither of these routes was available to women. Though the National Sculpture Society accepted female members, it deterred their competing for public commissions, long considered a male province. Nonetheless, at the time Gertrude took up sculpting, dozens of other women around the country were similarly breaking the barriers and succeeding in making careers as sculptors. Those who were well-to-do went abroad for the education they needed. Gertrude's fellow classmate from the Brearley School, Malvina Hoffman, went to Paris, where Rodin accepted her as an apprentice. "He took my hand and looked at me very intently. I felt I was discovered."[34] Harriet Whitney, of a prominent Philadelphia family, studied happily with Rodin as well, and she was apprenticed in the studios of other European sculptors. On the other hand, Anna Vaughn Hyatt, of a distinguished Boston family, was virtually self-taught. Women from more modest means, such as Janet Scudder, fought to be accepted at traditional art schools to learn their craft. There, however, women were excluded from essential life-modeling classes and anatomy lessons because of the issue of nudity, hence sexuality.

Gertrude was fortunate to have always known male artists who did not descriminate against her on account of her sex and who provided the initial education. Despite her having exhibited small works and obtained a few private commissions, it was not until 1907 that she defined herself fully as an artist.

The precipitating factor was a remark made by a friend, a "Mrs. L.," in mid-April of 1907. This woman's tattling made clear that all these years Harry had never given up his lover, indeed was even more bound to her than ever. Gertrude was furious and called her informant a fool, yet she suddenly understood it was true, which meant *she* had been the fool not to accept what so many clues had been telling her. All those efforts to appease, to comply, to satisfy, had been useless from the start. All those puzzling times of despair, of sobbing and nervous fits, had been warning signals that something tragic was actually occurring.

Following several months of hellish anguish and a host of physical ailments, Gertrude at last was able to act in accord with her reformulated values. She made so many changes that a year went by before she returned again to her journal, because "one does not write when one is cheerful, and when one's life is crowded to overflowing."[35] Her attitude toward Harry was to return his graciousness and cordiality, to accompany him to important racing events and host the parties he enjoyed but otherwise to design her life as though he had no claims. She let him know her discovery of the infidelity. He was semirepentant and grateful for her lack of vindictiveness; what he never expected was that she would now herself find love elsewhere.

She did not take long to find other partners. She had two brief affairs, which she found "a natural almost necessary development" that taught her the complexities of dealing with people. ("Be careful of burning others, you may get your own fingers in the fire!"[36]) She felt hard headed, ready to play with love, to cultivate excitement.

Rebellion Foments in
the Art World

In the process of her private redefinition, circumstances fostered Gertrude's future role as a major patron of American artists. It started when she organized an exhibition for the exclusive Colony Club, a woman's social, artistic, and physical club she had helped found in 1903. (Prior to then, the notion of women having private clubs had been considered indecent because it was feared they would use the facilities as men did theirs: for private assignations. Consequently, its founders tended to be reformists, suffragists, or political liberals.) Much of the display consisted of miniatures, antique lace, and portraits of members, but it included contemporary American paintings, including several by artists at odds with the ruling National Academy of Design. Because the show was private, it drew little attention from press or public. For the artists, though, it established Gertrude's commitment to their new ideas.

The most important consequence for Gertrude was her hiring a woman who would become her lifelong assistant in the service of American art. Juliana Rieser, a year younger than Gertrude, had the vividly theatrical personality to match her auburn hair and green eyes. Daughter of an angry, abusive mother and a father whose Pennsylvania hat-making business fell off when factory methods destroyed the craft, she had an unstoppable drive to compensate for the loss in family fortunes. A natural actress, she had acquired the patina of a lady from great wealth. She cultivated a slightly British accent and the distinctive poise that marks a private school education. Consequently, when she signed up with a secretarial agency in New York, she was soon popular with society women, eventually becoming full-time social secretary for Helen Hay Whitney, wife of Harry's brother Payne.

Juliana knew nothing about art, but she was eager to learn. Gertrude identified with her high energy, discipline, and inherent taste. As an adolescent Juliana had concluded, "Love of beauty is the only decided good one; for the rest, I have to fight hardest against a tendency to dictate [as well as] temper, uncharitableness, selfishness, pride, pessimism, and a sharp tongue."[37] Her self-assessment was accurate. While smartly dressed, well mannered, and at ease in any situation, she did not suppress her unorthodox views, a tendency to be outlandish, shocking. "Life was her meat," recalled painter Guy Pene du Bois. "She loved to report on how badly it could behave and stir it out of any angelic pose it might momentarily adopt. In conversation she preferred the bite, even of calumny if a substitute was wanting, to the toothlessness of a considered and polite statement."[38] That this successful wedding of convention and bohemianism was just what Gertrude was trying to achieve in her own life made Juliana all the more appealing. When the Colony Club project was over, Gertrude engaged Juliana at times to type her novels and assist her in artistic matters.

Though a social climber at heart, Juliana was not purely self-interested. Like Gertrude, she had a strong drive to serve artists, to apply her talents and resources so that they could concentrate more on creativity than on paying the rent. Little could these women, now in their early thirties, imagine the ultimate result of that shared ambition.

During these years, American art was stagnant, dominated by the academic traditionalism of the National Academy, whose juried exhibits excluded anything other than a pallid Impressionism and portrayal of a limited array of noble subjects. Only a handful of galleries in the country sold or showed the work of living Americans. The attitude was captured by a trustee of the Metropolitan Museum of Art: "What do you mean by American art? Do you mean English or

French or what? There is nothing in American art worth notice."[39] More pithily, painter John Sloan commented, "Artists, in a frontier society like ours, are like cockroaches in kitchens—not wanted, not encouraged but nevertheless they remain."[40]

Told Europe was the font of True Art, young artists begged or borrowed to travel abroad, where they confronted the works of the Fauves ("wild beasts"), the German Expressionists, the Italian Futurists, and the Cubists, all a far cry from what the National Academy taught or what millionaires were bringing home to hang on their walls. Inspired by their European comrades, these young American artists innovated in two directions. As has been noted, one direction was taken by Henri's comrades, with their trend toward earthy realism, fuller color, and zesty brushwork, an expressive extension of photography. This revolt was primarily in choice of subject, an announcement that the most casual scene was worthy of memorializing. A bar or a policeman were as fitting subjects as the academy's preference for a rainbowed landscape or a political hero. The other response was toward increasing subjectivity and intuition, a reaction to the scientific naturalism and growing materialism of the time. This revolt, which came to dominate after World War I, led to questioning the very idea of what art was and could be.

Before 1907, only one person offered any public acknowledgment of these rebellious artists. In 1905 photographer Alfred Stieglitz opened three small rooms in a brownstone off Fifth Avenue, better known by its street address of "291," where he exhibited experimental works and provided artists a place to gather and share their new ideas. Critics, however, informed the public that such shows were trivial, the work of lunatics, anarchists, nihilists, and foreigners. If Gertrude was not so harsh in her opinion of these experimenters, she was nevertheless unattracted to Stieglitz. A "mystagogue," as Van Wyck Brooks cleverly put it, Stieglitz demanded unquestioned devotion to his creed, which Gertrude was not inclined to do. Nor was she, as one dissatisfied with the narrowness of her social class, ready to exchange it for an equally narrow-minded artistic coterie. And the fact of Stieglitz's Jewishness might also have repelled her, as it would most white Protestants of her day.

In a move with historic consequence, in 1908 several artists finally rose up. When the National Academy rejected the work of George Luks, John Sloan, and William Glackens for its annual exhibition, Robert Henri, whose works had been accepted, withdrew in protest. Eventually, with others they formed a group of like-minded artists, The Eight, who assembled their own show at the MacBeath Galleries. The critics responded with horror, maligning it as the "Ash Can Show" and the "Revolutionary Black Gang." Some charged the work was a deliberate attempt to blacken the eye of America by deigning to portray subjects outside the "proper" domain of art.

Only three patrons bought seven paintings; Gertrude wrote a check for $2,225 to purchase four. John Sloan later commended her audacity for buying what were considered to be highly unfashionable, ugly, black illustrations. (This praise came some years later—immediately following the event he sniped about her choices, probably because his work had not been among her selections.) Gertrude's purchase was not just for collecting purposes. She wanted to patronize artists without condescending to them, or putting them into a position of begging for charity. They would ask, of course, as when later that year Hendrik Andersen explained the nearly $40,000 cost of finally casting a fountain he had been working on for eight years. More often Gertrude would be sensitive enough to anticipate a particular artist's need, thus contributing the expenses so that he could have a summer with his family in the country or she could have her rent covered. The gifts were made graciously, with no attachments other than that they be kept quiet, a practice she would adhere to from that point.

Consuelo Seeks Her
Purpose as Well

J ust as marital separation, though in spirit, freed Gertrude, so, too, it allowed Consuelo to solidify her identity. Now free of Sunny's taunts, she established her own country retreat, Crowhurst, a Tudor manor house in the fold of the North Wolds. She quickly impressed her personality on it by adding rooms, filling them with chintzed-covered chairs and period furniture polished to a honeyed sheen, and surrounding it with gardens of herbs, roses, irises, and spring color. Compared to Blenheim's endless hallways and cavernous salons, it was cozy, domestic, of the humane scale she wanted her boys to enjoy on their visits from school.

She needed its calming refuge, for she filled her London weekdays with benevolent work. Though less affected by immigration than the States, Londoners were in the midst of something akin to a Progressive movement. Its philosophy, combined with Consuelo's innate compassion, set Consuelo to improving the health, housing, and education of poor women and their children. Her first project was the Home for Prisoners Wives, who were left without any resources from the state while their husbands were incarcerated. This institution included a laundry and sewing shop where the women could work for the small standard wage while their children were cared for in the adjoining nursery. Consuelo acted as informal social worker, interviewing the women and their husbands when released and dispensing financial aid when she deemed it worthy, which was often. She also officiated over the prayers that were required at the end of the workday. The success of this venture would lead to other philanthropies, including a recreation home for working girls, the Mary Curzon Lodging House for Poor Women, and upon hearing the difficulties women doctors faced getting hospital appointments, a hospital staffed by female physicians.

During the Boer War, the English were stunned to learn that sixty percent of their men were judged unfit for service, hence could not defend the empire. They became preoccupied with such signs of "deterioration and degeneracy" of their "race." It was the poor, of course, whose malnutrition made unfitness. At the same time, the birthrate among middle and upper classes was falling. Consequently, many commentators, including Socialists, pressed for an investigation. Consuelo was the only layperson appointed to a national commission of inquiry on the problem. Three subtexts underlie the national concern: the reduction in taxes that would follow if the poor propagated less, the decline in "good Anglo-Saxon stock," which was being outpopulated by the working class, and the assertion of more independence by women. Herbert Spencer's race consciousness was rampant in England as well as in the United States, provoking the rise of eugenicists (those expounding the "science" of being well born) who attacked the upper-class's low birthrate for "race suicide" and selfishness.

The reason for the drop in fertility by the better-off was birth control. Although illegal—indeed referred to as the "American sin" by English medical moralists of the 1880s—physicians catering to the wealthy provided the necessary information nonetheless. Notwithstanding the particular method (withdrawal or condom) could involve the male partner, critics blamed women alone for the lower fertility rate. Many British would have seconded Theodore Roosevelt's assertion in this regard, "The woman who flinches from childbirth stands on a par with the soldier who drops his rifle and runs from battle."[41]

Consuelo was sympathetic to eugenics because she daily saw underfed and chronically ill children at her various charities. She advocated maternity and infant care services to ensure that poor children would start off life in better condition. A supporter of racial theories, she spoke out publicly that despite "the need to preserve and increase the Anglo-Saxon stock of the world" Christian ethics dictated "the preservation of infant life."[42] The obvious implication of her plea was that some of her audience believed poor children should be neglected and allowed to die.

During winters in London she sought out the companionship of intellectuals, Socialists, and reformers. Although she later intimated she frequently dined with such figures as George Bernard Shaw, novelist John Galsworthy, poet W. B. Yeats, playwright James Barrie, and writer H. G. Wells, she was not discussed in the diaries and letters of the set. In 1905, Consuelo had taken Sunny with her to hear social activist Sydney Webb speak, and she invited him and his partner Beatrice to Blenheim. Despite her Socialist leanings, Beatrice Webb was a snob who was attracted to titles and deplored bad table manners. Nonetheless, she found Consuelo and Sunny "somewhat futile young persons floating aimlessly on the surface of society . . . swayed to and fro by somewhat silly motives."[43] She suspected Consuelo was using her as a means of meeting Shaw. On the other hand, Shaw did have sufficient contact with Consuelo to inspire her to do fundraising on behalf of a national theatre. Yet even if these figures played a small role in her life, their conversations would have reinforced her impluse toward social reform.

Struck by the poor education of even the wealthiest and most aristocratic women in Britain, another of Consuelo's causes was female education. Schooling would result in better mothering, hence better eugenics, she inferred. In accepting the unpaid post as treasurer, actually fund-raiser, of Bedford College for women, she compared America to England favorably in this regard. Musing why Englishmen should have such rooted objections to their sisters' and daughters' learning, she quipped, "There must be some secret fear that, hard as they found it to understand a woman now, it would be absolutely beyond their ken were she highly educated."[44] A well-known humorist for *Punch* replied with four verses from a man's viewpoint, which included the following:

> I was never schooled at Bedford College,
> I was nursed at Balliol's homely knee;
> Therefore make allowance for the mental
> Lapses which invite your lips to laugh,
> And, as you are strong, be very gentle
> To your better half.[45]

Consuelo took no offense; she had learned Alva's technique that a sense of humor can be more persuasive than ridicule.

Her social causes allowed Consuelo publicly to play the Vestal Virgin, the all-good and pure woman, while in her private life she explored the Cleopatra side she had once shared with Gladys. One of Consuelo's lovers was Reginald Fellowes, who happened to be a first cousin of Sunny's. He was also six years younger than Consuelo, and his parents were put out that she was tying him up during a time when he should be selecting a wife. Although Sunny was now involved with Gladys Deacon, and had even informed his lawyers to take care of her in case anything happened to him, he complained to friends about Consuelo's romances, which he felt reflected badly on the family name.

The Feminists
Strike Out

Consuelo's particular interests imply that she was a feminist. Although she later disclaimed a strong commitment in this regard, her actions prove otherwise. This was a time in England of a clamorous and tenacious outcry by women seeking the right to vote. As in the United States, two factions acted simultaneously. The smaller but more visible bloc was the Women's Social and Political Union. This organization had been started in 1903 by Emmeline Pankhurst, widow of a prominent Manchester lawyer, and her daughter Christabel. Their motto was, "Deeds not words."[46] Thus the Pankhursts disputed the majority of suffrage activists, known as the Constitutionalists, whose strategy was to work within the law to change the law.

The Pankhurst minority, which called themselves suffragettes, at first used their Women's Political and Social Union to influence elections. Their first major effort was to unseat Winston Churchill, who in late 1905 was running for Member of Parliament representing North-West Manchester. The Pankhursts were from Manchester, and they fingered Winston as scapegoat for their attack on the Liberal party. Consequently, wherever he appeared, Winston sputtered more than usual before a crowd dotted with white banners reading, "Votes for Women," whose bearers would take any interruption in his speech to heckle. After one such meeting, Annie Kenney and Christabel Pankhurst were arrested. Winston went over to Strangeways Gaol to pay the prisoners' fines, but they chose a night behind bars instead. Despite his conciliatory move, the women persisted in disrupting Winston's speeches, no doubt aware his action was not heartfelt. One evening in exasperation he sputtered a taunt that most accurately revealed his position: "Nothing would induce me to vote for giving women the franchise. I am not going to be henpecked on a question of grave importance."[47]

While the Pankhursts failed to unseat Winston, they gained in both morale and momentum for their actions. In time, they would move to more radical tactics, beginning with protest marches and soapbox speeches, and when these mild challenges brought only police strong-arming and government threats, they moved to more assertive tactics. Knowing the devotion of parliamentarians to golf, they uprooted the sacred greens. They smashed windows in plant conservatories, poured acid into mailboxes of prominent men, set unattended homes of politicians on fire, blew up fuse boxes, cut telegraph lines, and even attacked members of government with whips or bare hands. These actions resulted in repeated arrests. While jailed, the women went on hunger strikes, which compelled the government either to force-feed the women or release them. This continual embarrassment of the government gradually won sympathizers from the larger and once-antagonistic public.

In her memoir Consuelo particularly discredited the radical tactics of the Pankhurst crew, whom she intimated were man haters. That criticism had two implications. One was the common accusation that the suffragettes were sexually embittered or atrophied, hence contributing to race suicide. When Emmeline Pankhurst proclaimed, "Votes for women and chastity for men," she upset the eugenicists. "Man hater" also had another meaning, one Consuelo would have known about, for several prominent suffragettes were lesbians. In fact, Emmeline Pankhurst had an affair with composer Ethel Smyth. A woman who espoused sexual purity, Consuelo was personally repulsed by these aspects of the suffragettes.

Yet while this upheaval was going on, she wrote a long article for *The North American Review* that belies her utter rejection of the radicals. "The Position of

Women" is an erudite review of woman's status over time to "follow her through the gradual narrowing and restricting of her sphere to the present day, when woman is at length attempting to re-establish the balance of primitive rights."[48] Referring to others' research, she noted that women "became an unfree class" at that point in history "when chronic militancy developed an organization among the males."[49] She concluded from her extensive reading into different cultures and times that women were the first social organizers, the constructive element of community that was driven out by men, who "robbed woman of the power, strength, and influence she could have exerted."

Examining particular cases, she drew pointed conclusions. Of Asian societies, she said, "[S]urely blind obedience is not the school to produce a sense of responsibility or a moral code to fit for others than slaves." In the Old Testament she found women of individuality, such as Miriam, "not a female cipher," honored among her people though an agitator. Noted Greek women, such as Sappho and Aspasia, had come down "slandered by the Comic [Greek] writers of the time" because they "wrote chiefly for men." Roman women did not hesitate to poison "a ferocious or undesirable husband." And she saw a parallel between one Roman woman, Hortensia, and the Pankhursts, for both "demonstrated" for woman's enfranchisement.

Consuelo squarely placed the source of Western woman's restrictions on early Christianity, whose leaders overturned the early sexual equality of the church to force women out of leadership. Rather, they reviled women as carnal, with only virgins, deaconesses, and martyrs being exempt from male condemnation. As a result woman's experience became more cramped and narrow, one of pure domesticity.

Following woman's achieving the vote, her first reform must be "to establish a moral standard for women in which every iota will not be relative to the sex question." In other words, she urged equal rights, a notion very few moderate activists were considering. With these rights should go a rejection of the imagery of "meekness and docility." More specifically, women needed to band together, whatever their class. Working women should quit selling "their work at half its worth and in blind perversity [lower] the standard of wages." Instead, they should join the trade union movement. As for the suffragettes: "It is because womanly measures have failed to open the gates that they have resorted to more masculine ones. Not because they enjoy going to prison or making themselves objectionable, but because they know that no great reform has ever been brought about without public agitation of a more or less aggressive character on the part of those directly concerned. If you have a sore and hide it, you are not likely to be admitted to a hospital." And it was particularly incumbent upon educated, independent women, self-supported or well-to-do, to fight for "the great class of struggling, suffering, unvoiced womanhood, too weak to cry out, too downtrodden to rebel, too uneducated to understand, but not too insensitive to suffer." These are hardly the words of one who claimed later to have professed the Pankhursts and their ilk were "distressing exhibitions of martyrdom."[50]

This was a remarkable essay for the duchess of Marlborough, and had any such words been expressed at the dinner tables of most aristocrats, she would have faced an embarrassed silence followed by a sudden change of topic. It was even a strong statement for most feminists of the day. For one, rather than perpetuate the commonly held canard that women were somehow very different from men, she implied women could express masculine virtues. Also, at a time in the United States when moderation was the rule among suffragists, she forthrightly supported her "aggressive" British sister activists.

In fact, Consuelo had always leaned toward feminism, and her unhappy marriage with Sunny stirred a veiled hostility toward patriarchal men. Remember that Alva not only supported women's rights, but, if anything, believed in the natural superiority of the female. Certainly Consuelo's perception of the various needs of British women was colored by this parental philosophy. (It is hard to imagine a Gertrude or Grace in her position responding in kind.) Indeed, Consuelo had only to look to her mother's own social projects in New York City for models and guidance. There Alva went daily to the soup kitchen she had started, where she helped feed women clothed only in a skirt, ragged coat, shoes with bare toes sticking out, old straw hats, and newspapers for underclothes. The frequent insults of the prostitutes did not deter her, for she understood their struggles. She spoke with the girls, such as the four who shared a closet in a tenement as their sole abode, meaning they must sleep on a rotation basis. It was not long before the kitchen was giving away more than food.

Christ Calls,
Alva Follows

In 1908, a tragedy befalling Alva further strengthened the bond between mother and daughter and their mutual work on behalf of women. That summer, while Harry and Alva were packing to spend the summer in England, he was struck down with appendicitis and as had happened with William Whitney succumbed to the ubiquitous killer, peritonitis following the operation. (One of the cruelest claims repeated in references mentioning Alva is that she drove him to death with her overpowering manner. This bizarre misrepresentation, so easily disproved, illustrates the extreme caricaturing of her in the literature of the time.)

Alva lost no time ordering a permanent resting place for Harry and eventually herself. She chose a spot at Woodlawn, New York's society cemetery, on a slight rise near the west gate, where she commissioned Hunt and Hunt to create a chapel inspired by the fifteenth-century Saint Hubert's Chapel of Amboise in the south of France, built for Charles VIII.[51] (In 1878 the bones of Leonardo da Vinci, who died in Amboise, were moved to rest within its walls.) The forests of

Amboise had long been the site of royal hunts, consequently the chapel's decorations emphasized horses, stags, and hounds. Since Harry had been an ardent follower of the hounds, he particularly admired this architectural beauty and visited it whenever they were in France.

It would be almost four years before the limestone structure was completed. Its spire rose sixty-five feet from the ground, capping a Gothic roof replete with crosses, staghorns, and fierce animal gargoyles. Typical of such designs, the ground plan was a Greek cross. The interior was lit through sixteen stained-glass windows designed and created by Helen Maitland Armstrong, who followed Alva's orders that they be done in a fifteenth-century technique, wherein images are painted on clear glass of the same thickness, the leads of various sizes. (American glass of the period was using layers of colored glass connected by uniform leading, with an emphasis on realism in the design.) When the interior was completed, artisan William Mackay worked for over a year transforming the cement interior into a smoke-incensed, weather-stained appearance, following Alva's plan to include even stains from simulated leaks in the roof. This aging process was applied to polychromed altar statues as well.

After the burial, Alva fled to Europe, accompanied by a nurse, her son William, and his wife. "I was ill for a long time," her only comment on that period, was a tremendous understatement for her grief.[52] She went into seclusion at Consuelo's home.

Eleven years later, in a letter to a friend who had lost a young son, Alva reflected upon her loss of Harry. It was a rarely stated expression of how her religious faith directed her social action. With the loss of "the light of my life," she faced "a dreadful doctrine but, Oh! so wise so perfect," namely that Christ had determined she could no longer have earthly love but must "work for all mankind." Thus her friend should follow her model, "Weep, weep and weep—and rise from those tears the New Woman. For women are to grieve no more, we have borne the sorrows of the world, we have lived, that others might live and now this shall not be." Only a few are chosen to do the work so that "woman will one day come into the open, more fortified, more what the future calls for."[53] Arriving in London when the Pankhursts' rebellious actions were on the front pages, she clearly saw her future.

10

1908-1914

Greenwich Village Beckons
Alva and Gertrude

It was a time, as Gertrude Stein noted, "when everything cracks, where everything is destroyed, everything isolates itself." If Alva Belmont or Gertrude Whitney now went out in the city for a luncheon date, instead of clambering into a horse-drawn carriage, each easily slid into the seat of a chauffeured automobile. Their clothes were more comfortable, the skirts fuller for ease of walking and hemmed a few inches above the ground so there was no need to lift them away from mud or puddle. Their lingerie had fewer bones to poke and restrict. If need be, they could cancel the appointment at the last minute by telephone instead of by the slower footman messenger. While placing the call they could use safer and brighter electric light (gas being still in use among the middle class and the poor).

During a trip down the avenues, the women would see the swing of wrecking balls, hear their thud followed by the crash of brick. Where the Madison Square Presbyterian Church once stood was a fifty-story life insurance building. The Singer Building and Woolworth Tower, now under construction, commemorated the glories of capitalism, while other towers rose over Wall Street in adoration of finance and banking. Templelike train stations disgorged crowds of commuters from Connecticut and New Jersey. The women's old haunts, certain exclusive restaurants and hotels, had fallen as well, to be replaced by larger, grander versions. At night, they might ride down Broadway, whose brilliant lights earned it the epithet Great White Way, to see the throngs of society, financiers, playboys, gold diggers, celebrities, chorus girls, gangsters, pickpockets, prostitutes of both sexes, and dope peddlers. Their long dead ancestors would have considered this display of hedonism proof the world was coming to an end, and to be sure, neither Alva nor Gertrude would stop at any of the hot spots.

They might, however, order their cars south, down to a section of the city that resisted modernization. Their destination was Greenwich Village, that neighborhood surrounding Washington Square, which included the onetime home of the Commodore. In recent years the now-seedy spacious Georgian mansions and town houses of earlier society had been divided into apartments and shabby rooming houses. Artists were attracted to the alley carriage houses, whose ample open spaces provided perfect studios. Writers and social radicals moved in for the cheap and simple fare of the spaghetti houses and cafés, the humane scale of the street scene. Among these rebels were many children of the affluent, graduates of Ivy League schools hell-bent for change in art, politics, gender definitions, and sexuality. Thus the papers decried Max Eastman, son of noted Congregationalist minister, and Ida Rauh, an escapee from the uptown brownstone elite, for the scandalous act of marrying yet retaining separate names.

Women were major catalysts of this change. The chief formal intellectual center was the Liberal Club, which met at Polly's Restaurant on MacDougall Street, south of the square. There leading spirit Harriet Rodman, in cropped hair and sandals, stunned authorities with her cries for woman's suffrage, free love, and socialism. There artists, writers, and political activists stirred continual fervor to toss out the old order where two percent of the families controlled 60 percent of the wealth of the nation while over a third of the families lived close to starvation. (The radicals were not unique to New York. During this time, Socialists all over the country were garnering the highest percentage of votes for their party ever in U.S. history, as well as controlling some city councils.)

These rebels were as much devoted to play and self-expression as to political upheaval, taking as their rallying cry Walt Whitman's *Song of the Open Road* with its paean to "health, defiance, gayety, self-esteem, curiosity." They produced plays, magazines, poetry readings, exhibitions, books, and manifestos laden with such words as *emotion, intuition, experiment, freedom,* and *liberation.* They created frolicsome Pagan Routs, where they dressed as nymphs and satyrs to thumb their nose at uptown "Puritans."

In 1913, another female Village leader emerged, Mabel Dodge, whose salon "Evenings" in her beautiful white French drawing room launched the latest cause, be it birth control, free speech, modern art, psychoanalysis, labor unionism, or anarchism. Dodge, a wealthy woman of the same creative instincts as Gertrude, took a more common path for women of their type, that of restricting her imagination, intensely concentrating on her self-presentation, and attaching herself to vital, creative men. While we do not know if either Gertrude or Alva ever attended Mabel's soirees, they would have known of her through friends. While appreciating Mabel's enthusiasms, they would have understood her unstated frustration and sense of unfulfillment that came from playing the social matron role, though to a more raggedy and polyglot set of guests.

It had not taken Gertrude long to notice the vitality of life around Washington Square. In 1907, following her revived commitment to art, she bought an old carriage house on MacDougall Alley. This charming gaslit cul-de-sac with its ivy-colored houses was a favorite of artists, whose doors were often open for the painter next door or sculptor across the way to stop in and chat, for parties to form spontaneously. They included James Earle Fraser, her onetime teacher, and Daniel Chester French, her good friend who was also the most popular sculptor of the day. These and others on the block were however, not artistic experimenters but traditionalists whose work would have found ready home in the National Academy expositions.

With the purchase of the MacDougall studio, Gertrude came into her own professionally. Instead of working alone on her imposing cloistered estates, she was now among her colleagues, sometimes even staying over at the studio, and as equal with them as could be possible given the curious circumstance of her wealth. Some in the neighborhood resented her, thought her a dilettante, an opinion furthered by their ignorance that she had been exhibiting for several years, though under an assumed name. If she knew of this condescension, she closed her eyes to it. Her critics may also have mistaken her shyness for snobbery, and they would have been astonished to learn that this carefully groomed woman was a playful practical joker among her closest friends. For example, she would dress up as a hobbling old woman for an appointment to surprise the companion who of course would not recognize her.

Most important, MacDougall was grand, spacious, allowing her to imagine large, monumental sculptures, the format she admired in Hendrik Andersen. No more puttering over little things! Malvina Hoffman, who also sculpted at a studio in the Alley, stopped by and was impressed by, and possibly envious of, the array of glistening saws and chisels, turntables, benches, and full lighting. "The whole atmosphere of the place excited me and filled me with awe. Mrs. Whitney herself, tall, thin, and fragile in appearance, worked tirelessly but was never too busy to help young sculptors."[1] More cynical was painter John Sloan, who referred to her as "the rich sculptor—at least she has a fine studio for the purpose," although he would soon change his tune.[2]

One of her first creations in McDougall was a fountain figure of Pan that was submitted to the Architectural League of New York, where it won first prize. The exhibit was part of a collaboration with mural painter Hugo Ballin and architect Grosvenor Atterbury, and the award was unfortunately disputed when it was revealed that Atterbury had himself headed the judging committee. This irregularity with its hint of favoritism brought further discrediting of Gertrude, who was humiliated to find herself the brunt of a satirical poem in *Town Topics,* one verse of which went as follows:

> But a studio is a proper thing,
>   And I'm primed chock full with bids;
> My praises all the journals sing,
>   I'm great on carytids;
> I love the appreciative stare

Of critic friends and lauders
'Tis facile for a millionaire
To be assure of orders.[3]

If some tittered, architects did not. This was a time when sculpture was an essential component of building design, and these designers were the gatekeepers for major commissions. While painters had to face the judgment of gallery owners, sculptors had to confront the blunt opinion of architects, and there was considerable competition for their assignments. Gertrude was at a disadvantage not only because of the disparaging gossip that she was an amateur but because many expected her to work for free, which she would not do. Overcoming these obstacles, she found herself with steady work for fountains and bas-reliefs.

Gertrude Becomes a
Part-time Expatriate

Gertrude's other artistic base was Paris, which had fallen on such hard times in recent decades that its population had actually stagnated and the city grown disheveled. Perhaps for those very reasons, along with its cheap living costs, it was attracting foreign composers, writers, artists, and political thinkers who shared a passion for experimentation and liberation. Desiring a break from what they called "patriarchy," "bourgeois values," and "central authority," they created a subculture venerating youth, homosexuality, sensuality, the unconscious, and the primitive. This spirit of this avant garde tantalized Gertrude, who went alone to expose herself to the stimulating challenge as well as to gain more distance from the pull of family and society in the States. Paris would provide her most significant mentors.

During a visit in 1908 with her model Edgar McAdams, whom she now helped in his own career as a sculptor, she went to a café hangout where she was introduced to another improverished young artist, Jo Davidson. Davidson had started out as a pyrographer, burning artistic landscapes and portraits onto leather or wood. Following a brief stay at Yale Medical School, he returned to New York, where he attended art school and apprenticed himself at a sculpting studio where he met English sculptor John Gregory. Recently involved in an unconsummated flirtation with the ruggedly handsome Gregory, Gertrude was delighted to learn that Davidson knew him as well.

The differing accounts of that evening show how a strong friendship can emerge from very disparate and self-centered aims. Like most ambitious young male artists, Davidson's talk was all about himself and his creativity. It was easy to sell himself, as he later recalled, because Gertrude "was extraordinary, how she gave one the feeling that what you did was the only thing that mattered."[4] Although he thought she was fascinated with his sculpting, she was titillated to be in the company of someone else who would talk warmly of her secret love. (After the meeting she wrote a long amorous letter to Gregory describing the encounter and how it aroused her desire for him.) Fortunately, once the subjects of sculpture and John Gregory were exhausted, the ebullient, bearlike Davidson entranced her with his songs and poems in various languages, his well-formed ideas on many topics. The next day she visited his studio and bought a bust of a young woman. He would be a steady colleague (but never a lover) over the years, the relationship never imbalanced by the fact of her continuing patronage.

Another friend was the duchesse de Choiseul, who, though not an artist, was the lover of the aged master Rodin. The American-born duchesse was known for her exotic dress, feathers, and readiness to break into a striptease dance. In other words, she enacted some of Gertrude's secret fantasies. Attracted by Gertrude's money, the duchesse permitted Gertrude to meet Rodin. The visit to his studio was a success, and not only because Gertrude purchased one of his most erotic statues of lovers kissing. As Rodin later commented to a friend, he found Gertrude an exception among his foreign artist visitors, for she "has the true vocation: and she has the gift, that mysterious gift, in order to hold within herself, by faithful work every day."[5] Rodin visited Gertrude's studio several times, and he left her with small models for study purposes.

Interestingly, there is no evidence that Gertrude associated with other artistic American women expatriates in Paris. It is not surprising that she would ignore Edith Wharton, who, though critical of American Society, settled for the rarified and narrow French salon scene. More curious is her apparent lack of contact with Gertrude Stein and Alice B. Toklas, for Jo Davidson was part of their circle (and would sculpt one of the most famous portraits of Stein). Nor are there signs she crossed paths with writer Natalie Barney's lesbian set. She may have met such women, but found there were too many demands on her time to develop close connections with them.

Despite Gertrude's passion for sculpture, she carved out time for creativity by segmenting her year into discrete periods for Harry and the children and others for work. During the winter she continued her frequent attendance at opera, dinner parties, and hosting of weekends at Westbury. In the summer she would relax for at least several weeks with the family at the Adirondacks camp, doing no art, often not even writing. This period of fishing and picnicking was the only time she was freed of schedules and pressures from work or others. Harry preferred sporty England to France and went there usually twice a year, often with the children. Gertrude would leave Paris to join them, albeit unhappily, for she could sense the English repugnance toward her bohemian style. Only in Paris was she relatively free of her family, yet even there she would have visits from one or another of them. Consequently, Gertrude could not work consistently at her art as her many male friends could. It was the familiar story of the woman artist.

Unlike most women artists, however, she could afford to arrange her work environment to her convenience. All of her studios followed the model of her first one in Paris, at 72 Boulevard Flandrin. Spare and simple, its largest space was the studio room, off of which was a tiny dining room for intimate dinners with a few artist friends, a spacious bedroom, and modern bath. The furniture was eclectic, combining antiques from various periods with Chinese panels, art of varying styles, and her own sculpture. The impression was not one of clutter but of a mind that knew itself and had selected and placed each object with unquestioned authority. If anything, the impression was one of underdecorating, of regal monasticism.

Gertrude's daily schedule in Paris was similarly monastic. Taking only a cook and a maid, who kept out of her way during the day, her daily schedule seldom varied: studio work predominating, with breaks for a roller-skate in the Bois, lunch, and a daily massage. If the children were in town, she would have them stay in another apartment with their caretakers, who would take them out during the day for cultural activities and play. She particularly enjoyed her oldest, Flora, who shared her interest in art, and Gertrude kept her nearby for longer periods. As soon as Flora was old enough to converse with adults, Gertrude introduced her to her many artist friends, further instilling in the girl a passion for contemporary art. (When Gertrude was in New York, she would have Flora brought down to her McDougall studio to join in the small gatherings there.) Harry would show up in Paris as well at times. Nevertheless, she guarded her schedule, preferring her time in the studio to be solitary, apart from the visit of an artistic adviser or lover.

Harry was so busy with his own sporting passions that while he still belittled Gertrude's art, he no longer interfered. In 1909 he had achieved his youthful goal of taking his polo team, The Big Four, to win the America Challenge Cup back from the British, who had held it since 1886. This victory brought him a national acclaim that, combined with his successful horse racing stable, would keep him on the front of the sports pages for years. Despite Harry's selfishness, Gertrude knew he wanted her alongside at key matches and races, and she often attended, making his sports their one shared activity. Her presence was, however, a personal act of loyalty, perhaps partly to maintain in public the facade of a successful marriage, for she had little interest in either polo or in racing.

Harry's success on the polo field did bring them a common friend. He commissioned the most accomplished sculptor of horses of the day, Herbert Haseltine, to do a statue of The Big Four, and he brought Haseltine to live at Westbury for the purpose. Urbane, witty, and Continental in style, he fit in so well with Gertrude and Harry that he eventually had to insist upon eating with the children and the French governess if he was to get any work done. When he was done, he went abroad, where he married an Englishwoman and settled in Paris. His correspondence and company when she was at her Parisian studio were a steady delight over the years.

Gertrude's Secret
Life Thrives

It is remarkable that Gertrude throughout this time sustained a lively array of affairs. One reason is she managed these episodes so carefully that they fell into a predictable pattern. Gertrude understood she had a special power, that even though plain looking, her complexity and mystery could attract anyone who interested her, and from her adolescent days she was practiced in setting the lure. She had no lack of objects: her models, fellow artists, even men in her social set. Once brought in, the lover would be disarmed by her surprising intimate revelations, her soul baring as it were, and hints at her readiness to bare herself in other ways. Meetings must necessarily be furtive; conveniently, her studios included couches or bedrooms. In some cases she would tease, refuse to consummate the relationship, yet continue to express passion. In other cases she would agree to sexual activity but would firmly regulate the circumstances. Naturally, it was she who broke off the relationship.

Most of her lovers accepted her having the upper hand. If artists themselves, they had wives or lovers who were likely to be bohemian feminists who praised free love for treating women more fairly than marriage (often described in their circles as "legalized prostitution"). In that set, one went into a relationship understanding it may not be permanent, nor would it imply fidelity on either one's part. Similarly, adultery had a long history among men of her class, though it would be less common to take as a lover a friend's wife. Nonetheless, Gertrude successfully flirted with Harry's friends. And when Gertrude put an end to the sexual intimacy, any preexisting friendship normally continued.

An example would be sculptor Andrew O'Connor, Jr., whom she had known since he made the doors in memory of her father, and she eventually had an affair with him in Paris in 1910.[6] A rugged, stocky redhead, he had since married and had four sons. The sexual relationship began when she asked him to her studio to advise her on a statue.[7] During that first visit he posed and strutted so outlandishly while declaiming his theory of art that she thought him a bit mad. At the next visit she sensed he wanted something from her ("money?"), yet "what difference does it make if I get what I want from him [artistically]." She felt he had "something big to give me" and told a friend she was going to make him fall in love with her. She admired his talent, his sincerity, and his critical approval of her work.

Late one afternoon she showed him nude photographs of herself, poses for another artist, and he responded that they were "among the most beautiful things he had ever seen." She realized his comment was a code for indicating his attraction to her sexually. As the sun set and the room darkened, she reclined on her sofa, he hovering above as he spoke. She felt compelled to reach up and pull him down and had a feeling "it will come—we will care, it *must* be." After a while she felt frightened, and when he turned to leave, she asked him to take her along to the cafés. By evening's end she sensed from him "that of all the things in the world that one might do being with me like that was the best." It was not a feeling she had known with Harry.

Besides becoming her lover, O'Connor became her unpaid teacher, directing on the construction of muscles, the play of light, the way to carve vitality into a piece. He said if she worked hard she could become the greatest woman sculptor. To Gertrude he was a "Dream Man," the "lost complement of myself that I have found." She returned to the States "changed and softened."

On her next visit to Paris she hardly saw him and the next time hardly at all because his family was sick and he not well either. She did not care; she had gotten what she wanted, a new approach to her modeling and acceptance both sexually and artistically. They remained lifelong friends.

It was a different matter with John Gregory, who, after three years of being very much second place in her life, terminated the affair. He observed astutely, "You offer me the sincere contact of one third of your life, for which you have told me there are three worlds in which you dwell, in exchange for my completeness—I think that an imposition. Do you think I'm flattered to escort you to Bohemia?"[8] Suddenly aware their relationship would never be as exclusive or complete as he wished, he bowed out, though they maintained their friendship. The only man with a chance of playing a role in more than a third of Gertrude's life remained the elusive Harry, and when he showed no interest in that third, she would allow no other men as much space as she offered her husband.

Gregory's withdrawal occurred just as Gertrude was getting ready to attend Dorothy Whitney's wedding on September 7, 1911. Dorothy's choice of husband, Willard Straight, had left Harry sputtering, but she was of age, now independently wealthy, and he could not interfere. A *New York Times* subhead best summarizes Straight's apparent deficiency: "A Career That Leads Like Romance Is That of the Missionary's Son Who Became a Figure in Finance, Politics, and International Affairs, and Who Won the Love of Two Haeiresses."[9] A fortune hunter, in other words. The heiress had been Mary Harriman, whose father, railroad magnate E. H. Harriman, encouraged the young man's diplomatic career, yet squelched his romance with his daughter. Straight's taking up with Dorothy so soon after did not endear him to Harry, who was proved wrong, for the marriage resulted a rich intellectual communion. (Dorothy and Willard Straight would two years later join with writer Herbert Croly to found *The New Republic*.)

Gertrude's major fiction from the period depicted her secret erotic life as well. In 1911 she handed Juliana Rieser the manuscript of a novella, *White Voices,* and asked her to explore its publication. To ensure an unbiased opinion, she put the pseudonym "Phyllis Lane" on the cover page. The story was so close to certain actual incidents that some of Gertrude's artist friends who read it worried that the characteristics of the heroine would too readily reveal the author of this tale of sexual arousal and repression and cause her great damage if it did appear. (This was, it must be remembered, a time when one of the country's most famous writers, Jack London, was accused of "erotomania" for even hinting at sexuality. Mrs. Grundy ruled the editorial boards.)

The plot of *White Voices* indeed matched Gertrude's life closely. It concerns a wealthy woman tired of her social life who conceives of posing nude, though masked, for a sculptor who will not seek to learn her identity. She confesses this impluse to an artist friend of hers, modeled after Howard Cushing, who after weighing the sexual and economic dangers involved, agrees to set up the arrangement. As a "Miss Smith" she models for a sculptor named Burns, a fictional version of John Gregory. Burns becomes aroused by her lithe, lily white body, her lovely hands and feet. When the heroine, who has been stirred sexually as well, withdraws from his declaration of love, he destroys the statue. At the conclusion, she coolly invites him to visit her and her husband sometime, to which he replies, "Goodbye forever—elusive, lovely, impossible—goodbye Dream Girl."

Despite Juliana Rieser's tireless attempts to sell the manuscript, it found no home, and understandably so. As with so much of Gertrude's fiction, *White Voices* successfully limned the nuances of particular encounters, but it lacked in most other literary regards. Quite simply, she was never good at disclosing motives, so her characters moved around stories like puppets. This inability to see inside the minds of different personalities suggests a reason for the difficulties Gertrude encountered in her own relationships, particularly that with Harry, namely, a lack of empathy. This failing also accounts for the common perception of her as cold, much like the heroine of her story. All those years of secretly reproaching her mother's remoteness, all those pages of astute self-analysis in her journals, had failed to unthaw Gertrude's own chilly demeanor.

The Sculptor
Matures

By 1911 a new, larger studio was also going up on Gertrude's Westbury property, providing a hideaway from even her bohemian friends. Of Italian Rennaissance design, it proved to be one of the most successful creations of architects Chester Holmes Aldrich and William Adams Delano. Returning from

Paris that year she was annoyed by New York City, the impassiveness of its buildings, streets and people, the tone of "winter, coldness, mental & moral frugalities."[10] The sight of flowers in an expressman's wagon brought to mind Parisian markets with their fat-stomached women and playful children, the purple and pink anemones she always bought. Paris was life, color, the representation of beauty.

Approaching Westbury, she ordered her driver to let her out so she could walk the last mile and a half through the woods alone. She yearned to be naked, imagined herself a Diana taking "long, long strides" off to play a trick on Pan and the nymphs. Hiking the rough muddy road toward her new studio she thought how certain words possess charm because of vibratory sound or association. The word *studio* "represented joy, freedom—the delicious intimate life of myself, my being in secret places." It was the place where "one risked much, and finally, as controlling a large expense, even a possible life, freedom to move without consideration for the world. And in the end, a place with no limitations except one's own." Reaching the stone steps of the building, she threw herself down in supplication, sensing "no other lover ever embraced me more passionately than the emotion that overcame me. I gave up my lips, my eyes, my hands."

Had her lovers read Gertrude's letters to them more carefully, they would have readily seen her placing art before all else. Most important during this period was the fountain she was constructing for the New Arlington Hotel, versions of which would be made in other sizes and materials for other locations. Like many sculptors constructing large works, her main role was to sketch, plan, and create models that skilled craftsmen (*practiciens*) would recreate under her guidance.[11] For a large marble piece, for example, she would establish key placement points on the block to direct her Italian stonecutters. If the work involved casting a bronze, she would oversee the process and make changes along the way as needed.

Up to this point her work was inspired by two disparate influences, the classical sculpture of Greece and Rome and that of Rodin. Her technique quickly matured and her bust *Spanish Peasant* was accepted for the prestigious Paris Spring Salon in 1911. By 1912, primarily due to the urgings of Andrew O'Connor, Gertrude was ready to explore other styles. O'Connor had argued that the classicists had exhausted the possibilities of their aesthetics, that contemporary sculptors needed to find their own aesthetic to make new statements.

Chinoise was her first clear break with the past. A gilded Buddha-like figure of a woman, its highly stylized fluid lines reflected both the orientalism and modernism in vogue then in Paris. This was the heyday of the Diagilev's Ballet Russe, whose colorful expressionist costumes and scenery influenced fashion and interior design. (Other sculptors of the day, similarly influenced, also turned out Oriental themes. Both Ida McClelland Stout and Lucy Ripley created Chinese female Buddha figures reminiscent of Gertrude's.) The exoticism of the Oriental particularly appealed to the Parisian artists, who dressed variously in highly patterned caftans, harem pants, kimonos, robes, and even turbans for parties where they reclined on pillows and struck meditative poses. For Gertrude, this vogue meant a new, more comfortable, and colorfully dramatic wardrobe, much of it designed by Paul Poiret and even the noted ballet costumer Leon Bakst.

The most important and best-known expression of Gertrude's shift in style, however, originated in tragedy. On April 12, 1912, the *Titanic* sank, taking down with it men she had come across socially, such as John Jacob Astor and Benjamin Guggenheim. Soon afterward Natalie Hammond, wife of a mining engineer who had been associated with Harry's and Guggenheim's ventures, organized a committee of women to raise money for a memorial to be placed in Washington, D.C. Gertrude helped with a theater benefit and eventually received a commission to create the sculpture.

For this purpose she conceived the cruciform figure of a nude youth (later a drape was added over arms and genital area), the outspread arms expressing both sacrifice and grief. Rather than follow the more realistic expression of musculature in her earlier work, she streamlined the figure as it moved into larger versions. As with most of her monuments, negotiating with the ruling committee, which had its own internal delays, meant the work was ready well before it saw its public. In this case it would be 1930 before the monument was dedicated on the Potomac Parkway.

Gertrude Turns Down the
Fires of Passion

During 1912 a particularly tempestuous affair gave Gertrude second thoughts about her libertine ways with men. The lover was William Stackpole, a stockbroker friend of Harry's whom she had flirted with periodically since 1907. By late 1912 they had a fiery affair, too much so for Gertrude, who referred to him in her letters as "dear child" (he was not that much younger).[12] This was clearly a more erotic relationship than previous ones. She once wrote him, "You have a way, dear, of sweeping aside the conventionalities and of putting the petty out of sight. I accept that in you. I will be a beast with you, I will be a saint with you, I will be low and high, broad and narrow, and that is because we must whether we want it or not be all things to each other. I feel the body of you against my poor quivering soul." As intensely jealous as he was passionate, Stackpole complained that her work and other social appointments took time away from him. She tried to push him away, but despite her effort, she remained drawn to him.

Then she went off to Paris to concentrate on her sculpture, writing him frequently, urging him to follow. While longing for him, she reminded him she

Phebe Hand Vanderbilt, the Commodore's mother, was the only person he respected and honored.

Brilliant, visionary, and audacious, the Commodore was as brutal toward his wife and children as he was toward his competitors.

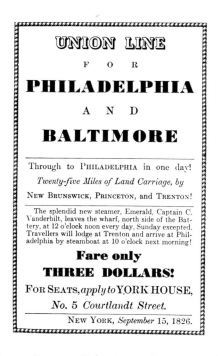

The Vanderbilt fortune began with the Commodore commanding the steamer, while wife Sophia managed the Bellona Inn in New Brunswick.

Although the Commodore thought son William Henry to be inept, he proved even wilier than his father at multiplying the family's fortunes.

Gertrude's father, Cornelius II, was pious, disciplined, and charitable, and expected the same from his children.

Fun-loving on the surface, Willie K. was cruel to Alva, and even brought his mistresses into their homes.

Alice Vanderbilt dressed as
"Electric Light" for sister-in-law
Alva's famous masquerade ball.
(Brown Brothers)

Alice chaperoned daughter Gladys
until her marriage to Count
Szechenyi of Hungary in 1908. *(Brown
Brothers)*

Catherine Hunt believed her husband's early and sudden death was due partly to Alice Vanderbilt's demands and insults during the building of the Breakers. *(Courtesy of Flora Biddle)*

The Breakers featured opulent and ornate rooms such as the music room. *(Preservation Society of Newport County)*

At her 1883 costume ball, Alva managed to do what no other Vanderbilt had done: Get the family accepted into Society. *(Brown Brothers)*

Through 660 Fifth Avenue, designed by Richard Morris Hunt, Alva challenged the rich to express their wealth tastefully rather than vulgarly or ostentatiously. Few could match her. *(Brown Brothers)*

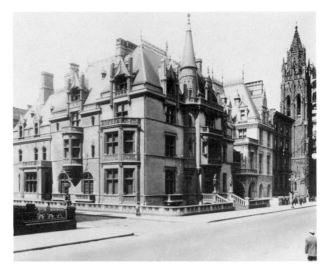

Alva and Richard Morris Hunt's collaboration on Marble House, inspired by the Petit Trianon, reflected their mutual love of French architecture. *(The Preservation Society of Newport County)*

Alva fought with Hunt over every detail of a building, but the results, as with the Gold Ballroom at Marble House, could be extraordinary. *(The Preservation Society of Newport County)*

Alva commissioned this Chinese Tea House to hold fund raisers for suffragism. The porcelain service she designed said "Votes for Women." *(Preservation Society of Newport County)*

Alice Paul proved the perfect partner for Alva's radical suffragism. *(Edith Derwent)*

During a later cruise, O.H.P. Belmont (far left) and Alva (lounging) would fall in love. Consuelo nestles in her father's lap. *(The Vanderbilt Museum)*

Alva at the time of her marriage to O.H.P. Belmont. *(Culver Pictures)*

Even in her seventies, Alva inspired young feminists with her "Valkyrie" stance on behalf of women's rights.
(The Bettmann Archive)

Gertrude in a flower costume, perhaps for Alva's famous 1883 ball. *(Courtesy of Flora Biddle)*

Gertrude (right) and her cousin Adele Sloan Burden, who accepted the social matron role of her class, yet tolerated Gertrude's refusal to conform. *(Courtesy of Flora Biddle)*

Knowing she was not beautiful, Gertrude learned early to attract through her expressive eyes. *(Photograph by Edward Steichen, Courtesy of Flora Biddle)*

Unlike her cousin Consuelo, Gertrude was ecstatic during her honeymoon (here in Japan) and felt she had found the perfect mate in Harry Whitney. *(Courtesy of Flora Biddle)*

Gertrude's sensuality and eroticism bloomed in Paris. Here she wears a costume by Bakst at an Oriental feast in 1913. Sculptor Herbert Haseltine sits at far right. *(Courtesy of Flora Biddle)*

Gertrude's sculpting of nude forms brought censorial comments from Harry, her mother, her friends, and some memorial committees. *(Courtesy of Flora Biddle)*

Sculptor Jo Davidson was one of Gertrude's closest artist friends, but she did not follow her practice by having an affair with him. *(Courtesy of Flora Biddle)*

Gertrude's *The Scout,* in Cody,
Wyoming on the way to Yellowstone,
is the only of her memorials on
prominent view today. *(Courtesy Buffalo Bill
Historical Center, Cody, Wyoming)*

Gertrude's last completed sculpture was her hopeful *Spirit of
Flight,* which was featured at the 1939 World's Fair. By then
her style of sculpture was considered banal. *(Courtesy of Flora Biddle)*

Flora Whitney's sober face during her 1920 marriage to Rod Tower
foretold its unhappy outcome. Sister Barbara (far left) suffered
emotional illness all her life. *(Courtesy of Flora Biddle)*

Gertrude's daughter, Flora Miller, and
granddaughter, Flora Biddle, both served
long terms at the Whitney Museum to
continue the tradition. *(Courtesy of Michelle Evans)*

Gertrude's partnership with the flamboyant and audacious Juliana
Rieser Force secured the reputation of contemporary American
art. *(Whitney Museum of Art, photograph by Cecil Beaton)*

Following years of adultery and
frustrations, Gertrude and Harry grew
devoted in middle age. *(Courtesy of Flora
Biddle)*

was there to work and he must "try not to absorb me too much, for when one's mind is entirely wrapped up in someone, one does not have anything left to put into one's work." When he finally arrived, her response was hardly encouraging: she was very busy on that day but she could manage to see him between four and six. Whether he acceded to that brief encounter is unclear.

That evening she went out to dine with another man—whose identity is unknown—and accepted his invitation to an apartment.[13] A struggle ensued when the man tried to rape her, but she subdued him. On their way out, the concierge reported that two men in a taxi had followed them to the building and asked for her host's name. She suspected Stackpole had sent detectives, and when confronted, he did not deny the story. Apparently this was not the first time he had violated her trust, for she referred to a "dirty trick in N.Y." when she should have ended the affair. She insisted he burn all her letters and leave Paris. He just as furiously attacked her for failing to admit that she was hardly innocent either, behaving like "a spoiled child who has committed the cardinal sin of having been found out." With his usual dramatic overstatement, he pronounced himself "broken, wretched, utterly miserable, insulted, deserted and wronged."

The Stackpole affair was a rare example of Gertrude's getting burned, a situation against which she had warned herself several years earlier. In fact, they continued to be friends. (It would be interesting to know just how they resolved this nasty argument.) Following this tumultuous episode, she grew more cautious and circumspect in her choice of lovers. Perhaps, too, now that she was making a name for herself as a sculptor, she felt less need to seek excitement and a sense of power through these triflings. Such trysts dwindled in frequency, until one day she no longer sought such excitement.

Despite her growing recognition and prominence in the American art world, Gertrude's own work was missing from the show that became a landmark in American art history, the Armory Show that opened on February 17, 1913. Gertrude had been in on the planning for this event since its conception in 1911, when Clara Davidge and Henry Fitch of the Madison Gallery sought a way to bring recognition to progressive, nonacademic artists. Out of this group evolved the Association of American Painters and Sculptors, which organized the show. This exhibit of more than 1,600 paintings, sculptures, drawings, and prints from both European and European-influenced American artists emphasized the Fauves and Cubists, Matisse and Picasso especially dominating. Although Gertrude's bias was for the realists, the Ash Can school and sculptors like Jo Davidson (who were also included), she and Harry's sister Dorothy Straight contributed about a fifth of the total budget.

Today the show is so often discussed in terms of the impact of the Europeans, notably Duchamps *Nude Descending a Staircase,* that the importance of the rebel Americans being included is underplayed. Just why Gertrude was not exhibited is not known. But the work of many of her male friends, whose efforts she certainly matched and in several cases exceeded, was. It may well be, as her granddaughter later argued, "she would have been included as an artist, but frequently wealthy artists pay twice for their patronage, and sometimes wealthy women artists pay a third time when they are subjected to male condescension."[14]

Gertrude was not the sort of woman to let such slights stifle her. She would soon be able to run her own exhibits. Overrun by uninvited visitors, begging artists, tourists, and cranks at her 19 MacDougall studio, she acquired a town house in back of it on 8 West Eighth. This would become the official Whitney Studio, a gallery space, with an office for Juliana, who kept unwanted guests from interrupting Gertrude during her private hours with the clay.

Alva Dons the
Suffrage Mantle

During these formative years as a sculptor, Gertrude could not open a New York newspaper without reading about her estranged Aunt Alva, who had become one of the most prominent women in the nation as well as in the city. Praised or vilified, depending upon the political bent of the paper, Alva had at last found a socially useful outlet for her formidable energy and intelligence. While Gertrude and her mother respected Alva's efforts, they were relieved she no longer bore the name Vanderbilt, but signed herself in honor of Harry, "Mrs. O. H. P. Belmont."

Alone for the first time in her life, Alva's rise to fame was also linked to Greenwich Village, though through a different crowd and under different circumstances than Gertrude's. Upon her return to New York in 1909, she resumed her various charities on behalf of poor women and children. While she acknowledged her efforts "did ameliorate the hardships" of these needy immigrants, she "was forced to come to the conclusion that the amelioration of the slums would, at best, be ephemeral unless the very conditions which created the slums were overcome."[15] The problem, she decided, was that only one-half of the human race was participating in government. The woman at home had no role in directing the cleanliness of streets, in deciding the proximity of saloons, in overseeing the safety of the water coming into her home. "There is no more cruel fallacy of democratic government than that all men are born free and equal. Men and women are equal only when their opportunities for doing good are equal."[16]

Thus one evening she decided to attend a lecture by Ida Husted Harper on the suffrage cause, and she met with Harper soon afterward. As Susan B. Anthony's biographer and a longtime suffrage activist, Harper was an expert on the history of the movement. That night she confessed her concern to Alva that the suffrage cause had "sunk into almost perfect oblivion."[17] Harper's evaluation was only a slight exaggeration. Since 1896 only six state referenda had been held on woman suffrage, and all had lost. No debate on woman suffrage had occurred in the U.S. Senate since 1887, and a suffrage bill had not received a favorable report in committee since 1893.

The major lobbying body of the cause, the National American Woman Suffrage Association, NAWSA, was moribund. Its national headquarters was in Warren, Ohio, simply because that was the residence of the treasurer. Its officers did little between conventions to spark grassroots action. The current president, Dr. Anna Shaw, was a captivating and convincing public speaker, but an inept administrator with a hostile, paranoid bent. Women loved to listen to her and were inspired by her call, yet they found working with her so troublesome that they would quickly quit their volunteer duties.

Alva found much to support Harper's claim the evening she attended a meeting of NAWSA at the Martha Washington Hotel in New York. The audience was "old and convinced suffragists. I could see that this was poor propaganda."[18] Making known her interest in helping the association, she met with Dr. Shaw, who appointed Alva as alternate delegate from New York to the upcoming International Woman's Suffrage Association meetings in London. The women meeting there struck her as serious, respectable, yet too placid. She did not see how the goals of the movement could be accomplished by such politeness. She changed her mind when she heard Emmeline Pankhurst say, "The hour of pleading is past. Now we demand our rights."[19]

She called reporters and began to speak out. In one of her earliest interviews, she said she would esteem it a privilege to go to jail if it would hasten woman suffrage by a single day. Other expressions were equally defiant. Headlines blasted: "Rifle Would Aid Suffrage, Hints Mrs. Belmont"; "All Women Hate Men But Few Fear to Say So, [Says] Mrs. Belmont"; "Mrs. Belmont Expects War Between Men and Woman."

Despite her inflammatory rhetoric, Alva was not yet ready to ape the Pankhursts. While she admired their courage and befriended them, initially Alva was like other American suffragettes of the day, which is to say a constitutionalist, committed to change through law. Thus when she returned, she decided to put both her money and her energies behind NAWSA, and its equivalent New York state organization. Recognizing the importance of sufficient office space, she bought 505 Fifth Avenue, providing it virtually rent free to the two organizations, furnished it, and underwrote the majority of the operating expenses. She also established the National Press Bureau, in the same building, to serve as a major public relations branch of the suffrage movement. This latter creation in itself was to be a significant boost to the cause because it centralized suffrage publicity and sent it out to papers and magazines throughout the country.[20]

In the remaining space she set up her own organization, the Political Equality Association, and made herself president. Her focus was New York City, and her tactic was to establish "suffrage centers" in various neighborhoods, houses, or halls to attract young people by holding meetings, concerts, readings, and discussion groups. Her plan was to broaden the base of the suffrage movement by becoming more accessible to working-class women. (In a clever move, she advertised that women who, for reasons of their own, did not actively desire to be affiliated with the cause, could ask for secret membership. Dues were also whatever women wanted to contribute.) These Suffrage Settlement Houses offered well-appointed and flexible settings where women could support one another both socially and through formal activities. They also included dances and tea rooms to attract men to the cause.

Very unconventionally, Alva's first choice for one of these centers was Harlem. There she bought and remodeled a four-story house at 84 East 111th Street and expressed publicly the importance of including black women in the movement. As she explained to the press, "These efforts cannot be confined to any one locality or class of people because the matter will have to be decided by a majority of all. I have been very glad therefore to help the colored men and women form a suffrage league. Colored men will have a vote on the amendment when it is submitted by the Legislature and this race should be able to use its influence understandingly."[21] What is unusual about this stance is that it recognized that an underlying racism infected suffragism at the time.

It may seem strange that a movement originating with the abolitionist cause had grown to accept the ideology of white superiority. Many changes had fed this odd reversal in civil rights stance. Following the Civil War, original suffrage leaders such as Susan B. Anthony became less convinced that the woman's issue and that of ex-slaves, was tied together, for, after all, the black male had gotten the vote. Since white women were the movement leaders, they gradually narrowed their interests to white concerns. Their efforts opened the doors of colleges to young white women, who were taught social Darwinism and accepted its "scientific" proof of racial superiority. These women being the new blood of the movement, they saw no problem in excluding black women from their activities or program.

Furthermore, if suffrage were to succeed on a federal level, the southern states must be brought in. For this reason, at its 1903 convention, NAWSA created a "states rights" position for the organization, which meant southern chapters could keep black women out of their membership and its speakers could state racist views openly at meetings. Consequently, some NAWSA strategists consciously played off the racism issue in various ways. They would suggest it was unfair for white women to be placed in a subordinate position to black men at the voting booth or that the enfranchisement of white women could ensure white supremacy in the South. Thus Alva's move was a highly visible repudiation of NAWSA policy.

Much can be seen of Alva's political astuteness in her organizing the Harlem branch. Her method was to begin through a meeting at that most important black cultural institution, the church. She organized a program at which the main speaker was Mrs. Henry Villard, daughter of abolitionist William Lloyd Garrison, who had walked out of a World Anti-Slavery Convention held in London in 1840 when he learned women delegates were not being allowed to speak. Included on the dais were presidents of leading black organizations, such as the head of the New York State Federation of Colored Women's Clubs. More than two hundred community women filled the church to see both the famous socialite and the many noted black women leaders.

As the service was about to start, the pastor of the church called for an opening song by the church choir and was embarrassed to discover the singers were not present. Alva arose, went to the podium, and said she would be happy to do the honors, provided I. L. Moorman, president of the Negro Women's Business League, join with her. Their duet, "Jesus, Lover of My Soul," surely warmed any suspicious hearts in the audience.

Alva's introduction of Villard was brief. Like many speeches she was to give over the years, it made its point in simple and powerful argument: "Washington, with his army of patriots, fought for the liberty of all the people, and later the States enfranchised some classes of men, but forgot all the mothers of the race. Lincoln gave freedom to the negro people, and the Republican Party later enfranchised the negro man, but ignored both the white and colored mothers of this land. The woman suffrage movement has higher aims than any that even the greatest of these men ever attained, for it demands the emancipation and freedom of all human beings—women and men of every race, creed, and station."[22]

Villard rose to remind the women that her father had helped black women find pulpits from which to speak against slavery, then appealed to the women present to join in the battle, which was not just for women's rights, but for human rights, because "the weak will be helped." Over half the women at the meeting joined the Political Equality League that night.

Yet it must be remembered that Alva had been raised a southerner, a girl who had accepted slaves as normal, so she was not totally free of racism. She could mix with the Harlem Club women because they were educated, successful women of their race. When it came to poor black men, however, she saw them as inferior, the fact that they had the vote a slap in the face to all women. In this regard she shared the views of NAWSA, and in her addresses before well-to-do men she played upon racist fears. And somewhat later she would secretly contribute $10,000 to the Southern Woman Suffrage Conference because "I plead guilty to so strong a desire for the political emancipation of women that I am not at all particular as to how it shall be granted."[23] Her point was that, as a southerner, she understood that organization's narrowness, but she was grateful for its contribution to the cause.

Nonetheless, Alva continued to appear often to work with the Harlem women and introduce special events she brought in, including classical music concerts and suffrage speakers. One of the first speakers was Dora Montefiore, the first of several English radicals Alva would bring over to share their stories with American women. Montefiore told of how she refused to pay income tax as a protest for not getting the vote and watched bailiffs, by order of the king, tear down the doors of her home, remove the furniture, and sell it. In the course of this speech, a small boy approached the podium and shot water at her from a squirt gun. This hostility was a mild omen of what the more outspoken suffragists in the country were to face.

Alva also included the Harlem women in her suffrage weekend retreats at her Long Island home, paying for their transportation as she did for the other women. Opening her sumptuous home to black and immigrant women was final evidence of her conviction that they were women first, who must identify on that basis and ignore class or race.

With Alva attending to poorer women, NAWSA's more affluent members could continue their work, relieved that someone else was paying attention to the immigrants. The old-time suffragists were also put off by Alva's emphasis on action. Because she had played no role in the sharing of the movement's traditions, she was not bounded by them either. And her brash manner, her use of the press, was too unfeminine for longtime suffragists, who subscribed to the belief that women were different from men and should behave accordingly.

During this initial activity, a tiny, sprightly woman once linked to the Vanderbilt family reappeared on the scene for the suffrage cause. Tennessee Claflin, the Commodore's "little sparrow" turned stockbroker, was now the wealthy Lady Cook in England. She appeared one day in New York, promising to give the American suffrage cause a million dollars, which, characteristically, never materialized. Rejecting violent opposition, she urged the suffragists to ridicule men, trick them, bewilder them, but never lose her temper. Following this brief appearance, she disappeared from suffrage history.

The Socialite Joins Hands
with the Union Women

In her other major activity, supporting union women, Alva had much more conventional suffragist company. Indeed, much of the eventual success of suffragism would come from united activity across class lines.

Following a long dispute with management over the formation of a union, the seamstresses at the the Triangle Shirtwaist factory walked out. Others in the garment trade soon followed, provoking what has been called the Uprising of the Twenty Thousand (or Ten or Thirty, depending upon one's source). Eventually Local 25 of the International Ladies Garment Workers Union demanded a general strike, and tossed its entire four dollar treasury behind the effort. For three months police arrested, fined, and jailed the strikers, while hired thugs ambushed and beat them. These young workers, mostly Jewish, were inspired by an old

Jewish oath, "If I turn traitor to the cause I now pledge, may my hand wither from this arm I now raise."[24] The strikers behaved so courageously in light of this repeated abuse that they quickly captured the sympathy of middle-class and wealthy women. (Also moving to these supporters must have been stories like those of Gussie Perk, who tried to kill herself by gas inhalation and cried out angrily on being revived. "Even if we girls were not on strike and I had work, I couldn't live long on the $5 a week I sometimes earn. Let me die!"[25]) As soon as Alva heard about the jailings, she went down to the night courts, where she would sit through the early morning hours, available to bail out each striker as her case was brought up. These personal appearances won Alva quick support from unionists, who saw her as being on the lines with them.

In December, to raise money for their support, she hired the massive Hippodrome, where Anna Shaw mesmerized the audience of seven thousand. Then she began to pressure her wealthy women friends. In January 1910 she hired a room at the Colony Club and sent out invitations to her best friend, Mamie Fish, along with the likes of Drexels and Morgans, to hear an appeal from Ida Husted Harper. Alva's opening comments there resembled an article she published that year on "Woman's Right to Govern Herself":

> If in this great battle of life you do not need the power, the strength, that Suffrage will give, what right, you, in your plenty, have you to raise your voice against the cry of the needy? You of the luxurious, educated class, know well, or if you do not, shame upon you! that the working-woman vitally needs the help of the ballot. Men at the head of large systems of industries, you know, and know well, that you are not the protectors of women! . . . I shall write the truth, and men to whom it comes home may cry out against me, but the overworked, underpaid woman, the mother toiling for hungry children, the drunkard's wife, the woman of the scarlet letter, the wife replaced by one younger and fairer, and saddest of all, the unprotected girl, these will bear me out.[26]

While she brought some wealthy women into the cause with such pleas, she also became "quite literally an outcast with my family and friends."[27]

Though the rejection hurt, Alva did not let it slow her down. She dove into the fray of the suffrage battle with the same enthusiasm she had given to architecture. Her published articles hint at her sharp mind and rhetorical ability; she knew how to pitch an argument to the readers. To the society women at *Harper's Bazar* (as it was spelled then) she disproved the claim that wealthy women are ladies of leisure. After listing the responsibilities and activities of these women in home and community, she suggested they needed a larger say in the world. She chided the male readers of *World Today* for educating their daughters, then denying them the opportunity to exercise their acquired wisdom.[28] For the more serious readers of *Forum,* she delineated the sociological forces behind the rebirth of the suffrage movement and predicted its success.

Still continuing direct social welfare, she established a hospital in Hempstead in honor of Harry, to be operated and staffed solely by women, except for the janitors. She set up a "suffragette farm" on her Long Island property, where she housed fifty-six troubled city women in the hope that farming would prove ameliorative. It was an experiment that failed—Consuelo later put the blame on the character of the women—but it exemplified her willingness to try any solution.

Alva Urges
Militancy

Experiences during a trip to England in 1910 shifted Alva's position to a more radical one. As she became more acquainted with the Pankhursts, she decided radical tactics were a necessary move if purely political action failed. She concluded that these women were no more anarchists than Paul Revere or Nathan Hale had been during the Revolution. She saw a double standard concerning militancy: despite the fact that men were taught to revere war and blood, they burnt Joan of Arc at the stake. She considered Susan B. Anthony the most militant woman in U.S. history for her fearless attack on any obstacle facing women's rights, and she felt that contemporary suffragists had unwisely accepted men's definition of women as accommodating. When interviewed about her views by a London paper, she predicted correctly that Englishwomen would gain the vote before American women. In the United States, she decided, an acute situation, a militancy, would be required before the vote came about. The current evolutionary tactics would not work.

Alva also introduced Consuelo to the Pankhursts and their comrades. Consuelo must have been more than casually involved with them because later, when speaking of Emmeline, she confessed, "I sometimes saw her during visits to Paris, which were secret and surreptitious, for she was wanted by the police."[29] Alva also told others of how Consuelo was secretly helping the English militants. Why would the duchess of Marlborough jeopardize her own reputation unless she were sympathetic? It seems she was.

Aligning herself with the Pankhursts did not make Alva popular with the public at home. When it was learned that she was setting up lecture tours in the States for English suffragettes, scores of anonymous letter writers sent angry protests to her for harboring anarchists. Also disagreeing with the Pankhursts were many American suffragists, who based their argument on the belief that England was a backward country where men treated women worse than in the United States. Here, they claimed, American men would give women what they wanted without a struggle. They were to be proved wrong, and some time later suffrage activist Doris Stevens would acknowledge that Alva "was the one suffrage leader who foresaw a militant battle here whenever women should determine to ask for their freedom immediately. In a great measure she prepared the way for that battle."[30]

Always in the forefront, Alva was soon seen in conspicuous positions in the suffrage parades that became a common ritual in New York and other cities. Within a few short years, as the size of the marches grew, so did the approval of onlookers. It was during these public demonstrations that the women began to wear white dresses as a unified symbol of their commitment. During a major march down Fifth Avenue in April 1912, one reporter noted the presence of Alva alongside Rebecca Goldstein, a sewing machine operator in a sweatshop. He observed how, unlike several years earlier, the crowd now responded to the women's intensity and purpose with admiration.[31]

What the reporter did not realize was the connection of Alva to a sweatshop girl was more than symbolic. With beloved husband dead, family avoiding her, friends dropping off, her social contacts became the more radical activist women of the Greenwich Village. Her intimates were now activist women, some of them becoming substitute daughters, others, closer to her in age, substitute sisters. If the woman were poor, then Alva would hire her for secretarial work for several months and pay her exorbitant wages to set her on a more self-sufficient path. This way Alva could contribute to the woman's welfare without compromising the recipient's self-respect.[32] What is remarkable about these connections is that while initially wary of their patron, they quickly came to admire her sheer gutsiness. The suffrage movement helped focus the belligerent side of her personality on her political foes, thus freeing her to enjoy more satisfying private relations. She discovered "a passion for giving women opportunity."[33]

One of her earliest companion-in-arms and half-adopted daughters was Inez Milholland, a wealthy Vassar graduate with a fanatical devotion to suffrage and socialism. The word most associated with her was *Amazon*. It referred to the impression she made on others of strength, due to her height and large bones; her beauty, comprised of large aquamarine eyes, ivory complexion, and long sable hair; and her fearless honesty. When she took the podium to speak on behalf of the vote, weary and impatient crowds hushed. During marches, she was a Joan of Arc figure riding a white steed and carrying a banner with a suffrage motto. Her charisma came across in photographs as well, making her an attractive, courageous image: an icon in the movement.

Milholland had once been romantically attached to Max Eastman, earnest Socialist and writer. In 1912 Eastman had been appointed by friends to edit a new magazine, *The Masses*. While it had an office, the rent some months in arrears, and a subscription list, *The Masses* had little else but enthusiasm and conviction. Eastman, a new father, figured he would need to be a business executive, promoter, and entrepreneur if he were ever to see the publication on the stands and a salary in his pocket. His first experimental issue was not a help. Its cartoon depicting the capitalist press as a whorehouse, with some of the participants being recognizable portraits of newspaper editors, alienated even some of the most ardent leftists.

In a stroke of fate, Eastman ran into Inez in the lobby of the Manhattan Hotel. While sharing recent news, he confessed his pecuniary needs. Inez suggested he try Alva. "She isn't a socialist," he replied. "What of it? You're a militant—that's all that matters," she replied.[34] An invitation to Alva's Madison Avenue town house soon followed.

Like other Socialist men of his set Eastman was very loving toward women, and yet, while welcoming their activism, he was often oblivious to their accomplishments. Thus he approached Alva's dinner table expecting to bamboozle this woman from the capitalist heights. He found her a "henna-haired, pug-nosed, and pink-painted old lady" who "liked to conceive herself in the role of noble-born patron to people whom some talent had raised, not up to her height to be sure, but above the common level."[35] He left feeling smug, thinking that he had outwitted her, gratified "that our super-revolutionary magazine owed its send-off to a leader of New York's 400—to the fortune of old Public-Be-Damned Vander-bilt." In fact, Alva had cleverly set up the dinner so that a best-selling author of the day, fellow southerner John Fox (*The Trail of the Lonesome Pine*) felt impelled to add $1,000 to Alva's $2,000 donation. Eastman had a lot to learn about bamboozling.

Eastman was to see later that Alva knew very well what she was supporting. When *The Masses* later ran into distribution problems and libel suits, Alva made herself available as moral support. One day she even appeared at a legislative investigation of the Interborough Rapid Transit to join in questioning August Belmont, her onetime brother-in-law, about why he supported removal of the magazine from the subway stands.[36] Then there was the time she led a group of working women in a protest on Gimbel's department store. Eastman was later to respect her as a leader among feminists for her indomitable willpower.

Further evidence of Alva's growing radicalism appeared in the New York Senate that same year. By now her Political Equality Association had eleven branches, including houses in Brooklyn and the Bronx, as well as interest clubs of nurses, artists, and physicians that probably met at the major headquarters. With all these women organized for suffrage, she needed to give them a goal that would have a clearly measurable outcome. Once again in the forefront, she decided upon a tactic never before used by suffragists: she would put her association to work to defeat antisuffrage politicians in the voting booth. Although her workers could not vote, they could inform male voters through speeches, posters, and handbills.

As if her assault on the office holders was not enough, she increased her use of violent metaphors. During a discussion of the suffrage bill, one senator arose and quoted Alva as saying the women of America were going to surpass their English sisters, by using not only rocks, but guns, and that they would shoot. Another day a legislator complained how Alva did not take the Sabbath off but stood in church doorways in his district distributing flyers urging parishioners to vote against him. This fact, he averred, was proof that women as a species were deadlier than the male. He lost the election, the first New Yorker ever tossed out on the basis of his suffrage stand.

Influenced by Kit Hepburn's work in Connecticut to eliminate prostitution,

Alva pressed for an interpretation and solution that even today strikes too close to the truth for some people's comfort.[37] For example, when she learned the governor of New York State wanted to budget $700,000 for refuge for young women caught in the "white slave trade," she wrote against the proposal. Instead, she proclaimed: "Arrest every man, rich or poor, young or old, who traffics in human bodies; fine him heavily according to his means, and the $700,000 necessary to provide an enlarged refuge for his victims will soon be raised. There is no difficulty in arresting the woman of the streets or the inmate of the house of ill repute; therefore the task of detecting men of the same caliber should not be among the impossibilities, and according to statistics, they outnumber women probably twenty to one."[38] She did not succeed here.

A Remarkable Partner
Comes on the Scene

Alva did succeed in finding activists more willing to go along with her heightened militancy. During 1913, NAWSA was infused with feisty new talent in the form of Alice Paul. Raised a Quaker, following graduation at Swarthmore, Paul went to England to pursue further studies at the London School of Economics. There she came in contact with Emmeline Pankhurst and soon joined in that group's sensational activities. Paul was among those arrested and imprisoned, and in the process she met another young American, Doris Stevens. Returning to the States in 1910 to complete a Ph.D. at the University of Pennsylvania, she wrote her dissertation on the legal status of women.

Paul's fervor and sincerity obtained Shaw's approval to organize for passage of the Susan B. Anthony suffrage amendment. This consent meant a deviation from NAWSA's belief the vote should be won in individual states first. Toward this new aim Paul was made chair of the Congressional Committee of NAWSA, but had to raise her own funds rather than be financed by the mother organization. Moving to Washington, she garnered about her a small cadre of committed women, including Lucy Burns, a Vassar graduate who had also helped the Pankhursts. Though fragile, even frail looking, Paul's stamina was legendary. She believed the most successful activist organization was built around a small group of the committed rather than a large membership with less than full-time to give to the cause. Paul also tolerated competition for leadership and could be dictatorial, but in her followers' eyes her self-sacrifice and charisma compensated for those weaknesses. For those who stayed, she was "a joy to work with"; for those who left, ungrateful and demanding.

Paul's ability to get what she wanted became myth making. A man appearing to complain about suffrage would find himself stamping envelopes. A woman expecting to donate a morning's work would be told to give all her time or none. When one avid worker protested that her history of tuberculosis should exempt her from a particularly stressful duty or else she would die, Paul as much as said the cause could use a martyr.[39] Accordingly, unlike most of her followers, Paul never married or had children, and she was impatient with those who claimed family duties as equal to political work. She refused no volunteer, however unsuitable she seemed to others in the office, and she would patiently shift the new worker from one job to another until she fit into the scheme.

One member of her cadre was a young sociologist, Max Eastman's sister Crystal, whose accomplished researches on urban workers and accidents in the workplace were already advancing improvements in workers' compensation laws. She had just returned to New York after spending two years directing the state suffrage efforts in Wisconsin. Her beauty matched her intelligence, and she carried her almost six-foot frame with great poise. It was a combination certain to attract Alva, who crossed paths with her at various immigrant aid activities and union rallies.

Eastman kept telling Paul to get Alva involved in the Congressional Union. She said Alva liked to be known by everybody and enjoyed being conspicuous, so she would probably enjoy the prominence of sitting on a float for the parade they were planning in Washington. Sit on a float? Paul was delighted, because no one liked to sit on a float. Apparently Alva didn't either, because she never responded to Paul's invitation, which smacked of condescension, a refusal to believe a wealthy woman could play a leadership role in the cause.[40]

The parade, chosen to be held March 13, 1913, in Washington the day before Wilson's inauguration as president, drew five thousand marchers whose presence, unlike in New York, brought jibes, jeers, spitting, and bullying. Police failure to protect the marchers resulted in its chief's eventual firing and much sympathy for the suffragists. Wilson himself did not see the display. Arriving by train at Union Station, he was surprised to find no public welcome. "Where are the people?" he inquired. "Over on the Avenue watching the Suffrage Parade," was the explanation. It was a warning he neglected.

Although Alva did not participate in this march, accompanied by Consuelo she did attend the International Woman Suffrage convention in Budapest that year. There she met with leaders from other countries and brought their ideas back to infuse the movement in the States. She had invited Emmeline Pankhurst to follow and offered to sponsor a speaking tour to rally support behind the British women. When Pankhurst reached the port, however, she was ordered to Ellis Island and detained on the basis of a dossier sent ahead by Scotland Yard warning the immigration officers she was of doubtful character. Alva sent a soliciter to represent Pankhurst's appeal, but he was refused. She may have pulled some other strings, for on the third day President Wilson ordered the suffragette's immediate release. (Pankhurst was not so lucky on the return trip. As the *Majestic* anchored in the harbor outside Plymouth, a police tender appeared and eight police boarded the ship to forcibly carry her off to prison.)

With the crusade picking up strength, in late 1913 Alva urged NAWSA to move its headquarters to Washington, D.C., where she saw it would be better placed toward influencing federal legislation. Her usual candor defeated her, however, for she mentioned her plan ahead of time to her opponents, the ruling board of the organization, which had time to set a strategy to defeat her. The rank-and-file delegates favored the move, but the officers used parliamentary procedures to shut off discussion.[41] This determination to keep NAWSA out of Washington reflected its leaders' commitment to gain woman suffrage on a state-by-state basis before pushing it on the federal level.

Alice Paul ran into similar rejection at that convention when her Congressional Committee demanded that NAWSA make an all-out commitment to the federal suffrage amendment. When the officers announced this program was premature, Paul held firm. They then removed her as chair of the committee in a fruitless move to quiet her dissension.

Somewhere during this period of splintering from NAWSA, Alva called up Paul and invited her to Long Island for dinner and to stay overnight. Paul found Alva effusive and single-minded, keeping her up until two in the morning with talk about the movement. In the course of her monologue, Alva decided to break with NAWSA as well. She immediately cut off relations with NAWSA and brought the membership of her Political Equality Association over to the Congressional Union. Concerned that Paul earned no salary for her work, she offered to pay her $1,000 a month. A woman of simple needs, Paul simply passed the money on into Congressional Union coffers. It was the start of a remarkable partnership.[42]

In June of 1914, Consuelo arrived to spend the summer with her mother and participate in a suffrage conference Alva had planned to be held at Marble House. She told reporters that she supported suffrage for England but not the violent tactics of the Pankhursts. Still, she excused the militants, explaining that the English male was more obstinate than the American male. Her overall thrust was that she was a humanist.

On the day of the affair, Consuelo sat on the podium with twelve working women, behind her a banners with such notices as "Telegraph Companies Pay Men $21.70 a Week. They Pay Women for the Same Work $14.75 a Week." Resplendent in black velvet, the Duchess surprised her audience with her speech. In a veiled criticism of Sunny and an endorsement of her mother, she explained, "Many persons wonder why wealthy women want the ballot. There would be little wonder if they knew the story of women whose sons-in-law have squandered the last penny. Legislation is the only protection for the wealthy mothers-in-law of a young spendthrift."[43] Little could she guess that as an Englishwoman she would have the right to cast a ballot before her mother would, for there was scant sign in Congress of the blatant hostility found among British politicians. She then changed into an antique Chinese robe to join her mother at her latest addition to Marble House, a tea house Alva built for the purpose of entertaining suffragists and raising funds for them. The service was designed specially by Alva, white china with blue trim, decorated with "Votes for Women." While mother and daughter had often had their differences in the past, they were now united.

11

1914-1919

War Fails
to Deter Alva

On August 3, 1914, the Germans invaded Belgium; on August 4, England entered the war to defend her allies. The only war on Alva's mind was that with the United States Congress. Plans were under way for a Congressional Union convocation at Marble House later in the month, which she would not cancel because the Europeans happened to be in battle. (Consuelo could not stay, of course, and was harried for some days trying to find ocean passage home.) Years later the women present during those sultry, sunny August days would claim this event to be a turning point in their organization, and in suffragism overall.

The group's immediate cause was defeat of a new bill in Congress, one favored by NAWSA, that would force a referendum on woman suffrage in any state where eight percent of those who voted in the last election signed an initiative to that effect. It was a cumbersome plan that continued to avoid forcing the federal government on the issue. Paul noticed Alva standing at the back of the room, listening intently. "She was just a born fighter. Whenever there was a fight she took the leadership, so she arose and said she wanted to do what she could to further this and she gave us $5,000, which was the biggest gift we ever had."[1]

Along with the money she introduced a political program, that the Congressional Union hold the Democratic party responsible for the failure of suffrage.[2] Consequently, it should enter the political arena and work to defeat Democratic candidates in the upcoming election, particularly in the nine states with women voters. It was the first time women activists chose to use political tactics on a nationwide scale to make their point. No doubt Alva pointed to her success on the state level in applying this approach. (Because of her position here, some commentators later wrongly identified her as a Republican; Alva had long voted

Democrat.) Crediting Alva for this tactic, Sara Bard Field observed how this wealthy socialite "had come over to us heart and soul. She was a woman of the most strange ability to grasp such a situation as holding the party in power responsible with clarity and fearlessness."[3]

It is supposed to have been at this event that Alva came forth with her most famous suffrage remark. The story may be apocryphal, for while it appears in a variety of nonsuffrage sources in various wordings, none of the memoirs of suffrage activists who knew Alva ever mention it. The supposed incident involved one young activist, who, feeling discouraged by the lack of response in Washington, expressed her despair to Alva, who reassured, "Trust in God. *She* will help you!"

War Inconveniences
Grace

Grace Vanderbilt did lose some of her trust in God. Women's rights mattered not at all to her, but war disrupted her life. For one, her good friend the Kaiser had become the Hun, the enemy. This loss was a particular blow because her husband had just inherited William H. Vanderbilt's mansion at 640 Fifth Avenue, and she was so looking forward to showing off her titled friends at parties there. (Over years to come she would never understand how so many of her royal and aristocratic associates would be tossed out of power, left to drift about Europe clinging to their meaningless titles.)

In fact, when war struck, she was in Paris stripping the stores of suites of furniture (some of it from Versailles), Louis XVI boiseries, Gobelin tapestries, and Savonnerie carpets to fill the six stories of seventy rooms and thirty-three bathrooms. On August 4, her two children were stranded in St. Moritz, for the trains had stopped running and communications were frozen between Switzerland and the Allies. Through his influence, Neily was able to get special gasoline supplies to drive to the children's lodgings. He had on him enough gold supplied by the American embassy to bail out all Americans trapped in Switzerland. Before leaving for England, he ordered his beloved *North Star* stripped of its portraits of Prussian aristocracy, then turned it over to the Allies, who used it as a mercy ship.

Oblivious to the conflict, once home Grace put her efforts to "important" matters, such as giving her children lessons in the seating of guests around the sixty-foot-long banquet table. She distressed Neily by refusing to cool her friendship with the German ambassador, Count von Bernstorff. Consequently, when he pointed out to her that her nephews, Belle Herbert's sons, were on the front, and the count's presence was an insult to their valor, she only laughed. Even her staff dared to rebuke her. One evening in Newport she placed the Count in the position of honor at her right. After the soup was served, no other course appeared, and she sat anxiously tugging at her flame-colored chiffon gown, wondering why the delay. Finally an Irish kitchenmaid skittered in with a heavy silver tray holding a small white note. After reading it, Grace announced to her guests, "Most of my servants are English or Irish. My chef is French. I regret to say that they refuse to serve the German Ambassador. Please accept my apologies."[4] Several good-humored male guests took over the serving and saved the evening. Still, it was not until the United States entered the war that Grace ended her friendship with the count.

Gertrude Rises
to Duty

While Grace considered the war to be a personal inconvenience, Gertrude, as might be expected, saw it as a call to service. On August 4, she was in the Adirondacks, whose protective isolation for once proved vulnerable to world affairs. While canoeing alone one afternoon she contemplated the fact of the battling, particularly the assault on her beloved France. She thought of the many working people she knew there, the gaiety of life, the tenderness and beauty of the country. As the moments passed she felt a growing and irreversible impulse to go there, to provide some direct service. Her sister Gladys was already assisting Austro-Hungarians through the Red Cross (and would later provide a retreat for 300 orphans at her home in Budapest). Could she do any less for her adopted second homeland?

Harry of course did not want her to become involved—just "send a cheque" being his refrain—but his objections no longer swayed her the way they once had. Fortunately, she knew Robert Bacon, former ambassador to France, who was organizing the American Ambulance Service, a field hospital on the outskirts of Paris staffed entirely by Americans who wanted to help their allies in a noncombatant way. Another Vanderbilt woman, Willie K.'s second wife, was already assisting him in France in setting up the first project. Harry agreed with Gertrude to contribute a quarter million dollars to this venture, but she wanted to do more on her own. Out of conversations with Bacon she decided to fully staff, supply, and fund a second field hospital closer to the lines. As she explained to Flora, now boarding at the Foxcroft School, she would send "8 doctors, 25 nurses, 20 ambulances. There goes with them everything necessary for their maintenance, assistants, chauffeurs, medical supplies, instruments, stretchers, blankets, linen, underclothes for soldiers, certain foods."[5] All this had to be gotten together for departure in early November. This she managed along with a fund-raiser fashion show featuring Parisian designers and an art exhibit at her new Whitney Studio for war relief.

When the time came to depart, she left Harry behind, as she so often had in the past, and entered her staterooms on the *Lusitania,* a ship she had often used, with mixed feelings of exhaustion and excitement. The one advantage of foreign travel then was its relaxed pace. The days on the ocean, as with all her numerous crossings, would be devoted to seldom-known solitude, a chance to reflect on recent events, to write in her journal, to write to friends, to exercise, and to savor daily massages. She needed all the rest she could for the months ahead.

Gertrude hobbled into her room at the London Ritz: her money belt was so loaded down with gold that it pained her to move. Her arm ached from a new typhoid vaccination. Her carrying case included a large supply of chocolate in case she ran into a situation where food would be unavailable, and a cache of medicines for "every known and unimaginable disease." A waiter's abrupt entrance to secure her drapes tight against light leaks reminded her that indeed war was on, that it was, as he noted, a splendid night for a zepellin raid. (Within months newspaper editors would receive coded telegrams from England about "red silk ties," the number attached referring to the deaths incurred by the latest attack from the silver monster.)

War had healed the breach between Harry and his sister Pauline. With husband Almeric Paget, she came by to recount how in just a few short months the trench warfare had been so bloody that already families had seen all their young males killed. She expressed some resentment that the French were expecting too much of the British troops, who were fighting in the muddy graves for days at a stretch with half rations. Very sympathetic to Gertrude's plan, Almeric offered to be her representative at the hospital after she returned home, saying he would go to France several days each week to oversee the project. In light of Harry's protests, their support boosted her resolve.

Possibly Gertrude also heard from them about Consuelo's activities. As soon as war had been declared the duchess quickly agreed to chair the American Woman's War Relief Fund and would raise more than $300,000 during its first year. She was also a key figure in setting up an American-sponsored military hospital of 400 beds in Devonshire. As if these activities were not enough, she helped administer the Woman's Emergency Corps. With hundreds of thousands of women now needed to fill the men's jobs in factories and offices, many odd duties remained unfilled, such as caring for horses, feeding Belgian refugees, or even making toys to supplant those once imported from Germany. Despite the zeppelin bombing, Consuelo refused to escape to the country but lived alone on the third floor of Sunderland House, giving over the basement as a bomb shelter and the large lower rooms as meeting spaces for the many organizations springing up around the war effort. She worried less for herself than for eldest son Blandford, now at Sandhurst, the Military College. (Upon reaching eighteen, he would be sent directly to the First Life Guards as second lieutenant but survive the years of bloodshed that wiped out so many young men.)

During a stormy channel crossing Gertrude lay in bed and hallucinated that a man was pressing up against the glass while she showered, then that he was in the next room with a strange clicking machine. She smelled an odd odor emanating about the room, and she was convinced he wanted to suffocate her. Determined he would not do so, she noiselessly removed her bedding, crept into her adjoining sitting room, and slept there on a chaise. It was the kind of nerve-shocked episode many people must have shared as they approached the battle area.

The sight of a beleaguered Paris—the Champs-Elysées deserted, houses shut down, pedestrians with troubled faces, a few buildings with Red Cross flags waving—led her closer to the reality of the slaughter. While the site and details for her hospital were being negotiated, she went daily to the American Ambulance hospital at Neuilly-sur-Seine, where she served tea, assisted on changes of dressings, and talked with the soldiers and staff. She did not feel very useful; the tasks were too much like the social matron role she disavowed.

Impatient, she dressed excitedly the day she could join in a caravan to inspect the sight of Hospital B, "her" hospital, located in Juilly, a hundred miles northeast of Paris, quite close to combat. There stood a medieval college, charming with its massive stone walls, pigeon tower, lake, and immense shade trees standing sentinal along the roadways.[6] While showing her around, the head abbé explained that the origin of the institution rested with St. Genevieve. The story went that one day while out walking the saint grew very thirsty. Upon praying for relief, a spring burst out of the ground, and in gratitude she started the college on that very spot. Gertrude was quite pleased with this meditative setting, especially its size, which could hold many more beds than had been originally planned. In fact, recently more than five hundred wounded men had been treated there briefly before being sent on to a regular hospital, so its suitability and practicality were already proven.

She returned to Paris to pack further supplies, hire additional staff, and work at Neuilly until Hospital B was ready to take patients. On the wards she noted the extreme fatigue of the nurses, and she began to share the frustration and anxiety that resulted from constant exposure to death. She was haunted by the memory of a family standing watch over their son dying of gangrene. The eyes of the men stared out from the beds to her, seeming to say, "Will I be the next?" Riding back to Juilly she saw a line of French soldiers, bright in their red-and-blue uniforms, metal polished, boots shined, horses fed, and thought how differently the Germans in gray would blend in the landscape, with their faces set, determined to kill the smiling Frenchmen somewhere further down the road.

Once the hospital was under way she had to leave—that third of her life still ruled by her family compelled her to go home for the holidays. But it was "so dull, so depressing when one longs to be over there with the sufferers. Not that there are no sufferers here—still it's not the same, is it?"[7] She could not stay away, and in January she returned once more to Juilly. Sulking, Harry nagged her with guilt-provoking letters preoccupied with his own latest physical ailments and the children's latest colds. She soon returned home.

While Gertrude did not work directly in the hospital from that point, she did receive frequent telegrams, letters, and reports from the medical chief, who shared the smallest problem. Should dancing be allowed, he asked, when it might insult the French, who would see it as a violation of their mourning? The local French doctors were all dead, so how should they handle the local townsfolks' needs for medical care? Could she send more gloves size 7, 7½, and 8? Ambulance drivers shared their experiences—of the young woman who hid in a cesspool to avoid rape by the Germans, of the peasant whose hand got caught in a threshing machine, of a playful little girl who was suddenly blown up, half her head landing on top of the nearby driver. Fourteen French soldiers prepared a book complete with photographs in which each wrote out his personal history as a sign of gratitude for her caring. (In November of 1916 President Poincaré dispatched France's Foreign Office gold medal to Gertrude in gratitude for her service.)

The needs of her family, war relief fund-raising, and efforts on behalf of other artists meant little time for the studio. Although in 1912 Juliana had married her longtime lover, dentist Willard Force, she did not intend to recede from the world of art, and in fact she gave more of herself over to her work with Gertrude. Gertrude trusted Juliana utterly and found her faith repaid in all regards. Juliana adeptly handled the public functions that made Gertrude so uncomfortable: the selling, the talking to reporters, the nurturing of artists. Together they planned themes for exhibits, selected artists, designed the displays and invitations, chose selections for Gertrude's private holdings, and decided which artists Gertrude should quietly help out. They were both women who enjoyed a drink (though Juliana more than Gertrude), sharp, crackling conversation, skewed humor, the practical joke. Throughout the many years of this extraordinary friendship neither gossiped nor spoke ill about the other.

Many of their early exhibits were tied to war relief. In December of 1914 the women sponsored a "50-50 Exhibit" at the studio at which half the proceeds of artists' works would go to the American Ambulance Hospital. In January of 1915 they arranged a competitive showing of works by student artists only, Gertrude providing the award money, with proceeds from admission to benefit families of French artists whose lives had been disrupted by the war. Similar fundraisers followed.

In 1915, Gertrude also led in the formation of an organization called the Friends of the Young Artists. This was a group of patrons who backed her in sponsoring other juried shows with competitive awards. (The practice would continue until 1917, when she announced a change in policy for the studio. Rather than provide an award, Gertrude concluded it would be wiser for direct sale of works to be encouraged, so the artist would benefit directly from knowing his or her work was actually desired.) The studio also held exhibits for established artists, including solo shows for Andrew O'Connor, painter John Sloan, and Gertrude herself. Sloan, unable until then to place much of his work in New York galleries, attributed the prestige of his exhibit at the Whitney Studio to setting a new stage in his career. In addition, Gertrude was a major underwriter for the annual shows by the Independents, that group of artists which had broken away from the National Academy following the Ash Can show in 1908.

The significance of her contribution should not be underestimated. Despite the breakthroughs of the Independents and the Armory Show, well beyond this decade the modern artist in America had little hope for survival. There were no teaching jobs, and few collectors of American art. Nor could commercial illustration promise a steady and adequate income. As for the major purchasers, the millionaire collectors, they "went on buying art from Paris, it being so much easier to spot greatness across an ocean."[8] Besides Gertrude, there was only Stieglitz. Particularly striking was her support of women artists. No collector of her time would buy and show more American art by women than Gertrude. They were as likely to receive a check for a trip abroad as their male colleagues, or find, to their astonishment, that Gertrude would pay for the private schooling of a child. Among women who benefited from her support and largesse were Isabel Bishop, Peggy Bacon, Katherine Schmidt, Dorothy Varian, Dorothea Schwarcz, Molly Luce, Nan Watson, Lucile Blanch, and Georgina Klitgaard.

Gertrude's own writing and sculpture were further thwarted by events in her private life. On May 7, 1915, a frightful news item flashed over the headlines: the Germans had sunk the *Lusitania* off the coast of Ireland. Among those on the ship was her older brother Alfred. For several days she and Alice waited for news of his fate, at first receiving hopeful rumors, then the terrible, final word that he was among the 1,198 dead. The one solace was in survivors' reports of his heroism in assisting women off the ship, how he had given his life jacket to an elderly traveler. "Come on and let us save the kiddies," he had been heard to shout midst the chaos.

Mourning this loss of a third child, Alice joined Gertrude at Westbury for several months, the shared grief rebuilding a bond between mother and daughter. As if Alfred's widow did not have enough sorrow, that July she received anonymous threats to kidnap her sons and had to hire guards to patrol the estate. One healing consequence of Alfred's death was Alice's recognition of Neily as head of the family. His mother and sisters increasingly admired and depended upon his mature, responsible outlook, which so contrasted with the dissolute Regi. Neily needed them as well, for Grace's frivolity and triviality drove him out of the house most evenings.

That August, Gertrude suffered appendicitis and was operated on at home. Although the recuperation began uneventfully, her chronic phlebitis recurred, preventing her from working in her studio. Apart from some sketches on war themes, she was able that fall to complete only one piece, a version of the head from the *Titanic Memorial* to be exhibited at the Gorham gallery.

Alva Composes an Operetta
and Builds Once More

War had not slowed down Alva's suffragism. She was now involved with the
Feminist Alliance, whose purpose was "the removal of all social, political, economic, and other discriminations which are based upon sex."[9] Started in 1914
by Crystal Eastman and other Greenwich Village radicals, its activities included
pressuring Harvard and Yale Medical Schools to admit women, to change the law
by which American women marrying foreigners lost their citizenship (as had happened to Consuelo), and to provide child care for working women. It urged
President Wilson to support a constitutional amendment that "no civil or political
right shall be denied to any person on account of sex," thus anticipating the
Equal Rights Amendment.[10]

Among Alva's fund-raising efforts was the case of Harriet Rodman, who
besides being a major force in the Liberal Club was a New York City school
teacher. In those days only single women were allowed to teach, consequently
married women usually hid their change in status until visible pregnancy forced
their firing. Though not a mother herself, Rodman was suspended for two years
after writing a letter critical of such "mother baiting" to a local newspaper. As
a result of Feminist Alliance pressure, the school board eventually gave way, and
New York City became only the fourth district in the country to allow married
women to work and obtain a leave of absence during pregnancy.

At this time Alva met another talented young woman and brought her in
to raise money for the cause. Elsa Maxwell was in many ways a young version
of Alva: sharp tongued, witty, mocking of convention, energetic, and built like a
bulldog. A talented musician, she earned her keep by playing piano at socialite
parties, where her clever, sometimes devastatingly witty banter added to her
appeal.

Maxwell could not have appeared at a better time. Somehow amid all her
activities Alva had written a suffrage operetta, *Melinda and Her Sisters,* and needed
someone to write music for the tunes. Maxwell was pleased to comply, and she
quickly completed the job. Meanwhile Alva arranged for a benefit performance
of *Melinda* at the Waldorf Astoria, with box seats going as high as $125, a hefty
price for those days. She next lined up what the press described as "a ten-
million-dollar cast" that included actress Marie Dressler, Metropolitan Opera
singer Frances Alda, and with architect Addison Mizner, who had built Palm
Beach out of a Florida wilderness. The chorus included Maud Kahn and Kitty
Bache, daughters of prominent Wall Street bankers.

The story of Melinda was slight, that of the Peppers, a *nouveau riche* couple
with eight daughters about to debut before society. Seven of the daughters have
become dilettantes in the arts and sports. The eighth, Melinda, is the family

skeleton, a suffragist who urges her sisters at the end to "Put away your curls," your vanity, and prepare for full political participation.

In the first half of the play Alva let loose with numerous witty epigrams and jabs at her own class:

Society is the key to the higher life—publicity.

They say that in New York women can have their hair any color so long as it suits the color of the dog they're wearing.

A perfect lady should know absolutely nothing. It gives an illusive charm.

America is really the greatest monarchy of all. Our society is the most expensive to get into.

It is so nice to be born in a position which enables one to cut others. That is the real higher education for women: to know just who and where and when to cut people. . . . If you know a woman on Fifth Avenue, you must not recognize her on Sixth.

The Peppers subscribe to such notions, and are fearful Melinda will spoil the coming-out occasion.

Melinda's appearance turns the skit into propaganda. Alas, she lacks a sense of humor, and throws off the sprightly rhythm of the work:

We fight, it is true, but we fight with good deeds, with love of humanity as our sword and justice as our shield. . . . We want you—and by you, I mean all women—to help each other, to be kind to each other, to throw off your shackles of servitude and become free—all equal, all great, all working together for the common cause—equal rights, equal responsibilities, equal rewards, equal punishments.

She then parries with the town mayor, accuses him of insulting his wife by not allowing her to vote, when "any farm hand or railroad laborer, even if he can't spell or write" or "old black Joe, the negro stable boy" are able to do so. Allowing "every Tom, Dick, and Harry" the vote means the mayor is placing every man "mentally and economically in a position superior" to that of his wife. "The country has been going to the dogs for quite a while now. Why not give it to the cats for a change?"

Melinda accomplished its purpose, filling the coffers of the suffrage treasuries. Maxwell claimed the resulting publicity brought a deluge of 10,000 membership applications into the Congressional Union. Though this figure is certainly an exaggeration, the scheme kept up publicity for the cause.

Alva never passed up an opportunity to raise money for the vote. When a silverware company asked her for a personal endorsement, she indignantly refused. Upon learning Elsa Maxwell had only Woolworth utensils, she called up the advertising agency and agreed—provided her protégée get a set of the service and the Congressional Union got to collect the standard fee. In accepting such arrangements, she introduced a new advertising gimmick, the socialite endorsement, a method other Vanderbilt women would use later.

During this period, Alva focused her energies in directions other than just needy women and the vote. She was once again "knee deep in mortar" with the Hunt brothers in the construction of a house. The site was on the water near Sands Point, Long Island. The Hunt sons, alas, did not possess the talent of their father. Dubbed Beacon Towers, its exterior was a carnivalesque adaptation of a Norman fortress. Unadorned with embellishments or detailing, its turrets, towers, and castellations later inspired the fictional home of Scott Fitzgerald's Jay Gatsby.[11] The interior was just as strange, six levels holding more than 140 rooms, easily twice that found in Alva's earlier homes. There were more than a dozen servants' rooms, three ladies' dressing rooms, a recreation room, a two-story tower for silver storage and polishing, soundproof telephone booths, and two elevators, one of them round to fit a turret.

Though lavishly appointed, Beacon Towers marked a break with Alva's past. It meant, for one, a farewell to Newport and all its associations. The inclusion of guest rooms also signified a change. This was after all the woman who assiduously protected her family life, who built mansions where guests came to dine or talk but were put up in a hotel at evening's end. That addition, along with the three ladies' dressing rooms (only one for men), and a space marked "Mrs. Belmont's office," point to a primary purpose for this immense house—to service the suffrage cause. Indeed, the interior resembles a conference center, with its large public rooms (not marked as in the past "salon" or "ballroom") and space for support activities.

In case anyone might miss the feminist connection, Alva chose as the major decorative motif Jeanne d'Arc. Wall-sized murals painted by Italian artist Vincent Aderente depicted the warrior saint's life. Alva's fabled medieval armory collection, wrought-iron Gothic sconces and chandeliers, and *fleurs de lis* motifs added to the effect. While some found Beacon Towers bizarre and forbidding, Alice Paul and other Congressional Union members would find it a secluded retreat where they would come for rejuvenation.

Gertrude and Alva Have
Curious Intersections

Alva's continual financial support and fund-raising success set the Congressional Union in high gear. While NAWSA was floundering under inept leadership and lack of funds, the Congressional Union sent organizers into the nine Western states with the woman's vote to swing it against Democratic candidates. By 1915 it was organizing in all forty-eight states. As a focal point, Alva sponsored a suffrage headquarters in the Palace of Education at the Panama-Pacific Exposition in San Francisco, and she paid for speakers to appear throughout that summer. At the booth, beneath a large picture of Alice Paul were arrayed dolls represent-ing each of the states on which placards indicated whether or not the women therein would vote.

On September 13, 1916, impeccably groomed in a jade green jersey travel-ing suit, Alva stepped down from a train in Oakland to meet reporters who had come to see "the woman who made suffrage fashionable."[12] Her purpose was to chair a political convention of women voters to be held at the Exposition site from September 14th through the 16th. Alva opened the proceedings, which had international delegates, with her usual inflammatory rhetoric. "We women of the North, of the South and of the East, branded on account of sex, disfranchised as criminals and imbeciles, come to the glorious West, where the broad vision of its men has seen justice."[13] On the final evening, before a crowd of ten thousand holding golden lanterns, noted San Francisco civic leader M. H. de Young, editor of the *San Francisco Chronicle,* on behalf of the directors of the Exposition presented Alva with a bronze medal in recognition of the work of the Congressional Union. (Both de Young's wife and Phoebe Hearst, mother of Randolph, were leaders in the suffrage movement in California.)

Throughout the week, Alva gave interviews that made front-page stories in the city papers, her picture and that of other party members were prominently displayed as well. Her vigor, efficiency, and determination impressed the report-ers, who also appreciated her clear, powerful rhetoric. Her biggest coup, however, was convincing the editor of the *San Francisco Bulletin* to allow her and a group of party members to edit a special edition of the paper, which appeared on September 18, 1915.

While Alva was at the Exposition, she must have seen Gertrude Vanderbilt's sculpture, the *El Dorado Fountain,* for it was prominently located. Sculpture was much favored at that time in the public landscape, in private interior design, in garden decoration, and in community fairs or exhibitions. Thus when San Francis-cans decided to plan the Exhibition to demonstrate to the world that the 1906 earthquake had not destroyed the city, its organizers included a Department of Sculpture to provide fountains, flower boxes, panels, friezes, and monuments to enhance the buildings and express the character of the event. Its mood was "irresistibly romantic . . . [a] wonderful assemblage of all races, this oasis of peace and beauty in the midst of a world gone mad with the awful realism of war."[14] One of the few non-San Francisco invitees, Gertrude was asked to prepare a 75-foot-long arched high relief frieze for placement in the Tower of Jewels colon-nade.[15] Opposite from her fountain would be Edith Woodman Burroughs's Foun-tain of Youth. Burroughs interpreted her theme literally, with a nude girl in the center sided by panels depicting ships of babies and aged. It was a pedestrian and uninspired presentation.

Gertrude approached her theme of the tale of El Dorado more sardonically.

According to this story, once in Mexico lived a golden king named El Dorado who scattered treasures along his path, inspiring later adventures to search for the lost cache. Gertrude's version placed a set of doors, slightly open, through which the king presumably has passed. Two impersonal Aztec figures guard the opening, and two trees have grown over part of the opening. On either side long panels with nude figures represent the striving of humanity for power and possession. Some rush gaily, some stumble, some press, some linger. One figure faints and another stops to assist, while a third figure pushes past. The overall impression, though, is of fatality and anguish. It became one of the most controversial pieces of the dozens of sculptures shown. (Gertrude attended the Exposition to view her work several weeks following Alva's appearance.)

The Woman Voters' conventioneers in San Francisco were too busy with their cause to bother with artistic debate. They easily passed a resolution calling upon the Sixty-fourth Congress to pass the Susan B. Anthony Amendment. With little trouble the Congressional Union filled a suffrage petition with half a million signatures of Exhibition visitors, which it later took to President Wilson, who made his first public declaration on behalf of suffrage. Yet he adamantly refused to pressure the Democratic party to place suffrage on its platform. Consequently, during its 1916 convention, the Congressional Union created the Woman's party to organize women in the suffrage states to vote against Wilson. Alva took the platform to pledge $50,000 to defeat every Democrat running.[16] Paul later credited Alva, "who was an *eastern* woman [whose monies would go to western campaigns]," for contributing "more than anybody else did" in this endeavor.[17]

To defeat Wilson, Alva also organized the Woman's Campaign Train, which carried dozens of women of wealth out to stomp for Republican presidential candidate Charles Evans Hughes. The itinerary included stops in Rochester, Cleveland, Toledo, Detroit, South Bend, Chicago, Miles City, Billings, Spokane, San Francisco, and Los Angeles. Among those who traveled parts of the journey were Millicent Hearst, Mrs. W. H. Crocker of banking, and Mrs. Daniel Guggenheim of finance. In a rare show of political expression, Alice Vanderbilt and Gertrude Whitney were also aboard. (Gertrude had also given a fund-raiser for Hughes at her Greenwich Village studio.[18]) Perhaps they did not know the project was Alva's domain, although that seems unlikely. More plausibly, their support of woman suffrage and Hughes impelled them to overlook their personal feelings toward the onetime family pariah.

Also known as the Billion Dollar Hughes Special, it marked the first entry of women into a national campaign purportedly separate from the suffrage issue, which was not quite the case. While many socialites aboard were sympathetic to the Republican philosophy, others like Alva, were Progressives who would have voted Democratic were it not for Wilson's refusal to move on suffrage. During stops, which understandably drew much heckling from working men, the women argued that Hughes was better suited to handle such problems as prison labor, increasing drug use, and the education of immigrants. It was not one of the Woman's party's better ideas.

Gertrude's participation in the Hughes campaign came on top of months of exceptional stress. Early in 1916 she had her first "one-man" show, featuring twenty-five works displaying her versatility. That spring, she had hosted five war relief benefits. In late April, Howard Cushing died suddenly, and she used her influence to organize a memorial exhibition of his work at the Knoedler Gallery. Invited to mount another show for the Art Association in Newport that summer, she scribbled twenty-eight pages of instructions describing the placement of the works, which included her own sculpture and works of other artists from her growing private collection. In addition to Juliana Force, she now had a most capable private secretary, Irene Givenwilson, to aid her volunteer work.

Flora's approaching debut brought other demands. Despite her secret discomfort with society rituals, Gertrude was highly conventional when it came to her children. Ironically, in light of her own experience, she viewed private schools and social rites of passage as necessary to rein in her youngsters' signs of nonconformity. Thus she felt impelled to have a ballroom quickly added onto the Newport house for the coming-out party and numerous related social activities. That event in August attracted five hundred guests, none artists. For weeks leading up to the event, Gertrude and Harry entertained as they had not done before in their twenty-year marriage. Their more frequent companionship was not, however, the expression of social obligation, but of renewed fondness.

Now in their early forties, Gertrude and Harry had passed through the hurt and bitterness caused by earlier infidelities and disenchantments. Possibly frightened by the intensity and melodrama of her affair with Stackpole, Gertrude was no longer toying with others' affections. Having never fully recovered from the loss of his father, Harry was not dallying much either. Years of hard athletic activity on the polo field and the drinking celebrations afterward were revealed in his body, now weakened by chronic cirrhosis of the liver. Certainly he was needy, and Gertrude was always drawn to nurture those less fortunate. More to the point, Harry's good-heartedness and his devotion to the children simply won her over during this time of so much historic and personal turmoil. As of this time he would return to the status of her first and best love, though her nurturing was more maternal than conjugal.

The tie between the couple tightened in November when news came that Harry's younger sister Pauline Paget had died suddenly in England. Pauline had inherited her mother's weak heart, so her death at an early age was not fully unexpected. Yet it devastated Harry, making him more reclusive and preoccupied with his own health. Indeed, he never bounded back to the virile, jovial Harry of his youth. Instead he grew more wary and anxious, and in letters to Gertrude, now his "Dearest," he alluded to himself at age forty-four as an old man. He did not have much to offer her now, but she did not refuse or discount his small gifts.

The Woman's Party
Challenges the President

Although the Woman's party campaign for Hughes was not successful—Wilson won ten out of twelve suffrage states—its participants simply claimed to have been outnumbered by male Progressives, workers, and farmers. More likely the cause was insufficient organizers and resources, as well as an animosity on the part of western women that eastern women were telling them what to do. Nonetheless, it was a public relations success in that the challenge brought numerous opportunities to present the party views in the newspapers. It had also put a scare in the minds of some of the Democratic leadership, who realized the women were gaining momentum.

By 1916, Carrie Chapman Catt had regained control of NAWSA, and through her exceptional organizational acumen she revitalized it. She developed the "Winning Plan," a highly coordinated and carefully administered program to ensure approval for the suffrage amendment in thirty-six states. Having been frustrated by this traditional route, Alice Paul decided Alva was right, the only path to suffrage must be a militant one aiming at the federal government.

If Paul had any problems convincing her workers of the need to become more aggressive, they found reason to abandon their objections later that year. Although she had married Jan Eugen Boissevain, Inez Milholland went off to stump about the west that fall, traveling alone from town to town with little rest. In late October, she mounted a podium before a crowd of several thousand in Los Angeles. Late in her speech, she quoted Wilson's promise to women, "The tide is rising to meet the moon; you will not have long to wait," then responded, "How long must women wait for liberty?" Upon saying the word *liberty*, she collapsed to the floor. Within a month she was dead, her undiagnosed pernicious anemia having been exacerbated by exhaustion. Hence the party proclaimed her a martyr, one of "the human sacrifices on the altar of woman's liberty," her comrades would charge. Previously tentative members were now ready to act.

The first move was a sensational protest. On December 4, 1916, President Wilson spoke before Congress. Entering the gallery was a pregnant-looking Sara Bard Field, whose heavy form caused a page to give her his chair. Just as Wilson introduced the importance of granting more freedom to Puerto Rican men, five women stood up in the balcony and snapped open a banner, Sara's "baby," which read "MR. PRESIDENT, WHAT WILL YOU DO FOR WOMAN SUFFRAGE?" Wilson looked up, so did the Congressmen. The page tore the banner away. Although Wilson returned to his text without comment, the politicians began to buzz over the demonstration. The women made front-page news, relegating the president's message to second place.

They followed this dare up with memorial meetings held throughout the country in honor of Inez Milholland, but also to reconsecrate activists to the suffrage cause. The most moving of these events, taking place on Christmas in Statuary Hall of the Capitol, was the result of Alice Paul's brilliance in creating moving spectacle. As the mourners came in, they faced a sea of several hundred chairs each supporting a flag of purple, white, and gold, the tricolor of the feminists. While boy choristers sang, young girls bore crusading banners. Speeches and music were interwoven. Just when the audience thought the service was over, the *Marseillaise* burst from the organ, stirring everyone to stand and sing, replacing the words with a feminist cry composed by poet Sara Bard Fields. It was a hypnotic rite, combining the rhetoric of both the American and French revolutions with the strong visual symbolism of the suffragists.

Several days later a deputation of three hundred women carried memorials from the various services honoring Milholland to President Wilson. They repeated earlier pleas, that he openly urge woman suffrage. They were hopeful because they knew Wilson was not an aloof academic but "a very human, sympathetic personality."[19] Tiny Sara Bard Field moved many women in the room to tears with her eloquent and courteous entreaty to Wilson to act "in the name of all women who have fought and died for this cause."[20] But, they noticed to their dismay that Wilson suddenly grew stone faced. When their presentation was done, he did not offer assurances, but argued that he could not change his inauguration speech because it had already gone out to the press. Stunned, the women returned to their headquarters to discuss the situation. Wilson had made clear his decision to do nothing on their behalf. As for his suggestion that they stir up more public opinion on their behalf, they were at a loss. For more than fifty years women had been making speeches, holding meetings, pressuring politicians, and marching in parades. They needed a new method. Already anticipating the outcome, Alice, Alva, and other members of the board of directors had a plan ready.

On January 10, 1917, several Woman's party members gathered to form the first picket of the White House in U.S. history. Throughout that Washington winter, daily they appeared with their first signs: "MR. PRESIDENT, WHAT WILL YOU DO FOR WOMAN SUFFRAGE?" and "HOW LONG MUST WOMEN WAIT FOR LIBERTY?" The police ignored them, onlookers watched with curiosity, and Wilson was even seen to doff his hat to them on drives past the line. The pickets returned on later days with new banners:

"DENMARK ON THE VERGE OF WAR GAVE WOMEN THE VOTE. WHY NOT GIVE IT TO AMERICAN WOMEN NOW?"

"WHY ARE YOU BEHIND LINCOLN? AFTER THE CIVIL WAR WOMEN ASKED FOR POLITICAL FREEDOM. THEY WERE TOLD TO WAIT—THIS WAS THE NEGRO'S HOUR. IN 1917, AMERICAN WOMEN STILL ASK FOR FREEDOM."

Paul ably directed her troops. She devised special banners for special days, such as on Susan B. Anthony's birthday on February 15, or set up state days wherein picketers from a designated state would come to Washington. This tactic saved both the energy of local workers and gave women from other parts of the country an opportunity to participate in the demonstrations.

Probably because of the heart ailment she had suffered since Harry's death, Alva never participated in picketing. Rather, from New York she continued to raise the enormous funds to support the constant supply of marchers, which included their travel to and stay in Washington, and traveled periodically to Washington to lobby politicians, men from her class whom she well understood how to pressure. Thus on March 3, when five thousand women rioted in New York over rising food prices caused by the war inflation, Alva was busy creating food kitchens and serving soup. That month, at their annual joint meeting, she also convinced delegates to unify the branches of the Congressional Union under the Woman's party banner. Paul was not very interested in this switch, but she went along because Alva "was of course very influential in our board because she was giving us so much financial help and was also so much help in every possible way."[21] Thus she let Alva handle the job of communicating with all the local groups to convince them that the Woman's party had "so much more strength and more dignity" as a name.[22] At that convention the delegates also voted to make passage of the suffrage amendment its top priority.

U.S. War Entry Inspires
the Whitneys

On April 7, 1917, the United States declared war against Germany. Like so many families, that of Harry and Gertrude Whitney found their daily concerns suddenly unimportant.

Coming of age during the war, Flora faced courtship aware that the young suitors could one day go into battle. She became engaged to Quentin Roosevelt, son of Theodore Roosevelt, and shared the experience of so many young women then in watching her beloved depart in uniform for camp. To take up the time while waiting for his next letter to appear, Flora learned typing and shorthand and worked on various projects in support of the war effort as well as with her mother at the Whitney Studio Club. Inspired by her mother's creativity, she began to explore short-story writing and sculpting.

Sonny Whitney was not only of age to fight but anxious to do so. He had inherited the Vanderbilt men's love of speed, and, like his uncle Regi, had already made the news with spectacular automobile accidents. He had to wait another year, however, to finish his term at Yale. In 1918 he signed up with the Signal Corps and started flight training in Fort Worth, Texas. Nervous about his going abroad, Gertrude took Flora to live in a cramped bungalow near the base in order to "cultivate" the officers, while Harry used his personal connections with Theodore Roosevelt to protect his son.[23] Sonny remained in the States as a flight instructor, and he was eventually assigned to fly stunt exhibitions around the country to encourage the purchase of war bonds.

Harry's immediate response to the war announcement was to pledge a million dollars to the Liberty Loan and a hundred thousand dollars to the Red Cross, as well as to sponsor a special training unit of Yale-graduate flyers. Harry also signed up for the army and was commissioned as a major for special service with the air force. He had been a pilot for several years, owned a hydroplane, and was a director of the Wright-Martin Aircraft Corporation. In fact, like many well-to-do men he did not experience service the way working men did; for the most part he was a consultant between business and the military.

As for Gertrude, her long anxiety for her beloved France, for the sacrifices of the British, became frenzied, driving her into a maelstrom of creative activity toward the war effort. The sheer labor exhibited in the surviving papers is awesome, as just one brief period from this time indicates. With Rollie Cottenet and others, she arranged for a fund-raiser at the Metropolitan Opera House: a "Tableaux of Nations Assembled in Homage to the New Democracy." With the Friends of the Young Artists, she planned a war poster competition. She oversaw the planning of a Sculptors' Day at an Allies Bazaar fund-raiser, pulling together the participation of other women sculptors. She arranged for the exhibition of the model of a French memorial Jo Davidson had created for the French Heroes Lafayette Fund. She was also quick to agree to such requests as dressing as a nun at a medieval pageant or joining for four days in a MacDougall Alley Fiesta with her artist friends to sell more than half a million dollars worth of liberty bonds.

Gertrude's support for artists in general continued unabated as well. She corresponded with Henry McBride, critic of the *New York Sun,* over the possibility of a law providing artists a small percentage in the case of resale of their works. Hearing that composer Edgar Varese had broken his foot, she sent him to specialists and paid the bills. Her many donations included $1,000 toward the first performance of the Berlioz *Requiem* in America (conducted by Varese), $5,000 to a group of New York Dadaists, and $5,000 toward a projected exhibition of sculpture by Mestrovic.

This meager sampling of her organizational activities hints at how little time was left for her own art. Disputes over the *Titanic Memorial*'s installation left it homeless in her studio. Her writing was limited to letters, reports, plans relating to fund-raisers and short notes to family members. When sculpting, one theme obsessed her, that of soldiers in battle. The result was a series of quickly modeled, impressionistic poses, most eventually cast in bronze, some later developed into war monuments. Titles included *His Last Charge,* a man thrust back in response to the shock of a bullet, *Private of the Fifteenth,* a black soldier in salute, *Chateau Thierry,* a soldier clutching his rifle and looking anxiously into the distance, *Found,* one soldier finding his wounded comrade, and *The Blind Soldier,* a marble relief of one soldier tenderly guarding his blind friend. The impression of muddy boots, wrinkled and filthy clothes, fearful and exhausted bodies combined in her most emotionally expressive works. Given the large number of pieces, some were more successful than others, but overall it was a project she could feel maintained her place among sculptors of the day.

The Party Pickets, While Alva
Drums Up Money in Newport

Where at this time Americans typically set aside their personal goals for the war effort, as Gertrude did, members of the Woman's Party refused to temporarily defer their demands for suffrage. Since Alice Paul and other key members of the Woman's Party were Quakers, the declaration of war rankled their pacifist convictions. Its members could also do war work, Paul announced, but not under party auspices. Most stayed on with the cause, and as the weather warmed, so did the spirits of the pickets, whose signs broadcasted more inflamatory slogans. On June 20, when President Wilson received an envoy from Russia, where women had just received the vote, the pickets advertised:

"PRESIDENT WILSON AND ENVOY ROOT ARE DECEIVING RUSSIA. THEY SAY 'WE ARE A DEMOCRACY. HELP US WIN THE WAR SO THAT DEMOCRACIES MAY SURVIVE.'"

"WE WOMEN OF AMERICA TELL YOU THAT AMERICA IS NOT A DEMOCRACY. TWENTY MILLION WOMEN ARE DENIED THE RIGHT TO VOTE. PRESIDENT WILSON IS THE CHIEF OPPONENT OF THEIR NATIONAL FRANCHISE."

It was not long before male onlookers became inflamed as well, reading in such words being expressed during wartime the idea of "traitor." Young boys, men in uniform, and businessmen tore the banners away from the women and in some cases struck them, pushed them down, or tore at their hair.

On June 22, following several incidents of such violence, the government began arrests of the pickets, not their attackers. The charge was the only one that could be legally made, that of obstructing the sidewalk. On August 14, a particularly violent crowd of young boys, men in uniform, and others formed a mob that chased the pickets back to the party headquarters, tore down banners, including the American flag, and began tossing eggs, tomatoes, and apples. A shot rang out. Several pickets who arrived too late to be let in were dragged along the pavements. Police did nothing.

While the pickets marched on the Capitol, Alva retired to Newport, where she brought Sara Bard Field to serve as her ghostwriter on a proposed autobiography. Of modest means, Sara was so overwhelmed by the opulence of Marble House that against Alva's wishes she eventually moved out to live in a boarding-house. She could not comprehend how Alva, so fervent on behalf of working women, could abuse her servants, even strike her maid with a hairbrush. Nor could she understand why Alva continued to attend social events that frankly bored her. "How do you endure it?" she asked one night. "To get money for causes out of them," Alva replied.

As she came to know Alva better, Sara softened, for she sympathized with Alva's early circumstances, her abuse at the hands of Willie, her courage in di-vorcing him, her fearless defense of the powerless. Yet she felt contaminated amid the rich of Newport, who ignored the tragic meaning of the sailors and soldiers crowding the streets and continued their self-indulgent ways. Even the high-ranking military officers she met at social events exhibited a shocking lack of interest in the war or in their men.

Sara's private life was unconventional. She had married a minister and lived with him and their two children in Burma. Upon returning to the West coast, she realized she did not love him, left him with the children, and fell in love with lawyer and poet Charles Erskine Scott Wood, who was also married. She wrote Wood daily, and she shared some of his letters to her with Alva, who chided her for the affair because he had so little to offer. "You must bury Ro-mance for the Cold Facts of Life in which your children are bound up. You cannot help your children to advantages through sentimental romance but through money which alone has power."[24] Marry first for money, she advised, then for love. It had worked for her! She even tried to stir a romance between her son Harold, stationed nearby, with Sara, and he was smitten. Sara would have none of him, though she was surprised to find he shared many of her liberal political beliefs and was a thoroughly nice man.

A few days later Sara was shocked to hear Alva confess that she was in love as well, with a younger man. When speaking of him, she would bring up other cases of May-December marriages, such as that of Jennie Churchill and George Cornwallis-West. When Sara reminded her that he had deserted Jennie for an actress, Mrs. Patrick Campbell, Alva noted that it was for yet another older woman. Sara wrote Wood, "My heart aches for her—selfish to the core and weighted down from babyhood with the heaviness of too much possession. A sculptor could well use the idea of her as a model for 'Aspiration chained.'"[25] She was relieved to find that the swain, one Ralph Potter, a clean-living Harvard graduate, fond of sports and gardens, seemed attracted to Alva's "vigorous men-tality and uncompromising selfness."[26] Alas, Sara and Alva soon left Newport, and Ralph Potter disappeared from history, his full place in her life unknown.

The Women Are Jailed
for Freedom

Now it was September, 1917, and the legal appeals of the picketers had been exhausted; women arrested various times through the summer were finally sentenced to the workhouse. One of the judges pronounced the banners treasonable, but the only charge he could hold them to remained obstructing the sidewalk.

Those jailed left behind stark descriptions of the setting: the rough heavy clothes, pails for toilets, enforced silence during meals, no pencils allowed, only two letters permitted to be sent out a month. Playing off the racism common to the era, the warden moved a group of black women from their segregated quarters into the suffrage prisoners' wing. His ploy worked—they were deeply insulted to have to share space and such supplies as soap with sick, often syphilitic black women. Although the picketers were sympathetic to the plight of these prisoners, their sense of white superiority was greatly affronted.

As in many prisons, the food provoked rebellion. Women sickened as they sat down to face wormy beans, hominy, rice, corn bread, and cereal, with no butter, sugar, milk, or fresh fruit. One day a prisoner pulled fifteen worms out of her dish and laid them out on the table. Ada Davenport Kendall then chose to go on a hunger strike and was put in solitary confinement in a room with dirty linens and sent only bread and water. Others followed her protest in sympathy.

Then on November 14 occurred what was later called the Night of Terror. It began when a new group of suffrage prisoners refused to answer any questions during intake. After several hours, the door burst open suddenly, and the warden of the workhouse was followed by a large contingent of men who seized the women and began to drag them to the cells, cursing them in the process. No one was spared. A frail and lame seventy year old was dragged down the stairs despite her pleas. One woman was shoved against an iron bed so hard she suffered a concussion that left her unconscious all night. A third had a heart attack. A frail Dorothy Day, who was was to make a career out of helping the poor, was cursed and slammed about.

The women were thrown into a wing with filthy mattresses on the floors. The cell ventilators were closed, heating cut off. Toilets in cells required that one call for a guard to handle the flush, which was controlled from the outside. No toilets flushed that night. Guards roamed menacingly with large sticks.

The following day, though sick and often dizzy, the women refused food or prison clothes, claiming they were political prisoners. Refusing food, they were forced: "I was held down by five people at legs, arms, and head. I refused to open mouth. Gannon [the doctor] pushed tube up left nostril. I turned and twisted my head all I could, but he managed to push it up. It hurts nose and throat very much and makes nose bleed freely. Tube drawn out covered with blood. Food dumped directly into stomach feels like a ball of lead."[27] Sentenced to seven months' imprisonment, Alice Paul was thrown into the psychiatric ward, where it was decided that in addition to forced feeding her treatment should include shining a flashlight in her face hourly throughout the night.

The establishment press, holding the women's protest was traitorous during a time of war, supported the arrests and said little about the imprisonment. While tossing the party members into the same cast as anarchists and Bolsheviks, they neglected to deal with the fact that most of the women were from the privileged classes, well educated, professionals, or married to professionals and businessmen. They were all ages, and few were like Alice Paul, a virtual nun to the cause.

In a letter to the New York Times, Alva observed the women had "committed no violence, but have stood there quietly, peacefully, lawfully, and gloriously. In return they have been attacked by the metropolitan police and their property destroyed." She reiterated a point made in the banners, that if the country was fighting for democracy, that if it was an ideal worth dying for, then how could the president and Congress deny such to women? Kept out of the political process, women's only recourse was the public banner. As for the claim of militancy, "Why all this tenderness and delicacy about 'militancy' in the form of banner-bearing when the Governments of all nations are conscripting their men, including in our own nation, to be militant? . . . Why this horror of mild 'militancy' on the part of subject citizens?"[28] In truth, the women were hardly militant, merely expressing their First Amendment rights. Unlike the Pankhurst suffragettes, they never sabotaged property or assaulted politicians. Yet as was to happen at later points in the century, merely speaking out on an unpopular cause led to illegal jailing. They were America's first political prisoners.

Despite the sensibility of Alva's point, NAWSA took pains to distinguish itself from the pickets and ordered those on marches it sponsored to carry signs to that effect. Picketing, they warned, was absurd, ill timed, and susceptible to grave and demoralizing suspicion. Carrie Chapman Catt insisted her suffrage workers must align with war activity, be it nursing, selling Liberty Bonds, working in factories, farming, or any other service. This directive was not easy for her and her followers, many of whom also had pacifist leanings. Their hope was that by showing their willingness to support the war, men would grant them the vote and more economic rewards in return. Furthermore, they had considerable evidence that their steady pressure and bargaining with politicians over the years was about to pay off, that even the president was ready to give his imprimatur. Nonetheless, long after the press, public, and many politicians came forward to praise the jailed Women's party pickets, NAWSA continued its condemnation. It insisted then and in its histories afterward that the Women's party protests had been detrimental to the cause and served only to delay suffrage.

When on November 23 the prisoners finally appeared in court for a hearing, the judge was so appalled by their strained and worn appearance that he decided that they had been illegally committed to the workhouse and should be freed or placed in the city jail, presumably a more congenial environment. Following one day of freedom and food, the government decided to jail them again, where the women once again refused to eat. However, this time the public uproar was so loud that after three days they were set free.

In early December 1917, the eighty-one jailed pickets marched onto the stage of the Belasco Theatre in Washington for a fund-raiser Alva had organized in honor of their sacrifice. Silver pins depicting the cell doors were presented to each. Several days later she learned that Wilson was including suffrage as part of his administration's goals, the first time an American president had done so.

The vote for the amendment was due on January 10, 1918. It was a truly climactic count, for in order to pass four men had to leave sickbeds and a fifth the deathbed of his suffragist wife, who made him leave her for the cause. The amendment passed with exactly the two-thirds majority needed.

To keep the heat on the Senate, the Woman's party started another round of demonstrations, this time reading from various of Wilson's speeches those passages concerned with liberty. When each reading was done, the woman would light it afire and place it in an urn, a symbol that liberty did not yet exist for half the nation. These "Watchfires for Freedom" once again aroused physical assaults from male onlookers and arrests by police. Although the women were sent to the District of Columbia Jail this time, the abuse and forced feedings continued. In March of 1918 a judge determined that all the arrests had been illegal.

Following a year and a half of shabby delays in the Senate, the Susan B. Anthony Amendment would finally make its place in the Constitution. Its passage went far beyond the efforts of the Woman's Party. NAWSA's steady and pragmatic "Winning Plan" impelled seven more states to vote woman suffrage in early 1917, and following the end of World War I, Carrie Chapman Catt convincingly swayed key senators to the cause. The withdrawal of oppositions from the Tammany Hall machine in New York City and similar city machines was significant. Many politicians were inspired by women's contributions to the war effort, and they realized they could simply no longer treat them as second-class citizens.

Nonetheless, in Knoxville during August of 1920, suffrage workers were in despair. Money, liquor, appeals to racism, and every form of antifemale prejudice threatened to block the Tennessee legislature from being the critical thirty-sixth state to ratify the Susan B. Anthony Amendment. The two hang votes turned on August 18, one the result of the governor's arm-twisting, the other of his mother's pleas. On that day 26 million women were enfranchised.

In their separate histories, both the Woman's party and NAWSA would claim major responsibility for this important advance. Catt would omit any mention of Alva Belmont, the woman responsible for pulling NAWSA out of the doldrums in 1909. Alice Paul would remember her, but on the same level of other workers in her group, someone clearly secondary to Paul herself. Alva would not have cared—she had never been in the service for personal adulation. And as far as she was concerned, the fight had just begun.

12

1919-1925

The War Makes Its
Final Impressions

As if the decade had not brought enough challenges to Gertrude's serenity, sometime in 1919 Harry wrote in an unusually large and hurried scrawl how, "By the worst piece of luck in the world—I would have given ten million dollars if it had not happened—I ran across your Stackpole letters last night in the country. You are the only person I have ever really loved, the only person that means more to me than any one else, man or woman. . . . Now the bottom is knocked out of life. It's all lies. Are you all a lie? Are you all false?"[1] He had known about her flirtation with Jimmie Appleton in 1902, but he never imagined she had been unfaithful with other men. Given the passion in Stackpole's writing, he could see the affair was not a casual physical encounter, and he suspected there were others. It must have particularly hurt that Stackpole was one of his closest friends and especially that he had been a frequent guest in Harry's home during the cuckoldry.

Just how the couple settled the matter went unrecorded, but soon Harry was sending his usual affectionate, hypochondriacal letters to Gertrude. Perhaps she lied to him and claimed that Stackpole was an exception, or perhaps she told the truth, that she was no longer dallying with other men. Whatever, they remained one another's "Dearest" in their frequent notes about their various activities and discussions about the children.

Foremost on their mind was Flora. The war hit hard and personally on July 14, 1918, when Teddy Roosevelt came to the house to tell her that Quentin had been shot down behind German lines and killed. Perhaps to help her daughter through the awful mourning, Gertrude had her pose for a small sculpture. She sat stiff in grief, head bowed, eyes sunken. Flora then accepted T. R.'s offer to be his private secretary, which she did until his death in 1919. Moving in with Quentin's sister, the vivacious Alice Longworth, she worked as a secretary for the Navy Department and the Women's Republican National Executive Committee. Later she joined her aunt Dorothy, who had lost husband Willard Straight in the war as well. Only ten years older than Flora, Dorothy proved the healing salve for Flora's bereavement.

The war's end meant Gertrude could once again focus on her art. In November of 1919 she premiered at the Whitney Studio twenty-four of her battle portraits under the theme "Impressions of War." The show was well attended and widely covered in the press, though not always as she would have liked. The printed reaction to this show typifies the difficult and unequal position she was cast in compared to other artists. The difficulty came both from her being a woman, wealthy, and a patron, sometimes all three confounding the message being delivered.

Her gender resulted in her work, like that of other female artists of the day, being prejudged in stereotypical terms. If a woman created an object, then it must depict feminine qualities. "In the sculpture of Mrs. Whitney is revealed the personality of the woman. It is rare that sculpture is so autobiographical, so temperamental. Mrs. Whitney's art reveals an impulsive, generous nature, enthusiastic, impatient."[2] Another reviewer wrote a long preface about how "these were sculptures from the heart in almost every instance. I do not in any sense say this as a criticism of them technically, but what I felt was, not so much the anguish and the torture and the horror of the soldier facing death however splendidly, but rather how sensitive, generous hearted women felt about the men who were at war."[3] Yet another remarked that her work was "feminine in its inspiration . . . the vehicle, notably, for the expression of deep pity."[4] Another common reference would be to her "decorative" sensibility. The problem with such criticism and its interpretation of gender qualities is that it avoids the larger criticism of the art itself. The implication is that women are not truly artists, for they are not judged on the same level as men.

Classic here was Guy Pene du Bois, who mocked Rosa Bonheur for smoking cigars and wearing trousers. She "denied her sex and expressed the need she felt as an artist to emulate men." As for most women sculptors, they were "little women trying to be big men." Gertrude Whitney, however, "resolutely expresses her sex" through her "feminine whimsicality," yet evidence of "patient hours" at work. He admired Gertrude's battle poses for failing to reflect the influence of her sturdy masculine teachers, Fraser and O'Connor. His ultimate compliment: "She has learned to be a sculptor while remaining a woman."[5]

At the same time Gertrude's work confounded some critics because it so strongly exhibited a sense of what they called "virility." They found it difficult to conceive that this mere woman could elicit such feelings of strength and power through her technique. Consequently, references to the masculine features of her work, the sense of vigor and potency, were immediately accompanied by reminders of her essentially feminine inspiration. In other words, she might sculpt like a man, but she wasn't one.

While Gertrude was hardly alone in being subtly discounted—her work interpreted only insofar as it reflected on her womanliness—she was alone in being so wealthy an artist. This characteristic led to such commentary as that of the *New York Times:* "Poor Little Rich Girl and Her Art: Mrs. Harry Whitney's Struggles to Be Taken Seriously as a Sculptor Without Having Starved in a Garret." In some papers, society columnists, rather than the art critics, covered her work.

Having been patronized and criticized by her social set, to receive similar treatment from art critics was especially disheartening. "People would look at me, then at [a sculpture], then make the bland assertion that they could not understand how a woman my size could build up a statue of that height." Even worse, "[L]et a woman who does not have to work for her livelihood take a studio and she is greeted by a chorus of horror-stricken voices, a knowing lift of the eyebrows. And much more condemnatory."[6] The stereotype had elements of truth, she acknowledged, for the renting of studios had recently become fashionable among certain young women who "spend half an hour daily messing up a palette of paints or a lump of clay." She felt she did not deserve to be lumped with such women (and one must add, young male pretenders as well) who were mere dabblers in the Greenwich Village bohemian life-style.

On the other hand, artist colleagues indulged her in a different way. Few would give her a necessary yet unflattering opinion or constructive criticism. Andrew O'Connor was the exception, and she continued through the years to seek his counsel and appraisal. She greatly appreciated such evaluations, for she was hypercritical of her deficiencies in technique, but they did not come often from others. Also, most of the artists she associated with worked in other mediums, notably painting and drawing. This lack of frank advice from peers may account for some of the unevenness in her work.

It would be wrong to conclude she went unrecognized. For one, her *Titanic Memorial,* which was exhibited in various forms, drew repeated praise. She was featured favorably in all the articles on woman sculptors of the day (and with none of the pejorative references to her wealth). When her war series appeared at the MacLean Gallery in London, one reviewer ranked it "as high as any one-man show seen in London in five years," and declared her technique "beyond criticism." When it appeared next in Paris, another critic remarked how one work "evinces that so important sense for 'profile' the absence of which, in modern sculpture, Rodin used to deplore."[7] He also singled out her architectural vision and talent for monumental design. (One reason she preferred Paris, she once observed, was the utter lack of concern with her wealth, the absence of the "starving artist" myth.)

Yet it was as a patron that she was earning the most publicity and recognition. One reason was the cleverness and idiosyncracy of the exhibits she organized with Juliana. One of these, the "Indigenous Art" show, held in 1918, exemplified her unorthodoxy. Here they conceived of hanging variously sized and framed blank canvasses in the Whitney Studio and having artists create the best picture as quickly as possible on the spot. A table loaded with paints, brushes, whiskey, and cigars sat in the middle of the room. For several days the participants cavorted while they worked. George Luks, drinking more than painting, dabbed his brushes at other artists' canvasses. Robert Chanler had an assistant spray paint on the canvas, which he then pushed around. Unhappy with the proceedings, Leon Kroll decided the idea was antiart and walked out. The participants took his blank canvas and developed work so successfully modern that one critic reviewed the "new genius," Kudo du Simodach Bey Oghli (the first letters of the artists' names). At a follow-up show, "Indigenous Sculptors," the artists collaborated on the slender figure of a woman on a pedestal, a host of admirers at her feet. Their inscription read, "Erected in admiration of the woman and sculptress who can cage twenty sculptors without bloodshed resulting therefrom." It was a rare moment of levity in those battle-ridden days.

Gertrude
Draws Inward

Late in the war, learning that her artist and student friends had little to do in the evenings, Gertrude took 147 West Fourth Street and turned it into the Whitney Studio Club. Several artists and their families already lived in the building, one of several in the Village she rented out to artists at low cost or for no rent at all to provide studio space and apartments. The remainder included the club's art library, billiard room, and offices; a squash court was laid in the back. Juliana Force became director of this informal and open organization, and she made her distinctive mark by ordering brilliantly colored furniture and decor. Dues were five dollars a year, though, characteristic of that disorderly organization, not always paid.

The Whitney Studio Club was more than a place for socializing. Its lessons cost little, and even Gertrude attended the sketching classes. Two galleries displayed members' works. With Gertrude's approval, Juliana would at times sacrifice the quality of an exhibition by giving an impoverished artist a break, even if it meant the first and last appearance of his or her work. Similarly, when Juliana purchased for Gertrude's private collection, compassion at times overruled aesthetics. Some concluded as a result that Juliana's eye was poor, but Lloyd Goodrich, who was to observe her selection process over the years, disagreed. She would come into a room, scan the selections, and very quickly and unerringly point to the best works, he asserted.

With the Whitney Studio Club also came a new seriousness about the women's mission. From the start their exhibits, where enthusiasm and cleverness were often the hallmark, had properly drawn mixed reviews. Some critics and visitors found the show themes inane; others deplored the inclusion of untalented amateurs or vacuous commercial artists. Most outspoken was Forbes Watson, critic of the *New York Post*. So acerbic were his reviews that one day in 1917, Juliana collared him in a gallery for a frank discussion. His blunt, perceptive evaluation convinced Juliana their exhibition program must present itself more coherently and seriously. Gertrude and Juliana could not easily subdue their playful impulsiveness, but from this point they would eventually mature and refine their approach enough to throw Watson's words back in his face.

With the addition of the Studio Club galleries to the original Whitney Studio space, the two women were now even more pressed by the need to mount several exhibits simultaneously at their two locations. The variety of eventual exhibits at both testified to their catholic tastes, from Edward Hopper's social realism paintings, Edgar Curtis's photographic portraits of American Indians, and O'Connor's sculptures to European works such as Italian drawings and works by Picasso. Most daringly, they mounted a collection of Russian posters, this at a time when anti-Bolshevism and red scare tactics drummed loudly from a growing right wing. Accordingly, after the war's end, Gertrude immediately set a plan to send contemporary American art abroad in traveling exhibitions as evidence the States were not backward creatively.

The club was also a place for fun, with Juliana at the center. More naturally subdued, Gertrude receded into the background, leaving Juliana for the more public contacts, the parties, the dealings with artists concerning their exhibitions. A staircase connected Juliana's space at 8 West Eighth to Gertrude's studio in MacDougall Alley behind so that the two women could consult without others' awareness. Gertrude was after all an artist herself, and she needed time for her own creativity. Having lost much of her free-spirited ways of the earlier days, she now struck some young artists as cold and hard, like her sculptures. Others saw a different side, playful and joking, the way she was with Juliana, but she felt too compromised in her curious position as patron and peer to be intimate with many club members.

This division of duties also satisfied the strong egos of each, for Juliana could reign in the limelight, with no fear Gertrude would move into her realm. In return, she was utterly loyal to Gertrude, who needed a steadfast presence in her life. So complete and intermingled was their collaboration that it is difficult to attribute particular aspects of the Whitney activities to either one woman or the other.[8]

Harry was often absent—he would lead the list of racing stable owners in winnings in 1920. Adding to Gertrude's loneliness would be Flora's departure, for she married Rodney Tower of the Philadelphia Mainline in April of that year. Although Gertrude liked Rod, she confided privately to Harry that she thought he was not a good match for Flora and tried to discourage the arrangement. Like so many young women of her day, Flora wanted the war years behind her, and she quickly grabbed this opportunity to start a new life. The spirit of the decade to come presented itself in the bride's waistless chemise wedding dress and bobbed hair. While Flora was fully modern, she would find that choice did not bring all the easy abundance and fun it promised.

In an undated fictional work probably written around that time, Gertrude describes a wealthy woman painter, now past forty, "alone in N.Y. She had made a pretext of some philanthropic work in order to leave her family at the seashore. The children were grown and independent, her husband was off yachting, and she had grown so tired of tidying up the disorders everyone left behind them. She had wanted her freedom for a while."[9] In real life Gertrude expressed this need by escaping to Spain, alone. In October of that year she wandered about from city to city, using her journal to reflect on her changing self. The sense of split personality remained, of the "sensible middle aged woman with a family ... whom she loved" and the "restless person, a lonely, selfish weak person with violent desires and wild dreams of impossible things."[10]

As with her 1901 trip through the Mediterranean, she recorded such sensuous descriptions of the scenery and people that the reader can readily participate in the smells, sounds, and colors of that culture. The Moorish architecture and atmosphere stirred erotic fantasies. In one daydream she imagined sculpting in a garden amass with flowers, cypress, pomegranates, and magnolias, with an Arab servant who would bring other Arabs and gypsies to her as models. When the day's work was done she would bathe outdoors in a little pool in the garden. Gypsies would feed her, then dance and sing for her. A lover would linger, "Pan arrived from the woods," and they would make love under the stars enveloped in the scent of the oranges.[11] These daydreams only heightened her loneliness and desire for "strong arms" about her.

Each day's sights further excited her imagination: religious processions, bullfights, cathedrals, and peasants, each provoking a particularly intense feeling, sometimes of awe, more often of melancholy. Toward the end of the wandering she reflected increasingly on the theme of her life, her lust for experience and the repeated dampening of that desire. "Was life to be passed so—being something, trying to be something else." The thought of returning to normal life left her feeling "like the lost animal returning to its lair to die."[12]

A final visit to the Alhambra provoked a daydream in which she felt she had lived there before, that she had been one of the Sultan's favorites. The thought of leaving, of willingly returning "to the usual and the commonplace" horrified her. Afterward she ate and drank too much to deaden the fear.

This remarkable document on midlife passage was Gertrude's last significant journal writing. In a sense she left behind her "restless" and "violent" person by the fountain of the Alhambra. Though only forty-five, she decided that her age demanded a severing of passions. So, during the raucous and wild twenties, a time during which others would loosen their self-control, Gertrude would seldom loosen her own. She dressed more conservatively, drew less attention to herself, and embraced "the usual and the commonplace."

Consuelo Finds
Happiness

Consuelo was facing more pointed changes in her life. Late in the war she had been actively involved in politics. In 1917 she organized the Women's Municipal party in London to propose female candidates in local elections. This defiance of traditional parties again reflects the consistency of her attitudes with her mother's. In January of 1918, against all predictions, Englishwomen gained suffrage before their American sisters. Aware of her progressive views, political brokers asked her to run for the London County Council as representative of the working-class North Southwark district. Despite her wealthy upbringing, Consuelo readily convinced the working-class Selection Committee of her suitability to represent them. Already popular among the poor, she easily attracted large crowds to her campaign appearances, which were often accompanied by small children singing "Vote Vote Vote for Mrs. Marlborough." The liberal *Manchester Guardian* approved of her candidacy, praising her as "the most energetic of all our duchesses" and highly experienced in issues of child welfare, the needs of working women, and local politics. Squeezing out the popular preacher running for Labour, she won the election in March of 1919.

Her tenure with the Council would be brief. In March of 1920 the newspapers hinted at what was to come. The story concerned Consuelo's going to court to petition restitution of her conjugal rights, in other words, to force Sunny to live with her again.[13] Her lawyers presented evidence that the two had lived together the previous November at her Crowhurst home. They claimed that after several weeks Sunny left for Blenheim, leaving behind a letter stating he did not see how he and Consuelo could "live happily together again." Further letters presented to the court included Consuelo's request that he reconsider, which he refused. Based on this strong written evidence, the judge decided that her pleas for restitution was "a sincere request" and ordered Sunny to return to her bed within fourteen days.

The request was of course a sham, the first stage toward divorce, which required proof of the husband's desertion and adultery. Since Sunny and Consuelo had been legally separated for twelve years, they must first demonstrate a recurrence of the marital relationship, something from which Sunny could desert. In fact, one of Sunny's sisters had accompanied him to Crowhurst, and his stay may have been only an afternoon. Several weeks later he and Consuelo arrived separately to attend eldest son Bertie's marriage to Mary Cadogan, daughter of viscount Chelsea. (The attendance of George V and Queens Mary and Alexandra at the rite marked the return of the Marlborough line into the royal social circle.) And after writing her fictional plea that Sunny return to her, Consuelo quickly departed for Eze on the French Riviera under the pretext of not feeling well.

There Alva waited in her villa, yet another in the long line of extraordinary mansions, to sit out the humiliating process with her daughter.

Indeed, even before the restitution case was argued before the judge, Sunny had taken the remaining steps to ensure the divorce decree. On February 26, accompanied by an unknown woman, he went to the Claridge's Hotel on the Champs-Elysées in Paris and signed in the guestbook "Spencer et Madame Spencer." The next morning he was seen leaving the hotel alone, the strange woman departing soon afterward. Consuelo would later testify that the signature was Sunny's but the woman was not she. Mr. Reuben Butler, an English inquiry agent, a private detective hired by Consuelo, happened to take room 194 adjoining 193, Sunny's bedroom, and swore no one left the premises that night. Based on this "evidence" the court granted the divorce decree in November.[14]

Consuelo's joy over the final break was short lived. On April 15, while attending the races at Auteuil, Willie K. suffered a heart attack from which he never recovered. She rushed to be near her beloved father and remained there until his death on July 22. Following the funeral in Paris, she accompanied the body back to the States for burial in the Vanderbilt mausoleum on Staten Island. From there she moved into Beacon Towers to wait out the remaining divorce proceedings in her mother's comforting presence. Willie's will of $54 million (less than $2 million of which was removed for estate taxes) left merely $1.7 million for Consuelo, but she had just received $15 million from him earlier in the year, so faced no change in her life-style.

The absence from home was necessary for another reason: she was planning to remarry and could not chance the slightest hint of an involvement with another man, for it would jeopardize the decree. Her fiancé was Jacques Balsan, a cultured and gracious Frenchman she had met during her introduction to Parisian society in 1894. Following her marriage to Sunny, Balsan became a family friend who visited Blenheim several times. Then his interest in aviation took him off on adventure, and she did not see him until World War I brought Balsan together with her father.

Having moved to France following his marriage to Anne Rutherfurd in 1903, Willie K. had quickly adopted allegiance to his new home and seldom visited the United States. He was thus understandably incensed when President Wilson refused to provide arms and men to defeat the invasion of "the despicable Hun." While his wife took on establishment of the American Ambulance service, Willie sought to make a similar contribution. The answer came in hearing that American barnstormer and daredevil flyers desired to volunteer to skirmish with the German aces. Deciding to put up the money to bring the volunteers over and pay them, he knew he needed an experienced and well-respected aviator to train the squadron so it would be acceptable to the French air force. The choice was obvious: Balsan, a man with numerous ballooning records and who was among the first to take out a pilot's license once airplanes appeared in France. In 1913, Balsan had flown to suppress rebel Morrocans in North Africa and became captain of cavalry aviation for the air force. Balsan gladly accepted Willie's offer to run the Escadrille Lafayette, and grew fond of the older man. (No doubt their mutual love of racing and speed strengthened the friendship.)

When the squadron was placed under American command late in 1917, Balsan took his numerous medals to London, where he was assigned leadership of the French Aeronautic Mission. Consuelo found his Gallic warmth and graciousness a most agreeable contrast to the unemotional Englishmen she had known for the past twenty-two years. With his refined manners, his placing her first in his life, his constant romantic expressions, he resembled the young men of her girlhood. He opened doors for her, gave her little keepsakes of exquisite taste, inquired as to her comfort and increased it, however small the gesture. He could spend hours happily conversing about art and interior design. (His well-placed family owned fabric mills in Touraine.)

Balsan also had a history of womanizing. His final test for determining the spousal suitability of a woman was her behavior on a balloon ride; whether Consuelo ever took this test is unknown. He was divorced, although Consuelo fostered the fiction he was a bachelor.[15] She could ignore any previous marriage as easily as she overlooked his small stature and his less agile mind, but she preferred that others think she was his first love. Love for Consuelo had always meant worship, and Jacques was happy to oblige.

Perhaps conscious of the symbolic meaning, Consuelo chose Independence Day in July 1921 for the wedding. At 8:30 that morning her son Ivor escorted her to the registry office in Covent Garden, where Neily Vanderbilt stood in as the one witness for the civil ceremony required by French law, then accompanied her to the Royal Chapel where he gave her away. Saying good-bye to her sons, she climbed into a plane with Jacques and flew off to her third and final homeland.

Ironically, Sunny was also honeymooning in Paris at the time. He had recently wed Gladys Deacon, who had now achieved her adolescent dream of marrying the duke. Even Proust left his bed to appear in his sealskin dressing gown at a pre-nuptial dinner for the couple, where he shared stories of melancholy with Sunny. Sadly, Gladys soon discovered that being mistress of Blenheim would not bring her the honor due the title. Both tenants and local gentry, who felt Sunny had been unkind to Consuelo, treated Gladys badly, and other duchesses reacted scornfully. Her thoughtless ways eventually alienated those more sympathetic to her. Nonetheless, she took over her estate duties enthusiastically, even picking potatoes alongside tenants. While she could handle others' ostracism, she found Sunny's dark moods less tolerable.

Consuelo would find her union with Jacques the very opposite, and she settled into the second half of her life finding that the man of her dreams was indeed just that.[16]

Alva Discovers a
New Protégée

During that spring 1920 stay with Consuelo in France, Alva reconnected with Elsa Maxwell, who was grateful to use her friend's advice and introductions to further her own growing career as a creator of interesting parties for the wealthy. Both returned home on the *Olympic*.[17] Also on that ship was a slender honey-blond adolescent whose delicate blue eyes flashed with intelligence and vitality. Clare Boothe was returning from a trip to England, where she thought she had met her future husband, war hero and Oxford graduate Julian Simpson. The flush of new love only added to her allure.

Clare's ideas on many topics were original and indicated a depth of education unexpected in so young a woman. Her father, a violinist, had walked out on the family when she was a youngster, and her proud mother misled the girl into thinking he had died. She had only recently learned of her mother's deceit and left home as a result. But her mother had compensated for this lie with a determination that Clare and her brother should have the best of educations. Somehow she managed to place both in well-run private schools, and when at times that was not possible, she encouraged Clare to learn independently by exposing her to the classics in all fields. A voracious reader, by early high school Clare was doing college-level work in languages, literature, and history. At sixteen, she wrote in her diary that her life's ambition included competency in four languages, marriage to a publisher, and writing something that would be remembered. She was to succeed on all counts.

Clare must have conveyed some of this background to Alva, who rushed to Elsa Maxwell to enthuse, "She's only seventeen and she's poor, but she has the beauty and brains to go as far as ambition will take her. If she gets half the advantages she deserves, you'll be proud to know her twenty-five years from now."[18] Within a few verbal exchanges, Alva identified Clare's nascent feminism and decided to recruit her as another protégée for the cause. She had finally found someone with the magnetism of the martyred Inez Milholland, someone who by sheer physical presence could force a hostile crowd to listen to her champion cause and become converted to it.

Clare was just as taken with Alva, who was unlike anyone she had ever met in her life. Of course, Alva's social prominence and money helped, for Clare had been raised to think that she deserved the status of her wealthy classmates. Although she believed herself informally engaged to Julian Simpson, she accepted an invitation for a weekend at Alva's Beacon Towers estate to discuss the National Woman's party. Later she went with Alva to Washington to meet Alice Paul. Yet she would still not commit herself to volunteer.

In June, Julian Simpson came to visit, and he was in for a tremendous letdown. It seems that as a joke, he had been misled by a friend into believing that Clare was rich, and nothing in her poised and polished behavior had given away the truth. What he discovered was a comfortable but definitely middle-class home in a small Connecticut town. (Clare's mother had recently remarried, to a successful doctor who was more interested in cures than in an affluent life-style). Julian abruptly left, pleading unexpected family needs, and he later sent Clare a letter withdrawing his interest. Indeed, he callously admitted his only interest all along had been purely financial, an admission that lessened Clare's trust for men and thrust her actively into the women's movement.

Always quick to use a promising opportunity, Clare called Alva and said she would go with her after all to Seneca Falls to celebrate the seventy-fifth anniversary of the Women's Rights Conference. Her first public act for feminism was to don a leather helmet and goggles and go up in a World War I Jenny to scatter leaflets over nearby Schenectady, advertising the event. Alva hired Clare to be her personal secretary, but in fact the pay went more for activities on behalf of the cause. Clare appeared in a number of cities carrying National Woman's party banners, and newspapers were quick to print photographs of this frankly sexy feminist. Alva was delighted to have the image of youth and vitality replace the previous shots of women such as herself, stout and as angry looking as bulldogs.

Unfortunately for the movement, Clare eventually took to heart a lesson Alva often repeated to her younger assistants, that every woman should marry twice, first for money, then for love. Indeed, she tried to press divorced son Willie K. Junior on Clare, who found him charming but "rather an elderly gentle-man."[19] The money appeared in the form of playboy millionaire bachelor George T. Brokaw, who was not much younger than Willie, though much handsomer. Sources dispute who introduced Clare to this catch—Elsa Maxwell credits Alva—but whoever the source, in 1923 she accepted his seventeen-carat diamond ring. (Brokaw proved to be a sadist who deserted Clare and their small daughter and declined to support them. In 1935 she would remarry for love, to magnate *Time-Life* publisher Henry Luce, and later write a play, *The Women,* whose wit and bite still keeps it alive on the little theater circuit around the country.)

Alva Pumps for Equal Rights and Is Branded a Radical

Clare Boothe's desertion of the women's rights cause was part of a pattern. With the war over and the vote in hand, most women were relieved to just get on with their lives and enjoy the new consumer prosperity and fun of the twenties. No longer hostages in their homes, forced to be dreamy-eyed, corseted ladies, younger women in particular instead drove automobiles, smoked, plucked their eyebrows, spoke in slang, and wore very little under their slinky dresses. A good dresser and a pal to men, the flapper expected to combine a career with marriage and children. Those retaining an activist bent usually agreed with Carrie Chapman Catt that achieving suffrage meant they could now focus their energies on other social issues. More liberal women turned to reforms in child health, women's labor conditions, prison reform, birth control, and maternal endowment, while conservative women joined their husbands in campaigns against smoking, the teaching of evolution, immigrants, and radicals. Few objected in 1919 when Catt changed the name of NAWSA to the League of Women Voters and defined it as a nonpartisan organization. Women should choose membership in one of the two major political parties according to their own intelligent reflection, she preached. It was time to get along with men, and not do anything too radical, such as retain one's maiden name after marriage.

The few ex-suffragists disagreeing with Catt were primarily members of the National Woman's party. Alva was now president, overseeing the general planning and fund-raising from Beacon Towers, with Alice Paul commanding the troops from Washington. Since neither the Republicans nor Democrats backed women's issues, the nonpartisan stance of the League of Women Voters appeared to them as *nonfeminist.* Alice Paul agreed with Alva that the fight against inequality had just begun, and it could be won only by persistent feminist activism. Alva pursued the even more radical idea that the structure for such activism must be a separate woman's political party.[20] In a letter to the *Washington Times,* she instructed women readers to "husband your new power. Suffragists did not fight for your emancipation for seventy years to have you now become servants to men's parties."[21] The most liberal feminists agreed; Charlotte Perkins Gilman contended women's power lay in not joining the party system of men, who knew they could neutralize women's influence once they were in the organization.[22] During a meeting of the executive committee at Beacon Towers, Alva introduced the idea of a separate woman's party and convinced Paul of its rightness. That the other members did not all agree was irrelevant: though no longer titular head of the party, Paul remained its prime administrator . . . and dictator.

This separatist stance irritated the establishment press. The *New York Times,* for example, praised Catt as "perhaps the ablest and almost certainly the most tactful" leader of women "in advising her sisters to join the existing parties and in advising them with the utmost earnestness not to make the terrible mistake of trying to form a separate party of their own." Those who might recommend separatism—Alva and Alice by implication—were discrediting "the political competence of the whole sex these *misguided* ones would claim to represent."[23]

By this time Paul often lived with Alva on Long Island. The jailing and years of fanatical devotion to suffrage had weakened the tiny Quaker, who finally accepted a modicum of comfort in her life. They were a formidable team that continued to attract talented and single-minded workers. Their myopic mythology that they had single-handedly brought about suffrage further preserved loyalty to the party. Those who had suffered the ignominy of unfair and brutal imprison-ment also remained. These volunteers were experienced lobbyists, fund-raisers, and grassroots organizers. They had impeccable files on the foibles and prefer-ences of Washington congressmen and had used this intelligence data to persuade many politicians to sing their suffrage tune. Heady with success, self-confident, regenerated, they were ready for new challenges. Most were also free of family ties, being permanently single, widowed, divorced, or with husbands fully sup-porting their work.

In early 1922 the party held a convention in Washington, inviting activists from throughout the country. Although Alva was overseas, Alice Paul represented her wishes concerning establishment of a separate political party. The recommen-dation fanned the dissent that had been festering among the delegates. For exam-ple, Jane Addams argued their main goal should be alignment with the international peace movement. Social reformers such as Florence Kelley of the National Consumers League argued for protective work legislation for women. Ella Rush Murray wanted the organization to appoint a special committee to ask Congress for an investigation of the trickeries used in the South to prevent black women from voting. The membership voted down these various proposals, caus-ing their supporters to later condemn the proceedings in print.

The critics' slurs became encased in history. Most were along the lines of Kelley, who accused the party of being a group of rich and professional racists who ignored the needs of working women.[24] (That many of the critics behaved in similarly racist ways was overlooked.) The party was unable to defend itself, partly because it was deeply in debt, and partly because it lacked its own publica-tion. (Its *Suffragist* had terminated with passage of the amendment, and it would be 1923 before it would again have its own bulletin, *Equal Rights*.) Consequently, women not present at the meeting believed the antagonists, who were further backed up by the establishment press.

One criticism was accurate: the party was now explicitly racist. During this convention, Paul assured southern women that there would be no active recruit-ment of black members, and she refused to allow prominent black women to present speeches. Although Inez Milholland had been active in black civil rights, Paul refused black speakers at a memorial in her honor. At the end of the cere-mony, Inez's father stormed the podium and delivered a stinging rebuke of the party's discrimination (the text of which was later widely published). Even in her final years, a time of tumultuous civil rights activity, Paul continued to express racist stereotypes, her concern, for example, that she did not want the party archives to go to the Smithsonian because "colored women" would handle the materials.

The breaking issue dividing those who became known as social feminists from the party was protective legislation. Its constituents included Women's Clubs, the Women's Christian Temperance Union, and the League of Women Voters, all of which had worked with organized labor to institute protective work laws. These women held that their sex needed such safeguards as no night shifts or exclusion of women as operators of certain machinery. They had in their defense surveys and studies that poignantly documented the plight of factory women, the injuries and abuses relating to the job. How could a mother work all night and properly care for her children, they asked. At first the party agreed with these laws, but as it developed its policies, it decided that such protections should apply to men as well as to women. If a piece of machinery was dangerous, then why should men be forced to use it? And were not the protection laws a ploy so men could keep women out of the better-paying jobs? Although the party was conciliatory and sought several times to arrange conflict resolution meetings with their critics, Kelley and her ilk adamantly refused to talk. The breakdown in communication was to seriously hamper the further implementation of women's rights in the nation.

The final break with moderate feminists came during that 1922 convention, when members heard the results of attorney Burnita Shelton Matthews's survey of state laws regarding their inequalities toward women. She had found great inconsistencies, with many states wherein women could not be jurors, could not hold office, could not sue or be sued, could not have the power to sign contracts, could not retain guardianship of children, and so forth. In response, Alva and Alice developed a 29-point "Declaration of Principles" for the party's first platform. It addressed not only the numerous legal discriminations women faced but argued for such radical ideas as the inclusion of women in the ministry, equal pay for equal work, elimination of the double standard in sexuality, elimination of white-slave traffic, "the same right to control their persons as men," shared headship of the family with the husband, and the maintenance of independent identity after marriage.[25] Men, in return, would be exempt from the requirement that they support their wives; rather her "mutual contribution to the family maintenance shall be recognized." Given that some of these notions raise hackles of sizable numbers in the 1990s, they seemed pure lunacy to many readers in 1922. Yet many of the ideas had been expressed in 1848 at that first women's rights convention in Seneca Falls.

It did not help the party's image when Alva, now the group's leading ideologue and theorist, rose to give her notorious speech on "Women as Dictators."[26] Contrary to common pattern, the firebrand was growing yet more radical with age. Almost seventy, she inspired her followers: "By excluding women men have interfered for too long with the development, interests, and intelligence of humanity. Men have always kept women in subjection. To acknowledge them as equals would have destroyed their own pedestals. They have opposed an even partially woman-governed world, fearing a limitation of their own undisputed freedom. Men have insisted not only that we live in a man-governed world but that we worship in man-dominated church, and we can no longer accept this." Astutely, she pointed to men's isolation of women in the home and away from the community, "like the harem." In politics, it was "a crime for this country to be represented by some of the men who are there," meaning decrepit or stupid politicians. Her recommendation was that women unify by refusing to support either major political party, that they fight current attempts to close coeducational colleges to women, and that they refuse to accept the subordinate position forced in churches, because "Christ did not acknowledge man" as superior over woman. To speak of women as dictators, then, was to speak of their working for the entire human race.

More practically, to achieve these goals, Alva and Alice argued, the legal system needed a general principle of equality; otherwise it would be necessary to revise the code books item by item, state by state. They noted Wisconsin's recent success in enacting an equal rights statute to remove gender barriers throughout their legal code. The party wanted a similar federal statute, but without the qualifying clause allowing for labor protective regulations. Florence Kelley took a strong stand against all "blanket bills," as they were called, because they would remove too many necessary protections. She lobbied successfully for the support of such diverse power blocs as the American Federation of Labor and the League of Women Voters to fight such Equal Rights bills on both the state as well as federal level.

An even more powerful enemy was Mary Anderson, head of the new Woman's Bureau of the Department of Labor, who used her prominence and position in an undisguised vendetta against the party. "If the women in the Woman's Party would work in industry for just a few months, they would realize that [a woman] is not fit to do the work a man does. Most of them, as I understand, are women of leisure and professional women and they do not know the hard work that the woman in industry has to do."[27] Anderson stacked government hearings to support protective legislation, and she kept up her public ridicule of the Equal Rights Amendment.

A later objective look at labor protection laws suggests both sides were correct. Whether laws helped or hindered women depended upon the industry. Women printers, for example, were clearly obstructed from advancement once they were forbidden to work night shifts, a major work time for typesetting and printing for certain publications. In such cases labor protection really meant protecting males from further female incursion into the craft or profession. But in a few industries the laws did not affect women's participation and may have been a boon to working mothers in freeing them from late work or long shifts. As is often the case in politics, however, reality was irrelevant in lawmaking.

Undeterred by their attackers, the party had its legal team to come up with an appropriate wording for their federal Equal Rights Amendment. Dubbed the Lucretia Mott Amendment, contrary to recent historical claims, it was not the creation of Alice Paul. Many women in the party collaborated with the attorneys on the more than 180 versions. Among the eminent jurists asked to participate were Felix Frankfurter and Roscoe Pound, who advised them that the final wording would effectively wipe out all protective legislations, which meant any hope of reconciliation with the moderate feminists was lost. They decided to go along with it anyway.

The informal launching of the ERA occurred at the Seneca Falls celebration in July 1923. Clare Boothe's air pamphleting brought crowds of local women to join the conventioneers in a banner-ladden march across a field to sing women's anthems. Afterward, the women made a pilgrimage to the grave of Susan B. Anthony, where they vowed to continue the struggle she had started. Charles Curtis, the party's strongest supporter in the U.S. Senate, introduced the amendment in December of 1923, and it languished for five decades before rejuvenation, remaining to this day unenacted. To rouse support, Alva toured the Midwest, where she was highly successful in recruiting new members to the party.

By 1924 every other important feminist organization had refused to support the ERA and fought it outright. Still a relentless adversary, Carrie Chapman Catt branded the party "the cuckoo which laid its eggs in nests that had cost much to build."[28] Although the party had been on record against a piecemeal approach to equal rights, they were essentially pragmatists and followed that strategy while seeking the federal amendment. Consequently, throughout the 1920s they kept teams of lawyers busy throughout the country chipping away at specific statutes, gaining jury duty for women in some, eliminating discrimination against women teachers in others, and securing the right to sue in yet others. Still, by the end of that decade, in more than half the states, women were still prevented from jury duty; in a third, a mother's rights were less than a father's; and more labor protection laws kept women from better-paying jobs. Overall, of six hundred pieces of legislation introduced by their efforts, more than three hundred made the law books.

All this lobbying and legislating required large budgets, and the party was probably the smallest national women's organization in the country. Just as Alva rejuvenated the party's ideology, so she filled its treasury.

For years, the pressing need had been space. The party had been renting quarters in Washington, but not very adequate ones at that. Alice Paul had lived in a virtual cell in the basement, her bed and telephone the main furnishings. By 1922 the party was so in debt its very continuance was in question. Alva responded by paying more than $200,000 to purchase, repair, and furnish the Old Brick Capitol, really a joining of three old town houses comprising about a hundred rooms. It had become the temporary location of the Congress after the British ransacked and burned government buildings during the War of 1812. "Within the walls of these buildings," she proclaimed, "we shall handle questions long neglected by those in power from the neglect of which humanity is greatly suffering."[29] It would provide common ground to the "woman of wealth and the woman factory worker, the titled aristocrat of the old world and the labor woman of the new, clasp hands as equals and see in one another light of the new kinship."[30] A curious stipulation of her deed was that the party not hire any men or allow them to hold office.

Alva also donated her feminist library and some furniture to the headquarters, which was soon permanent residence for as many as forty workers, as well as temporary shelter to visitors from state womens' organizations. Besides serving as a residence and hospitality house, it contained offices and meeting halls. In keeping with the belief that nothing should come in the way of active service, a staff of servants handled the housekeeping and cooking. To inspire the workers, the house was decorated with paintings and busts of earlier feminists. Alva even gave up the precious Jeanne d'Arc wedding present from Harry as an inspirational model. It was not, however, a sign of waning fervor.

Gertrude Honors an
American Icon

Aging was harder on Gertrude than on her onetime aunt. Besides being a chain-smoker, she thought four or five drinks a day of bootleg liquor was modest. When added to her severe underweight—she would plummet to ninety pounds during one troublesome period—these addictions diminished her stamina and sense of well-being. Thus it is all the more remarkable that she continued her hyperactive schedule unabated and entered a decade of high productivity in both her sculpting and her Whitney Studio matters, as well as maintaining her strong devotion to her family.

Now Gertrude's most noted sculptures were to be large memorials, through which she demonstrated her versatility in design and technique. These commissions required much more than just studio work. Each involved negotiating with a memorial committee, a collection of otherwise unrelated individuals who had their own specific purposes in mind for the design. Since she demanded the same commission as any artist to cover the considerable expense of constructing a large monument, she would be hampered by fund-raising delays. Politics also entered in, as when, following several years of negotiations toward a commission, architects in Providence successfully lobbied to stop her going forward with the War Memorial for that city.

These byzantine negotiations sent her out of the studio on trips to meet with various authorities, to place pressure here, to pacify there, with Juliana handling the massive correspondence on the details, and representing her at some meetings as well. Gertrude's war relief experiences served her well here, and she saw projects completed that would have caused others to throw up their hands. She also got her way most of the time when petty censors or self-appointed art critics attempted to reshape a design. She even found the ceremonials surrounding the unveilings amusing, and she never took herself as seriously as the various speakers on the platform honoring her work.

The first such major commission was for a statue of Buffalo Bill to be erected in Cody, Wyoming. The state of Wyoming had set aside $5,000 for this project in 1917, yet by 1922 nothing had come to pass, not even a committee to arrange the project.[31] That year a friend of Gertrude's with a vacation home in Cody informed her of the opportunity. Inspired by the thought of such an all-American hero and mythic figure, she wrote Cody's niece and immediately received the commission. Afterward followed two and a half years of reading histories of the West, studying others' equestrian statues, and viewing photographs of Buffalo Bill and other cowboys in action. The final pose was inspired by a Western horse and rider she brought eastward to pose for a series of photographs. (The Paris Salon granted her its highest award for foreign artists for a working model of the project.)

Unfortunately, the people of Cody complicated the situation by exploiting Gertrude's reputation in hopes of getting her to fully fund the project. "The happiest two hours of Mrs. Whitney's life were spent in Cody," claimed Buffalo Bill's niece to the Wyoming papers.[32] Gertrude sent Juliana to the town to remind them they would have to come up with the finances to complete the statue. Juliana's magnetism captivated the townsfolk, and she flattered them by saying that "good Americans when they live should come to Cody."[33] The monument, she explained, was not simply of Buffalo Bill the man but of "the spirit of every American whether he was known or not, which contributed to this country's success."

The final three-ton, thirteen-foot-high statue was unveiled on July 4, 1924, in the midst of coast-to-coast news coverage. Unaffected by the publicity, Gertrude sent a telegram thanking the governor of Wyoming for "the honor paid me in having been chosen to make your statue."[34] Too busy to attend the unveiling, Gertrude approved the final base and site, a fifteen-foot-high, almost two-hundred-foot-long stone plinth designed by Albert Ross, positioned to overlook the Shoshone River with the snow-covered mountains of Yellowstone Park behind. The road leading to the monument was renamed Gertrude Vanderbilt Whitney Drive. There *Buffalo Bill* stands today, the only one of her monuments to remain a tourist attraction.

Buffalo Bill exuded the energetic, free-formed realism of her war sculptures, a contrast to her next major project, a memorial to the American soldiers who fought in France. Named after the town in which it was placed, St. Nazaire, this design was more symbolic. The central figures were an American eagle with wings outspread almost forty feet, atop which stood a helmeted American soldier, fifteen feet high, arms outstretched, an ancient sword in his right hand. Thus, as with the *Titanic Memorial,* cruciform shapes represented sacrifice. To add to the monumentality, Albert Ross fashioned a stone base of about seventy feet high. Gertrude selected for the site in that crowded port a rugged, commanding promontory. The technical problems of bringing this massive construction to completion fascinated and preoccupied her for two years.

Gertrude Sponsors
The Arts

While working on major commissions and smaller sculptures, Gertrude was no less involved with her continuing passionate service to American art. One of her most significant contributions was saving the young magazine *The Arts*. Launched by Hamilton Easter Field (an inspired amateur collector, teacher, and critic), from its first issue, the magazine offered an important new voice against the dominant academic art establishment. When Fields died of an infection in 1922 at age 49, critic Forbes Watson approached Gertrude and convinced her to sponsor the publication. A leading liberal and champion of artistic freedom, he was a favorite of Gertrude's, who took out her checkbook and established him as editor.

Forbes was by then hardly a stranger. His frank advice having won the women's admiration in 1917, he had become an informal consultant on their projects. In 1920, with wife, painter Nan Watson, he had moved into an apartment two doors from the Whitney Studio and two blocks from Juliana and Willard Force's residence. Born to a genteel Boston family, as a youth he had traveled often to Europe, where his erudition in art appreciation crystallized. Trained in law, he never practiced, but went into journalism instead. A feminist, he thoroughly supported and assisted Nan's career, and he publicly decried the common state of artist marriages where the husband insisted the wife set her talent aside.

He also had one quality that increased his glamour in the eyes of both Gertrude and Juliana: he was an unabashed sensualist, whose dapper dress and bright eyes helped him to successfully bed down women artists, gallery workers, and art aficionados he met in the course of his day. Soon after his move near the Whitney Studio, he entered into an affair with Juliana, who found him a perfect partner for her hours of chatty drinking in Village speakeasies, where, as John Dos Passos noted, "The waiter smiled with sympathetic understanding at your lady friend . . . [T]here were no rules and regulations, no yesterday and no tomorrow, no husbands to complain, no private entanglements with other women, only this moment."[35]

In 1922, for a brief period Juliana even rented an apartment of her own across the hall from the Watsons. Long tolerant of Forbes's past dalliances, Nan once again pretended to turn a blind eye. She had little to lose, for Forbes remained otherwise loyal to the bond, and his influence on Juliana assured Nan's favored presence in Whitney Studio exhibits. For Juliana, nearing fifty, the affair compensated for the loss of passionate feeling for her husband.

Although admiring the European modernists, Watson's primary sympathy was with contemporary American art. Toward that end he enjoyed skewering the more pompous pronouncements and decisions of the National Academy of Art.

And, like Gertrude and Juliana, he sometimes praised too quickly or liberally or failed to draw obvious lines between talent and fashion. But he also shared Gertrude's strength, that of letting the artists themselves provide direction, and consequently, many contributions to *The Arts* were written by the artists themselves. His editorial policy even expanded its definition of art to include interior design and the movies. As with Gertrude's other philanthropies, she exercised no censorship. "To my knowledge neither Mrs. Whitney nor Mrs. Force ever tried to influence what we said," remarked assistant editor Lloyd Goodrich.[36] Although some gallery owners withdrew advertising in protest over various articles, Gertrude underwrote all the yearly deficits for the life of the publication.

Gertrude and Juliana were also accomplishing much on the gallery front. Reviewers wrote more about Whitney Studio and Whitney Studio Club exhibitions, frequently praising them and they were less likely to make snide comments about "Bolshevik" or "socialist" artists. The Whitney Studio Club reviews in particular applauded the variety in viewpoint and method as well as the freshness and vitality of the work of upcoming American artists. For example, a typical 1923 review observed, "It used to be the Independents to which one went on a tour of discovery for new talent [where] now it is the Whitney Club show. The impression that the Whitney Studio Club favors a certain type of modern art, an off-shoot of the Bellows-Luks-Glackens group, is erroneous. A glance around the galleries is enough to disprove such an opinion."[37] Another in 1924 remarked, "It is one thing to mean to do good and another to achieve it. This institution provided an excellent gallery and all sorts of enticements to young artists for a number of years before it finally caught on. The young artists who now belong are talented."[38]

In addition to the annuals, Gertrude and Juliana mounted several dozen solo and limited shows that brought a number of deserving artists into the spotlight. One that occurred in January of 1923 hints at their personal involvement with the artists. Featured were fifty watercolors and gouaches of the industrial city by John Dos Passos, thirty-one paintings by Adelaide Lawson, and six carvings by Reuben Nakian. Modestly proud of his first major exhibit, Dos Passos scribbled on the back of his invitation to Scott Fitzgerald, "A desperate tea will be held at the Whitney S Club Friday afternoon Jan 5—Contestants are advised to wear masks and raincoats. Lost articles such as happy phrases, critical conundrums et al will be confiscated by the management."[39] Nakian was not even expecting a show. He had been overwhelmed the day the women turned over to him the garage studio of a stonecutter who had once worked for Gertrude. The man had quit the business, leaving behind all his tools, pulleys, and turntables. After some time, Juliana called Nakian over and told him to bring by some of his works, that they were giving him a show.

Juliana's own collecting preference expressed itself in an exhibition of American folk and primitive art mounted in 1924. "The Cigar Store Indian has found a home," one critic approved, for the American primitives on view "serve as the much-needed first link in the chain of American art."[40] She also worked with Gertrude in creating traveling exhibitions that took Whitney Studio Club works across the country, from Boston west to Minneapolis, Denver, San Francisco, and south to New Orleans.

During this time, a subtle competition ensued between the Whitney galleries and Stieglitz's 291. Gertrude and Juliana saw themselves as facilitators for many views in modern art, and they fully expected time would separate the works of quality and the noteworthy experiments from the less significant ones. Stieglitz nurtured a tiny select group of artists he had determined (correctly as it turned out) were the current equivalents of Old Masters. They included Arthur Dove, Marsden Hartley, John Marin, Georgia O'Keefe, Paul Strand, and himself. He was also adamantly modern, and he rejected any American artist whose style was not directly descended from recent revolutionary European art. Although Gertrude and Juliana's catholic taste included the avant garde, they did not count it superior to others. (Significantly, the one medium they excluded was Stieglitz's own—photography.) Given the extreme egotism of the two women and Stieglitz, none of the works of Stieglitz's group hung on Whitney walls during this time.

Two Glorias Bless the
Vanderbilt Family

As if all the deadlines, letters, exhibition planning, travel, and sculpting related to her own art and that of other artists were not complicating her life enough, Gertrude's family was a source of frequent irritation during the twenties. Indeed, one of the children would get the family name on the scandal sheets, while another would cause gossip in society circles. The Literary Digest had proclaimed, "Society is not only undergoing a revolution, it is experiencing a devil-ution. Not only is it undergoing, it is going under." The Whitney children were prime examples of this change.

The first scandal occurred in the summer of 1922 when dancer Evan Fontaine, who claimed to have been engaged to Sonny, charged him with being the father of her child and sued for a million dollars. What may have provoked her was announcement of his plans to marry socialite Marie Norton, so Evan included breach of promise in her complaint. Over a period of weeks she and her mother fed reporters ever more fantastic stories, such as one identifying Flora as the bearer of secret love letters between her brother and Evan, another blaming Gertrude for preventing the marriage, and yet another describing an attempted kidnapping of the child. While the tabloids repeated these tales, Gertrude kept her silence and set the lawyers to work.

While it is tempting to think wealth bought the eventual judgment of innocence to Sonny, the facts imply he was victimized by an emotionally unstable woman and her mother. Evidence appeared that "Miss" Fontaine was in fact married to one Sterling Adair at the time Sonny reputedly proposed. Furthermore, it seemed Evan had committed perjury during a later annulment hearing in claiming her husband consented to the legal proceedings, which he had not, and that her mother also perjured herself in testifying that the couple had lived together for only three hours, whereas they had actually cohabited for a year. Eventually a letter from Evan to her ex-husband was produced in which she asked him to swear that they had not lived together. Despite the fact that the judge tossed out the annulment and voided the suit against Sonny as well as the two perjury indictments, the two women continued to use the court to harass Sonny and the family. They were utterly unsuccessful.

In the midst of this brouhaha, Alice called Gertrude one day to say Regi was engaged to Gloria Morgan, the sultry daughter of minor American career diplomat Harry Hays Morgan. She insisted that Gertrude and Harry attend the family reception to meet the fiancée.

Regi had continued to be a disappointment to Alice. He had deserted his wife and his eight-year-old daughter without money in Europe, and continued his gambling and womanizing. When his wife finally divorced him in 1919, his longtime mistress, discovering he had no interest in making her the next Mrs. Vanderbilt, took an overdose of opium and Veronal and survived only because a bellboy happened to hear her screams. If Regi was not the only man in the Vanderbilt line to be a wastrel, he represented a nadir. His corpulence, puffy hands, and haggard, heavy-lidded eyes made him appear ten years older than his forty-two years, and his mother knew that his life was threatened by liver disease. Nonetheless, Regi was *the* catch of the day. For many women in that set that partied endlessly, his fun-loving nature and recklessness only added to his obvious financial appeal.

Alice was above all a practical woman, who was relieved to see Regi show an interest in any commitment, even to a seventeen-year-old girl of doubtful lineage. Several years of convent school (and a social-climbing mother) had at least taught Gloria Morgan the fine points of demeanor and bearing. She could pass in society, her charming stammer, her odd accent with its touch of several European countries distracted the curious from asking too many questions of background.

If Alice was cool to the match, Gertrude and Harry must have been downright disapproving. They would have known what Alice might not, that Regi's fiancée had been dubbed "Glorious Gloria" by Maury Paul, writer of the Cholly Knickerbocker column. Since her sudden appearance in New York with her equally bewitching twin sister Thelma, she was the topic of frequent gossip, published and otherwise. (Their older sister Consuelo, another brunette beauty, was in Europe at the time.) Released from the eternal vigilance of a hysterical and abusive mother, Gloria and her twin strode blasély into the center of that part of society centered around speakeasies with their bootleg liquor, and found themselves welcomed particularly by the men within. They were like the flappers in

Fitzgerald novels, "the best thing a girl can be in this world, a beautiful little fool."[41]

Ironically, most of the midtown Manhattan speaks were in old brownstone residences once inhabited by the Knickerbocker society. It amused many New Yorkers that the greatest concentration was not far from Grace Vanderbilt, still reigning from her part of the old Triple Palace. Virtually every house along Fifty-second street was a speak, the most exclusive being the Twenty-one Club, known to habitués as Jack and Charlie's. There society mixed with celebrities of stage and screen in a mansion renovated to hold two bars, restaurants, lounges, and a dance floor with orchestra. The real activity occurred around midnight, after the Broadway shows had closed. More notorious and popular were the various speaks of Texas Guinan, "Queen of the Night Clubs." Mixing racketeers and debutantes, showgirls with intellectuals, call girls with stock market financiers, she invented the setting for what would be called café society.

Attending such spots, the Morgan twins became enamored of celebrity, be it evangelist Aimee Semple McPherson, Lord and Lady Mountbatten, aspiring mayor Jimmy Walker and his mistress Betty Compton, racketeer banker Arnold Rothstein, and actress Mae West. Lithe and stunning, they easily found companions to take them in their own handmade dresses to the Lido, Ciro's, or the Trocadero, where they could see Fred and Adele Astaire dance, Beatrice Lillie do her comic songs, or Paul Whiteman and his band perform. In the early hours of the morning, the raucous party would board a taxi for Harlem and the jazz clubs. While fun and entertaining, these venues were not the sort of schools to inculcate character, virtue, and purpose.

The Morgan twins did, however, keep their sexual virtue. Despite the new freedoms, sexual activity in the twenties retained some of its Victorian undertones. And raised as Catholics, though not devout, the girls further valued the preservation of virginity until marriage, especially if the man was rich. This belief may explain Thelma's hasty marriage to James Vail Converse, grandson of the founder of the Bell Telephone Company. Thelma had not been smart enough to check him out and learn he had very little of his own money. He was also an alcoholic and turned out to be a wife beater as well.

Deserted by her twin, Gloria set her sights on Regi, using his daughter Cathleen to insinuate her way into his life. Cathleen was delighted. Following many years of neglect, her father was now paying attention to her, sponsoring parties for her—and Gloria was frequently part of the gathering. Yet it had taken over a year for Regi to propose with a sixteen-and-a-quarter carat heart-shaped diamond ring. When he told Cathleen of his engagement to Gloria, she burst into tears, distraught that she had been used by both her father and Gloria, and she fled to her mother in Palm Beach. Two weeks later Regi and Gloria staged a proposal scene in Regi's apartment for Maury Paul, who bought the charade. There Regi informed Gloria that every cent of his personal fortune was tied up in a trust fund that would go to his daughter upon his death. Only if she had a child, who would share the trust fund with Cathleen, would Gloria's financial future be secure. Gloria apprised Regi it was he, not his name or the Vanderbilt money, that she loved.

Despite their objections, Gertrude and Harry were proper and behaved civilly, if not warmly, to their prospective sister-in-law. They had too much else on their mind to pursue their doubts about Regi's choice of mate. They had to get to France, where Sonny was marrying socialite Marie Norton on March 5. (They were not happy about this match, for Gertrude saw in Marie the same qualities she had seen in Grace thirty years earlier.) Consequently, they missed the wedding of Regi and Gloria Morgan that took place on March 6, 1923.

Nor were they around when Gloria M. gave birth to a daughter, also named Gloria, on February 24, 1924. The delivery, a cesarean, was hard on the mother, who also came down with phlebitis. Worried about her daughter's health, Mrs. Morgan, who lived with the couple (and was known to wheedle large amounts of money from Regi), hired a nurse, Emma Keislich. On doctor's orders, Regi took Gloria M., as we shall distinguish her from this point on, abroad to recuperate, leaving the baby behind. Thus the child was six months old before it was reunited with its mother, six months critical to the development of a maternal bond.

When not abroad at the various seasonal hot spots, the couple spent most of their time at Regi's Rhode Island horse farm, Sandy Point, so Gertrude and Harry had almost no contact with them. When they were in the States, Regi was often drinking or sick from drinking, while his wife went out shopping or joined in bridge marathons with her mother. Consequently, baby Gloria had little acquaintance with her parents even when they were around, for she was often left with her nurse.

Fortunately for the baby, Emma Keislich was not a follower of Dr. John B. Watson, the psychologist Dr. Spock of his day. Watson's theories demanded firmness: feeding on schedule by the clock, not giving into crying, not allowing arguing back. Trained in Switzerland, with references from top society families, the plain, pudgy nurse had a fierce maternal drive that expressed itself in constant affection, indulgence, and protection. The infant came to think of this comfortable soft form as her mother.[42]

13

1925-1932

Walls Come
Tumbling Down

By the mid-twenties, Fifth Avenue was no longer synonymous with mansions and millionaires. Prohibition had brought the closure of the city's most celebrated restaurant, Delmonico's, and another popular meeting place, Sherry's, was transformed into a financial institution. The march of business steadily northward meant a doyenne of society would walk out her door one day to discover a gaping hole next door, where the foundation for another business tower was replacing her neighbor's palace. Not only would the light of the sun be blocked, but she would have to share her sidewalk with streams of office workers.

The rich had no choice but to move. Some sought out penthouses on the summits of the new buildings, or duplexes, even triplexes, within exclusive buildings, apartments so large with rooms so spacious that they felt like small mansions. Others, tired of managing large staffs, fled to suites in luxury hotels, where they redecorated with the family heirlooms and found life free of servant troubles much easier. (When the war began, servants fled for better-paying war work, and few wanted to return to the subservience afterward.) Still others noted a slum area on the East Side near the river, and rehabilitated the decaying brownstones into charming town houses. There Mrs. William K. Vanderbilt, Jr., took over a corner on East Fifty-seventh Street and built a handsome Georgian residence. Soon other millionaires became her neighbors, and the once-blighted area, known as Sutton Place, replaced Fifth Avenue as the exclusive address.

In 1925, Alice Vanderbilt, now eighty, was saddened by the change in the neighborhood around her home, as well as the cost of running it. She was sorry to learn that as a residence, the house, which had cost more than $3 million, was assessed at $100,000. The land, however, was valued at $4.7 million. After putting the house on the market, she began the long job of sorting through its contents and reducing them to fit the smaller white marble mansion she would move into at the corner of Fifth and Sixty-seventh Street. Before moving out, she opened the house for a brief period to benefit the Association for Improving the Condition of the Poor. Thousands of people she considered beneath herself paid twenty-five cents to gape at the opulent 137 rooms. Before the demolition, theater tycoon Marcus Lowe purchased the colonial room and bizarre Moorish smoking room for a movie theater in Kansas City. Gertrude saved the ornate iron gates and later gave them to the city for the entrance to the Conservatory Gardens in Central Park. Alice eventually got $6.6 million from the developers, who put the Bergdorf Goodman department store on the parcel.

Richard Morris Hunt's masterpiece, 660 Fifth, also went on the market that year, and it was torn down in 1926 to make way for a skyscraper. It had sat vacant since Willie K.'s death in 1920 because neither his second wife nor his children were interested in taking it over. Its most significant paintings, including Alva's favorite *Toilette of Venus* by Boucher, now hung in the Metropolitan Museum of Art. Soon Caroline Astor's mansion would tumble as well, with a new building, the Empire State Building, said to be the world's tallest, built to stand where the Mystic Rose once ruled the Four Hundred. Although Gertrude seldom stayed at 871 Fifth, preferring to live in her carriage house instead, it was still used by Harry and their adult children during their stays in the city.

The wrecking balls, the disbursement of treasures to museums, the contracts of sale—all mirrored the disintegration occurring on a more private level throughout the family. When society breaks as new forms emerge, people find their own ties to one another more fragile, more vulnerable to the larger cataclysm.

An exception was Grace Vanderbilt, who continued her increasingly anachronistic form of entertainment at 640 Fifth. She still had her servants wear the Vanderbilt maroon livery, and she ordered a red carpet rolled out over the sidewalks when guests were expected. Although she spent over a quarter-million dollars a year on entertaining, an expense that was eating into her capital, she blithely ignored the changes about her. Her guests included not only presidents, cabinet members, heads of state, and those royalty who had survived recent cataclysms, but actors, classical musicians, and conductors.

Once the war was over, Grace resumed her involvement with English society, and hoped to find an aristocrat for her daughter, Grace junior. Close to the royal family, she was responsible for bringing together a notable pairing in that line. Both Prince Albert (later George VI) and the prince of Wales were frequent guests on the yacht *Sheelah*. One evening in 1921, Wales presented Grace to a tall and handsome young man in a naval uniform and introduced him as his cousin, Dickie Mountbatten, son of the marquess and marchioness of Milford Haven. Shortly thereafter they held a ball at Claridge's Hotel and invited Edwina

Ashley, a slender intelligent blond with bright blue eyes. Noting that Dickie and Edwina were attracted to each other, Grace invited both for a ten-day cruise to Belgium and the south of France. The match took, and little could the couple have guessed the future ahead of them, including Dickie's reign as the last viceroy and first governor-general of India.

However much Grace tried to duplicate the ways of her childhood, her children were rebelliously modern. Rejecting British suitors, Grace junior eloped with a Princeton graduate and mining engineer, her brother Neil the only family member present. In a curious echo of an earlier family tragedy, Grace and Neily virtually cut themselves off from Neil when he insisted upon a career in the disreputable field of journalism. He lost not only their allegiance, but that of the rest of the family when he started a left-leaning newspaper in Los Angeles. (He went through life a charming and happy-go-lucky man, and as his six marriages testify, an optimistic one. He was one of the few men in the Vanderbilt line to break the iron bonds successfully.)

The Younger Vanderbilts Find a Name
Cannot Protect Them

Nineteen twenty-five was a bad year for Gertrude. That spring, her youngest child, Barbie, who had married Barklie "Buz" Henry the previous summer, became very ill during her pregnancy. The couple were living in England, where Buz was going to Oxford. Following her delivery of a daughter, Barbie had so profound a nervous collapse that doctors ordered her isolated in a bright and cheery room away from any house noise or street traffic. Gertrude nursed Barbie for many months, although doing so meant neglecting her *St. Nazaire* commission and other valued work. Then Harry wrote from the States that he had suffered a bad fall playing polo and had broken his collar bone; following this accident, he would never return to full health.

Worse, Flora's marriage was breaking up, and in none too calm a manner. Soon after the marriage, Rod had left his seat on the New York Stock Exchange for oil exploration, settling with Flora first in Los Angeles, then in Mexico. Caught up in the excitement of his new adventure, he had little time for Flora, who suffered through his long absences comparing him unfavorably to Quentin Roosevelt. The appearances of daughter Flora and son Whitney provided a diversion, but by the couple's fourth anniversary, they "dine alone in [her] room & talked & talked—dreadful—& decided it definitely—what hurts! what hurts—."[1]

Although Flora and Rod agreed to divorce, they fought over the arrangements. Distraught, Flora found solace in a married man, and people in the States were passing rumors about the adultery. Unhappy with the situation, Rod threatened to seek full child custody. Flora fled to England to join Gertrude and Barbie, only to be followed by both her lover and Rod. Back in the States, Harry agreed to work with the New York lawyers on Flora's behalf. Consequently, he and Gertrude wrote long and thoughtful letters designing strategies to solve their children's various problems.[2] Gertrude prodded Flora, her lover, and Rod to come to a resolution, but the negotiations changed daily. Gertrude's main worry was that Flora's lover would throw her over once she was divorced, for the man gave sufficient hints he would not follow through with his own divorce and then marry Flora. She succeeded by getting Flora to procrastinate—Flora decided she should wait until Rod found someone he was interested in so he would be less touchy about child custody. Eventually the situation cooled down, and Flora did get custody of the children.

While still embroiled in Barbie's and Flora's troubles, another event set in motion a drama that would eventually mark the Vanderbilt family for scandal one more time. Early in the morning on September 4, 1925, Regi Vanderbilt died wretchedly of internal hemorrhage, the result of his chronic alcoholism. So bloody was the bed scene that when his wife arrived (she had been on her way to see her ailing grandmother in Chile), Alice held her back from the room to spare her the sight. Gloria M. misinterpreted that concern, and she was angry that she could not view her husband until his body and surroundings had been cleaned up. She also misconstrued Harry's gift of $15,000 to pay for the funeral as evidence he liked her. These were the first of many wrong conclusions that were to haunt her for life.

To evade the press following Regi's burial in the Staten Island mausoleum, Gloria M. sent her small daughter to stay with the aged Alice at the Breakers, while she moved in with her mother at a New York hotel. With bill collectors descending, she took her mother's recommendation and went to the Morgan family law firm, that of Cadwalader, Wickersham & Taft. One of their staff, Thomas Gilchrist, explained that Regi was essentially insolvent at the time of his death, that his bequest to her of a half million dollars along with the New York town house and Sandy Point Farm were meaningless. Her only hope for any money would be to sell the properties, which by dower right claims would leave her with one-third the proceeds before creditors could fight over the rest. Until then, she was destitute, but Alice Vanderbilt had promised to support her in the interim. Fortunately, the child's trust of $2.5 million was sacrosanct, to be managed by a guardian until her twenty-first birthday. As Gloria M. was not of age herself, she also required a guardian to handle her financial affairs. Gilchrist recommended George Wickersham to handle that role, and Gloria M. quickly agreed. In fact, Gilchrist would actually handle the daily activities of guardianship as Wickersham's representative.

Surrogate Justice James Aloysius Foley approved the arrangement whereby Gloria M. would receive $4,000 a month for the support and maintenance of her child. None of this was identified as for the mother's personal use. Although

Gloria M. eventually received about $85,000 for the sale of the two properties, she felt impoverished. It had not helped that, at the auction of the furnishings, she watched people stroll around the grounds eating hot dogs and making pointed comments about the merchandise. Even the baby's carriage went, for $1.50. Alice Vanderbilt sent an agent to buy Regi's horse show trophies, as well as heirloom rugs, silver, linen, tapestries, and family portraits.

Gloria M. could not seem to grasp the fact that $4,000 a month was twice the *yearly* income of the average American at that time. Now, Regi's death thrust her more under her mother's manipulative guidance, especially since Regi's friends immediately excluded her. Lost and isolated only two weeks after his burial, she sought solace by going to Paris to buy clothes against Gilchrist's advice. Two more trips to Europe followed shortly thereafter. Gilchrist deduced that this was a woman who needed to be strongly controlled, if only for her child's sake, and he had one weapon, the child's trust. Consequently, when Gloria M. expressed an interest in moving to Paris, he warned her that her allowance could be reduced. She then appealed directly to Surrogate Foley, who agreed with her that Europe would be a suitable place for the child until she was old enough to go to school, at which point she must be brought up in America.

At the end of May 1926, Gloria, her child, Mrs. Morgan, and Emma Keislich sailed for France on the *Leviathan*. Before leaving, however, she acquiesced to her mother's insistence that the child, who had already been christened in an Episcopalian service, be baptized Catholic at the Convent of the Sacred Heart. They were careful not to let Alice Vanderbilt know, for fear of offending her and her generous pocketbook. Gloria M. must have felt great relief as the boat left New York City. She had won the first round with Gilchrist, but she was unaware it would be her only victory.

Consuelo
Faces Scandal

Nineteen twenty-six was a difficult year for Consuelo. Because he had married a divorcée, not only had Jacques been forbidden the sacraments of the Catholic Church, but Consuelo had been excluded from gatherings held by his conservative family. (Presumably Jacques' first marriage had been civil only; hence its dissolution would not have affected his status as a communicant.) To correct this situation, her marriage to Sunny must be annulled by the Catholic church so she would no longer be a divorced woman and could remarry Jacques in a Catholic ceremony.

Conveniently, Sunny wished to convert to Catholicism himself. In 1922, the Anglican Bishop of Oxford informed him he could not attend the Oxford

Diocesan Conference because he had divorced and remarried.[3] From that time Sunny was observed by his tenants to have changed his place of worship to the Catholic St. Aloysius Church in Oxford. Religion playing a large role in his life now, he wanted the peace of mind that would come with full acceptance into the Church of Rome and the sanctification of his marriage to Gladys through a religious rite. Once Sunny was assured that the legitimacy of his sons by Consuelo would not be affected, he agreed to the proceedings. Most significantly, Consuelo could provide the "evidence" for this matter, just as he had contributed to the charades at Crowhurst and the Savoy hotel in Paris.

The hearings occurred early that year before a diocesan court in Southwark, a summary later appearing in the official Vatican proceedings, the *Acta Apostolicae Sedis*.[4] There Consuelo's lawyers made the case that she had been coerced into the marriage, hence the ceremony had not been valid. Her brief testimony outlined what would be filled in by her ghostwriter three decades later: that Alva tore her away from Winty Rutherfurd, prevented her from seeing him, threatened to kill him, and demanded she marry the duke. Sunny's statement asserted that early in the marriage Consuelo had repeated the same story to him. Alva, Alva's sister Jenny, Consuelo's English governess, and Alva's good friend Mrs. William Jay all testified with corroborating evidence.

In accepting the tale, the priests reviewed how Consuelo was seventeen when she became engaged to Marlborough, despite "amore flagrare," blazing love for "M. R.," presumably Rutherfurd. It was her mother, who strongly opposed that match, who commanded her to marry the duke, using such intimidation as the threat of a heart attack or shooting M. R. Imagine Consuelo, they implored, endowed with every womanly grace with nobody to turn to and finding a guard placed at the door of her room on the day of her wedding. Consider, too, they argued, how shortly after the ceremony the unhappy bride confessed to her husband that she married him only because of her mother's violence. On February 9, 1926, the court declared the marriage annulled on the basis of the coercion.

That July the Church Rota in Rome accepted and validated the diocesan court decision and asked Consuelo to pay for all the expenses of the proceedings. Consuelo studied with a priest for a conversion of convenience, necessary for her remarriage to Jacques, and to gain full acceptance from her in-laws. For once she had managed to keep a sensitive aspect of her life hidden from public view.

Imagine her shock in November to learn of a news report that Sunny had applied to the pope for reception into the church and was seeking an annulment so he could remarry Gladys in a religious ceremony. The next day the Vatican claimed no request for annulment had been made. The day after that, however, the Vatican announced the annulment had already occurred, with both Consuelo and Sunny having been so notified. By the fourth day the papers disclosed that although all judges had been bound under fear of excommunication not to reveal any information on the case, "an excellent source [tells] that the verdict in this case was based on the fact that the marriage with the Duke of Marlborough was not freely given, but was wrested from her by undue influence on the part of her mother and other relatives."[5]

The buildup to this announcement of the annulment suggests the entire sequence of stories had been carefully planned by the papers. One possibility is that there had been a leak concerning the hearings, very possibly by a noncleric in the diocese, a secretary or char perhaps, who saw a way of making a few dollars or of simply stirring up trouble. (Perhaps a reporter had seen a copy of the material scheduled to appear in the *Acta Apostolicae Sedis,* but that is unlikely because none of the news stories provide the detail of that document.) The principals all went into hiding and refused to comment.[6]

The Anglican clergy in both England and the United States, however, picked up the story and kept it on the front page for another week. In New York, Bishop Manning departed from his prepared Sunday text to refer to the nullification as "amazing and incredible," and preached the "sacredness and permanence of marriage."[7] (The *New York Times* reminded readers how Alva had recently chastised that bishop for not hesitating to ask her for money while refusing to allow her, a divorced woman, to be listed as a contributor to church charities.) In London, Canon Carnegie said that it was scandalous that a marriage that had endured twenty-five years from which two children had been born could be annulled.[8] The Bishop of Ripon deplored the clear insult to the Anglican church that the Catholics would declare invalid a ceremony entered into by two Protestants administered by an Episcopalian bishop.

Bishop Manning saved his best volley for another Sunday: "That any woman of middle age, after years of married life, should be willing to swear that her parents sold her for worldly gain, and against her will, is in itself a scandal, and the more so when one of the parents [Willie K.] is not here to deny such an accusation."[9] There was no mention of forced consent during the English divorce trial, he added, so how could it be a valid issue for marital dissolution later? Further doubts were cast by Dr. Arthur Kinsolving, a clergyman who had attended the wedding. He reported Consuelo had been a "happy, radiant bride" and that after the wedding Bishop Littlejohn commented about her joyful appearance.[10] Adding that he knew the Vanderbilts personally, Kinsolving declared he knew firsthand that Consuelo had not been under compulsion "from any quarter" before the wedding.

By now rumors were spreading that Vanderbilt money had bought the annulment from the Vatican. Reprinting the original marriage agreement with its munificent awards to Marlborough, as well as the state of Consuelo's current wealth, more than $10 million, made the rumors more credible. This charge, combined with the criticism exposing Catholic doctrine as hypocritical, sent Catholic priests scurrying to defend.

The Catholics in the States were particularly pressed to act. The divorce rates, which had escalated greatly since the end of the war, were provoking much moral discussion in popular magazines, press, pulpit, and legislature concerning the imminent collapse of the family. For the church, long conservative in this regard, to have displayed what seemed to many a curious leniency in this case, was a public embarrassment. Worse, the revived white Protestant supremacist Ku Klux Klan was experiencing a revival, so much so that one in three Anglo-Saxon men in the nation were members. More than the South was involved: 10,000 appeared to burn a sixty-two foot cross during a klavern in New Brunswick, New Jersey. Catholics, as well as blacks and Jews, were the brunt of this bully organization's floggings, tar-and-featherings, brandings, castrations, and lynchings. When Alfred Smith that year tested the waters for a presidential nomination, Methodist bishop Adna Leonard of Buffalo, also president of the Anti-Saloon League, warned "No Governor can kiss the papal ring and get within gunshot of the White House."[11] Unfortunately for Smith, the Bishop proved right about the mindset of Americans.

The Catholic case was weak. The Vatican Rota pointed out numerous past instances where couples married under Protestant rites had applied for and received annulments, usually for the purposes shown in the Marlborough case, to have a later marriage sanctified. The requirements were rigid and "for one case of annulment that is decreed, hundreds fail."[12] As for buying an annulment, they observed that not even Henry the VIII had been able to purchase one—nor, more recently had the wealthy Goulds. Furthermore, the cost of the court, only $240, would be defrayed for couples who could not afford that modest fee. "Our Church does not do the sort of thing the Duke desires unless there is really just cause. Nothing more can be done for a Duke than for a tramp."[13] "Show us the tramp," the critics dared. None was forthcoming.

In another rebuke, a Catholic paper asked where Bishop Manning had been when the marriage occurred. Why had he not ensured that "a mere child of 17 and not of precocious stock was [not] cowed by the insistence of her family that she should become a duchess?"[14] This was a time, it reminded its readers, when coronets were known to be for sale. And as for the complaints that the church was being hypocritical, Protestant churches all over the world were recognizing divorce, hence it was the Catholics who really upheld the sanctity of marriage, they averred.

Hindsight argues that money did not sway the diocesan court and the Rota. Charges that priests were corrupt were and remain a common theme of anti-Catholic propaganda both in the United States and England. None of the critics considered the possibility that the clerics' judgment had been undermined by the duplicity of the witnesses with their story of a virgin despoiled by cruel parents. "The Catholic Church rejects the heathen practices of marriage by capture and of marriage by purchase, however plausible their renaissance may be dissembled by professing Christians of vast wealth and high position," explained one priest.[15] Nor should one judge the applicants and their witnesses too harshly. They were required to dissemble in the English courts to gain a divorce, so why should it be any different in a church court? And since no one testifying was a Catholic, the oaths of honesty would not bother their consciences. Also, the story was not totally false—Alva's objections to Winty Rutherford had been public knowledge.

In the midst of this religious mudslinging, Sunny hid at Blenheim, while Alva remained uncharacteristically incommunicado during her ocean crossing to join Consuelo in France. The reporters even looked up Winty Rutherfurd, now married to Lucy Mercer, Franklin Roosevelt's past (and future) mistress.[16] He maintained his gentlemanly silence, admitting only, "Yes, some thirty years ago I knew Miss Vanderbilt and I was one of her great admirers."[17]

Shocked by the gossip and attacks, Consuelo gave the New York Times an emphatic denial that she had been forced into the marriage. Such an intimation was "the foulest slander that could have been uttered against my father and mother, both of whom thought only of my happiness." She "may have been a little romantic and consequently over-enthusiastic at the time" with regard to Winty. "I want you to be clear that the step was mine and that I alone was responsible for it."[18] That rebuttal stopped the personal stories and calls from reporters. Unfortunately, Consuelo did not know that the proceedings were being set into type, that she would not be able to further discredit the story without perjuring herself.[19]

In 1927, Sunny knelt joyfully for his conversion and his remarriage in the Catholic Church to Gladys, but apart from religion he gained little additional happiness. Despite the steady influx of Vanderbilt money, which according to the prenuptial agreement continued following the breakup with Consuelo, he found maintenance of Blenheim ever more difficult. Worse, his relationship with Gladys had deteriorated. At first the differences were of interest: he liked jazz, she preferred Bach; she savored tramping through the Alps, he found such exercise excessive. The major break came after Gladys suffered a series of miscarriages. Terrified of having a child, Gladys refused Sunny's sexual overtures and kept a gun on her bedside table as a warning that she was serious. Frustrated by the "Hyperboria" of Blenheim, as she put it, Gladys drank. One evening at dinner when Sunny was discussing politics with guests, she yelled at him to shut up, that she had slept with all the prime ministers in Europe and most kings. She also took up the breeding of spaniels, which she would do the rest of her life, except she kept the kennels in the grand salons of the palace and let the dogs run about the halls.

In June of 1931 Sunny moved to Carlton House, deserting Gladys in a shut-up Blenheim. When she would not leave, he ordered the gas, electricity, and phone cut off, then sent private detectives in to evict her in May of 1933. Then signs of stomach cancer afflicted Sunny. Winston Churchill brought comfort, observing how his cousin "faced this universal ordeal with dignity and simplicity, making neither too much nor too little of it."[20] Death came swiftly in 1934, and to Winston's relief, with little pain.

Ever the historian, Winston's eulogy examined how changes in English society during Sunny's life "cast a depressing shadow." The several hundred leading families, including the Marlboroughs, had lost not only land and property in many cases, but were almost entirely relieved of political responsibilities and power. Unlike Winston, who moved with the times, Sunny had identified with the old system "and he foresaw with not ill-founded apprehension that the world tides which were flowing would remorselessly wash away all that was left. He resigned himself to this. He acquiesced and even aided the process." But despite his efforts to contribute to the more democratic England, Sunny nonetheless spent his final years saddened and frustrated in his attempts to preserve Blenheim and its treasures for the national culture.

What a contrast to Consuelo's life! The war was over. Away from England with its hungry children and tired mothers, she resumed life as though the Gilded Age still existed. Following her mother's example she acquired a collection of houses to decorate. In Paris, an imitation eighteenth-century house at 2 rue du General Champ de Mars was set behind lawns spreading out to the Seine. To escape gray Parisian winters, she and Jacques bought the tiny properties of fifty-two small holders to acquire an estate of 150 acres near Alva's Villa Isoleta in Eze. On this steeply banked property architect Achille Duchene created a version of a twelfth-century Cistercian Abbey named Le Sueil, or the Hearth. Desiring a place to escape Parisian summers, they bought a pink-brick, moated four-hundred-year-old chateau by the Forest of Dreux and restored it to its original design. (Alva bought her own fifteenth-century chateau nearby at Augerville-la-Riviere and began her usual endless construction, which included a bowling alley and cutting back the banks of the river flowing nearby to double its width.)

The estates provided a purpose for Consuelo, who could spend her days roaming through art and antique galleries with Jacques, a skillful haggler, and her evenings ruling over dinner and conversation. Invitations to her home were sought after by celebrities as well as all sectors of society. She created a clever ambiance by inviting a cosmopolitan mix of guests, filling them with delectable food, and directing the conversation with deftness. The result was much like the famed salons of such women as Madame Recamier. In the same room might gather French aristocrats such as the Duc du Gramont, old friends such as Winston (who appreciated Dreux for painting holidays), British politicians such as Lord Curzon, and entertainment figures such as Charlie Chaplin. There were fancy dress balls in Paris, horse races at Nice, and yachting off Monaco.

Consuelo also acquired the reputation of a Grande Dame. She refused to speak to reporters, who were inevitably told by her maids that "Madame Balsan is not at home." Given her deafness and her solid belief that wealth had its privileges, the criticism may be accurate. Although Consuelo often proclaimed herself a fervid American democrat, she idealized her charitableness, ignored its patronizing elements. Like many of the rich she was quick to announce her sympathy for the plight of the ill-fated poor and hungry, yet wrote most of her checks for her own comfort.

Though she had grown more vain, more preoccupied with the superficial, Consuelo flourished as a grandmother to son Bertie's growing brood and as a make-believe aunt to other children. Children from the countryside were allowed to join the young Marlboroughs on the estate for trout fishing, walks through the woods, and bicycling. She was permissive, doted on the children, perhaps to make up for her own restricted childhood and lack of opportunity to mother her own sons. In time, she would focus her charities upon less-privileged children.

Overall, it was a most convivial life. Her husband spoiled her, her friends fascinated her, and her family, both mother and children, brought pleasure. She could buy anything she wanted; she could order a servant to do anything she wanted. For a Vanderbilt woman she was doing very well.

Alva Takes the Feminist
Cause International

From the point of Consuelo's annulment in 1926, although remaining president of the National Woman's party, Alva would reside most of the time in France. Back home, the party was not doing well. The continued criticism from other women's organizations and the lack of movement toward the Equal Rights Amendment disenchanted some volunteers. Others could no longer take the semi-monastic vows demanded by Alice Paul. Some activists agreed with critics that the party had lost touch with the needs of working women, especially with regard to child care and family health issues. But likely just as disabling was Alva and Alice's splitting their energies between the United States and Europe.

Once Consuelo had remarried and moved to France, Alva began to spend more time overseas. Her purpose was to have a headquarters for organizing suffragists and feminists on a worldwide level. Though now in her seventies, she did not relax. As one party member observed of her at this time, "Like the Vikingess she was, she burned for action. Where her presence was necessary, a call brought her immediately across the Atlantic Ocean or the American continent, or both."[21] Toward that end, in 1921, Alva had invited Alice Paul to stay with her in Europe to establish ties with women's rights leaders overseas. Throughout the decade the two would spend many months each year together and separately overseas consulting with organizational leaders from throughout Europe.[22] By 1923, the pair set up two formal international arms of the party. An International Advisory Council was to provide the organization information and liaison with overseas organizations, while the Woman's Party Auxiliary of American Women offered expatriates continued affiliation with the homeland organization.

Decisions by the League of Nations had produced the same conflict among feminists over labor protection legislation in Europe as occurred in the United States. In 1919 the International Labor Conference of the League prohibited night work for women, a recommendation many nations had quickly ratified into law. Alva naturally gravitated to those feminist groups which agreed with her that equal rights meant equal responsibilities and that a work environment unhealthy for women should not be foisted upon men. Strongest here was the British Advisory Committee led by Lady Rhondda, who joined with Alva to provoke other European feminists into becoming more assertive and demanding about women's rights. Lady Rhondda was the daughter of a Welsh coal-mine owner who not only inherited his holdings but his place in the House of Lords. Obviously, she was not very popular with conventional aristocracy, but she was just the sort of upper-class renegade Alva admired. Lady Rhondda's group opposed labor protection and supported lobby leaders in Washington in behalf of the party's stance.

At that time feminists from different countries were coordinated under the auspices of the International Suffrage Alliance. Carrie Chapman Catt's organization, the League of Women Voters, had served as the American representative for some years, but in 1926 the Alliance's president, Mrs. Corbett Ashby, invited the National Women's party to apply for affiliation as well. Mrs. Ashby's main motive may have been financial, for Alva voiced her intention to make a big gift to the Alliance upon acceptance. Pleased by the prospect of this important recognition, Alva funded a contingent of party workers to come to France and make the case before the Alliance board. The afternoon of the presentation went well, and the workers left certain of certification.

What they did not know was that Catt had been working behind the scenes to discredit the group, and vowed to withdraw the League of Women Voters with their considerable financial contributions if the party were accepted. This threat was sweetened by the pledge of woman publishing magnate Frank Leslie to give the Alliance one million dollars. Consequently, the Alliance board met in secret session to discuss Catt's objections, and they decided to refuse the National Woman's party membership, based on such blatantly contrived reasons as an accusation the party used public relations too often. A subsequent public session during which the party workers made an impassioned plea for reversal was unsuccessful.

The next day the party held a luncheon in honor of Alva and Lady Rhondda, who astutely explained to the disappointed group that not all suffragists had been feminists, they had simply wanted women's votes for their special causes. What upset the other women's groups was that the National Woman's party was purely feminist. When Alva stood to speak, she made no reference to the recent slap in the face from the Alliance but emphasized future action, the need for all international councils to include the voices of women (who were just as absent from League of Nation's councils as from national governments). "We ought to be more impatient than we are," she urged.[23] Her refusal to look backward to this recent disappointment inspired those attending, who found their energies directed forward rather than mired in talk of revenge or useless after-the-fact analysis. Instead, Alva gave her money to a French feminist organization unaligned with the Alliance.

Just when party members back in Washington were taking their permanent home for granted, Congress stepped in to condemn the property so it could be torn down to make way for the new Supreme Court Building. Despite the objections of historic preservation groups as well as the party, the condemnation went through. Consequently, Alva bought the Sewall House, a much smaller brick home at 144 Constitution Avenue still in walking distance of Congress. This building was also a historic structure, having served as residence of Albert Gallatin, secretary of the Treasury in the first decade of the 1800s, during which time he financed the Louisiana Purchase. Having lost much of its vitality, the party found the small building sufficient, for it became primarily a home for Alice Paul and her few remaining devotees.

Gertrude Builds
More Monuments

In June of 1926, family troubles behind her, Gertrude took Alice, Flora, and Juliana to France to attend the unveiling of the *St. Nazaire* memorial. As she rode in an open car to the event past the admiring crowds of thirty thousand, the house and shop windows decorated with both French and American flags, she was moved to tears, visibly so when the French Legion of Honor was pinned on her. But "what really pleased me was that for once in my life I couldn't have done more. The difficulty of deciding the proportion, the difficulty of standing up against real opposition, and the fact that it is done & over make me much happier than decorations & all the rest of the tomfoolery."[24] In fact, the *St. Nazaire* memorial was her least successful monument, praised more for its sentimentality than its artistic achievement. Overblown and melodramatic, it could not match the emotional impact of her smaller war sculptures and memorials, nor the vitality of *Buffalo Bill*.

By 1926 it was also apparent that Gertrude and Juliana's scheme for the Whitney Studio Club had been so successful that ironically artists were breaking away. Surveying that year's Annual exhibition, critic Forbes Watson noted that some of the older painters had not sent their most important work and that some younger talents also held back their most recent best creations. The reason, colleague Henry McBride explained was that "alas, some of the artists [of the Whitney Studio Club] are beginning to forsake the parent institution for the more precarious [and profitable] delights of uptown recognition."[25] Yet the women continued to mount shows with significant new work, and they added a shop on the premises for the sale of graphic works. Artists could put what they wanted in the shop—it thus provided needed free storage for some—and the club took no commission on the sale.

That fall Gertrude made another important contribution to modern art when she became embroiled in a battle with the government. It began when photographer Edward Steichen brought Brancusi's polished bronze sculpture *Bird in Space* into the country. A customs inspector denied it was a work of art, classifying it instead as "kitchen utensils and hospital supplies" with a duty payable of $240. Hearing of the case, Gertrude told Steichen she would intercede legally and pay all costs to get his duty returned. Before *Brancusi v. the United States* reached the court in October of 1927, Gertrude held meetings at her studio to stir up support against this threat to artistic expression. Those attending included not only visual artists but musicians, such as the renowned conductor Leopold Stokowski. The coverage surrounding the case further educated the public to the cause of less traditional modern art. The court ruled *Bird in Space* was indeed art, although afterward customs officials, spurred by certain traditionalists unhappy with the new wave, continued to harass importers of the avant garde.

The victory was not foremost on Gertrude's mind. Underweight and exhausted, she had, at one point that fall, been rushed to a hospital. Following many tests, the doctors diagnosed phlebitis and insisted on complete rest to prevent formation of a fatal blood clot. This order excluded, in particular, visits from the effervescent Juliana and Gertrude's other high-spirited artist friends, who were thought too stimulating for the patient's welfare. In January of 1927, when she was well enough to get about, she left for a cruise through the Mediterranean that would include several weeks in Egypt so she could study the sculpture there. Harry was too weak to go along, but Flora and her family accompanied her. Her health remained unstable, requiring daily shots and bandaging of her phlebitic legs. Jo Davidson and his family joined them in Egypt, for the leisurely trip through Italy to Paris.

With Andrew O'Connor's assistance, she worked on her latest commission, a memorial to Columbus to be set in Huelva, Spain. Modeled after the development of the Statue of Liberty, the concept of the sponsoring committee was to solicit popular subscriptions so everyday Americans could contribute this evidence of appreciation to the people of Spain for sponsoring the "founding" voyage. Gertrude also found this was an opportunity to show her very private appreciation for that country's influence and inspiration in arousing her creativity.

Just as Spain sparked her secret, sensual side, so Gertrude created for it a monument within a monument. Columbus, embracing a shoulder-high cross, stood staring out to sea; the four sides of his pedestal were decorated with reliefs representing the four hemispheres his travels opened up. The pedestal was itself a small building, holding within stylized statues of Queen Isabella and King Ferdinand. Andrew O'Connor retained his influence, taking on many day-to-day duties in overseeing the final construction during those times Gertrude was in the States.

It was not an easy job. As a friend remarked, O'Connor "had been in his element playing uncanny politics, injecting the virus of speed into languid Spaniards, accomplishing the impossible."[26] As with all her monuments, Gertrude was present as much as possible to supervise the stone cutting, the moving of the carved blocks on dredges, the search for cement and competent stone workers, the final joining in Huelva. "To see suddenly before you the real dream in great blocks of stone is overpowering. The cloud shapes one visualized come down to earth. God! The fascination of building, of creation!"[27]

Still not in the best of health, once home she set to work on a design for a *Daughters of the American Revolution Memorial,* which would eventually be placed in Washington, D.C., and for another, *Pioneer Woman,* that would not be installed. But her blood count was rising, her legs still swelling up, and by summer she had sworn off alcohol.

Ill-health made Gertrude emotionally fragile, and she turned for comfort to a young man she had met on the ocean liner to New York. Paul Clayton was an aspiring artist with a drinking problem whose mother was trying to curb his habit and wanted him placed in a sanitarium. Gertrude gave him $2,000 to cover him while he found his way, and she showed his sketches to Juliana. In May he decided to go to a ranch in Montana, after which Gertrude's letters became more intimate, with the tone she had used with her lovers of twenty years earlier. "I loved hearing about the ranch & wish you needed a maid of all work to look after you! I would be so useful."[28] She wrote almost daily, expressing dismay when she did not hear from him as frequently in return.

Her dependency grew as she revealed her closest feelings. She wrote of "a little girl who was very sad," who treasured something she could never find, then found it "because it had come through the air from the heart of the person she wanted it from."[29] In July she returned to France, where one night she dreamed of having an appointment to meet Paul, but obstacles kept getting in the way. She shared with him the problems of quitting alcohol. "It used to be so easy, if you didn't want to face something just exactly as it was to take a cocktail."[30] She wished he would love her, hold her tight, and she wrote fairy tales that inspired cloying responses from him. It was overall a pathetic correspondence, hinting at some deep, unresolved loneliness. When Gertrude returned to New York that winter, she realized he had not stopped drinking after all, and cut him off abruptly with a cold note.

Perhaps as a result of frequent illness and isolation, Gertrude considered the state of the Whitney Studio Club and came to a hard conclusion. In 1928 she decided to disband the organization, for it had achieved its aim of obtaining recognition for modern artists so well that they no longer needed the protective philanthropic environment. There were too many members, more than three hundred, for too little gallery space, and so many careers had been launched that the artists were finding other galleries anxious to exhibit and sell their work. Supplanting the Whitney Studio Club was their new organization, the Whitney Studio Galleries, which would operate in competition with the uptown Fifth

Avenue galleries and would not limit itself primarily to American works.

In fact, the galleries program over the next three years would function much like the old Studio Club, except for the absence of the social program. Of forty-four exhibitions, forty were solo shows, almost all featuring American artists. Replacing the Annuals were Christmas holiday sales of small works. Gertrude and Juliana's wit and cleverness demonstrated themselves once again in the 1929 exhibition of paintings devoted to the Circus and Circus Life. To enhance this display they stripped the walls of the old house on Eighth Street, installed bright colors, playful dadoes around the doorways, and balloons in clusters on the ceilings. An organ grinder with a monkey and free peanuts added to the circus ambience. The display itself was comprehensive, reaching back to Watteau and Hogarth, Degas and Toulouse-Latrec and forward to Picasso. Once again these remarkable women proved that fun and serious art could be companions. Reviewers, reporters, and gallery goers agreed.

Gertrude and Juliana Launch
the Whitney Museum

Despite its change in direction from Studio Club to for-sale galleries, Gertrude and Juliana continued to be dissatisfied. During 1929, Harry Whitney joined their discussions about new directions. Now in her mid-fifties, Gertrude sought simplification of her life, along with more time to spend with her ailing husband. (Though a shadow of his athletic self, feeble really, Harry roused himself to watch his prize horses win yet further trophies, and he managed trips to Canada for salmon fishing.) Through Juliana's partnership she had acquired more than six hundred works of recent American art, well beyond the ability of the current setup to put on display. Believing art should hang on walls to be viewed, not left to dusty storage for the eyes of mice and spiders, Gertrude saw only two choices: to give the collection to a museum with enough space to display it or to start a museum herself. She preferred the former.

Consequently, one morning Juliana visited the office of Dr. Edward Robinson, director of the Metropolitan Museum, to convey Gertrude's offer of her collection, along with a munificent endowment to build a wing to house it. The Metropolitan had already accepted numerous gifts from the Vanderbilts in recent years as family members had scaled back their living and taken down the large houses. To Juliana's astonishment, Dr. Robinson refused the collection so acerbically, quipping that his basement was full of such American art stuff, that she never had an opportunity to tell him of the accompanying building endowment.

A furious Juliana returned to meet Gertrude and Forbes Watson for lunch; the latter, expecting a celebration, were not disappointed. If the Metropolitan was so foolish as to reject Gertrude's gift, then Gertrude would make her own museum. Watson watched in delight as the two women rose to the challenge, this opportunity to move them from the class of "gifted amateurs" to professionals. Gertrude demanded that Juliana, despite her lack of academic credentials, be director, and that the preliminary advisers consist not of society and business types or academicians but of fellow artists. It was a bold and revolutionary conception of how to run a museum.

Gertrude held off announcement of the museum until the start of 1930. The reason may have had to do with Black Friday, October 24, 1929, when the stock market crashed. It would have been neither wise nor tasteful to remind the public of the considerable capital her family controlled while others around them throughout every social class were losing everything. The Vanderbilts and Whitneys suffered little from the debacle. While their portfolios lost value, the reduction was from many millions to fewer millions, a paper loss for people who were not forced to sell the holdings. Many of the investments were in blue chip companies that would bounce back when the economy rebounded years later. To Harry's great fortune, his recent investment in a hydroelectric plant began to pay off soon after the crash, as did new mines and metallurgical plants. Utterly oblivious to the change in the economy, Grace Vanderbilt continued to spend a quarter of a million dollars a year on entertainment alone, while Neily, now separated from her, lolled about in his yacht off the Florida coast. Another noted Vanderbilt yachtsman, Alva's son Harold, successfully defended the America's Cup, a victory that brought cheerful distraction to an unhappy populace.

When Gertrude did break the news about the new museum, the papers expressed astonishment, for in the past year Mrs. John D. Rockefeller, Lizzie Bliss, and Mrs. Cornelius Sullivan had announced their creation of the Museum of Modern Art. Accomplished collectors, they brought into their plan a fashionable board of trustees that imbued the Modern's mission with historicism, professionalism, and—some might say—elitism. Their first director was Alfred H. Barr, Jr., an art history professor from Wellesley College. Gertrude announced no such eminences. More shocking, she explained the Whitney mission as a democratic one, that of discovering fresh talents and working with artists rather than waiting until the artist has "been deadened by old age" or accepted "within their [other museum's] scared portals."[31]

Gertrude was in Paris during the final show of the Whitney Studio Galleries, one by forty artists on the theme of flowers. As in previous exhibitions, she and Juliana paid special attention to framing, ordering simple wood frames painted in hues that harmonized with the image within. Although Juliana was given major credit for the display, Gertrude had put a strong hand to it. As Forbes Watson later remarked, "Only [after Gertrude's death] did Mrs. Force play the part of museum director. She was the dynamo that moved Mrs. Whitney's activities in art forward and Mrs. Whitney controlled the dynamo."[32]

Unfortunately for Watson, his own relationship with the women was about to change, with serious consequences for *The Arts*. His incendiary affair with Juliana was burning out; he began to appear in public with a onetime member of the Whitney Studio Club, who now lived above her antique store across the street from Juliana's apartment. Consequently, the ever-jealous Juliana could sit at the window and watch for her former lover's visits with his new paramour. The final break came at a dinner party in 1930, when in full view of everyone at the table he leaned over to her and loudly remarked, "Everything you know, I taught you."[33] Whereas Juliana stood up and cursed him, Nan Watson made a polite excuse and pulled her husband away from the table.

Juliana then attacked Forbes where she knew it would hurt him the most. The expenses for the museum had already caused Gertrude to cut back some of her support for *The Arts,* so Juliana had a reason to convince her to eliminate its subsidy completely. Unaware of Juliana's vituperative motive, Gertrude complied, forcing Forbes to search for other funding. He responded with a generous letter, praising her museum plans for "encouraging the American artist and showing the great public that life isn't merely material."[34] Lincoln Kirstein, who was to be the major donor for George Balanchine's ballet company, helped for a while, but the magazine did not survive. Worse, in March of 1931, Watson lost his art critic job when the *World* merged with the *Telegram.* Following two threadbare years, he was forced to take an appointment with the federal government in Washington, where he became a bitter and frustrated man. After the fight, Juliana went about for weeks crying, and from then on relied upon "professional bachelors," the term then for homosexuals, for escorts. Although she and Forbes eventually reconciled as friends, both had suffered terribly as a result of their outburst that fateful evening, and the art world lost out as well.

Gertrude Loses Harry
and Gains a Lover

Gertrude was also preoccupied during much of 1930, with several memorials that would never come to fruition due to political pressures and changes in public sentiment. For example, plans for a monument to Marshall Foch were later terminated when the organizers learned the public was resentful that France had not paid its World War I debts to the United States. Nor was that part of the public afflicted by the depression very sympathetic to the notion of scarce dollars being paid out for such luxuries as monumental sculptures.

Early that October, Gertrude joined Harry for a weekend in Westbury, but he came down with a cold and was so ill that he could not even take a walk around the grounds. On Tuesday they went to the city so he could be examined by close friend and family doctor, Josh Hartwell. During his subsequent consultation alone with Gertrude, Josh made frightening references to pneumonia, hardening of the arteries, and liver damage. Unable to comprehend how sick Harry had been in recent years, Gertrude denied Josh's intimations. That weekend the children came by to join her in caring for their father, who fought valiantly through the futile treatment. Lapsing into unconsciousness, he died without final words. He was fifty-eight.

More than twelve hundred mourners filled St. Bartholemew's for Harry's funeral. Despite Gertrude's own fame, Harry had often been even more celebrated during much of their life together. His leading the "Big Four" to defeat the long invincible British polo team in 1909 had made him an American hero. His brilliant racing stable had won the Pimlico Preakness and Kentucky Derby repeatedly, and he had played a major role in upgrading the quality of the sport. Handsome and photogenic, courageous and clever, he represented an image of the rich that average Americans could admire. The list of his charity and business boards ran into the dozens, and his role in his racing stables included all aspects of breeding, training, and management, not just writing the checks and turning over the work to someone else. Gertrude was now grief stricken to lose the companion she had once avoided. Harry had proved to be a caring spouse and father, who despite his own disapproval of some of her artistic endeavors ultimately backed her up, particularly concerning the Whitney Studio Club, Gallery, and Museum. With their repeated reference to his generosity and kindness, the sympathy letters must have added to her sorrow.

Rather than stay near her children in Westbury or go to her studio in Paris to be with friends there, Gertrude chose to isolate herself at a modest villa in Havana. She was not well; the years of heavy smoking, drinking, and poor nutrition were now catching up with her. While visitors came and went, much of the time she was alone, connecting with others through long letters.

With no hope of commissions for monuments, Gertrude transformed her grief through a mystery novel, eventually titled *Walking the Dusk*.[35] The plot concerns a young woman, Mabel Randolph, who comes out of nowhere to live with a socialite couple, Stephen and Katharine Osmund. On the very day she privately announces her engagement to marry, Mabel dies, a possible suicide. The first person narrator, a party guest at the home named Diana, explores the mystery of the causes and motives for Mabel's death. If she did not commit suicide, then who murdered her, and why? The shocking truth is that Katharine Osmund had been Mabel's secret lover. Upon that discovery, Diana decides not to pursue the matter any further.

Similar to Gertrude's other fiction, the characters, settings, and situations so resembled her real life circle that she created a pseudonym, L. J. Webb, and used an intermediary to locate a publisher. Coward-McCann accepted the manuscript and brought it out in 1932, where it languished on the booksellers' shelves. Although the advertising department planted items with gossip columnists to perk interest in the real identity of the author, the subject matter, with its world of the idle rich and its lesbian subplot were hardly what readers desired then.

Walking the Dusk was a rather daring book for its time. Several years earlier

Radclyffe Hall's novel of lesbian love, *The Well of Loneliness,* became "the book that must be suppressed" in England. The sensation of the subsequent obscenity trial had led the normally liberal Blanche and Alfred Knopf to cancel their intended publication of the work, on grounds it would be considered a "dirty book" in the States. It was eventually banned in both countries. It was not just homosexuality that was under attack; the looser behavior of the twenties seemed terribly self-indulgent during a time when paying the rent was hard for so many. Perhaps to bolster overburdened families during these depression years, society viewed sexuality as legitimate only within the confines of a monogamous marriage. Former flappers now urged virginity upon their daughters.

While completing her novel, Gertrude also wrote frequent, detailed letters to Juliana, whose responsibility it was to ready the museum for its opening. The task of converting the buildings at 8, 10, and 12 Eighth Street into a coherent interior was left to G. MacCulloch Miller, Gertrude's son-in-law. Cully, as he was known, had met Flora soon after her divorce and married her in 1927. Forty years old at the time, he was still a bachelor, a man whose impeccable sense of style had kept him patiently waiting for the absolutely perfect match. Though still in her twenties with two small children, Flora easily fit the mold. She had her mother's emotional depth and artistic sensibility combined with her father's warmth and wit. In a family of troubled marriages, theirs was an exception, their temperaments as compatible as that of Cornelius and Alice.

Cully unified the buildings with a facade of pink stucco, adding such art deco touches as aluminum outer doors with a design of five-pointed stars. The foyer featured a stylized American eagle to alert visitors to the mission of the museum. Unlike the severe and cold walls typical of most other museums then, the eleven Whitney rooms offered variety in both color and surface, with one room even painted canary yellow and another covered in cork. The atmosphere was more one of a home than of an institution. To pay for the renovations, Gertrude had to borrow $1.6 million.

On November 16, 1931, dressed in black velvet and chiffon mourning clothes, Gertrude nervously approached the CBS radio microphone. First a message from President Hoover was read, one line of which must have particularly pleased Gertrude: "It [the Whitney Museum] should quicken our national sense of beauty and increase America's pride in her own future." Agreeing, Gertrude responded in a shaky voice, "In making this gift to you, the American public, my chief desire is that you should share with me the joy which I have received from these works of art. It is especially in times like these that we need to look to the spiritual. In art we find it."[36] Then several thousand guests pushed in, shook hands with Gertrude and pressed into the galleries to examine the collection.

The reaction was predictably mixed. Those critics favoring the abstractionists and modernists affiliated with Stieglitz found the collection "puny and gray . . . yards of uncreative canvasses."[37] The general press was nonetheless enthusiastic that for the first time the United States had a museum devoted entirely to contemporary American art. It reassured a country proud in its isolationism, resentful of an ungrateful Europe, that native artists now had a prominent vehicle for recognition. The Whitney, the message implied, proved America was neither a country of mindless and parochial Sinclair Lewis Babbits nor of H. L. Mencken's Boobocracy.

The museum meant a new spree of purchasing. The major goal was to fill in gaps. Consequently, Gertrude and Juliana submitted themselves to Stieglitz to negotiate purchase of two paintings by his wife, Georgia O'Keefe, which they recognized were essential to their collection. Yet their buying was also to relieve the suffering individual artists experienced during the depression. Moses Soyer wrote, "Who can describe the hopelessness that its victims knew? Perhaps no better than the artist taking his work to the galleries. They were at a standstill. The misery of the artist was acute."[38] Much of the public considered artists deadbeats, unwilling to "work" for a living. Besides expanding the Whitney holdings, the women's other major assistance to hungry artists was to send out traveling exhibits to develop a nationwide audience for contemporary American art. When offered the opportunity to head the New York region of the federal Public Work for Arts Project, Juliana naively thought this a wonderful chance to rescue artists, but she found herself embroiled instead in politics and accusations that would result in some disgruntled artists picketing the Whitney in protest of her policies.[39]

These plans were all in the future. Soon after the opening of the museum, Gertrude's health once again failed rapidly. She had a mastoid operation followed by a painful period of recuperation. Because her resistance was so low, infection set in and she almost died.

Chronic illness meant frequent visits from family doctor Josh Hartwell, who had even traveled to attend her when she was staying in Cuba. Sixty-five, at the height of his medical career, Hartwell was bored with both his professional routine and his wife. Free spirit Gertrude was an irresistible temptation. An affair ensued and, as usual, Gertrude was careful to control the pace and circumstances. Her datebook now referred to meetings with "X," Hartwell that were as frequent as with her ailing mother. His passion for Gertrude was evident in the letters, some more than a dozen pages long, extolling her importance to him. The casual encounters soon grew into a mature love relationship.

In June of 1932, two days after he and Adele had been over for lunch, Jay Burden died. Only sixty-one, he had fractured a hip the year before and was left crippled. His eventual death resulted from an embolism traceable to the injury. In a sympathy letter to Adele, Gertrude reviewed how similar the course of Harry's and Jay's lives had been, how they had in the final years been cut off from sport, club life, and most normal pursuits. "Then our function came—to love and cherish them. It wasn't that they had not loved us, but now we had to keep full those hours which other pursuits & friends had kept occupied."[40]

Gertrude's words were wise. Adele had never understood Jay's devotion to his family's failing ironworks, and like Gertrude she had taken to going off alone to Paris. Lacking Gertrude's artistic bent or talent, Adele thrived in the world of charity boards, fox hunts, and bridge. She would find a more congenial mate in her later marriage to musician and amateur artist Richard Tobin. But at her request, she was buried in the plot next to Jay.

Gertrude Moves to
Protect Her Niece

On June 9, 1932, Gertrude had yet another family member to console: Regi's daughter Gloria, who was in the hospital with tonsillitis. Now eight, Gloria had been living in New York City since March, with Emma Keislich and Mrs. Morgan. (Her fun-loving mother had not wanted to remain in New York until July, the time doctors originally recommended for the surgery, so she had taken the next ship back to Europe.) The child's guardians had been disturbed by Gloria M.'s nonchalance—the Lindbergh baby had just been kidnapped and young Gloria was worth much more money if someone were to hold the child for ransom. Viewing young Gloria for the first time in six years, guardian Tom Gilchrist was astonished by her wan appearance, stammer, and fearfulness. He also ordered a detective service to protect Emma Keislich, Mrs. Morgan, and the child, who was ignorant of the Lindbergh incident because the adults around her controlled her access to the radio and the press.

What Gilchrist did not know at the time was that the child's timidity was provoked by the person closest to her, the nurse at the direction of the grandmother. Since infancy, Emma Keislich had been so protective that the child never slept a night alone without her. Now eight, Gloria had never been to a school and had only minimal lessons from her nurse. Whereas some adults might disapprove of such a sheltered life-style, the child felt no deficiency. Lacking a father and ignored by her mother, the child clung to the buxom nurse happily. She was Dodo, the friendly Big Elephant, who with the fiery yet doting Little Countess, Mrs. Morgan, substituted for real parents.

Mrs. Morgan was a mercurial, domineering woman who had neglected her own children, then when they reached adulthood hovered around to exploit them financially. Gloria M. was the weakest emotionally of the four siblings, and, as the Vanderbilt widow, drew the worst of her mother's sick and perverse attention. Mrs. Morgan had moved in with her and Regi soon after the marriage, and she continued to live in Paris with the two Glorias after his death. When Gloria M. became involved with Prince Friedrich Hohenlohe in 1927, Mrs. Morgan became fanatical in her determination to destroy the relationship she feared would separate her from the Vanderbilt money. From that point on she began to feed both the child's guardian lawyers and the members of the Vanderbilt family with her distorted and paranoid views: Her daughter wanted to steal the American heiress away to a hideous German castle! Fearful herself she would be separated from the child, Emma Keislich collaborated with Mrs. Morgan and projected her own insecurities onto the suggestible youngster.

Unfortunately for Gloria M., besides his love, Prince Hohenlohe could offer her only aristocratic blood and a family estate much in need of cash to repair the castle and keep the fields fertile. Aware that after her marriage, she would need to continue to collect income from her daughter's estate and that, legally, she did not have the right to do so, she appealed personally to Gertrude and Alice to intercede with the guardians. Disturbed over rumors they had been hearing, both women stood back while the lawyers delivered the bad news: Marry the foreigner and give up your income. In 1929, learning that her mother had conspired to ruin her engagement to the prince, Gloria M. sent her packing from her home at 14 rue Alfred Roll in Paris to a small house nearby. Mrs. Morgan never forgave this eviction from her daughter's house.

Destined to make the worst choices throughout her life, Gloria M. further left herself vulnerable by leaving her daughter for months at a time in the care of Keislich and Mrs. Morgan. Twin sister Thelma, divorced and now remarried to Lord Furness, had become mistress to the prince of Wales. Consequently, Gloria M. was frequently in England with the prince's frivolous social set or on the Riviera with an even faster crowd. Her friends included the "Palace Gang," the prince's cousin and wife, Dickie and Edwina Mountbatten, along with Dickie's brother, George Milford Haven and his wife Nada. Both Edwina and Nada discovered an emotional comfort in each other they had not found in their career-minded husbands. Both women relished adventure, even danger, and eventually took trips together through wild and seldom-visited parts of the world. Rumors of bisexuality followed them. (George's idea of adventure was running the train collection that filled his estate house's theater or browsing through his fabled pornography collection.)

Seductive and domineering, Nada had little difficulty attracting the suggestible Gloria M. into her bisexual life-style. Edwina was attracted to the raven-haired beauty as well and had visited her in the States in 1928, where they explored the nightclubs of Harlem to enjoy the bustling jazz scene. In 1930, Nada joined Gloria M. on a trip to California for part of the winter, where they met such friends of Edwina's as Fred Astaire and Douglas Fairbanks, and were guests of William Randolph Hearst at San Simeon. During this trip, young Gloria spent the holidays with her octogenarian paternal grandmother, Alice.

By 1932, Gertrude probably knew about Gloria M.'s connections to the disreputable Milford Havens, for Mabel Randolph of *Walking the Dusk,* the opportunistic society girl with a secret lesbian life physically resembles her sister-in-law Gloria. Yet having so often lived a secret life of adultery herself, and having known lesbians in her own artistic circle, Gertrude was not inclined to make a charge of loose morals against her.[41] What mattered was the possible neglect of the child. Despite her own absences from her children, particularly when they were small, Gertrude had been attentive to their very different needs, and she knew Harry was often home playing the role of paterfamilias. She was puzzled that Gloria M. exhibited so little bonding to her daughter. Having grown up in a close family, Gertrude could not conceive of the bizarre upbringing the Morgan children had known.

Even if Gloria M. had suddenly determined to be more maternal, she would have found her role impossible. For three years now Emma Keislich and Mrs. Morgan had manipulated young Gloria's mind against her mother. This was not difficult. When Gloria M. was home, she slept until midday, permitting her daughter to see her usually when she was dressing for an evening out. The child hovered nearby in admiration as her mother sat in custom-made robe with matching slippers at her boudoir table arranging her makeup, hair, and jewels. "My mother—her face softer than any flower, hair gentle dark and waved as I touched it, the petal of her skin pulling at me with its beauty. How I longed to merge into her.[42] But then she would go away, down the long corridors of hotels, down staircases, along avenues in her pale furs, snow-sprinkled, disappearing into the velvet caverns of waiting cars and borne away, away, away."[43]

Then there were the everpresent Morgan aunts, the twin Thelma, whom the child sometimes mistook for her mother, and Consuelo, towering, stern. Her mother always had time to lounge afternoon hours away chatting and laughing with her sisters before going off for another evening's adventures, while the child lingered in the hallway, longing to be in on the fun. Or she would lean against her mother's bedroom door to overhear the murmurs of Nada's voice, straining to hear the secrets they shared. And there were the men, of course. One night, the child, longing for her mother, entered the bedroom to discover "the long arms and legs of praying mantises battling with the other. I do not know what I will do when I reach them; maybe I will kill them."[44]

It was from Thelma's home, Melton Mowbray, in England in late 1931 that Emma Keislich instructed Gloria to write letters to her grandmother. By then Thelma had given Lord Furness a son, Tony, to whom she, too, showed little attention. "Toney's mother said I can't have any birthday presents because it is so near Christmas," went one letter to Mrs. Morgan. "My mother is so bad to me I wish I could run away to New York to you," went another. Forced to misspell on purpose so the letters would look genuine, she described her mother as "a rare bease" in one, and noted "I love the cards that you sent me my mother was in Paris enjoying herself while poor me was unhappy in Englan," in another.[45]

If the child did not find life at Melton Mowbray pleasant compared to France, one incident there made a significant change in her life. Her aunt Consuelo was visiting and, in a rare moment of affection, sat down to read from *Alice in Wonderland* to Gloria. The vision of Alice escaping down the hole after the rabbit aroused the child's interest in fantasy and fairy tale. What you see is not necessarily what is, such stories seemed to say. The world can change magically, and it has possibilities that strict attention to reality can obstruct. Fairy tales aroused her innate sensuality, inspiring her to examine the world for signs of underlying wonder. And because such fantasies often involved mysteries, she was impelled to solve the puzzle of the life around her.[46]

By spring of 1932, the child's legal guardians were troubled by the stories coming from abroad. Thelma's affair with the Prince of Wales was widely known, and pointed to a less than moral atmosphere for the girl. The constant outcries from Mrs. Morgan concerning her granddaughter's threatened well-being impelled the lawyers to force Gloria M. to bring the child to New York. Their reason, that the girl had not been to the States in two years, was a ploy.

Gloria was often sickly, and arrived in the States with a severe case of tonsillitis. Despite her daughter's illness, Gloria M. left her with Gertrude and went back to Europe.

In late May of 1932, when the child's condition became serious enough to require surgery, at the guardians' insistence Gloria M. returned from Europe to be with her daughter. Once the operation was over she seemed more interested in the name of a Parisian hat designer than her daughter's recuperation. On June 17 she informed her daughter she would be returning to Europe the next day, then went out for the evening.

While her mother was out, Gloria began to scream about stomach pains. To the doctor examining her, she shouted, "Don't let me die!" Determining the problem was psychological in origin, he suspected that suggestions from anxious Emma Keislich were the source of the hysteria. In fact, Mrs. Morgan had been the stronger influence in persuading the child that her mother was dangerous, would kidnap her and take her away forever to the mysterious castle overseas, away from her beloved Dodo and Little Countess.

Arriving home that evening to learn of her daughter's stomach cramps, Gloria M. agreed to postpone her departure for a week. During that time Gertrude offered to bring the girl to Westbury, where she could be with her cousins in the healthy setting of the estate. Gloria M. quickly assented, unaware her daughter would live there without her for the next two years.

Despite an erosion of wealth during these depression years, the Whitney estate remained intact, with its sprawling central mansion, where Gloria moved in with her aunt. Also located on the property were the houses of Gertrude's children and grandchildren. A large pool, stables, indoor tennis court, and separate gymnasium provided athletic diversions. Gertrude's daughter Barbie had a child, Gerta, who was Gloria's age, and the two became fast friends, attending the Green Vale School together and sharing fantasies during private times on the estate. Although Gloria remained nervous and spoke with a stammer, Gertrude observed improvements in her demeanor and mood.

Gertrude placed Gloria next to her in Harry's old bedroom, still decorated with his trophies and sporting regalia. Though nearing sixty and in troubled health, Gertrude found her niece's intelligence and vivaciousness rejuvenating. Her daybook now added appointments at Green Vale to watch Gloria and Gerta in a play, trips to the beach, parties, and camping in the Adirondacks, along with consultations with the guardians and doctors concerning Gloria's welfare. Meanwhile Gloria M. traveled about Europe on the money from her daughter's trusts, making brief visits to America now and then to check in on her child. She didn't seem to realize that the Vanderbilts would see the many photographs of her and Thelma in the latest fashion at various social functions and read items about them in the gossip columns.

14

1932-1936

The Indefatigable Alva
Meets Her Maker

During 1932, Consuelo Balsan and her brothers were reunited in France, for Alva was ailing. Since 1924, Alva had lived almost entirely in that country to continue her work on behalf of international women's rights. In 1927 she sold Beacon Towers to her friend Millicent Hearst, the wife of the publisher, who stripped the interior of its numerous St. Joan motifs. (Despite extensive remodeling, the Hearst family made little use of the house and tore it down in 1945.) In 1932 she sold Marble House to Frederick Prince, president of Armour and Company. She probably felt little sadness, for she had always found the act of building design and construction much more interesting than living in the finished product.

Her Chateau d'Augerville-la-Riviere became as noted in France as her previous homes had been in the States. Considered perhaps the best example of the French Gothic period, its many previous owners had kept it virtually uncorrupted by renovation since its building in 1495. Its white stone walls were surrounded by a swan-filled moat formed by the river Essonne. Its tract of almost four hundred acres included forest, meadow, hills, winding paths, and tiny tributaries of the river. Alva removed out-of-period embellishments and restored the brightly colored designs to the heavily beamed ceilings. Then she filled the rooms with rare fifteenth- and sixteenth-century tapestries, wrought-iron chandeliers, and carved chests and cabinets from the original period. In achieving these ends, she took on the traditional role of chateleine, hiring local villagers whenever possible, and providing for the recreation, education, and health needs of residents of the nearby hamlets.

Redoing a house was, of course, never enough to occupy her. In 1930, Consuelo joined Alva and feminists from around the world to attend the League of Nations conference establishing an international code of laws.[1] Of particular concern to the women was the topic of nationality. In many countries a woman lost her citizenship upon marrying a foreigner, as had happened to Consuelo upon marrying Marlborough. When in 1922 American women forced removal of the objectionable law known as the Cable Act, Consuelo resumed her U.S. citizenship. Nonetheless, a foreign woman marrying a U.S. citizen could not apply for naturalization papers until a year afterward; she would be without a country during that time. In some countries, a woman lost citizenship if she merely moved to her husband's homeland. The inconsistencies and inequities being obvious, the women hoped the League would make one clear and equitable standard.

Unfortunately, the Hague conference refused to correct the discrimination but instead included numerous clauses throughout its report that retained all varieties of inequities based on gender. By then the National Woman's party had sufficient clout with the Hoover administration to induce it to order the U.S. delegation to the conference to vote against the new code and refuse to sign it. The reason stated by the acting secretary of State was that U.S. laws made few differences between men and women. This was, of course, not true, but at the time the United States was far ahead of other countries with regard to women's equality. (Unfortunately, the later New Deal policies would authorize pay inequities and other unfair treatment of working women, practices that would remain legal until the late 1960s.)

Working closely with Alva then was party member Doris Stevens, who lived for periods of time at the Augerville estate. Doris had been a tireless and loyal full-time party member for many years, and she suffered nervous collapses several times as a result, but some time in 1930 she alienated Alva.[2] Anticipating she did not have much time left, Alva called Elsa Maxwell to the chateau to witness a revision of her will, which included the revoking of a substantial bequest to Doris. Maxwell reported later that Alva also wanted to leave money to her, but she refused it. Events would later prove the wisdom of her decision.

Alva also invited Elsa, Consuelo, Jacques, and son Willie to accompany her on a tour of Egypt, "to take a last look around."[3] Millicent Hearst joined up with another group of friends. For seven weeks the two parties sailed the Nile in large river boats, stopping to visit the various tombs so popular in the imagination of the American public. It was Alva's final excursion.

After a stroke paralyzed the feisty feminist in April of 1932, she refused to slow down, and instead ordered the servants to push her about in her wicker wheelchair so she could oversee the latest revision of the gardens. She hired Matilda Young, sister of one of the party's jailed hunger strikers, to take down a new version of her memoirs. Young wrote home how Alva was "so valiant. I took hold of her paralyzed hand, which has feeling in it now" and a strong grasp. When Alva tried to release her grip, nothing happened, leading her to joke about her "funny hand." Young was moved to tears by Alva's courage.[4]

For weeks Alva remained in high spirits, comforted by the frequent visits of Consuelo, Jacques, and son Harold. Slightly built, shy, Harold Stirling Vanderbilt was by then not only a noted yachtsman but the inventor of contract bridge. Alva had no interest in cards, and even less in the dominoes he tried to teach her. She wanted nothing of the life of an invalid, and she insisted on being taken out to fetes in the local community she often graced with numerous gifts.

One day Elsa Maxwell arrived to find Alva fretting that the nurses had allowed her dyed red hair to go gray. "I don't want to die with white hair," she complained, "It's so depressing." Then she reflected, "It makes no difference now. The important thing is learning how to live. Learn a lesson from my mistakes. I had too much power before I knew how to use it and it defeated me in the end. It drove all sweetness out of my life except the affection of my children. My trouble was that I was born too late for the last generation and too early for this one."[5]

In late August the doctor advised Matilda Young that "a very untoward event would carry her [Alva] off suddenly."[6] She died five months later, following a siege of pneumonia. Consuelo took the body back to New York for burial. Alva's crypt was already in place next to Harry's in the chapel at Woodlawn Cemetery.

In one of her last conversations with Alice Paul, Alva had requested that the party oversee her funeral. She said any man who had been of service to his country got a public ceremony, while "nobody ever pays any attention to the death of a woman who has made a great gift to her country in the way of working for some reform."[7] Alice kept her promise. All around the perimeter of St. Thomas Episcopal Church in New York stood young girls bearing the purple, white, and gold suffrage banners. The music included suffrage tunes and a hymn composed by Alva. One of the faded banners echoed Alva's philosophy of life: "FAILURE IS IMPOSSIBLE."

Doris Stevens delivered a stirring memorial address, tracing Alva's vision from rebellious early childhood in Mobile to her final years, when she dreamed of joining "to Europe and the Americas the women of Asia and Africa."[8] She praised Alva's relentless determination, her intensity, which could sometimes result in ruthless leadership, along with her vitality, gayness, and tender side. "But hers was a lonely road which more compassion, more loving approval would have made less lonely. Had she lived in a world without galling inequalities on every side, in a world more welcoming of women's abilities, gentleness would have been her predominant trait."

The party received Alva's largest charitable bequest: $100,000. It was perhaps curiously small in view of the size of the estate, but Alva had given many times that amount to the party while she was alive.

Discovering she had been cut out of the will, Doris Stevens concluded that Alice Paul was behind her failure to receive the $50,000 Alva had once promised. Matilda Young got wind of this and warned Paul, who quickly obtained legal support and successfully rebutted Doris's claims. Hearing that it was Elsa Maxwell who actually witnessed the codicil's signing, Doris sued the estate directly. Paul later heard that Consuelo settled with Doris quietly out of court for five or ten thousand dollars.[9]

Doris Stevens would never trust Alice Paul after this point, and she worked within the party to undermine her leadership. (Paul would later tell Elsa Maxwell that Stevens was anti-Semitic and unhappy with the presence of Jewish women in the organization; however, Jewish women had been there from the start, so that accusation is not very credible.) During World War II, Stevens even stole the organization's mailing list and advertised a convention competitive with the party, which by then was almost moribund. By the 1970s, it consisted of a tiny coterie so conservative that its staff turned away young hippie-looking women's liberation activists who wanted to volunteer. The building Alva gave to the cause of women became a mere memorial, not the center for women's political power she had planned it to be.

Gloria M. Decides
to Seek Custody

In March of 1933, Gloria M., who had been overseas with her sister Thelma and the prince of Wales, arrived at the Milford Havens to find a letter from her daughter's guardian indicating the surrogate was unhappy with sending her $4,000 a month when the child was not living with her. Panicked, she returned to the States, where she was told that the guardians believed the child would be better off living with Gertrude for the time being. Although Gertrude objected, the child went to spend several hours with her mother, their first time together in five months. Despite her pleas, the lawyers cut Gloria M.'s support allowance down to $750 a month and agreed to pay for her New York house and servants. (At that time, the monthly income for eight out of ten American families was $200 or less. Keislich, for example, received $125 a month for full-time care of Gloria, whereas the chauffeur earned $160.)

In need of a protector, Gloria M. turned to A. C. Blumenthal, the dwarfish showman who had taken over Ziegfeld's Follies following the originator's death. Tainted by his connection to gangsters and to Jimmy Walker's corrupt mayoral administration, he was a terrible choice. Used to selecting men for their celebrity and not their character, Gloria M. overlooked that Blumie, as she called him, was married, an accused criminal, and a publicity seeker. For the next few months Gertrude read with increasing dismay about the couple's latest appearance at this nightclub or that prizefight. The worst headline was on June 16, when she read "Blumenthal-Vanderbilt Board Ship Secretly." They had gone off to Europe, partly so Blumenthal could escape being served papers from a lawsuit.

That summer was particularly memorable for young Gloria, as she was to spend two months at Oakland Farm in Rhode Island with Alfred's son, William H. Vanderbilt, his wife Anne Colby, their three daughters, one of them Gloria's age, and four dogs of assorted sizes. It was the first time in her childhood Gloria would live with a loving couple who were affectionate parents. "They were happy all the time," she discovered.[10] Also new in her experience, Anne "talked right to me and really listened to things I said."[11]

One day Mrs. Morgan showed up, and the eavesdropping child could hear her grandmother behind the door "hissing, hissing" with Emma Keislich. When Gertrude also appeared at lunch, the girl picked up other intimations that a plan was under way. Now nine and a perceptive child, Gloria knew she was included in the plan, that she was supposed to pretend to be sick on visits to the doctors. Although she wasn't clear on the details, she "was in too deep . . . that if I went along with it, Dodo Elephant and Naney Morgan would not be sent away. Without them I would be nothing."[12]

In September, when the wayward lovers returned, Gertrude telegraphed Gloria M. to meet her to discuss young Gloria's school plans for the coming year. The response read, "Will be very happy to see you. Thursday noon. Love. *Blumie* [emphasis added]."[13] With no better proof of her sister-in-law's submission to a bad influence, Gertrude nonetheless ignored mentioning the slipup during the two women's meeting. Once again, temperamentally unable to say no to anyone, Gloria M. quickly agreed to leave her daughter in Westbury so she could continue her education at the Green Vale School with her cousin Gerta. When she suggested renting a place nearby so she could see her daughter more often, Gertrude discouraged the idea by saying Gloria M. was welcome to stay at Westbury any time she wished to visit.

Blumie was furious. Having been a poor Jew from New Jersey, he was quick to interpret the situation as implicit class warfare, the eminent Vanderbilt tribe closing in to protect its own, young Gloria, and keep out the intruder, Gloria M. His lawyer, Nathan Burkan, another son of immigrant Jews, saw the case as an opportunity to make a personal vendetta against the WASP lawyers who had excluded him from their offices, clubs, and homes, even though he had become more successful than many of them with his client roll of celebrated stage and movie stars. Over the years Burkan had intimidated conservative opposition by resorting to dramatic scenes in court (such as a tearful, demurely dressed Mae West defending an obscenity charge) and sharing files with reporters to win public support through the press. He was brilliant, fearless, and unfazed by criticism. Although he had no partners in his firm, he had a network of talented and expert investigators to do his footwork.

Burkan's response to Gloria M.'s story was so obvious one wonders why she and her many supporters hadn't thought of it sooner: she should take possession of her child.

On September 17, 1933, when Emma Keislich and Gloria stepped off the train returning from the Adirondacks, Gloria M. was there, ordering them to return to *her* home, not the Whitneys. Emma Keislich grew hysterical that the place was not fit for a child. (It did not help that she was later awakened at two in the morning by an anxious Gloria M., who was looking for salve for a guest whose face had been seared when the oven blew up on her.) Over the next few days the child's guardians applied pressure to force Gloria to send her daughter back to Westbury. As usual, money preoccupied the discussions. Gloria M. had outstanding debts in Europe, which the guardians would pay only if she agreed to comply with their instructions. Not yet deeply involved in the case, Burkan advised her to accept the agreement. "Gloria and school," Gertrude entered in her daybook on September 26.

The story continued. Gloria M. and Blumenthal remained in New York, their evening exploits splashed about the gossip pages. Gertrude returned to her schedule of work, staying in New York during the week to manage the Whitney, sculpt, visit with her ailing mother, and sneak off with lover Josh Hartwell, afterward returning to Westbury on weekends to relax with her children, grandchildren, and niece.

Themes of violence and destruction appeared in some of her sculpture, which was now more introspective and dark. Unable to build monuments, she sculpted private and personal works, such as a bust of Josh Hartwell (*John*) or of a black servant (*Gwendolyn*). A plaster model of a man holding a paper, head downcast, titled *Unemployed,* echoed the vibrancy of her war pieces. One of her most stunning works was *Woman and Child,* carved in a golden russo antico marble. Here a figure, nude from the waist up, despairs over the dead infant form she holds stretched over the folds of her long skirt. Yet in counterpoint to this Gertrude also modeled visions of strength and serenity. The quiet meditation of *Nun* with rosary was further proof of her technical growth and emotional expression. Two lover poses, *Devotion* and *The Kiss,* evinced a tenderness she had not been able to achieve in earlier work.

That winter Thelma joined Gloria M. on a trip to California, where they met Hollywood friends that Gloria had made during her previous trip with Nada Milford Haven. It was during this time that Wallis Simpson took up with Thelma's "little man," the prince of Wales, but Thelma assured the break when news of her flirtation with the Aly Khan reached the prince's home, Fort Belvedere. This well-publicized affair further hardened Gertrude's conviction that the Morgan sisters could not provide a healthy family life for Gloria. On April 12, 1934, Blumenthal's twenty-two room mansion in Larchmont, which had been part of the public warfare between him and his estranged wife, mysteriously burned to the ground. He collected the insurance money. This incident hardly enhanced his standing with Gertrude.

On April 22, 1934, Alice Vanderbilt died at age eighty-nine. During the 1920s, Gertrude had taken a more solicitous attitude toward her mother, including her on some voyages abroad and speaking with her or visiting with her daily when she was in New York. Alice had remained healthy and mentally alert; she even took language lessons while in her eighties. In 1931 she began to fail, spending most of her days in her room on the second floor of her home overlooking Central Park.

Alice's will, drawn up in 1928, left about $14 million to Gertrude, the Breakers and a trust of several million to daughter Gladys, and the Gwynne building in Cincinnati, worth many millions of dollars, to son Neily. Regi's daughters, Cathleen and Gloria, received $1 million each. To Gloria M. she bequeathed what was in her mind a token gesture of $100,000. She would have been shocked to know how the money would be spent.

Gertrude Decides to Fight

On the strength of Alice's expected legacy, Gloria M. borrowed $20,000 for legal fees and delivered the money to Nathan Burkan. (That Blumenthal, who could easily have helped her financially, never did, hints at the weakness of their relationship.) Now that she was of legal age, Burkan advised, she could apply for guardianship of Gloria. Indeed, success was likely because the surrogate judge, James Aloysius Foley, was not only a personal friend of Burkan's but noted for his sympathy toward widows. A hearing was set for July 3, 1934.

Hearing of the filing, Mrs. Morgan rushed to Gertrude. As long as Alice was alive, Gertrude had felt it necessary to keep her concern over her sister-in-law's dissipated life-style out of discussions and negotiations with the guardians.[14] Consequently, she relied upon the doctors' reports to demonstrate the need for Gloria to remain at Westbury. Unaware the child was being primed by both her nurse and Mrs. Morgan to fake illness, Gertrude had further reason to believe she was acting wisely. With Alice dead, Gertrude agreed with counsel that the truth could come out, but the case would be strongest if the objections were stated by Mrs. Morgan. Consequently, when Gloria M. confidently entered the courtroom on the morning of the hearing, she was dumbfounded to hear a stranger, a lawyer for Mrs. Morgan, jump up and object to the petition "on the grounds of unfit guardianship." Thus Gloria M. learned the extent of her mother's revenge.

Over subsequent weeks Surrogate Foley and the lawyers on both sides tried to work out an agreement to avoid a trial with its consequent public exposure. By summer's end, an informal deal was struck: during the next year Gloria would continue to live at Westbury and attend Green Vale School and could visit with her mother for one month. Gertrude assumed the guardianship question would be reopened again after that year; Gloria M. assumed she would get full custody of her daughter at that point. With both sides distrustful of the other, the lawyers continued to collect affidavits as evidence in case of an eventual trial. Partly for this reason, Gloria M. went abroad to obtain a character statement from Prince Hohenlohe, now married to Princess Margarita of Greece and Denmark, sister to the future Prince Phillip. Her sister Consuelo returned with her to the States. In turn, Gertrude's lawyers hired detectives to follow Gloria M. and planted spies in her house staff.

The child herself was growing more nervous. Though unaware yet of the custody battle, her cooperation with her nurse and grandmother Morgan in "the plan" went from pretense to belief. She was no longer simply following their instructions when she stated she was unhappy with her mother. She believed it. Adding to her fear was her isolation. That summer she went to Oakland Farms again, where she figured out that another plot was under way. The telling clue emerged when word came that her mother was to visit her at the farm, but then a doctor suddenly appeared and announced all the children were on strict quarantine, not to leave the premises. Yet no one was sick. Thus Gloria inferred her mother was going to come and take her away to that strange country overseas with Prince Hohenlohe's gloomy castle and mean-spirited inhabitants. Despite this fear, she had moments when she would long for her mother, even run into the woods, hug a tree as though it were her mother. "But I could not sustain it. Tree of oak was not my mother."[15]

In August, when the child joined the Whitney family camp in the Adirondacks, Gloria M. arrived with her older sister Consuelo, determined to go there and take the girl away. Their father had died recently, so they were dressed in somber black with mourning veils over their faces. Alerted that the sisters were on their way across the lake and fearful that the women had come to abduct Gloria and take her to nearby Canada, Gertrude sent Emma Keislich and her niece off in another boat. As the women's boat approached the child's, Gloria recognized the "two nuns, hooded and joined together . . . the One with the Nose [Consuelo] and The Beautiful One [her mother]," and shook in terror. Convinced they had come to take her away, she pleaded to her nurse, "Don't let them take me please please please!"[16] Later that afternoon, when Gertrude allowed the women to see her, Gloria resisted and consented only under duress.

During that summer, the girl was repeatedly examined by doctors. In one case, she was even required to strip naked and pose for photographs taken by Keislich. Gloria grew so anxious that she had trouble eating, with the result that doctors ordered her already sparse exercise cut back. In the afternoons, while her cousins ran about the woods and splashed in water games, ten-year-old Gloria was put to bed to take a nap. She was also given medicines to force her bowel movement, which were judged to be irregular.

A month later, after Gloria's mother returned from Europe, Gertrude agreed that the child should spend several days with her in New York before school started. Once again, the two sisters dressed in mourning were unaware of their ominous impression on the child. (Apparently no one had bothered to tell the girl of her maternal grandfather's death.) Much of Gloria M.'s talk was of the house she had found near Old Westbury, where she hoped to take custody of her child, for Gertrude could not argue over the healthiness of the setting or the proximity to Green Vale School. A key feature of her plan was to get rid of Emma Keislich, whom she correctly saw to be a spy and provocateur.

One stormy morning the child was playing her favorite game, Invisible, sneaking about to spy on the mother she both feared and desired, to observe and listen. Quietly positioning herself outside the living room, she watched a common and harmless scene, her mother and Consuelo play bezique. What she heard, however, was not harmless. Consuelo was talking about getting rid of Keislich, replacing her with "a German fraulein." Gloria's mother responded by saying she would call Prince Hohenlohe for such a person, and she looked at her watch to determine what time it was in Germany.

Hysterical, Gloria ran up to her nurse, who advised her to calm down. Keislich advised she would take her to Mrs. Whitney, but they must pretend they were going out to skate in the park, for the rain had just ended. Safely out of the house, the child felt "body and face were coming apart, and everything was exploding."[17] Her fit continued after they arrived at Gertrude's, who heard the child say she was afraid of her mother. Gloria's shrieking continued when one of the guardians arrived. He was astonished to hear the child say "If you send me back to her I will kill myself."[18]

In the midst of this turmoil, Consuelo and Gloria M. burst into the home, dashed upstairs, and pushed their way into the bathroom where Gertrude and Keislich were preparing Gloria for a bath. "Get out of this room!" they shouted to Keislich, who obeyed. Gloria clung to Gertrude and screamed, "Don't let her come near me, don't let her kill me!"[19] Finally persuading Gloria M. and her sister to leave, Gertrude returned to the child and stayed at her side while she sobbed herself to sleep. Any hesitation she had felt about her determination to protect Gloria disappeared.

The next day Gloria M. and Consuelo appeared with their own doctor and demanded he be allowed to examine the child and report his independent opinion concerning her health. To their dismay, he informed them he agreed with the other physicians that the child needed calm and rest and should not be moved from Gertrude's care. Assured she would be returning to Westbury with Keislich, Gloria agreed to see her mother briefly. Just before that encounter, Mrs. Morgan came in to spend a minute alone with Gloria, who "felt her wings around me . . . the love spreading through me." Gloria, her grandmother Morgan advised, must kiss Aunt Gertrude a lot and show her love for her. Objecting she didn't truly know Aunt Gertrude, so it was hard to know if she loved her, Gloria eventually capitulated to her grandmother's repeated urgings.

Down in the huge salon, the child found her mother and Consuelo, again in black with veils over their faces, and at Gertrude's prompting sat between them. Frightened, "to my horror—my mother reached out to take my hand. I left [it] as if it were a dead thing."[20] Caught between Consuelo's angry eyes and her mother's beauty, she was torn, wanting to both throw herself into her mother's arms and tear her hand away so fiercely it would bring her mother's soft fingers with it. Asking to be excused, Gloria crept away, leaving her mother distraught and humiliated.

Within hours a process server appeared at 871 Fifth Avenue to serve Gertrude with a writ of habeas corpus to present to Judge John Carew "the body of Gloria Laura Morgan Vanderbilt by you imprisoned and detained."[21] The compromise had broken down.

Justice Produces
a Travesty

The story of the trial was retold to a popular audience in 1980 with the appearance of Barbara Goldsmith's meticulously researched book *Little Gloria ... Happy at Last,* recast in a four-hour television miniseries in 1984 that still runs periodically. The book's most accurate and useful feature was that it captured the bizarre and byzantine qualities of the hearings: Keislich was so hostile and vindictive toward Gloria M. that both counsels secretly agreed she must go; Maria Caillot, Gloria M.'s personal maid for five years, revealed that she had seen Nada Milford Haven in her mistress's bed "kissing her like a lover"; Mrs. Morgan, clutching a large gold crucifix, portrayed her daughter's lack of maternal instinct; Charles Zaug, butler and paid Whitney spy, testified to the presence of lesbian pornography in Gloria M.'s home; maid Olga Wright claimed there were no unseemly books present in the house; various doctors' gave confused and ambiguous medical testimony; Thelma attempted valiantly but unsuccessfully to portray her sister as an excellent mother; Gertrude Whitney claimed that she considered Gloria M. to be a perfect lady with no objectionable personal characteristics; Burkan claimed that Gertrude's sculpture and art collection was obscene. Overseeing all was Carew, a flawed jurist and a fanatical Catholic who was hiding his own secret: a drinking problem.

Goldsmith did not, however, have access to Gertrude's private papers, nor would Gloria Vanderbilt talk to her about the case. Consequently, it was not until Gloria wrote her own account, *Once Upon a Time,* that her perspective was revealed.

Since Gertrude had to take Gloria to the first court session, she could no longer keep the fact of the trial from her. Although Gloria still did not feel she knew her aunt, she appreciated how she spoke calmly to her in the car on the way to the courthouse, how in the crowd pressing in on them on the steps, Gertrude inspired her. "In all that pushing and shouting, in all that hullabaloo, she took each step, on her thin long legs in their elegant green shoes, up and up, just as if she did not have a care in the world. If she can do it, so can I."[22]

If there was ever a time Gertrude could have formed a bond with Gloria, it would have been these frightening initial days of the proceedings. But she was preoccupied with the trial, caught up in the role of avenging angel to protect the girl whose health and mood had clearly improved during the two years under her care. Also, Gloria was too young to understand the pressures brought on her aunt by the scurrilous press coverage, much of it brought on by William Randolph Hearst.

Hearst's venom toward Gertrude was ironically connected to the Whitney Museum activities. Earlier that year, the Whitney sent more than a hundred works from its collection to represent the United States at the Venice Biennale, the most important exhibition of contemporary art. While it was being packed, Hearst offered to pay the shipping provided one more oil be included, Polish artist Tade Styka's portrait of the magnate's lover, Marion Davies. Juliana Force refused, only to learn later the picture was in place with the Whitney collection, and in the most prominent spot in the pavilion at that. Hearst had used his friendship with Mussolini to get his way with Biennale officials.

Juliana sent a representative to Venice to negotiate removal of the Davies portrait, under threat that the entire Whitney exhibit would be dismounted and sent home. If the officials did not agree, then the museum would break the story to Hearst's publishing rival, the Associated Press. Knowing Hearst hated any reference to him and Davies, whose reputation he scrupulously protected, Juliana felt confident of their position. Out of her league, she was stifled by Italian bureaucrats, who, when sued to release the art, saw that the case was delayed until the close of the exhibit. Their one concession was a placard below the Davies portrait on which it was stated that the work was not part of the Whitney collection. As a result of this dispute, Juliana lost face with Gertrude for failing to salvage the situation, and worse, she made an enemy of Hearst. As Gloria M.'s longtime friend, Hearst would naturally have defended her in his presses, but now he had personal revenge to express as well.

Each day Gertrude went to court to observe the proceedings; sometimes Flora joined her mother. Hearst's slanted coverage was facilitated by Judge Carew's grandstanding. When, during her testimony Marie Caillot broke the story of lesbianism, the judge closed the courtroom to all but the principals. From that point he gave daily reports to the press on the trial highlights, not all of which were accurate. When the day's testimony was over, Gertrude would consult with lawyer Frank Crocker, who had been Harry's adviser for many years. As she felt more isolated from her normal life and vilified by the press, Gertrude leaned more on Crocker for direction. Thus when the lesbianism tale broke, she asked him to stop the trial, and she was upset when he explained Gloria M. had brought the suit, and she alone could halt it.

Gloria went off to school daily, aware teachers and classmates were discussing "It," the trial, but refusing to allow any discussion of It in her presence. On weekends, when Gertrude appeared, none of the cousins or aunts and uncles mentioned the matter either, and while Gloria ached to talk about her mother with Gertrude, she sensed the topic was taboo. (Their silence was probably motivated to prevent Gloria from worrying.) The people who did discuss the matter with her were the "Three Wise Men," the lawyers who prepared her for her eventual meeting with Judge Carew. It was their job to carefully plan and teach her the script she would use to such devastating effectiveness. And Keislich and Mrs. Morgan continued their pressure: Gloria must always show Gertrude how much she loved her.

If Gertrude had any doubts about the correctness of her position, however, they were probably destroyed by information she received concerning the state of Gloria's education. She learned that when Gloria first entered Green Vale in 1932, her aptitude on the Stanford Achievement Test was so low that it could not be scaled. Consequently, the girl was placed a year below her age group and given extra tutoring. A year later, she had shown much improvement. Still, although a year older than her classmates, she was behind in spelling and about four months behind the average of her class overall.[23]

She also pasted in her picture album photographs of a Gloria much different from the nervous child who had arrived two years earlier. She laughed at the camera, showed off on stilts, and sat affectionately beside Gerta. There were also pictures the girl had made for her aunt to show her love. One showed a robed fairy reclining in a crescent moon; another, an ocean liner with a figure, presumably Gloria, sending her love; and a third, a bird carrying a thank-you for some books, and with many XXXs and OOOs. That Keislich may have been behind these drawings is suggested by an obvious misspelling on one of them, reminiscent of "rare bease."[24]

In late October of 1934, one of the Wise Men, lawyer Frank Crocker, came to Westbury and informed Gloria that her mother was coming to visit the next morning and that Keislich would be going away for the day. While waiting for her mother's arrival she was to go riding with her uncle Buz Henry—Bozo Bean to her. Gloria became hysterical again, partly because she had seen this uncle punish one of his children in the Adirondacks by chaining him to a tree like a dog. Keislich calmed Gloria down and promised she would return to Westbury. During the ride Uncle Henry said nothing, leaving Gloria frustrated that no one would explain to her the presence of police and guards all over the estate. She was still unaware of the Lindbergh case and family fears she could be kidnapped.

Arriving back at Gertrude's house, Gloria jumped off her horse, dashed into the house, locked herself in her room, threw the key in the fire, and sat down in the bathroom, her back against the door. Soon her uncle Henry and aunt Consuelo were pounding on the door shouting threats to her: They would call the police to break it down, they would call a doctor. "Why were doctors always being brought in? What I needed was simple—what I needed was Big Elephant [Keislich]."[25] Eventually making their way in, they convinced Gloria the court required her to see her mother. Compliant, she found her mother in another room, prostrate under the covers, her eyes closed. "Hello, Mommy," she said. Gloria M. did not answer. The child left the room and stood on the landing to watch as Thelma and Consuelo drifted down the stairs, supporting Gloria M. between them.

The day came for Gloria to face Judge Carew. This time Herbert Smyth, the lawyer who had worked most closely with her in creating her responses, accompanied her in the Rolls Royce. The crowds, an "ocean of seaweed," taunted "You treat your ma good, Little Gloria" and "You be nice to your ma?" Others jeered, "Down with Gertrude! Down with her millions! Down with the aunt, up with the mom!" Hearst's propaganda was working its charm too well.

During the two and a half hours in the private chamber, Gloria played her part exquisitely, all the while knowing she was telling a story: She loved the country, hated the city. She liked dogs, but her mother took them away. Her Aunt Thelma was not nice. Her mother was always too busy for her. No one ever told her to say anything about her mother. Her mother never read to her. She never said in her prayers "God bless Mummy." She did not recognize her mother in a photograph. She *hated* her mother. Her loving letters to her mother were to fool her. She was afraid of her mother. She liked Aunt Gertrude.

Throughout, Gloria's heart pounded, desperate to tell the judge the truth, that "he would know it was not Aunt Gertrude I was afraid of being taken from—it was [my nurse] Dodo!"[26] What she did not know is that Keislich's testimony had guaranteed the worst would happen.

Returning to school that afternoon, Gloria felt naked. She knew something had come out in the papers during the trial, something about her mother, yet no one would tell her. "If it was so terrible and she was my mother, then it must mean I was in some ways terrible too. [I] might be so terrible a thing that I would no longer be able to live. I would be struck dead."[27] She could not know that the charge, the reputed lesbianism, was something the most well-meaning adult would have had difficulty explaining to a ten year old. Confused, she fantasized "melting into the skin" of her mother, penetrating so deeply into the center of her that she would have "no more of me left." Then she recalled her terror the day she saw the two black figures on the boat in the Adirondacks, and the pleasant daydream ended abruptly.

On November 21, 1934, Judge Carew handed down his Solomonic compromise. Frustrated by the child's intransigent stand against her mother, he could not see a way to give Gloria M. full custody. What was needed, he decided, was to create a situation where the mother could gradually regain the daughter's affections. Consequently, Gloria was to be a ward of the court, placed in Gertrude's custody at the Westbury residence, attend the Green Vale School, and be raised in the Catholic faith of her mother's. She was to be delivered to her mother on Saturdays at 10:00 A.M., to stay until Sunday sundown; she was also to stay with her for the month of July, and for eight hours on Christmas Day. She was not permitted to leave the state of New York. What was not stated was the mutual agreement of both sides that Keislich be let go.

Soon afterward, lawyer Frank Crocker appeared once again in the living room at Old Westbury to speak with Gloria. While running his fingers over the piano, he explained, "This is your lucky day. The Judge has handed down his decision, *and* he has decided in favor of your Aunt Gertrude!"[28] Her mother could appeal the Judge's decision, he advised, but that was unlikely. Happy that "the plan" had worked, Gloria got up to leave. Crocker reached over to stop her. He had almost forgotten to mention that Nurse Keislich would be leaving, just before Christmas. "Run run upstairs. I ran into the soft mountain of Big Elephant. My heart broken and the blood of it gushed from me into the soft sweet love of her. And from that moment to this—nothing has ever been the same again."[29] Several weeks later she returned from school to find Nurse Keislich gone, in her place a Mademoiselle Ruel, "hard, fat, with hair in a fisted bun. I hated her."[30]

Gloria M. and Gertrude
Turn to Writing

Gloria M. was to continue to press appeals and changes in the ruling for the next two years, always unsuccessfully. Although she had lost her guardianship bid, she had gained in a way curiously satisfying—the public had supported her throughout. It was only recently (much thanks to the National Woman's party) that women were being granted equal consideration in custody hearings against their estranged husbands, who as breadwinners had typically gained control. Although no man was involved in the dispute in this case, Gloria M.'s case signified a change in public attitude. Motherhood was a holy status not to be disrupted except under the most extreme circumstances. Furthermore, the depression had turned many against the rich. That Gertrude was of great fortune increased public sympathy for Gloria M. For if money could buy this child, then it meant millions of Americans were similarly powerless, victims of the well-to-do.

To take advantage of this popularity, Gloria M. hired a ghostwriter to prepare a book, *Without Prejudice,* documenting her life story and position in the trial. It was an opportunity to expose the villain in her life, her mother, whom she portrayed as pathologically impulsive, mercurial, and domineering toward the four children and their often-absent father. Alternately seduced and abandoned, the twins responded by worshiping, clinging to, and always obeying this fierce figure. (It is a case codependency theorists would describe as classic.) Given Mrs. Morgan's behavior as noted by others and exhibited in court, the depiction is probably accurate, and her abused daughters deserve sympathy.

Where the story goes askew, however, is in its account of Gloria's relationship with the Vanderbilts. Highly idealized, she portrays herself as pursued by Regi, not the pursuer, and she distorts her relationship with his daughter Cathleen. If she joined readily in his compulsive nightlife, she rationalizes, it was because she was used to bending to her mother's whim. She idolizes Alice Vanderbilt for her kindness, which was genuine, but misrepresents Harry Whitney as her champion, "one of my truest and most steadfast friends," which he was not.[31] (She admits to admiring Gertrude at first for the characteristics that made her similar to Regi, her charm, keen mind, and quick wit.) Similarly, she portrays Nada Milford Haven as a charismatic friend and Hohenlohe as the Prince Charming she gives up in a scene worthy of a Hollywood costume drama. With a hint of hostility, she remarks, "But there was the child—and I sacrificed my marriage for her."[32] Tellingly, she discloses it would not have been fair for her to have Gloria grow up in Bavaria "seeing that her income would be cut to such a nominal allowance that it would prevent my bringing her to America for six months of every year."[33]

The most revealing feature of the book is how its pages are jammed with details of clothes, of the decor of a house, of the names of illustrious guests at parties, of conversations with celebrities, of life at San Simeon, of the thrill of being presented to the English royalty, yet it says virtually nothing about the person whom she claims meant most to her, her daughter. There are hardly any discussions of the child's development and achievements for the simple reason she was not around to observe them.

While Gloria M. worked with her ghostwriter, Gertrude also turned to writing. Reviled by the press, she struggled to return her life to its old order. One result was a novel published posthumously in 1984 under the title *A Love Affair*. The heroine, Sandra Fane, once a wealthy Bostonian now widowed, designs clothes in Paris under the curious name of Madama Nada. Her lover, American lawyer Stanley Marston, has a semiinvalid wife, Eileen, whom he will not leave. Each highly successful in their separate careers, Sandra and Stanley have a congenial arrangement, with frequent meetings at Fleuris, a modernized Norman chateau similar to Gertrude's own, Le Boulay. One day, disturbed by the comments of a guest, Sandra muses on the "malevolent force about and around her. Men doing things against beauty; men being grotesque; men deliberately destroying themselves, and dragging women with them to destruction when with Marston there was joy and loveliness to be taken."[34]

Sandra's best friend, the unhappily married Bea, appears. They are depicted as two women who are affectionately devoted to one another through the years. Bea is deeply moved by Sandra and Stanley's devotion and wishes to see them permanently together. One day she accidentally meets Eileen and discovers she is a malingerer who manipulates her husband for her own selfish purposes. Repulsed by her, Bea arranges to be alone with Eileen one night and then poisons her in such a way that it appears to be suicide. In the final pages Sandra recognizes what Bea has done, the sacrifice she has made for her. The two women realize they can never meet again, for fear of exposing the truth.

Certain elements of Gertrude's relationship with Josh Hartwell were incorporated into the story, and one wonders about his relationship with his wife, whether she had any of the characteristics of Eileen. Josh even playfully indulged

Gertrude by pretending he was Stanley and writing letters to her as though she were Sandra.

A Love Affair has many elements of an effective romance. The nonerotic love between the women is as powerful as the romantic love between Sandra and Stanley. Both are set against the background of fashionable Paris in the thirties, with its collection of fun seekers and degenerates. The castle hideaway with its tower, den for Stanley, and studio for Sandra, evokes romantic hope. Successfully woven into the story is Gertrude's real-life experience when William Stackpole had detectives follow her to an apartment where she had almost been raped. The moral issues surrounding Bea's murder are provocative even to today's readers.

Yet the novel does not work. As in her other fiction, Gertrude's characters lack depth and motivation. We have no sense of how Sandra came to design in Paris. There is no explanation for the great loyalty between her and Bea. Stanley is too perfect, too noble. Features that should become metaphorical, such as the chateau or a well-placed lightning storm, fail to transform. The lengthy cocktail conversations that should illumine Paris in the thirties are simply boring. The prose is flat, lacking the rhythm and meter to carry the reader forward. Gertrude set the manuscript aside following a year's attempts to publish it, and when it did appear posthumously, it earned negative notice in its few reviews.

Gertrude also worked on a play during this time, *The Hand*. Although *The Hand* went through many versions, the basic plot remained as it developed originally from a short story.[35] A poet has another man's hand reattached following an accident that has mangled his own. He is a jealous man who beats his wife, and in the end he kills her. "It [the hand] controlled me. I wanted to keep on. It gave me sensations of power I never had," he justifies. In the dramatic version, the poet is replaced by a painter whose art turns degenerate and obscene following the operation. Friends learn the source of the hand was a strong, boastful Mexican peasant reputed to have killed a woman. Aware the painter has become possessed in a way by the peasant's spirit, just as they seem to have convinced him to go to the hospital, he suddenly turns and stabs his long-suffering wife (or in a later version, his doctor). This theme of murderous rage out of control obsessed Gertrude for the next eight years, perhaps channeling all the anger she wished to express toward others in her life, but could not.

Gloria Tries to
Find Her Place

Meanwhile young Gloria was left bereft with little comfort apart from Mrs. Morgan, with whom she talked on the phone every evening before bedtime. In one of the more perverse medical decisions forced on this hapless youngster, she was required to go to bed at seven, lights out, no activity until breakfast. Thus while her cousins in neighboring houses finished their homework, read, and in spring hours played outside after dinner, Gloria lay alone, wide awake, nervous because the door would not be opened even a crack to let light through. Accompanied by bodyguards to school, she put up a brave front against the continuing publicity surrounding her, just as Gertrude had taught her to do that day climbing the courthouse steps.

In public, reporters and photographers tracked along, following her and Gertrude on a shopping trip to a department store, and to mass, where they spied the ten-cent piece Gloria dropped in the collection basket. Worse, Gloria's childhood "hate letters" to her mother were printed in the newspapers for all her friends to read. It was right after these appeared, December 22, 1934, that Gloria was scheduled for her first weekend visit with her mother. "G. went to town. Terrible scenes," wrote Gertrude in her daybook.

Carew's hope that the mother and child could reconcile was impossible under these circumstances. Their first day together, Gloria M. took her daughter to F.A.O. Schwartz, the toy store, to buy Christmas presents, and begged the cars of reporters and cameramen to leave the two alone. When they refused, she realized she and her daughter could not go out publicly. Yet privately she was not able to cultivate a relationship with Gloria, which is not surprising in light of her own mother's model. (Certainly she deserves credit for at least not perpetuating Mrs. Morgan's actual abuse.)

In another autobiography written years later with Thelma, *Double Exposure,* Gloria M. once again idealized this time. What good times she and her daughter had in movie theaters together, sitting in the dark away from the staring eyes of strangers, sharing in the wonderful celluloid fancies of the thirties! Not so, said the child. "The best thing about weekends at my mother's was that she let me go to the movies. It was Tootsie Eleanor [the weekend nurse] who sat beside me because, always, at the last minute, my mother was too tired to go."[36] Accompanying her daughter to noon mass on Sunday, Gloria M. had a tendency to grow faint during the service and draw the parishioners' attention to them because it meant the two would have to get up and move to the balcony, where it was less crowded.

Gloria was, for all purposes, a child without a mother, and there was no consistent, caring male adult to fill the role of her dead father. The uncle she saw most frequently, Buz Henry, did not like her. Her mother's lovers were hardly paternal, and Gloria M. was peeved that all her weekends were tied up by the child's presence. One of Nathan Burkan's associates agreed, "Gloria didn't know what to do with the kid. She'd ask me—what am I going to do with her this weekend, Jim?"[37] Sometimes lunch at the Sherry Netherland would follow, but Tootsie Eleanor would be at the table as well, and Gloria M. would dawdle so that there would be no time for an afternoon visit to the movies. Gloria knew of A. C. Blumenthal, present in the form of lavish gifts, but she saw him only in passing—his going down the stairs from her mother's house while she went up. She wondered if he would marry her mother, what it would be like to go to the house and find him greeting her instead of hurrying away.

In July of 1935, Gloria went to stay for her appointed month with her mother at a rented house near Nissequogue on the north shore of Long Island Sound. The house was large, filled with Gloria M.'s friends (but no Blumenthal), who spent the mornings sleeping until lunchtime, forcing the child to tiptoe around and whisper with Tootsie Eleanor. Also present was Thelma with son Tony, as were the daughter and son of guest Melba Melsing Meredith, a radio singer. A Mr. Gardner was said to return home to the city after dinner, or so the grown-ups said, but the children knew he kept his clothes in a room over the garage and slept in Thelma's room. For Gloria, this duplicity was just one more facet of the "pretend business" so characteristic of the adults around her.

The singer, who had the room next to Gloria, did garner the child's admiration. In the dusk she would bend over her guitar, "laughed her beautiful poppy-red laugh and plunged into one song and then on into another, lovelier than the one before."[38] During these moments, the child would gaze at her mother whispering to Thelma, and make up stories about her. Imaginary tales were all she had—Gloria M. remained so aloof the child did not know which room her mother slept in.

Even this isolated spot did not protect Gloria from reminders of the custody fight. One day a small plane appeared, and the children took turns going up. It would return another day, they were told when they begged for further rides. But it did not come back. Tootsie Eleanor confided the reason to Gloria. Frank Crocker had learned, perhaps from servant spies, that the plane's appearance was just part of another plot, this one concocted by a sympathetic William Randolph Hearst, to take Gloria and her mother away to Canada. "Kidnapping by my mother and Mr. Hearst so he could use it for publicity in his tabloids," was the explanation.[39] With Crocker now wise, Gloria M. aborted the plan.

If Gloria longed for her mother's affection, she also longed for Gertrude's. Although Gertrude was now spending more time at Westbury, and wrote affectionate letters to the girl when they were separated, Gloria came up against the same wall others confronted in dealing with her elusive aunt. Naturally timid, Gloria kept waiting for the adults around her to bring up topics of interest to her. Characteristic of an orphaned child her age, she was desperate to know about her father and waited hopefully for Gertrude to have a talk with her about him. Learning a bust in Gertrude's bedroom was of her father, she hoped it would stimulate her aunt into describing him. When Gloria pointed it out one evening, Gertrude said only that it was sculpted by Jo Davidson, and left Gloria to finger the face, probing for information that was not forthcoming. Perhaps Gertrude found it hard to explain a father famous for his gambling and womanizing.

Gloria was not the only child being overlooked at Westbury. Gerta was also left in the company of staff for long periods of time. Despite frequent medical care, her mother Barbie had not improved since her postpartum depression in

1925. In fact, Buz had informed Gertrude that the doctors had come to the conclusion that the case was apparently hopeless, and he assured her he would never leave Barbie because of it. Consequently, to protect Barbie's nerves, he took her off to health resorts and away from the pressures of the family when he could.

Gerta and Gloria loved to poke about the estate, searching for clues about Gloria's father. One day they sneaked into Gertrude's studio and pulled the cloth off a pedestal to find the head of a girl. Gloria was elated—the head suggested her own, so Gertrude must be coming to the studio secretly to do the bust as a surprise for her. "And if this was so, it must mean she really liked me a lot. Not only liked me but, yes! *loved* me!"[40] This proof lifted her up for days, had her excited in anticipation of the day Gertrude would unveil this most complimentary expression of her love. Then one afternoon Gloria happened to overhear that the statue was the head of an unknown girl, a bust Gertrude had worked on years before and never finished.

In her memoir of this period, Gloria presented a view of her relationship with Gertrude as distant and unsatisfying. For example, she writes of how, one night, Gertrude came into Gloria's bedroom, sat beside her on the edge of the bed, and took her hand. "I hope you know how much I love you, Gloria?" she asked. Gloria wanted to say she did, she knew her aunt loved her, but "words hard to come by are always too late."[41] Gloria's letters to Gertrude, which she did not refer to in preparing her book, suggest a more complicated relationship, in which Gloria was not as neglected as she later portrayed.

Gertrude loved her niece yet was somewhat hampered in her ability to meet her needs. Most inhibiting was her own inability to express her feelings directly to people—that WASP temperament she had for so long deplored. The age difference certainly played a role. Gertrude was now in her sixties. At Gloria's age Gertrude was growing up in a household with brothers and sister, father and mother ruling all with their regular, firm, and united presence. Her French governesses had been emotionally secure, cultured companions. Gloria had no siblings, no father, and had been exposed to an array of adults placing competing pressures on her for their own selfish interests. Her education had been spotty prior to attending Green Vale School, and she was not the dedicated student Gertrude had been. Both aunt and niece were of passionate temperament, but where Gertrude's sensuousness forced her inward, toward narcissism and fear of relating too closely to others, Gloria's impelled her outward, to imagine herself bonded with the other, to become the other.

It is not surprising that during Gloria's visit to the Adirondacks during the summer of 1935 she became smitten with a young boy visiting the Whitney camp. If she could not find affection from the adults who should be giving it to her, she would turn to boys instead. The romantic music of Gershwin and Porter fed her fantasies of male rescue, a fairy tale that would rule her life well into adulthood.

Crocker Comes Between
Gertrude and Juliana

Living on Long Island, Gloria was aware of her aunt's lively professional life in New York City, but she could not understand its demands. Gertrude had been managing the Whitney Museum as a private concern, meaning it had no legal existence, hence no tax deductibility, and questionable perpetuity following her death. Consequently, with Frank Crocker and Juliana Force she spent months developing the nonprofit corporate structure and ensuring its financial security through a contribution of 20,000 shares of R.J. Reynolds Tobacco Company and $100,000 in cash. The two women oversaw renovation of the galleries as well. They also agreed to a policy adopted by the Society of American Painters, Sculptors and Gravers to pay exhibited artists a modest rental fee. The incorporation was finally approved by the state of New York on February 26, 1936.

With Juliana she also created the World's Fair Five Organization, a group committed to seeing that the upcoming 1939 exhibition would not be limited to scientific and commercial displays but would include art in the form of murals, memorial sculptures, and inspiring architecture. Toward that end Gertrude paid four architects, including son-in-law Cully Miller, to create a plan for the proposed site. Although their work was not used, the World's Fair Five must have swayed some minds on the Fair board, for eventually thirty-six commissions were handed out for free-standing sculptures, fountains, and murals. One of these went to Gertrude.

Despite these shared activities, Juliana's position with regard to Gertude was weakened as a result of the custody trial. Having served Gertrude so well through that period, Frank Crocker became her major adviser. A man used to protecting his own class, he looked over the Whitney Museum accounts and decided Juliana was another Gloria M., an unworthy leech on the family fortune. Gertrude knew that Juliana was padding her considerable salary by charging many items to her open-ended expense account, but she did not care. Juliana's inability to control her spending was well known. Partly it was a refusal to deny herself any luxury, but part, too, was her generosity. She supported two spinster sisters, the family of an alcoholic brother, and was the benefactress of other siblings with special needs, such as a nephew's education. She also paid $200 a month out of pocket to a couple she had asked to research the Shaker arts. In other words, her personal and Whitney expenses commingled in a way Crocker found to be proof of fraud.

His animosity for Juliana forced two changes upon the museum. First, Juliana was to be on salary only, with no expense account, in effect cutting her income by two-thirds. Second, he convinced Gertrude to reorganize the museum as a nonprofit corporation, of which he by default became the key board member, because Sonny and Flora, also appointed to the board, acted as rubber stamps for his decisions. Juliana was dumbstruck and aggrieved: "I have devoted myself to Mrs. Whitney, and now they are doing this to me."[42] Worse, it turned out Crocker believed the museum should run like a business, without loss, making up all its costs through whatever means possible other than Gertrude's charity. Besides placing unrealistic demands on Juliana, his philosophy meant cutbacks in both acquisitions and traveling shows. While she lost these battles, she fought him successfully, however, when he wanted to eliminate the fees paid to exhibited artists.

Crocker's pettiness grew nastier. He pronounced Juliana's expense accounts to be compensation and made the decision retroactive, which made her liable to past income taxes and penalties. He also said he would report a portion of the museum building insurance as part of her compensation, for it included Juliana's apartment. Pressed, she had to sell her beloved Bucks County farm and many of her treasured works of folk art. The relationship between the two women naturally suffered, although Juliana remained loyal and did not blame Gertrude for the ordeal.

During this time Gertrude also spent many days at her New York studio directing artisans in the carving of her models for an exhibit at the prestigious Knoedler's Gallery. It was her first solo show since 1923. Although consisting of only fourteen pieces, it represented the various lines of her diverse output during these confusing and conflicted years. Because Gertrude's work lacked a single, strong expression or theme, the critics were understandably divided. They found it hard to place an artist who could create both a cool, stylized, modern "Nun," a romantic and expressionistic "Daphne," and a forthright "John." Where some felt that her reputation as an artist grew because of the event, others thought that it revealed the weakness of her work, a decorative conception of sculpture. Nonetheless, even less favorable critics acknowledged her technical skill and facility.

Gertrude must have known that any representational sculptor at that time would be facing a difficult audience, for the art form was in flux. The most recent (and what proved to be final) major exhibition of traditional representational American sculpture had been in 1929 at the Legion of Honor in San Francisco. Since then, the depression had forced many sculptors to teach or make commissioned portraits to supplement their incomes. Her good friend Jo Davidson, for example, was hired by the publishing firm of Doubleday, Doran & Co. to model portraits of ten authors, including James Joyce, Aldous Huxley, and D. H. Lawrence. Others found contracts for public buildings, such as zoos and museums. Yet another major source of sculptural commissions, architects, was declining as they adopted the streamlined Bauhaus style, with its machine aesthetic that called for a minimal use of decoration on and within buildings. Not coincidentally, abstract sculptors such as David Smith and Isamu Noguchi were drawing praise from gallery owners and museum curators.

Gertrude herself obtained only two major commissions during the thirties.

In 1936, the Netherland-American Foundation ordered a statue of Peter Stuyvesant placed in Stuyvesant Square at Second Avenue and Sixteenth Street, once part of that city founder's farm. Told there would be no fee apart from casting expenses, Gertrude demurred, for it had long been her practice to refuse such opportunities for fear she was taking a potential commission away from a needier artist. Assured no other artist had been offered a fee, she finally agreed, and she sent an assistant to gather information from various local historical societies on Stuyvesant. The resulting full-body representation of the crafty, peg-legged Dutchman was not among her better works.

More inspiring would be her World's Fair Commission for a major work to be installed in a dominant location, just in the gateways used by visitors arriving by the Long Island Railroad and the IRT-BMT subway lines. Conceiving of the Spirit of Flight as her theme, she placed the nude figures of a man and woman before three soaring bird's wings, the highly arched and soaring pedestal adding to the suggestion of takeoff. The problem was the construction. She conceived the arc to be a rainbow and was uncertain how to produce the colored effect. Fortunately, she met Buckminster Fuller, a brilliant young engineer and inventor, who introduced her to neon tubing, lucite, and plexiglass and thus inspired creation of the first of many neon-lighted rainbow designs to appear in public.

Although the world's fair sculpture was just a dream in 1936, its vision of romantic optimism may have reflected her wishes for her relationship with Josh Hartwell, a future that his marriage made impossible. He had proved to be the confidante and passionate lover she had hoped Harry would be. He was the model of the mature, tender male lover in her draft of *A Love Affair*. When separated by travel, he continued to write her lengthy letters expressing his longing for her. But those letters now came in shaky hand, for his health was failing, and his steady decline over the next few years would break her heart. She still attracted men—business executive George Wharton Pepper in Philadelphia was strongly infatuated with her and visited New York to accompany her places—but Josh brought her the emotional fulfillment she had been denied for most of her life.

P A R T 3

One could say with accuracy of Gloria Vanderbilt that she is superlatively self-made. Like Yeats, and with something like the same intensity of effort, she has come to know that her soul is self-delighting.

—BRENDAN GILL

15

1936-1942

Gloria Searches
for an Anchor

That Gertrude was interested in Gloria's activities is evident in the girl's letters to her.[1] She described books she was reading, movies she saw, friends she was making, and dreams. Signs of her artistic and sensual personality appeared early. In one letter she wrote of planning a book that would consist of descriptions of imaginary paintings, which she would try to paint as illustrations, although she thought she would not do well.[2] She would also describe her deep emotional response to a snowy landscape or sunset and hope her aunt did not think she was silly to respond so. Of similar temperament, Gertrude could hardly think so.

Meanwhile, Gertrude protected Gloria from the continuing litigation, her mother reappearing in court to argue the girl had been "shuttled back and forth each week like a tennis ball."[3] Although her second appeal on March 30, 1936, to the New York Supreme Court failed, Gloria M. vowed to continue. Ever quick to use Hearst's free banner to persuade the public of her victimization, she had fewer advocates, however, now that her daughter's nasty letters had become common knowledge. Also, the Surrogate Court was not pleased to see that she had spent almost $35,000 of Gloria's trust money to maintain a house the child saw only on weekends. Among the items charged to the account were fifty dozen cartons of cigarettes, ten cases of beer, fourteen dozen bottles of White Rock Soda, and ten dozen bottles of ginger ale. Her personal allowance having been cut back to $9,000 a year, a generous allotment for those days, Gloria M. promptly put up for sale Regi's silver horse show trophies, goblets, and trays, which Gertrude's agent promptly bought at the auction, to give her niece at the appropriate time, she indicated to reporters.

That July, Gloria visited her mother at a house near Gertrude's estate. To her great displeasure, Consuelo was present—Consuelo, the aunt despised for her vindictive and cruel taunts during the months leading up to the custody battle. Soon after arriving, Gloria's first menstrual period began, and like other ignorant girls, she was terrified until she confessed her situation to Tootsie Eleanor, who consoled her about "the Curse." Her discomfort with the changes in her body was amplified by the thoughtless remarks of Consuelo and her mother, who teased her about her weight. Like so many chubby young adolescents Gloria suffered a common problem, but she imagined that she alone was fated to be heavy. "I hated my fatness with every day that dawned, and I dreamt hated dreams of my fatness with every night that darkened."[4] Always there was the image of her mother's favorite actress and friend, Constance Bennett, so thin that, according to her mother's admiring claim, if she swallowed an olive it would show.

That year, Blumie did not appear at her mother's side; only Roberto Mendoza, who appeared for lunch on weekends. Gloria was hurt, because when his presence was expected her mother would dress up in print silks and seem happy, whereas in the long absences in between she would drift into languor.

By the end of 1936, Gloria M. had finally convinced the court to agree to a new arrangement. She would see her daughter less often, but for longer periods of time, including most of the summer. Ailing and exhausted, Gertrude was grateful for the change, for it meant she would be free to return to Europe during the summer of 1937. Because of her responsibilities toward Gloria, she had not been able to go abroad for over five years.

The trip was also a means for her to be kinder to Juliana. By now Gertrude recognized Frank Crocker's animosity toward her good friend and insisted that Juliana's salary be raised significantly. To assuage Crocker, Gertrude increased her annual contribution to the museum. But the travel was not relaxing for either woman. Gertrude found the usually cheerful Jo Davidson unconsolable over the recent death of his wife. She also felt guilty for leaving behind an ailing Josh Hartwell. Gertrude was in such poor health herself that Juliana became upset. "I told her," Gertrude wrote to a friend, "that I was going to be quiet here and that unless she would go ahead and do her own things I didn't want her to stay with me. Instead she worries all the time (even if she doesn't say anything) and appears with red eyes etc., etc.,"[5] In Hungary, while visiting sister Gladys, Gertrude contracted bronchitis and went to a spa for a water and massage cure, repeated at a health resort in France. She had arrived in Paris weighing ninety-one pounds and was not much heavier when she boarded the ship for her return.

Another trip followed from January to late March of 1938. This time Flora, husband Cully, and a friend of theirs, socialite Schuyler Livingston Parsons, formed the party with Gertrude. One suspects Flora was worried about her mother's health and talked her into this relaxing voyage, during which, Parsons noted, Gertrude "gave me diversion in my loneliness."[6] The cough she had brought back from Europe continued despite the warm climate and lack of pressure.

That August, Gloria was stunned to learn she had a half sister, a woman as old as her mother. Why had no one told her before? Cathleen, now Mrs. Lawrence Lowman, impressed Gloria with her Sabu turban, black dress, jangly bracelets, and long, tapering fingers. (The girl became desperate for a black dress herself after that visit.) Filmstruck, she equated Larry and Cathleen to Nick and Nora Charles. Their Park Avenue apartment with it dachshunds and Gauguin only heightened the image. The couple took her to Jimmy's Oyster Bar, where she sat listening to Larry talk, wishing all the while that Cathleen would tell her about their father. Her wish was not granted. She could not know that her father had neglected his first daughter, who also resented Gloria's mother's use of deception in marrying him.

Around that time Gloria faced yet another sudden and emotionally traumatic separation. One day she and cousin Gerta Henry decided to go riding and asked Gerta's mother, Barbie, if they could do so. "We'll see," she said repeatedly while absentmindedly pulling out blades of grass from the lawn. They ran into the library, where Gerta's father worked, but he barked at them so loudly that Gloria skulked out to wait in the hall while her cousin made the request. Gerta rushed out of the room sobbing, threw her arms around Gloria, and said she was forbidden to ever see her again, that her father said Gloria was a bad influence. She could never even write Gloria again. Just why Buz Henry chose to ostracize Gloria is unclear. Perhaps he was overwrought from his caring for Barbie, or he may have been overly sensitive about appearances and foresaw that Gloria was headed for trouble.

Consequently, in the fall of 1938, Gloria entered Miss Porter's School in Farmington, Connecticut, alone, without the comfort of her dearest companion. Aunt and niece wrote to one another frequently, Gertrude attempting to instill the values she had been raised on; for example, Gloria should not see a boy without Gertrude's knowing about it. And when Gloria was home and off at a party, Gertrude saw that a chaperone was always present, which made Gloria feel even more out of place. Gertrude's protectiveness was not an unthinking anachronism. Not only must she behave scrupulously in the eyes of the Surrogate Court, she must consider the real danger of a kidnapping for ransom. Also, before admitting her, the head of Miss Porter's had expressed concern about ensuring Gloria's safety. Oblivious to these pressures, Gloria resented her aunt's rules, which her friends did not experience with their parents.[7]

Gloria wrote of liking the school, but not too convincingly. Apart from periodic delights, such as making the school glee club, she was unhappy. She wrote Gertrude of home sickness, and as holidays approached she would count the days to return to her aunt.[8] A frequent plea was that Gertrude write back soon. She often requested money, for Crocker had not understood the girl's need for a reasonable allowance. And despite Gertrude's sternness on some points of behavior, Gloria showed a desire to please.

That fall she also felt close enough to Gertrude to beg her assistance in being allowed to see Keislich. Gertrude complied, and Gloria was very grateful for the chance to have her Dodo visit her. She also asked Gertrude if she could have a pup from a Westbury litter to give to Keislich for Christmas. In these letters, Gloria's affection for her nurse is expressed in a way one would expect from a child of say, seven, not one of fourteen.

During that school year, a small scandal brought to Gloria's attention the stories of her mother's alleged lesbianism. A young man she'd gone to a dance with at the Northchurch Academy suddenly grabbed her during the ball and took her running with a male friend to hide in an attic. Crowds appeared below taunting the boys about something she did not understand. Several days later at Miss Porter's she learned from a classmate the boys had been expelled because they were "pansies." Totally ignorant of what that meant, the informer sneered that Gloria of all people should know, given the stories about her mother in the paper. Although the word *lesbian* was stated, she still did not fully understand its meaning.

Adolescence Strikes
with a Vengeance

In early May of 1939, Gloria came down with appendicitis, a relief because it meant she could not finish the term, hence she would be away from her whispering classmates.[9] She wrote her aunt how one day she would have the last laugh on all the people talking about her.

On a lovely sunlit May 25, 1939, Gertrude sat happily near Mayor Fiorello LaGuardia, who dedicated *To the Morrow,* as she finally named her World's Fair monument, praising her "creation of these two youthful, unarmed and unhelmeted figures ... the expression of the hope of all intelligent people that this new destroyer of time and distance, aviation, will be used only for the bringing about of peace in the future."[10] On that joyous occasion no one thought about the hundreds of planes lingering on German air bases, anxious to make their death runs. Rather, the odd third wing in her sculpture brought much discussion in the press. It is, explained Gertrude, the Wing of Tomorrow (while Jo Davidson quipped it was the equivalent of a spare tire).

Two other dedication ceremonies later brought Gertrude back to the fair. One was for the exhibit of *Devotion* installed in the Contemporary Arts Building, the other for her *Arlington Fountain,* placed in the Memorial Gardens. This would be the last public setting at which she appeared as a sculptor.

Gloria did not attend these events. As soon as she recuperated from her operation, she clambered up the steps of the Super Chief with her mother to spend the summer in California, Hollywood no less. The good part was meeting the movie stars the twins had come to know on earlier visits: Maureen O'Sullivan by her pool, Joan Crawford in her dressing room, Constance Bennett—as skinny as her mother had described—and Gilbert Roland coming down the curving staircase of their mansion. The bad part was being patronized by her mother, who embarrassed her by dressing her in dotted Swiss, a childish fabric in Gloria's mind, who wanted something glamorous, like the crepe de chine cut on a bias her mother wore. Then there was the constant presence of Ketti Keven, introduced to Gloria as an actress, but whose presence reminded her of Nada, "only of course nowhere as elegant and bewitching."[11] With Ketti around, Gloria had almost no time alone with her mother, but worse, she felt left out when she did not understand Ketti's jokes that made her mother giggle so freely.

Gloria M.'s inability to relate to her child reappeared during the long drive north, past Santa Barbara and Cambria to San Simeon. For once Eleanor was not along, as Gloria's chaperone, and Gloria sat wondering which of the tons of things she had to say to bring up. But her mother "ran out of conversation," so they "sat silently for miles and miles" until she asked the limousine driver how to turn on the radio in the back. (Reading of the trip in the papers, Gertrude wrote to her sister Gladys, "A visit to Hearst & Marion Davies among other things!"[12]) Their last night together, a visit to the Trockadero, Gloria admired how much more beautiful her mother was than the great cinema beauties nearby, Dolores Del Rio and Loretta Young. During that evening, she caught her mother leaning over and talking to a stranger, then realized "that *I* was the stranger," who wanted to belong to her mother.[13]

Gloria returned to Gertrude, in July of 1939, understandably more difficult to manage. The frustrated aunt determined to fill up as much of her niece's time as possible, hence stayed in Westbury with her the rest of the summer. Meanwhile, she appealed to Mrs. Keep, head of Miss Porter's School, who had also read the newspapers and pronounced Gloria *persona non grata* for being publicly associated with the notorious Hearst, to reconsider her decision. "Her mother had arrived unexpectedly from abroad and the child was being pulled in various directions by the people whom I do not consider have her best interests at heart," Gertrude explained. "The plan was to go to Catalina but they never got there and stayed in Hollywood for a month getting some rather unpleasant notoriety from my standpoint."[14]

For once Gertrude could not change someone's mind. When she explained the situation to Gloria, the girl could hardly contain her glee that she would not have to return to Miss Porter's, but she pretended she was sad about it. Gloria ended up at the Mary C. Wheeler School in Providence, Rhode Island, where she adapted easily to that more relaxed atmosphere. It was schools such as Wheeler that had *Fortune* magazine sputtering over the "casual, even untidy, appearance" of such girls, whose tweed skirts, handknit sweaters, and low-heeled shoes replaced the more formal wardrobes of just a few years prior. One of Gloria's first letters home was to beg to have all her Brooks Brothers sweaters shipped off immediately.

Gertrude's major difficulty with Gloria, apart from her mother's permissiveness, was the atmosphere away from school. Society had undergone a rapid change, with what was known as Café Society displacing the Old Guard. The reason for the change was economic and practical—wealthy families no longer had the large mansions in which to entertain, so they met instead at select restaurants and clubs.

Grace Vanderbilt remained the exception. While skyscrapers overshadowed her Fifth Avenue mansion, Grace continued to live in Gilded Age style, with twenty-six to thirty servants to see that her superb parties went on effortlessly. These included the butler, who changed his attire three times daily to match the hour, six liveried footmen, a social secretary, a chef with kitchen staff, various maids, and three laundresses to handle the bed linen, which, with guests, could run to two hundred sheets a week. As many as ten thousand guests a year dined at her request, or one should say, her command, for when the great hurricane of 1938 struck Newport, twenty-seven of the thirty invited braved the dangerous gale to appear at Grace's table that evening.

Few New Yorkers could either afford to live like Grace or, if they had the money, wanted to. Furthermore, partly due to Grace's influence—she being among the first to include theatrical performers and musicians among her guests—society now broadened to include members of the entertainment world. It was stage actors and movie stars whose activities were filling the gossip columns, and the younger members of society preferred the more public, fun-loving, performers. They no longer held that the only proper times to have one's name in the paper were at one's birth, marriage, and death.

Mass circulation magazines such as *Life* and national radio columnists such as Walter Winchell helped to create society and entertainment celebrities, and social-climbing mothers cultivated the press on their daughters' behalfs. It was one such mother who was responsible for seeing her daughter become the symbol of the ascendancy of Café Society. The girl, Brenda Frazier, had the dramatic high contrast coloring that made her stand out in photographs. Brenda had become another notorious Poor Little Rich Girl in 1933 when her father died and left her $4 million to be held in trust until her twenty-first birthday. Her mother, having been divorced from Frank Frazier in a contentious battle, was left nothing, so sought guardianship, which she was granted. In 1934, upon moving to New York, she petitioned Judge Foley, then busy with Gloria's custody suit, for authorization to spend $30,000 a year on household expenses, which he granted.

As he had done with the Morgan twins, gossip columnist Maury Paul focussed on Brenda Frazier as an up-and-coming beauty who would be "THE belle of her season."[15] That was two years before her debut, during which time teenage Brenda's appearance at a nightclub would be dutifully recorded by the photographers. Actors such as Errol Flynn, Mickey Rooney, and Bruce Cabot soon learned that appearing in public with Brenda brought attention to themselves as well.

Brenda's fame was assured at the opening of the Metropolitan Opera on November 21, 1938. For that annual event the "star" had always been Grace Vanderbilt, who would arrive late, after the first act had started, emerging from her limousine ablaze with her jewels and furs. "Here she comes, boys. The season is open!" a photographer would shout. That year the frenzy was not for Grace but for seventeen-year-old Brenda Frazier, who appeared in a simple white satin dress, over which was draped a white ermine jacket with a spray of white orchids. Maury Paul was quick to remind his readers how two years previously he had been the first to realize she "was a 'Glamour Girl' in the making," who belonged to the public as much as a movie star or operatic diva. Brenda's debut several weeks later made a *Life* magazine spread. In accord with her role as Queen of Society, one of the first guests to arrive there was Grace Vanderbilt, with son Neily.

Gloria could not help but be aware of Brenda Frazier's impact. Not only were they both famous heiresses, they shared the same dramatic high contrast coloring, that ivory skin made whiter by white powder, mouth stark in deep carmine, almost black lipstick, and lustrous dark hair. Although Gloria was still struggling with her "fatness" and her desire for more sophisticated clothes, the kind her mother and Brenda wore, she was getting a taste of Café Society and found it addictive. When her mother returned east for a visit, she took Gloria to the Stork Club, where she could try out the rhumba and conga she had learned at ballroom dance classes in Providence. She also had fights with Gertrude over clothes she could buy, such as a black dress or high, high heels.

Gloria's face became commonplace in the social pages and magazines. Since the custody trial she had become accustomed to camera flashes going off in her presence, her various moves published in the daily papers. While her mother said the girl grew hungry for the attention, her cousin Gerta knew the truth, that it was an act. To protect herself, Gloria learned how to pose artfully to avoid being caught in a clumsy or embarrassing stance; she cultivated a broad smile to cover her true feelings. (She was not always successful; sometimes the camera caught a frightened grimace.) An exception was when Diana Vreeland, editor of *Harper's Bazaar,* met Gloria and asked Gertrude if she would allow the girl to pose for a portrait by the noted Louise Dahl-Wolfe. Made up to look much older than her fifteen years, Gloria struck a pensive, haunting pose that showed off the exotic beauty seldom evident in news shots of her with gangly boyfriends. "And although the girl in the photograph on the page of the magazine is said to be me," she mused, "it really has nothing to do with me at all."[16] It was in fact a remarkable prevision of the adult woman in her future.

She also fell in love for the first time, with Geoffrey Jones, a Princeton man she met at a tea dance.[17] It was through him that she met a Dalton student who would become a lifelong friend. Carol Marcus was a stunning Jean Harlow blond with lustrous full lips and a zany, madcap streak to her personality. She also had a secret in her background with which Gloria could identify. Carol's mother, Rosheen, was sixteen when she gave birth to her illegitimate daughter. Forced by her family to marry a philosophy professor, who was not the father, she had a daughter by him, Elinor. When the professor then insisted Carol be put up for adoption, Rosheen walked out. But she had to place her girls in a foster home while she found a way to support herself. When she was eight,

Carol's mother appeared at the home one day, packed her bags, and took her to her new home on Park Avenue. Rosheen had married Charles Marcus, a top executive with Bendix aircraft, who then adopted the girl. (Rosheen had not told him about Carol until after the marriage, and she waited two more years to let him know about Elinor, who had also ended up in a foster home. He adopted her as well.) Although she loved her warm and doting stepfather, Carol shared with Gloria the status of Poor Little Rich Girl, only in her case no one knew the truth about her troubled past. They must have confided in each other about the difficulties of vain, self-centered, sometimes eccentric mothers.

Carol also introduced Gloria to another friend, Oona, daughter of the playwright Eugene O'Neill. Oona's mother was O'Neill's second wife, Agnes, and he had deserted both when the girl was quite young to take off with his eventual third wife, Carlotta. Highly possessive, Carlotta disapproved of Oona's New York ways and swayed O'Neill against his daughter. Oona seldom saw him, and when she did, she faced a fearsome patriarch rather than a wise and supportive father. A classically beautiful brunette, Oona's serenity was a good counterbalance for Gloria's dramatic appeal and Carol's sprightliness. She agreed with the other two that they made a great team because none was jealous of the others or likely to steal the others' beaux; Gloria also felt they liked her for herself, not her name. (One day she overheard a dance partner accuse Carol of only liking famous people. When Carol came back, "That's right. They're all terrific, and you stink," Gloria realized the strength of Carol's loyalty to her.[18])

At Wheeler, Gloria discovered painting, and she began to define herself as an artist. There the art teacher allowed her to spend off-hours in the studio, where she could spread out her work and concentrate without bumping into other girls. During these solitary creative hours she felt the same security she had always felt with Emma Keislich, only it was better because it would never be lost, could never go away the way a person could. She shared her discoveries with Gertrude, who wrote that she looked forward to visiting the school to see Gloria's artwork.

During spring break from Wheeler, Gloria went to Havana, where her half sister Cathleen was now living. Cathleen had separated from her husband and was having an affair with a Cuban. Once again Gloria tried to extract information about her father and the custody trial, but Cathleen was evasive and turned the discussion back to nail polish. (After Gloria returned home, Cathleen divorced Larry and married a prominent Cuban newspaper publisher, Martin Arostegui. In 1942, when Brenda Frazier, then married to first husband, former football hero John "Shipwreck" Kelley, moved to Cuba, Cathleen, an alcoholic, took the young woman under her tutelage, encouraging the heavy drinking that would eventually undermine Brenda's life as well.)

Taught to pretend and manipulate as a child, Gloria did so with skill as a teenager. When she wanted the restrictions on her visitations with her mother loosened, she played up to Juliana Force, who interceded for her with Gertrude. When she wanted to transfer to the Spence School to be closer to Geoff, she pressured her Grandmother Morgan, who wrote Gertrude to ask that she comply. According to her, Gloria wrote "Quoting, 'I am so worried that I cry myself to sleep every night, not having any assurance as yet, from Auntie Ger, about my going to Spence school next year, which means such a lot to me. If Auntie Ger, keeps me *away from her,* even to the very last year of my school days, may I ask, how in heavens name, can I ever get to know her, and be close to her?'"[19] The language sounds more like Mrs. Morgan than a direct quote from a letter of Gloria's, but the message was probably accurate. Gertrude responded by noting all the times Gloria came home but seldom stayed around to spend any time with her. Furthermore, "If her own way was the right way I would want her to do it. All she wants is to have her freedom and I don't like her reasons for it. If she came out and told the truth it would be much better."[20] Clearly, Gertrude was not only aware of Gloria's manipulations, she was disgusted by the girl's lack of candor.

Gertrude was fooled at times, however. When Gloria and Geoff wanted to spend a weekend alone together at his family's summer home, Gloria told Gertrude she was spending the weekend with Emma Keislich, while informing Keislich she was off to visit the Jones family. Whenever Gloria stayed as a guest at the Joneses, Geoff would find a way to sneak into her bed, even though her chaperone would be sleeping in a room nearby.

Gloria also decided she wanted to marry Geoff. Although sixteen was a young age to be considering marriage, she was in line with the cultural message of the thirties. *Life* magazine said it most succinctly: "Boy's goal: a profession . . . Girl's goal: still a home." Journalists wrote about the "old days" when women set out for Greenwich Village and a career, whereas for the "modern girl," work no longer held glamour. She assured her aunt that Geoff was the source of perfect fulfillment and happiness, and of course she would wait until he graduated from Princeton. Her mother was so supportive of the idea that she told Gloria of states where the two could marry despite the girl's age.

If Gloria felt the need to be manipulative, so, too, did her aunt, if it meant preventing trouble. To prevent the marriage, Gertrude and Mrs. Morgan collaborated to befriend Mrs. Jones. One day, while watching the three women chat congenially over tea, Gloria concluded from her aunt's demeanor that she would never be allowed to marry Geoff. At that point he began to pressure her, to coach her on how to talk to Gertrude to win her over to accepting the marriage. He gave her exact phrases to use and forced her to practice them. In light of her previous experience with plots and conspiracies, it was not a wise move. Pressured all her life to dissemble, pretend, and misrepresent, Gloria began to feel the same anxieties, she had known as a child, around Geoff.

In fact, as Gertrude held firm and refused Gloria's various demands, the girl seemed to respect her more and draw closer. By the spring of 1940, Gloria was angry at her mother and decided to spend the summer in New York at an acting school, a plan of which Gertrude approved. Gloria's letters were lengthier, more sincerely affectionate, and more expressive of her feelings. In one revealing reply, Gertrude explained, "I don't think happiness comes without frankness. Do you? The only time I am unhappy with you is when I feel you are shutting me out." She explained that superficialities such as chaperones and social conventions were not related to "fundamental truths," but one had to conform, accept them, and forget them. In concluding, she showed her awareness of Gloria's curiosity concerning her father. "You, Gloria darling, are like your father and he and I were alike. . . . He was a completely loveable man, and how proud he would be to know that you are going to be worthy of him."[21]

German Invasion
Threatens Consuelo

Like many Americans in 1940, Gloria hardly noticed the war in Europe; it was the Europeans' problem, one with which the United States should not concern itself. But Gertrude was very troubled by the news from overseas, for she still had friends living there, and her sister Gladys, now widowed, had already fled Hungary with her family and moved to the States. As with World War I, stories about the fighting aroused in Gertrude images of new patriotic sculptures, themes such as Victory, Freedom, and Liberty.

For one Vanderbilt, Consuelo, the war was very real. Since Alva's death she had devoted her life to Jacques and to needy French children. On a hillside overlooking the village of Saintes Georges-Motel she built a sanitarium to accommodate eighty children, ages twelve months to five years, complete with wards, playgrounds, playrooms, and quarters for staff. To achieve this, she had to meet the needs of the federal social welfare bureaucrats in Paris, who were so impressed with her accomplishment that in time they requested she add fifty beds for young tuberculosis patients. This she did, along with establishing a school for nurses and a kind of summer camp for village youth. As with her earlier social work in London, she took a strong role in management of the facilities, making rounds daily with notebook in hand, breaking away from administrative detail for a few minutes to play with a child. Denied much of a role in the rearing of her own children, now, whenever possible, Consuelo treated these dozens of wards as her own, dispensing hugs, or crouching down to hear the latest tale.

During the thirties, while Hitler bullied his neighbors, Consuelo grew fearful that France would not survive any act of aggression on his part. Her intuition was proven correct in 1939 when the Red Cross sent refugee children from Paris. Told to salute the French flag, they would ball their fists and shout, "Heil Hitler, who comes to deliver us."[22] Although the teachers were able to change the children's behavior, Consuelo knew it reflected a pro-Nazi influence popular among certain French elements. Government leaders visiting her chateau themselves confessed doubts that the country could unite against Hitler, indeed some admitted their private inclination to capitulate if that dictator drew his sword. And from her long experience with French bureaucrats used to bending with the latest political wind, she doubted their capacity to maintain a strong center of resistance.

A visit to Blenheim in 1939 only further added to her apprehensions. In the midst of the splendor surrounding her granddaughter Sarah's coming-out ball, she felt the same unease she had experienced years before at the court of the Russian czar just before revolution struck him down. Conversations with Winston Churchill did not reassure her—not even his apparent satisfaction over the defenses the French government had established. His description of the Maginot Line—pillboxes and wire—left her feeling desperate, particularly in light of America's "living in a halcyon world where even the shadow of war never cast its gloom."[23] On August 23, Hitler and Satlin came to terms in Moscow, guaranteeing Russia's neutrality in case of war. Eleven days later Consuelo read the headline, "C'est la Guerre." Hitler had invaded Poland.

In the bitter winter that followed, one with little fuel to warm the chateau or the children's wards, Consuelo awoke each day fearing the worst. Then her maid would appear to say, "There is nothing to report," and life would go on as normally as possible under the circumstances. Refugees escaping the battlefields in border areas filled the churches, inns, and makeshift lodgings of local towns of the department. One evening her car was pulled over suddenly in the dark by several figures with a large field gun, members of an English regiment on its way to Evreux, the largest town nearby. Jacques, now seventy-one, donned a uniform and went off to serve on what missions he could. The Red Cross conveyed word that, due to her wealth, Consuelo had been targeted by the Germans for capture and ransom. Friends urged her to flee the country, but she would not leave the children.

On May 10, 1940, Consuelo's maid awoke her with the terrible message that Hitler had invaded Holland, Belgium, and Luxembourg, and that his troops were moving swiftly south and west. German planes were dropping bombs on French cities as far south as Lyons. As Consuelo went out, she saw refugees appearing in the lanes about Saintes Georges, first the chauffeured limousines of wealthy Parisians, then horse-drawn wagons of farmers, finally peasants on foot, carting what they could on their backs. Weaving in and out the procession were packs of bicyclists. Consuelo arranged for mattresses to be laid out wherever possible and food dispensed to the exhausted travelers, some of whom had been on the road for two weeks.

On May 17, the mayor of Evreux asked her to prepare food and lodging for 45,000 refugees expected to arrive that evening by train. Consuelo called her staff and somehow managed to devise a plan to distribute the arrivals among local villages, locate lodgings in schools and meeting halls, commandeer food and people to prepare it, and set up a clinic for the wounded—all in a day. After night fell, the train station remained quiet, and no train appeared. Instead, the next morning its travelers straggled into Evreaux, some on foot, others in automobiles, for the Germans had bombed the rail lines. Many were wounded from strafing attacks. One woman told Consuelo how she had watched her two children gunned down by an aviator who had kept his eyes aimed at them as he swooped down toward them. Consuelo wondered how the afflicted could remain so calm and composed through it all, so quick to give thanks for the smallest assistance.

The children's sanitarium remained her greatest concern. The Ministry of Health sent orders that the children were to be evacuated in small groups so as not to panic local villagers. (The idea was inane—villagers knew Germans had already parachuted into nearby forests, disguised themselves as priests, peasants, or French soldiers, and had begun their rampage of mass shootings to undermine the local resistance movement.) On June 6, Jacques put two small overnight valises in their Citroen, took the wheel, and drove Consuelo to Pau in the southernmost department of Pyrenees Atlantiques to locate a suitable place for those children who could not be reunited easily with their parents. There they leased a villa suitable for their purpose.

Throughout the journey at stops in cafés they listened to the buzz of rumors: Paris had fallen, Paris was secure; Hitler had won; America had declared war. On the return home, in a café they overheard news that Germans had taken over Saintes Georges. Jacques said the story was nonsense and, ignoring the ominous sign of heavy traffic in the southbound lane, continued northward. Suddenly Consuelo spotted one of their own family cars heading south as well, their butler behind the wheel. Signaling his attention, they pulled over, and sat in disbelief as he verified the worst. Indeed, Germans had bombed the village and evacuated the area, but the chateau and sanitarium remained intact. Fortunately, anticipating the attack, painter Paul Maze, who had been a houseguest at the time, had managed to organize and lead a convoy that was carrying the children south to Pau. No one from their institution was hurt, although some of the villagers they knew had been killed in the bombardment.

Initially determined to return home and face being shot by the Germans, Consuelo accepted reality and had Jacques turn the car around to meet the children in Pau. Once the youngsters were settled in their new sanitarium or sent to their parents, she faced a worse decision. With France under enemy hands, her income would be frozen, and she could not maintain herself, let alone the sanitarium. For their own safety, everyone urged, she and Jacques must leave. But the American consulate in Pau refused them a visa because they lacked birth certificates and other papers, so they could not exit for the United States directly from France. There followed several harrowing days, obtaining visas in Bordeaux to pass through Spain to Portugal, where they hoped to be more successful with the American consulate there. Knowing the border could close at any time, Consuelo pushed ahead of lines when necessary. (She was later ashamed of her action.) For the first time in her life, with little money and few clothes, Consuelo was reduced to a commoner, a position she did not always handle gracefully during those hectic and fearful hours.

The results were what mattered—she succeeded in getting the necessary documents and wired her brothers in the States to see that airline tickets were available for them to pick up in Lisbon. On their last night, the duke of Kent, the king of England's brother, invited them to dinner. Saying all she had was the plain and wrinkled traveling dress she had been wearing for several days, the duke told her to come anyway. During the meal he made her feel welcome, "brought England and my children closer to me" through his consideration, while several others disapproved of her shabby appearance.[24] "How odd it seemed to sit at a formal dinner again free of anxiety and care—how little these people knew of the storm and stress of a country overrun by a ruthless enemy."[25] She would never see the duke again; two years later he died in an airplane accident.

Consuelo and Jacques made their way to Florida, where both her brothers had homes. Perhaps anticipating that the need would one day arise, she had previously bought a home fifteen miles from Palm Beach, a secluded villa she called Casa Alva in honor of her mother. There she set up a life of anonymity. Once he was convinced of her comfort, Jacques returned to Europe to join Charles deGaulle's resistance government. Although German Luftwaffe used her chateau as headquarters, her faithful majordomo, Basil Davidoff, managed to preserve its treasures, even when the greedy Hermann Goering made an appearance. (Regrettably, Consuelo failed to recognize Davidoff's impressive role as guard. After the war she sold the chateau, sending granddaughter Rosemary to arrange the final closing. When Davidoff refused to leave the premises, Rosemary discovered it was because Consuelo's monthly pension was insufficient for him to live on, and, without informing her grandmother, she added a monthly stipend of her own to recompense him honorably for his duty.)

Gertrude's Life Threatens
to Unravel

If Gertrude heard any word of Consuelo's harrowing escape, she never noted it; the rift in the family remained unbridgeable. She herself had been in Florida that spring to see Neily, who had been ailing for years with heart trouble. Although a semi-invalid, often suffering considerably, he retained a sense of humor, and Gertrude had grown fond of his company. (Grace remained in the Fifth Avenue mansion, oblivious to the tumult in the world about her.) Gertrude's lover Josh Hartwell was terminally ill as well. Of her children, only Flora was content. Sonny's latest marriage was breaking up, and Barbie continued to suffer from melancholy.

Despite her own troubled health and concern for her loved ones, Gertrude pressed on with her usual busy schedule. Honors continued to accumulate, requiring her appearance at ceremonies. In 1940, these recognitions included election as an associate of the National Academy of Design, the Medal of Honor from the National Sculpture Society, and a fourth honorary doctorate, this one from Russell Sage College. With no sculpture commissions in sight, and less stamina to work on models, Gertrude returned to fiction for her primary creative expression. Thus in the fall, at age sixty-five she signed up for a Columbia University evening seminar on professional writing under Helen Hull.

Hull had made her way from constant rejection to seasoned professional, and she understood the short-story market well. A conscientious teacher, she wrote numerous and precise comments on Gertrude's many assignments.[26] In turn, Gertrude was a determined and obedient student, faithfully submitting weekly stories. Despite Hull's meticulous direction and her own dogged persistence, Gertrude did not advance much in the craft. Her stories continued to exhibit the weaknesses of her earlier writings: flat prose, absence of motivation, failure to distinguish characters through their speeches, and excessive use of dialogue over action. Part of the deficiency was temperamental, based in Gertrude's rather naive understanding of human nature, but part was also self-censorship, a reluctance to report on the narrow and conventional society she had known. These later works contained few of the bohemian characters and *outre* episodes of *Walking the Dusk* or *A Love Affair;* possibly she did not want to expose that unconventional side of herself to Hull.

Besides writing short stories, Gertrude continued revisions of her play *The Hand.* Neighbor and play producer Richard Myers described the story line as "perfect" but said the dialogue needed to be gone over "with a fine tooth comb." Once this editing was accomplished, he advised, he would definitely consider taking the play on for production.[27] Toward this end, Gertrude hired a friend, Major Ronald Victor Courtenay Bodley, a slim, blond, charming writer in his late forties. They worked so harmoniously that Gertrude was soon addressing him as "Ronnie" and inviting him to work at Westbury. Despite daily revisions over months, they were unable to correct the fundamental weakness of the work, its inability to give a fresh and vital dramatization of the theme of spirit possession.

The Whitney Museum finances continued to nag. As in past years, Gertrude had to come up with a way to infuse more money into the institution, which now required $100,000 a year for its exhibitions and purchases. Besides making outright gifts over the years, she had also made a loan. To ease the burden on both her and the museum, Frank Crocker suggested she give the institution some tangible assets which it could sell as the need arose, and in the process repay its debt to her. Instead, she sold off a block of stock, but conscious of her failing health, she worried about the viability of the museum beyond her lifetime.

Despite the darkening clouds on the world scene, Gertrude was often good humored. On a visit to Neily in Florida, she stopped at Marineland, which Sonny had developed with a cousin. Watching two porpoises play and mate, she giggled heartily, "*Now* I understand why Marineland is so popular."[28]

Gloria
Goes Hollywood

Gertrude seemed resigned to her life. If she could not cure Josh or Neily, she would comfort them. If she could not sculpt, she would write. If she could not guarantee the Whitney Museum's perpetuity, she would see to the next year's viability. With reduced control of so many areas, she pressed hard to control Gloria, yet even there she was forced to withdraw.

Swayed by pressure from Geoff, Gloria still longed to be married—her first hope always having been to find a man and set up "a home for two," the "blue heaven" of a favorite song lyric. She wrote Gertrude to help her in getting court approval to let her live in an apartment with her grandmother and be on her own in a way while Geoff finished his senior year at Princeton.[29] Gertrude disapproved of the plan and answered that while she would always let Gloria see a lot of Mrs. Morgan, even encourage their taking trips together, it would not be appropriate for a girl Gloria's age to be on her own. "Until the time you get married it is up to me to see you are protected against evil tongues. I feel that G. [Gloria's mother] agrees with me. Stories from Cal. are again appearing in the papers—lies and slanders against your family on both sides."[30] Holding firm, she made Gloria return to school.

Gertrude was rapidly loosing her patience with her niece, whose behavior, following visits with her mother in California, seemed increasingly out of control. (And had she known the full extent of Gloria's sexual life, she would certainly have disciplined the wayward girl more assertively.) Gertrude wanted to go on with her work, untroubled by personal problems. But Josh Hartwell finally died, Neily was rapidly failing, and her own undiagnosed heart condition was dispiriting to her. Thus she may have felt relieved that summer of 1941 when Gloria left for the airport to visit her mother in California.

Gloria approached "the Emerald City" of her fantasies in high spirits. She was fleeing her stodgy aunt and nagging boyfriend, and felt no fidelity to either. For the flight, she wore her new V-necked black dress, one Gertrude very much disliked. Adding to the flash of the outfit were high heeled black pumps and black fishnet stockings à la Alice Faye in *Rose of Washington Square*. The usual disappointment followed. Instead of greeting her at the air terminal, her mother sent a chauffeur to take her and her chaperone to 719 North Maple Drive in

Beverly Hills, where Gloria M. was sleeping in late as usual. (Gloria was excited to learn it was an area where movie stars lived; George and Gracie Allen owned the house across the street.) Worse for her, Thelma was also living at Maple Manor, as they called it, and had brought her son Tony over from England for the duration of the war. Nearby was Melba Melsing, the singer Gloria admired so during her stay with her mother in Long Island. Harry Morgan, the twins' brother, also lived now in Los Angeles with his new wife.

If Gloria M. was oblivious to her daughter's need for affection, she understood how to delight a starstruck teenager. The night of her arrival, mother and daughter went to a party at actor Basil Rathbone's house, and the following night Gloria had a date with Phil Kellogg, a film cutter from MGM she had met during a previous visit. (She did not tell Geoff she was dating someone else.) Best of all, her mother said she could go out without her chaperone, that the idea of being so protected was the most *ridiculous* thing she had ever heard of. And then there was the cocktail party Gloria M. arranged for June 21, invitations explicitly noting it to be "in honor of her daughter." Gloria enjoyed watching her chaperone's lips purse as she sulked over the confused state of the household, which was hardly run according to Whitney standards.

The dispute as to when Gloria was to be allowed the independence of an adult was over in fact, if not in law. The court had control until she was twenty-one, argued Gertrude, who had major responsibility to that point. Her mother, who had escaped her own family at age sixteen and fled Europe for New York, naturally considered Gloria already mature. Consequently, she not only removed all restrictions, she encouraged profligacy. Gertrude soon heard from the chaperone how Gloria was going out at all hours to nightclubs and talking with male callers on her private phone line while taking bubble baths. Used to receiving $300 a month in spending money from Gertrude (close to $2,000 in 1990 dollars), Gloria had no sense of expenses. While her mother could not afford such extravagance, neither could she refuse her daughter, for fear she would once again lose her. And since the courts would not let her have legal custody, she must gain possession of her daughter through alternative means, by making life so pleasant that the girl would insist upon staying with her. However, rather than admit she was coddling the girl, she blamed her daughter for the financial excesses and saw herself as victimized by her own child.

To Gloria M., motherhood meant custody, possession; to Gloria, motherhood meant intimacy, revealing one's self to the mother and being listened to compassionately. Gloria M. got her daughter to be with her for the summer, but Gloria did not gain a mother. Most significant, an incident soon occurred when the daughter finally recognized her longing for her mother would never be fulfilled, that her mother was incapable of loving her as she wished. The situation developed when her Aunt Thelma announced she was off to spend the weekend with lover Edmond Lowe, and Gloria M. said she would go do the same with her lover, Ketti Keven. Desperate for some time alone with her mother, Gloria suggested that Ketti come and spend the weekend there at Maple Manor. Her

Consuelo was a strikingly beautiful young woman. *(The Bettmann Archive)*

Although Consuelo claimed to have been virtually imprisoned in her Marble House bedroom in 1895, other evidence suggests she was not fully truthful. *(The Preservation Society of Newport County)*

Consuelo was considered one of the most beautiful women in America, as this drawing by Paul Helleu, featured in *Cosmopolitan Magazine,* reveals. *(Culver Pictures)*

Carolus Duran's portrait of Consuelo (lst State Room, Blenheim Palace) captures the pride and stubbornness cloaked by a contrived innocence. *(His Grace the Duke of Marlborough, photograph by Jeremy Whittaker)*

In his 1905 family portrait for the Red Drawing Room at Blenheim Palace, John Singer Sargent clearly thought Consuelo more important than Sunny. *(His Grace the Duke of Marlborough, photograph by Jeremy Whittaker)*

Blenheim, the ancestral home
of the Marlborough family.
(Culver Pictures)

Consuelo in her royal robes.
(Culver Pictures)

After delivering her "heir and spare," Consuelo (third from left) took up the adulterous ways of the Prince of Wales, who glanced at her admiringly during an 1896 house party at Blenheim. Jennie Churchill sits to her left. *(His Grace the Duke of Marlborough)*

Consuelo, like her mother, was devoted to social reform. Here she inspects a group of railroad engineers. *(Culver Pictures)*

Consuelo and Sunny drifted apart steadily. *(Culver Pictures)*

Consuelo with Jacques Balsan. *(Culver Pictures)*

Grace Wilson was too much of a fortune-seeker for Cornelius and Alice, but she won their son anyway. *(Brown Brothers)*

Neily defied his family to marry Grace, only to find her selfish and utterly unsupportive of his considerable talents. *(Brown Brothers)*

Grace gave birth to
her first child in
1912. *(Bettmann Archive)*

Grace became known as the "Queen of Society." Here she opens the Metropolitan Opera season. *(The Bettmann Archive)*

Although Grace and Neily appeared together at the Easter Parade in 1932, they were informally separated. *(The Bettmann Archive)*

Gloria Morgan and husband Regi
Vanderbilt on one of their
numerous trips, typically taken
without infant Gloria. *(Brown
Brothers)*

Contrary to her recall in *Once
Upon a Time,* Gloria was closely
bound to her aunt Gertrude,
who was loving yet unable to
show much emotion. *(Courtesy of
Flora Biddle)*

Visiting her mother in 1939, Gloria found herself losing out to her mother's female lover. *(The Bettmann Archive)*

Only seventeen, Gloria married Pat di Cicco to escape both her mother and Gertrude. Di Cicco proved to be abusive and dissolute. *(The Bettmann Archive)*

Stokowski's friends were taken by Gloria's shyness, vulnerability, and artistic sense. *(The Bettmann Archive)*

Though Leopold Stokowski was a deceitful egomaniac who played upon Gloria's naivete, he encouraged her development as an artist. *(Brown Brothers)*

After years of isolation demanded by Stokowski, Gloria (with Marlene Dietrich and John Ringling North) went public by organizing a charity circus show. *(Brown Brothers)*

Devoted to one another in later years, Gloria's mother (left) and twin Thelma never understood how their actions brought on their difficulties. *(The Bettmann Archive)*

Though from opposite ends of the class ladder, Gloria and
director Sidney Lumet shared a devotion to the theater and a
highly disciplined approach to work. *(Brown Brothers)*

In a publicity shot to save the Calder Circus at the Whitney, Flora Irving Biddle displayed her grandmother Gertrude's spunk. *(Courtesy of Michelle Evans)*

At age 55, wealthy of her own doing, and alone, Gloria preferred work over the jet set life. *(The Bettman Archive)*

hope was to find some spare minutes when Ketti would not be around so she could get to know her mother.

On the eventful Friday, Gloria sat by the pool waiting for the sun to go down and her mother to wake up. Finally her mother appeared in the distance on the porch, a white chiffon robe flowing about her like a cloud, a fan of rice paper fluttering in her hand. Gloria rose and ran toward her mother to let her know "I am the breeze that cools her face" and watched as the fan waved in greeting.[31] Then, as she approached, she realized the figure was not her mother, but Thelma. Rushing past in tears, she felt her aunt grab her and ask what was wrong. "Where is my mother?" Gloria asked. There was a change in plans, explained Thelma—Edmond was sick and her mother had decided to go off for the weekend with Ketti anyway. "Sunday or Monday or Tuesday or Wednesday, Thursday's child has far to go, and if I did see her on Friday or on any of those other days, whom would I see."[32]

Nor did it help when her mother did not seem to provide the usual protectiveness a child expects from a parent. One evening she accompanied her mother and Thelma to a cocktail party at the Jules Stein home, and she realized no one there cared that she was too young to be drinking and smoking. Heady with the insight, she casually took one cocktail, then another, then went into a fog. When her senses returned, she found herself in a strange nightclub dancing with a strange man. After concentrating, she recognized the brillantined hair as belonging to Broadway actor George Metaxa. Dressed in her black V-necked sheath and fishnet stockings, Gloria appeared to be in her twenties, so Metaxa felt no inhibition about suggesting how nice she would look dressed *only* in her big white hat and black garter belt and black fishnet stockings. The frightened girl shoved him aside and ran outside where another family friend happened to be leaving and offered Gloria a ride home. Once there, she realized no one had noted her departure from the party nor cared to ask what had occurred afterward. The episode left her ashamed and upset over what Hollywood boyfriend Phil Kellogg might think of her.

Her mother did satisfy her in one regard. After much begging from Gloria, she called Gertrude and the lawyers and arranged for Gloria to stay on through the entire summer. Gertrude was actually relieved to be free of Gloria's problems and even dismissed the chaperone. She no longer needed a spy to inform her of her niece's comings and goings in Hollywood—the newspapers were providing that service for free.

Gloria liked Phil Kellogg, and she would have been contented dating only him, except for his introducing her to certain Hollywood stars he knew thorough his work. One day Phil took her for a poolside lunch at the Beverly Hills Hotel. Sitting in her strapless shocking-pink swimsuit, she soon attracted the eye of actors Van Heflin, Bruce Cabot, and their friend Pat di Cicco, all three striking in their "vanilla-on-vanilla" suits. Of the three, Pat caught her eye, "the most movie-starrish of them all . . . sure of himself, but in a much too conceited way."[33] All three men called her afterward, but she held back and continued to see Phil Kellogg. Eventually she switched to Van Heflin, and she found herself in considerable trouble when she wrote to half sister Cathleen that they were looking at houses and planning to marry. It was a pretend engagement, the kind of joking arrangement couples sometimes make up. But Cathleen took it seriously and informed Gertrude, who called Gloria M., who had Thelma berate the girl for causing such an uproar. Gertrude was further upset to read about Gloria dating other older movie stars such as Errol Flynn, Franchot Tone, and George Montgomery, but she kept quiet.

Meanwhile Pat di Cicco was constantly calling and sending orchids, although Gloria refused to talk to him and resisted his pressure for dates. She was getting mixed messages about him at home. Her mother seemed to admire him and encourage Gloria's going out with him. Then one day a drunken Ketti Keven called Gloria up to warn her about Pat, that his ex-wife, actress Thelma Todd, had been found murdered after their divorce and that no one knew who had murdered her. Gloria's mother backed up Ketti, so Gloria was confused. Ketti and her mother pointed out that Pat's job was not so hot—although he called himself an agent, he was a kind of gofer for Howard Hughes, which seemed to involve playing gin rummy most of the time. (They did not tell Gloria that many people in Hollywood considered Pat to be a procurer of women for Hughes.)

In fact, di Cicco had been a talent scout for MGM in 1939 when Hughes introduced him to Brenda Frazier to arrange a screen test. Brenda had met Hughes in Nassau, where, proving his reputation for wooing young beauties, he had taken her to bed by the third day. Hughes thought Brenda combined the glamour of a movie star with the polish of a socialite, that she could be a second Kate Hepburn, and di Cicco agreed. Naturally shy, Brenda did not want to act, nor had she the talent, and following the screen test she was relieved when her mother announced to the papers that they were turning down MGM's contract. Hughes continued to pursue Brenda with his curious humor, which included sending a fancy Cartier ring box that contained two aspirins. She wisely turned down his eventual proposal because he seemed a little too mysterious.

It did not take long for Hughes to learn about Gloria from Pat. His approach was identical to that used with Brenda and dozens of other young women during those years. He let it be known he was casting the lead for a new movie and sent a photographer over to take stills of her. Then he took her out in his plane and to dinners with his standby meal of steak, peas, and baked potato. When Pat continued to call and send flowers, Gloria complained to Hughes, who sent him to Kansas on a business trip. Then Hughes invited her to his house in Santa Barbara, ostensibly for Fiesta Weekend, though really for an assignation. Gloria's mother did not object, even though she had initially presumed it was *she* and not Gloria in whom he was interested. Still a dreamy-eyed teenager, Gloria easily succumbed to Hughes's line, which always included a form of a marriage proposal, though rarely meant seriously.

When Gloria wrote Gertrude that she intended to marry Hughes, Gertrude drew up a clumsy plan to short-circuit the venture, and she commanded her niece to return to Westbury to discuss the matter.[34] Gloria went, unhappily accompanied by both her mother and Ketti Keven, who had decided to enjoy New York City for a few days. Once Gloria reached her old home on Long Island, she was stunned to learn that Geoff Jones had been invited for the weekend. Although she had maintained contact with him, even before leaving for California that summer she had lost interest in him as a lover. The final disillusionment had come when he insisted she be his caddy on the golf course. By now Gloria found very little appeal in young men of her class when compared to "grown-ups" such as Van Heflin, di Cicco, or Hughes. When Geoff arrived, Gertrude left both young people speechless by announcing she had agreed to their getting married after all. Fortunately, although he had hoped to marry Gloria one day, Geoff was gracious and did not press his cause. While he left the room to unpack, Gloria reminded Gertrude about Howard Hughes and his intentions to marry her. On cue, Hughes called Westbury and asked to speak to Gertrude, who, following a long and secret discussion said afterward that everything would work out for the best. Gloria smelled a plot.

Early the next morning Gloria called a taxi to sneak away but was caught by Gertrude, who spoke to her as never before, raising her voice passionately. Gloria was thrilled, because for the first time Gertrude was showing her feelings, even though they were angry ones. Gloria felt a bond to her, a connection she had never felt before. Then it became evident Gertrude was letting her go, for she ordered the car to take Gloria back to the city. There Gloria told her mother she wanted to go to Chicago where Pat di Cicco was on business. Whether they went or not is unclear.

Back in California, Gloria stayed by the phone at all hours waiting for Hughes to call, but he never did. He was probably grateful to have Gertrude's objections as an excuse to bow out. Instead, aware all along that the relationship would not last, Pat moved in to fill the void. Visiting the still-hopeful Geoff in Princeton one afternoon, Carol Marcus watched him pick up the phone. It was Gloria, and he immediately lit up with delight, then suddenly seemed hurt, wounded. Carol knew the message was an eventful one, and she felt her heart pounding while she waited for it to end. When he hung up, he was silent for a while, then very quietly looked up and asked Carol, "Do you know who Pat di Cicco is?"[35]

Rejected by Gertrude as well as by her mother, and not wanting to finish her last year at Wheeler, Gloria chose the only route to freedom: marriage to the one person waiting for her, "someone dark and unkind."[36] While longing for Howard to step in again, and hoping Gertrude would "get so furious at me she'll send a bolt of lightning to prevent the wedding," Gloria pretended to everyone that Pat was the greatest man alive. She succeeded so well that Carol and Oona were inspired to follow her model, to find not a boy, but a *man*. You feel protected with a man, Gloria had told them, pretending to even her best friends. So one day, when Geoff Jones appeared at Maple Manor, Gloria had her mother send the boy away without allowing him in the house.

In a repeat of her mother's experience, Gloria gave columnist Maury Paul the exclusive on the engagement. Paul had referred to di Cicco in an earlier column as from the "wrong side of the tracks," the son of a successful broccoli farmer who was a ballroom exhibition dancer during his marriage to Thelma Todd. Now he presented Pat as a movie executive making a sizable salary. On December 3, Gloria wrote her aunt in an agitated handwriting to apologize for not having been in touch for so long. She explained that California had shown her that what she thought was her happiness, Geoff, was not so. She said she wanted to bring Pat to see her, and she begged Gertrude to set her prejudices aside because he was where her true happiness lay. They did not meet, however, probably because of the Pearl Harbor attack on December 7, which caused so many in the country to change their plans.

Instead, Gertrude let it be known through her lawyers that Gloria would be cut out of her will. It was an idle threat. Gloria really wanted her aunt to come and kidnap her to Westbury, to save her from herself, and especially from the fiancé whose volcanic expressions of violence terrified her and had her waking up in the middle of the night with heart palpitations. By not being truthful, as Gertrude had often urged her to be, Gloria lost any chance of being saved. How could Gertrude possibly read between the lines of a letter that extolled Pat as the perfect mate?

The December 7 attack on Pearl Harbor had caused the cancellation of Carol Marcus's debut at the St. Regis as well. Papers had been playing it up for weeks, announcing Errol Flynn was going to play Prince Charming by riding into the room with her in a Cinderella coach. Following that sudden letdown, Rosheen Marcus was delighted when Gloria provided a consolation prize by inviting Carol to be a bridesmaid at her December 28 wedding in Santa Barbara, where Errol once again appeared, this time as an usher. Sunny California would sooth any leftover pain from the loss of Carol's big event.

On the eventful day, rain fell on the thousand spectators hoping to get a glimpse of the famous heiress and her movie industry husband. Gloria was stunning in an elegantly plain gown of white satin with a coronet of old lace and tulle, but in the windy and damp weather the crowd saw little of her, usher Errol Flynn, or Gloria M., dressed in the silver gray gown she had worn for her marriage to Regi Vanderbilt. By the end of the ceremony, however, the sun broke through the clouds to spotlight the wedding party as it came down the steps following the nuptial mass. Emma Keislich and Mrs. Morgan stood approvingly on the steps outside the Santa Barbara Mission as Gloria, unkissed by her husband during the ceremony, came out with her reflex smile, all the while secretly wishing her windblown veil would turn into a sail and carry her away from everyone.

Carol Marcus caught the bouquet, and she soon found her man. Because Charles Marcus had Bendix company matters in the area, Rosheen rented the family a penthouse at the Sunset Towers, where she gave parties for Carol to meet other young people from Los Angeles. Bandleader Artie Shaw came to one with a friend of Rosheen's and was quickly taken with Carol, but he was smart enough not to become entangled with a sixteen year old. Shaw knew playwright Bill Saroyan, and he somehow brought the two together, not realizing his thirty-three-year-old friend would go right after Carol and succeed. Inspired by Gloria's model, Carol quickly fell for this darkly handsome, romantic-looking, intense man who quickly seduced her. She would later learn, as Gloria was beginning to learn, that a domineering man extracts a high price for his protection, that what seems like security is actually enslavement.

The Son of a Broccoli
King Is Hardly a Prince

While Carol and Oona idealized Gloria's marriage, the bride found from the first night that Pat was even worse than she had anticipated. Arriving in their suite at the Everglades Club in Palm Springs, Gloria took a long bath and prepared herself for her wedding night. Pat had gone out, and he was away so long she fell asleep. In the morning she found him in the living room at a card table with Zeppo Marx, movie mogul Joe Schenck, and a friend, so engrossed in the game he did not notice when she changed into a suit and went out to the pool. (Though explicit about her sex life with other men, in later writings Gloria omitted any mention of her life with di Cicco, other than a reference to the fact he was sterile as a result of a polo accident.) From Palm Springs the newlyweds drove to Palm Beach, Pat mocking her along the way, calling her "Fatsy Roo." When a reporter asked how her aunt Gertrude felt about the marriage, Gloria lied. Gertrude sent a one-sentence letter in response: "How *could* you have said to the press that I am happy about this terrible thing you are doing?"[37] Gloria was ashamed by her action but had set herself a trap and was unable to tell anyone the truth.

With the country now at war, Pat had planned to sign up for the cavalry, but unknown to Gloria, he sent a telegram in her name to her cousin Bill Vanderbilt asking his assistance in getting a commission. When that failed, he pestered her to get him $5,000 for an unknown purpose. Since she received only $750 a month from her trust, she capitulated to his demand that she pressure Mrs. Morgan to lend her some rings so she could pawn them. Later she learned the money went for bribes in an unsuccessful ploy to get his commission. While in New York to get the rings, Gloria visited Gertrude in hope of a reconciliation. Instead, she sensed her aunt was still angry and unapproachable, so she continued to pretend she was perfectly happy with her new marriage. Once again her passivity, combined with Gertrude's reserve, made what could have been a moving reunion, a breakthrough to intimacy, impossible. That night, sleeping in her old room, Harry's room, next to Gertrude's, Gloria was kept up all night by a coughing she only later realized was her aunt's.

Pat did manage to be stationed for Officer Training School at Fort Riley, so the couple settled in Junction City, Kansas, in the heartland of the state along the Kansas River. There she quickly adapted to the popular role of good little service wife. Not one to think of herself as above domestic chores, Gloria took up house cleaning, laundry, and decorating with enthusiasm, but she hired a local woman to cook. Pictures of her from the time show a strikingly different Gloria Vanderbilt from any before or after that time. On a windy day she poses behind a clothesline, her hair blowing the same as the laundry. For another, dressed in plaid skirt and sweater she stands in the backyard, bending over as she dries her hair, smiling at the photographer over the pose. In a third, she wears a flowered cotton dress, her arms enclosing a baby, her look so proud one would think it hers, but it is a godchild. Pat stands beside her, tickling the child's foot. Perhaps most charming is a scene of her sitting on the ground near a sidewalk, dressed in a sailor jumpsuit with oxfords and anklets. At normal weight, not her later excessive thinness, she looks like a happy, healthy, patriotic Kansas farm girl. What stands out is her smile, which is natural, not the forced grin more characteristic of earlier and later years.

Magazines of the time urged cleverness and thrift in housekeeping. Gloria complied by painting orange crates with many layers of white paint to give them a lacquered look and turned them into night tables, and she made a dining room table out of a piece of plywood on top of two green-painted barrels. She idolized Gene Tierney, who lived nearby with husband Oleg Cassini, but she could not get the courage to speak to her. When she felt Pat was safely gone, she would paint for a few hours, leading him upon his return to mock her as Fatsy Roo Van Gogh. And there were trips to the doctor for black eyes she said were caused by falls.

What she didn't recognize then or later was her impact on the community. What she saw as "the coziest house ever" was the nine-room pride of a local leader who had moved out of what was considered to be a very fine house to inferior quarters so Gloria Vanderbilt would have proper shelter. The town was so excited by her presence that a special traffic cop had to be assigned to her street to manage the steady stream of gawkers driving by. But that soon ended because the community wanted to welcome her into their social life, their clubs, their sidewalk conversations, their encounters in stores, their church worship. They felt it important to show her they were not intimidated by her celebrity and glamour, that she could feel at ease among them. The prevailing hope was that she would go to the drugstore and have Cokes with other women like herself, young wives of servicemen. They had no understanding that Gloria had never known smalltown life, had seldom been able to go anywhere unchaperoned, let alone gone to the local drugstore. At Westbury, Newport, and Hollywood, the Cokes had come to her.

Instead, she stuck to the house, partly out of shyness, partly out of lack of interest in the local people, partly because wife beaters like Pat purposely isolate their spouses. She put in the only unlisted phone the town had ever known.

When she pushed and pulled the furniture around, made new curtains, and created tables out of scraps, she in effect mocked the taste of the family who had sacrificed its comfort for her.

Unpaid bills brought lawsuits. "They're not suing me because I owe them money; they're miffed because they rolled out the red carpet and I wouldn't walk on it," she complained to reporters. She said the townspeople treated her like a freak, when she was just a young bride ignorant of money and budgets. "We were like young birds preyed upon by hungry hawks. Why it cost us $17,500 just for food and rent for five months."[38] What she couldn't conceive is that $17,500 would provide food, clothing, and shelter to three or four middle-class families for a year at that time, so her defense only contributed to the town's conclusion that it was *she* who was doing the snubbing.

Townspeople also did not know that Gloria was not yet wealthy. In addition to her allowance, which the guardians may have increased now that she was married, on Pat's urging she regularly begged money from her grandmother Morgan. Yet these monies, combined with Pat's army salary, could not meet the bills for a simple reason: on weekends he turned the house into a gambling center, and he was often the loser.

Still a teenager, Gloria looked around for someone to save her from an abusive husband. Her first move was unwise. Not many months into the marriage, during a leave in New York City, Gloria and Pat went to Twenty One, where Orson Welles joined their table, noodling with Gloria's knee throughout the evening. Although she knew his wife Rita Hayworth was pregnant, she flirted back, even kissed him at a party later that evening. Several nights later Pat beat Gloria up so badly and banged her against the wall so hard that she passed out. When she awoke, Pat was asleep, so she fled the hotel room and went to her guardians' law firm, where Gilchrist called Gertrude, who was unsympathetic. Gloria slammed down the phone and fled back to Pat, who during her absence had just learned his mother had died. Gloria forgave him.

16

1942-1959

Gertrude's Heart Gives Out,
and the Whitney Almost Succumbs

W hat Gloria didn't know during those weeks she had been trying to reconnect with Gertrude was her aunt's illness and distress over Neily, who finally died in Florida while she was at his bedside. She had brought the body back for burial with a service at St. Thomas' Episcopal on March 5, 1942. Following his death, she was listless and unable to eat, further weakening her own fragile health. On April 7, her doctors recommended she go to the hospital, where tests revealed the worst, bacterial endocarditis. She remained there, her children often at her bedside, until her death on April 18.

Unaware that Gertrude had even been sick, Gloria was stunned when Gilchrist called to give her the news. Her shock increased when Emma Keislich met her at the hotel dumbstruck and furious because Gertrude did not leave her any money. Pat sulked because all Gloria would receive was a Cartier pearl and diamond bracelet and her father's trophies. (In fact, Gloria found the jewelry bequest proof Gertrude loved her after all, because it was one Gertrude almost always wore.) At 60 Washington Mews, where Gertrude was laid out on her bed, Gloria faced a cool response from her relatives, and she searched the room for her cousin Gerta, who was mysteriously absent.

Pat decided he was not going to the funeral, delaying her so that she was the last to arrive. Her tardy appearance in three-quarter length mink coat and wide-brimmed hat seemed contrived to some. Now resettled in the States, Consuelo had apparently decided the old family feud best forgotten, and appeared with her husband at the church. So when Gloria reached the full family pews, Jacques Balsan graciously gave her his seat. From there she gazed at the back of the head of Gerta's father, the fearsome Uncle Buz, and thought how "pleased *he* must have been, proving all along how right he was . . . because, as he said—I might turn out like my mother."[1]

The service, attended by 1,400, was brief, a half hour, with readings from the bible and the singing of Gertrude's favorite hymns. Then the cortege went up to Woodlawn Cemetery, where Gertrude was laid to rest next to Harry. Her aunt Alva was the other Vanderbilt woman in Woodlawn.

Of the many editorials and memorial essays on Gertrude to appear in subsequent weeks, among those that would have most pleased her was that of art critic Henry McBride:

> Gertrude Vanderbilt Whitney was an artist by vocation and at the same time, by an accident of fate, a very rich woman. Spectacular riches . . . present so many hazards to character that not all who have been tried in that way have surmounted the test; and the possession of what is known as artistic temperament is almost as fatal to good citizenship.
> But Gertrude Vanderbilt Whitney was a good citizen. . . . It was not enough to put her thoughts into concrete, stone, and bronze, she wished the entire country to share her pleasure in the arts, and from the moment of her first emergence into public life she began a system of philanthropies that finally placed the entire country in her debt. It is not an exaggeration to say that there is not a contemporary artist of note in America who has not been helped by her.[2]

Thus in death her full contributions to American culture were recognized.

If Gertrude's estate of $11 million seemed small in view of her various inheritances, it was because she had in recent years made large gifts to her children as well as to the Whitney Museum. Gloria was not alone in receiving jewelry; it was the common bequest to her nieces and granddaughters. Most of the real estate and stock was left to Flora, Barbie, and Sonny. As the one most interested in art, Flora received the Whitney Museum properties (subject to its leases), the Paris studio, and Le Boulay chateau. Of Gertrude's most valuable paintings, Flora chose Turner's *Juliet and Her Nurse,* which she would find a near-priceless gift at a later time. The Whitney Museum received $2.5 million dollars and the forgiveness of its debts. Juliana Force received $50,000 as well.

Though griefstricken over the loss of her friend and colleague of over thirty years, Juliana immediately moved on two fronts in behalf of Gertrude's causes. First, she arranged for a memorial exhibition of her sculpture, which was presented for a month in early 1943. Most of the works had not been shown at the Whitney before.

Her other effort, along with Flora and Frank Crocker, was to see whether the Whitney Collection could become part of the Metropolitan Museum of Art. Gertrude had already explored this possibility with them before her death, so they knew she would approve. In January, a plan was announced publicly.[3] The Whitney collection would move to the Metropolitan to be established in a separate wing paid for by the Whitney assets. The Whitney trustees would be an advisory council in the development of the Metropolitan's American art collection, and Juliana Force would be an advisory director. The immediate response from the art world was cautious support. While centralization of the two collections was thought to be advantageous, artists feared the loss of informality and intimacy characteristic of the Whitney. Others mourned the loss of the old house-galleries and the unique identity Gertrude and Juliana had brought to the institution. Accordingly, praise was great when the Whitney galleries, closed for more than a year, reopened in November 1943 with its traditional Annual.

Negotiations between the two museums continued for several years without an agreement. Stripped of the autonomy of her position, Juliana was dismayed when the Metropolitan ordered her to vacate her treasured apartment, rich with memories, over the galleries. Nor did Francis Henry Taylor, director of the Metropolitan, share her sympathy for unknown but promising artists. Juliana's recommendations for purchase had to go through Taylor's office, where the acquisitions committee could further stall or obstruct her choice. When Juliana one day asked what he thought the trustees' attitude toward a particular purchase would be, Taylor responded, "I think they will puke."[4] His animosity was more public in the form of articles attacking modern art for what he considered its lack of redeeming value and significance.

To the art world, the merger appeared on line. In September of 1946, the Whitney Museum opened its season with a collection taken from both the Metropolitan and its own holdings as a preface to the final union. On September 15, 1947, an agreement was struck between the Metropolitan, the Whitney, and the Museum of Modern Art defining areas of interest and coordination among the three institutions. However, during a dinner discussing this division of territory, a Metropolitan representative spoke out strongly against the Whitney's policies toward artists, implying they would not be carried out under the reorganization. Suffering from cancer, Juliana was told about the remarks from the staff member she had sent to the meeting in her place. When informed by her of the situation, the Whitney trustees, much influenced by Flora, called off the merger.

Thus when Juliana died on August 28, 1948, she did so relieved that her and Gertrude's mission, with its commitment to new American artists, would continue uninterrupted. Her children raised, Flora had more time to commit to the maintenance of the Whitney tradition. In honor of her mother's partner, Flora arranged a Memorial Exhibition to reflect Juliana's taste in developing the collection, along with a memorial booklet that provided vivid portraits of her written by artists and critics.[5] In later years, Flora worked to widen the base of the museum by developing a nonfamily Board of Trustees (who would strengthen its financial base) and by locating the collection in a larger building uptown.

The art world gained in a more curious way following Gertrude's death. The Whitney mansion at 871 Fifth Avenue was demolished and a forty-five story apartment building would eventually take its place. The Metropolitan purchased scores of tapestries and pieces of furniture from the auction, and the Walters Art Gallery in Baltimore obtained the entire grand ballroom—floor, paneled walls, and ceiling, originally part of the chateau of Baron D'Albert from the time of Louis XVI. Museums would similarly benefit with the demolition of 640 Fifth

Avenue. Neily had sold the mansion in 1940 to William Waldorf Astor with the stipulation that Grace be allowed to live there, paying rent, until one year after his death. She in fact stayed until 1945, at which point the wrecking balls appeared. She then moved uptown to a smaller, elegant mansion. Even then she did not seem to realize that she was a queen without subjects.

Gloria's Friends Find
Their Perfect Mates

With her aunt dead, Gloria Vanderbilt was essentially cut off from her father's family. They did not ostracize her so much as pay little attention, for it appeared she had willfully chosen her path of rebellion, and they were willing to let her suffer its consequences. Her play acting that everything was wonderful disguised the wreckage of her marriage.

The day Pat came home to say he had been ordered overseas brought secret relief to Gloria. Then fate intervened, striking him down with a case of blood poisoning that almost killed him. While it seemed that he was dying, Gloria received a call from her half sister Cathleen's son, who said his mother had just died and would be buried in Cuba. Gloria explained she could not attend her half sister's funeral and returned to Pat's bedside. There, in desperation, the doctors injected a new drug, penicillin. Pat miraculously recovered from the infection that had often meant certain death in the past and left the hospital with an honorable discharge. Gloria took him to their new home, a duplex apartment in New York City that Sonny Whitney had offered her at a miniscule rent.

Meanwhile, Bill Saroyan, now in the army in Sacramento, had told Carol he would marry her, provided she got pregnant first. She went to see him, "chaperoned" by Oona. Nervous because she did not consider herself a facile writer, Carol edited love letters she had received from another boyfriend, writer Jerry D. Salinger, and sent them to Bill. Since he knew Carol's English was rudimentary compared to the craft expressed in these letters, he readily determined they were fraudulent. Furious, he sent the girls away, but had reunited with Carol later. By 1942, he was stationed with the Army film studios in New York, and Carol was trying to get pregnant so he would marry her.

With Pat often away on various ventures, Gloria felt free to join Carol and Oona on rounds of the Stork Club, El Morocco, and other favorite café society haunts. This trio of distinctly different beauties drew much attention, and Oona was named "debutante of the year." One day Carol called Gloria to say she had just met the most amusing young man whose witty sense of humor complemented her screwball nature. He was fair, slight, short, with a Southern accent, and had the curious name of Truman Capote. During the winter of 1942, the trio would take Truman to lunch and introduce him to their other friends. For a young man planning to be famous, he was making the right contacts. His fascination with the three gorgeous socialites led him, years later, to use them for the basis of his most memorable character, the charming and scatter-brained Holly Golightly of his novel *Breakfast at Tiffany's*.

The trio's adventures ended in 1943. Carol became pregnant, and Bill, who had been transferred to Ohio, married her that February. Oona, who had a vague interest in acting, went to Northern California to visit her father and stepmother, but primarily to land a role in Hollywood. The visit to her father was tragic. Egged on by the jealous and vindictive Carlotta, he tore into his daughter for being a well-known debutante.

Down in Hollywood, Orson Welles took Oona out on a date, read her palm, and predicted that within a short time she would meet and marry Charles Chaplin. At that time, Chaplin was being falsely defamed by both red-baiting columnists such as Hedda Hopper and an emotionally disturbed actress, Joan Barry, who stalked him with a gun and eventually won a baseless paternity suit against him. (Blood tests proved he could not be the father, but a scandal-biased jury judged otherwise.) Orson Welles must have piqued Oona's curiosity, for through an agent, she arranged to meet Chaplin. The fact that he was fifty-one and she was seventeen intrigued her; Oona found her ideal paternal substitute and never spoke to her father again. She married Chaplin in June, and with him created a unique and successful union that drew the admiration of their friends over the years.

Gloria Meets Her Perfect Man

Deserted by her best friends, Gloria turned to more inner resources. By 1944, she had secretly rented a studio on the top of an old town house on East Fifty-third Street, her mother's old speakeasy neighborhood. In the afternoons she took a life drawing class at the Art Students League. Her mother, having broken off with Ketti Keven, lived in New York as well, with decorator Maurice Chalom, but Gloria avoided her.

That winter Pat was off to Hollywood on business, and Carol came into town, griefstricken over husband Bill Saroyan's orders to go overseas. Gloria felt as though she were on leave from school, free from the make-believe life she spent with Pat. On December 13, she went to the Saroyan apartment for dinner, and there she met a man "so tall, a tree rooted in beauty, stretching up into the sky above me with white clouds in a halo around his head."[6] A woman introduced him: Leopold Stokowski.

Stoki, as his friends called him, was quite taken with Gloria. Afterward, he asked someone, "Who was that wonderful girl I met last night? She had a Dutch name."[7] Upon finding out, he sent her a single ticket to his concert at the City Center, along with an invitation to dine with him in his home afterward. The meal was simple and elegant: soup in a pottery bowl, hors d'oeurves made with tiny pumpernickel squares and vegetables, and Chateau d'Yquem, a wine she had never heard of.

After the meal they sat on the sofa, where she listened to him describe the countries he had visited. Recalling the encounter later, she wrote: "He touches my face, my eyes, and I am no longer blind, my flesh is clay, his hands on my breasts and my nipples rise to meet his lips as he calls my name. I put my hand back against the wall, pushing it hard so that he can come deeper into me, yes, deeper, only him will it be, only him will I know, deeper each wave brings him closer to me."[8] Her first great love was on. "Make me worthy of him," she prayed, "and I'll give up desserts not just for Lent but for the end of time."

When Gloria Vanderbilt di Cicco met Leopold Stokowski she was still underage, twenty, and had experienced no stable emotional relationship yet in her life. She confused sexual attraction with love, and she defined love as a small child seeking protection would, a merger with the other, a loss of self into the other. So when Stokowski seduced her, she submitted with no thought of the consequences to herself.

Gloria was also blinded by Stokowski's fame. He was the world famous conductor, the man notorious for his escapades about the States and Europe with Greta Garbo during the late thirties. If he had loved Garbo, and now loved her, Gloria, then how could she refuse? She accepted him as a myth, unaware of how much of it was self-created. He misled her, as he had often done with the press, by claiming he was Polish, that his mother had died when he was small, and that he was raised in England by strangers.[9] It was the kind of story to appeal to orphaned Gloria. In fact, he had been born in the Marylebone section of London in 1882, son of an Irishwoman, Anne Moore, and Kopernik Stokowski, an English cabinetmaker whose father had emigrated from Poland. Stokowski's mother was still alive in a nursing home in London, and over the years he had successfully kept her existence from the press, and later kept it from Gloria as well.

Though born and bred in London, he now spoke with an exotic European accent of unspecific origin. At age 13 he had displayed such impressive organ skills that he was accepted at the Royal Academy of Music, and later he attended Queen's College, Oxford, where he performed so brilliantly that in little more than a year of part-time attendance he earned his bachelor's degree in music. He then went to America, where he saw a brighter opportunity for his skills.

Gertrude would have been aware of him, because his first job, obtained in 1905, was as organist at St. Bartholomew's Church. There he was so accomplished and charismatic that the priest thought he was taking too much attention away from the altar, and after a couple of years, fired the popular musician. It did not matter, for Stokowski had met a well-to-do concert pianist, Olga Saranoff, whose social connections led to his first conducting job, with the Cincinnati Symphony. He later married Olga and had a daughter by her, but she left him because of his preference "for any inconsequential flapper that comes along."[10] By the 1920s, his marriage had ended, but his career as director of the Philadelphia Orchestra was earning well-deserved praise. His second wife, socialite Evangeline Brewster, bore him two daughters and easily adapted to his nomadic temperament. Also inclined to infidelity, she had accepted his extramarital relationships until his affair with Garbo hit the newspapers. For the sake of their daughters, she left him. Both ex-wives maintained friendly relations with him, and he was known to be a doting father.

Gloria was also unaware that Stokowski's career was troubled. He was no longer associated with the Philadelphia Orchestra, the company he had turned into one the greatest virtuoso instruments in the country, some said in the world. A pioneer in advancing electronic recording techniques, he was now without a record contract as well. Since his work on *Fantasia* for Walt Disney in 1940, he had been floundering about for a permanent conducting position. His work on that picture and several other movies in Hollywood biased some music critics, who associated such activity with vulgarity and reviewed his later concert performances from that slant. While his grandiose and volatile personality contributed to the severing of his professional relationships, he was not fully to blame. In 1941, he had been appointed codirector of the NBC Symphony with Arturo Toscanini, who disdained Stokowski's free interpretation of scores and maneuvered to have him fired. This finally came about in the spring of 1944 after he insisted on performing the Schoenberg Piano Concerto, which was too much for the more conservative Toscanini and NBC corporate brass. That summer he found himself the brunt of much bad publicity after he rightfully walked away from a concert series in Mexico. The month Stokowski met Gloria he was working on the formation of the New York City Symphony, but following so many years of fame as guest conductor with major orchestras around the world, he found the job wanting. Worse, symphony hall managers in Europe, devastated by war, were not calling him. His friends were troubled that he had turned into a lonely, hurt, and antagonistic man.

If Gloria rejuvenated Stokowski, he proved the most ardent, mature, and accomplished lover she had ever known. As he came to know of her unsettled past, he grew very protective of her. In return, however, he was duplicitous about his past, even to the point of having nothing good to say about the two ex-wives who continued to support, even love him. This grievance only made Gloria all the more determined to make his life whole again. As a friend of his observed, they had "found each other because both are being constantly and unreasonably wounded by the world. They are a refuge to each other. For, certainly, any fool can see they are deeply in love."[11] The problem is, one of the two was exaggerating his wounds.

Gloria and Her Mother
Have Another Go at It

Gloria Vanderbilt's introduction of Leopold Stokowski to her mother is proof of what some might call her recklessness, others her youthful lack of sensitivity. She arranged the meeting to occur in public at a party at Rosheen Marcus's apartment. Gloria M. resisted—she didn't know Rosheen and felt she would be an intruder. When Gloria pressed, saying she had something wonderful to show her, her mother finally showed up. She stood dumbfounded while her glowing daughter brought over a pompous, much older man and introduced him as her fiancé. Her mother's scorn infuriated Stokowski, a man who took small slights to be major insults. Although Gloria was unaware of it, new battle lines were being drawn that put her in the middle of the fray.

When Pat returned and heard of Gloria's intent to divorce him, he reacted with disbelief, and he asked her to wait until he had some minor though necessary surgery that was scheduled upon his return to California. In the end, he behaved rather well for someone in his position, or perhaps Gloria had something on him. She was about to turn twenty-one, and take control of her inheritance, but rather than hang in and fight for a large cut, di Cicco returned to Los Angeles and eventually sent a message through Joe Schenck that $200,000 would buy her freedom. She quickly agreed and left for Reno.

While waiting in a lodge in Nevada, Gloria "reached her majority," as the law phrases it, and was now in charge of her fortune. During the period of her guardianship, Gilchrist and Wickersham had paid out $895,575 on her behalf, about a fourth of the original estate. Yet they had also made such wise investments that despite the depression the rise in the value of securities increased the estate by $1,367,000. Consequently, the estate value on Gloria's twenty-first birthday was $4,295,628. Very importantly, the annual payment of $21,000 to her mother, $6,000 to Mrs. Morgan, and $3,000 to Emma Keislich would now stop, and any contribution to them would now have to come from Gloria's generosity. When no money had come forth from Gertrude's will for Emma Keislich, Gloria had promised her disconsolate nurse she would continue to look after her. It was easy for her to do the same for Mrs. Morgan, a miser who lived frugally in one room in a hotel, and did not even spend Gloria's contribution to her support. Gloria was less certain about her responsibility to her mother.

Finances were at the moment the last thing on her mind, however. While waiting for her divorce, she was not fully certain that Stoki intended to marry her. To her relief, he appeared a week before her residency period was up. Meeting him at the rail station, she had a minor auto accident in the parking lot, thus drawing reporters' attention to the couple. Having made headlines nationwide, they eloped to Mexico the day after the divorce was made final. (On the way down, their small plane ran into engine trouble and had to make an emergency landing in a field, frightening Stoki away from most flying afterward.) The groom lied about his age, claiming to be 58 when he was in fact 62, and claimed his mother's name on the marriage certificate as Czartorieska.

There was no time to honeymoon, for Stokowski had rehearsal commitments for a summer season at the Hollywood Bowl. Consequently, he took Gloria to his home high up Beverly Crest in Los Angeles. As had been the case with Pat, Gloria eased into the housewife role, bringing him picnic lunches and overlooking any signs of conflict or incompatibility. There they often entertained Stoki's friends. A frequent visitor was composer George Antheil, who was stunned upon first meeting Gloria, "tall, slender, but utterly beautiful . . . one of the two most beautiful women we had ever seen, the other being Heddi Lamarr."[12] Another friend was struck by her "sensitive face," that of one "who, over a long period, had been hurt and hushed. I could not reconcile the young girl sitting there to her [sensational] newspaper publicity."[13]

At first it was a good match. Gloria rejuvenated the aging conductor and worshiped him as a genius. In return, he gave her a sense of security she had never known, broadened her knowledge of music, art, and literature. When she mentioned her interest in painting, he urged her back to the easel, and visitors soon noted the house covered with her colorful canvasses. When she admitted her creative bent toward poetry, he encouraged her, even took a pile of her poems and sent them to editor Blanche Knopf, who did not accept them for publication. When she described her childhood dream of becoming an actress, a desire she had shared only once before, with Gertrude, who had belittled the idea, he listened thoughtfully, then called movie contacts about screen tests and arranged lessons for her with a dialogue coach.

Stokowski's admiration of creative women held not only in his choice of wives but in his work as well, for he fought to put talented minority and women instrumentalists in orchestras at a time when they were entirely composed of white males. In the early 1930s, during a trip to India with Evangeline, he met Annie Besant, head of the Theosophical Society, and Krishnamurti. As a result of this trip he also subscribed to Shakti worship, a Hindu cult placing Shiva's wife, Parvati, as superior to her husband. Whenever Gloria was troubled, he would encourage her to pray to the Divine Mother. Although his discussions of *karma, dharma, papa, punya,* and *moksha* confused her, she told him she did understand the *suttee* funeral pyre, that if he should die she would want to also.

If Stokowski encouraged Gloria's intellectual and artistic maturation, he was less able to nurture her emotional growth. Building his reputation on a false history, over the years he had become more pompous and demanding of others. Gloria was his Trilby; the light shining on her would brighten him standing alongside. She must appear remarkable, for he could only have a remarkable wife. Yet she was to create only as her own time, when he was rehearsing, for example, and never allow her interests to threaten his primacy in her life. One afternoon when she came home, he took her in his arms and described how in her absence everything in the room reminded him of her. Then he drew an L with the lower stem looping around to enclose the L in a G. While Stokowski felt Gloria encircling him emotionally, the fact was just the opposite, with his rules restricting her sphere of movement.

His rigid patriarchy agreed with Gloria, who just wanted a home, children, and the chance to be artistic on the side. Carol Marcus Saroyan now had a son, Aram. After lunching with Oona, now pregnant with her first child by Charlie, Gloria was "wishing, wishing—praying, soon it will be me."[14] Stoki agreed, and expressed his hope for a girl.

Instead of a home and infant, Gloria she found herself constantly on the road with Stoki, who had guest engagements all over the country. On one such trip they stayed at Rananim, the late D. H. Lawrence's community in Taos, now centered around his widow Frieda, painter Dorothy Brett, and Mabel Dodge Luhan who had left Greenwich Village in hopes of creating a new artistic Eden in New Mexico. Stoki had first come to Taos in 1931 and sought out Mabel, who had married Tony Luhan, a full-blooded Tiwa, in hopes they could help him learn about Native American ceremonial chants. He visited several times over the next few years to study the music, and he tried to sell a movie script Mabel had written on Spanish-American history.

Mabel also wrote an insightful and charming essay on him, "Bach in a Baggage Car." The reference was to a time he overcame a radio broadcasting problem by placing his orchestra in the baggage car of the train they were traveling in. She astutely identified his noted appeal to women, how he was "living proof that men may exist on this earth who understand Everything: everything about Beauty, Spirituality, Art and Consciousness."[15] Dorothy Brett agreed, describing his having "one of the most finely chiseled, sensual faces I ever saw . . . I just gaped."[16] Mabel so admired Stoki that she had even provided him and Greta Garbo with a hideaway in 1937 and 1938, although their presence also significantly increased tourist traffic to that small town.

Given this long history of friendship, the three women catered to Stoki and ignored his new wife. To Gloria's consternation, they thoughtlessly repeated the name of his second wife, Evangeline, causing her to stew "in silent battle to hold on to Leopold body and soul."[17] She had little to worry about. Brett thrust her brass ear trumpet into his face and enthused for hours about his nose, how many portraits of him she could paint, while blowzy Frieda dropped cigarette ashes over her deceased husband's manuscripts. During subsequent months tracking back and forth across the country in a Chevrolet, with "home" reduced to lookalike hotel rooms and restaurants suggested by Duncan Hines *Adventures in Good Eating,* this colorful episode stood out in her memory.

Stoki was known among his friends for his exotic and sometimes eccentric dress. Shaping herself to his fantasy, Gloria let her hair grow long, until it went to her waist, and wore clothes with an ethnic flare, such as Austrian folk costumes or gypsy blouses with sandals, long skirts, and silver belts. Stoki's friends were the great composers, musicians, and actors of the day, who found Gloria's charm and native intelligence a welcome addition to their circle. With her socialite background, she had the refined manners and graciousness to meet his demanding level of formality, those precisely staged dinners with elaborate settings of porcelain, crystal, silver, impeccable flower arrangements, fine-honed conversation (with any opinions she expressed being his, of course).

Their semipermanent home was in New York City, but they were generally there only in the winters. In March of 1946, while traveling in Mexico, Gloria decided to cut her mother off from all future support. Looking back on this decision years later, she said Stoki filled the role her Grandmother Morgan once had in feeding her mind against her mother. From what he could see, the matter was simple: Gloria M. had never given the child any love; only Emma Keislich had. So Gloria brought her aging nurse to live with her in the penthouse, gave her $12,000 a year, an affluent income for those days, and a mink coat. She sent her mother a cable:

> LOOKING THROUGH MY BOOKS AND ACCOUNTS, OWING TO HEAVY EXPENSES, I CAN NO LONGER CONTINUE YOUR MONTHLY ALLOWANCE.[18]

In a follow-up letter, she pointed out that Thelma, who had recently won a lawsuit over Lord Furness's estate, had plenty of money for both of them. (This was not so—the money was Tony's—but truth was not the point here.) While Stoki's secretary typed up the response, Gloria had an eerie feeling she was back in England the day she was told to write a letter describing her mother as a "rare bease."

Yet in suggesting years later that Stoki was the primary source of this move, that she was a helpless pawn in his nasty scheme, Gloria continued to disavow her own rightful *hostility* toward her mother. Her greatest shortcoming, she would say, was her inability to express anger, her storing it up, "and often it will reappear over a more trivial but related subject."[19] This financial severing was hardly a trivial expression of years of withheld fury, but it was both cathartic and effective in severing Gloria's romantic childhood desires for an eventual merger with her mother. Cutting off her mother would channel all her passion into Stokowski alone, though she was not aware of it at the time. He was isolating her just as effectively as Pat had, though the jail was sweeter.

What Gloria or Stoki certainly never counted on was her mother's habit of using the press to argue her position and garner public support. Crestfallen, Gloria M. took to her bed, gathered reporters around, and dramatized how she was being abused by her child. To raise money, she sold the diamond engagement ring Regi had given her, making the sale public knowledge.

It was an ugly story with neither side behaving well.

The couple had to sneak back from Mexico to New York City. To elude the press, they left most of their luggage in the car outside their apartment and rushed inside. Before their help could bring up the belongings, a thief burgled the car. "The best laid plans often go screwy," wrote a tabloid reporter, "like last night when Gloria Vanderbilt Stokowski, America's parent-ditching money-bags, and her ever-loving Leopold, the orchestra man, tried to ease quietly into town and failed only because a thief tried to swipe their baggage and Gloria's jewels."[20] Stoki, always hypersensitive to newspaper criticism, grew enraged to find himself ridiculed as "Stokie-wokie."

To minimize further mockery, he consulted with lawyers. First he appeared in court and refused to press charges against the apprehended suspect, saying he sympathized with all underprivileged persons. Then he arranged a press conference at which he had Gloria remind reporters that "when the U.S. Supreme Court in the *Vanderbilt* case judged her [mother] unfit, the Court had to be closed because some of the evidence was so terrible that it could not be made public."[21] Mrs. Morgan tried to be the peacemaker and arranged a visit between mother and daughter, at which Gloria offered $500 a month support. Gloria M. responded that she would accept the money provided it came from a trust that was to revert back to Gloria's control upon her death. According to Gloria M. some years later, her lawyer called the next day to say a clause had been added to the contract, that she would have to collect the money personally wherever her daughter specified. In other words, if Gloria wanted her to collect the money in China, she would have to go there to get it. The fight returned to the courts.

In another statement to reporters, Gloria argued that her "filial regard" for her mother remained, but "I am certain she can work as she has done in the past and as I am doing at present."[22] The "work" was a foundation Stoki had devised she could say the purpose of her money that had formerly gone to her mother would go to help blind, homeless, and starving children around the world. (Ironically, Gloria M. was going blind from glaucoma.)

Following repeated nasty references to this episode in the press, Gloria relented four years later and agreed to give her mother $500 a month. By this time the Morgan twins had fallen on hard times, having failed at both a doll company, "Pooks," Gloria M.'s nickname for her daughter, and a fragrance concern. Just as the twins' naivete had so often gotten them into trouble, so it plagued them when times were bad. And times would get worse for them.

Gloria Plays at Being the Perfect Wife, Again

Fortunately, it was time again to return to Los Angeles for another season at the Hollywood Bowl. Gloria could return to her painting and privacy. Reporters in Los Angeles hounded her much less than those in New York City. Yet her insecurity regarding his previous marriages brought unhappiness to his children, for he had much less contact with them. On June 8, 1946, Stoki's eldest daughter,

Sonya, was married at St. Bartholomew's. Her bridesmaids were her half sisters, the daughters of Evangeline, who also attended. Certain her father would give her away, Sonya was stunned to receive a telegram stating he would not appear, and she walked down the aisle unescorted. When asked who would give the bride away, her mother Olga stood up and walked dramatically to the front of the church.

While Stoki demanded Gloria's fervent devotion, he was not sexually faithful. Among his several homes his favorite was a ranch high in the hills in Santa Barbara, where he oversaw the planting of its seventeen acres with fruit orchards and exotic trees. (Asked how a group could honor him, he would request that an unusual specimen be added to his arboretum.) Gloria wanted nothing to do with this ranch, for not only had he lived there with second wife Evangeline and their two children, but, more importantly, it had been the hideaway for his trysts with Greta Garbo in 1937. Consequently, soon after the marriage, Stoki had allowed his friend Beryl Markham, famous aviator and writer, and her husband, writer Raoul Schumacher, to live rent free as caretakers on the ranch. Wildly promiscuous, Markham had already bedded Stokowski earlier in their friendship and continued to do so when he showed up alone to check on his beloved trees. Schumacher was used to his wife's sexual voraciousness and absented himself whenever one of her other lovers appeared.

When these arrangements were being made, Gloria must not have yet met Markham, a willowy, enchanting blond whose reputation for infidelity was well known in Los Angeles. Certainly she would never have imagined Stoki cheating on her with his caretaker. And if Stoki was ready to accept Markham's charms with her husband under the same roof, then he must have done the same on those trips he made without Gloria. Age never eroded his appeal to worshipful women fans or his willingness to satisfy them.

Gloria's happiest times were their intermittent stays at one of the homes. In the east, they split their time between a small hideaway home in Greenwich, Connecticut, and a penthouse they acquired in 1948 at 10 Gracie Square in the city. Their apartment faced north, looking out over the mayor's mansion, and included a roof garden, large rooms, and much changing light as the day passed. While Gloria was constantly redecorating, one room remained sacrosanct, Stoki's study, in which everything was pale blue, including walls, ceiling, upholstery, and even grand piano. The neighbors on the south side of the floor were opera star Lily Pons and conductor André Kostelanetz. Both couples visited one another and had a stream of visitors from the arts. One, soprano Lucia Albanese, was impressed by the beauty of the apartment and the fact that Gloria had made dessert herself. "I saw many beautiful paintings that she did. The colors were so bright, so alive, so striking. Maybe that's what she had in her heart, and it never came out."[23]

Another recent resident of 10 Gracie Square was Flora Miller, Gertrude's daughter and Gloria's first cousin, who had taken a duplex which she decorated with her mother's sculptures and the paintings she had inherited. Society had changed, much due to the influence of Grace Vanderbilt, so that Flora could do what her mother had not, and included artists at the same parties and dinners with socialites. She had also taken on the role of matriarch, making her home the center for family reunions and gatherings. Although Gloria lived in the same building, she had little contact with her cousin, who was twenty-seven years older.

One reason Gloria saw little of her father's family was that she was seldom in New York for long periods of time. That she was not an avid traveler is evident in her later description of this period in her book *Black Knight, White Knight* (and the fact that in later years she was not part of jet-set society). Although tours with Stokowski took her all over the United States and most of Europe, she was apparently untouched by these voyages. That she saw Europe in its wartorn state seemingly made no impression, for she describes this aspect of their life together curtly and without detail.

The reason for Gloria's lack of connection with the cultures and historical change around her may not have been solely lack of interest on her part. Stoki wanted her at his side as much as possible. During rehearsals, she was to stay in the hotel; during performances, she was to sit in the audience. Consequently, what for a more independent person would have been a remarkable opportunity was for Gloria a procession of hotel rooms whose banal interiors only depressed.

Another striking absence from Gloria's memoirs is any commentary on the music. She experienced some of the most important musical performances of the day, for Stokowski continued his commitment to premiering contemporary compositions and was often brilliant in producing old works in new form. Gloria not only heard this music, but met the most eminent musicians and composers of the time. Stoki's other wives had been highly knowledgeable about classical music, and Gloria's ignorance, perhaps even indifference, must have provoked him.

Gloria's dissatisfaction was tempered in 1950, when she discovered she was pregnant. On August 22, 1950, she gave birth to a six-pound, fourteen-ounce boy, Leopold Stanislas III, called Stan. Like other women of her time, she had been influenced by Dr. Grantley Reed's *Natural Childbirth,* which urged the refusal of anesthesia, but during the delivery she called for gas. Despite her checking into New York Lying-In Hospital as "Mrs. Laura Green," the press soon learned about her presence. Cholly Knikerbocker reported she was guarded at the hospital with "as much secrecy as if she were the formula for the A-bomb."[24]

Despite the appearance of an ideal life, Gloria was lonely. Stoki was showing the first sign of an antisocial and slightly paranoid outlook that would increase in later years. For example, in 1949, following his conducting performances in New York, he would whisk Gloria down a hallway of garbage cans to a limousine waiting by a secluded entrance. Both fans and reporters resented his unavailability.

Worse, he decided he was through with being the regular conductor for any orchestra and signed with Andrew Schulhof to manage his worldwide bookings as guest conductor, and went on the road. He demanded Gloria accompany him as well, which she did at first, with Stan, but the baby was cranky on the road. Thus Gloria was thrilled to learn she was pregnant once again because it would give her a reason to stay home in New York.

In June of 1951, Gloria left Stan with a nurse and flew to England to spend some time with Stoki. One day he said he wanted to take her to meet someone but would not say who it was. On the train, he explained they were going to a nursing home where the woman who took care of him after his mother died was staying. Gloria was shattered: "What a fool to believe I was close to him, possessed him in some small measure, when I did not know until this moment that this person so dear to him was alive."[25] She refused to go, and she waited on the platform while he made his visit. Years after she understood the foolishness of her reaction, which reflected how essentially insecure she remained to be so jealous of Stoki's old nurse. And too late she realized with sadness and humiliation that the woman was actually his mother.

Gloria spent much of that summer on the road, traveling through Holland, Germany, Austria, England, Spain, and Portugal, and returned when the late stage of her pregnancy demanded that she do so. Stoki had placed only one free week in the schedule around the second baby's due date in January of 1952, which made Gloria angry. The baby did not come, he went off, then canceled a concert to return for a possible delivery. Still the baby did not arrive, and Stoki's impatience grew more visible with each hour. Finally Christopher arrived, and with his birth Gloria sensed that she and her two boys were a separate and distinct unit from her husband.

Despite her desire to be at home with the boys during the early years, as Dr. Spock clearly wrote was essential for their healthy development, Gloria capitulated to Stoki's demands that she be with him. Consequently, the children were raised more by governesses, as she had been. She even tried Emma Keislich at one point, but soon realized their views on childrearing were incompatible. "As the years passed, my life went in directions different from the ones she had in mind, and it ended badly and it broke my heart."[26] She continued to support Keislich, but was no longer emotionally attached to her.

When days were bad, Gloria had Carol Saroyan and Oona Chaplin with whom to compare herself. Oona's life was totally domestic, Charlie her benevolent master, the growing flock of children her joy. While Gloria admired domesticity, she could not consider it the sole expression of her self. Carol, now with two children, was similarly homebound in San Francisco, but by a cruel and jealous Saroyan. A gambler, in 1948 he had lost their house to betting debts. Her mere acceptance of a dance from an acquaintance at a social club led to his picking at her for weeks. She excused his dark, angry moods as passion, a necessary companion of his art. Because he expected more beauty in life than it could provide, she must do everything to compensate for his constant disappointment.

Despite the continent between them, Gloria and Carol maintained a telephone and letter lifeline that the husbands begrudgingly tolerated. If one friend needed the other, no one could interfere. Thus when Bill once took over the top flat of their San Francisco house and refused any communication with Carol, she asked Gloria to come out and help her. Although Gloria was terrified of Bill, who resembled Pat di Cicco, she volunteered to approach him and attempt a reconciliation. She did, and within a few minutes he appeared downstairs ready to live once more with his family.

The reconciliation did not last, and in 1949 he suddenly deserted Carol when she happened to mention she was Jewish. Claiming she had been lying to him all along, he went off to Nevada for six weeks of gambling, drinking, and a divorce, losing every penny of the more than $50,000 he made that year, so that Carol and her children were evicted for nonpayment of rent. When the court decree gave her full custody of the children, Saroyan was so enraged that he had her shadowed in hopes of getting evidence to have her declared an unfit mother. Although Carol dated, she remained bewitched by Saroyan, and saw him as her only love. Then, as he so often did in his life, he reversed course and determined to win her back. They remarried in 1950, but in 1951, following a fight where he tried to strangle her, she walked out. Even then she could not sever her dependence upon him, even doing his laundry and other chores for a period.

It is tempting to think these three young women were so compliant and docile because they had all lacked father figures, and certainly that psychology must have played some role. But many other women were homebound during these years, subservient then as well, women from more traditional family dynamics. These were the women who bore the baby boom, and their experiences at this time, regardless of class or race, exuded domesticity. They shared the "expert" advice of Marynia Farnham and Ferdinand Lundberg, whose best-selling *The Modern Woman* insisted that true fulfillment of female sexuality was in motherhood. Movie stars, depicted as glamorous in the fan magazines of the thirties, now appeared in picture spreads surrounded by their children and gave interviews, as Maureen O'Hara did, extolling pregnancy for "the completeness of being a woman, a warm human being."[27] Movie plots showed fewer of the career women of earlier years, and when they did have careers, they dropped them at the end of the story for love and family. The theme of *Ladies' Home Journal* and similar woman's magazines was the "absorbing, creative profession" of housekeeping and motherhood. In the larger context of the cold war, these women saw their adaption of this role as essential to citizenship, proof Americans had a superior way of life to spread throughout the world.

Thus it was not unusual that Stoki also came up with a plan unique to those cold war days: they should have a bomb shelter on their Connecticut land. Popular magazines were pouring out numerous articles on such home additions, which were touted as playhouses a harried mother could send her children to. (It may also have been real estate ads proclaiming "country properties for Atomic retreat" that impelled the couple, like so many New Yorkers at the time, to rush to buy rural retreats, be they beaten-down farms or estates like the Stokowskis' Innesfree.) Gloria thought it was a foolish idea, for what would one do when after the blast other desperate people came along. "Anyway—who wants to live in a world where a bomb shelter is called home?"[28] Gloria's objection was not politically fashionable, for most women followed the lead of Federal Civil Defense Administrator Jean Wood Fuller, who urged them to set up the equivalent of "Grandma's Pantries" and "make a game of it: Playing Civil Defense" with children.[29]

Her independent position on bomb shelters created a small problem in the marital relationship. Another occurred during a lunch with Betsy Close, a friend of Stoki's. During the meal Betsy raised the subject of a recent community conflict over the location of the U.N. building in their elite enclave. When she inquired, "What do you think of it?" Gloria felt at a loss. "Haven't you a mind of your own?" Betsy pressed. Gloria quickly said with pride, "Yes, Leopold's mind." Afterward she reflected that perhaps this boast was not healthy and, worse, that her lack of an independent opinion was tied to her isolation, her husband's increasing insistence they spend their time together without other adults around.

If Gloria had befriended Stoki's first wife, she would have found her situation repeated a pattern. Stoki had treated Olga similarly, demanding she be creative, though not too much so, with the result that she eventually dropped her performing career. The stresses had become so great that one day Olga left Philadelphia and found herself wandering the streets of New York in an amnesiac daze. It was upon giving birth to Sonya that she was forced to choose between independence or at least twenty more years of unsatisfactory life with Stoki, who loved children but could not bear losing his wife's attention to them. As we have seen, she opted for independence, yet to her dying day remained in love with her impossible ex-husband.

Similarly torn between Stoki's demands of her as a wife and society's strictures as a mother, Gloria came down with what was then called a nervous breakdown, periods of choking and dizzy spells. Fortunately, psychoanalysis reached new prominence in the fifties and provided an answer. Through four years of therapy, for the first time in her life Gloria began to make her own major decisions and, more important, work through the consequences. Most symbolic, she went out one day and had her hairdresser cut off her hair. She took it home in a bag and showed it to Stoki. She regretted the move afterward, but not for long. "I like long-hair music and long-hair girls," he petulantly noted to Edward R. Murrow during a television interview in their home.[30] She told reporters long hair represented the "Arab wife" and pointed to friend Oona Chaplin, now self-exiled in Switzerland with Charlie as a result of the Red Scare hounds in Hollywood, as "the *perfect* Arab wife." With each trip to the beauty parlor the cut became shorter, until she had the chic Italian look popular then, a sleek and glimmering cap. Just to prove her point, she returned to the pages of *Vogue* as a celebrity model for such noted photographers as Cecil Beaton and Horst. With her expressive dark eyes and sylphlike figure, as slim as Constance Bennett's in the thirties, Gloria was an ideal mannequin for the body-hugging Parisian fashions of the day.

Tired of being kept out of the social scene, in 1953 Gloria organized a circus benefit in Madison Square Garden for Cerebral Palsy of New York, accepting "the spotlight she has avoided since her marriage to Stokowski" noted *Look,* which found the event worth a several-page spread. On that evening, which was really Gloria's long-delayed social debut, Stokowski was absent, and good friend Gian-Carlo Menotti sat in the box with her during the show. This event also marked recent changes in society's rituals. No longer able to afford the opulent grand balls of the past, smart social matrons entertained through sponsorship of a charity function held at a hotel, theater, or other public setting. As the number of these events increased, socialites found themselves in a situation at which their Gilded Age ancestors would have been amazed: wishing for fewer invitations, because one ended up "paying one's way" through the social season.

Gloria then arranged the first solo exhibition of her paintings, which was politely reviewed but not taken too seriously. A talented amateur, was the implicit meaning, but in need of further development. "Dreamy romanticism" was the theme, a reflection of her own internal view of the world during those eight years of solitary work in the studio. The images of fragile-looking girls in flowered landscapes or playing with pastel-colored balloons on a beach were a curious contrast with the abstractions and dark colors of Jackson Pollack or Mark Rothko. Although the serious art world did not include Gloria, others found her sentimental works touching. (One must wonder what direction she might have taken had she been closer to Flora, who could have introduced her to contemporary artists who might have shaped her craft and vision in new ways.)

Grace Dies, and Consuelo Tells Her Story

In 1953, Gloria's aunt Grace died alone in her twenty-eight room house at Eighty-sixth and Fifth. Having moved there after the demolition of 640 Fifth, she had disappeared from the society pages and had little company beyond her faithful servants. The people who mattered now in society were not inclined to be impressed by an invitation from an elderly woman who missed the passing of aristocracy in Europe. With failing health she had become cantankerous and difficult, throwing hairbrushes at her maid. Her final years had been spent bedridden, her sight and hearing impaired. Although few family members had been in contact with her during those lonely days, the Vanderbilt clan appeared *en masse* to provide a cortege of limousines for the trip to the mausoleum on Staten Island. There Grace had her final rest among those who had rejected her earlier in life.

That same year a book appeared reviving an old family scandal. Just why Consuelo Balsan agreed to publish *The Glitter and the Gold* is unclear. In accord with the *grande dame* role she had put on since returning to the States, she had scrupulously avoided the limelight; this pose may have been a cover for her deafness or her inability to adjust to modern times. So important was maintaining an illusion of continued grandeur that twice a year she moved her entire household—furniture, carpeting, tapestries, and fine arts—from Long Island to Palm Springs and back again. Asked to pose for major magazines, she carefully adorned herself in sumptuous silk gowns and sat regally amid her museum-decor surroundings of gilded French antique furniture and oriental rugs. Fortunately, the woman who had so loved her grandchildren when they visited her chateau in France, found them paying back the affection in her final years.

The book was a highly sanitized, ghostwritten view of her life, constructed to portray her as a valiant and abused young woman who matured to make significant contributions to the welfare of others. Although she had known great historical figures of her age intimately, she said almost nothing about them. Her feminism went unmentioned, as though to disown her earlier courage, independence, and political principles. The story of her first marriage and divorce was copied from the annulment proceedings, and its truth value remains unclear. It would have been outlandish during the fifties for a woman to have admitted to love affairs, however many decades past, and she did not break the pattern. What remains most curious, though, is the amount of vitriol expressed toward Sunny, his family, and his country, all presented as though she were utterly victimized by them. This fury must have had some impression on her sons Ivor and Bertie (now the tenth duke of Marlborough) and his children, however sympathetic they were to her.

Her loathing for England even affected her relationship with her children. Since moving back to the States, she had never returned there to visit them. As the tenth duke, Bertie had found a way to preserve Blenheim, by opening it to tourists, some of whom had the delight of buying an illustrated guidebook from him. As the heir, Bertie had been given much more attention from nannies and family than Ivor, who blamed his mother for the emotional deprivation he felt. More like his sensitive father, Ivor had become an aesthete, spending his days studying and buying French art. Fearful of flying, he refused to cross the ocean to see his mother. When he died of a brain tumor on September 17, 1956, Consuelo had not laid her eyes on her youngest son since 1940. She could not attend the interment because Jacques was bedridden and failing as well. In fact, he died in early November of that year. Consuelo accompanied his body to France, and she would return there at intervals to visit his relatives and old friends. But she stayed away from England, so Bertie and his family would have to come to her.

Gloria
Breaks Away

While Gloria would have seen *The Glitter and the Gold* in New York bookstores, and may well have read this story of a relative from an estranged branch of the family, Consuelo certainly never saw Gloria's first publication effort. Her *Love Poems* was not an auspicious debut ("childishly conceived . . . full of artificial thoughts," judged *Saturday Review*).[31] The poor response to her writing did not matter; she sublet her studio and returned to acting lessons. (Composer Alan Hovhaness, who worked closely with Stokowski, set three of her works to music, which were performed by the CBS Orchestra and singer Nell Tangemann in 1954.)

A social event provided the breakthrough for her acting career. Producer Gilbert Miller had been impressed by Gloria's dramatic ability during the pageant at the April in Paris Ball, where she stepped in for the last minute to replace an ailing Audrey Hepburn in the role of John Paul Jones. What he saw was tremendous potential: "an electric presence, dignity, poise, intelligence, and beautiful speech," qualities that would serve her well on a different stage later on. He admitted she needed training, but he cast her in Molnar's *The Swan* for the 1954 summer season at the Pocono Playhouse.

That spring, Stoki went to Europe alone, while Gloria stayed behind to study the play. When he returned, he took the boys to Lake George, while Gloria went to the Poconos for rehearsals. Her fellow actors found her less the pampered socialite than a highly disciplined worker. The same determination that kept her five-foot-seven frame down to 110 pounds, that had her walking fifty or sixty New York blocks at a clip for exercise applied well in rehearsals. Before she set foot on the practice stage for the first day, she had her lines and blocking down. She was terribly nervous opening night and had difficulty controlling the stammer she had suffered during anxious moments since childhood. The reviewers were gentle, acknowledging her weakness in the love scenes, yet praising her poise and enunciation.

Jealous and hurt, Stoki never appeared in the audience. When she could, Gloria drove home to Connecticut to be with the boys. When the Pocono show was over, she finished the summer with a run at the Falmouth Playhouse on the Cape. Her husband ignored these performances as well. Gloria was absorbed by the theater, by the camaraderie of those creating the show, by the way playing a role seemed to inform on an unknown part of herself. Although she loved Stoki, she realized "in the doing I merged with him, became him," yet what she had believed in, that this act would signify love, was untrue. She could no longer depend upon others to bring her the answers, no "White Knight to rescue me—I would rescue myself."[32]

Gathering her resources for her intended independence from Stoki, she acquired an agent, small television acting jobs, and a new boyfriend, Frank Sinatra. On December 30, 1954, she announced to the press that she had left Stokowski and moved with the boys to the Ambassador Hotel. Friends were quick to support her. "It must have been like living with Mount Everest," said one. "For a girl as warm, vital, and vulnerable as Gloria, it was a life too rigid, austere and secluded," commented another.[33] Stoki stayed close by to see the boys as much as he could. When he saw reporters out in the snow outside the Gracie Square home, he ingratiated them by inviting them in and serving them tea in fragile porcelain cups.

By the time Gloria announced the separation, Sinatra was out of the picture. She had never seen him as any more than a bridge, a sign that she was still attractive and desirable. Not one to be tied down, Sinatra must have found the arrangement congenial as well. Contrary to his sometimes rough reputation, he could be thoughtful, kind, and gentle toward the objects of his affections, thus was a good choice for her purpose. It was a further sign of her maturity that she could distinguish that a flirtation need not mean a long-term commitment.

Alone now, she could rearrange her social life to her purposes. When married to Stoki, she shared the same split Gertrude had experienced: a requirement that she play the social matron at formal, sit-down dinners, while preferring and seeking out rare informal, playful evenings with friends from the art world. As Gertrude had done, she used her studio for the latter events, which Stoki avoided. By now she had friends throughout the arts, including actresses Judith Anderson and Joan Blondell, painter Rufino Tamayo, writers Budd Schulberg and Truman Capote, composers Jule Styne and Harold Arlen. Pink, a favorite fifties color, dominated the walls, candles, and invitations. Although she was hard to know, mercurial, withholding, her friends also found her exceptionally thoughtful and warm. She was that rare confidante who knew just how and when to surprise someone, how to lift them out of a depression or hurt.

One of the plays was a particular delight for Gloria. In 1955 the New York City Center wished to produce a revival of *The Time of Your Life* and consulted with Bill Saroyan, who had through his authorial rights some control over casting. Although he and Carol were on the verge of their second divorce, he saw that she was hired to play Mary L., the role Celeste Holm had originated on Broadway, while Gloria was given Elsie Mandelspiegel. Cheered to be in New York near her oldest friends, Carol decided to resettle there permanently. Following this run, Carol was made understudy to Jayne Mansfield in *Will Success Spoil Rock Hunter?* Since leaving Saroyan, Carol had been having an off-and-on affair with English critic Kenneth Tynan. At one rehearsal, she met a struggling young married actor, Walter Matthau, and entered into an off-and-on affair that would eventually result in a highly successful marriage, one of which Gloria disapproved.

At this point, however, Gloria enjoyed the return of Carol, and the two took up some of their old practical joking. A particular target was Billy Rose, who lived across the street from Carol's apartment. The two women took to spying on him. One night Gloria cooked up a plan where they dressed up in old raincoats, appeared at his door, and said they were collecting money for Czechoslovakian refugees. The short but gruff Rose boomed back that he was a very busy man and didn't ever want them to ring his bell again. Gloria whipped off her coat to reveal the dress underneath and yelled out her identity. Rose took the women inside, where Carol noticed Gloria's fascination with the original Renoir he had hanging in the living room.

Gloria showed more stage presence during *The Time of Your Life*, and she was soon cast in William Inge's *Picnic*. The director was a vibrant man her own age, Sidney Lumet. She was just his type, a thin, gorgeous, talented brunette.

Cupid Strikes Again, and Brings a Director

At the time Gloria met Lumet, he was coming out of a marriage to actress Rita Gam. At first it is hard to imagine the attraction between a member of one of the country's notable families and the son of Polish Jewish immigrants. Upbringing proved less important than temperament.

Lumet's parents had been actors in Yiddish theater, which had twelve companies working nearly year-round in New York during the twenties. At age four he made his own acting debut in a production with his father, who also cast him in some radio productions. Throughout his childhood he performed in Yiddish on a weekly radio show, *The Rabbi from Brownsville*, alongside his mother, the leading lady, his father, the leading man and writer. The $35 a week earned by all three saw the family well-fed through the worst days of the depression. With Yiddish theater dying out, the family then successfully made the transition to the Broadway stage. By adolescence Sidney had acted alongside Lotte Lenya, played the role of a young Jesus in two productions, and performed in Bill Saroyan's first drama, *My Heart's in the Highlands*.

Sidney's talent was evident, but his small stature hampered his getting certain roles. In describing him, acquaintances inevitably referred to his size: tiny, short, small, elfin, a leprechaun. He saw new possibilities in 1939, when two plays in which he was performing were also filmed. He hated acting in front of the camera: "The third eye. It's going to see something you don't want known."[34] The war interrupted his dramatic career, and because of bad eyesight he spent his service repairing radar devices. When it was over, he realized "that if I stayed in acting the best I could hope for was getting the part of the little Jewish kid from Brooklyn who got shot down by the mean Japs or Nazis, and then Clark Gable would pick me up and then tears in his eyes would rush forward and single-handedly wipe out their machine gun nest. That was an area of drama that didn't particularly interest me."

In reaction to the philosophy of the trendy Actors Studio, in 1947 he founded one of the first off-Broadway acting groups. Realizing he had a large collection of actors and no one to direct, he took over the job. During the fifties, he directed several hundred live dramatic presentations at CBS television during that medium's golden age. At the time he met Gloria, he was also directing off-Broadway.

Lumet was taken by Gloria's devotion to the theater, her quick mind and technical understanding. She was attracted to this vital, articulate personality who would go on to create the most telling and perceptive modern movies depicting the grittier features of life in New York City. They shared a commitment to hard work based on careful research and planning, as well as an impassioned curiosity about the world about them. Although they fell in love, she did not obtain her divorce, this time in Mexico, until October of 1955, and they did not marry until August 28, 1956.

Friends noted a change in Gloria's demeanor during her marriage to Lumet. She had typically been shy, placid, withdrawn, gently floating on the surface of life. Where strangers took her to be aloof, an "iceberg," intimates understood she was in fact constantly monitoring herself so that no expression of feeling or hostility come out. She was watchful and cautious among others and would disclose her deeper thoughts through oblique phrases and indirection. Exposed to the more expressive and open Lumet, she became more relaxed in social situations, more ready to trust.

Unlike Stokowski, Lumet respected Gloria's drive and concentration and did not complain when she went off to the studio to paint for ten hours or work alone on a play. Several years into the marriage he proudly explained, "I honestly think that Gloria's got more guts than anybody I've ever known because, don't you see, it would have been so easy for her to just throw up her hands and walk out on the whole damn struggle of making it in the theatre."[35] He also suggested that her lyric, delicate quality would make her "a magnificent Ophelia."

Her devotion included a determination to earn her reputation on her efforts rather than her name. Consequently, for a time she hired a press agent whose job was to keep her name out of papers. Thus she refused interviews when on the road with a show, a rejection that did not bring her favor with regional drama reviewers who had expected her cooperation in a special feature article. Her eschewing publicity may also have been encouraged by Sidney, who obsessively refused to appear on television talk shows or give interviews to the press. Where some of his fellow directors in television moved to Hollywood, he determined to stay in New York and began to shoot movies on location there.

Incapable of frivolous leisure, Gloria put herself through a tough daily schedule, including workouts in a gym, classes at Sanford Meisner's Neighborhood Playhouse, and constant reading of classical drama on her own. Some fellow actors wished she had a bit less determination and a bit more friendliness. She appeared in such diverse productions as *Peter Pan,* Molnar's *Olympia,* and live television plays on such shows as "Studio One" and "Kraft Television Theatre."

When she was good, she was "luminous," a favorite word critics applied to her. As with the reviews of Gertrude Whitney's artwork, it is hard to find comments that are not colored by the commentator's knowledge of Gloria's wealth and history. No matter how she performed, she was a novelty evaluated apart from her peers, either given kid-glove treatment or taken not quite seriously. Her agent complained that producers were not giving Gloria a fair shot at roles because they believed she was not serious about her work.

Despite Gloria's efforts, she may not have been fully satisfied. Some years later, in writing about collage, she observed, "It's not like getting up on a stage and performing. You're in control, and if it's not successful the first time, you simply keep experimenting until you're ready to let your friends and family see it."[36] Despite her imaginative bent, she had difficulties giving up control, and that pulling back from the edge may account for her mercurial behavior. Just as she acquired the level of craft in a particular art, be it painting, writing, or acting, where it was necessary to let go of some control, she would brake. She apparently could not often tolerate the accidents and disorder necessary to produce illuminating surprise. And nowhere are these necessary accidents more unsettling to the insecure artist than on the stage in front of an audience.

Gloria's Mother
Strikes Back

Gloria's sons were now old enough to go to private school in New York. True to her theory that each child's individualism should be nurtured, she sent Stan to the Rudolf Steiner School, with its unconventional theory of education. He was complex and commanding, more like his father, she acknowledged, whereas Chris was more like her. The boys had come into their own inheritance in February 1956, when Mrs. Morgan died and her will named Stan and Chris as main beneficiaries of her residuary estate. Daughter Thelma received $45,000 and Gloria M., her jewels, furs, and $80,000 with "my thanks for the time that I lived with her." Her granddaughter received $100,000 in appreciation for the gifts she had made since turning twenty-one, an amount larger than Gloria had given to her grandmother over the ten years since receiving her inheritance.

Gloria M. and Thelma were clearly unhappy with the bequest, for they set out to write a joint autobiography, *Double Exposure*. Written with the assistance of numerous ghostwriters, its appearance in 1958, and its accompanying publicity, prevented any possible reconciliation between mother and daughter. Much of the book repeated the theme of *Without Prejudice*, blaming their mother for much of the troubles of their early years but adding an attack on Gloria for the woes of their later years. The resentment oozes off the pages:

Of the visitation periods: "And she was also bound, whether she liked it or not, *whether I liked it or not,* and whether Mrs. Whitney liked it or not, to spend weekends with me—those famous, horrible weekends—and the month of July."[37]

Of Gloria's stay in Kansas: "I suspect that Gloria only enjoyed play-acting the simple life; as a novelty it was fun. Marie Antoinette for a single afternoon enjoyed the role of a milkmaid."[38]

On why she never remarried: "What man who called himself a man would accept a life of court-supervised weekends—and the month of July—when I was legally bound to be a combination of real mother, proxy, mother, nursemaid, and companion."[39]

On seeing a television clip about Gloria's marriage to Lumet: "I couldn't help but think back to that memorable time when Gloria, then about to marry Stokowski, expressed a desire not to have me go with her to Reno, saying, 'Please, Mummy darling, think of the publicity.'"[40]

The longest episode described concerns a time when Gloria M. was hospitalized in the early 1950s. According to the twins, when Gloria finally showed up at the hospital, she was primarily concerned with what clothes to take to Europe. The tale recalls the time when the child Gloria, very ill with tonsillitis, was ignored by her mother, who went shopping for hats and planned to leave for Europe. If the story is true, perhaps Gloria was finally getting her revenge on her mother for that abandonment.

The twins' extraordinary obliviousness to their own behavior and the harm they had brought upon others remained. Locked in a vision of victimization they could not give up, they clung to one another, Thelma substituting for Gloria M.'s useless eyes as they went from one city to another to hawk the book. Yet they had managed to remain survivors, and they conveyed a sense of courage and nobility to interviewers unaware of how difficult their lives had become in recent years.

17

1959-1990

Another Vanderbilt Custody
Trial Ensues

It was the Stokowski sons who became the focus of yet another Vanderbilt custody trial, this one in 1959. It seems that in old age Stokowski had wanted his sons to fulfill the role Gloria once played and apart from his music talked only of them. Since her departure from his life, his loneliness and isolation had been exacerbated upon his becoming the conductor of the Houston Symphony. He hoped to buy a ranch in Texas where the boys could play and enjoy the outdoor life. He ended up living in a residential hotel. Worse, in 1955 he had lost the wise and supportive guidance of his manager, whom he fired because a photographer had taken his picture during a rehearsal.

Were it not for two women, he may well have gone into a suicidal despondency. His visiting angels were Natalie Bender and Faye Chabrow, who had been high school groupies during his tenure at the Philadelphia Orchestra. So enamored were young women then of Stokowski that they would compose witty songs of praise during the long hours in the standing-room ticket line, and after performances they would stand in the parking lot next to his house and serenade him. Always a great supporter of youth, he entertained the girls and encouraged their various musical careers. In admiration, his two greatest fans renamed themselves Natasha and Feodora. Natasha went on to become a composer, organist, and administrative assistant on various of Stokowski's youth projects. Upon his marrying Gloria, they had departed from his life (whether at his doing or hers is unclear), and they had returned just as swiftly upon her departure, finding him a new apartment in New York, decorating it, and visiting daily to tend to his needs.

Yet even Natasha and Feodora could not satisfy Stoki's longing for family life. Taking advantage of the liberal visitation agreement, he had the boys dine at his house alternate nights, while he joined them and their governess in the penthouse at 10 Gracie Square, which remained Gloria's property, on the other nights. Gloria accepted his demands and his somewhat meticulous childrearing ideas until he asked to have them for longer periods as well to be able to take them to Europe with him. When she balked, on May 13, 1959, while out walking, a process server placed in her hands a show-cause order as to why visitation rights should not be revised. When she tried to contact Stoki, she learned he had left for a European tour.

In an eerie repeat of the 1934 custody hearing, Stokowski's statement to the court accused Gloria of keeping strange hours, of partying too much, and of not spending enough time with the boys. Gloria was furious, and she used the papers to garner sympathy for her case. Consequently, for several days she allowed parts of her affadavit leaked to the press, noting she would fight all the way to prevent the tyrannical, despotic power he exerted while they were married to continue to assert itself. Through these releases she criticized his "overanxious, harassing and harassed great-grandmother" behavior that created "neurotic explosions over minutiae."[1] (In fact, visitors were surprised he would make the boys take afternoon naps in separate rooms while he did the same. But Gloria did not understand that some of his protectiveness was a result of the Lindbergh kidnapping, for his daughters had been threatened by an extortionist during that time.) She noted his refusal to let the boys fly, and she pointed out the comparative safety of planes compared to trains or an automobile driven by a "driver of 85." (He was, in fact, 87.)

Further, the presence of Natasha and Feodora unleashed a fury that was likely a suppressed anger toward her mother and Nada Milford-Haven or Ketti Keven. Without identifying the women by name, she hinted at lesbianism as making them unsuitable companions for their boys. "It would be hard to imagine two women less qualified to provide a proper influence over the children," she argued in her statement for the court in the euphemistic style of the day.[2]

Although the hearings were closed, the arguments on both sides quickly leaked out to become public knowledge as each fed information to the press. In the end Stokowski found his visitation rights curtailed instead of increased. Gloria won full custody, with Stokowski getting annual four-week holidays and a split of school vacations and weekends. But the judge saved his real thoughts for a closing commentary, noting how sad it was that a month of court time had been devoted to the resolution of a problem that mature and intelligent adults should have been able to work out for the sake of their children. Neither Gloria nor Stoki was present in the courtroom to hear this indictment of their behavior.

Her assertiveness during the custody dispute undermined Stokowski's self-confidence even further. Consequently, he took pains to keep himself out of the public spotlight even more, for fear of further alienating Gloria. Thus, when he fell while playing football with his sons and broke his hip, he insisted he be hospitalized under a false name so Gloria would not find out.

Despite the dramatic and destructive courtroom conflict, Gloria soon backtracked and allowed Stoki to take the boys overseas for some of his tours. Consequently, their relationship with their father was not cut back severely, and as teenagers they were able to appreciate the travel adventures, made more memorable by Stoki's talent for creating a daily life of style and good taste.

Despite her dramatic endeavors, Gloria was a less visible figure during her marriage to Lumet. The stage and television roles were fewer, and she returned to painting. She became a fashion personality, noted for her ability to mix *haute couture* with dimestore accessories. In 1961 she allowed *Vogue* to follow her through a day at the House of Revlon, where she posed in curlers, getting a pedicure, and being made up. Although this and a *Vogue* article the next year mentioned she was preparing for a role in a new Lumet-directed movie based on F. Scott Fitzgerald's *Rich Boy,* the project never materialized. She also spoke of writing a play, which never appeared. The marriage was in trouble.

At Last Prince
Charming Arrives

Gloria Vanderbilt has yet to publish the third installment of her autobiographies, which would begin with her marriage to Lumet, so her perspective on the relationship is not available. A very private person, Lumet has predictably kept silent. In the many articles on Gloria since then, the only remark concerning this marriage is from a close onlooker, who states that their ambitions clashed. Truman Capote, who had come to dislike Gloria in later years and was known for his cruel gossip, said she had expected Lumet to make her a star and was upset when he failed to do so. Breakups can seldom be reduced to such simple formulae. Curiously, when Gloria published "A Few Biographical Facts," a detailed chronology of important events in her life as an appendix to *Woman to Woman* in 1979, she omitted any mention of this marriage (or of that to Pat di Cicco).

One evening in 1962, Sidney Lumet confessed the break to a sympathetic Carol Matthau. She had not spoken with her girlhood friend ever since an incident that occurred one afternoon at the Lumets. Carol's husband Walter Matthau, in a state of distracted boredom, perched on a glass table and broke it, gashing his leg. When they returned from the emergency room, Gloria's too-gushing show of sympathy made Carol angry. Carol was beginning to feel that Gloria gave parties "not to see her friends, so much as to allow her friends to see *her.*"[3] She was tired of Gloria's perfection—everything about her being so beautiful, including Gloria, who despite it all remained very sweet. Carol lent the distraught Lumet the keys to her New York apartment so he could use it temporarily. What she didn't know was that he then left them in a drawer in their original envelope, aware that Gloria would one day come across them, and recognize Carol's distinctive handwriting. Gloria would see how her best friend had shifted her loyalty.

Lumet was not disconsolate for long. That summer at a house in East Hampton he was beguiled by another willowy beauty, Gail Jones, daughter of singer Lena Horne. Gail was a recent Radcliffe graduate and liberal activist working at *Life* magazine, where she clipped wire presses and delivered them to the appropriate editors. Lumet was her idea of "the perfect older man."[4]

In August of 1963, the Vanderbilt-Lumet marriage was dissolved. A week later he denied to a reporter that his overdose of sleeping pills with alcohol had been on purpose. It was merely "idiocy," he remarked, and he was likely right.[5] He was pleased with his current movie project, *The Pawnbroker,* and planned to marry Gail Jones.

Gloria was not alone either. Truman Capote knew all about her latest affair because she had visited him in Corsica. Writing friends, he spread the gossip: "There *is* a new man in her life. It's supposed to be a great secret, but I will tell you because I must just tell somebody, it's so fantastic: Nelson Rockefeller. Heaven knows what will come of it—it would certainly be a strange thing if they married."[6] In fact, Gloria had told her real lover to be discreet in the letters he sent to her, while she misled the loose-tongued writer, for she knew her nosy host would find one way or another of reading her mail.

Gloria wanted to share her news with Carol, to strike a reconciliation, but she needed a reason to reinitiate contact. It came when Carol and Walter chose not to attend the Lumet-Jones wedding because President Kennedy had just been shot. Gloria misread Carol's behavior, thinking that the Matthaus had not attended the wedding out of loyalty to her. When Carol received an endearing, though misplaced thank-you note from Gloria, she rushed to her apartment to chat. Confessing their individual hurts and grievances, as the day ended, they quickly forgave one another and fell into their girlish chatter. Gloria boastfully described the new man, a handsome, debonair, nattily-dressed bachelor named Wyatt Cooper. In the course of her description, she mentioned that Wyatt knew Carol's mother Rosheen. A month later, when Rosheen called her daughter from Rome, where she was staying, Carol happened to mention Gloria's engagement. Following a telling and uncharacteristic silence, Rosheen remarked, "Yes, I know Wyatt Cooper, and all I can tell you is that Gloria is going to be a very happy woman."[7]

Wyatt was very different from the men Gloria had been attracted to in the past. He was three years younger than she, a onetime actor turned writer and magazine editor. He had been born into a large farm family in Quitman, Mississippi, and venerated the values he had learned in that rural community, seemingly old-fashioned virtues such as honesty, loyalty, dignity, and moral integrity. Atypically for a southern boy, he went to college in California, to Berkeley and UCLA, where he became a liberal in both the broad and narrow sense. He was that rare student who left college having understood the mission of a liberal arts education, that literature, philosophy, history, and other studies are to guide one's way to finding a noble purpose in life. He read extensively, questioned, and struggled for his own personal meaning of life. Politically, he became a strong supporter of civil and human rights, and he predicted that the kind of tolerance for eccentricities present within southern families would one day transfer to racial problems, that southern whites had within them the potential to accept blacks as part of the human family.

Wyatt's own family was rich with a history of eccentricity. There was the aunt who painted angels on the ceiling above her bed, the face on each her own; Uncle Jesse, the senile and deaf civil war veteran; a "fallen woman," Myrtle, whose fate was not considered polite conversation; egomaniacal Uncle Woodrow, whose face was scarred from numerous car crashes; fat, tobacco-spitting "Tiny" who would briefly break out of his indolence to sing in a lilting tenor. When Wyatt read Homer, Shakespeare, or Tolstoy, he had no difficulty locating their heroines, heroes, and villains among his various relatives. With family ties so important, he took Gloria to Mississippi to meet her future in-laws. He had already told her about the relative who had shot her mother and sawed the body into sections, distributing them so well that only a pair of thighs were ever found, and the cousin murdered by his wife, who was not prosecuted because the two small children would be left parentless. Gloria thought these were amusing tales, the typical exaggerations of writers. Then she met his brother-in-law, the town marshal, who proceeded to describe the latest death in the family, in which the wife died during a struggle over a gun and the husband was left with two bullets in his head.

Wyatt gave Gloria no reason to think such violence was part of his makeup. Despite his nostalgia for the family life of his childhood, he did not cling to its rigid sex roles, and he appreciated how changes during the sixties supported men who found fault with aggressive masculinity. He was excessively modest, believing humility in a person to be more desirable than perfection, and shamelessly emotional, feeling free to cry while listening to a piece of Brahms. An adept conversationalist, he was a prominent member of the social scene, attending premieres, opera debuts, society parties, and fashion shows. Yet he had little patience with the small talk at such events, and he searched out partners of substance. He was taken by Gloria's creative expression and would refer to her as "the artist Gloria Vanderbilt." Overall, he was a man secure in himself who had no special claims on Gloria, no need to dominate her or demand her adoration.

On Christmas eve of 1963, with cousin Gerta as witness, Gloria married Wyatt in a Virginia lawyer's office in a quiet civil ceremony. Rosheen Marcus's prediction proved true. If ever there was a Prince Charming for someone with the sentimentally romantic tastes of Gloria Vanderbilt, it was Wyatt Cooper. Despite her age, she was enthusiastic about providing him the children he had always wanted, and she gave birth to Carter Vanderbilt Cooper in January 1965. She was thus much ahead of her time in consciously having a child at an age when it was considered unnatural, even dangerous.

They continued to keep the Greenwich, Connecticut, home, Faraway, Gloria had shared with Lumet, except now it took on a new vitality. The onetime gate house, romantic in association with its stone Norman tower, sat on sixteen acres along the shallows of the Mianus River. Swans and peacocks, lilacs, roses, lilies-of-the-valley, and ferns perfected the romantic aura. Bricks curving around an ancient apple tree formed a dining patio. Inside she arranged the casual yet studied interior design look she would soon make famous: ginghams, wicker, collections of shells, old family photographs mixed with contemporary ones. A cottage held the child's bedroom and guest rooms, while her studio sat on the highest point of the land. With sheepdog to finish the portrait, her life was finally settled into the familial bliss the vision of which she had carried about in her mind for so many years.[8]

Making the home so perfect was not an illusion; for once history and mate matched her nature. It was the time of women's liberation, an imprimatur for separate identity in a career, and Wyatt Cooper totally supported that philosophy. She also found the perfect metier for her artistic and dramatic expression: business. Cooper took no embarrassment in being a journeyman writer, one who applied his craft in the popular culture of movies and magazines. Although he worked at a novel now and then, he understood his gift was not for serious literature. (The closest he got to that was cowriting a television play with friend Truman Capote, whom he met through Gloria.) Once Gloria made the similar analogy, that she need not compete in the realm of fine art or the legitimate stage, she was able to forge years of discipline and preparation into a career as a formidable decorator of people and homes for the middle class.

In moving into fashion and interior design, Gloria was asserting her final independence from Gertrude Whitney, who would have considered appearances in *Vogue* and *House and Garden* publicity seeking, a terrible fault. In analyzing these activities, so belittled compared to serious art, Gloria argued for their importance in women's lives in establishing personal identity. "Men are provided with certain masks for their roles and they can live contentedly within them. Women are more tortured by conflicting demands."[9] Fashion and interior design provide women a means for discovering and communicating the fantasies that are clues to their individual identity, she explained. She realized how in her own youth, having been given "no opportunity to find out about myself through the supportive base that a rounded family relationship can provide," she made contact with her private side through dress. As she changed the style of her clothes and the rooms about her, she could reflect on her own maturity and growing insight, and she encouraged middle-class women to do the same.

Wyatt Cooper was a great believer in family sanctity, and it was possibly his urging that led to a reconciliation between Gloria and her mother. After that meeting, Wyatt remarked that her mother and Thelma never really understood one thing that had happened to them. Now more emotionally mature than her mother, Gloria saw that he was right and was able to forgive her parent's inadequacies. She found her mother "touching and vulnerable and not at all the ephemeral being who floated on the periphery of my childhood."[10] Gloria Morgan

Vanderbilt died soon after of cancer in 1965 at age 60, after which Gloria made a shrine of a picture of the two of them taken in the 1920s.

Consuelo had died of a stroke the year before, in 1964. In her final years, taxes had forced her to sell off Casa Alva in Palm Beach and move from her large Southampton home to a smaller one. Accordingly, precious antiques and works of art disappeared from the rooms, sent quietly to the auction houses to pay the bills. There were stories of servants taking advantage of her. A granddaughter, Sarah, was so fond of her that she spent much time keeping her grandmother company and watching out for her interests. When the end came, Sarah accompanied the body to its final resting place, which was neither with Jacques in France nor with her mother in America. Instead, at her request the coffin was placed in the cemetery at Bladon, in the Marlborough family plot next to Ivor, the son from whom she had been estranged. The body of the first husband she so came to disdain was a convenient distance away, in the family chapel. Once one of the wealthiest women in the world, less than a million dollars remained of Consuelo's fortune.

The Gloria Vanderbilt
Industry Takes Off

I n 1966, Gloria took up the first decorative expression that would become shaped into marketable products: collage. It began accidentally, shortly after a solo show of her characteristically romantic acrylic paintings at the Hammer Galleries in New York. Dawdling in her studio, she picked up a lace placemat and suddenly saw how she could cut it out to form the headdress of a portrait of an Alsatian girl she had been sketching. Suddenly her mind was crowded with visions of assemblages from everyday materials. She was attracted to the notion she could incorporate not only the trivial, but unique loved objects into a composition. Consequently, many of her creations were intensely personal, based on items her sons brought to her or family photographs. Her early works were meant as gifts for those around her, not as art for display and sale.

At the same time she took an interest in quilts and the use of multiple patterns in decorating a room. The relation was not accidental. Patchwork and collages both reflected "that intricate, amazing process called 'memory,'" a more intuitive reflection of the past than a simple photograph album or diary. They also revealed her need for creating order out of disorder, for controlling even the seemingly most unrelated objects.

One of the inspirations for her interior design concept was Juliana Force. Gloria recalled the childhood pleasure of entering the apartment above the Whitney Museum to walk upon Juliana's "primrose path," created by laying cloth flowers on the floor and shellacking over them for protection. Actually, Juliana's decorator, Bruce Butfield, had invented the idea of lacquering fabrics to the floor as decoration, and Gloria not only followed that practice, but attached fabrics to practically every surface of a room and its furniture.

Juliana more directly inspired Gloria's eclecticism. Juliana had been fearless about combining patterns, textures, and seemingly incongenial decorative objects into an original statement, one proclaiming a determined individuality of intelligence and curiosity. Her suite of rooms on the top two floors of the Whitney, which Gloria had visited as a child, placed unmatched chairs and loveseats covered in satins, brocades, velvet, and fringes partnered by tables of various heights and period, all set upon richly patterned, dramatic carpets. Swags, American eagles, gilded sconces, crystal candelabra, tiny sculptures, needlepoint pillows, folk objects, and modern paintings all competed for one's attention. Though Gloria was not as fearless or eccentric as Juliana had been, she nonetheless took more chances than her peers.[11] Reporters familiar with photo spreads of her rooms expected to be overwhelmed by the busyness when they actually got to see them; instead, they found the actual effect more one of playfulness, curiosity, and intrigue.

For the next several years Gloria continued to paint, construct collages, and try her decorating ideas on a new country home, this one in Southampton, Long Island. (Faraway was sold, a move she later regretted.) The media featured her now impeccable and fastidious fashion taste. The *New York Times* preview of her Hammer Galleries show was covered by style editors, who noted the appearance of designer Pauline Trigere's cape and Gloria's Mainbocher sheath, as well as by art critic John Canaday, who remarked on her "interior decorator's sense of color. . . , but beyond that her confections [were pointless]."[12] Adolfo announced his 1968 collection as having been inspired by Gloria's use of rich fabrics in her harem pants and jumpers. *Vogue* featured her collection of rare Fortuny dresses, which, as Gloria explained turned women "into something more than woman . . . a flower . . . an urn . . . a statue."[13] In 1969 both she and Wyatt were placed on the International Best Dressed List, dressing up being a controlled expression of their dramatic impulses.

Despite this public persona of glamour, she and Wyatt tried to lead a quiet life, although this was not fully possible given their mutual enjoyment of social events. She gave birth to her fourth child, Anderson, in June of 1967 at the age of forty-three. Wyatt was an exceptional stepfather, and his devotion to parenting was a forceful influence upon Gloria. As her son Stan later observed, "He [Wyatt] had a great influence on my mother; she was different before. She didn't spend as much time with me and my brother Chris. We were with governesses a lot. Carter and Anderson grew up differently."[14] Her affection for and closeness to her husband and sons was reflected in both public and family photographs, as well as in her collages and decorating, which often incorporated memoirs of family life, such as a child's drawing.

Starting with 1969, Gloria's business career had grown more earnest. As a result of an appearance with some of her collages on the Johnny Carson Show that year, Hallmark Cards commissioned her for a designs of calendars, cards, puzzles, memorandum pads, and address books, as well as collage kits. There soon followed contracts with other companies for designs of sheets, yard goods, glassware, scarves, wallpaper, and table linen. Her use of commonplace fabrics, such as gingham, was immediately popular with women of average income: Gloria Vanderbilt was saying chic could be affordable.

She also put together an instruction book, *Gloria Vanderbilt's Book of Collage,* which revealed the streak of discipline and perfectionism in her work. Photographs of her at work, nails short and unpainted, in simple cotton jumpsuit recall those of Gertrude in her sculpture studio. Throughout, her tone is one of optimism and enthusiasm. Everyone has imagination, she assures, and the timid can simply experiment secretly until they are ready to show their projects to their friends and family. And she may have been talking to herself when she concluded the book, "Don't worry about whether or not you are an artist. It's for you to do what you must do; leave it to others to decide whether it's art or not. . . . You will find great satisfaction in trying to set down the truth of your reactions to that which you consider beautiful."[15]

It was Wyatt who urged her to use her own name with her keynote signature on her creations, so by the mid-1970s she was headlined once more as "Gloria Vanderbilt," not "Mrs. Wyatt Cooper." Wyatt's pride could be seen in his Foreword to her collage book. There he praised her "tremendous appetite for life, her quick response of delicate sensibility, her instinctive grasp of whatever is new or vital, her immense curiosity about all things, . . . her willingness to face experience, her openness to change, and her restless quest for perfection." He also compared her to Snow White, Earth Mother, American Beauty Rose, Wicked Queen, a unicorn, an Egyptian temple cat, and more. At work, he explained, she used such concentration that he had to go to the studio to remind her to eat or to come home, a service he implied he was clearly delighted to provide.

Gloria's early business contracts were no mere selling of a name. Every morning she was up early to see the boys off, then take the elevator to the top of their apartment in United Nations Plaza, where she had a design studio. As the products developed, she traveled around the country on behalf of manufacturers to place the lines in stores. It was here her natural poise and years of dramatic training paid off and made her a convincing salesperson. Having traveled so much in her childhood, she found hotel rooms and the temporary life oddly satisfying. (Also, she did not travel alone. Her longtime personal assistant, Nora Marley, would arrive on an earlier plane and prepare the hotel suite with scented candles, Porthault sheets, and family photographs.) As word of her marketing effectiveness spread through the business community, china, flatware, stemware, eyeglasses and scarves now added to the list of Gloria Vanderbilt Ltd. with its destinctive swan motif. Overall, the results were moderate success. The lines did not flop, nor did they take off.

In 1975, she was able to take special pride in Wyatt as well. He published his only book, *Families,* a thoughtful evocation of the significance of family ties in a society where some experts were claiming the institution to be outmoded and finished. It was in a way a love letter to both his southern family and the family he made with Gloria. He wrote proudly of his sons, how he fostered their admiration of her art, of the educational sightseeing trips he took all over the country with Gloria and the boys.

Gloria was taken aback in November of that year, when a story by Truman Capote appeared in *Esquire* magazine. Called "La Cote Basque" after the restaurant of that name, its lead character, Lady Ina Coolbridge, modeled after socialite Slim Keith, recounts salacious gossip about characters those in the know quickly recognized to include such notables as Bill Paley, the head of CBS, and his popular wife Babe. Truman was furious at Paley for cheating over the years on gorgeous Babe, and he described an adultery scene wherein a WASP governor's wife bedded a man modeled on Paley, who was Jewish, while she was having her period as a way of insulting him. Babe was dying of lung cancer when the story appeared, and to Truman's naive surprise she stood by her husband. Another character in the story was Ann Woodward, who had killed her husband, was spared punishment when his family protected her afterward (the story later retold by Dominick Dunne as *The Two Mrs. Grenvilles*). Hearing that Truman was reviving the tale again after so many years, Woodward took a fatal dose of Seconal. Although confidantes had warned Truman not to publish the work, he scoffed at them, saying those involved would be too stupid to recognize themselves.

In one section of the story, Carol Marcus and Gloria, identified by their real names, are overheard recounting their various marriages. At one point, Pat di Cicco comes over to say hello, and it is only after he leaves that Gloria realizes the strange man had been her first husband. Apparently this actually happened once in a restaurant. After reading the story, Gloria vowed to spit at Truman if she came across him. As Wyatt explained, "After all, they've known each other a long time. It's not that a secret has been betrayed, it's that a kind of trust has been betrayed."[16]

Quickly putting Capote behind her, Gloria moved on to yet a new venture, which would be her most noted failure. In May of 1976 she debuted her line on Seventh Avenue. For this endeavor she signed on as an associate designer Jesper Nyeboe, previously an assistant to Geoffrey Beene. At this hopeful occasion, Wyatt fretted that the models weren't showing off the versatility of the clothes, while Chris in white suit and Stan in blue jeans offered moral support. Gerta, herself an artist, stood by and diplomatically avoided making personal remarks about her famous cousin, whose privacy she guarded fiercely. Although the review was favorable, one editor noted a distinctive signature silhouette was missing, nothing akin to the Diane Von Furstenburg wrap dress popular then.

A year later a small announcement was sent out that the business had been sold to Schrader Corporation because Gloria had been on the road too much to handle the daily needs of the firm. Her business agent said the goods had not been delivered to her standard of quality. But assistant Nyeboe had a different story. He said he was "taken aback by her extremely commercial attitude, even 'at the expense of the details and refinement she believed in."[17] In other words, Gloria had learned about the bottom line.

She soon made up for the loss by signing up with Murjani in 1977 to market jeans. Murjani had come up with the perfect fabric and fit to produce a jean for normal American women whose hips were too broad to fit comfortably into the ultra-slim cuts of other manufacturers. The company knew it had developed a winning product and wanted a celebrity salesperson. Of about twenty names, including Lee Radizwill and Charlotte Ford, they chose Gloria, partly for her artistic experience. Although it cost $2 to place her swan logo on the front coin pocket and stitch her signature on the back of the jeans, they went ahead in hopes of following the success of the Lacoste alligator logo. While Gloria played no role in the design of the jeans, she was consulted for later color and style variations.

The resulting marketing campaign became a case study of extraordinary success. Gloria posed with her rear end to the camera, in throaty Long Island upperclass voice informed the viewer that these jeans "really hug your derriere." Even though Gloria was pencil thin, every woman knew the real message, that the pants would fit their fuller figure. The combination of television spots, print advertising, and Gloria's personal appearances in stores thrust Murjani into the major competition, with only Calvin Klein and Levi's beating them in sales. During department store appearances, career women, housewives, and teenagers crowded around to seek her advice on makeup, decorating, and fashion. Even though she was obviously not one of them, and peppered her speech with private school exclamations—"Kind of divine!" and "Sort of marvelous!"—she made them feel part of her life for a few minutes. An events coordinator for Macys who had to work with her found she was very natural and friendly, with no celebrity pretenses.

Mourning Brings
Renewal

In September of 1977, Gloria said goodbye to her two oldest boys before they flew off to London for their father's funeral. Stokowski had moved to England five years earlier, to settle in Hampshire. His faithful fan Natasha accompanied him there and continued to look after his daily needs. Although he seldom conducted in public, he continued to produce recordings, and he impressed engineers with his ear and technical knowledge of the process. With few exceptions he had been vigorous until that day on September 13 when he went to take a nap and quietly died. His will gave equal shares to his five children, with a special bequest for the faithful Natasha. The Curtis Institute of Philadelphia received his library and scores. Yet, most fitting for this man who created a mystery about his life, the ship container filled with his correspondence, mementos, photographs, souvenirs, and other personal ephemera washed overboard in an Atlantic storm, taking many details of his intimate life with it.

Gloria's sorrow would be for her older sons, not herself. What she could not imagine is that in just a few short months she would be mourning the loss of her younger sons' father as well.

Wyatt's family line possessed a gene not only for eccentricity but also for heart failure. His youngest sister had died suddenly of a heart attack on her thirty-eighth birthday. The theme of death weaves throughout his *Families*. Its opening anecdote concerns son Carter asking, "When I get to be as old as you are now, will you be very old and getting ready to die?"[18] Wyatt is stunned by the realization, and by Carter's easy return to his toys after considering the question. "It's a strange way of doing it," the precocious three-year-old observes. After further rumination upon the fact that his children's "rise is my decline," Wyatt sees how critical his role is as a father for passing on to his sons "the piled-up wisdoms, instincts, skills, and acquisitions of customs."

But Wyatt would not live to the decline Carter foresaw. On January 5, 1978, he was rushed to the hospital with heart failure and immediately sent to surgery. Much in character, facing the likelihood of death, he apologized for leaving Gloria and the boys in such a spot. While in the waiting room, Gloria held the hand of a stranger, another woman in a similar position, and pressed her eyes closed to pretend it was years earlier, that she was a child on the beach. The doctor appeared in the early morning hours to tell her Wyatt had died. He was only 50.

Practiced in survival, Gloria used work to transform her grief (and later wondered how Oona, following Charlie's death, had become a permanent widow, shrouded and by choice isolated in her home, a kind of psychological suttee). By 1979, the Vanderbilt jeans surpassed even Calvin Klein's in sales, and surveys showed that seventy-four percent of New Yorkers were aware of the Murjani label. Women attending her appearances that year also brought a copy of her latest book, *Woman to Woman,* for personal inscription. Dedicated to Carol Marcus, it used the patchwork quilt as a model for its structure, incorporating autobiography and personal philosophy with practical advice on beauty, fashion, and interior decorating. (She even included household tips and recipes from her assistant, Nora Marley.) While some of the suggestions are out of touch with the realities of middle-class budgets, for the most part the book succeeds in appealing to average women through its unabashedly romantic attitude, its conviction that one can construct a world that combines both intimacy and independence. Its expression is the frank, commonsense speech of women's private conversations. Although she denied it was autobiography, more than in her later two memoirs she revealed regrets, mistakes, and perceived faults, such as her inability to express anger.

It also helped that since her marriage to Wyatt, Gloria found her previously tenuous connections with her Whitney relatives strengthened. Three women in the family had continued Gertrude's work in support of art, though with much less public fanfare. Flora Miller had served as president of the Whitney Museum Board of American Art until 1966. That year she cut the ribbon to the new building designed by Marcel Breuer on Madison Avenue and donated Aristide Maillot's *Jeune Fille Qui Marche dans L'eau* to an auction for the benefit of the new building. Flora's activity on behalf of the museum waned somewhat, however, following the death of her beloved husband Cully in 1972, although she never lost her commitment.

Flora's daughter, also named Flora, had married architect Michael Irving, who had assisted in the planning of the Madison Avenue building. In 1977, this Flora assumed presidency of the Whitney Museum, a position she would hold for eight years. Flora Irving was middle aged and had raised her family. To prepare for her new role, she went to college for a degree in art history. In need of a senior thesis topic, she happened one day to come across a trunk filled with her grandmother's diaries, letters, and manuscripts. Realizing she had the basis for a larger project, she asked novelist B. H. Friedman, who was also a museum trustee, to write a biography of Gertrude with her assistance. Published by Doubleday in 1978, it was dense with details and interpretation. Flora Irving did not act as a censor and the book candidly presented her grandmother's life with all its virtues and peccadilloes. Unfortunately, its structure, a yearly chronology written in the present tense, made it rather inaccessible to the reader expecting more narrative and drama. Consequently, although this was a time when books on "forgotten women" were popular, Gertrude remained forgotten to women's history.

Gloria did not often appear with the other family members at the various ceremonies and parties relating to Whitney functions. She did, however, show up for an event organized by her cousin Gerta. A very private person, Gerta was also a painter and designer, whose works were reproduced for interior design. She participated in some Whitney activities, and added to her daily schedule committee and board meetings for numerous other organizations, including the Musicians Emergency Fund, the Junior Council of the Museum of Modern Art, the Asia Society, the Citizen Exchange Corps with the Soviet Union, and the Morgan Library. Gerta's major interest, however, was in art education, perhaps because her parents had objected to her own desire to obtain one. Her favorite institution here was the Skohegan School of Painting and Sculpture, for which she organized its major annual fund-raiser, the Gertrude Vanderbilt Whitney Awards Dinner. Gloria retained her special devotion to Gerta and publicly supported her in this endeavor.

While Gloria did not often see her Whitney relatives, she valued their acceptance of her and for giving her "a sense of family and belonging."[19] Flora Miller held an annual Thanksgiving dinner, at which, Gloria later recalled, that family matriarch would appear like an Oriental ruler, dressed in colored silks, Chinese lacquer fingernails, pearl earrings, resplendent jewels. She would sit on a sofa near the fireplace in Gertrude's Westbury Studio, draw each family member over to hear the latest gossip, and receive homage from them.

These connections were even more important now that Wyatt was gone. She felt confidant of her ability to continue raising the two younger sons on her own. Other men quickly appeared to vie for her affections. Sidney Lumet, whose marriage to Gail Jones had collapsed, escorted her for a while. Then she was seen often with singer and pianist Bobby Short, famous for his renditions of the thirties classics she adored; he appeared with her in one of the Murjani commercials. If she knew Truman Capote was spreading malicious rumors that she had been responsible for Wyatt's death, that Cooper had come to hate her, she rose above them. Having publicly injured his friends, Capote wandered about drunk and drugged, full of venom for those from his past.

It was her relationship with Short that caused another scandal, this one brought upon a Vanderbilt rather than by one. Gloria's closest friends understood the ambition behind her work, her desire to have a high-status apartment bought with her own earnings. (She had, for some time, been unable to maintain her life-style on what remained of her original inheritance.) In New York City, the premiere apartment building is the exclusive River House on East 52nd Street. Built as a cooperative in 1929, a typical suite had twelve rooms, six baths, and two fireplaces. Maintenance charges ran $2,000 a month. Among the Social Register occupants were some Vanderbilt relatives, including Gloria's cousin Carter Burden.

In 1980, when a duplex became available, Gloria applied but was turned down by the board of the cooperative, which criticized the "unwelcomed publicity" her presence would bring. They were put off by "the ceaseless flow of gossip column items . . . where she eats and with whom, what parties, what she wears and where she lives."[20] Gloria lodged a complaint with the city's Commission on Human Rights, charging the true reason for the exclusion was her relationship with Short, who was black. The seller's attorney apparently asked if she intended to marry him, and she grew furious at the racist intimation.

As the brouhaha continued, one wondered why Gloria would want these people for neighbors. "Gloria's tapioca," one resident told writer Anthony Haden-Guest, which he learned meant "broke."[21] She was not, but the River House board did not like the way she earned her money. Carter Burden discounted the rumor that racism was involved. He said his neighbors were actually worried that denizens of Seventh Avenue would be hanging about the place, people like Liza Minelli and Halston. Burden, a liberal, observed he had brought people of all shapes, sizes, and colors to his place, and received no complaints. However, one resident advised Haden-Guest that, "[His bringing such guests] was all we talked about." When it was pointed out that Henry Kissinger, hardly a private person, was also a resident, the protesters answered that his fame was based on public service. And, they reminded reporters, they had put thumbs down on President Richard Nixon after he left office. Even Russell Baker came to Gloria's defense in a witty editorial essay in which he noted celebrities were "just as human as women and blacks and people who worship by handling rattlesnakes."[22]

Although Gloria swore to pursue the suit to a satisfactory end, after several weeks she withdrew her complaint and injunction. When she refused to comment on the matter, the president of Murjani volunteered that the publicity had become too much and was interfering with her home life with her children. Bobby Short let it be known that he went along with her wishes.

Another Writer Stirs
Gloria's Competitiveness

In the summer of 1980, Barbara Goldsmith published her meticulous documentation of the custody trial of 1934, *Little Gloria . . . Happy at Last*. Gloria was very unhappy with its appearance and its subsequent success as a best-seller. As she later explained to Dominick Dunne, Goldsmith "called me, which fascinated me, and said, 'I'm ready to interview you.' I said, 'From one personal writer to another, why should I give you material? Someday I am going to write my own book.'"[23] Nor was she delighted to be labeled *Little* Gloria throughout, the childhood name she disliked then and at age 56 certainly found inappropriate. She implored her friends not to read the book, refused to appear at a dinner when she learned Goldsmith would be present, and later terminated her friendship with actress Maureen Stapleton when she learned she had accepted the role of Keislich for the television miniseries. She also canceled some business appearances because she was so frustrated by reporters' questions about the book instead of her work.

Married to film director Frank Perry, Goldsmith selected a highly cinematic style, producing a smashing read in which one could almost picture the camera angles. Hollywood did not bite, however. The eventual television miniseries based upon the book depicted characters much unlike their real counterparts. A gangly Christopher Plummer portrayed the portly Regi with a gentlemanly panache that boozy rebel would have found highly amusing. Directed to emphasize Gertrude as the villain, Angela Lansbury created a one-dimensional portrayal considerably off the mark. One scene of a party in Gertrude's Village studio had Lansbury blowing smoke in the face of a model, an insulting gesture totally out of character for a woman who befriended and coddled her own models. As Alice Vanderbilt, Bette Davis gave one of the unintentionally campy performances she was prone to in her later years. The actresses playing the Morgan sisters better captured those fey, confused, helpless beauties. In its favor, the series emphasized the trial, which, having been based on the actual transcript, was the most accurate section of Goldsmith's book.

It may have been *Little Gloria . . . Happy at Last* which provoked Gloria's decision to write a series of her own autobiographies. Like other members of her family she was a lifetime diarist and datebook keeper. One of her favorite writers was Anaïs Nin, whose many published diaries had touched and inspired so many women during the early years of the women's movement. Gloria corresponded with Nin, and she took from both her and earlier writer Katherine Mansfield inspiration to explore her inner world through use of fantasy and intuition. Thus she was well-prepared to write about herself.

Once Upon a Time covered her childhood up until her move to California in 1941. Unfortunately, at age 25 she had destroyed her childhood diaries and was forced to rely upon memory. Except for some confusion in chronology, it served her well, perhaps freed her to make the audacious move of writing from a child's perspective. To capture youthful innocence successfully without appearing false or cloying is very difficult, but Gloria succeeded ably by casting events in the fairy tale imagery she held at the time. By writing in a child's voice she could unfold the tremendous emotional deprivation she experienced free from the resentment and anger that later developed. The result is a chilling document of abuse without the vindictiveness typical of such later parent-bashing books as Cheryl Crawford's *Mommie Dearest*. And despite her being a child of wealth, class barriers fade as she transforms her story into a universal tale.

If women readers loved it, reviewers were not universally in agreement. Men in particular had difficulty with its intense emotionality. Walter Clemmens of *Newsweek* called it "pretty vapid," while Stefan Kanfer of *Time* described it as "the literary equivalent of sequins on a party dress." Understanding its position in the tradition of women's journal-based writing, Barbara Grizzutti Harrison praised the "vivid freshness" of this story of "the child who is wounded and carelessly wounds, the child who has surges of surprised joy and is afraid of the dark, and most terribly afraid of those she loves."[24] Harrison put her finger on the book's appeal to women of much more modest means, its expression of the pain American girls so often feel in the presence of unfeeling, disparaging adults.

Gloria quickly followed this book up with *Black Knight, White Knight*, which covers her marriages to di Cicco and Stokowski. The voice changes from private school enthusiasms to starker prose as she faced the demands and abuse each man presents. Once again, she recounts a haunting tale of distorted relationships with men with which many women, not necessarily of her class, could identify. Although the story is very selective, the omissions are necessary to maintain the primary theme, her error in confusing submission and compliance with love. Gloria also omits many details of life among the very wealthy and, in doing so, she helps the middle-class reader identify with her plight. Wife beaters and abusive husbands cross class boundaries.

Although the book sold well for several months, it did not draw the readership of *Once Upon a Time*. Once again reviewers were divided over its effectiveness. Her vagueness concerning the actual course of events is confusing, such as the question of whether Pat continued to beat her once they settled in a luxurious life in New York City, whether she confided her abuse to Carol and Oona, why he did not fight more for money in exchange for the divorce. Similarly, the relationship with Leopold Stokowski consists of key emotional episodes with little connection from one to the other. Vagueness about childhood memories is to be expected, but not about adult relationships.

Curiously, though autobiography is popular as a text in courses on women, Gloria Vanderbilt's works were not to be found on college bookshelves. This neglect is regrettable because despite their literary weaknesses both volumes concern popular themes of female oppression and the struggle for autonomy. One suspects that she has faced the same dismissive attitude Gertrude often did, the belief that because she is well-to-do her work cannot be of much consequence. In fact, of all her creative achievements, it is her depiction of her life story that is most likely to survive as memorable and significant.

When the jeans market went into decline in the 1980s, Gloria found success placing her name on yet another product, perfumes named Glorious and Vanderbilt. Linking up with Warner Cosmetics for the project, its outcome was doubtful. Launching a new fragrance requires an enormous investment to establish the market, but Warner had already succeeded with several Ralph Lauren brands and felt confident that Gloria's promotional draw would succeed. Their risk paid off, with Vanderbilt rocketing to become the most popular fragrance on the market. This time Gloria was used for public appearances, while a swan represented her in the television and print advertisements.

Yet some other moves in the area of food marketing were less successful. Houston foods produced a Vanderbilt chocolate line that failed when the company realized a confectionary's reputation for quality could not be imposed through a name. Seligco discontinued Gloria Vanderbilt Glacé, a tofu frozen dessert that also ran into trouble when a rabbi complained that his endorsement of its being kosher was not valid. Gloria then tried unsuccessfully to move into a field only one celebrity, Paul Newman, had conquered, salad dressing. Since she had never been associated in the public eye with gourmet food, one wonders why she attempted this shift in emphasis.

Signs the Vanderbilt name was losing its cachet could be seen in other areas as well. In May of 1988, Murjani said it planned to relaunch Gloria Vanderbilt jeans, but several months later sold the use of the Vanderbilt name to the Gitano group, a company having earnings difficulties. For some years the elegant Gloria Vanderbilt signature had appeared on clothes in which the label was the only quality component. Shapeless bathing suits, blouses of crude cut, and dresses of uninspiring fabrics, hardly styles the noted best-dressed woman would wear, were the norm. It was not surprising to come across them in discount stores with other lower-end brands. Somehow Gloria had lost sight of the need to preserve the value of her signature with well-chosen products congruent with the image of Vanderbilt.

If Gloria seemed moving in too many directions, she was typical of celebrities of her time. *Spy* magazine would later look over the 1980s and characterize it as a period of chameleon personalities: so many public figures readily transforming themselves to the most current idea or potential source of fame. Not only were the efforts in various endeavors short lived, they were usually marked by superficiality, the absence of craft. It was an era, after all, when a onetime Vietcong supporter turned aerobics capitalist, politicians became hawkers of television products, and a B-grade movie star could head, if not exactly lead, the country.

While Gloria was more sincere, less cynical than some other celebrities, she was at a disadvantage because of her curious childhood. Her education had been spotty, and the person who could have best inculcated in her the slow, steady path to craft and expertise, her aunt Gertrude, had not done so. The private schools of the thirties focused less on preparing girls intellectually than in earlier years. And where the governesses of earlier Vanderbilt women had spoken to their charges in French and taken them to museums, Gloria's had taken her to the movies.

Gertrude's Legacy Is
Threatened

By the 1980s, the Whitney Museum had a very different appearance and organization from the days of Gertrude and Juliana. Marcel Breuer's stark, hard-edged, granite building was much more assertive than the institution's previous two homes. That assertiveness reflected in the shows as well, as new curators frequently mounted controversial shows. The new vitality was assured once Tom Armstrong came on as director in 1974. He succeeded in placing the Whitney at the center of the international contemporary arena, and the board, now composed of business giants who knew how to raise millions of dollars, gave the museum a strong financial basis as well. By the early 1980s, in a most unusual move, the museum opened four self-sustaining branch galleries in New York and Connecticut, so that overall attendance as well as staff size had greatly increased. Gertrude's and Juliana's wish that contemporary American art become accessible to many people was being fulfilled.

Armstrong admired Flora Irving, Gertrude's granddaughter who became president of the Museum in 1977. She was committed to her grandmother's mandate that the Whitney be devoted to living American artists, and was open to all ideas, urged Armstrong to represent the most challenging new directions. More natural and relaxed than her mother or grandmother, Flora easily mixed with artists, befriending them to create a bond between them and the museum, as had happened during the days of Gertrude and Juliana. She invited Jasper Johns, Rich Tuttle, and others into her home and made them feel welcome. Armstrong thought her enthusiasm and integrity created a bond with the artists that created a special period for the Whitney during her tenure.

A serious problem for Armstrong, however, was the same one Gertrude had faced in 1928: the gallery space permitted showing only a tiny amount of the holdings, which had become a significant representation of twentieth-century American art. Thus he persuaded the trustees that the institution should expand into the block surrounding it. In support, Flora Miller made a most extraordinary gift to start off the fund-raising campaign by donating *Juliet and Her Nurse* to Sotheby's for auction, the proceeds to go to the Whitney. It was her favorite painting, which she always moved with her when she went to spend summers in Westbury. She expected the price would be high, but as she sat in the auction room with her daughter Flora Irving beside her, she was stunned to watch the bidding go in six minutes to its final price, $6.4 million, the highest bid ever to that date for an artwork.

Then the troubles began. The trustees commissioned architect Michael Graves to design the addition, and his first model, a pink-and-gray wedding cake atop the stark Breuer, struck most people as wrong. It was 1988 before he came up with a version that satisfied most people. In the subsequent controversy, staff, trustees, and volunteers became exhausted by the disputes and fund-raising.

The unhappiness over the building provoked further animosities concerning the Whitney exhibits. The longtime accusations of trendiness, superficiality, and favoritism became more heated. Most disputed were the Biennial exhibits, where the most important new work was supposedly exhibited. On opening night, the lines of artists, dealers, and curious stretched out the doors to see what had been honored by the curators. In a way, the museum's success had spawned its problems, for its cachet had increased, and artists who were omitted banded together to criticize that for which they secretly longed. The artists who were included praised the Whitney's commitment to the avant garde, those excluded accused it of narrowness and partiality. More reasoned observers argued the Whitney had lost a sense of clarity and purpose, that it took interesting risks but ones that too often were questionable. Armstrong in particular was accused of failing to provide direction to the institution.

Yet the Whitney was also hampered, in part, by the change in the contemporary art scene. In Gertrude's time, artists were true Bohemians, struggling in most cases to make a living. But, by the 1980s, artists were competing for wealth and privilege in an atmosphere of affluent faux-Bohemianism. Art had become an investment. Trustees were also collectors who wanted to boost the value of their holdings. With tremendous inflation occurring in the galleries and auction houses, large profits were possible. The Whitney Board became particularly divided during the 1980s, both over personal social slights and decisions about the exhibits. In time, an anti-Armstrong faction evolved, composed of the very CEOs he had brought onto the board to strengthen its fund-raising ability. Rumors started to spread that the board was out to replace Armstrong.

One of the most aggrieved was Laurence Tisch, who visited Flora Irving, now remarried to a Biddle, to accuse Armstrong of anti-Semitism and insisted she get rid of Armstrong or else he would spread the story all over town.[25] Tisch had been offended when his son applied to buy into the same co-op building that Armstrong lived in but was turned down by the board. Ignoring that other

Jews lived in the co-op, Tisch continued to make his attacks. Although evidence is strong that Armstrong is anything but anti-Semitic, stories to the contrary spread throughout the art world, and remain today. In New York City, where wealthy Jews are also prominent art patrons, such gossip had devastating implications for the Whitney endowment.

Flora was caught up in the maelstrom that had grown out of control by the late 1980s. She resigned as president in 1985, and expected to take a less active role in the museum's affairs. But as the only family member now closely connected to the institution, and a supporter of Tom Armstrong, she felt impelled to keep her hand in and try to prevent his firing.

She failed. On November 3, 1989, trustee William Woodside demanded that Armstrong resign, and he added that the consensus of the board was behind the request. Armstrong began making calls, and he discovered that of fourteen trustees he was able to contact, only two knew of Woodside's proposal. Choosing to confront his critics, Armstrong refused to resign. During the ensuing months, the press detailed the "war at the Whitney," thus adding to the image of the institution as divided and rudderless. The simple principles Gertrude and Juliana had operated upon had vanished, as they necessarily would now that the organization was being run not by two compatible and determined individuals, but by a cumbersome nonprofit bureaucracy contaminated by art market capitalism.

Armstrong lost and was let go. Rather than remove her allegiance from the museum in support of him, Flora devoted virtually all her energy to healing the breaches. It was not clear that others were as willing to compromise for the sake of Gertrude's vision. By the end of 1990, Flora was making plans to move away from New York, which meant Gertrude's legacy was now fully in the hands of nonfamily members.

Further Tragedy Fails
to Defeat Gloria

I am no longer frightened by the word loneliness," Gloria had written in *Woman to Woman*. Rather, she would follow the model of Katherine Mansfield's first husband, "who scratched out 'lonely' in one of her early poems and substituted the word 'solitary.'"[26] She remained unmarried, tending to her sons as she thought Wyatt would want them raised. Her penthouse apartment at 10 Gracie Square now reflected a serenity not visible during her quilts-and-collage days. The walls were less cluttered, some simply lacquered to highlight the elegant classic carving of the woodwork. The patterns on the drapes and upholstery were fewer. These were rooms in which Gertrude, Alva, or Consuelo would have felt comfortable. Only her bedroom with its Victorian splendor of roses and lace, elaborate silk embroidered spread and French needlepoint rug retained some of the busyness of earlier interiors. Yet the swirls, circles, and curves of patterns and furniture formed a pleasing rhythm, a lively dance, like the personality of its owner.

"It's important to me to feel that home is always going to be here," she explained for a *House and Garden* spread. "That it has roots and stability."[27] Entering her sixties, her drive to succeed continued unabated, and she spoke proudly of her latest assignment, design work for J. P. Stevens. The interviewer agreed she had accomplished her aim, observing how the apartment, while high off the ground with the East River and Triborough Bridge gleaming below, the place felt "firmly rooted. Its occupant is held in place by these walls, by glittering collections, by paintings and collages, by snippets of the past."

The remark was tragically ironic in light of a subsequent event. During lunch on July 22, 1988, her 23-year-old Carter grew agitated over his problems. He had been under treatment for depression, which runs through and afflicts scattered members of the Vanderbilt line, and recent troubles with a girlfriend had reversed the progress of his cure. During his troubled outbreak, to her horror he clambered upon the ledge of the terrace fourteen floors above the sidewalk. In the course of pleading with him to come down, her hand reaching out to his, he suddenly slipped and fell over the side, his hand extended out helplessly for her.

The family doubted he intended suicide, and they wondered if the antidepressant drugs had been in some way responsible. His behavior made no sense in light of his temperament, even if he were depressed. He had been a handsome, principled young man, daring to go against conventional beliefs, the kind of man Wyatt would have admired. Gloria entered a period of mourning so private that even some of her closest friends and family members did not hear from her for many months. There were rumors of her buying property in New Mexico and resettling there. What few knew about were her secret visits with Nancy Reagan, by then another of her special women friends who provided great comfort.

As after Wyatt's death, she grasped onto work, this time a novel. *Never Say Good-bye* attempts to celebrate Gloria's devotion to friendships with women. Concerned with four successful career women whose lives are linked through ties with certain lovers, the effort fails. The key figure is Jessica, a widower and art gallery manager with a dancer daughter. Jessica's married lover, television journalist Maclin Hollis, has a fiesty wife, Billie, who "hangs in there like a lockjawed terrier." While Jessica was still a child, her mother Delores mysteriously disappeared but is later shown to have been locked up in a Russian sanitarium since 1934. There, another inmate, Brillianta Vosvi, protects her. Two other women connect to Jessica through their being lovers of her previous amour, Grafton Davis, a commercial artist. Garnet is a New York painter and Jane a London actress.

The structure of the novel shifts among the viewpoints of the six adult women, the disconnected plot concerns their relationships with their lovers and

Dolores's eventual discovery in the asylum. The collage fails to cohere into a gestalt, a discernible theme. Much of the problem concerns the material itself, which takes patches of biography from the life of Gloria and those around her without transforming it to fit the characters. Consequently, the impression is that she has taken the impulse behind her collage constructions, where she uses photographs and personal mementos, and transferred it to words. For example, Dolores's reminiscences are lifted directly from Gloria Morgan's life, including early widowhood, a German prince, and a card-playing sister. In one curious episode she relates a dinner with Kaiser Wilhelm that was in fact the experience of Grace's son Neil as he described it in his *Queen of the Golden Age*. Jane's childhood experiences resemble those of Carol Marcus. A particularly curious intrusion is Billie's lengthy description of her mother's infatuation with Indiana Ku Klux Klan leader David Stevenson, who fell from power when charged with the rape and murder of school teacher Madge Oberholzer. The reader senses Gloria had Come across this real-life story one day and appropriated it with little accommodation to the needs of her plot.

Furthermore, the tone conveyed is one of a self-absorbed, shallow woman. That all were accomplished in their careers is never made apparent. Instead, their conversations center upon appearances: their Laszlo skin treatments, Revlon makeup, body waxings at Elizabeth Arden, the color of their toenail polish, details of the design of their rooms. When Jessica meets one of Mac's ex-lovers, they titter about his giving them scarves that he then used to tie them to the bed during lovemaking. Mac also likes Jessica to dress up as a man, which she does so successfully that they win a dance contest at a gay nightclub. Grafton is a bully, who beats up his lover and tosses a cat out a window. The men are insensitive, brutish, and unfaithful; why these supposedly fabulous and talented women remain with them is never clear. The overall conclusion seems to be that the writer accepts her characters' values and relationships—no hint of irony or satire is present.

Late in the book Jessica goes to meet her daughter Kate outside Lincoln Center. Kate runs toward her in great excitement and is hit by a car, "an instant—it's not bad, it's going to be all right—but she fell reaching her hand out to me as the wheel crushed her head."[28] This episode is followed by snatches of expressions of grief, which constitutes the only segment of the book with any feeling. The book's title resonates in the last line, "for the love that is lost is the love that is found and the love that lasts forever." Yet even this heartfelt material loses power because the relationship between Jessica and her daughter has not been developed; indeed, the death appears another ill-fitting scrap from the quilt. In the final pages, Gloria attempts to show the value of women's friendships, yet she fails because the key character, Jessica, is looking forward to reviving her relationship with the feckless Mac.

It's natural to make a comparison to Gertrude's writing, which also tended toward *roman a clef,* her characters caught up in complex, often erotically charged relationships. Although she was not an accomplished fiction writer either, Gertrude's expression of the subtleties and undercurrents of intimacy was more polished. She was also better able to weave real-life incidents into the plot without disrupting its integrity and reshape people she knew into autonomous characters whose behavior was not a mere distillation of real actions. For all its flaws, Gertrude's *A Love Affair* unfolds more pointedly the theme of one woman's platonic devotion to another. *Never Say Good-bye* portrays women's culture as vapid, cynical, and devoid of spiritual basis.

Never Say Good-bye quietly appeared on the store shelves and quickly disappeared back to the publisher's warehouses. The reviews were not sympathetic and, possibly out of kindness, Knopf did not stage a publicity campaign to play off her name. The book jacket stated that she was working on another novel, a worrisome sign she was moving on once more, leaving her memoirs unfinished like so many other endeavors she has stopped midcourse.

Like her fictional Jessica, Gloria did not give up. She decided not to move to Santa Fe. After more than a year's seclusion, she began to let friends know through her secretary that she was ready to see them.

The Legacies

I n 1990, Gloria's place in American social history was marked by no less than the Smithsonian Institution in Washington, D.C. There its Museum of American History featured an exhibit on gender and style, in which viewers would find the derriere-pose of Gloria Vanderbilt's in her famous jeans. In addition, she was placed on a lifetime fashion industry list, along with designers Coco Chanel and Bill Blass, for her contributions to style.

That year as well, a new line of Gloria Vanderbilt clothing appeared in the stores, most items with fabrics and construction that promised long wear to cost-conscious middle-class buyers. In place of the swan logo were her initials, a large GV. The line included three styles of jeans, cut in varying degrees of shapliness to custom fit women from hipless to full bodied. A variety of cotton-knit tops sported attractive paisleys and stripes. A feminist clothing cooperative featured one in its catalogue: "Now you know we're not heavy into designer labels, but we couldn't resist you, Gloria." She probably never saw this particular praise, but it was proof she had not lost her touch with women.

Above all, one can see that Gloria Vanderbilt was an exemplar of the contemporary American character, recreating herself, achieving success on her own merits. She has been a painter, model, actress, writer, and designer for home and fashion. She taught women that the decoration of self and home need not be trivial, but a way of exploring one's own being and celebrating its uniqueness. While some feminists might see this view as reactionary, they might reconsider her philosophy in a different light, that of honoring what has been denigrated by society in recent years. One can look back to the often-misunderstood period of the 19th century when women's lot was narrowly domestic, but the home was venerated, so women were not "just homemakers." Gloria is in kinship with the women novelists and essayists of that time who sought deeper values in the running and decorating of a house.

Raised on movies, and drawn to the stage, Gloria urges a model of sets and costuming for the presentation of one's self. Her form-fitting jeans were presented as fun, as celebration, not as a sexual attractant. The implicit message was, "Other companies' jeans are designed by men who just don't understand women's bodies. I do." Similarly, her interior designs assiduously avoided what has commonly been associated with the masculine: earthtones, modest plaids and stripes, symbols of sport. It is the feminine signs that dominated: light or bright color, flower motifs, family memorabilia, collections of natural objects such as shells, sentimental art. Home is woman's stage, designed and controlled by her, with man the guest.

Whether one agrees with Gloria Vanderbilt or not, her assertions continue a long debate concerning the relation of woman to decoration and fashion. They remind us of the complexity of the discussion, for it encompasses subtleties of sexuality, power, and control. She prefers flaunting the traditionally-feminine, of increasing its value, rather than aping the masculine.

The limitations of gender are also evident in Gloria Vanderbilt's story. Though she developed a career in the design industry, her role has been subsidiary. She did not, for example, find doors to high-level management open. She does not sit on boards of directors of companies, as successful men in one field are called upon to serve in another. Her role was carefully circumscribed in design and marketing, the way women in many organizations today are segregated in "less important" functions. She did very well for herself financially, but a man in a comparable situation would have gone much further. He would have eventually owned his own company and developed business connections unavailable to Gloria as a woman. Never one for political analysis, she has not shown awareness of the obstacles placed before her.

Her aunt Gertrude was only too aware of such obstacles. Throughout her journals she struggled with what she considered to be a split nature. She was not split: she was essentially passionate and artistic, but society demanded she be subdued, the social matron. What is interesting is how Gertrude analyzed her problems in terms of class; it was the awful WASP requirements that bound her and stifled her impulses, she thought. That image of a bird with clipped wings so haunted her that she never imagined the source of the mutilation to be gender as well. But many of the criticisms she faced, from family and elsewhere, were for failing her feminine duties. Only a man can be an artist, only men are permitted excessive expression, they implied.

The exception here was the friendship of artists such as Andrew O'Connor and Jo Davidson, who accepted Gertrude as a peer and assisted in the development of her craft. Yet, for the most part, the artists of her time viewed her as a wealthy woman patron, even an amateur dabbler. Consequently, when mentioned in art history books at all it is for her establishment of the various Whitney art organizations and the museum. These were in themselves extraordinary contributions to American culture. However, it should be noted that when preparing this volume, the writer a number of times came upon people who thought the financial backing for the museum was Eli Whitney!

Gertrude as an artist was much silenced by history. During World War II the Germans bombed and destroyed her memorial at St. Nazaire. The *Columbus Memorial* in Spain has been falling apart due to lack of maintenance. When the Kennedy Center was built along the Potomac, the *Titanic Memorial* was moved to an obscure setting. Gertrude's other memorial statuary shared the fate of other comparable pieces all over the country, ignored by passing citizenry, of use only to pigeons. Even the Whitney Museum has seldom exhibited studio works of hers that it owns. Curiously, the upsurge of women artists in the seventies and eighties overlooked Gertrude (and many other women sculptors as well.)

This is not to say Gertrude's art was exceptional, that a major artist has been ignored. Because of the many competing pressures on her, she could not give the consistent concentration necessary for the best work. Still, her oeuvre deserves recognition, and her proper place in the history of sculpture should be given consideration.

Very recently, small signs suggest renewed interest in her achievements. In *American Women Artists,* Charlotte Rubenstein has included several pages on Gertrude's work as a sculptor, not only as a patron, and concluded she had a secure history of American art as a conservative sculptor of public monuments. Paying more attention to her studio pieces, Janis Conner and Joel Rosenkranz included Gertrude in their highly selective review of sculptors of the period, and praised her original point of view, particularly as expressed in her quickly modeled works. Finally, the Art Institute of Chicago, upon receiving a gift of six of Gertrude's sculptures, kept five for its collection.

The legacies of Gertrude's aunt Alva are also underappreciated. If people know of Alva at all, it is less by name than by awareness of Marble House in Newport. This home, the only of her architectural projects virtually intact today, well exemplifies her belief that the wealthy have a responsibility to contribute visions of beauty and higher values to the public. Live comfortably, she urged, but with exquisite taste. Alva would deplore many of the "Lifestyles of the Rich and Famous" as vulgar, narcissistic, and uninformed. Certainly it is difficult to think of many of the estates shown on that television show as popular tourist sites a hundred years from now.

Alva's greatest legacy was of course her radical feminism, her unrelenting critique of sexism in all spheres of life, her belief women must do more than work within the system to gain their full rights. She went to her grave full of hope for the National Woman's Party. Today its offices are in the basement of the Sewall-Belmont House at 144 Constitution Avenue NE in Washington, D.C.

Although the organization still publishes pamphlets in support of the Equal Rights Amendment, it is essentially moribund. The women belonging to the organization are very different from the likes of the brazen Alva, Alice Paul, Doris Stevens, and Inez Milholland.

The National Parks Service maintains the main rooms upstairs. There visitors will find sculpture and memorabilia relating to suffragism, along with furnishings and household goods donated by Alva when she bought the building for the party. She would be dumbstruck today to find it a museum instead of a beehive of political activity. She would also be astonished to walk to the Capitol nearby and see so few names of women legislators listed.

Consuelo's legacy is greatest in England, where her reform work and sincere charity provided an exemplar of the Good Duchess, a model for other aristocrats to follow. But the aristocracy continues to lose ground, and the people would like more than the old *noblesse oblige.*

What she also leaves behind is a tantalizing mystery, questions concerning the misrepresentations and omissions from *The Glitter and the Gold.* When other evidence is addressed, clues to a secret life emerge, hints of a more complex personality than she revealed in public. We will never know the truth of her feelings toward Sunny, her exact connection with Gladys Deacon, her adulteries, her involvement with the Pankhurst women. Consuelo hints of having the same passionate nature as Gertrude, yet in her writing she obliterated signs of its expression. One must wonder if she was truly so happy in her later life when she succumbed to the role of grand dame. Where Gertrude valiantly and continually faced the struggle between self and a disapproving society, Consuelo was often confused, unable to clarify what mattered to her, to stand up for it consistently. In the end, she could not be candid, but portrayed herself as she wished to be remembered, as a victim and a charitable person.

This criticism is not to dismiss her. Consuelo was just a teenager when she was wrenched from her protective and demanding mother and thrust into a very different culture. She used her American traits of adaptability and practicality to succeed eminently in the demands placed upon her, and in her time stirred among the British renewed good feelings for our nation. Her reform efforts improved the lives of poor women and children in England and France. One merely wishes she had more of her mother's forthrightness in discussing her life.

Despite the uncovering here of these women's individual encounters with the strictures of their gender and class, it may not be apparent how unusual they were. Their stories continue in the lives of similarly inclined upper-class women today. Their first duty is to their husband and family, their associates limited to the proper sort found in private clubs and select communities. To appear useful to the community, they volunteer in appropriate organizations, where they gain some power from their fund raising. They seldom have economic power: their inheritances are typically trusts managed by brothers, husbands, or other males. Segregated from the other classes, they can have curiously skewed perceptions about how others live. An example of this old money view is Barbara Bush, an astute and intelligent woman, who speaks of the woman's role as if all wives are free of financial worries and have household staff.

For these women to challenge family and friends would be to confront some of the most powerful people in their community, in some cases the country. Given the material benefits of keeping silent, most women remain so. As long as the wives and daughters of powerful men refuse to speak out, then the rights of all women will remain hampered.

The contrary can be seen in Miche Evans, one of Gertrude's great-great-granddaughters. In adulthood, she left the East Coast to live modestly while raising horses in Oregon, and later became a musician singing in small clubs in California. In mid-life she returned to college to complete her bachelor's degree with thoughts of teaching children with disabilities. She called one day to discuss her next semester's course plans. "I've never understood the need for women's studies," she explained, "but now I see that is because I come from a family where the women are so creative and active. I never understood until recently how different it was for other women. Now all I want to study is women writers and musicians." Through Miche and other women in her family line, the legacy of their self-affirming women ancestors lives on.

ACKNOWLEDGMENTS

The initial impulse for this book belongs to the Newport Preservation Society, which maintains the Breakers and Marble House, among other estates. During 1977, I spent a year in Rhode Island, during which time I often returned to these sites and thought of writing a book about the servants, crafts workers, and townspeople of the time. That idea was put aside when I decided to return to California, but I retained the memories of that organization's efforts to preserve a part of the American past.

Some years later I happened upon James Brough's *Consuelo,* which refers briefly to Alva Smith Vanderbilt Belmont's work as a suffragist, and became curious about her actual contributions. In the course of that exploration, I came across Gertrude Vanderbilt Whitney's papers as well, and the project expanded to include her. Although I intended to end the history with Gertrude's death, I found my growing file on Gloria Vanderbilt could not be ignored for its reflection of changing social history. My major debt is to these women, whose private and public writings form the groundwork for this study.

It was my great fortune to be introduced to several members of the family, who were unfailingly generous with their assistance and quick to bolster me during difficult periods of research. My first contact was with Gerta Conner, Gertrude's granddaughter, who directed me to the location of certain materials and discussed the contributions of more private family members in the art world. Another granddaughter, Flora Miller Irving Biddle, had collaborated on the first biography of Gertrude, which proved a constant, encyclopedic reference. Both Flora's candid and incisive conversations and letters and her assistance in connecting with other people were most valuable. It was my great delight one day to receive a note from Miche Irving Evans, Gertrude's great-great-granddaughter, who happened to live nearby. From that point of meeting, my work was made much easier by Miche's encouragement, loans of materials from her own collection on the family, and feedback on various drafts.

My hope was to interview Gloria Vanderbilt concerning her artistic and business endeavors, but she had withdrawn from social life following her son's death and I did not want to press my case too hard in light of that tragedy. I thank those who sought to intercede on my behalf here, and I want to emphasize that these individuals did not compromise her wishes for privacy in their discussions with me about the family.

Among informants in the art world who were of great assistance in enhancing my understanding of Gertrude Whitney, the Whitney Museum, and art of the period were Tom Armstrong, Avis Berman, Nancy Boas, Janis Conner, Joel

Rosencranz, and Patterson Sims. Their views sometimes conflicted, so my interpretation is totally my own, and any errors are mine as well.

The most significant improvement for scholars in recent years is the wider availability of microfilms and interlibrary loan. This, however, places heavy burdens on librarians. At Reuben Salazar Library, Sonoma State University, Gail Cosmo handled dozens of interlibrary loan requests with speed, while Barbara Beibush and Jean Day assisted with reference concerns. Sherry C. Birk was gracious and informative during my visit to the American Institute of Architects in Washington, D.C., to examine the Richard Howard Hunt drawings. Abigail Yasgur at the Arthur and Elizabeth Schlesinger Library at Radcliffe College assisted me in determining what materials in their extensive holdings would meet my needs, as did Peter Blodgett of the Huntington Library in San Marino. Mrs. Leonard Panaggio of the Preservation Society of Newport was quick in responding to requests. Also helpful were staff from the Bodleian Library at Oxford University, the William R. Perkins Library at Duke University, the Richard A. Gleeson Library at the University of San Francisco, the New York Historical Society, the Museum of the City of New York, the Bancroft Library of the University of California, the Newport Public Library, the Long Island Historical Society, and the Staten Island Historical Society. My thanks as well to staff of the Archives of American Art at the three branches I visited, in New York, Washington, D.C., and San Francisco.

Special help in locating photographs was provided by Mary Ruthsdotter of the National Women's History Project, Susan Boone of Sophia Smith Library, Mrs. Harold Tinney of Belcourt Castle, and Paul Duffie of Blenheim Palace. When word came certain photographs could not be provided by deadline, Flora Biddle and Miche Evans graciously loaned me material from their personal collections.

Both my agent, Elizabeth Frost Knappman, and Toni Lopopolo encouraged my original interest and provided direction on organizing a multi-generational biography. Toni also introduced me to a member of the family who alerted me to materials of which I was unaware. At St. Martin's, my editor Charles Spicer, boosted my spirits and in the final stages corrected the more egregious prose. My gratitude also to his assistant, Blake Spraggins, and my copy editor, Juli Barbato, who made such helpful queries.

A summer travel stipend from Sonoma State University enabled me to collect research materials on the East Coast that could not otherwise be obtained. My good friend Nona Schwartz gave me a base in New Jersey to work from while there.

My work would have taken much longer were it not for the research assistance of Connie Williams, who developed bibliographies, located sources, developed leads on her own, while Donna Beddingfeld located a mass of material on Gloria Vanderbilt. My daughter, Kendra Stoll, an amateur social historian, filled in helpful details on high society.

Four friends took on the awesome task of reading a draft of the book: Candy Donnelly, Barbara Lesch McCaffry, Sal Noto, and J. J. Wilson. Their frank comments served me greatly in the final stages. A special thanks to Jim Donnelly, who appeared one day with a gift of *Double Exposure* he had found in a used bookstore. My colleagues in the Department of History at Sonoma State University continually inquired on the progress of the work and by their curiosity reinforced my own. Fellow writers ready with special emotional boosts were Elizabeth Herron and Suzanne Lipsett.

As usual, my husband, Michael Orton, chauffeured me on research trips, protected my private writing hours from intrusion, and did not complain too much when the den we share became overrun with piles of photocopies and stacks of books. (I must also thank his mother, Virginia Murche, for teaching him to cook and iron his own clothes.) I would have dedicated the book to him, but he would have found that inappropriate for a work that honors women previously lost to history.

NOTES

Research Note

I hope my overview of the contributions of the women discussed in this volume will inspire specialists to look more closely at particular aspects of their lives. The extent and depth of the primary materials on Alva Smith Vanderbilt Belmont and Gertrude Vanderbilt Whitney in particular promise much for scholars. Since the endnotes do not indicate fully the richness of this material, I offer the following.

Those interested in the life of Cornelius Vanderbilt will find three sources most useful. The first biographer, Andrew Croffut (1886) knew members of the family, so he provided firsthand knowledge of individual personalities. Wayne Andrews's (1941) history expands on Croffut through extensive use of newspapers of the time, that reliance on journalism being its weakness as well. The only serious work by a historian is Wheaton Lane's (1942) balanced study of the Commodore's contributions to the growing economy of the country. Many other volumes are pastiches that build off of Croffut, Andrews, diatribes, and questionable journalistic works.

My discussion of Alva Smith Vanderbilt Belmont's contributions to the National Woman's Party could be much expanded. To do so here, however, would have been perhaps to mislead. Although she was a significant figure, so were others besides herself and Alice Paul, and a fair picture must look at the collectivity. The full story of the party, both nationally and on a state level, has been little studied, Geidel (1980) and Cott (1984) being recent exceptions. The addition of the Alice Paul papers to the Elizabeth and Arthur Schlesinger Library (which were unavailable at the time of my work) should fill out the enormous archival material on this organization. Those reading firsthand accounts of party members, however, such as Irwin (1921), should remember they were prone to think of themselves as the only suffragists of the time.

Alva left two sets of memoirs. In 1917 she hired Sara Bard Field to take down her reflections on her life and compose a biography. Both Field's rough notes and typed draft are in the C. E. S. Wood Collection, Henry E. Huntington Library, and are referred to her as "SBF notes" for handwritten material, or "SBF typed notes" for the draft. Sometime later Alva wrote her own version, which she had typed in 1932. This typescript is in the Matilda Young Papers, William R. Perkins Library, Duke University, and is referred to as "ASVB memoir" here. Unfortunately, both say little about her marriage to O. H. P. Belmont or her suffrage work. For the latter, check the mass of materials she left with the National Woman's party.

Gertrude Vanderbilt Whitney's place in American art as a sculptor has yet to be examined. Those interested in the Whitney Museum's role with regard to particular artists over the century should start with Avis Berman's (1990) lively and meticulous study, which builds upon primary materials and personal interviews with key survivors of the period. Berman's extensive notes will guide those concerned with particular artists into the appropriate locations in the Archives of American Art. Feminist scholars interested in autobiography may also find Gertrude's various unpublished journals worth examining.

Gertrude Whitney's papers come on microfilm in two versions. When Flora Irving Biddle was working on the biography of Gertrude with B. H. Friedman (1978), she had significant portions of Gertrude's diaries and correspondence typed up for easier study. She included these with her contribution of the originals to the Whitney Museum of American Art. In preparing this volume, I found a high degree of accuracy between the typed and handwritten versions, so in most cases I referred to the former in my notes. Scholars will of course want to examine the originals as well, for these rolls include much correspondence and some journal material that was not transcribed.

My hope in preparing this study was to combine scholarly standards of research for a story written for a lay audience. Consequently, I eliminated ellipses in quotations in most cases after nonspecialist readers informed me they found such usage interruptive. Those referring to the original sources will, I hope, find my deletions have not changed the meaning.

Abbreviations Used
in the Notes

AAA	Archives of American Art
ASVB	Alva Smith Vanderbilt Belmont
BKWK	*Black Knight, White Knight* by Gloria Vanderbilt
GG	*The Glitter and the Gold* by Consuelo Balsan
GVW	Gertrude Vanderbilt Whitney
GVW	*Gertrude Vanderbilt Whitney* by B. H. Friedman
OUT	*Once Upon a Time* by Gloria Vanderbilt
RES	*Rebels on Eighth Street* by Avis Berman
SBF	Sara Bard Field
WW	*Woman to Woman* by Gloria Vanderbilt

Prologue

1. In an 1893 diary Gertrude enters a poem in which she suggests a kiss with Elliot Shepard in Bar Harbor, but that is likely all it was, a poetry kiss. GVW papers, AAA, roll 1903, frames 489–90.

2. *GVW*, 91.

3. Henry James, *The American Scene*, 65.

4. Edith Wharton, *The Age of Innocence*, 1050.

Chapter 1: 1647–1849

1. The list of patents issued by the Dutch government between 1630 and 1664, the time of the initial settlement, lists no van der Bilt. For the list of patents, see Pamela and J. W. Smit, *The Dutch in America, 1906–1970*, 100–109. A member of "the other branch of the family," Philip Vanderbilt Schneider, provided me with a family tree, developed by a great aunt, which shows Jan Aetsen arriving in 1650.

2. The best sources on van der Bilt family lineage are Lane, *Commodore Vanderbilt*, chap. 1, and W. A. Croffut, *The Vanderbilts and the Story of Their Fortune*, chap. 1. I substituted the original names of towns for the modern ones.

3. Letter of the Dutch magistrates of New Orange to the States General in Holland, as quoted in Gerald de Jong, *The Dutch in America, 1609–1974*, 38.

4. Several sources that reproduce this cottage, such as Robert King, *The Vanderbilt Houses*, and Jerry Patterson, *The Vanderbilts*, show a photograph of a later version, after it had been doubled in size and the attic area expanded into bedrooms. This renovation was likely arranged when the Commodore gave the home to Alva and Willie K. Vanderbilt in the 1870s.

5. Wayne Andrews, *The Vanderbilt Legend*, 6.

6. Wheaton Lane, *Commodore Vanderbilt*, 36.

7. The personalities of Ogden and Gibbons and the background to this major Supreme Court decision are charmingly recounted in Lane, chap. 3.

8. Philip Howe in his diary in the late 1830s, as quoted in David Black, *The King of Fifth Avenue*, 26.

9. This description of the house is from "A Noted Mansion Burned," *New York Times*, 14 January 1882. Although the house was gutted by the fire, contrary to Robert King, *The Vanderbilt Houses*, it was not destroyed. The shell was renovated, and the house still stands, a current photograph appearing in Jerry E. Patterson, *The Vanderbilts*, 24.

10. In *All-American Girl*, Frances B. Cogan identifies another model of femininity in the popular culture of the day, the "Real Woman." She was neither the lady of leisure

nor the revolutionary feminist but rather physically active, committed to education, and determined to pick her own mate. This model does not seem to have influenced women of the upper class during this period.

11. Within the family, William Henry was called Billy into adulthood. However, to prevent confusion later on in the story, when another William appears, I use the name by which he became publicly known.

12. Andrews, 27.

13. Ibid., 28.

14. Ibid., 20.

15. Although these families often claimed to be descendants of patroons, the early large land-grant holders, that was not the case in most instances. In fact, the patroon system was short lived, and too heavily colors the story of early Dutch settlement in America, which more often followed the pattern of the first Vanderbilt, that of a small land holder farming his own land.

16. Knickerbocker Abram Dayton, as quoted in David Black, *The King of Fifth Avenue*, 29.

17. As quoted in Pauline Maier, "Boston and New York in the 19th Century," *Proceedings of the American Antiquarian Society* 91, part 2 (October 21, 1981): 177–95.

18. Andrews, 23.

19. From her treatise, *Woman in the Nineteenth Century*, as quoted in Glenda Riley, *Inventing the American Woman*, 114.

20. As quoted in Riley, 115.

Chapter 2: 1849–1869

1. As quoted in David Black, *The King of Fifth Avenue*, 59.

2. Wayne Andrews, *The Vanderbilt Legend*, 38.

3. As quoted in Croffut, *The Vanderbilts and the Story of Their Fortune*, 285.

4. Andrews, 46.

5. Alva refers in her memoirs to a Desha County in Kentucky being named after someone in the family. No such county exists today, although one may have in the past.

6. *New York Herald*, 27 June 1857. This is a prediction that came true later that year.

7. Dixon Wechter, *The Saga of American Society*, 152.

8. ASVB memoir, 24.

9. Ibid., 44.

10. Ibid., 34.

11. Ralph G. Martin, *Jennie: The Romantic Years*, 25.

12. It is unclear when the family went to Europe. In the ASVB memoir she mentions the mother putting bunting up when Lincoln died, yet in the SBF notes she says the family left when the war began. This is a rare inconsistency between the two sets of memoirs.

13. ASVB memoir, 64.

14. SBF, typed notes.

15. Ibid.

16. Ibid.

17. Ibid.

18. Croffut, 182.

19. Gustavus Myers, *History of the Great American Fortunes,* 2: 130.

20. Ibid., 90.

21. Andrews, 92.

22. Ibid., 102–3.

23. Henry Nash Smith, *Popular Culture and Industrialism, 1865–1890,* 96. This collection includes a reproduction of the monument taken from *Harper's,* two contemporary and contrasting views of the installation, and excerpts from both Croffut's biography and a *Herald* biographical sketch written in 1877 after the Commodore's death.

24. "The Vanderbilt Memorial," *Nation* 9 (18 November 1869): 431–32.

25. From a *New York Tribune* article as quoted in Andrews, 145.

26. Again, the actual dates of return are unclear. In the ASVB memoir she states the year as 1869, while in the SBF notes she says it was when the war was over, which would be several years earlier. The 1869 date seems very late in light of other events discussed.

27. This date is an inference. I was unable to locate death notices on either Phoebe or Murray Smith.

28. Although several sources claim Alva's mother ran a boardinghouse, I was never able to find any firsthand sources for this claim. The closest I found was her statement in the SBF notes that the possibility was discussed following her mother's death.

29. SBF interview notes.

Chapter 3: 1870–1879

1. Although Alva in her memoirs never mentioned paying attention to Susan B. Anthony's activities during this time, she so often later invoked Anthony and the early women's rights leaders that their having made a significant impression is evident.

2. Johanna Johnston, *Mrs. Satan,* 20.

3. Wayne Andrews, *The Vanderbilt Legend,* 145.

4. Andrew Croffut, *The Vanderbilts and the Story of Their Fortune,* 122.

5. For a lively and detailed examination of this event, known then as Black Friday, see John Steele Gordon, *The Scarlet Woman of Wall Street* (New York: Weidenfeld and Nicolson, 1988). It is also an extremely partisan rendition that somewhat mocks moral critics of the time.

6. Johnston, 59.

7. Another significant figure in opening the podium to women was Quaker Anna Dickinson. She shocked during the war when she held lectures on politics, military affairs, and antislavery, as well as stomped for political candidates. After the war, she became known as the "Queen of the Rostrum," to some a term of praise, to others of derision.

8. M. M. Marberry, *Vicky,* 19. Anthony anticipated Woodhull would be "a lady quite déclassée in any society which calls itself polite" and led a delegation to request the Senate refuse her appearance. Once Anthony met Woodhull, she changed her mind and became an avid supporter.

9. Marberry, 23.

10. Johnston, 116–17.

11. Marberry, 99.

12. Alva's memoirs mention friends from Knickerbocker families—Jay, Livingston, Schermerhorn—but it is dubious she would have been accepted by them at this time. She was marginal as it was among the upstart group.

13. Sara Bard Field to her lover, Charles Erskine Scott Wood Collection, 31 July 1917, Huntington Library.

14. SBF interview notes.

15. Andrews, 174.

16. Ibid., 177.

17. Frank Clark [Frank Kintrea], "The Commodore Left Two Sons," *American Heritage* 17 (April 1966): 81.

18. Clark, 83.

19. Ibid., 86.

20. Ibid., 86.

21. Ibid., 90.

22. Ibid., 92.

23. Ibid., 101.

24. Ibid., 102.

Chapter 4: 1880–1885

1. As quoted in Stephen Bedford, "Country and City: Some Formal Comparisons," from The Parrish Art Museum, *The Long Island Country House: 1870–1930*, 46.

2. Catherine Howland Hunt memoir, American Institute of Architects, 1.

3. In her memoirs, Alva says she worked with Hunt and his draftsmen at his office. "He was my instructor and dear friend for many years, and the work we did together was for me a great delight, and a great resource." ASVB memoir, 92.

4. SBF, typed notes.

5. The architectural sketches for these many buildings can be viewed at the American Institute of Architects in Washington, D.C.

6. ASVB memoir, 111.

7. Ibid., 111.

8. Exactly who in the family devised this affectation is unclear, as it appears in all the mansions being built in the 1880s.

9. Wayne Andrews, *The Vanderbilt Legend*, 221.

10. "W. H. Vanderbilt's Pictures on View," *New York Times*, 4 May 1902. The article refers to an exhibit of the paintings at the Metropolitan Museum of Art, which eventually received them.

11. Edith Wharton, *A Backward Glance*, 55.

12. *RES*, 44.

13. Andrews, 244. The speaker is Ward McAllister, a southern swell who was entrusted by Mrs. Astor to maintain the list of Ins and Outs.

14. Anonymous guest, as quoted in Allen Churchill, *The Upper Crust*, 126.

15. Edith Wharton, *The Age of Innocence*, 1055.

16. Ibid., 1017.

17. John Briggs, *Requiem for a Yellow Brick Brewery*, 6.

18. David Black, *The King of Fifth Avenue*, 635.

19. Ibid., 637.

20. Ibid., 663.

21. As a result of this investigation, William H. sold a large block of New York Central to a British syndicate to give the impression he was giving up some power. In fact, he retained a large number of shares and an immense block of the railroad's bonds. With the $35 million he made on the sale, he bought government bonds, which gave

him respectability and four percent a year interest to invest further in his businesses. Through collusion with others, the Vanderbilts ended up with such holdings as a large part of the anthracite coal region in Pennsylvania.

22. For more detail on this incident, see John Steele Gordon, "The Public Be Damned," *American Heritage* (September/October 1989): 18–20.

23. To be accurate, the body was laid temporarily with that of the Commodore, as workmen had not yet completed the Romanesque Chapel that was to become resting place for many Vanderbilts.

24. "Carried to the Grave," *New York Times,* 12 December 1885.

Chapter 5: 1885–1893

1. "My History," AAA, roll 1903, frame 584.

2. GVW papers, AAA, roll 1903, frame 246.

3. Florence Adele Sloan, *Maverick in Mauve,* 20.

4. GVW papers, AAA, roll 1903, frame 464.

5. *GVW,* 30.

6. GVW papers, AAA, Washington, box 5.

7. *GVW,* 47.

8. *OUT,* unnumbered introductory page.

9. Sloane, 128.

10. *GVW,* 42–43.

11. Ibid., 42.

12. As I note later in discussing Consuelo's marriage, she may have overstated Alva's negative qualities as a mother in order to boost the drama of her claim that she was forced to marry the duke of Marlborough. I accept these stories here because they make sense in light of Alva's own descriptions of herself.

13. GVW, "Travels in Foreign Countries and in the Mind," volume I, Washington branch of AAA, box 5.

14. Ibid.

15. ASVB papers, 135.

16. David Black, *King of Fifth Avenue,* 717.

17. *GG,* 20.

18. Ibid., 22.

19. Sloane, 26.

20. Most of these details on the background of Marble House come from Catherine Hunt's memoir, American Institute of Architects.

21. The stained glass was replaced after the house was sold because the later owners, the Frederick Prince family, found it too dark. They also stripped the polychrome from the vaulted ceiling. Consequently, today's visitors do not experience the original, more haunting atmosphere.

22. Catherine Howland Hunt papers, 422.

23. GVW papers, AAA, roll 1903, frame 577.

24. Esther Hunt to GVW, January 11, n.d., AAA, role 1903, frame 857.

25. GVW, AAA, roll 1903, frame 709.

26. Esther Hunt to GVW, Wednesday, n.d., AAA, roll 1903, frames 859–60.

27. Sloane, 174.

28. GVW papers, AAA, roll 1903, frame 479.

29. Ibid., frame 502.

30. Ibid., frame 549.

31. *GVW*, 72.

Chapter 6: 1893–1895

1. Wayne Andrews, *The Vanderbilt Legend*, 284–5.

2. In a rare error, Wayne Andrews states the party returned to Paris immediately upon reaching Bombay (*The Vanderbilt Legend*, 269).

3. SBF, typed notes.

4. "O.H.P. Belmont Dead After Brave Fight," *New York Times*, 11 June 1908.

5. James Brough, *Consuelo*, 58.

6. ASVB memoir, 143.

7. Alva reflected extensively on her mindset at the time in her discussions with Sara Bard Field. See SBF notes.

8. For a sprightly review of these and other early weddings, see Gail MacColl and Carol McD. Wallace, *To Marry an English Lord*, chapter 1.

9. McColl and Wallace, 87.

10. ASVB memoir, 153.

11. Ibid., 151.

12. See SBF notes on Alva's relation with her lawyer, Mr. Choate.

13. SBF notes.

14. *GG,* 29.

15. Since this is a postdivorce recall of the meeting, and Consuelo had no good word to say about Sunny by that point, she may in fact have had a more positive impression.

16. GVW papers, AAA, roll 1903, frame 563. Gertrude spelled his name in her journal as the more pronounceable "Garwick."

17. This proposal has never been corroborated by other sources.

18. *GG,* 33.

19. McColl and Wallace, 127.

20. Jennie Churchill's role in the courtship of Sunny and Consuelo is unclear. It would seem natural that she encourage it, for she took strongly to Consuelo. Whether she actually did so is unknown, along with the rest of Sunny's side of the story.

21. Maureen E. Montgomery, *Gilded Prostitution,* 175. The paper quoted is the *New York Morning Journal.* I had already concluded Consuelo's story lacked credulity when I came across Montgomery's study, which independently drew the same conclusion from other evidence she uncovered.

22. Brough, 73.

23. Ibid., 74.

24. *GG,* 42.

25. Ibid., 42.

26. Ibid., 46.

27. Ibid., 57.

28. MacColl and Wallace, 199. Lady Curzon was the previous Mary Leiter, a belle from Washington, D.C.

29. *GG,* 65.

30. Ibid., 66.

31. Ibid., 95.

Chapter 7: 1895–1899

1. Grace's son Cornelius said he never had written proof of his mother's relationship with Bill Vanderbilt, but the servants around Newport claimed it to be so. Servants being in the best position to know, I am inclined to accept the arrangement as true. It also explains the strength of Alice's and Cornelius's antipathy toward Grace.

2. GVW papers, AAA, roll 1903, frame 793.

3. Ibid., frame 795.

4. Cornelius Vanderbilt, *Queen of the Golden Age,* 49.

5. *GVW,* 74.

6. GVW papers, AAA, roll 1903, frame 782.

7. Ibid., frame 623.

8. Ibid., frame 638.

9. Ibid., frame 626.

10. *GVW,* 76.

11. GVW papers, roll 1903, frame 721.

12. *GVW,* 87.

13. Ibid., 110.

14. GVW papers, AAA, roll 1903, frame 817.

15. *GVW,* 129.

16. Henry Adams, *The Education of Henry Adams,* 378–80.

17. *GVW,* 114.

18. GVW papers, AAA, roll 1903, frame 821.

19. *GVW,* 116.

20. C. Vanderbilt, 52.

21. Ibid., 56.

22. Ibid., 140.

23. This account comes from Grace's ever-sympathetic son Cornelius, so it may be an invention conveyed to him to impress upon him his grandparents' animosity. It seems credible, however, that Alice and Cornelius would want to make a public sign of their defeat of the Wilsons, and for that reason I include the story.

24. *New York Journal,* n.d., as reprinted in C. Vanderbilt, 67.

25. C. Vanderbilt, 75.

26. *GVW,* 140.

27. Ibid., 142.

28. Ibid., 142–43.

29. C. Vanderbilt, 78.

30. GVW to Esther Hunt, 21 July 1896, AAA, roll 1903, frames 882–83.

31. W. A. Swanberg, *Whitney Father, Whitney Heiress,* 149.

32. C. Vanderbilt, 104.

33. Andrews, 353.

34. C. Vanderbilt, 138.

35. Ibid., 139.

36. Ibid., 136.

Chapter 8: 1900–1908

1. A careful reading of Veblen's *Theory of the Leisure Class* shows he saw the women as victims, relegated by their husbands to play the role of conspicuous consumers as a way of demonstrating masculine achievement. He understood the sexual power relation, unlike many critics of upper-class women, who greatly misconstrue the power these women actually hold, which is very small.

2. Belcourt today is privately owned by the Tinney family. Its contents, a veritable jumble of antiquities and art objects from various periods and cultures, belong to that family. The house shows considerable wear, and among design changes made since the days of Alva was the removal and redesign of the stairway to the second floor. The house is open more as a presentation of the Tinney collection than as a historical preservation, and depending on the docent available, the information provided on Hunt or the Belmonts has varying accuracy. The contrast of Belcourt with the pristine condition of Marble House and the Breakers, under the care of the non-profit Newport Historical Society, hints at the great difficulty of private owners with good intentions to maintain such mansions. Not surprisingly, many other of Newport's palaces are now part of Salve Regina College.

3. This statue now stands in the foyer of the Sewall-Belmont House in Washington, D.C., which is open to the public under the auspices of the National Park Service.

4. "Consul, Chimpanzee, Mr. Belmont's Guest," *New York Times,* 27 July 1907.

5. ASVB memoirs, 158.

6. Ibid., 162.

7. "Belmont's First Speech," *New York Times,* 14 October 1900.

8. *GG,* 103.

9. James Brough, *Consuelo,* 140.

10. *GG,* 103.

11. A. L. Rowse, *The Churchills,* 363.

12. Hugo Vickers, *Gladys, Duchess of Marlborough,* 41.

13. Ibid., 112.

14. "American Women in English Society," *Harper's Bazzar,* (July 1905): 602–9.

15. "A Friend's Tribute," *London Times,* 2 July 1934.

16. See Brough, 164, for one newspaper item. Brough, who takes Consuelo's late-life memoir to be utterly true, believes Consuelo's claim the story was false.

17. Gail MacColl and Carol McD. Wallace, *To Marry an English Lord,* 273.

18. Philip Magnus, *King Edward the Seventh,* 406.

19. W. A. Swanberg, *Whitney Father, Whitney Heiress,* 208.

20. Cornelius Vanderbilt, *Queen of the Golden Age,* 165.

21. Henry James, *The American Scene,* 66.

22. For more on the early years of Neily and his sister Grace, see the early pages of his *Farewell to Fifth Avenue.*

23. C. Vanderbilt, *Farewell to Fifth Avenue,* 5.

24. C. Vanderbilt, *Queen of the Golden Age,* 159.

25. Ibid., 171.

26. For James on dinner parties, see *The American Scene,* 183ff.

27. C. Vanderbilt, *Queen of the Golden Age,* 214.

28. GVW, 155.

29. GVW papers, AAA, roll 1903, frame 1236. This is the beginning of an autobiography probably written in the 1930s. Notes on this typescript between Flora Miller Irving and B. H. Friedman indicate their first impression was that it was written much earlier, but as they worked through it they realized it must be from a later date. The tone and sweep of the writing suggests many years have passed since discussion of the events mentioned.

30. GVW papers, AAA, roll 1903, frame 1237. Gertrude's estimation of Andersen was apparently correct, as his very brief mention in contemporary books on sculpture singles out his use of tinting.

31. *RES,* 58.

32. GVW papers, AAA, roll 1903, frame 1237.

33. *GVW,* 173.

34. Ibid., 174–5.

35. Ibid., 176.

Chapter 9: 1900–1908, Continued

1. GVW papers, AAA, roll 1903, frame 951.

2. GVW papers, AAA, roll 1903, frame 698. Gertrude made this evaluation in 1895 when they were seeing each other socially.

3. GVW papers, AAA, roll 1903, frame 952.

4. Ibid., frame 981.

5. Ibid., frame 953.

6. Ibid., frame 954.

7. Ibid., frame 987.

8. Ibid., frame 987.

9. Ibid., frames 1044–45.

10. Ibid., frame 989.

11. Ibid., frame 954.

12. Ibid., frame 1005.

13. Ibid., frame 1045.

14. In her journals, Gertrude at times refers to the participants with pseudonyms developed out of a parody Cushing had written. Gertrude is the Queen, Harry the Prince Consort, Adele the Duchess, J. the Duke, Cottenet the Gold Stick or the Thug, Cushing the Caterer or Alice, and Appleton the New Acquisition, Little Man, Siegfried, or the Dago.

15. GVW papers, AAA, roll 1903, frame 1051.

16. Ibid., frame 1104.

17. Ibid., frame 1065.

18. Ibid., frame 1087.

19. Ibid., frame 1101.

20. This image of the Eastern woman is of course a stereotype, one that is perpetuated today in reports of Islamic culture. Because the life of Islamic women is so private, Western observers have constructed a simplistic analysis of male-female relations based on what little is observable. The view is more understandable in Gertrude's time, for it was consistent with the social Darwinism of the era, hence the superiority of the Anglo-Saxon to the browner Arabs.

21. GVW papers, AAA, roll 1903, frame 969.

22. For these plot notes, see GVW papers, AAA, roll 1903, frames 972–79. These were loose sheets placed in the 1901 travel journal, so their time of composition is unknown. The style and psychology expressed suggest their being done c. 1901–02.

23. GVW papers, AAA, roll 1903, frame 1210.

24. Ibid., frames 1116–17.

25. *GVW*, 205.

26. GVW papers, AAA, roll 1903, frame 1163.

27. Ibid., frame 1190.

28. Ibid., frame 1193.

29. Ibid., frame 1209.

30. As quoted in *RES*, 74.

31. *RES*, 74.

32. *GVW*, 232.

33. Ibid., 233.

34. From her unpublished diary, as quoted in Janis Conner and Joel Rosenkranz, *Rediscoveries in American Sculpture: Studio Works, 1893–1939*, 54. Hoffman's and other women sculptors' experiences prove that Rodin's manipulation of Camille Claudel was not the case with all women.

35. GVW papers, AAA, roll 1903, frame 1215.

36. Ibid.

37. *RES*, 30.

38. Whitney Museum of American Art, *Juliana Force and American Art*, 47.

39. Avis Berman, "The Force Behind the Whitney," *American Heritage* (September/October 1989): 103.

40. Berman, 103.

41. Maureen Montgomery, *Gilded Prostitution*, 188.

42. "Wasted Child Life," *London Times*, 30 June 1916. This was her Lady Priestly Lecture before the National Health Society. Consuelo was the first woman granted the opportunity to speak in this forum.

43. Beatrice Webb, *Our Partnership*, 311.

44. *GG*, 152.

45. Sir Owen Seaman, as quoted in *GG*, 153.

46. Crystal Eastman, *On Women and Revolution*, 121.

47. Morgan, 180.

48. Duchess of Marlborough, "The Position of Women," 11.

49. Consuelo's prescience is seen in that this theory is taken seriously by current feminist historians. See for example, Gerda Lerner, "Reconceptualizing Differences among Women," *Journal of Women's History* (Winter 1990): 106–122.

50. *GG*, 156.

51. For illustrations and plans, see L. R. McCabe, "A Revival of French Gothic Architecture," *Architectural Record* (September 1913): 202–12.

52. ASVB memoir, 166.

53. Alva Belmont to Sara Bard Fields, 1–5–1919, C. E. S. Wood Collection, Huntington Library.

Chapter 10: 1908–1914

1. *GVW,* 246.

2. *RES,* 77.

3. Ibid., 78.

4. Jo Davidson, *Between Sittings,* 49.

5. Camille Mauclair, "L'art de Mme Gertrude Whitney," Whitney Museum papers, AAA, roll N578, no frame numbers. This is the only extensive essay on Gertrude's sculpture I came across.

6. The date may be otherwise. Gertrude did this recounting of the affair in early 1912, and the timing is inferred from other remarks within the document.

7. All quotes relating to this episode are from GVW papers, AAA, roll 1903, frames 13–20.

8. *GVW,* 298.

9. W. A. Swanberg, *Whitney Father, Whitney Heiress,* 322. In fact, Straight's father had been a normal school teacher in Oswego, New York.

10. GVW papers, AAA, Washington, D.C., untitled notebook beginning "I had just come back from Paris . . . ," box 6.

11. During this time Jo Davidson, Malvina Hoffman, and Anna Hyatt Huntington were among those artists who carved stone as well as modeled it. Those who relied on *practiciens* included Mario Korbel, Max Kalish, and Herbert Haseltine. For centuries artists have used assistants to complete or refine their works; in modern times there are well-known cases where the artist does no more than give instructions to his or her crafts workers.

12. Letters to William Stackpole here were copied over into Gertrude's journal 1912–13, AAA, roll 1904, frames 162–83.

13. Gertrude's only account of this encounter is vague and hints at a certain hiding of the truth. She goes with the man, whom she does not like, to some unknown address. She hints of more complicity in the episode than she admits to.

14. *GVW,* 326.

15. "Why I Am a Suffragist," 1172. I was unable to locate many particulars concerning

Alva's pre-1908 social service activities, which she later intimated included hospitals and settlement houses.

16. Ibid, 1174.

17. ASVB memoirs, 167.

18. Ibid.

19. SBF notes.

20. For more details on her activities here, see "What Mrs. Belmont Has Done for Woman," *New York Times,* 9 March 1910.

21. "How Can Women Get the Suffrage," 688.

22. "Negro Women Join in Suffrage Fight," *New York Times,* 7 February 1910.

23. Ida Harper, *History of Woman Suffrage,* vol. 5, 672.

24. William O'Neill, *Everyone Was Brave,* 153–4.

25. "Suffragists to Aid Girl Waist Strikers," *New York Times,* 2 December 1909.

26. "Woman's Right to Govern Herself," 665.

27. ASVB memoir, 4.

28. This is her only publication that hints at acceptance of social Darwinist ideas, when she asks how fathers can let "that alien who cannot read or write" vote, yet not their educated daughters. This position is contradictory in light of her more frequent inclusion of women of all classes and races in her suffrage call, but Alva was never one for fully consistent positions.

29. *GG,* 170.

30. Doris Stevens, *Jailed for Freedom,* 31.

31. For more description, see Eleanor Flexner, *Centuries of Struggle,* 259.

32. A classic example of the beneficiary is Sara Bard Field. In 1915, Alva learned the poet was divorced with two small children and later arranged for her to live in Newport for two months to assist in the writing of her memoirs. Field wrote her lover Charles Erskine Scott Wood that she intended to "stick her for $250" a month salary. (Letter of 8–31–1915, C. E. S. Wood Collection, Huntington Library.) Belmont paid her $1,000 a month.

33. SBF notes.

34. Max Eastman, *Enjoyment of Living,* 403.

35. Ibid., 404.

36. Ibid., 474.

37. Katherine Hepburn's mother was instrumental not only in eliminating flagrant prosti-

tution but started an organization that became the League of Women Voters. For an introduction to this other neglected reformer and feminist, see Christian Andersen, *Young Kate*, 1988.

38. Extract of a letter to the Committee on Criminal Courts, April 1913, as printed in *GG*, 171.

39. The worker was Sara Bard Field, who sought exemption from picketing duty in 1917. Field had been in a tuberculosis asylum and had a history of nervous breakdowns as well. See her oral history.

40. See Alice Paul, oral history, 320, for details.

41. See "Congressional Committee Archives, NAWSA Convention, Washington, D.C., November 29–December 5, 1913" in Mari Jo Buhle and Paul Buhle, *The Concise History of Woman Suffrage*, 417–21. The anonymous writer of account notes that the delegates were more in favor of Alva's stand than the final vote tally showed.

42. See Alice Paul's oral history, 86–8, for a discussion of Alva's joining the Congressional Union. Paul's refusal of a salary does not mean she lived impoverished. Since the Congressional Union paid her living expenses, her basic needs were well met, including the provision of staff to shop, cook, and clean. Until the 1920s, she lived austerely in a basement at headquarters with a phone by her bed, and she worried staff with her neglect of personal need. In later years, after Alva bought a comfortable home for the organization in Washington, Paul enjoyed a more gracious living amid antiques and maids. It was a late, deserved reward for her sacrifices.

43. James Brough, *Consuelo*, 161.

Chapter 11: 1914–1919

1. Alice Paul, oral history, 331.

2. For a full statement of this position, see Doris Stevens, *Jailed for Freedom*, 33–4. Sara Bard Field (oral history, 301) also credited Alva for having "the most strange ability to grasp such a situation as holding the party in power responsible."

3. Sara Bard Field, oral history, 301.

4. Cornelius Vanderbilt, *Queen of the Golden Age*, 229.

5. GVW papers, AAA, roll 1904, frame 270. The letter is undated but written likely in September or early October 1913.

6. GVW papers, AAA, Washington, D.C., box 8 contains all the materials on Juilly, including photographs Gertrude took, letters from the staff, and other ephemera.

7. GVW papers, AAA, roll 1904, frame 62.

8. Rudi Blesh, *Modern Art USA*, 96.

9. June Sochen, *The New Woman*, 47.

10. Ibid., 48.

11. Sherry Birk, curator at the American Institute of Architects suggested the descriptive "carnivalesque," a telling and accurate portrayal of this oddity with its turrets, windows in the form of crosses, and absence of the elegant finish details found at 660 Fifth Avenue. The Gatsby connection was identified by Jerry E. Patterson, *The Vanderbilt Homes*, 164. This is also the only reference I came across showing interior shots of the building.

12. "Battle for Suffrage Is Biggest Job," *San Francisco Bulletin*, 13 September 1913.

13. "National Campaign Begun for Suffrage," *San Francisco Chronicle*, 15 September 1915.

14. Benjamin Ide Wheeler, president of the University of California, as quoted in Nancy Boas, *The Society of Six*, 56. Boas also shows how this romanticism and idealism resulted in a selection of art that was so unadventurous that it retarded the development of modernism in California.

15. For information on sculpture at the exhibition, see John D. Barry, *The City of Domes* (San Francisco: John J. Newbegin, 1915) and A. Stirling Calder, *Sculpture and Mural Decorations of the Exhibition* (San Francisco: Paul Elder, 1915).

16. Alice Paul is contradictory in her reporting here. She claimed when first interviewed that Alva pledged the money but did not deliver it (153), yet in later discussion on the same contribution credits her help (347–48). Since there is no other record of Alva being the sort to make public pledges and not deliver, it is likely she came through in this instance.

17. Alice Paul, oral history, 346.

18. Gertrude saved a clipping from the *Toledo News Bee*, 4 October 1916, which informed here.

19. Congressional Union member Maud Younger, as quoted in Inez Hayes Irwin, *The Story of the Woman's Party*, 195.

20. Doris Stevens, *Jailed for Freedom*, 56.

21. Alice Paul, oral history, 209.

22. Alice Paul, oral history, 346. This is Paul's version of Alva's words.

23. For their frequent letters of concern about Sonny, see GVW papers, AAA, roll 2361. A man with his father's bonhomie, Sonny Whitney has always been candid about his enjoyment of life. He once quipped how he was never further than third from the bottom of his classes at Yale.

24. SBF to Charles Erskine Scott Wood, C.E.S. Wood Collection, Huntington Library, 31 July 1917.

25. Ibid, August 1917.

26. Ibid, 16 August 1917.

27. Doris Stevens, *Jailed for Freedom*, 201–2. The quote is from a diary of Lucy Burns's that was smuggled out of the prison.

28. *New York Times,* 9 July 1917.

Chapter 12: 1919–1925

1. GVW papers, AAA, roll 2361, frames 746–48. The letter, undated, was filed in Gertrude's 1919 correspondence.

2. *GVW,* 417. The critic quoted is from the *Brooklyn Eagle.*

3. "Sculpture of War: The Work of Gertrude Whitney," *Touchstone,* January 1920. This article includes several reproductions from the exhibit.

4. "Mrs. Whitney's Sculptures Winning Europe," *Literary Digest* 2 (July 1921). The quotation is from a reviewer for *The American Art News* concerning the exhibit of her war sculpture in Paris.

5. "G. V. W.," Whitney Museum papers, AAA, roll N587, frame numbers not indicated.

6. *GVW,* 415–16.

7. "Mrs. Whitney's Sculptures Winning Europe," *Literary Digest* 2 (July 1921).

8. Here I differ from Avis Berman's exceptional history of the Whitney, *Rebels on Eighth Street.* Berman attributes much of what went on at the Whitney to Juliana. Looking at the residue of that activity, the letters and papers, one could well conclude such. But this ignores that the operations were the result of unrecorded personal interactions. To argue such is to present Gertrude simply as the patron, the moneybags, when this was clearly not the case.

9. GVW papers, AAA, roll 1904, frames 503–4.

10. Ibid., frame 512.

11. Ibid., frames 518–19.

12. Ibid., frame 536.

13. "The Duchess of Marlborough: Restitution Suit," *London Times,* 23 March 1920.

14. "The Marlborough Divorce Suit," *London Times,* 10 November 1920.

15. Brough, *Consuelo,* describes Balsan as a bachelor, yet the *New York Times* states he was previously married and divorced ("Duchess Obtained Annulment Decree in Marlborough Suit," 14 November 26). In her own book, which Brough relies so much upon, Consuelo implies Balsan was a bachelor. In light of the episode discussed here, she would certainly not want it known that he also was divorced. Alva's suffrage scrapbooks include a clipping from an unknown London paper dated July 5, 1921, that describes Balsan as previously married to one Marie Adele.

16. Although the claims for this great romance come only from Consuelo, no evidence is found from observers that the relationship was otherwise. For example, Mary Younger, who was Alva's secretary, gave no indication to the contrary in her comments about Consuelo in her gossipy letters home. Despite Consuelo's tendency to

rewrite history, it seems likely her marriage to Balsan was in fact most congenial.

17. Sources disagree as to whether the episode discussed here occurred during the trip to Europe or on the way back. That fact being irrelevant to the main point, and both sources having equal problems in accuracy of details, I have chosen one version for narrative's sake. Compare Maxwell, *R.S.V.P.*, with Shadegg, *Clare Boothe Luce*.

18. Maxwell, 106.

19. Ibid., 107.

20. In her oral history (451–53), Paul corroborates that it was Alva who originated the idea of a separate party.

21. *Washington Times*, 9 July 1920.

22. *New York Call*, 9 July 1920.

23. *New York Times*, 26 August 1920.

24. Most histories of this period accept the critics' views as reality and portray the National Woman's party accordingly. For significant counter evidence, see Peter Geidel, "The National Woman's Party and the Origins of the Equal Rights Amendment, 1920–1923," *The Historian*, 44 (1980): 557–82. Geidel examined the actual proceedings and observed that the NWP had a difficult time presenting an accurate picture because it lacked a publication at that time.

25. Alva E. Belmont, "What the Woman's Party Wants," *Collier's*, 23 December 1922, 6.

26. Mrs. O. H. P. Belmont, "Women as Dictators," *Ladies' Home Journal*, September 1922, 7ff.

27. As quoted in Mary Anderson and Mary Winslow, *Woman at Work* (Minneapolis: University of Minnesota Press, 1951): 164.

28. Dorothy M. Brown, *Setting a Course*, 63.

29. *Equal Rights*, 3 March 1923.

30. Ibid., 8 May 1926.

31. Based on a remark from Sonny Whitney, Avis Berman (*RES*, 179–80) suggests that Gertrude bought the land, hence guaranteed this commission. Flora Biddle, in an interview, responded to me that the history of the work is not so clear-cut, that she and B. H. Friedman were unable after exhaustive research to prove or disprove a connection.

32. *RES*, 204.

33. Ibid., 206.

34. *GVW*, 463.

35. *RES*, 188.

36. Lloyd Goodrich, "'The Arts' Magazine: 1920–31," *American Art Journal* 5 (1973): 79–85.

37. *Brooklyn Eagle*, 8 April 1923.

38. *New York Evening Sun*, 16 May 1924.

39. *RES*, 184.

40. *Brooklyn Eagle*, 17 February 1924.

41. F. Scott Fitzgerald, *The Great Gatsby*, 11.

42. Keislich claimed her love for Gloria was an expression of that lost on a son who had died. Barbara Goldsmith, who checked into this matter extensively, was unable to come up with any evidence of such. See her *Little Gloria . . . Happy at Last*, 134–35. If Goldsmith is correct, then Keislich was much more mentally unstable than ever came out at the later trial.

Chapter 13: 1925–1932

1. From Flora's unpublished diary, as quoted in Whitney Museum of Art, *Flora Whitney Miller, Her Life, Her World*, 20.

2. These letters can be found in GVW papers, AAA, roll 2362.

3. "Marlborough Seeks the Aid of the Pope," *New York Times*, 11 November 1926.

4. "Sacra Romana Rota: Southwarcen. Nullitatis Matrimoii (Vanderbilt-de Marlborough), *Acta Apostolicae Sedis*, 1926: 501–506. The proceedings are written in the official church language, Latin, except for quotes from the testimony, which is presented in French. In *Consuelo*, 215–21, James Brough incorrectly dates this appearance as 1932. Brough does give fair translations of sections of these proceedings, however.

5. "Duchess Obtained Annulment Decree in Marlborough Suit," *New York Times*, 14 November 1926.

6. In *Consuelo*, James Brough claims Sunny went to Rome in November but presents no evidence. He may have been misled here by the early news stories, which suggested such a visit, yet later denied it.

7. "Vanderbilt Decree Sought to Validate Second Marriage," *New York Times*, 15 November 1926.

8. "Marlborough Stays Secluded in Castle," *New York Times*, 18 November 1926.

9. "Bishop Manning Attacks Rome's Vanderbilt Decree as Impertinent Intrusion," *New York Times*, 26 November 1926.

10. *London Times*, 18 November 1926.

11. Geoffrey Perrett, *America in the Twenties*, 310.

12. "Clergy Uphold Bishop Manning," *New York Times*, 27 November 1926.

13. "Marlborough Gets Marriage Annulled," *New York Times,* 13 November 1926.

14. "Catholics Defend Vanderbilt Decree," *New York Times,* 20 November 1926.

15. Ibid.

16. In 1902 Rutherfurd married Alice Morton, youngest daughter of New York's governor Levi Morton. It was a happy union, producing five children. She died only fifteen years later. In 1920 he married Lucy Mercer, who had become Franklin Roosevelt's lover when Eleanor refused him conjugal rights. That affair was over when Lucy married Winty, but the liaison would revive in the 1940s, and she was with Roosevelt when he died.

17. "W. Rutherfurd, 82, Leader in Society," *New York Times,* March 21, 1944. I could not locate the original source for this quote from his obituary.

18. "Says Ex-Duchess Denies Coercion," *New York Times,* 21 November 1926.

19. It is of course possible that Consuelo's interview was a fake or a contrivance. The language and motive seems to be in character, however, and gives further credence to the coercion story being a convenient exaggeration of the facts.

20. "A Friend's Tribute," *London Times,* 2 July 1934.

21. Inez Hayes Irwin, *Angels and Amazons,* 358.

22. Unfortunately, Alice Paul said little about this activity in her extensive oral history. The full story of this international cooperation among feminist groups is yet to be written, so Alva's and Alice's full roles remains sketchy. Much of this discussion is pieced together from the articles of Crystal Eastman, written during this time, columns in *Equal Rights,* and dabbles of information available in the histories of the women's movement.

23. Blanche Wiesen Cook, *Crystal Eastman on Women and the Revolution,* 208.

24. *GVW,* 484.

25. Henry McBride, *The Dial,* May 1926.

26. *RES,* 247.

27. *GVW,* 520.

28. GVW to Paul Clayton, 30 May 1927, GVW papers, AAA, roll 1904, frame 641. The originals of the correspondence are in roll 2362.

29. GVW to Paul Clayton, 13 June 1927, GVW papers, AAA, roll 1904, frame 647.

30. GVW to Paul Clayton, c. August 1927, GVW papers, roll 1904, frame 696.

31. *New York Times,* 3 January 1930.

32. Whitney Museum of American Art, *Juliana Force and American Art,* 60.

33. *RES,* 294.

34. Forbes Watson to GVW, GVW papers, AAA, roll 2363, frame not visible.

35. My discussion of this novel is based upon the summary provided by Flora Irving Biddle to B. F. Friedman for *GVW*, 549–53. My attempts to locate a copy of this book proved futile, for even family members had lost their copies over the years. Flora Biddle's own copy disappeared after lending it to someone, but she had already prepared the precis.

36. *GVW*, 559.

37. Paul Rosenfeld, *The Nation* (30 December 1931).

38. *RES*, 309.

39. For a spirited description of the internecine battles here, see *RES*, chapter 9.

40. *GVW*, 567.

41. Given the lesbian theme of *Walking the Dusk*, I looked for any sign of such a relationship in Gertrude's adult life but saw none. Flora Irving Biddle shared with me that she had done the same search during her research and had explored the topic with her mother. She stated that Flora Whitney MacCollough resisted such discussion, and she had never been able to determine whether it was out of her mother's personal discomfort with the topic or because she may as a youngster have heard a rumor of Gertrude's involvement with a woman. From all evidence, both Gertrude and her closest woman associate, Juliana Force, were utterly heterosexual.

42. *OUT*, 4.

43. Ibid., 27

44. Ibid., 15.

45. Barbara Goldsmith, *Little Gloria . . . Happy at Last*, 220–22, provides texts of these and other letters, which became part of the public record during the 1934 custody trial.

46. See *WW*, chapter 2, for her elaboration of this insight.

Chapter 14: 1932–1936

1. See Mrs. O. H. P. Belmont, "Are Women Really Citizens?" *Good Housekeeping*, September 1931, 99ff.

2. This is not the first time Doris's behavior upset Alva. In 1928 she misrepresented her authority at a Paris conference, and Alva berated Jane Norman Smith, then secretary of the party, concerning the action. She quickly forgave Doris then, however. See correspondence in the Jane Norman Smith papers, the Schlesinger Library, Radcliffe College.

3. Elsa Maxwell, *R.S.V.P.*, 212.

4. Matilda Young to her mother, Matilda Young papers, Duke University Library, 13 August 1933.

5. Maxwell, 110.

6. Matilda Young to her mother, Matilda Young papers, 31 August 1932.

7. Oral interview with Alice Paul, Bancroft Library, 564.

8. "Tribute to Alva Belmont," *Equal Rights,* 15 July 1933.

9. For more details, see the oral interview with Alice Paul, Bancroft Library, 560–68.

10. *OUT,* 36. Gloria dates this as 1932, but she was at Westbury recuperating much of that summer.

11. *OUT,* 38.

12. Ibid., 46.

13. Barbara Goldsmith, *Little Gloria . . . Happy at Last,* 299.

14. A set of notes in unidentified hand spell out the argument in favor of Gertrude's obtaining custody. "Not advisable at this hearing to refer to indifference [,] neglect or dislike, by mother." GVW papers, AAA, roll 2363, frames, 853–56.

15. *OUT,* 46.

16. Ibid., 48.

17. Ibid., 58.

18. Goldsmith, 61.

19. Ibid., 63.

20. *OUT,* 65.

21. Goldsmith, 64.

22. *OUT,* 79.

23. Letter of Barklie Henry to Mrs. G. MacCulloch Miller (Flora), 18 October 1934, GVW papers, AAA, roll 2363, frames 873–75.

24. I refer the interested to GVW papers, AAA, roll 2363, frame 540.

25. *OUT,* 86.

26. *OUT,* 109. Barbara Goldsmith's main theme is that Gloria had been aware of the Lindbergh and other kidnappings, hence was afraid her mother was going to kidnap and *kill* her. Gloria did use the word *kidnap* several times over the months, but the fear was such abduction would mean separation from Dodo. Although Goldsmith, herself growing up at the time, shared this fear with other youngsters (as I did with friends when a child nearby fell into a well and eventually died), she erred in assuming Gloria was similarly exposed to newspapers and radio. Everything in Gloria's memoir points to her not being aware of these well-known events, that indeed she knew little about anything going on in the country at the time.

27. *OUT,* 112–13.

28. Ibid., 115.

29. Ibid., 116.

30. Ibid., 119.

31. Gloria [Morgan] Vanderbilt, *Without Prejudice,* 111.

32. Ibid., 157.

33. Ibid., 158.

34. GVW, *A Love Story,* 94–5.

35. For some of these versions, see the GVW Collection, AAA, Washington, D.C., box 1.

36. *OUT,* 134.

37. Goldsmith, 647. Quote taken from an interview Barbara Goldsmith had with Jim Murray.

38. *OUT,* 152–53.

39. Ibid., 152.

40. Ibid., 141.

41. Ibid., 167.

42. *RES,* 382.

Chapter 15: 1936–1942

1. These letters may be found in GVW papers, AAA, roll 2364. They cover a period between 1935 and 1941.

2. Gloria Vanderbilt to GVW, GVW papers, AAA, roll 2363, frames 177–80.

3. *GVW,* 614.

4. *OUT,* 171.

5. GVW papers, AAA, roll 2364, frame 273.

6. From his autobiography *Untold Friendships,* as quoted in GVW, 622.

7. Robert Porter Keep to Frank Crocker, GVW papers, AAA, roll 2464, frames 390–1.

8. Gloria's letters to Gertrude are scattered throughout GVW papers, AAA, roll 2464.

9. Gloria says in *OUT* that because of her appendicitis she missed the entire spring term. This is another error in chronology, for Gertrude's diaries put the operation on May 7, with Gloria leaving the hospital in an ambulance on May 17.

10. As quoted in *GVW,* 632.

11. *OUT*, 190.

12. GVW to Gladys [Sechenyi], GVW papers, AAA, roll 2464, frame 662.

13. *OUT*, 193.

14. GVW papers, AAA, roll 2464, frame 667. This is a handwritten draft of the letter presumably sent to Mrs. Keep.

15. Gioia Diliberto, *Debutante,* 94.

16. *OUT*, 283.

17. In *OUT*, Gloria renames Jones as Winston Smith II to cover his identity, which had already become public knowledge in B. H. Friedman's biography of Gertrude. Aram Saroyan also identified him in *Trio,* which appeared in 1985, so I do the same here.

18. Aram Saroyan, *Trio,* 33.

19. Laura [Morgan] to Gertrude [Vanderbilt], GVW papers, AAA, roll 2464, frame 762.

20. GVW to Laura [Morgan], GVW papers, AAA, roll 2464, frame 764.

21. Notes for a letter from GVW to Gloria, GVW papers, AAA, roll 2464, frame 664.

22. *GG*, 253.

23. Ibid., 237.

24. Ibid., 259.

25. Ibid.

26. Gertrude's dozens of short story assignments with Hull's comments may be seen in the GVW collection, AAA, Washington, D.C.

27. *GVW*, 648. For full correspondence from that time concerning the play, see GVW papers, AAA, roll 2464, particularly letters from Ronnie [Bodley].

28. *GVW*, 643.

29. Gloria omits mention of this desire in *OUT*. The evidence comes from letters between her and Gertrude as found in GVW papers, AAA, roll 2464.

30. GVW notes for a letter to Gloria, GVW papers, AAA, roll 2464, frame 519.

31. *OUT*, 335.

32. Ibid.

33. *BKWK,* 29.

34. In *OUT*, Gloria omits that the trip was from the start to discuss the Hughes proposal and says simply that Gertrude had ordered her back home for a visit.

35. Saroyan, 24.

36. *BKWK,* 85.

37. Ibid., 112.

38. Maurice Zolotow, "Gloria Vanderbilt's Search for Happiness," *Cosmopolitan*, July 1958, 50.

Chapter 16: 1942–1959

1. *BKWK*, 155.

2. Henry McBride, *New York Sun*, 24 April 1942.

3. See *New York Herald-Tribune*, 19 January 1943.

4. Avis Berman, "Juliana Force," *Museum News* (November/December 1976): 61.

5. *Juliana Force and American Art*, 24 September 30 October 1949, Whitney Museum of American Art.

6. *BKWK*, 178. Gloria states she and Carol went off to a party together, where they met Stokowski. His datebook indicates otherwise, that he met her at the Saroyan apartment.

7. Oliver Daniel, *Stokowski*, 484.

8. *BKWK*, 181.

9. Stokowski's success at rewriting his biography was so effective that even so scrupulous a source as the *Grove's Encyclopedia of Music* until very recent editions duplicated common errors. For a discussion of these errors, see Daniel, especially chapter 1.

10. Daniel, 189.

11. Boski Antheil, as quoted in Daniel, 488.

12. Daniel, 487.

13. Ibid., 488.

14. *BKWK*, 221.

15. Lois Palken Rudnick, *Mabel Dodge Luhan*, 270. On Stowkowski's request, "Bach in a Baggage Car" was never published. The manuscript is in the Mabel Dodge Luhan Collection, Beinecke Library, Yale University.

16. Rudnick, 269.

17. *BKWK*, 226.

18. Ibid., 233.

19. *WW*, 182.

20. Daniel, 503.

21. *New York Journal-American*, 13 March 1946.

22. *New York Times*, 4 April 1946.

23. Daniel, 546–47.

24. Ibid., 532.

25. *BKWK*, 255.

26. Ibid., 299.

27. As quoted in Elaine Tyler May, *Homeward Bound*, 141.

28. *BKWK*, 248.

29. May, 104.

30. Maurice Zolotow, "Gloria Vanderbilt's Search for Happiness," *Cosmopolitan*, July 1958, 51.

31. *Saturday Review*, 8 October 1955. Carol Marcus's novel was also reviewed in this article, entitled "Eight Ways to Become an Authoress." Though a nasty sexist bite at young women authors, "ladies" in the quaint language of the day, the review of Gloria's poetry was more accurate than that of the polite *New York Times* (8 April 1956), which calls them "surprisingly good . . . childlike . . . gently touching," yet slips at the truth in saying she "*artlessly* convinces one she has the poet's right to speak [emphasis added]."

32. *BKWK*, 299.

33. Laura Berquist, "Gloria Vanderbilt Starts a New Life," *Look*, 12 July 1955, 95.

34. *New York Times*, 20 January 1974.

35. Zolotow, 46.

36. *Gloria Vanderbilt Book of Collage*, 111.

37. Gloria Vanderbilt and Thelma Furness, *Double Exposure*, 318. Emphasis is added. Although she adds, "the existing arrangement was as hard on Gloria as it was on me," the emphasis is on Gloria M.'s own inconvenience.

38. Vanderbilt and Furness, 336.

39. Ibid., 339.

40. Ibid., 367.

Chapter 17: 1959–1990

1. *Time*, 6 July 1959.

2. *New York Mirror*, 15 May 1959.

3. Aram Saroyan, *Trio*, 180.

4. Gail Lumet Buckley, *The Hornes*, 248.

5. *New York Times*, 27 August 1963.

6. Gerald Clarke, *Capote*, 336–37.

7. Saroyan, 189.

8. For pictorial evidence of this description, see "Private World: Connecticut House of Mr. and Mrs. Wyatt Cooper," *Vogue*, 1 February 1966. See also chapter 13, *WW*, for her description of decorating Faraway.

9. *WW*, 67.

10. *WW*, 31.

11. For photographs of Juliana's brilliant creation, see *RES*, 2–3. For comparison to Gloria, see illustrations to *Gloria Vanderbilt Book of Collage*, 1970, or "Gloria the Great's Patchwork Bedroom," *Vogue*, 1 February 1990, 206–9.

12. *New York Times*, 9 April 1966.

13. "Kore-Sculpture in Cloth: Mrs. Wyatt Emory Cooper in her Fabled Fortuny Dresses," *Vogue*, December 1969, 243.

14. Francesca Stanfill, "The Marketing of Gloria Vanderbilt," *New York Times Magazine*, 14 October 1979, 137.

15. *Gloria Vanderbilt Book of Collage*, 111.

16. Gerald Clarke, *Capote*, 469.

17. Stanfill, 124.

18. Wyatt Cooper, *Families*, 1. Subsequent quotes are from chapter 1.

19. Whitney Museum of American Art, *Flora Whitney Miller*, 116.

20. "River House Rebuttal in Vanderbilt Case," *New York Times*, 28 May 1980.

21. "'Little Gloria' Vs. That Co-op," *New York*, 9 June 1990.

22. "Take a Celebrity to Lunch," *New York Times*, 11 June 1980.

23. Dominick Dunne, *Fatal Charms*, 193.

24. Barbara Grizzutti Harrison, review of *Once upon a Time*, *New York Times*, 14 April 1985.

25. For more particulars, see Kay Larson, "War at the Whitney," *New York*, 12 February 1990, 35.

26. *WW*, 195.

27. Barbara Lazear Ascher, "A Personal Tradition," *House and Garden* (February 1984): 76.

28. Gloria Vanderbilt, *Never Say Good-bye*, 142.

BIBLIOGRAPHY

Publications by the Principals

Balsan, Consuelo Vanderbilt

Marlborough, Duchess of. "The Position of Woman." Parts 2, 3, 10. *North American Review.*
89 (1909): 180–93, 351–59, 11–24.

————. "Hostels for Women." *The Nineteenth Century and After,* 1911, 858–66.

Balsan, Consuelo. *The Glitter and the Gold.* London: William Heinemann, 1953.

Belmont, Alva Smith Vanderbilt

PRIMARY SOURCES

National Woman's Party Papers, Microfilming Corporation of America. (Rolls 113, 116,
164–65: Alva's correspondence, speeches, and news clipping scrapbooks covering
her suffrage activities.)

Jane Norman Smith Papers, Elizabeth and Arthur Schlesinger Library, Radcliffe College.
(Box 5, folders 101–3: Correspondence concerning the National Woman's party
during the late 1920s.)

C. E. S. Wood Collection, Huntington Library. (Sara Bard Field's handwritten notes of
interviews with Alva and typescript of biography, prepared in 1917.)

Matilda Young Papers, William R. Perkins Library, Duke University. (Typed memoir
prepared by Alva, c. 1932.)

ORAL HISTORIES

Sara Bard Field, *Poet and Suffragist,* an interview by Amelia R. Fry, Regional Oral History
Office, The Bancroft Library, University of California.

Alice Paul, *Woman's Suffrage and the Equal Rights Amendment,* an interview by Amelia R.
Fry, Suffragists Oral History Office, The Bancroft Library, University of California.

Mabel Vernon, *Speaker for Suffrage and Peace,* an interview by Amelia R. Fry, Suffragists
Oral History Office, The Bancroft Library, University of California.

PUBLICATIONS

"Woman's Right to Govern Herself." *North American Review.* 190 (November 1909):
664–74.

"Belief in Woman Is Belief in Woman Suffrage." *The Woman's Magazine,* December 1909.

"Farewell to the Doll Age." *Paris Modes,* February 1910.

"How Can Women Get the Suffrage?" *Independent.* 68 (31 March 1910): 686–89.

"Why the Women Should Have the Ballot." *Searchlight Magazine,* March 1910.

"Woman Suffrage as it Looks Today." *Forum.* 43 (March 1910): 264–68.

"Woman and the Suffrage." *Harper's Bazaar.* 44 (March 1910): 170.

"Why I Am a Suffragist." *World Today.* 21 (October 1911): 1171–78.

Chicago Sunday Tribune Series:

"How Suffrage Will Protect Women from Men Who 'Sow Wild Oats,'" April 28, 1912.

"Why Women Need the Ballot," May 12, 1912.

"Votes for Women Will Improve Existing Conditions," May 26, 1912.

"A Son Loses Respect for His Mother the Day He Votes," June 2, 1912.

"A Girl? What a Pity It Was Not a Boy!" June 9, 1912.

"In What Respect Do Women Differ from Slaves or Serfs?" June 16, 1912.

"Women Can Tell from Intuition an Honest Man from a Grafter," June 23, 1912.

"Woman's Suffrage Raises the Quality of Electorate," June 30, 1912.

"Women Suffragists Ask for Progressive Constitution," July 7, 1912.

"'Do Not Let the Women Vote'—Slogan of Political Bosses," July 14, 1912.

"In Nonvoting States Women Are Classed With Lunatics," July 21, 1912.

"Man Has Failed to Care for Women and Children," July 28, 1912.

"Are Politicians Seeking a Flirtation with Suffragists?" August 4, 1912.

"Men Will Forget the Rosenthal Murder; Women Will Remember It," August 11, 1912.

"The Country Always Progresses Despite Politicians, Not on Account of Them," August 18, 1912.

"Shall the Market Basket of America's Poor Be Filled?" August 25, 1912.

"We Read Sign Posts Along the Road That Leads to Votes for Women," September 8, 1912.

"What Place Will Women Take in Our Political Life?" September 15, 1912.

"We Have to Take What We Can Get in the Company It Comes," September 22, 1912.

"We Have Gone Back to the Worship of the Golden Calf," September 29, 1912.

"The Ballot Is the Scepter of Sovreignty in America," October 13, 1912.

"Do the Candidates Now See the Light?" October 20, 1912.

"Equal Suffrage Not National Question?" November 3, 1912.

"The Liberation of a Sex." *Hearst's Magazine*. 23 (April 1913): 614–16.

"Jewish Women in Public Affairs." *The American Citizen*. (May 1913): 181ff.

"Foreword" to "The Story of the Women's War." *Good Housekeeping*. 57 (November 1913): 571a–71b.

"New Standards for Business Women." *Business Woman's Magazine* (January 1915): 7–9.

"Women as Dictators." *Ladies' Home Journal*. 39 (September 1922): 7ff.

"What the Woman's Party Wants." *Collier's*. 70 (December 23, 1922): 6.

"Are Women Really Citizens?" *Good Housekeeping*. 93 (September 1931): 99ff.

Vanderbilt, Gloria

PRIMARY SOURCES

Gertrude Vanderbilt Whitney Papers, Whitney Museum of American Art, Archives of American Art. (Rolls 2363–64: Correspondence from Gloria to Gertrude.)

PUBLICATIONS

Gloria Vanderbilt Book of Collage. New York: Van Nostrand Reinhold, 1970.
Woman to Woman. Garden City, N.Y.: Doubleday, 1979.
Once upon a Time. New York: Knopf, 1985.
Black Knight, White Knight. New York: Knopf, 1987.
Never Say Good-bye. New York: Knopf, 1989.

Whitney, Gertrude Vanderbilt

PRIMARY SOURCES

Gertrude Vanderbilt Whitney Papers, Whitney Museum of American Art, Archives of American Art. (Rolls 2356–71: Original journals, datebooks, correspondence, sculpture files, party books, drafts of fictional works; rolls 1903–04: Typescripts of major portion of original writings and correspondence prepared for B. H. Friedman's biography.)

Gertrude Vanderbilt Whitney Papers, unmicrofilmed portion. Archives of American Art, Washington, D.C. (six boxes: Drafts of fiction and plays, photographs and correspondence concerning hospital at Juilly, journals, ephemera.)

Whitney Museum Papers, Archives of American Art. (Roll N586: Clippings, articles, reviews.)

PUBLICATIONS

"The Useless Memorial." *Arts and Decoration*. (April 1920): 421.
"The End of America's Apprenticeship in Art." Series run in *Arts and Decoration* issues of June 25, 1920, October 1920, November 1920.
"Fear—The Destroyer." *Ladies' Home Journal*. (February 1923): 27ff.
Walking the Dusk. [Pseudonym L. J. Webb] New York: Coward, McCann, 1932.
A Love Affair. New York: Richardson and Snyder, 1984.

Selected Bibliography

Adams, Henry. *The Education of Henry Adams*. New York: Modern Library, 1918.
Allen, Frederick Lewis. *The Big Change*. New York: Harper & Row, 1952.
Armory, Cleveland. *The Last Resorts*. New York: Harper & Row, 1952.
Andersen, Christopher. *Young Kate*. New York: Henry Holt, 1988.
Andrews, Wayne. *The Vanderbilt Legend*. New York: Harcourt Brace, and Co., 1941.
Auchincloss, Louis. *The Vanderbilt Era*. New York: Scribners, 1989.
Baker, Paul R. *Richard Morris Hunt*. Cambridge, Mass.: MIT Press, 1986.
Barrett, Richmond. *Good Old Summer Days*. New York: Appleton-Century-Crofts, 1941.
Becker, Susan. *The Origins of the Equal Rights Amendment*. Westwood, CN: Greenwood, 1981.
Beebe, Lucius. *The Big Spenders*. Garden City, N.Y.: Doubleday, 1966.
Benstock, Shari. *Women of the Left Bank*. New York: University of Texas Press, 1986.

Berman, Avis. *Rebels on Eighth Street*. New York: Macmillan, 1990.

Birmingham, Stephen. *The Secret Aristocracy*. New York: Little, Brown, 1987.

Blatch, Harriot Stanton, and Alma Lutz. *Challenging Years*. New York: Putnam's, 1940.

Breuning, Margaret. "Gertrude Whitney's Sculpture." *Magazine of Art*. (February 19, 1943): 62–65.

Briggs, John. *Requiem for a Yellow Brick Brewery*. Boston: Little, Brown, 1969.

Brown, Dorothy M. *Setting a Course: American Women in the 1920s*. Boston: Twayne, 1987.

Buckley, Gail Lumet. *The Hornes*. New York: Knopf, 1986.

Buhle, Mari Jo, and Paul Buhle. *The Concise History of Woman Suffrage*. Urbana: University of Illinois Press, 1979.

Capote, Truman. *Answered Prayers*. New York: Random House, 1987.

Churchill, Allen. *The Upper Crust*. Englewood Cliffs, N.J.: Prentice-Hall, 1970.

Churchill, Peregrine, and Julian Mitchell. *Jennie: Lady Randolph Churchill*. New York: St. Martin's Press, 1974.

Clark, Frank [Frank Kintrea]. "The Commodore Left Two Sons." *American Heritage*. 17 (April 1966): 5–13, 81ff.

Clarke, Gerald. *Capote*. New York: Random House, 1988.

Cogan, Frances B. *All-American Girl*. Athens: University of Georgia Press, 1989.

Conner, Janis and Joel Rosenkranz. *Rediscoveries in American Sculpture: Studio Works, 1893–1939*. Austin: University of Texas Press, 1989.

Cook, Blanche Wiesen. *Toward the Great Change: Crystal and Max Eastman on Feminism, Antimilitarism, and Revolution*. New York: Garland, 1976.

————. *Crystal Eastman on Women and Revolution*. New York: Oxford University Press, 1978.

Cott, Nancy. "Feminist Politics in the 1920s." *Journal of American History*. 71 (June 1984): 43–68.

Croffut, A. *The Vanderbilts and the Story of Their Fortunes*. New York: Belford, Clarke & Company, 1886.

David, Oliver. *Stokowski*. New York: Dodd, Mead, 1982.

Davidson, Jo. *Between Sittings*. New York: Dial, 1951.

deJong, Gerald F. *The Dutch in America, 1609–1974*. Boston: Twayne, 1975.

Desmaroux, Helene. *L'Oeuvre du Sculpture O'Connor*. Paris: Librairie de France, 1927.

Diliberto, Gioia. *Debutante*. New York: Pocket Books, 1988.

Dorr, Rheta Childe. *What Eight Million Women Want*. Boston: Small, Maynard, 1910.

Dowling, Antoinette, and Vincent J. Scully, Jr. *The Architectural Heritage of Newport, Rhode Island*. New York: American Legacy Press, 1982.

Dubbert, Joel. *A Man's Place: Masculinity in Transition*. Englewood Cliffs, N.J.: Prentice-Hall, 1979.

du Bois, Guy Pene. "Andrew O'Connor and His Sculpture." *International Studio*. (January 1927): 55–61.

Eastman, Max. *Enjoyment of Living*. New York: Harper & Row, 1948.

Eksteins, Modris. *Rites of Spring*. New York: Doubleday, 1990.

Felsenthal, Carol. *Alice Roosevelt Longworth*. New York: Putnam's, 1988.

Fitzgerald, F. Scott. *The Great Gatsby*. New York: Scribner's, 1953.

Flexner, Eleanor. *Century of Struggle*. New York: Atheneum, 1970.

Foreman, John, and Robbe Pierce Stimson. *The Vanderbilts and the Gilded Age: Architectural Aspirations, 1879–1901.* New York: St. Martin's Press, 1991.

Friedman, B. H., with the research collaboration of Flora Miller Irving. *Gertrude Vanderbilt Whitney.* Garden City, N.Y.: Doubleday, 1978.

Geidel, Peter. "The National Woman's Party and the Origins of the Equal Rights Amendment, 1920–1923." *The Historian.* 42 (1980): 557–82.

Gill, Brendan. "Gloria Vanderbilt Updates." *Vogue.* 165 (June 1975): 106–109.

Goldsmith, Barbara. *Little Gloria . . . Happy At Last.* New York: Knopf, 1980.

Gooch, Stapleton Dabney IV. "Richard Morris Hunt and the Vanderbilts." M.A. thesis, University of Virginia, 1966.

Hartmann, Susan M. *The Home Front and Beyond: American Women in the 1940s.* Boston: Twayne, 1982.

Healy, Daty. *A History of the Whitney Museum of American Art: 1930–1954.* Ph.D. dissertation, New York University, 1960.

Hills, Patricia and Roberta K. Tarbell. *The Figurative Tradition and the Whitney Museum of Art.* New York: Whitney Museum of Art, 1980.

Hoogenboom, Ari and Olive Hoogenboom, eds. *The Gilded Age.* Englewood Cliffs, N.J.: Prentice-Hall, 1967.

Hough, Richard. *Edwina: Countess Mountbatten of Burma.* New York: Morrow, 1983.

Hynes, Samuel. *The Edwardian Turn of Mind.* Princeton: Princeton University Press, 1968.

Irwin, Inez Haynes. *The Story of the Woman's Party.* New York: Harcourt, 1921.

James, Henry. *The American Scene.* New York: Horizon, 1967.

Johnston, Johanna. *Mrs. Satan: The Incredible Story of Victoria C. Woodhull.* New York: G. P. Putnam's Sons, 1967.

Josephson, Matthew. *The Robber Barons.* New York: Harcourt, 1934.

King, Robert B. *The Vanderbilt Homes.* New York: Rizzoli, 1989.

Kraditor, Eileen S. *The Ideas of the Woman Suffrage Movement, 1890–1920.* Garden City, N.Y.: Doubleday Anchor.

Lane, Wheaton. *Commodore Vanderbilt.* New York: Knopf, 1942.

Larkin, Jack. *The Reshaping of Everyday Life, 1790–1840.* New York: Harper & Row, 1988.

Lewis, R.W.B. *Edith Wharton.* New York: Harper & Row, 1975.

Lovell, Mary. *Straight on Till Morning.* New York: St. Martin's Press, 1987.

MacColl, Gail and Carol McD. Wallace. *To Marry An English Lord.* New York: Workman, 1989.

Maher, James T. *The Twilight of Splendor.* New York: Little, Brown. 1975.

Magnus, Phillip. *King Edward the Seventh.* New York: E.P. Dutton, 1964.

Manchester, William. *The Last Lion: Winston Spencer Churchill, 1874–1932.* New York: Little, Brown, 1983.

Marberry, M. M. *Vicky: A Biography of Victoria C. Woodhull.* New York: Funk and Wagnalls, n.d.

Martin, Ralph G. *Jennie: The Life of Lady Randolph Churchill,* 2 volumes. New York: New American Library, 1970.

Maxwell, Elsa. *R.S.V.P.: Elsa Maxwell's Own Story.* Boston: Little, Brown, 1954.

May, Elaine Tyler. *Homeward Bound: American Families in the Cold War Era.* New York: Basic Books, 1988.

Montgomery, Maureen E. *Gilded Prostitution: Status, Money, and Transatlantic Marriages, 1870–1914*. London: Routledge, 1989.

Morgan, Ted. *Churchill: Young Man in a Hurry—1874–1915*. New York: Simon and Schuster, 1982.

Morris, Lloyd. *Incredible New York*. New York: Random House, 1951.

Munro, Eleanor. *Originals: American Women Artists*. New York: Simon and Schuster, 1979.

Myers, Gustavus. *History of the Great American Fortunes*. Chicago: Kerr, 1908–10.

Nelson, Marjory. *Ladies in the Streets: A Sociological Analysis of the National Woman's Party, 1910–1930*. Ph.D. dissertation, State University of New York at Buffalo. Ann Arbor Mich.: University Microfilms, 1976.

O'Neill, William L. *Everyone Was Brave*. Chicago: Quadrangle, 1969.

Ostrander, Susan A. *Women of the Upper Class*. Philadelphia: Temple University Press, 1984.

Pardo, Thomas C., ed. *The National Woman's Party Papers, 1913–1974: A Guide to the Microfilm Edition*. Sanford, N.C.: Microfilming Corporation of America, 1979.

Parkes, Kineton. *Sculpture of Today*. New York: Scribners, n.d. (c. 1920).

Patterson, Jerry E. *The Vanderbilts*. New York: Abrams, 1989.

Perrett, Geoffrey. *America in the Twenties*. New York: Simon and Schuster, 1982.

Riley, Glenda. *Inventing the American Woman*. Arlington Heights, IL: Harlan Davidson, 1986.

Robinson, David. *Chaplin, His Life and Art*. New York: McGraw-Hill, 1985.

Rose, Kenneth. *King George V*. New York: Knopf, 1984.

Rowse, A. L. *The Churchills*. New York: Harper & Row, 1957.

Rubenstein, Charlotte Streifer. *American Women Artists*. Boston: G. K. Hall, 1982.

Rudnick, Lois Palken. *Mabel Dodge Luhan*. Albuquerque: University of New Mexico Press, 1984.

Rybczynski, Witold. *Home: A Short History of an Idea*. New York: Viking Penguin, 1986.

Saroyan, Aram. *Trio*. New York: Linden/Simon and Schuster, 1985.

Shadegg, Stephen. *Clare Boothe Luce*. New York: Simon and Schuster, 1970.

Simon, Kate. *Fifth Avenue*. New York: Harcourt Brace Jovanovich, 1978.

Sinclair, Andrew. *The Emancipation of the American Woman*. New York: Harper & Row, 1966.

Slater, Philip. *Wealth Addiction*. New York: Dutton, 1980.

Sloane, Florence Adele. *Maverick in Mauve*. Garden City, N.Y.: Doubleday, 1983.

Smit, Pamela, and J. W. Smit. *The Dutch in America: 1609–1970: A Chronology and Source Book*. Dobbs Ferry, N.Y.: Oceana, 1972.

Smith, Henry Nash, edit. *Popular Culture and Industrialism, 1865–1890*. Garden City, N.Y.: Anchor, 1967.

Smith-Rosenberg, Carroll. *Disorderly Conduct: Visions of Gender in Victorian America*. New York: Knopf, 1985.

Sochen, June. *The New Woman: Feminism in Greenwich Village, 1910–1920*. New York: Quadrangle.

Stevens, Doris. *Jailed for Freedom*. Freeport, N.Y.: Books for Libraries Press, 1920.

Swanberg, W. A. *Whitney Father, Whitney Heiress*. New York: Scribner's, 1980.

Taft, Loredo. *The History of American Sculpture*. New York: Macmillan, 1924.

Tomkins, Calvin. *Merchants and Masterpieces: The Story of the Metropolitan Museum of Art, Revised Edition*. New York: Henry Holt, 1989.

Vanderbilt, Arthur T. *Fortune's Children: The Fall of the House of Vanderbilt.* New York: Morrow, 1989.

Vanderbilt, Cornelius Jr. *Farewell to Fifth Avenue.* New York: Simon and Schuster, 1935.

————. *Queen of the Golden Age.* Maidstone, England: George Mann, 1989.

Vanderbilt, Gloria Morgan. *Without Prejudice.* New York: E.P. Dutton, 1936.

Vanderbilt, Gloria and Lady Thelma Furness. *Double Exposure.* New York: Donald McKay, 1958.

Veblen, Thorstein. *The Theory of the Leisure Class.* New York: Modern Library, 1934.

Vickers, Hugo. *Gladys Duchess of Marlborough.* New York: Harcourt Brace Jovanovich, 1979.

Ware, Susan. *Holding Their Own: American Women in the 1930s.* Boston: Twayne, 1982.

Webb, Beatrice. *Our Partnership.* London: Longmans, 1940.

Wecter, Dixon. *The Saga of American Society.* New York: Scribners, 1937.

Wharton, Edith. *A Backward Glance.* New York: Appleton-Century, 1934.

————. *The Age of Innocence.* New York: The Library of America, 1985.

Whitney Museum of American Art. *Gertrude Vanderbilt Whitney: Memorial Exhibition,* January 26 to February 28, 1943.

————. *Juliana Force and American Art.* 1949.

PERMISSIONS AND ACKNOWLEDGMENTS

Grateful acknowledgment is made to the following: Whitney Museum of American Art, for excerpts from its journals and letters from the Gertrude Vanderbilt Whitney Papers (a gift of Flora Miller Irving Biddle); Regional Oral History Office, Bancroft Library, University of California at Berkeley, for excerpts from the oral histories of Sara Bard Fields and Alice Paul; The Huntington Library, San Marino, California, from the C. E. S. Wood collection for excerpts from letters by Sara Bard Field, and from Field's notes and drafts of the Alva Smith Vanderbilt Belmont biography; William R. Perkins Library, Duke University, for excerpts from the Matilda Young papers, memoir by Alva Smith Vanderbilt Belmont.

INDEX